W9-CBI-001

NORTHERN IRELAND
Pages 246–277

ndonderry   ANTRIM

LONDONDERRY

**NORTHERN
IRELAND**

YRONE   BELFAST

ARMAGH   DOWN

MONAGHAN

AN   Dundalk
              LOUTH

IDLANDS

        MEATH

TH

    D U B L I N

KILDARE

      WICKLOW

IS

    CARLOW

UTHEAST
RELAND

KENNY   WEXFORD

terford   Wexford

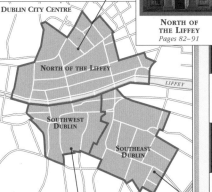

DUBLIN CITY CENTRE

NORTH OF THE LIFFEY

LIFFEY

SOUTHWEST
DUBLIN

SOUTHEAST
DUBLIN

**NORTH OF
THE LIFFEY**
Pages 82–91

SOUTHWEST DUBLIN
Pages 70–81

SOUTHEAST DUBLIN
Pages 54–69

SOUTHEAST IRELAND
Pages 116–143

THE MIDLANDS
Pages 228–245

EYEWITNESS TRAVEL GUIDES

IRELAND

EYEWITNESS TRAVEL GUIDES

IRELAND

Main Contributors:
LISA GERARD-SHARP AND TIM PERRY

LONDON, NEW YORK,
MELBOURNE, MUNICH AND DELHI
www.dk.com

PROJECT EDITOR Ferdie McDonald
ART EDITOR Lisa Kosky
EDITORS Maggie Crowley, Simon Farbrother, Emily Hatchwell,
Seán O'Connell, Jane Simmonds
DESIGNERS Joy FitzSimmons, Jaki Grosvenor,
Katie Peacock, Jan Richter
RESEARCHERS John Breslin, Andrea Holmes
PICTURE RESEARCHERS Sue Mennell, Christine Rista
DTP DESIGNERS Samantha Borland, Adam Moore

CONTRIBUTORS
Una Carlin, Polly Phillimore, Susan Poole, Martin Walters

PHOTOGRAPHERS
Joe Cornish, Tim Daly, Alan Williams

ILLUSTRATORS
Draughtsman Maps, Maltings Partnership, Robbie Polley

Reproduced by Colourscan, Singapore
Printed and bound in China by Toppan Printing Co. (Shenzhen Ltd)

First published in Great Britain in 1995
by Dorling Kindersley Limited
80 Strand, London WC2R 0RL
**Reprinted with revisions 1996 (twice), 1997, 1999,
2000, 2001, 2002, 2003, 2004**

A CIP CATALOGUE RECORD IS AVAILABLE FROM THE BRITISH LIBRARY.
ISBN 1 4053 0498 7

**The information in this Dorling Kindersley Travel Guide
is checked regularly.**
Every effort has been made to ensure that this book is as up-to-date
as possible at the time of going to press. Some details, however,
such as telephone numbers, opening hours, prices, gallery hanging
arrangements and travel information, are liable to change. The
publishers cannot accept responsibility for any consequences arising
from the use of this book, nor for any material on third-party
websites, and cannot guarantee that any website address in this
book will be a suitable source of travel information. We value the
views and suggestions of our readers highly. Please write to:
Publisher, DK Eyewitness Travel Guides,
Dorling Kindersley, 80 Strand, London, Great Britain WC2R 0RL.

CONTENTS

An evangelical symbol from the
Book of Kells (see p62)

**Georgian doorway in Fitzwilliam
Square, Dublin *(see p67)***

IRELAND REGION
BY REGION

Detail of the Chorus Gate at
Powerscourt *(see pp126–7)*

Lighthouse at Spanish Point near Mizen Head *(see p159)*

TRAVELLERS'
NEEDS

SURVIVAL GUIDE

TRAVEL
INFORMATION *350*

Façade of a pub in Dingle *(see p149)*

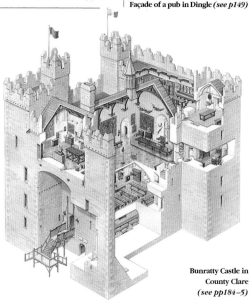

Bunratty Castle in
County Clare
(see pp184–5)

How to Use this Guide

This guide helps you to get the most from your visit to Ireland. It provides both expert recommendations and detailed practical information. *Introducing Ireland* maps the country and sets it in its historical and cultural context. The seven regional chapters, plus *Dublin Area by Area*, contain descriptions of all the important sights, with maps, pictures and illustrations. Restaurant and hotel recommendations can be found in *Travellers' Needs*. The *Survival Guide* has tips on everything from the telephone system to transport both in the Republic and in Northern Ireland.

DUBLIN AREA BY AREA

Central Dublin is divided into three sightseeing areas. Each has its own chapter, which opens with a list of the sights described. A fourth chapter, *Further Afield*, covers the suburbs and County Dublin. Sights are numbered and plotted on an *Area Map*. The descriptions of each sight follow the map's numerical order, making sights easy to locate within the chapter.

All pages relating to Dublin have red thumb tabs.

A locator map shows where you are in relation to other areas of the city centre.

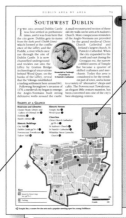

Sights at a Glance lists the chapter's sights by category: Churches, Museums and Galleries, Historic Buildings, Parks and Gardens.

1 **Area Map**
For easy reference, the sights are numbered and located on a map. Sights in the city centre are also shown on the Dublin Street Finder *on pages 110–11.*

2 **Street-by-Street Map**
This gives a bird's-eye view of the key area in each chapter.

A suggested route for a walk is shown in red.

Stars indicate the sights that no visitor should miss.

3 **Detailed information**
The sights in Dublin are described individually with addresses, telephone numbers and information on opening hours and admission charges.

Story boxes highlight noteworthy features of the sights.

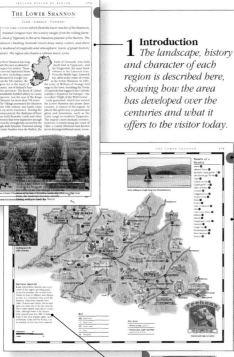

IRELAND REGION BY REGION

Apart from Dublin, Ireland has been divided into seven regions, each of which has a separate chapter. The most interesting towns and places to visit in each area have been numbered on a *Pictorial Map*.

1 Introduction
The landscape, history and character of each region is described here, showing how the area has developed over the centuries and what it offers to the visitor today.

Each region of Ireland can be quickly identified by its colour coding, shown on the inside front cover.

2 Pictorial Map
This shows the road network and gives an illustrated overview of the whole region. All interesting places to visit are numbered and there are also useful tips on getting around the region by car and train.

Getting Around gives tips on travel within the region.

3 Detailed information
All the important towns and other places to visit are described individually. They are listed in order, following the numbering on the Pictorial Map. Within each town or city, there is detailed information on important buildings and other sights.

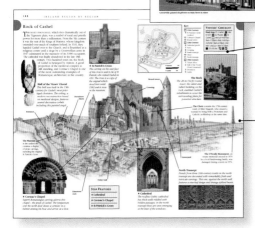

The Visitors' Checklist provides all the practical information you will need to plan your visit to all the top sights.

4 Ireland's top sights
These are given two or more full pages. Historic buildings are dissected to reveal their interiors. The most interesting towns or city centres are shown in a bird's-eye view, with sights picked out and described.

Introducing
Ireland

Putting Ireland on the Map

THE ISLAND OF IRELAND covers an area of 84,430 sq km (32,598 sq miles). Lying in the Atlantic Ocean to the northwest of mainland Europe, it is separated from Great Britain by the Irish Sea. The Republic of Ireland takes up 85 per cent of the island, with a population of 3.9 milllion. Northern Ireland, part of the United Kingdom, has 1.7 million people. Dublin is the capital of the Republic and has good international communications.

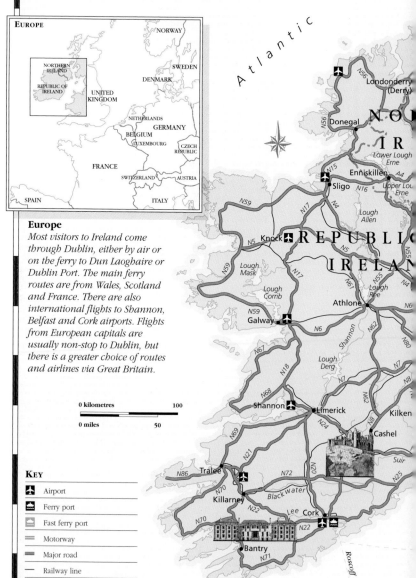

EUROPE

NORWAY

SWEDEN

DENMARK

NORTHERN
IRELAND

REPUBLIC OF
IRELAND

UNITED
KINGDOM

NETHERLANDS

GERMANY

BELGIUM

LUXEMBOURG

CZECH
REPUBLIC

FRANCE

SWITZERLAND

AUSTRIA

SPAIN

ITALY

Europe
Most visitors to Ireland come through Dublin, either by air or on the ferry to Dun Laoghaire or Dublin Port. The main ferry routes are from Wales, Scotland and France. There are also international flights to Shannon, Belfast and Cork airports. Flights from European capitals are usually non-stop to Dublin, but there is a greater choice of routes and airlines via Great Britain.

0 kilometres   100

0 miles   50

KEY

✈	Airport
⛴	Ferry port
⛴	Fast ferry port
━	Motorway
━	Major road
—	Railway line

Atlantic Ocean

Londonderry
(Derry)

N O

I R

Donegal

N56

Lower Lough
Erne

Enniskillen

A4

Sligo

N16

Upper Lou
Erne

N15

N59

N17

N4

Lough
Allen

Knock

R E P U B L I C

N5

Lough
Mask

N5

N55

Lough
Ree

I R E L A N

N59

N17

N61

Athlone

N6

Lough
Corrib

Galway

N6

N59

Shannon

N62

N80

Lough
Derg

N7

N67

N18

N7

N8

N68

Shannon

Limerick

N24

Kilken

N69

N20

Cashel

N21

Suir

N86

Tralee

N72

N25

N70

Killarney

Blackwater

N22

Lee

Cork

N70

N22

N71

Bantry

Roscoff

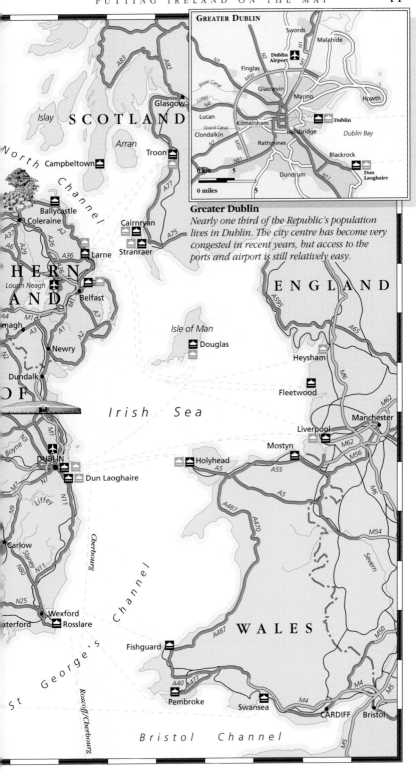

Greater Dublin

Nearly one third of the Republic's population lives in Dublin. The city centre has become very congested in recent years, but access to the ports and airport is still relatively easy.

A Portrait of Ireland

*M*ANY VISITORS *see Ireland as a lush green island, full of thatched cottages, pubs, music, wit and poetry. Like all stereotypes, this image of the country has a basis in truth and the tourist industry helps sustain it. The political and economic reality is, of course, rather less ideal, but the relaxed good humour of the people still makes Ireland a most welcoming place to visit.*

Ireland, at least for the time being, is a divided island. History and religion created two hostile communities in North and South. The IRA ceasefire of 1997 and the subsequent Good Friday Agreement brought new hope, however. John Hume of the SDLP and David Trimble of the Ulster Unionist Party were jointly awarded the Nobel prize for peace for their work in the peace process, and the inaugural meeting of the Northern Ireland Assembly took place on 1 July 1998.

Ireland has had more than its fair share of wars and disasters, culminating in the Great Famine of 1845–8, since when poverty and emigration

Cathleen ni Houlihan, personification of Ireland

have been part of the Irish way of life. More people of Irish descent live in the USA than in Ireland itself. Suffering and martyrdom in the cause of independence also play an important part in the Irish consciousness. The heroine of WB Yeats's play *Cathleen ni Houlihan* inspires young men to lay down their lives for Ireland. Her image appeared on the first banknote issued by the newly created Irish Free State in 1922.

Yet, the Irish retain their easy-going attitude to life, with a young, highly educated population working hard to make its way in today's European Union. In the Republic, over 50 per cent of the population is under 30.

Façade of Trinity College, Dublin, the Republic's most prestigious university

◁ Thatching a traditional cottage in Adare, County Limerick

Young first communicant in County Kerry

Despite its high birth rate, rural Ireland is sparsely populated. The Industrial Revolution of the 19th century barely touched the South and for much of the 20th century the Republic seemed an old-fashioned place, poorer than almost all its fellow members of the European Union.

ECONOMIC DEVELOPMENT

In recent years, tax breaks and low inflation have attracted more foreign investment to the Republic and many multinationals, especially computing and chemical companies, have subsidiaries here. Ireland joined the single European currency on 1 January 1999, and the Republic's economy continues to grow while unemployment is falling. Another important industry is tourism. The South receives over 3 million visitors a year and visitors to the North are now steadily increasing.

Traditionally, Northern Ireland had far more industry than the South, but during the 25 years of the Troubles, old heavy industries, such as shipbuilding, declined and new investors were scared away. However, the election of members to the new Northern Ireland Assembly in June 1998 ushered in a new political and economic era for the North. For both parts of Ireland, geography is still a barrier to prosperity. Located on the periphery of Europe, the island is isolated from its main markets and thus saddled with high transport costs. Fortunately, subsidies from the EU have helped improve the infrastructure in the Republic.

RELIGION AND POLITICS

The influence of Catholicism is strong. In the Republic, the Church runs most schools, along with some hospitals and social services. Irish Catholicism runs the gamut from missionary zeal to simple piety. According to some

Pavement artist on O'Connell Street, Dublin

estimates, over 90 per cent of the population goes to Mass. Religion plays an important role in the politics of the Republic and moral conservatism is evident in attitudes to divorce, contraception, abortion and homosexuality.

The election of liberal lawyer Mary Robinson as President in 1990, the first woman to hold the post, was seen as a sign of more enlightened times by many people, an attitude reinforced by the election of Mary McAleese as her successor in 1998. A new political climate has favoured the quiet spread of feminism

Traditional Irish dancing

Traditional farming: a field of haystacks overlooking Clew Bay, County Mayo

and challenged the old paternalism of Irish politics, not only in social issues but also in helping break down the clannish cronyism of the traditional parties Fianna Fáil and Fine Gael.

LANGUAGE AND CULTURE

Ireland was a Gaelic-speaking nation until the 16th century, since when the language has declined. Today, however, the Republic is officially bilingual. Knowledge of Irish is a requirement for university entrance and a career in the public sector, although only 11 per cent of the population speaks Gaelic fluently.

Connemara pony show

Irish culture, on the other hand, is in no danger of being eroded. The people have a genuine love of old folk legends and epic poetry and songs. Festivals, whether dedicated to St Patrick or James Joyce, pubs or oysters, salmon or sailing, are an important part of community life. Music is a national passion – from the rock of U2 and the Cranberries to the folk music of Clannad, the Chieftains and Mary Black.

Another national passion is horse racing. Ireland's breeders and trainers are masters of their trade and enjoy astonishing international success for such a small country. Other sports are followed with equal intensity, as witnessed during the 1994 football World Cup. Drinking also plays an important part in Irish culture: social life centres on the pub and the "crack" (convivial chat) to be enjoyed there. When the Republic introduced stricter drink-driving laws in 1994, many rural publicans said traditional Irish society would collapse. Given the attachment to Guinness, gossip and music, this is extremely unlikely.

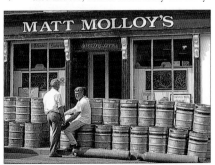

Matt Molloy's pub in Westport, County Mayo

The Landscape and Wildlife of Ireland

Corncrake

T HE LANDSCAPE is one of the Ireland's greatest attractions. It varies from bogs and lakes in the central lowlands to mountains and rocky islands in the west. Between these two extremes, the island has abundant lush, green pastureland, the result of plentiful rainfall, but little natural woodland. Parts of the far west, where the land is farmed by traditional methods, are havens for threatened wildlife, including the corncrake, which needs undisturbed hayfields in which to nest.

THE FAUNA OF IRELAND

Natterjack toad

Many animals (including snakes) did not make it to Ireland before the Irish Sea rose after the Ice Age.

Other surprising absentees are the mole, weasel and common toad (the natterjack, however, can be seen). The wood mouse is the only small native rodent, but the once common red squirrel has now been virtually taken over by the grey.

ROCKY COASTS

Chough

The Dingle Peninsula *(see pp150–51)* is part of a series of rocky promontories and inlets created when sea levels rose at the end of the Ice Age. Cliffs and islands offer many sites for sea birds, with some enormous colonies, such as the gannets of Little Skellig *(pp156–7)*. The chough still breeds on cliffs in the extreme west. Elsewhere in Europe, this rare species of crow is declining in numbers.

Thrift grows in cushion-like clumps, producing its papery pink flowerheads from spring right through to autumn.

Sea campion is a low-growing plant. Its large white flowers brighten up many a cliff top and seaside shingle bank.

LAKES, RIVERS AND WETLANDS

Great crested grebe

This watery landscape around Lough Oughter is typical of the lakelands of the River Erne *(pp262–3)*. Rainfall is high throughout the year, which results in many wetlands, especially along the Shannon *(pp176–7)* and the Erne. The elegant great crested grebe breeds mainly on the larger lakes in the north.

Water lobelia grows in the shallows of stony lakes. Its leaves remain below the water, while the pale lilac flowers are borne on leafless stems above the surface.

Fleabane, once used to repel fleas, thrives in wet meadows and marshes. It has yellow flowers like dandelions.

Grey seals are a common sight in the waters off the Atlantic coast, feeding on fish and occasionally on sea birds.

Otters *are more likely to be seen in the shallow seas off rocky coasts than in rivers and lakes, though they live in both habitats.*

Pine martens, though mainly nocturnal, may be spotted in daytime during the summer.

Red deer *have been introduced into many areas, notably the hills of Connemara.*

MOUNTAIN AND BLANKET BOG

Wheatear

As well as the raised bogs of the central lowlands *(p244)*, much of Ireland's mountainous ground, particularly in the west, is covered by blanket bog such as that seen here in Connemara *(pp198–201)*. On drier upland sites this grades into heather moor and poor grassland. The wheatear, which inhabits rocky scree and heathland, is a restless bird with an unmistakable white rump. It flits about, dipping and bobbing in pursuit of flies.

Bog myrtle is an aromatic shrub, locally common in Ireland's bogs. Its leaves can be used to flavour drinks.

Bogbean, a plant found in fens and wet bogland, has attractive white flowers splashed with pink. Its leaves were once used as a cure for boils.

PASTURELAND

Rook

Rolling pastureland with grazing livestock, as seen here in the foothills of the Wicklow Mountains *(pp130–31)*, is a very common sight throughout Ireland. The traditional farming methods employed in many parts of the island (particularly in the west) are of great benefit to wildlife. Rooks, for example, which feed on worms and insect larvae found in pasture, are very common.

Meadow vetchling uses its tendrils to clamber up grasses and other plants. It has clusters of pretty pale yellow flowers.

Marsh thistle is a common flower of wet meadows and damp woodland. It is a tall species with small, purple flowerheads.

Architecture in Ireland

Window of an Irish cottage

IRELAND'S TURBULENT HISTORY has done incalculable damage to its architectural heritage. Cromwell's forces, in particular, destroyed scores of castles, monasteries and towns in their three-year campaign against the Irish in the mid-17th century. However, many fascinating buildings and sites remain, with Iron Age forts being the earliest surviving settlements. Christianity in Ireland gave rise to monasteries, churches and round towers; conflict between Anglo-Norman barons and Irish chieftains created castles and tower houses. The later landlord class built luxurious country mansions, while their labourers had to make do with basic, one-roomed cottages.

LOCATOR MAP

	Iron Age forts
	Round towers
	Tower houses
	Georgian country houses

IRON AGE FORT

Ring forts (raths) were Iron Age farmsteads enclosed by an earth bank, a timber fence and a ditch to protect against cattle-raiders. Inside, people lived in huts with a souterrain (underground passage) for storage and refuge. Some were in use as late as the 17th century, but all you can usually see today are low circular mounds. In the west, stone was used for cahers (stone ring forts) and promontory forts (semi-circular forts built on cliff tops using the sea as a natural defence).

Thatched hut

Entrance   **Souterrain**

ROUND TOWER

Lookout window   **Conical roof**

Round towers, often over 30m (100 ft) tall, were built between the 10th and 12th centuries on monastic sites. They were bell towers, used as places of refuge and to store valuable manuscripts. The entrance, which could be as high as 4 m (13 ft) above ground, was reached by a ladder that was hauled up from the inside. Other moveable ladders connected the tower's wooden floors.

Wooden floor

Moveable ladder

TOWER HOUSE

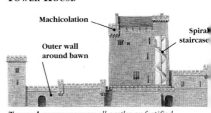

Machicolation

Outer wall around bawn

Spiral staircase

Tower houses were small castles or fortified residences built between the 15th and 17th centuries. The tall square house was often surrounded by a stone wall forming a bawn (enclosure), used for defence and as a cattle pen. Machicolations (projecting parapets from which to drop missiles) were sited at the top of the house.

COTTAGE

One-roomed cottages, thatched or slate-roofed, are still a common feature of the Irish landscape. Built of local stone with small windows to retain heat, the cottages were inhabited by farm workers or smallholders.

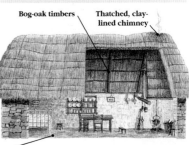

Bog-oak timbers   **Thatched, clay-lined chimney**

Clay floor

Iron Age Forts

① Staigue Fort *p156*
② Dún Aonghasa *p206*
③ Craggaunowen *p182*
④ Grianán of Ailigh *pp218–19*
⑤ Hill of Tara *p240*

Round Towers

⑥ Kilmacduagh *p204*
⑦ Ardmore *p137*
⑧ Clonmacnoise *pp242–3*
⑨ Devenish Island *p263*
⑩ Kilkenny *pp136*
⑪ Glendalough *pp132–3*

Tower Houses

⑫ Aughnanure Castle *p201*
⑬ Thoor Ballylee *pp204–5*
⑭ Knappogue Castle *p181*
⑮ Blarney Castle *p163*
⑯ Donegal Castle *p222*

Georgian Country Houses

⑰ Strokestown Park House *pp210–11*
⑱ Castle Coole *p264*
⑲ Emo Court *p245*
⑳ Russborough House *pp124–5*
㉑ Castletown House *pp122–3*

The well-preserved round tower at Ardmore

Georgian Country House

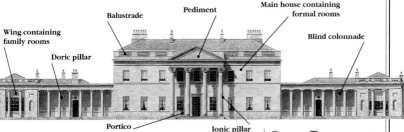

Wing containing family rooms

Doric pillar

Balustrade

Pediment

Main house containing formal rooms

Blind colonnade

Portico

Ionic pillar

Between the 1720s and 1800, prosperous landlords commissioned palatial country mansions in the Palladian and Neo-Classical styles popular in England over that period. Castle Coole (above) has a Palladian layout, with the main house in the centre and a colonnade on either side leading to a small pavilion. The Neo-Classical influence can be seen in the unadorned façade and the Doric columns of the colonnades. Noted architects of Irish country houses include Richard Castle (1690–1751) and James Wyatt (1746–1813).

Stucco

Stucco (decorative relief plasterwork), popular in the 18th century, is found in many Georgian country houses as well as town houses and public buildings. The Italian Francini brothers were particularly sought after for their intricate stuccowork (notably at Castletown and Russborough) as was Irish craftsman Michael Stapleton (Trinity College, Dublin and Dublin Writers Museum).

Trompe l'oeil detail at Emo Court

Ceiling at Dublin Writers Museum

Stucco portrait at Castletown House

Stuccowork at Russborough House

Other Terms used in this Guide

Beehive hut: Circular stone building with a domed roof created by corbelling (laying a series of stones so that each projects beyond the one below).

Cashel: Stone ring fort.

Crannog: Defensive, partly artificial island on a lake. Huts were often built on crannogs (*see p31*).

Curtain wall: Outer wall of a castle, usually incorporating towers at intervals.

Hiberno-Romanesque: Style of church architecture with rounded arches highly decorated with geometric designs and human and animal forms. Also called Irish-Romanesque.

Motte and bailey: Raised mound (motte) topped with a wooden tower, surrounded by a heavily fenced space (bailey). Built by the Normans in the 12th century, they were quickly erected in time of battle.

Tympanum: Decorated space over a door or window.

Literary Ireland

FOR A LAND the size of Ireland to have produced four Nobel prizewinners in Shaw, Yeats, Beckett and Séamus Heaney is a considerable feat. Yet it is not easy to speak of an "Irish literary tradition" as the concept embraces rural and urban experiences, Protestant and Catholic traditions and the Gaelic and English languages. Irish fiction today, as in the past, is characterized by a sense of community and history, a love of storytelling and a zest for language.

A first edition of Ulysses

WB Yeats – Ireland's most famous poet

The Blasket Islands, which provided inspiration for several writers

GAELIC LITERATURE

IRISH LITERATURE proclaims itself the oldest vernacular literature in Western Europe, dating back to early monastic times when Celtic folklore and sagas such as the epics of Cúchulainn *(see p24)* were written down for the first time. The disappearance of Gaelic literature followed the demise, in the 17th century, of the Irish aristocracy for whom it was written. Gaelic literature has had several revivals. Peig Sayers is famous for her accounts of the harsh life on the Blasket Islands *(see p150)* in the early 20th century.

Novelist Maria Edgeworth

ANGLO-IRISH LITERATURE

THE COLLAPSE of Gaelic culture and the Protestant Ascendancy led to English being the dominant language. Most literature was based around the privileged classes.

An early Anglo-Irish writer was satirist Jonathan Swift *(see p80)*, author of *Gulliver's Travels*, who was born in Dublin in 1667 of English parents. Anglo-Irish literature was strong in drama, the entertainment of the cultured classes, and owed little to Irish settings or sensibilities. By the 1700s, Ireland was producing an inordinate number of leading playwrights, many of whom were more at home in London. These included Oliver Goldsmith, remembered for his comedy *She Stoops to Conquer*, and Richard Brinsley Sheridan, whose plays include *The School for Scandal*. Near the end of the century, Maria Edgeworth set a precedent with novels such as *Castle Rackrent*, based on the class divide in Irish society.

The 19th century saw an exodus to England of Irish playwrights, including Oscar Wilde, who entered Oxford University in 1874 and later became the darling of London society with plays such as *The Importance of Being Earnest*. George Bernard Shaw *(see p98)*, writer of *St Joan* and *Pygmalion*, also made London his home. This dramatist, critic, socialist and pacifist continued to write until well into the 20th century.

Playwright George Bernard Shaw

20TH-CENTURY WRITERS

IN 1898, WB Yeats and Lady Gregory founded Dublin's Abbey Theatre *(see p86)*. Its opening, in 1904, heralded the Irish Revival, which focused on national and local themes. Playwright John Millington Synge drew inspiration from a love of the Aran Islands and Irish folklore, but the "immoral language" of his *Playboy of the Western World* caused a riot when first performed at the Abbey Theatre. Along with contemporaries, like Sean O'Casey and WB Yeats, Synge influenced subsequent generations of Irish writers, including novelist Seán O'Faolain, humorous writer and columnist Flann O'Brien, and hard-drinking, quarrelsome playwright Brendan Behan. The literary revival also produced many notable poets in the mid-20th century such as the gifted Patrick Kavanagh and Belfast-born Louis MacNeice, often considered to be one of the finest poets of his generation.

The writer Brendan Behan enjoying the company in a Dublin pub

Caricature of protesters at Dublin's Abbey Theatre in 1907

THREE LITERARY GIANTS

FROM the mass of talent to emerge in Irish literature, three figures stand out as visionaries in their fields. WB Yeats *(see p225)* spent half his life outside Ireland but is forever linked to its rural west. A writer of wistful, melancholic poetry, he was at the forefront of the Irish Revival, helping forge a new national cultural identity. James Joyce *(see p88)* was another trailblazer of Irish literature – his complex narrative and stream of consciousness techniques influenced the development of the modern novel. *Ulysses* describes a day in the life of Joyce's beloved Dublin and shaped the work of generations of writers. Bloomsday, which is named after one of the novel's characters, Leopold Bloom, is still celebrated annually in the city. The last of the three literary giants, novelist and playwright Samuel Beckett *(see p60)*, was another of Dublin's sons, though he later emigrated to France. His themes of alienation, despair, and the futility of human existence pervade his best-known plays, *Waiting for Godot* and *Endgame*.

The poet Patrick Kavanagh celebrating Bloomsday

CONTEMPORARY WRITERS

IRELAND's proud literary tradition is today upheld by a stream of talented writers from both North and South. Among the finest are Cork-born William Trevor, regarded as a master of the short story, and Brian Moore, whose stories of personal and political disillusionment are often based in his native Belfast. Similarly, Dubliner Roddy Doyle mines his working-class origins in novels such as *The Snapper* and *Paddy Clarke Ha Ha Ha*. Other established Irish writers are Brian Friel and Edna O'Brien. Out of Ireland's contemporary poets, the Ulster-born writers Séamus Heaney and Derek Mahon are considered among the most outstanding.

IRELAND IN THE MOVIES

Ireland has long been fertile ground for the world's film makers, and its people have been the subjects of major films, notably *The Crying Game* (1992), *In the Name of the Father* (1994) and *Michael Collins* (1996). Another popular film was *The Commitments* (1991). Filmed on location in and around Dublin with an all-Irish cast, it was based on a novel by Roddy Doyle. More recently, parts of Co Wexford doubled as the beach heads of Normandy in Steven Spielberg's World War II epic *Saving Private Ryan* (1997).

Cast of *The Commitments*, written by Roddy Doyle

The Music of Ireland

IRELAND IS THE ONLY COUNTRY in the world to have a musical instrument – the harp – as its national emblem. In this land, famous for its love of music, modern forms such as country-and-western and rock flourish, but it is traditional music that captures the essence of the country. Whether you are listening to Gaelic love songs that date back to medieval times or 17th- and 18th-century folk songs with their English and Scottish influences, the music is unmistakably Irish. Dance is an equally important aspect of Irish traditional music, and some of the most popular airs are derived from centuries-old reels, jigs and hornpipes. Nowadays these are mainly performed at *fleadhs* (festivals) and *ceilís* (dances).

An Irish jig

Turlough O'Carolan *(1670–1738) is the most famous Irish harper. The blind musician travelled the country playing his songs to both rich and poor. Many of O'Carolan's melodies, such as* The Lamentation of Owen O'Neill, *still survive.*

Piano accordion

The *bodhrán* is a hand-held goatskin drum that is usually played with a small stick. It is particularly effective when accompanying the flute.

Flute

Two-row button accordion

John F McCormack *(1884–1945) was an Irish tenor who toured America to great acclaim during the early part of the 20th century. His best-loved recordings were arias by Mozart. Another popular tenor was Derry-born Josef Locke. A singer of popular ballads in the 1940s and '50s, he was the subject of the 1992 film* Hear My Song.

THE CURRENT MUSIC SCENE

Mary Black

Ireland today is a melting pot of musical styles. The resurgence of Irish traditional music has produced many highly respected musicians, such as the pipe-players Liam Ó Floin and Paddy Keenan from Dublin, while groups like the Chieftains and the Fureys have gained worldwide fame by melding old with new. Ireland is also firmly placed on the rock'n'roll map, thanks to singers such as Van Morrison in the 1970s and later bands like Thin Lizzy and the Boomtown Rats. The most famous rock band to come out of Ireland is Dublin's U2 who, in the 1980s, became one of the world's most popular groups. Other international successes include singers Enya, Mary Black and Sinéad O'Connor; and, more recently, bands like the Cranberries and the Corrs.

Bono of U2

Traditional Irish dancing is currently enjoying renewed popularity. From the 17th century the social focus in rural areas was the village dance held every Sunday. From these gatherings, Irish dancing became popular.

LIVE TRADITIONAL MUSIC

Wherever you go in Ireland, you won't be far from a pub with live music. For the Irish traditional musician, there are few set rules – the improvisational nature of the music means that no two performances of any piece are ever likely to be the same.

Violins, or fiddles, can either be tucked under the chin or held against the upper arm, shoulder or chest.

The New National Song —

ERIN
Remember
1916

PRICE 2d NET

Published by
QUINN & COMPANY,
20 UPPER ABBEY ST,
DUBLIN.

Irish folk songs, such as this one about the 1916 Easter Rising, tend to have a patriotic theme. But some of the most powerful songs have been written not just about the national struggle, but also about hardship, emigration and the longing for the homeland.

TRADITIONAL INSTRUMENTS

There is no set line-up in traditional Irish bands. The fiddle is probably the most common instrument used. Like the music, some instruments have Celtic origins – the uillean pipes are related to the bagpipes played in Scotland and Brittany today.

The melodeon is a basic version of the button accordion. Both these instruments are better suited to Irish music than the piano accordion.

The uillean pipes are similar to bagpipes and are generally considered to be one of the main instruments in Irish traditional music.

The harp has been played in Ireland since the 10th century. In recent years, there has been a keen revival of harp playing in Irish traditional music.

The banjo comes from the Deep South of the US and adds a new dimension to the sound of traditional bands.

Tin whistle

Flute

The flute and tin whistle are among the most common instruments used in traditional Irish music. The latter is often called the penny whistle.

The violin is called a fiddle by most musicians. The style of playing and sound produced varies from region to region.

Ireland's Celtic Heritage

Stone carving on Boa Island

IRELAND'S RICH TRADITION of storytelling embraces a folk heritage that abounds with myths and superstitions. Some stories have been in written form since the 8th century, but most originated over 2,000 years ago when druids passed on stories orally from one generation to the next. Like the Gaelic language itself, many of Ireland's legends have links with those of ancient Celtic races throughout Europe. As well as the heroic deeds and fearless warriors of mythology, Irish folklore is also rich in tales of fairies, leprechauns, banshees and other supernatural beings.

The formidable Queen Maeve of Connaught

Part of the 2,300-year-old Gundestrup Cauldron unearthed in Denmark, which depicts Cúchulainn's triumph in the Cattle Raid of Cooley

CÚCHULAINN

THE MOST FAMOUS warrior in Irish mythology is Cúchulainn. At the age of seven, going by the name of Setanta, he killed the savage hound of Culainn the Smith by slaying it with a hurling stick (one of the first times the sport of hurling is mentioned in folklore). Culainn was upset at the loss so Setanta volunteered to guard the house, earning himself the new name of Cúchulainn, meaning the hound of Culainn.

Before he went into battle, Cúchulainn swelled to magnificent proportions, turned different colours and one of his eyes grew huge. His greatest victory was in the "Cattle Raid of Cooley" when Queen Maeve of Connaught sent her troops to capture the coveted prize bull of Ulster. Cúchulainn learned of the plot and defeated them single-handedly. However, Queen Maeve took revenge on Cúchulainn by using sorcerers to lure him to his death. Today, in Dublin's GPO (see p87), a statue of Cúchulainn commemorates the heroes of the 1916 Easter Rising.

FINN MACCOOL

THE WARRIOR Finn MacCool is the most famous leader of the Fianna, an elite band of troops chosen for their strength and valour and who defended Ireland from foreign forces. Finn was not only strong and bold but also possessed the powers of a seer, and could obtain great wisdom by putting his thumb in his mouth and sucking on it. When they were not at war, the Fianna spent their time hunting. Finn had a hound called Bran which stood almost as high as himself and is said to be the original ancestor of the breed known today as the Irish wolfhound. Many of the

FAIRIES, LEPRECHAUNS AND BANSHEES

The diminutive figure of the leprechaun

The existence of spirits, and in particular the "little people", plays a large part in Irish folklore. Centuries ago, it was believed that fairies lived under mounds of earth, or "fairy raths", and that touching one of these tiny figures brought bad luck. The most famous of the "little people" is the leprechaun. Legend has it that if you caught one of these, he would lead you to a crock of gold, but take your eyes off him and he would vanish into thin air. The banshee was a female spirit whose wailing presence outside a house was said to signal the imminent death of someone within.

A banshee with long flowing hair

Fianna possessed supernatural powers and often ventured into the life beyond, known as the Otherworld. Among these was Finn's son Ossian who was not only a formidable warrior, like his father, but was also renowned as a wise and knowledgeable poet. Through time, Finn has come to be commonly portrayed as a giant. Legend has it that he constructed the Giant's Causeway in County Antrim *(see pp254–5)*.

A 19th-century engraving of Finn MacCool dressed for battle

THE CHILDREN OF LIR

ONE OF the saddest tales in Irish folklore involves King Lir, who so adored his four children that their stepmother was driven wild with jealousy. One day she took the children to a lake and cast a spell on them, turning them into white swans confined to the waters of Ireland for 900 years. However, as soon as she had done the deed, she became racked with guilt and bestowed upon them the gift of exquisite song. The

The children of King Lir being turned into white swans

king then decreed that no swan in Ireland should be killed – an act which is still illegal today. The end of the children's 900-year ordeal coincided with the coming of Christianity. They regained human form but were wizened and weak. They died soon afterwards, but not before being baptized.

SAINT BRENDAN

BRENDAN THE NAVIGATOR, like many other 6th-century monks, travelled widely. It is known that although he lived in western Ireland he visited Wales, Scotland and France. It is likely, though, that his most famous journey is fictitious. This story tells of a shipload of monks who, after seven years of all kinds of strange encounters designed to test their faith, found the Land of Promise. It is essentially a Christian retelling of the common tales of the Celtic Otherworld. The Feast of St Brendan on 16 May is celebrated in Kerry by the climbing of Mount Brandon.

Engraving showing St Brendan and his monks encountering a siren

ORIGINS OF IRISH PLACE NAMES

The names of many of Ireland's cities, towns and villages today are largely based on ancient Gaelic terms for prominent local landmarks, some of which no longer exist. Here are just a few elements of the place names the traveller may come across.

The fort on the Rock of Cashel that gives the town its name

Ar, ard – *high, height*
Ass, ess – *waterfall*
A, ah, ath – *ford*
Bal, bally – *town*
Beg – *small*
Ben – *peak, mountain*
Carrick, carrig – *rock*
Cashel – *stone fort*
Crock, knock – *hill*
Curra, curragh – *marsh*
Darry, derry – *oak tree*
Dun – *castle*
Eden – *hill brow*
Innis, inch – *island*
Inver – *river mouth*
Isk, iska – *water*
Glas, glass – *green*
Glen, glyn – *valley*
Kil, kill – *church*
Lough – *lake, sea inlet*
Mona, mone – *peat bog*
Mor – *great, large*
Mullen, mullin – *mill*
Rath, raha – *ring fort*
Slieve – *mountain*
Toom – *burial ground*
Tul, tulagh – *small hill*

St Canice's Cathedral in Kilkenny (the town's name means "church of Canice")

The Sporting Year

A LL MAJOR INTERNATIONAL team sports are played in Ireland, but the most popular games are the two uniquely native ones of Gaelic football and hurling. Most of the big games, plus soccer and rugby internationals, are sold out well in advance. However, if you can't get a ticket you'll find plenty of company with whom to watch the event in pubs. Horse racing, with over 240 days of racing a year, attracts fanatical support. For those keen on participatory sports, there are also Ireland's famous fishing waters and golf courses *(see pp332–3).*

***The North West 200** is the fastest motorcycle race in the world over public roads – held near Portstewart (see p252).*

Four-day national hunt racing festival at Punchestown

Round-Ireland Yacht Race – held every two years

The Irish Grand National *is a gruelling steeplechase run at Fairyhouse in County Meath.*

January	February	March	April	May	June

Irish Champion Hurdle, run at Leopardstown, County Dublin

Start of the salmon fishing season

The Six Nations Rugby Tournament, *between Ireland, Scotland, Wales, England, France and Italy, runs until April. Ireland play their home games at Lansdowne Road, Dublin.*

The International Rally of the Lakes is a prestigious car rally around the Lakes of Killarney *(see pp154–5).*

KEY TO SEASONS

	Hurling
	Gaelic football
	Flat racing
	National Hunt racing
	Rugby
	Association football
	Salmon fishing
	Equestrianism

Irish Football League Cup – Northern Ireland's final

The Irish Derby, *Ireland's premier flat race, attracts many of Europe's best three-year-olds to the Curragh (see p121).*

The All-Ireland Football Final *is held at Croke Park in Dublin. The top two counties play for this Gaelic football championship. More people watch the game than any other event in Ireland.*

Cork Week *is a biennial regatta, organized by Royal Cork Yacht Club, where crews and boats of all classes meet and compete.*

Greyhound Derby, run at Shelbourne Park, Dublin

The Dublin Marathon *is Ireland's foremost marathon event. It attracts a huge field including top-class athletes from around the world.*

Galway Race Week is one of Ireland's premier festival meetings and a popular social event.

Football Association of Ireland Cup – the Republic's football final

Millstreet Indoor International showjumping event

July	August	September	October	November	December

All-Ireland Hurling Final at Croke Park, Dublin

The Dublin Horse Show *is Ireland's premier horse show and a major event in the social calendar.*

The Irish Open Golf Champion-ship *is held at a different course each year and attracts a world-class field to courses such as Ballybunion in County Kerry.*

THE GAELIC ATHLETIC ASSOCIATION

The GAA was founded in 1884 to promote indigenous Irish sport. Today, despite heavy competition from soccer, the most popular sport in Ireland remains Gaelic football. Its rules are somewhere between rugby and soccer, though it predates both games. In it, the ball can be carried and points scored over the goalpost. Another intriguing GAA game is hurling, a fast and physical field sport played with sticks and said to have originated in ancient Celtic times. Both games are played at parish and county level on a wholly amateur basis. The season ends with the All-Ireland finals, which draw large and passionate crowds to Dublin.

Camogie, a version of hurling played by women

THE HISTORY OF IRELAND

IRELAND'S RELATIVE ISOLATION has cut it off from several of the major events of European history. Roman legions, for example, never invaded and the country's early history is shrouded in myths of warring Gods and heroic High Kings. Nevertheless, the bellicose Celtic tribes were quick to embrace Christianity after the arrival of St Patrick on the island in AD 432.

Until the Viking invasions of the 9th century, Ireland enjoyed an era of relative peace. Huge monasteries like Clonmacnoise and Glendalough were founded, where scholarship and art flourished. The Vikings failed to gain control of the island, but in 1169 the Anglo-Normans did. Many Irish chiefs submitted to Henry II of England, who declared himself Lord of Ireland. He left in 1172, and his knights shared out large baronies between themselves.

Matters changed when Henry VIII broke with the Catholic church in 1532. Ireland became a battleground between native Irish Catholics and the forces of the English Crown. Where

South Cross, Clonmacnoise

the Irish were defeated, their lands were confiscated and granted to Protestants from England and Scotland. England's conquest was completed with the victory of William of Orange over James II at the Battle of the Boyne in 1690. Repressive Penal Laws were put into place, but opposition to English rule continued.

The Famine of 1845 to 1848 was one of the bleakest periods in Irish history. Two million people died or emigrated, and many who stayed were evicted by English landlords. A campaign for Home Rule gathered strength, but it was 1920 before the Government of Ireland Act divided the island. The South became the Irish Free State, gaining full independence in 1937, while the North became part of the UK. For more than 25 years Northern Ireland has been a battleground, with both Loyalist and Republican paramilitary groups waging bombing campaigns. In 1998, the Good Friday Agreement was signed, paving the way for a new Northern Ireland Assembly and hopes of peace.

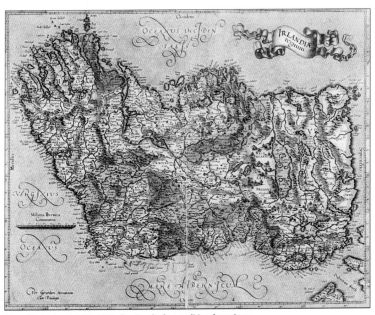

Map of Ireland, printed in 1592, showing the four traditional provinces

◁ *The Feast of St Kevin amid the Ruins of Glendalough* by Joseph Peacock (1813)

Prehistoric Ireland

UNTIL ABOUT 9,500 YEARS ago Ireland was uninhabited. The first people, who may have crossed by a land bridge from Scotland, were hunter-gatherers and left few traces of permanent settlement. The 4th millennium BC saw the arrival of Neolithic farmers and herdsmen who built stone field walls and monumental tombs such as Newgrange.

Early Bronze Age stone axe-head

Metalworking was brought from Europe around 2000 BC by the Bronze Age Beaker people, who also introduced new pottery skills. The Iron Age reached Ireland in the 3rd century BC along with the Celts, who migrated from Central Europe, via France and Britain, and soon established themselves as the dominant culture.

IRELAND c.8000 BC

- Former coastline
- Present-day coastline

Dolmens or Portal Tombs
These striking megalithic tombs date from around 2000 BC. Legananny Dolmen in the Mountains of Mourne (see p276) is a fine example.

The terminal discs were worn on the shoulders.

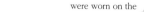

GLENINSHEEN GORGET
Many remarkable pieces of gold jewellery were created in the late Bronze Age. This gold collar dates from about 700 BC. The Iron Age Celts produced similarly fine metalwork and ornaments.

Three strands of ropework

Wooden Idol
This Iron Age fetish would have played a role in pagan fertility rites.

Celtic Stone Idol
This mysterious three-faced head was found in County Cavan. In Celtic religion the number three has always had a special significance.

Bronze Bridle Bit
Celtic chiefs rode into battle on two-horse chariots with beautifully decorated harnesses.

TIMELINE

c. 7500 BC First inhabitants of Ireland

Extinct giant deer or "Irish Elk"

5000–3000 Ireland covered by dense woodland dominated by oak and elm

2500 Building of Newgrange passage tomb *(see pp238–9)*

1500 Major advances in metalworking, especially gold

8000 BC	6000	4000	2000	1000

6000 Date of huts excavated at Mount Sandel, Co Londonderry; oldest known dwellings in Europe

3700 Neolithic farmers reach Ireland; they clear woods to plant cereals

2050 Beaker people (so-called for their delicate pottery vessels) reach Ireland at the beginning of Bronze Age

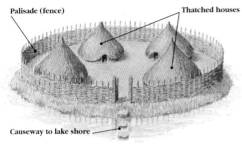

Palisade (fence)

Thatched houses

Causeway to lake shore

Reconstruction of a Crannog

Originating in the Bronze Age, crannogs were artificial islands built in lakes. At first used for fishing, they soon developed into well-protected homesteads. Some remained in use up to the 17th century.

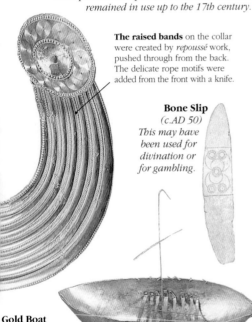

The raised bands on the collar were created by *repoussé* work, pushed through from the back. The delicate rope motifs were added from the front with a knife.

Bone Slip

(c.AD 50)
This may have been used for divination or for gambling.

Gold Boat

Part of a hoard of gold objects found at Broighter, County Londonderry, the boat (1st century AD) was made as a votive offering.

WHERE TO SEE PREHISTORIC IRELAND

Prehistoric sites range from individual tombs such as Newgrange, Browne's Hill Dolmen *(see p133)* or Ossian's Grave to whole settlements, as at Céide Fields *(p196)* and Lough Gur *(p186)*. The largest Stone Age cemetery is at Carrowmore *(p226)*. Good reconstructions of prehistoric structures can be seen at Craggaunowen *(p182)* and the Ulster History Park *(p261)*. The National Museum in Dublin *(pp64–5)* houses the finest collection of artifacts, including wonderful gold objects from the Bronze Age.

Newgrange (pp238–9) is Ireland's finest restored Neolithic tomb. At the entrance lie huge spiral-patterned boulders.

Ossian's Grave is a court grave, the earliest kind of Neolithic tomb (p259). An open court stood before the burial mound.

---

600 First wave of Celtic invaders

500 Intertribal warfare; chieftains vie for title of *Ard Ri* (High King)

AD 80 Roman general Agricola considers invasion of Ireland from Britain

367 Roman Britain attacked by Irish, Picts and Saxons

| 750 | 500 | 250 | AD 1 | AD 250 |

Bronze goad decorated with birds

250 Second wave of Celts, who bring La Tène style of pottery

c. 150 Greek geographer Ptolemy draws up map and account of Ireland

Bronze sword hilt imported from southern France

Celtic Christianity

CELTIC IRELAND was divided into as many as 100 chiefdoms, though these often owed allegiance to kings of larger provinces such as Munster or Connaught. At times, there was also a titular High King based at Tara *(see p240)*. Ireland became Christian in the 5th century AD, heralding a golden age of scholarship centred on the new monasteries, while missionaries such as St Columba travelled abroad. At the end of the 8th century, Celtic Ireland was shattered by the arrival of the Vikings.

Monk illuminating a manuscript

IRELAND IN 1000

▨ *Viking settlements*

☐ *Traditional Irish provinces*

Ogham Stone
The earliest Irish script, Ogham, dates from about AD 300. The notches correspond to Roman letters, like a form of Morse code.

CELTIC MONASTERY
Monasteries were large centres of population. This reconstruction shows Glendalough *(see pp132–3)* in about 1100. The tall round tower served as a lookout for Viking raiders.

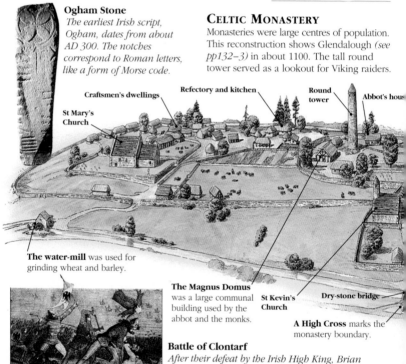

Craftsmen's dwellings

Refectory and kitchen

Round tower

Abbot's house

St Mary's Church

The water-mill was used for grinding wheat and barley.

The Magnus Domus was a large communal building used by the abbot and the monks.

St Kevin's Church

Dry-stone bridge

A High Cross marks the monastery boundary.

Battle of Clontarf
After their defeat by the Irish High King, Brian Ború, in 1014, the Vikings began to integrate more fully with the native population. Brian Ború himself was killed in the battle.

TIMELINE

430 Pope sends first Christian missionary, Palladius

455 St Patrick founds church at Armagh

St Patrick

563 St Columba (Colmcille), the first Irish missionary, founds monastery on Iona in the Hebrides

664 Synod of Whitby decides that Irish Church should conform with Rome over date of Easter

400	500	600	700

432 Start of St Patrick's mission to Ireland

c. 550 Beginning of golden age of Celtic monasticism

615 St Columbanus dies in Italy after founding many new monasteries on the Continent

c. 690 *Book of Durrow (see p61)* completed

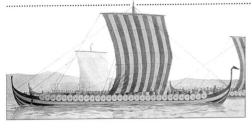

Viking Raids and Settlements
The first longships reached Ireland in 795. Though notorious for pillaging monasteries, the Vikings introduced new farming methods and coinage. They also founded walled cities such as Dublin, Waterford and Limerick.

Garryduff Gold Bird
Irish metalwork in the early Christian era was of very high quality. This gold ornament, possibly a wren, dates from around the 7th century AD.

WHERE TO SEE EARLY CHRISTIAN IRELAND

Important early monastic sites besides Glendalough include Clonmacnoise and Devenish Island. Churches from this period can also be seen at Gallarus (see p149), Clonfert (p205) and the Rock of Cashel (pp188–9), while High Crosses (p235) and round towers (p18) survive all over Ireland. Dublin's National Museum (pp64–5) has the best collection of ecclesiastical (and Viking) artifacts and Trinity College (pp60–62) houses the finest illuminated manuscripts.

***Devenish Island** has a fine 12th-century round tower and enjoys a peaceful setting on Lower Lough Erne (p263).*

Cathedral

Gatehouse

Guesthouse and stables

Monks' dwellings and barns

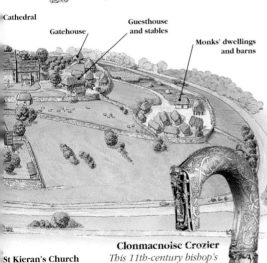

***Clonmacnoise** (pp242–3) lies on the east bank of the Shannon. This Romanesque doorway is part of the ruined Nuns' Church.*

St Kieran's Church and other important churches were built of stone, but most buildings were wood.

Clonmacnoise Crozier
This 11th-century bishop's staff is decorated with an ornate silver casing. The style of the incised patterns shows Viking influence.

Viking silver brooch

795 First Viking invasion of coastal monasteries

807 Work starts on Kells monastery (see p233)

841 A large Viking fleet spends the winter at Dublin

967 Irish warriors sack Limerick and begin military campaign against Viking overlords

999 Sitric Silkenbeard, the Viking king of Dublin, surrenders to Brian Ború

1014 High King Brian Ború of Munster defeats joint army of Vikings and the King of Leinster at Clontarf

Viking coin

1166 Dermot McMurrough, King of Leinster, flees overseas

1134 Cormac's Chapel is built at Cashel (see pp188–9)

1142 Ireland's first Cistercian house founded at Mellifont (see p237)

800 900 1000 1100

Anglo-Norman Ireland

13th-century gold brooch

ANGLO-NORMAN NOBLES, led by Richard de Clare (nicknamed Strongbow), were invited to Ireland by the King of Leinster in 1169. They took control of the major towns and Henry II of England proclaimed himself overlord of Ireland. In succeeding centuries, however, English power declined and the Crown controlled just a small area around Dublin known as the Pale *(see p124)*. Many of the Anglo-Norman barons living outside the Pale opposed English rule just as strongly as did the native Irish clans.

IRELAND IN 1488

☐ *Extent of the Pale*

CARRICKFERGUS CASTLE

The first Anglo-Norman forts were wooden structures, but they soon started to build massive stone castles. Carrickfergus *(see p267)* was begun in the 1180s and by 1250 had acquired a keep and a gatehouse.

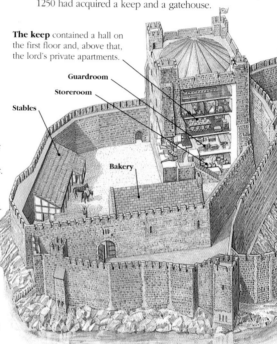

The keep contained a hall on the first floor and, above that, the lord's private apartments.

Guardroom

Storeroom

Stables

Bakery

Marriage of Strongbow
The King of Leinster gave his daughter to Strongbow for helping him regain his lands. Daniel Maclise's painting (1854) emphasizes Anglo-Norman power over the Irish.

Norman Weapons
These bows and arrows, unearthed at Waterford, may be relics of Strongbow's assault on the city in 1170.

TIMELINE

1172 Pope affirms King Henry II of England's lordship over Ireland

1177 John de Courcy's forces invade Ulster

Dermot McMurrough, King of Leinster, who invited Strongbow to come to his aid

1318 Bruce killed in battle

1315 Scots invade Ireland; Edward Bruce crowned king

1200	1250	1300

1169 Strongbow's Anglo-Normans arrive at invitation of exiled King of Leinster, Dermot McMurrough

1224 Dominican order enters Ireland and constructs friaries

1260 Powerful Irish chieftain Brian O'Neill killed at the Battle of Down

1297 First Irish Parliament meets in Dublin

Richard II's Fleet Returning to England in 1399
Richard made two trips to Ireland – in 1394 and 1399. On the first he defeated Art McMurrough, King of Leinster, and other Irish chiefs, but the second was inconclusive.

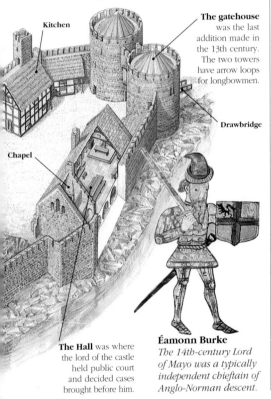

Kitchen

The gatehouse
was the last addition made in the 13th century. The two towers have arrow loops for longbowmen.

Drawbridge

Chapel

The Hall was where the lord of the castle held public court and decided cases brought before him.

Éamonn Burke
The 14th-century Lord of Mayo was a typically independent chieftain of Anglo-Norman descent.

WHERE TO SEE ANGLO-NORMAN IRELAND

The strength of Norman fortifications is best seen in the castles at Carrickfergus, Limerick *(see p183)* and Trim *(p240)* and in Waterford's city walls. Gothic cathedrals that survive include Dublin's Christ Church *(pp78–9)* and St Patrick's *(pp80–81)* and St Canice's *(p136)* in Kilkenny. There are impressive ruins of medieval Cistercian abbeys at Jerpoint and Boyle *(p211)*.

Jerpoint Abbey (p137) *has a well-preserved 15th-century cloister decorated with carvings of curiously elongated figures.*

Waterford's Anglo-Norman *city walls include this sturdy watchtower* (pp138–9).

Great Charter Roll of Waterford (1372) showing portraits of the mayors of four medieval cities

1394 King Richard II lands with army to reassert control; returns five years later but with inconclusive results

1471 8th Earl of Kildare made Lord Deputy of Ireland

1496 Kildare regains Lord Deputy position

1491 Kildare supports Perkin Warbeck, pretender to the English throne

| 1350 | 1400 | 1450 |

1366 Statutes of Kilkenny forbid marriage between Anglo-Normans and Irish

1348 The Black Death: one third of population killed in three years

English forces (left) confront Irish horsemen on Richard II's return expedition

1487 Kildare crowns Lambert Simnel, Edward VI in Dublin

1494 Lord Deputy Edward Poynings forbids Irish Parliament to meet without royal consent

Protestant Conquest

ENGLAND'S BREAK with the Catholic Church, the dissolution of the monasteries and Henry VIII's assumption of the title King of Ireland incensed both the old Anglo-Norman dynasties and resurgent Irish clans such as the O'Neills. Resistance to foreign rule was fierce and it took over 150 years of war to establish the English Protestant ascendancy. Tudor and Stuart monarchs adopted a policy of military persuasion, then Plantation. Oliver Cromwell was even more forceful. Irish hopes were raised when the Catholic James II ascended to the English throne, but he was deposed and fled to Ireland, where he was defeated by William of Orange (William III) in 1690.

Hugh O'Neill, Earl of Tyrone

IRELAND IN 1625

▨ *Main areas of Plantation in the reign of James I*

The first relief ship to reach Londonderry was the *Phoenix*. For three months English ships had been prevented from sailing up the Foyle by a wooden barricade across the river.

James II's army on the east bank of the Foyle attacks the ship.

Battle of the Boyne
This tapestry, from the Bank of Ireland (see p58), shows William of Orange leading his troops against the army of James II in 1690. His victory is still celebrated by Orangemen in Northern Ireland.

Silken Thomas Fitzgerald
Silken Thomas, head of the powerful Kildares, renounced his allegiance to Henry VIII in 1534. He was hanged along with his five uncles in 1537.

The artist's depiction of 17th-century weapons and uniforms is far from accurate.

TIMELINE

Henry VIII	**1541** Henry VIII declared King of Ireland by Irish Parliament	*Sir Thomas Lee, an officer in Elizabeth I's army, dressed in Irish fashion*	**1585** Ireland is mapped and divided into 32 counties	**1592** Trinity College, Dublin founded

1500 — **1525** — **1550** — **1575** — **160(**

1534 Silken Thomas rebels against Henry VIII

1504 8th Earl of Kildare becomes master of Ireland after victory at Knocktoe

1539 Henry VIII dissolves monasteries

1557 Mary I orders first plantations in Offaly and Laois

1582 Desmond rebellion in Munster

1588 Spanish Armada wrecked off west coast

The Siege of Drogheda
Between 1649 and 1652 Cromwell's army avenged attacks on Protestant settlers with ruthless efficiency. Here Cromwell himself directs the gunners bombarding Drogheda.

PLANTATION IRELAND

James I realized that force alone could not stabilize Ireland. The Plantation programme uprooted the native Irish and gave their land to Protestant settlers from England and Scotland. London livery companies organized many of the new settlements. The policy created loyal garrisons who supported the Crown.

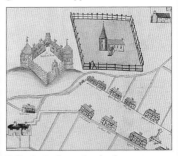

Bellaghy *in County Londonderry was settled by the Vintners Company. This map of the neatly planned town dates from 1622.*

The Walls of Derry have never been breached by any attacker and many of the original 17th-century gates and bastions that withstood the siege of 1689 are still in place *(see pp250–51).*

St George's flag

Ship Quay

Protestants emerge from the besieged city to greet the English relieving force and to engage the enemy.

Loftus Cup
Adam Loftus, Chancellor of Ireland, used his position to enrich his family. In 1593 he had the Great Seal of Ireland melted down and made into this silver-gilt cup.

THE RELIEF OF DERRY *(1689)*
Some 20,000 Protestants were besieged for 105 days in Londonderry by James II's forces. Thousands died from starvation, until relief finally came from English warships. This 18th-century painting by William Sadler II gives a rather fanciful picture of the ending of the siege.

1607 Flight of the Earls: old Irish leaders flee to the Continent; Plantation of Ulster

1632 Important Irish history, *The Annals of the Four Masters,* written by four Franciscan friars from Donegal

Protestant apprentice boys closing the gates of Derry before the siege of 1689

1690 William of Orange defeats James II at Battle of the Boyne; James's army surrenders the following year in Limerick

| 1625 | 1650 | 1675 | 1700 |

1603 Earl of Tyrone ends nine years of war by signing the Treaty of Mellifont

1641 Armed rebellion in Ulster opposes Plantation

1649 Cromwell lands in Dublin; razes Drogheda and Wexford; Catholic landowners transplanted to far west

1688 James II, deposed Catholic king of England, flees to Ireland and raises army

1695 Penal code severely reduces rights of Roman Catholics

1689 Siege of Derry

Georgian Ireland

Lacquer cabinet in Castletown House

THE PROTESTANT ASCENDANCY was a period of great prosperity for the landed gentry, who built grand country houses and furnished them luxuriously. Catholics, meanwhile, were denied even the right to buy land. Towards the end of the century, radicals, influenced by events in America and France, started to demand independence from the English Crown. Prime Minister Henry Grattan tried a parliamentary route; Wolfe Tone and the United Irishmen opted for armed insurrection. Both approaches ultimately failed.

IRELAND IN 1703

Counties where protestants owned over 75 per cent of land

State Bedroom

The saloon, the Casino's main room, was used for formal entertaining. It has a magnificent parquet floor.

Stone lions by Edward Smyth (1749–1812)

The Irish House of Commons
This painting shows Irish leader Henry Grattan addressing the house (see p58). The "Grattan Parliament" lasted from 1782 to 1800, but was then abolished by the Act of Union.

The basement contains the servants' hall, the kitchen, pantry and wine cellar.

Surveyors
The 18th century saw work begin on ambitious projects such as the Grand Canal, new roads and Dublin's network of wide streets and squares.

TIMELINE

Jonathan Swift (1667–1745)

1724 Swift attacks Ireland's penal code in *A Modest Proposal*

1731 Royal Dublin Society founded to encourage agriculture, art and crafts

1738 Death of Ireland's most famous harper, Turlough O'Carolan (see p22)

1710	1720	1730	1740	1750

1713 Jonathan Swift appointed Dean of St Patrick's Cathedral (see p80)

1731 First issue of the *Belfast Newsletter*, the world's oldest continually running newspaper

1742 First performance of Handel's *Messiah* given in Dublin

1751 Dublin's Rotunda Lying-In Hospital is first maternity hospital in the British Isles

Linen Bleaching
Ulster's linen industry flourished thanks to the expertise of Huguenot weavers from France. The woven cloth was spread out in fields or on river banks to bleach it (see p260).

(see p260)

WHERE TO SEE GEORGIAN IRELAND

Dublin preserves many fine Georgian terraces and public buildings such as the Custom House *(see p86)* and the Four Courts *(p91)*. Around Dublin, the grand houses at Castletown *(pp122–3)*, Russborough and Powerscourt *(pp126–7)* are fascinating reminders of the lifestyle of the gentry. Other 18th-century country seats open to the public include Emo Court, Westport House *(pp196–7)* and Castle Coole *(p264)*.

***Emo Court's** façade, with its plain Ionic portico, is by James Gandon, architect of many of Dublin's public buildings (p245).*

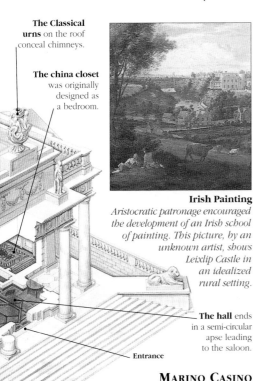

The Classical urns on the roof conceal chimneys.

The china closet was originally designed as a bedroom.

Irish Painting
Aristocratic patronage encouraged the development of an Irish school of painting. This picture, by an unknown artist, shows Leixlip Castle in an idealized rural setting.

The hall ends in a semi-circular apse leading to the saloon.

Entrance

MARINO CASINO

This frivolous summer house was built in the 1760s for the first Earl of Charlemont on his estate just north of Dublin *(see p98)*. Palladian architecture of this kind was popular among the Irish aristocracy, who followed 18th-century English fashions.

***Russborough House** (p124) was built in 1741 by Richard Castle. Elegant niches with Classical busts flank the grand fireplace in the entrance hall.*

1760	1770	1780	1790	
	Guinness Brewery Gate	**1782** Parliament gains greater degree of independence from Westminster	*The Irish Volunteers, a local militia which pressed Parliament for reform*	**1798** Rebellion of Wolfe Tone's United Irishmen quashed

		Custom House	**1791** James Gandon's Custom House built in Dublin	
1759 Arthur Guinness buys the St James's Gate Brewery in Dublin			**1793** Limited emancipation for Irish Catholics	**1795** Orange Order formed by Ulster Protestants

Famine and Emigration

Ration card from Famine period

THE HISTORY of 19th-century Ireland is dominated by the Great Famine of 1845–8, which was caused by the total failure of the potato crop. Although Irish grain was still being exported to England, around one million people died from hunger or disease, with even more fleeing to North America. By 1900, the pre-famine population of eight million had fallen by half. Rural hardship fuelled a campaign for tenants' rights which evolved into demands for independence from Britain. Great strides towards "Home Rule" were made in Parliament by the charismatic politician Charles Stewart Parnell.

IRELAND IN 1851

   Areas where population fell by over 25% during the Famine

The ships that brought the Irish to America were overcrowded and fever-ridden, and known as "coffin ships".

Daniel O'Connell
Known as "The Liberator", O'Connell organized peaceful "monster rallies" of up to a million people in pursuit of Catholic emancipation. He was elected MP for Clare in 1828.

Castle Clinton was used for processing new arrivals to New York prior to the construction of the huge depot on Ellis Island.

The Boycotting of Landlords
In 1880, troops guarded the crops of Captain Boycott, the first notable victim of a campaign to ostracize landlords guilty of evicting tenants. His name later passed into the English language.

TIMELINE

Charles Bianconi's coach service, 1836

1815 First coach service begins in Ireland

1817 Royal Canal is completed

1838 Father Mathew founds temperance crusade – five million Irish take abstinence pledge and whiskey production is reduced by half

1845 Start of Great Famine which lasts for four years

1800	1810	1820	1830	1840

1803 Uprising, led by Robert Emmet, is crushed after feared Napoleonic invasion of England fails to materialize

1828 After a five-year campaign by Daniel O'Connell, Catholic Emancipation Act is passed, giving a limited number of Catholics the right to vote

1800 Act of Union: Ireland legally becomes part of Britain

Father Mathew

Eviction of Irish Farmers
In the late 1870s, agricultural prices plummeted. Starving tenant farmers fell into arrears and were mercilessly evicted. Their plight spawned the Land League, which lobbied successfully for reform.

THE IRISH ABROAD

One result of the Famine was the growth of a strong Irish community in the USA. From the lowest rung of American society, the immigrants rose up the social scale and became rich by Irish Catholic standards. They sent money to causes back home, and as a well-organized lobby group put pressure on the American government to influence British policies in Ireland. A more militant group, Clan na Gael, sent veterans of the American Civil War to fight in the Fenian risings of 1865 and 1867.

New Yorkers *stage a huge St Patrick's Day parade, 17 March 1870.*

The Irish were widely perceived as illiterate peasants in the USA and often met with a hostile reception.

IMMIGRANTS ARRIVE IN NEW YORK
The Irish who survived the journey to America landed at Castle Garden in New York, seen here in a painting by Samuel Waugh (1855). Although mainly country people, most new arrivals settled in Manhattan, often enduring horrific living conditions.

Charles Stewart Parnell
A campaigner for the Land League and Home Rule, Parnell saw his political career ruined in 1890, when he was cited as co-respondent in a divorce case.

	Dublin Exhibition	**1884** Founding of Gaelic Athletic Association, first group to promote Irish traditions	**1892** Second Home Rule Bill is defeated
1853 Dublin Exhibition is opened by Queen Victoria	**1877** Parnell becomes leader of the new Home Rule Party		
1850	**1860**	**1870**	**1880**	**1890**
1867 Irish-Americans return home to fight in a rising led by the Irish Republican Brotherhood, also known as the Fenians		**1881** Parnell is jailed in Kilmainham Gaol, Dublin	**1886** British PM Gladstone sponsors first Home Rule Bill but is defeated by Parliament
1848 Failure of the Young Ireland Uprising – a spontaneous response to insurrections elsewhere in Europe	**1879–82** Land War, led by Michael Davitt's Land League, campaigns for the reform of tenancy laws		

War and Independence

Irish Free State stamp of 1922

IRELAND IN 1922

- Northern Ireland
- Irish Free State

PLANS FOR IRISH HOME RULE were shelved because of World War I; however, the abortive Easter Rising of 1916 inspired new support for the Republican cause. In 1919 an unofficial Irish Parliament was established and a war began against the "occupying" British forces. The Anglo-Irish Treaty of 1921 divided the island in two, granting independence to the Irish Free State, while Northern Ireland remained in the United Kingdom. There followed a civil war between pro-Treaty and anti-Treaty factions in the South.

The Unionist Party
Leader of the campaign against Home Rule was Dublin barrister Edward Carson. In 1913 the Ulster Volunteer Force was formed to demand that six counties in Ulster remain part of the UK.

The 1916 Service Medal, issued to all who fought in the Easter Rising, depicts, on one side, the mythical Irish warrior Cúchulainn.

Sean J Heuston

Thomas McDonough

Major John McBride

William Pearse

Patrick Pearse, a poet, read the Proclamation of the Republic from the steps of the GPO on Easter Monday.

The Black and Tans
Named for their makeshift uniforms, these British troops – mostly demobbed World War I soldiers – carried out savage reprisals against the Irish in 1920–21.

TIMELINE

The Titanic

1913 General strike in Dublin

1912 Belfast-built *Titanic* sinks on her maiden voyage

1918 Sinn Féin wins 73 seats at Westminster; Constance Markievicz elected first woman MP

1916 Easter Rising quashed

1919 First meeting of independent parliament (*Dáil Éire*

1905	1910	1915	192

1905 Sinn Féin (We Ourselves) party founded

1912 Edward Carson rallies Ulster Protestants; solemn covenant to defeat Home Rule signed by 471,414 people

1920 Government of Ireland Act proposes partition of the island

1904 Dublin's Abbey Theatre opens

Despatch bag carried by Constance Markievicz during Easter Rising

1921 Anglo-Irish Treaty signed; de Valera resigns; southern Ireland plunged into civil wa

The General Post Office, Easter 1916
What was supposed to be a national uprising was confined to 2,500 armed insurgents in Dublin. They managed to hold the GPO and other public buildings for five days.

This Mauser rifle, smuggled in from Germany in 1914, was used by rebels in the Rising.

EAMON DE VALERA (1882–1975)

After escaping execution for his part in the Easter Rising, American-born de Valera went on to dominate Irish politics for almost 60 years. The opposition of his party, Sinn Féin, to the Anglo-Irish Treaty of 1921 plunged the new Irish Free State into civil war. After forming a new party, Fianna Fáil, he became Prime Minister (*Taoiseach*) in 1932. De Valera remained in office until 1948, with further terms in the 1950s. Between 1959 and 1973 he was President of Ireland.

Tom Clarke

James Connolly

Joseph Plunkett

Mementos of the Rising at Dublin's Kilmainham Gaol (*see p95*) include this crucifix made by a British soldier from rifle bullets.

THE SHADOW OF THE GUNMAN

KEEP IT FROM YOUR HOME

VOTE FOR CUMANN NA nGAEDHEAL

LEADERS OF THE 1916 RISING

This collage portrait shows 14 leaders of the Easter Rising, who were all court-martialled and shot at Kilmainham Gaol. The brutality of their executions (the badly injured James Connolly was tied to a chair before being shot) changed public opinion of the Rising and guaranteed their status as martyrs.

Election Poster
Cumann na nGaedheal, the pro-Treaty party in the Civil War, won the Free State's first general election in 1923. It merged with other parties in 1933 to form Fine Gael.

1922 Irish Free State inaugurated; Michael Collins shot dead in ambush in Co Cork

Michael Collins (1890–1922), hero of the War of Independence, became chairman of the Irish Free State and Commander-in-Chief of the Army

1932 Fianna Fáil sweeps to victory in general election, and de Valera begins 16-year term as *Taoiseach* (Prime Minister)

1936 IRA proscribed by Free State Government

1939 Éire declares neutrality during World War II

1925	1930	1935

1923 WB Yeats wins Nobel prize for Literature

1926 De Valera quits Sinn Féin; sets up Fianna Fáil (Soldiers of Destiny) party

1925 GB Shaw also receives Nobel prize

1929 Work starts on River Shannon hydro-electric power scheme

1933 Fine Gael (United Ireland) party formed to oppose Fianna Fáil

1937 New constitution declares complete independence from Britain; country's name changes to Éire

Modern Ireland

Mary Robinson, Ireland's first woman President

SINCE JOINING the European Economic Community (now called the European Union) in 1973, the Irish Republic has done much to modernize its traditional rural-based economy. There have been social changes too, and laws prohibiting abortion and divorce have slowly been relaxed. Meanwhile, Northern Ireland has lived through more than 25 years of bombings and shootings. But recent peace agreements have brought new hope to the province, especially since the inauguration in 1998 of the new Northern Ireland Assembly.

1972 Bloody Sunday – British soldiers shoot dead 13 demonstrators in Derry. Northern Ireland Parliament is suspended and direct rule from Westminster imposed

1970 Reverend Ian Paisley, a radical Protestant Unionist, wins the Bannside by-election

1969 Violent clashes between the police and demonstrators in Belfast and Derry. British troops sent to restore order

1956 IRA launches a terrorism campaign along the border with Northern Ireland which lasts until 1962

1967 Northern Ireland Civil Rights Association is set up to fight discrimination against Catholics

NORTHERN IRELAND

1945	1955	1965

REPUBLIC OF IRELAND

1949 New government under John A Costello. Country changes name from Éire to Republic of Ireland and leaves British Commonwealth

1955 Republic of Ireland joins United Nations. Irish troops have played an important role in UN peace-keeping missions around the world ever since

1959 Eamon de Valera resigns as *Taoiseach* (Prime Minister) and is later elected President

1969 Samuel Beckett, seen here rehearsing one of his own plays, is awarded the Nobel prize for literature, but does not go to Stockholm to receive it

1963 John F Kennedy, the first American President of Irish Catholic descent, visits Ireland. He is pictured here with President Eamon de Valera

1947 Statue of Queen Victoria is removed from the courtyard in front of the Irish Parliament in Dublin

1973 Republic of Ireland joins the European Economic Community at same time as the UK. Membership has given the country access to much-needed development grants

74 Power-sharing experiment is ~~~ught down by a devastating ~~~ke, organized by Protestant ~~~rkers. Direct rule is reimposed

1976 Organizers of the Ulster Peace Movement, Mairead Corrigan and Betty Williams, are awarded the Nobel Peace Prize in Oslo

1982 De Lorean car factory in Belfast closes just four years after £17 million investment by British government

1981 Hunger-striker Bobbie Sands dies in Maze Prison

1985 Barry McGuigan beats the Panamanian, Eusebio Pedroza, for world featherweight boxing title

1986 Bitter Loyalist opposition follows the previous year's signing by the British and Irish governments of the Anglo-Irish Agreement

1987 IRA bomb explodes during Enniskillen's Remembrance Day parade, killing 11 people

1991 Peace talks instituted by Westminster between the main political parties of Northern Ireland (except Sinn Féin) and the British and Irish governments

1994 IRA and Unionist cease-fires. Gerry Adams, Sinn Féin leader, allowed to speak on British radio and television

1995 For the first time in 25 years, there are no troops on daylight patrols in Northern Ireland

1998 The Good Friday Agreement sets out proposed framework for self-government in Northern Ireland

NORTHERN IRELAND

| 1975 | 1985 | 1995 |

REPUBLIC OF IRELAND

1988 Dublin's millennium is celebrated, boosting the city's image

1991 Mary Robinson becomes first female President of the Republic, succeeded by Mary McAleese in 1998

1992 In a referendum, 62 per cent of the Irish vote in favour of allowing pregnant women to seek an abortion abroad. A vote in favour of divorce follows in 1995

1979 Pope John Paul II visits Ireland and celebrates Mass in Dublin's Phoenix Park, in front of more than a million people

1994 Republic of Ireland football team reaches quarterfinals of World Cup in the USA. Here, Ray Houghton is congratulated on scoring the winning goal against Italy

1999 Ireland joins the single European currency on 1 January

1985 Irish pop singer Bob Geldof organizes Live Aid concerts in London and Philadelphia; £40 million is raised for African famine relief

1987 Dubliner Steven Roche wins the Tour de France, Giro d'Italia and World Championship in one incredible season

IRELAND THROUGH THE YEAR

POPULAR MONTHS for visiting Ireland are July and August, though Belfast tends to close down in July for the marching season. June and September can be pleasant but never count on the weather, for Ireland's lush beauty is the product of a wet climate. Most tourist sights are open from Easter to September but have restricted opening hours or close in the low season. During spring and summer, festivals are held in honour of everything from food to religion. A common thread is music, and few festivities are complete without musical accompaniment. Ireland is at its best when it has something to celebrate, so is an inspired choice for Christmas and New Year. Look out for the word *fleadh* (festival) on your travels but remember, too, that the Irish are a spontaneous people: festivities can spring from the air, or from a tune on a fiddle.

Ladies' Day at Dublin Horse Show

Dublin's annual parade to celebrate St Patrick's Day (17 March)

SPRING

ST PATRICK'S DAY is often said to mark the beginning of the tourist season. Later, the spring bank holiday weekend in May, when accommodation is in short supply, is celebrated with music in most places. After the quiet winter months, festivals and events start to become more common.

MARCH

St Patrick's Day *(17 Mar)*. Parades and pilgrimages held at Downpatrick, Armagh, Dublin, Cork, Limerick and many other places.

Jameson International Dublin Film Festival *(Mar)*. International film festival.

Horse Ploughing Match and Heavy Horse Show, Ballycastle *(17 Mar, see p258)*. This popular annual competition is more than 100 years old.

A St Patrick's Day float advertising Guinness

APRIL

Feis Ceoil, Dublin *(end Mar or early Apr)*. A classical music festival held at many different venues throughout the city.

Pan Celtic Festival, Tralee *(mid-Apr, see p148)*. A lively celebration of Celtic culture, with music, dance and song.

Cork Choral Festival *(late Apr–May, see pp166–7)*.

MAY

Belfast Civic Festival and Lord Mayor's Show *(mid-May, see pp268–71)*. Street parade with bands and floats.

Royal Ulster Agriculture Society Show, Belfast *(mid-May)*. A three-day show with diverse events ranging from sheep-shearing competitions to fashion shows.

"A Taste of Baltimore" Shellfish Festival *(end May, see p162)*.

Fleadh Nua, Ennis, *end May, see p181)*. Four days of traditional Irish music, songs and dance.

SUMMER

FOR THE VISITOR, summer represents the height of the festive calendar. This is the busiest time of year for organized events, from music and arts festivals to lively local race meetings, summer schools and matchmaking festivals. Book accommodation if your plans include a popular festival.

Beach races at Laytown (June)

JUNE

Laytown Beach Races, Co Meath *(late May or early Jun)*. Horse races on the sand.

County Wicklow Garden Festival *(May–Jul)*. Held at private and public gardens around the county, including Powerscourt *(see pp126–7)*.

National Country Fair, Birr Castle Demesne, Co Offaly *(early Jun, see p245)*. One of Ireland's most popular country fairs.

Women's Mini Marathon, Dublin City *(early Jun)*.

Bloomsday, Dublin *(16 Jun)*. Lectures, pub talks, readings, dramatizations and walks to celebrate James Joyce's greatest novel, *Ulysses*.

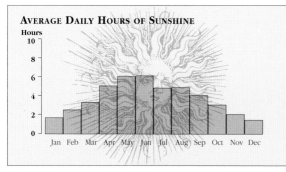

AVERAGE DAILY HOURS OF SUNSHINE

Sunshine Chart
The chart gives figures for Dublin, though conditions are similar around the country. The Southeast enjoys more sunshine hours than any other part of Ireland, while Northern Ireland receives marginally fewer hours of sun than the Republic.

Scurlogstown Olympiad Celtic Festival, Trim *(mid-Jun, see p240)*. Traditional Irish music, dance, fair and selection of a festival queen.
Music in Great Irish Houses *(first two weeks)*. Classical music recitals in grand settings at various venues.
Castle Ward Opera, Strangford *(all month, see p276)*. Opera festival in the grounds of 18th-century stately home.
County Wexford Strawberry Fair, Enniscorthy *(end Jun–early Jul, see p141)*. Includes a craft fair, music, street theatre and, of course, strawberries.

JULY

Battle of the Boyne Day *(12 Jul, see p236)*. Members of the Orange Order march in towns across Northern Ireland to celebrate the Protestants' landmark victory over King James II's Catholic army in 1690.
Galway Arts Festival *(third & fourth weeks, see pp202–3)*. Processions, concerts, street theatre, children's shows and many other events in the medieval city centre. Followed

Traditional sailing craft in the Cruinniú na mBád at Kinvarra (August)

immediately by Galway's popular five-day race meeting.
Mary from Dungloe International Festival, Dungloe *(last week, see p220)*. Dancing, music and selection of "Mary", the beauty queen.
Lughnasa Fair, Carrickfergus Castle *(end Jul, see p267)*. A popular medieval-style fair.
Ballyshannon International Folk Festival *(end Jul or early Aug, see p223)*. Three days of traditional Irish music.
O'Carolan Harp and Traditional Music Festival, Keadue, Co Roscommon *(end Jul or early Aug)*. Traditional music and dance celebrations.

AUGUST

Stradbally Steam-engine Rally, Co Laois *(early Aug)*. Many types of steam-engine join this rally.

Letterkenny Folk Festival, Co Donegal *(early Aug, see p219)*. A week of celebration.
Dublin Horse Show *(first or second week)*. A premier showjumping competition and social event.
Puck Fair, Killorglin, Co Kerry *(mid-Aug, see p157)*. A wild goat is crowned "king" at this two-day-long traditional festival.
Blessing of the Sea *(second or third Sunday)*. Held in seaside towns all over Ireland.
Oul' Lammas Fair, Ballycastle *(mid–end Aug, see p258)*. A popular fair that is particularly famous for its edible seaweed.
Kilkenny Arts Week *(middle of the month, see pp134–6)*. A major arts festival including poetry, film and crafts.
Rose of Tralee Festival, *(end Aug, see p148)*. Bands, processions, dancing and selection of the "Rose".
Cruinniú na mBád, Kinvarra *(end Aug, see pp203–4)*. Various types of traditional sailing craft take part in this "gathering of the boats".

Orangemen parading on Battle of the Boyne Day

Steam-engine at Stradbally Rally (August)

AVERAGE MONTHLY RAINFALL

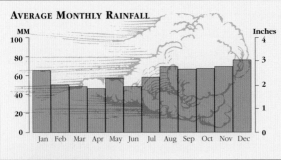

MM												Inches

Jan Feb Mar Apr May Jun Jul Aug Sep Oct Nov Dec

Rainfall Chart
*Ireland is one of the
wettest countries in
Europe, with rainfall
distributed evenly
through the year – the
figures displayed here
are for Dublin. The
West has the heaviest
annual rainfall, while
the Southeast receives
marginally less rain
than other regions.*

Galway Oyster Festival (September)

AUTUMN

O YSTERS AND OPERA are the
two big events in autumn.
There are also festivals devoted
to jazz, film and music. The
October bank holiday weekend is celebrated with music
in many towns; though it is
low season, it can be difficult
to find accommodation.

SEPTEMBER

Heritage Week *(early Sep).*
Special events countrywide.
All-Ireland Hurling Final,
Croke Park, Dublin *(first or
second Sunday, see p27).*

**Lisdoonvarna Match-
making Festival** *(all
month and first week of
Oct, see p180).* Singles
gather for traditional
music and dance.
**Waterford Interna-
tional Festival of
Light Opera** *(mid-Sep
–early Oct, see p329).*
Musicals and operettas
at the Theatre Royal.
All-Ireland Football Final,
Croke Park, Dublin *(3rd
Sunday, see p27).* Gaelic
football final.
Galway Oyster Festival *(end
Sep, see pp202–3).* Oyster
tastings at different venues.

OCTOBER

Octoberfest, London-
derry *(all month, see
pp250–51).* Dance,
poetry, film, comedy,
theatre and music.
Cork Film Festival
*(early Oct, see
pp166–7).* Irish and
international films.
**Kinsale International
Festival of Fine Food** *(early
Oct, see pp164–5).* Superb

All-Ireland Hurling at Croke Park, Dublin

food served in restaurants
hotels and pubs of Kinsale.
Ballinasloe Fair, Co Galway
(first week). One of Europe's
oldest horse fairs, staged amid
lively street entertainment.
Dublin Theatre Festival *(first
two weeks).* Features works
by both Irish and foreign
playwrights.
**Wexford Opera
Festival** *(last two
weeks in Oct, see
p329).* A festival of
lesser known operas.
**Hallowe'en (Sham-
hana)** *(31 Oct).* An
occasion celebrated
all over the country.
Cork Jazz Festival
(end Oct, see pp166–7).
An extremely popular festival,
with music throughout the city.

**Horse and trap at
Lisdoonvarna fair**

NOVEMBER

**Sligo International Choral
Festival** *(early Nov, see p226).*
Choirs from around the world
in concert and competition.
Belfast Festival at Queen's,
Queen's University *(end Oct
to early Nov, see pp268–71).*
Arts festival featuring drama,
ballet, cinema and all types of
music from classical to jazz.
Éigse Sliabh Rua, Slieverue,
Co Kilkenny *(mid Nov).*
Festival of local history and
music with special guests and
interesting talks.

Traditional horse fair at Ballinasloe in County Galway (October)

Average Monthly Temperature

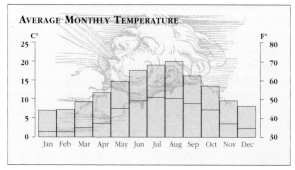

Temperature Chart
This chart gives the average minimum and maximum temperatures for the city of Dublin. Winter is mild throughout Ireland, except in the high mountain ranges, while the warmest summer temperatures are in the Southeast.

Winter

ALTHOUGH a quiet time for festivals, there's a range of entertainment including musical and theatrical events. Christmas is the busiest social period and there are plenty of informal celebrations. There is also a wide choice of National Hunt race meetings *(see p26)*.

December

Pantomime Season *(Dec–Jan)*. Traditional pantomime performed at many theatres throughout Ireland.
Leopardstown Races *(26 Dec, see p121)*. The biggest meeting held on this traditional day for racing. There are other fixtures at Limerick and Down Royal.
St Stephen's Day *(26 Dec)*. Catholic boys traditionally dress up as Wren boys (chimney sweeps with blackened faces) and sing hymns to raise money for charitable causes.

Young boys dressed up as Wren boys on St Stephen's Day

January

Salmon and Sea Trout Season *(1 Jan–end Sep)*. Start of the season for one of the most popular pastimes in Ireland.

February

Dublin Film Festival *(end Feb–early Mar)*. International films at various venues.
Belfast Music Festival *(end Feb–mid-Mar)*. Young people take part in music (and speech and drama) competitions.
Six Nations Rugby Tournament, Lansdowne Road, Dublin *(varying Saturdays Feb–Apr, see p26)*.

Public Holidays

New Year's Day (1 Jan)
St Patrick's Day (17 Mar)
Good Friday
Easter Monday
May Day (first Mon in May)
Spring Bank Holiday (Northern Ireland: last Mon in May)
June Bank Holiday (Republic: first Mon in Jun)
Battle of the Boyne Day (Northern Ireland: 12 Jul)
August Bank Holiday (first Mon in Aug)
Summer Bank Holiday (Northern Ireland: last Mon in Aug)
October Bank Holiday (last Mon in Oct)
Christmas Day (25 Dec)
St Stephen's Day (Republic: 26 Dec)
Boxing Day (Northern Ireland: 26 Dec)

Glendalough *(see pp132–3)* in the snow

DUBLIN AREA BY AREA

Dublin at a Glance

IRELAND'S CAPITAL has a wealth of attractions, most within walking distance of each other. For the purpose of this guide, central Dublin has been divided into three sections: *Southeast Dublin*, heart of the modern city and home to the prestigious Trinity College; *Southwest Dublin*, site of the old city around Dublin Castle; and *North of the Liffey*, the area around the imposing O'Connell Street. The map references given for sights in the city refer to the *Dublin Street Finder* on pages 110–111.

Christ Church Cathedral
was built by Dublin's Anglo-Norman conquerors between 1172 and 1220. It stands on high ground above the River Liffey. Much of the cathedral's present appearance is due to restoration carried out in the 1870s. (See pp78–9.)

NORTH OF THE LIFFEY
Pages 82–91

SOUTHWEST DUBLIN
Pages 70–81

Dublin Castle *stands in the heart of old Dublin. St Patrick's Hall is part of the suite of luxury State Apartments housed on the upper floors on the south side of the castle. Today, these rooms are used for functions of national importance such as presidential inaugurations. (See pp74–5.)*

St Patrick's Cathedral
has a spectacular choir featuring banners and stalls decorated with the insignia of the Knights of St Patrick. The cathedral also holds Ireland's largest and most powerful organ, as well as memorials to Dean Jonathan Swift and prominent Anglo-Irish families. (See pp80–81.)

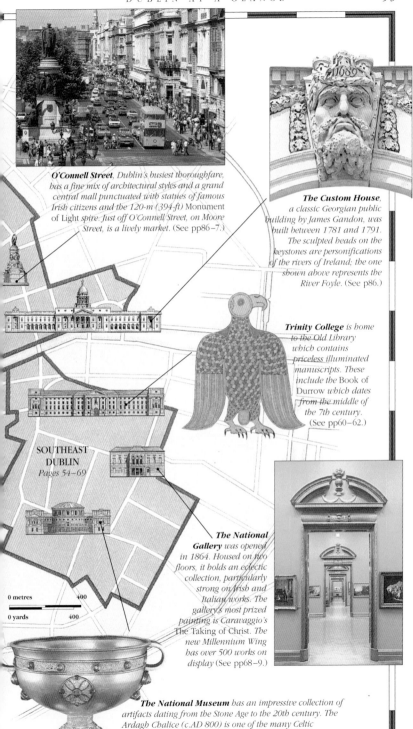

O'Connell Street, Dublin's busiest thoroughfare, has a fine mix of architectural styles and a grand central mall punctuated with statues of famous Irish citizens and the 120-m (394-ft) Monument of Light spire. Just off O'Connell Street, on Moore Street, is a lively market. (See pp86–7.)

The Custom House, a classic Georgian public building by James Gandon, was built between 1781 and 1791. The sculpted heads on the keystones are personifications of the rivers of Ireland; the one shown above represents the River Foyle. (See p86.)

Trinity College is home to the Old Library which contains priceless illuminated manuscripts. These include the Book of Durrow which dates from the middle of the 7th century. (See pp60–62.)

SOUTHEAST
DUBLIN
Pages 54–69

The National Gallery was opened in 1864. Housed on two floors, it holds an eclectic collection, particularly strong on Irish and Italian works. The gallery's most prized painting is Caravaggio's The Taking of Christ. The new Millennium Wing has over 500 works on display (See pp68–9.)

0 metres   400

0 yards   400

The National Museum has an impressive collection of artifacts dating from the Stone Age to the 20th century. The Ardagh Chalice (c.AD 800) is one of the many Celtic Christian treasures on display. (See pp64–5.)

SOUTHEAST DUBLIN

ESPITE ITS location close to the old walled city, this part of Dublin remained virtually undeveloped until the founding of Trinity College in 1592. Even then, it was almost a hundred years before the ancient common land further south was enclosed to create St Stephen's Green, a spacious city park.

The mid-18th century saw the beginning of a construction boom in the area. During this time, magnificent public buildings such as the Old Library at Trinity College, Leinster House and the Bank of Ireland were built. However, the most conspicuous reminders of Georgian Dublin are the beautiful squares and terraces around

Georgian doorknocker in Merrion Square

Merrion Square. Many of these buildings still have their original features, including doorknockers, fanlights and wrought-iron balconies.

Today, Southeast Dublin is very much the tourist heart of the city: few visitors can resist the lively atmosphere and attractive shops of Grafton Street. The area is also home to much of Ireland's cultural heritage. The National Gallery has a good collection of Irish and European paintings while the National Museum has superb displays of Irish Bronze Age gold and early Christian treasures. Nearby, the fascinating Natural History Museum has preserved its wonderful Victorian interior.

SIGHTS AT A GLANCE

Museums, Libraries and Galleries
National Gallery pp68–9 ⑪
National Library ⑧
National Museum pp64–5 ⑦
Natural History Museum ⑩
Royal Hibernian Academy ⑬

Historic Buildings
Bank of Ireland ①
Leinster House ⑨
Mansion House ⑤
Trinity College pp60–61 ②

Historic Streets
Fitzwilliam Square ⑭
Grafton Street ③
Merrion Square ⑫

Churches
St Ann's Church ⑥

Parks and Gardens
St Stephen's Green ④

KEY

◼ Street-by-Street map
See pp56–7

🚉 Railway station

DART station

🚊 Luas stop

🅿 Parking

ℹ Tourist information

0 metres 250
0 yards 250

◁ **Marble bust of Jonathan Swift in the Old Library, Trinity College**

Street-by-Street: Southeast Dublin

THE AREA AROUND COLLEGE GREEN, dominated by the
façades of the Bank of Ireland and Trinity College, is
very much the heart of Dublin. The alleys and malls
cutting across busy pedestrianized Grafton Street boast
many of Dublin's better shops, hotels and restaurants.
Just off Kildare Street are the Irish Parliament, the
National Library and the National Museum. To escape the
city bustle many head for sanctuary in St Stephen's
Green, which is overlooked by fine Georgian buildings.

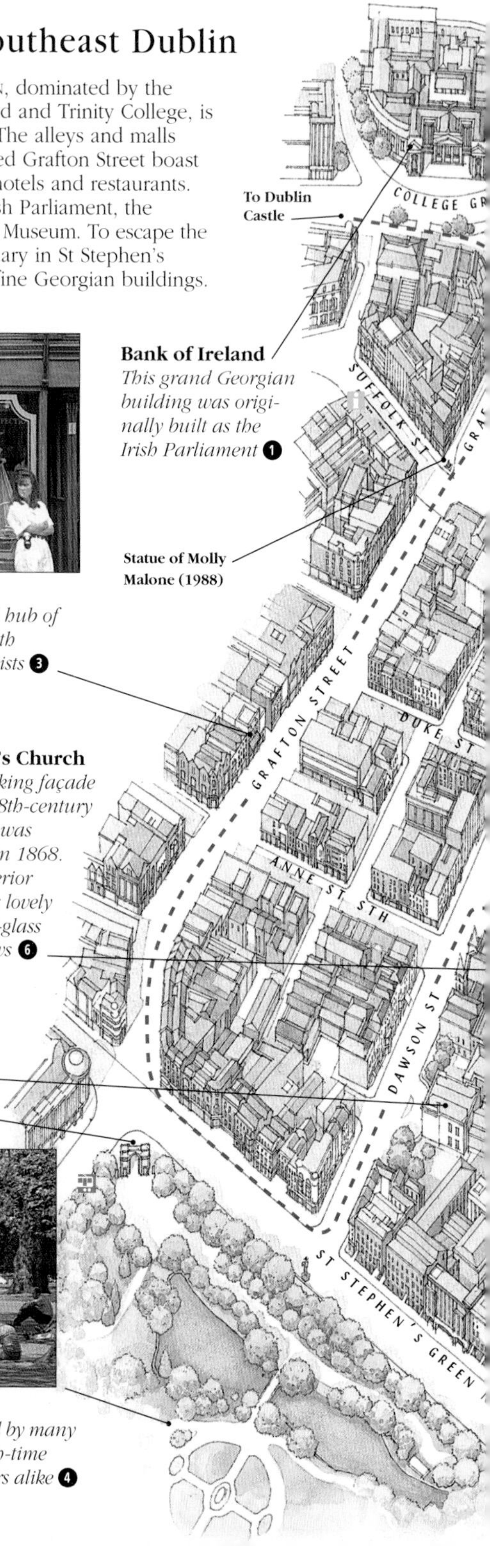

Grafton Street
*Bewley's Oriental Café is the social hub of
this busy pedestrian street, alive with
talented buskers and pavement artists* ❸

**To Dublin
Castle**

Bank of Ireland
*This grand Georgian
building was origi-
nally built as the
Irish Parliament* ❶

**Statue of Molly
Malone (1988)**

St Ann's Church
*The striking façade
of the 18th-century
church was
added in 1868.
The interior
features lovely
stained-glass
windows* ❻

Mansion House
*This has been the official
residence of Dublin's Lord
Mayor since 1715* ❺

Fusiliers' Arch (1907)

★ St Stephen's Green
*The relaxing city park is surrounded by many
grand buildings. In summer, lunch-time
concerts attract tourists and workers alike* ❹

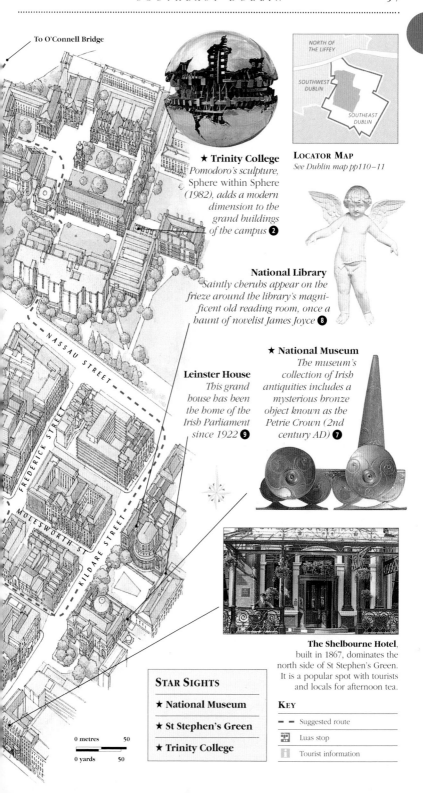

To O'Connell Bridge

NORTH OF
THE LIFFEY

SOUTHWEST
DUBLIN

SOUTHEAST
DUBLIN

★ **Trinity College**
Pomodoro's sculpture,
Sphere within Sphere
*(1982), adds a modern
dimension to the
grand buildings
of the campus* ❷

LOCATOR MAP
See Dublin map pp110–11

National Library
*Saintly cherubs appear on the
frieze around the library's magnificent old reading room, once a
haunt of novelist James Joyce* ❽

★ **National Museum**
*The museum's
collection of Irish
antiquities includes a
mysterious bronze
object known as the
Petrie Crown (2nd
century AD)* ❼

Leinster House
*This grand
house has been
the home of the
Irish Parliament
since 1922* ❾

NASSAU STREET

FREDERICK STREET

MOLESWORTH ST

KILDARE STREET

The Shelbourne Hotel,
built in 1867, dominates the
north side of St Stephen's Green.
It is a popular spot with tourists
and locals for afternoon tea.

0 metres 50

0 yards 50

STAR SIGHTS

★ **National Museum**

★ **St Stephen's Green**

★ **Trinity College**

KEY

– – Suggested route

Luas stop

Tourist information

Original chamber of the Irish House of Lords at the Bank of Ireland

Bank of Ireland ❶

2 College Green. **Map** D3. ☏ *671 2261.* ☐ *10am–4pm Tue, Wed & Fri, 10am–5pm Thu.* ● *Mon & public hols.* **House of Lords** ☒ *10:30am, 11:30am & 1:45pm Tue or by appt.*

T HE PRESTIGIOUS offices of the Bank of Ireland began life as the first purpose-built parliament house in Europe. The original central section was started by Irish architect Edward Lovett Pearce and completed in 1739 after his death. Sadly, Pearce's masterpiece, the great octagonal chamber of the House of Commons *(see p38)*, was destroyed by fire in 1792. The House of Lords, however, remains gloriously intact. Attendants lead tours that point out the coffered ceiling and oak panelling. There are also huge tapestries of the *Battle of the Boyne* and the *Siege of Londonderry*, and a splendid 1,233-piece crystal chandelier dating from 1788.

The east portico was added by architect James Gandon in 1785. Further additions to the building were made around 1797.

After the dissolution of the Irish Parliament in 1800, the Bank of Ireland bought the building. The present structure was then completed in 1808 with the transformation of the former lobby of the House of Commons into a magnificent cash office and the addition of a curving screen wall and the Foster Place annexe.

At the front of the bank on College Green – common grazing land in the 17th century – is a statue (1879) by John Foley of Henry Grattan *(see p38)*, the most formidable leader of the old parliament.

Trinity College ❷

See pp60–61.

Grafton Street ❸

Map D4.

T HE SPINE OF DUBLIN'S most popular and stylish shopping district runs south from Trinity College to the glass St Stephen's Green Shopping Centre. At the junction with Nassau Street is a statue by Jean Rynhart of *Molly Malone* (1988), the celebrated street trader from the traditional song "Molly Malone". This busy pedestrianized strip, characterized by energetic buskers and talented street

Bronze statue of *Molly Malone* on Grafton Street

theatre artists, boasts Brown Thomas, one of Dublin's finest department stores *(see p325)*. However, the street's most famous landmark is Bewley's Oriental Café at No. 78 *(see p306)*. Although not the oldest branch of this 150-year-old Dublin institution, this is Bewley's most popular location. It stands on the site of Samuel Whyte's school, whose illustrious roll included Robert Emmet *(see p75)*, leader of the 1803 Rebellion, and the Duke of Wellington.

Despite the removal of the old wooden pews, the café retains its Victorian ambience, especially in the James Joyce Room on the first floor.

St Stephen's Green ❹

Map D5. ☐ *daylight hours.* **Newman House** *85–86 St Stephen's Green.* ☏ *706 7422.* ☐ *Jun–Aug: noon–5pm Tue–Fri, 2–5pm Sat, 11am–2pm Sun (Sep–May: by appointment).* ● *public hols.* ◪ ☒ *obligatory.*

Royal College of Surgeons, which overlooks St Stephen's Green

O RIGINALLY one of three ancient commons in the old city, St Stephen's Green was enclosed in 1664. The 9-ha (22-acre) green was laid out in its present form in 1880, using a grant given by Lord Ardilaun, a member of the Guinness family. Landscaped with flowerbeds, trees, a fountain and a lake, the green is dotted with memorials to eminent Dubliners, including Ardilaun himself. There is a bust of James Joyce *(see p88)*, and a memorial by Henry Moore (1967) dedicated to WB Yeats *(see pp224–5)*. At

Dubliners relaxing by the lake in St Stephen's Green

the Merrion Row corner stands a massive monument (1967) by Edward Delaney to 18th-century nationalist leader Wolfe Tone – it is known locally as "Tonehenge". The 1887 bandstand is still the focal point for free daytime concerts in summer.

The imposing Royal College of Surgeons stands on the west side. Built in 1806, it was commandeered by rebel troops under Countess Constance Markievicz in the 1916 Rising *(see pp42–3)* and its columns still bear the marks of bullets from the fighting.

The busiest side of the Green is the north, known during the 19th century as the Beaux' Walk and still home to several gentlemen's clubs. The most prominent building is the venerable Shelbourne Hotel *(see p287)*. Dating back to 1867, its entrance is adorned by statues of Nubian princesses and attendant slaves. It is well worth popping in for a look at the chandeliered foyer and for afternoon tea in the Lord Mayor's Lounge.

Situated on the south side is Newman House, home of the Catholic University of Ireland (now part of University College). Opened in 1854, its first rector was English theologian John Henry Newman. Famous past pupils include Patrick Pearse, a leader of the 1916 Rising, former Taoiseach Eamon de Valera *(see p43)* and author James Joyce.

Tours reveal some of the best Georgian interior decor to survive in the city. The walls and ceilings of the Apollo Room and Saloon at No. 85 are festooned with intricate Baroque stuccowork (1739) by the Swiss brothers Paolo and Filippo Francini. The Bishops' Room at No. 86 is decorated with heavy 19th-century furniture.

The small University Church (1856) next door has a colourful, richly marbled Byzantine interior. Also on the south side of St Stephen's Green is Iveagh House, a town house once owned by the Guinness family and now the Department of Foreign Affairs.

Mansion House ❺

Dawson St. **Map** E4. ● *to the public.*

Set back from Dawson Street by a neat cobbled forecourt, the Mansion House is an attractive Queen Anne-style building. It was built in 1710 for the aristocrat Joshua Dawson, after whom the street is named. The Dublin Corporation bought it from him five years later as the official residence of the city's Lord Mayor. A grey stucco façade was added in Victorian times.

The Dáil Éireann *(see p63)*, which adopted the Declaration of Independence, first met here on 21 January 1919. The Fado Restaurant *(see p306)* in the old supper room is in period style.

St Ann's Church ❻

Dawson St. **Map** E4. 〖 *676 7727.* ◐ *10am–4pm Mon–Fri (also for Sun service, phone to check).*

Founded in 1707, St Ann's striking Romanesque façade was added in 1868. Inside are colourful stained-glass windows, dating from the mid-19th century. The church has a long tradition of charity work: in 1723 Lord Newton left a bequest to buy bread for the poor. The original shelf for the bread still stands next to the altar.

Famous past parishioners include Wolfe Tone *(see p39)*, who was married here in 1785, Douglas Hyde *(see p43)* and Bram Stoker (1847–1912), author of *Dracula*.

Detail of window depicting Faith, Hope and Charity, St Ann's Church

Trinity College

Trinity College coat of arms

Trinity college was founded in 1592 by Queen Elizabeth I on the site of an Augustinian monastery. Originally a Protestant college, it only began to take Catholics in numbers after 1970, when the Catholic Church relaxed its opposition to their attending. Among Trinity's many famous students were playwrights Oliver Goldsmith and Samuel Beckett, and political writer Edmund Burke. The college's lawns and cobbled quads provide a pleasant haven in the heart of the city. The major attractions are the Old Library and the *Book of Kells*, housed in the Treasury.

★ Campanile
The 30-m (98-ft) bell tower was built in 1853 by Sir Charles Lanyon, architect of Queen's University, Belfast (see p270).

Reclining Connected Forms (1969) by Henry Moore

Dining Hall (1761)

Chapel *(1798)*
This was the first university chapel in the Republic to accept all denominations. The painted window above the altar is from 1867.

Parliament Square

Statue of Edmund Burke (1868) by John Foley

Main entrance

Statue of Oliver Goldsmith (1864) by John Foley

SAMUEL BECKETT (1906–89)

Nobel prizewinner Samuel Beckett was born at Foxrock, south of Dublin. In 1923 he entered Trinity, and later graduated with a first in modern languages and a gold medal. He was also a keen member of the college cricket team. Forsaking Ireland, Beckett moved to France in the early 1930s. Many of his major works such as *Waiting for Godot* (1951) were written first in French, and later translated, by Beckett, into English.

Provost's House (c. 1760)

Examination Hall
Completed in 1791 to a design by Sir William Chambers, the hall features a gilded oak chandelier and ornate ceilings by Michael Stapleton.

Library Square
The red-brick building (known as the Rubrics) on the east side of Library Square was built around 1700 and is the oldest surviving part of the college.

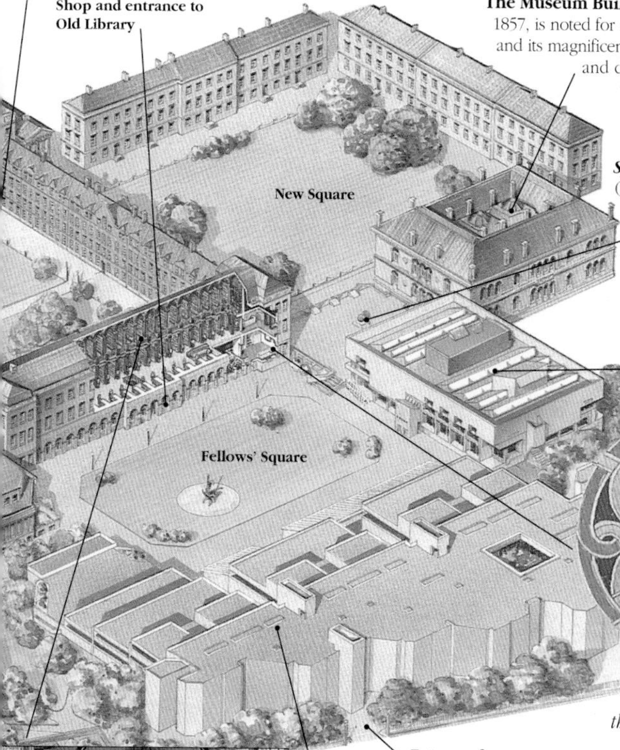

Shop and entrance to Old Library

The Museum Building, completed in 1857, is noted for its Venetian exterior, and its magnificent multicoloured hall and double-domed roof.

New Square

Sphere within Sphere *(1982) was given to the college by its sculptor Arnaldo Pomodoro.*

Berkeley Library Building by Paul Koralek (1967)

Fellows' Square

Entrance from Nassau Street

The Douglas Hyde Gallery was built in the 1970s to house temporary art exhibitions.

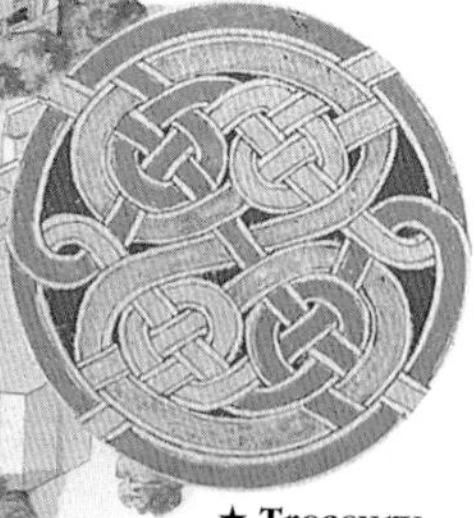

★ **Treasury**
This detail is from the Book of Durrow, *one of the other magnificent illuminated manuscripts housed in the Treasury along with the celebrated* Book of Kells *(see p62).*

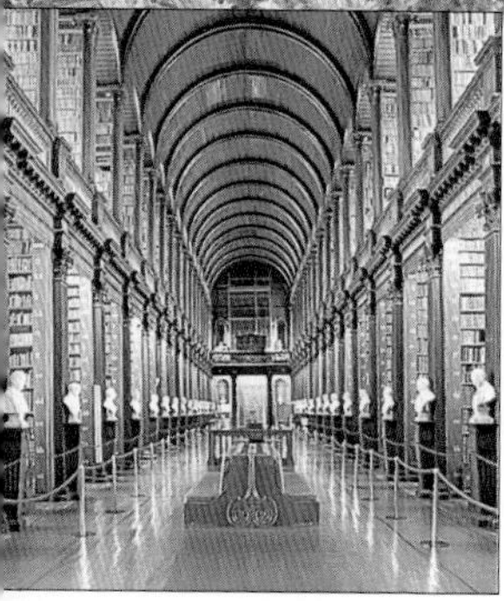

★ **Old Library** *(1732)*
The spectacular Long Room measures 64 m (210 ft) from end to end. It houses 200,000 antiquarian texts, marble busts of scholars and the oldest surviving harp in Ireland.

STAR FEATURES

★ **Campanile**

★ **Old Library**

★ **Treasury**

The Book of Kells

T HE MOST RICHLY decorated of Ireland's medieval illuminated manuscripts, the *Book of Kells* may have been the work of monks from Iona, who fled to Kells *(see p233)* in AD 806 after a Viking raid. The book, which was moved to Trinity College *(see p60–61)* in the 17th century, contains the four gospels in Latin. The scribes who copied the texts also embellished their calligraphy with intricate interlacing spirals as well as human figures and animals. Some of the dyes used were imported from as far as the Middle East.

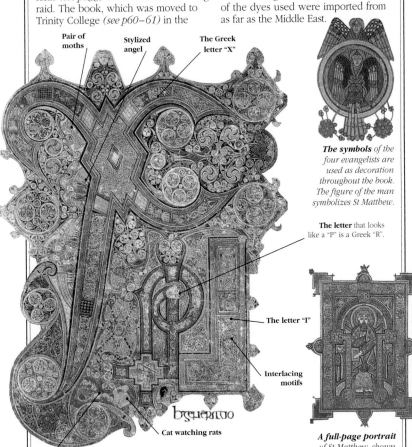

Pair of moths

Stylized angel

The Greek letter "X"

The letter that looks like a "P" is a Greek "R".

The letter "I"

Interlacing motifs

Cat watching rats

The symbols of the four evangelists are used as decoration throughout the book. The figure of the man symbolizes St Matthew.

A full-page portrait of St Matthew, shown standing barefoot in front of a throne, precedes the opening words of his gospel.

Rats eating bread could be a reference to sinners taking Holy Communion. The symbolism of the animals and people decorating the manuscript is often hard to interpret.

MONOGRAM PAGE

This, the most elaborate page of the book, contains the first three words of St Matthew's account of the birth of Christ. The first word "XRI" is an abbreviation of "Christi".

The text is in a beautifully rounded Celtic script with brightly ornamented initial letters. Animal and human forms are often used to decorate the end of a line.

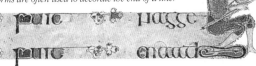

The magnificent domed Reading Room on the first floor of the National Library

National Museum ⑦

See pp64–5.

National Library ⑧

Kildare St. **Map** E4. ☎ *603 0200.*
☐ *10am–9pm Mon–Wed, 10am–5pm Thu & Fri, 10am–1pm Sat.*
● *public hols.*

DESIGNED BY Sir Thomas Deane, the National Library was opened in 1890. It was built to house the collection of the Royal Dublin Society, which was formed in 1731 to promote the arts and sciences and improve conditions for the poor. The Library contains first editions of every major Irish writer and a copy of almost every book ever published in Ireland. The list of distinguished Irish writers is well known and all are represented here. There is a huge collection of old maps, papers, and manuscripts by such names as playwright George Bernard Shaw and politician and liberator Daniel O'Connell *(see p40).*

The first-floor Reading Room (where Joyce sited the literary debate in *Ulysses*) has well-worn desks and green-shaded lamps. Simply ask an attendant for a visitor's pass. There is also a small genealogy exhibit; a more extensive display,

along with details on how to trace family trees, can be found at the Heraldic Museum in the Genealogical Office a few doors down at Nos. 2 and 3 Kildare Street.

Leinster House ⑨

Kildare St. **Map** E4. ☎ *618 3000.*
☐ *groups by appt only.*
◪ *phone for details.*

THIS STATELY MANSION houses the Dáil and the Seanad – the two chambers of the Irish Parliament. It was originally built for the Duke of Leinster in 1745. Designed by German-born architect Richard Castle, the Kildare Street façade resembles that of a large town house. However, the rear, looking on to Merrion Square, has the air of a country estate complete with sweeping lawns. The Royal Dublin Society bought the building in 1815. The government obtained a part of it in 1922 for parliamentary use and bought the entire building two years later.

To arrange a guided tour of the main rooms, including the Seanad chamber with its heavily ornamented ceiling, phone before you visit.

THE IRISH PARLIAMENT

The Irish Free State, forerunner of the Republic of Ireland, was inaugurated in 1922 *(see p42)*, although an unofficial Irish parliament, the Dáil, had already been in existence since 1919. Today, parliament is made up of two houses: the Dáil (House of Representatives) and Seanad Éireann (the Senate). The Prime Minister is the Taoiseach and the deputy, the Tánaiste. The Dáil's 166 representatives – Teachta Dála, known as TDs – are elected by proportional representation. The 60-strong Seanad is appointed by various individuals and authorities, including the Taoiseach and the University of Dublin.

Opening of the first parliament of the Irish Free State in 1922

National Museum ⑦

T<small>HE</small> <small>NATIONAL MUSEUM OF IRELAND</small> was built
in the 1880s to the design of Sir Thomas
Deane. Its splendid domed rotunda features
marble pillars and a zodiac mosaic floor.
The Treasury houses priceless items such as
the Broighter gold boat *(see p31)*, while *Ór –
Ireland's Gold*, an exhibition of Ireland's
Bronze Age gold, has fine jewellery such as
the Gleninsheen Gorget *(see pp30–31)*. Many
collections have now moved to the annexe
of the museum at Collins Barracks *(see p90)*.

Egyptian Mummy
*This mummy of the lady Tentdinebu
is thought to date back to c.945–716
BC. Covered in brilliant colours, it is
part of the stunning
Egyptian collection.*

★ Ór – Ireland's Gold
*This is one of the most extensive
collections of Bronze Age gold in
Western Europe. This gold lunula
(c.1800 BC) is one of many pieces
of fine jewellery in the exhibition.*

KEY TO FLOORPLAN

- ☐ The Road to Independence
- ☐ Ór – Ireland's Gold
- ☐ The Treasury
- ☐ Prehistoric Ireland
- ☐ Medieval Ireland
- ☐ Viking Ireland
- ☐ Ancient Egypt
- ☐ Temporary exhibition space
- ☐ Non-exhibition space

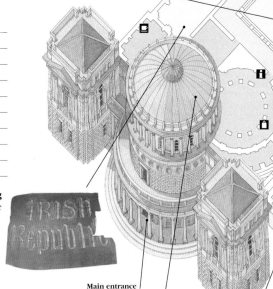

Flag from 1916 Rising
The Road to Independence
*exhibition covers historical
events between 1900 and
1921. This flag flew over
Dublin's GPO during the
Easter Rising (see p87).*

Main entrance

GALLERY GUIDE

The ground floor holds The Treasury, Ór – Ireland's
Gold *exhibition,* The Road to Independence *and
the* Prehistoric Ireland *display. On the first floor is
the* Medieval Ireland *exhibition, which illustrates
many aspects of life in later medieval Ireland. Also
on the first floor are artifacts from Ancient Egypt
and from the Viking settlement of Dublin.*

**The domed
rotunda**, based
on the design of
the Altes Museum
in Berlin, makes
an impressive
entrance hall.

The Treasury
houses masterpieces
of Irish crafts such as
the Ardagh Chalice
(see p53).

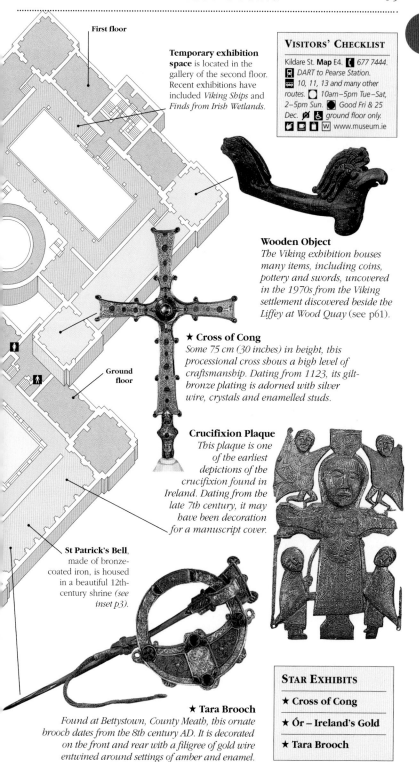

First floor

Temporary exhibition space is located in the gallery of the second floor. Recent exhibitions have included *Viking Ships* and *Finds from Irish Wetlands*.

Wooden Object
The Viking exhibition houses many items, including coins, pottery and swords, uncovered in the 1970s from the Viking settlement discovered beside the Liffey at Wood Quay (see p61).

★ Cross of Cong
Some 75 cm (30 inches) in height, this processional cross shows a high level of craftsmanship. Dating from 1123, its gilt-bronze plating is adorned with silver wire, crystals and enamelled studs.

Ground floor

Crucifixion Plaque
This plaque is one of the earliest depictions of the crucifixion found in Ireland. Dating from the late 7th century, it may have been decoration for a manuscript cover.

St Patrick's Bell, made of bronze-coated iron, is housed in a beautiful 12th-century shrine *(see inset p3)*.

★ Tara Brooch
Found at Bettystown, County Meath, this ornate brooch dates from the 8th century AD. It is decorated on the front and rear with a filigree of gold wire entwined around settings of amber and enamel.

STAR EXHIBITS

★ Cross of Cong

★ Ór – Ireland's Gold

★ Tara Brooch

Natural History Museum ⑩

Merrion St. **Map** E4. ☎ 677 7444.
◯ 10am–5pm Tue–Sat, 2–5pm Sun.
⬤ Mon, Good Fri & Dec 25. ♿
ground floor only.

Ｋ NOWN AFFECTIONATELY as the
"Dead Zoo", this museum
is crammed with antique glass
cabinets containing stuffed animals from around the world.
The museum was opened to
the public in 1857 with an
inaugural lecture by Dr David
Livingstone. The building has
barely altered since Victorian
times, and is now practically a
museum piece itself.

The Irish room on the
ground floor holds exhibits on
Irish wildlife. Inside the front
door are three huge skeletons
of the extinct giant deer, better
known as the "Irish elk". Also
on this floor are shelves
stacked with jars of bizarre
creatures such as octopuses,
leeches and worms preserved
in embalming fluid.

The upper gallery houses
the noted Blaschka Collection
of glass models of marine life,
and a display of buffalo and
deer trophies. Suspended from
the ceiling are the skeletons
of a fin whale, found at Bantry
Bay (see p159) in 1862, and a
humpback whale, which was
found stranded at Inishcrone
in County Sligo in 1893.

**Lawn and front entrance of the
Natural History Museum**

National Gallery ⑪

See pp68–9.

Georgian town houses overlooking Merrion Square gardens

Merrion Square ⑫

Map F4.

Ｍ ERRION SQUARE is one of
Dublin's largest and
grandest Georgian squares.
Covering about 5 ha (12 acres),
the square was laid out by
John Ensor around 1762.

On the west side are the
impressive façades of the
Natural History Museum, the
National Gallery and the front
garden of Leinster House (see
p63). However, this august
triumvirate does not compare
with the lovely Georgian town
houses on the other three
sides of the square. Many
have brightly painted doors
with original features such as
wrought-iron balconies, ornate
doorknockers and fanlights.
The oldest and finest houses
are on the north side.

Many of the houses – now
predominantly used as office
space – have plaques detailing the rich and famous who
once lived in them. These
include Catholic emancipation
leader Daniel O'Connell (see
p40), who lived at No. 58 and
poet WB Yeats (see pp224–5),
who lived at No. 82. The playwright Oscar Wilde (see p20)
spent his childhood at No. 1.

The attractive central park
features colourful flower and
shrub beds. In the 1840s it
served a grim function as an
emergency soup kitchen,
feeding the hungry during the
Great Famine (see p211). On
the northwest side of the park
stands the restored Rutland
Fountain. It was originally
erected in 1791 for the sole
use of Dublin's poor.

Just off the square, at No. 24
Merrion Street Upper, is the
birthplace of the Duke of

Wellington, who, when teased
about his Irish background,
said, "Being born in a stable
does not make one a horse."

Royal Hibernian Academy ⑬

15 Ely Place. **Map** E5. ☎ 661 2558.
◯ 11am–5pm Tue, Wed, Fri & Sat,
11am–9pm Thu, 2–5pm Sun.
⬤ Mon, public & Christmas hols. ♿

Ｔ HE ACADEMY is one of the
largest exhibition spaces
in the city. It puts on touring
exhibitions and mounts
shows of painting, sculpture
and other work by Ireland's
best young art and design
students. This modern brick-
and-plate-glass building does,
however, look out of place at
the end of Ely Place, an
attractive Georgian cul-de-sac.

Fitzwilliam Square ⑭

Map E5. **No. 29 Fitzwilliam St Lower**
☎ 702 6165. ◯ 10am–5pm Tue–
Sat, 2–5pm Sun. ⬤ Mon & 3 weeks
at Christmas. 📷 📷

Ｄ ATING FROM 1825, this was
one of the last Georgian
squares to be laid out in central Dublin. Much smaller than
Merrion Square, it is a popular
location for medical practices.

In the 1960s, more than 20
town houses on Fitzwilliam
Street Lower, a continuation
of the east side of the square,
were torn down to make way
for the headquarters of the
Electricity Supply Board. The
company has since tried to
appease public indignation by
renovating No. 29 as a
Georgian showpiece home.

Dublin's Georgian Terraces

THE 18TH CENTURY was Dublin's Age of Elegance, a time of relative prosperity when the Irish gentry, keen not to appear as the poor relations of Britain, set about remodelling Dublin into one of the most elegant cities in Europe. Terraced town houses were built, forming handsome new streets and squares. During the 19th century the city's wealth declined,

Doorknocker, Merrion Square

forcing some middle-class families to divide their homes into tenements. Many of Dublin's once grand streets slowly deteriorated. A century later the property boom of the 1960s threatened to rip out what was left of Georgian Dublin. Fortunately, much has survived and some of the city's finest architecture can be seen in Merrion Square and Fitzwilliam Square.

Playroom

Attic

Wrought-iron balconies gave added prestige to the Georgian house. Those still in place today are mostly later Victorian additions.

The drawing room was always on the first floor. The high ceiling was decorated with the finest plasterwork.

Architrave

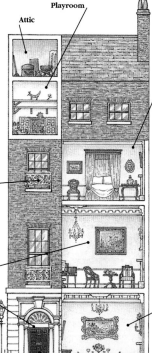

The bedrooms were usually on the second floor, while the upper floors contained the servants' quarters and children's rooms.

Lavish stuccowork was an important way of showing an owner's wealth during the 18th century.

The dining room was normally on the ground floor.

The kitchen contained a huge cooking range which was fired by either coal or wood. The adjoining pantry was used to store the household's groceries.

The doorway was usually crowned with a segmented fanlight. The principal decoration on the door itself was a heavy brass knocker.

GEORGIAN TERRACED HOUSE

While Georgian streetscapes may appear uniform, closer inspection reveals a diversity of styles in terms of details such as fanlights, architraves and balconies. The hallways usually had stone floors and, facing the hall door, a staircase rising to the upper floors. Many of the town houses did not have gardens – the railed-off parks in the centre of the squares were reserved for residents only and served as such.

National Gallery ⓫

T HIS PURPOSE-BUILT gallery was opened to the public in 1864. It houses many excellent exhibits, largely due to generous bequests, such as the Milltown collection of works of art from Russborough House *(see p124)*. Playwright George Bernard Shaw was also a benefactor, leaving a third of his estate to the gallery. A new wing has been added to

The Houseless Wanderer by John Foley

the gallery, which now has more than 700 works on display. Although the empha-

sis is on Irish landscape art and portraits, the major schools of European painting are well represented with works by Goya, El Greco, Vermeer, Titian and Monet.

GALLERY GUIDE

The main entrance is through the lofty Millennium Wing on Clare Street. Irish and British collections are housed on level 1, with the National Portrait Gallery on the mezzanine level. The European schools are located in the original gallery building on level 2, with changing special exhibitions installed in the adjacent Millennium Wing.

★ **Pierrot**
This Cubist-style work, by Spanish-born artist Juan Gris is one of many variations he painted on the theme of Pierrot and Harlequin. This particular one dates from 1921.

Mezzanine level

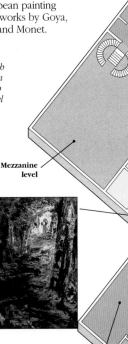

★ **For the Road**
The Yeats Museum houses works by Jack B Yeats (1871–1957) and his family. This mysterious painting reflects the artist's obsession with the Sligo countryside.

STAR PAINTINGS

★ **The Taking of Christ by Caravaggio**

★ **Pierrot by Juan Gris**

★ **For the Road by Jack Yeats**

The Shaw Room is an elegant hall, lined with full-length portraits, dating from the 17th century onwards, and lit by magnificent Waterford Crystal chandeliers.

Merrion Square entrance

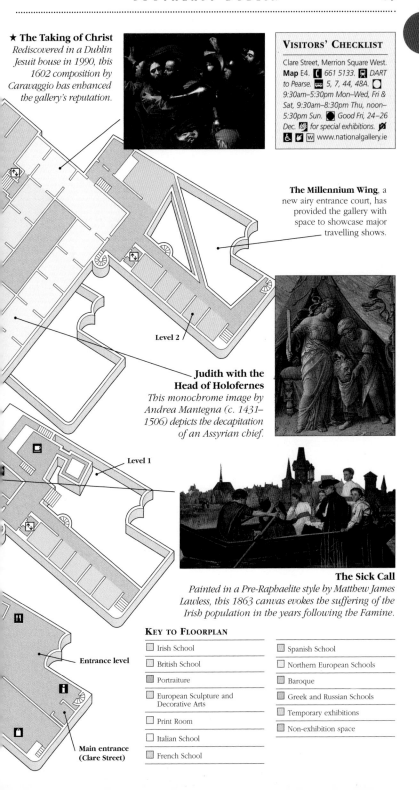

★ The Taking of Christ
Rediscovered in a Dublin Jesuit house in 1990, this 1602 composition by Caravaggio has enhanced the gallery's reputation.

VISITORS' CHECKLIST

Clare Street, Merrion Square West.
Map E4. [661 5133.] DART
to Pearse. [5, 7, 44, 48A.]
9:30am–5:30pm Mon–Wed, Fri &
Sat, 9:30am–8:30pm Thu, noon–
5:30pm Sun. [Good Fri, 24–26
Dec. [for special exhibitions. [
[[[w] www.nationalgallery.ie

The Millennium Wing, a new airy entrance court, has provided the gallery with space to showcase major travelling shows.

Level 2

Judith with the Head of Holofernes
This monochrome image by Andrea Mantegna (c. 1431–1506) depicts the decapitation of an Assyrian chief.

Level 1

The Sick Call
Painted in a Pre-Raphaelite style by Matthew James Lawless, this 1863 canvas evokes the suffering of the Irish population in the years following the Famine.

Entrance level

Main entrance (Clare Street)

KEY TO FLOORPLAN

- Irish School
- British School
- Portraiture
- European Sculpture and Decorative Arts
- Print Room
- Italian School
- French School
- Spanish School
- Northern European Schools
- Baroque
- Greek and Russian Schools
- Temporary exhibitions
- Non-exhibition space

SOUTHWEST DUBLIN

THE AREA around Dublin Castle was first settled in prehistoric times, and it was from here that the city grew. Dublin gets its name from the dark pool *(Dubh Linn)* which formed at the confluence of the Liffey and the Poddle, a river which once ran through the site of Dublin Castle. It is now channelled underground and trickles out into the Liffey by Grattan Bridge. Archaeological excavations behind Wood Quay, on the banks of the Liffey, reveal that the Vikings established a trading settlement here around 841.

Following Strongbow's invasion of 1170, a medieval city began to emerge; the Anglo-Normans built strong defensive walls around the castle.

Memorial to Turlough O'Carolan in St Patrick's Cathedral

A small reconstructed section of these old city walls can be seen at St Audoen's Church. More conspicuous reminders of the Anglo-Normans are provided by the grand medieval Christ Church Cathedral and Ireland's largest church, St Patrick's Cathedral. When the city expanded to the north and east during the Georgian era, the narrow cobbled streets of Temple Bar became a quarter of skilled craftsmen and merchants. Today this area is considered to be the trendiest part of town, and is home to a variety of "alternative" shops and cafés. The Powerscourt Townhouse, an elegant 18th-century mansion, has been converted into one of the city's best shopping centres.

SIGHTS AT A GLANCE

Museums and Libraries
Chester Beatty Library and Gallery of Oriental Art **2**
Dublinia **8**
Marsh's Library **12**

Historic Buildings
City Hall **3**
Dublin Castle pp74–5 **1**
Powerscourt Townhouse **4**
Tailors' Hall **10**

Historic Streets
Temple Bar **5**
Wood Quay **6**

Churches
Christ Church Cathedral pp78–9 **7**
St Audoen's Church **9**
St Patrick's Cathedral **11**
Whitefriar Street Carmelite Church **13**

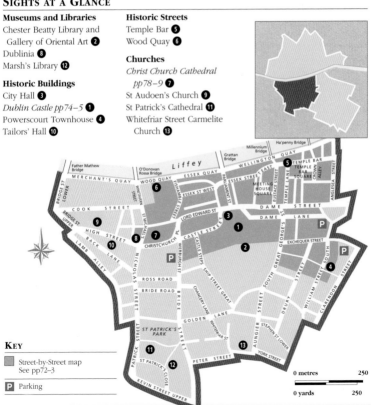

KEY

■ Street-by-Street map
See pp72–3

P Parking

| 0 metres | 250 |
| 0 yards | 250 |

◁ **Temple Bar, a centre for the arts and a popular meeting spot for young Dubliners**

Street-by-Street: Southwest Dublin

D ESPITE ITS WEALTH of ancient buildings, such as Dublin Castle and Christ Church Cathedral, this part of Dublin lacks the sleek appeal of the neighbouring streets around Grafton Street. In recent years, however, redevelopment has helped to rejuvenate the area, especially around Temple Bar, where the attractive cobbled streets are lined with interesting shops, galleries and cafés.

Sunlight Chambers were built in 1900 for the Lever Brothers company. The delightful terracotta decoration on the façade advertises their main business of soap manufacturing.

Wood Quay
This is where the Vikings established their first permanent settlement in Ireland around 841 ❻

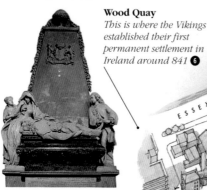

★ **Christ Church Cathedral**
Huge family monuments including that of the 19th Earl of Kildare can be found in Ireland's oldest cathedral, which also has a fascinating crypt ❼

St Werburgh's Church
An ornate interior hides behind the somewhat drab exterior of this 18th-century church.

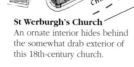

City Hall
Originally built as the Royal Exchange in 1779, the city's municipal headquarters is fronted by a huge Corinthian portico ❸

Dublinia
Medieval Dublin is the subject of this interactive museum, located in the former Synod Hall of the Church of Ireland. It is linked to Christ Church by a bridge ❽

★ **Dublin Castle**
The Drawing Room, with its Waterford crystal chandelier, is part of a suite of luxurious rooms built in the 18th century for the Viceroys of Ireland ❶

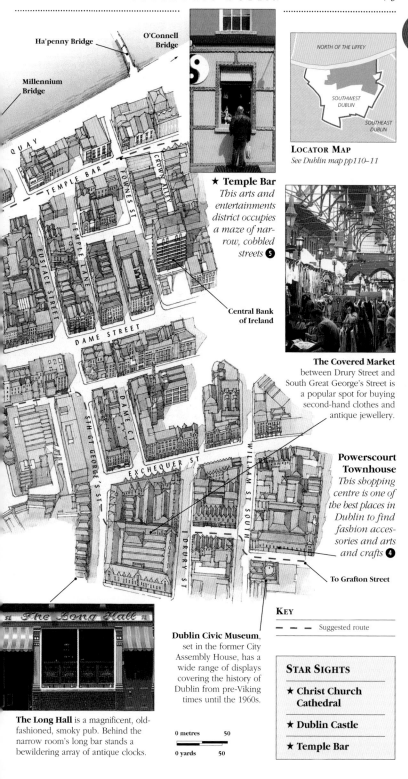

Ha'penny Bridge

O'Connell Bridge

Millennium Bridge

QUAY

TEMPLE BAR

EUSTACE STREET

TEMPLE LANE

FOWNES ST

CROWN ALLEY

DAME STREET

DAME CT

5TH GT GEORGE'S ST

EXCHEQUER ST

DRURY ST

WILLIAM ST SOUTH

LOCATOR MAP
See Dublin map pp110–11

NORTH OF THE LIFFEY

SOUTHWEST DUBLIN

SOUTHEAST DUBLIN

★ **Temple Bar**
This arts and entertainments district occupies a maze of narrow, cobbled streets ❺

Central Bank of Ireland

The Covered Market
between Drury Street and South Great George's Street is a popular spot for buying second-hand clothes and antique jewellery.

Powerscourt Townhouse
This shopping centre is one of the best places in Dublin to find fashion accessories and arts and crafts ❹

To Grafton Street

Dublin Civic Museum, set in the former City Assembly House, has a wide range of displays covering the history of Dublin from pre-Viking times until the 1960s.

The Long Hall is a magnificent, old-fashioned, smoky pub. Behind the narrow room's long bar stands a bewildering array of antique clocks.

KEY

– – –   Suggested route

0 metres   50

0 yards   50

STAR SIGHTS

★ **Christ Church Cathedral**

★ **Dublin Castle**

★ **Temple Bar**

Dublin Castle ●

FOR SEVEN CENTURIES Dublin Castle was a symbol of English rule, ever since the Anglo-Normans built a fortress here in the 13th century. Nothing remains of the original structure except the much modified Record Tower. Following a fire in 1684, the Surveyor-General, Sir William Robinson, laid down the plans for the Upper and Lower Castle Yards in their present form. On the first floor of the south side of the Upper Yard are the luxury State Apartments, including St Patrick's Hall. These rooms, with Killybegs carpets and chandeliers of Waterford glass, served as home to the British-appointed Viceroys of Ireland.

St Patrick by Edward Smyth

Figure of Justice
Facing the Upper Yard above the main entrance from Cork Hill, this statue aroused much cynicism among Dubliners, who felt she was turning her back on the city.

★ Throne Room
Built in 1740, this room contains a throne said to have been presented by William of Orange after his victory at the Battle of the Boyne (see p236).

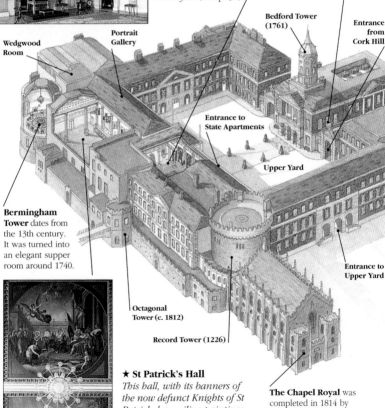

Wedgwood Room

Portrait Gallery

Bedford Tower (1761)

Entrance from Cork Hill

Entrance to State Apartments

Upper Yard

Bermingham Tower dates from the 13th century. It was turned into an elegant supper room around 1740.

Entrance to Upper Yard

Octagonal Tower (c. 1812)

Record Tower (1226)

★ St Patrick's Hall
This hall, with its banners of the now defunct Knights of St Patrick, has ceiling paintings by Vincenzo Valdré (1778), symbolizing the relationship between Britain and Ireland.

The Chapel Royal was completed in 1814 by Francis Johnston. The 100 heads on the exterior of this Neo-Gothic church were carved by Edward Smyth.

ROBERT EMMET

Robert Emmet (1778–1803),
leader of the abortive 1803
rebellion, is remembered
as a heroic champion of
Irish liberty. His plan was
to capture Dubl in Castle
as a signal for the country
to rise up against the Act
of Union (see p40). Emmet
was caught and publicly
hanged, but the defiant,
patriotic speech he made
from the dock helped to
inspire future generations
of Irish freedom fighters.

**Government
offices**

wer Yard

Dame Street

STAR FEATURES

★ **St Patrick's Hall**

★ **Throne Room**

**Manuscript (1874) from the Holy Koran written by calligrapher
Ahmad Shaikh in Kashmir, Chester Beatty Library**

Chester Beatty Library and Gallery of Oriental Art ②

Clock Tower Building, Dublin Castle.
(407 0750. ⬜ 10am–5pm Mon–
Fri (Tue–Fri Oct–Apr), 11am–5pm Sat,
1pm–5pm Sun. 🌑 Good Fri, 24–26
Dec & public holidays. 🅿 🚻 🍴
🖥 www.cbl.ie

THIS COLLECTION of Oriental
manuscripts and art was
bequeathed to Ireland by the
American mining magnate and
art collector Sir Alfred Chester
Beatty, who died in 1968. This
generous act no doubt led to
his selection as Ireland's first
honorary citizen in 1957.

During his lifetime, Beatty
accumulated almost 300 copies
of the Koran, representing the
works of master calligraphers.
Also on display are 6,000-year-
old Babylonian stone tablets,
Greek papyri and biblical
material written in Coptic, the
ancient language of Egypt.

Treasures from the Far East
include a collection of Chinese
jade books – each leaf is made
from thinly cut jade, engraved
with Chinese characters which
are then filled with gold.
Burmese and Siamese art is
represented by the collection
of 18th- and 19th-century
Parabaiks, books of folk tales
with colourful illustrations on
mulberry leaf paper. The
Japanese collection includes
paintings, woodblock prints
and books and scrolls from
the 16th to 18th centuries.
The illustrations were painted
by Buddhist monks. One
of the most beautiful
manuscripts in the western
European collection is the
Coëtivy Book of Hours, an
illuminated 15th–century
French prayer book.

City Hall ③

Cork Hill, Dame St. **Map** C3. (672
2204. ⬜ 10am–5:15pm Mon–Sat,
2pm–5pm Sun and public holidays. 🌑
Good Fri, 24–26 Dec. 📷 ♿ 🍴 📷

DESIGNED BY Thomas Cooley,
this imposing Corinthian-
style building was erected
between 1769 and 1779 as the
Royal Exchange. It was taken
over by Dublin Corporation
in 1852 as a meeting place for
the city council – a role it
keeps to this day.

The building has recently
been restored to its original
condition and a permanent
exhibition on the city's history,
Dublin City Hall - The Story
of the Capital, is housed on
the lower ground floor.

City Hall from Parliament Street

a centre of specialist galleries, antique shops, jewellery stalls, cafés and other shop units. The enclosed central courtyard, topped by a glass dome, is a popular meeting place with Dubliners. The centre can also be reached from Grafton Street down the narrow Johnson Court alley.

Interior of Powerscourt Townhouse Shopping Centre

Powerscourt Townhouse ❹

South William St. **Map** D4. ☎ *679 4144.* ⏰ *10am–6pm Mon–Fri (8pm Thu), 9am–6pm Sat, noon–6pm Sun. See also **Shopping in Ireland** pp322–5.*

COMPLETED IN 1774 by Robert Mack, this grand mansion was built as the city home of Viscount Powerscourt, who also had a country estate at Enniskerry *(see pp126–7)*. Granite from the Powerscourt estate was used in its construction. Today the building houses one of Dublin's best shopping centres. Inside it still features the original grand mahogany staircase, and detailed plasterwork by Michael Stapleton.

The building became a drapery warehouse in the 1830s, and major restoration during the 1960s turned it into

Temple Bar ❺

Map C3. **Temple Bar Information** ☎ *671 5717 (24hr info line). See also **Entertainment in Dublin** p106.* **Project** *39 East Essex Street.* ☎ *679 6622.* **Irish Film Centre** *6 Eustace Street.* ☎ *679 5744.* 🎬 *Diversions,* (May–Sep). 🌐 *www.temple-bar.ie*

SOME OF DUBLIN'S best night spots, restaurants and unusual shops line these narrow, cobbled streets running between the Bank of Ireland *(see p58)* and Christ Church Cathedral. In the 18th century the area was home to many insalubrious characters – Fownes Street was noted for its brothels. It was also the birthplace of parliamentarian Henry Grattan *(see p38)*. Skilled craftsmen and artisans, such as clockmakers and printers, lived and worked around Temple Bar until postwar industrialization led to a decline in the area's fortunes.

In the 1970s, the CIE (the national transport authority) bought up parcels of land in this area to build a major bus depot. Before building, the CIE rented out, on cheap leases, some of the old retail and warehouse premises to

young artists and to record, clothing and book shops. The area developed an "alternative" identity and when the development plans were scrapped the artists and retailers stayed on. Described by some cynics as the city's "officially designated arts zone", Temple Bar today is an exciting place with bars, restaurants, shops and several galleries. Stylish residential and commercial development is contributing further to the area's appeal.

Highlights include the **Project**, a highly respected venue for avant garde performance art; and the **Irish Film Centre**, which shows art house and independent films, and has a popular restaurant/bar and shop.

Nearby Meeting House Square is one of the venues for Diversions, a summer programme of free outdoor concerts, theatre and film screenings. The National Photographic Archive and

A pub in Temple Bar

Gallery of Photography are also on the square and there is an excellent organic food market here on Saturdays, where you can sample oysters, salmon, cheese and other local produce.

Wood Quay ❻

Map B3.

NAMED AFTER the timber supports used to reclaim the land, Wood Quay has undergone excavations revealing the remains of one of the earliest Viking villages in Ireland *(see p77)*. It is hoped that part of the excavated area will eventually be open to public view.

Viking artifacts can be seen at the Dublinia exhibition *(see p77)* and at the National Museum *(see p64–5)*.

Strolling through the streets of Temple Bar

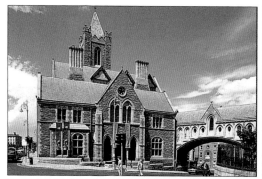
Former Synod Hall, now home to the Dublinia exhibition

Christz Church Cathedral **7**

See pp78–9.

Dublinia **8**

St Michael's Hill. **Map** B3. **C** 679 4611. **O** May–Sep: 10am–5pm daily; Oct–Apr: 11am–4pm daily including public hols. **●** 24–26 Dec. **✍** minimum charge to enter Christ Church Cathedral via bridge. **&** **W** www.dublinia.ie

MANAGED BY the non-profit-making Medieval Trust, the Dublinia exhibition covers the formative period of Dublin's history from the arrival of the Anglo-Normans in 1170 to the closure of the monas-teries in the 1540s *(see p36)*. The exhibition is housed in the Neo-Gothic Synod Hall, which, up until 1983, was home to the ruling body of the Church of Ireland. The building and the hump-backed bridge linking it to Christ Church Cathedral date from the 1870s. Before Dublinia was established in 1993, the Synod Hall was used as a nightclub.

The exhibition is entered via the basement where visitors walk through life-size reconstructions of the Medieval City. These depict major events in Dublin's history, such as the Black Death and the rebellion of Silken Thomas *(see p36)*. The ground floor houses a large scale model of Dublin in around 1500, a display of artifacts from the Wood Quay excavation, and reconstruc-tions including the inside of a late medieval merchant's kitchen. There are also infor-mation panels on the themes of trade, merchants and religion. A multi-screen presentation on Dublin's medieval history can be seen in the dark-wood panelled Great Hall on the first floor.

The 60-m (200-ft) high St Michael's Tower offers one of the best vantage points for views across the city.

St Audoen's Church **9**

High St, Cornmarket. **Map** B3. **C** 677 0088. **O** Jun–Sep. **✍** **✓**

Tower of St Audoen's Church

DESIGNATED a national monument and open for visitors in the summer months, St Audoen's is Dublin's earliest surviving medieval church. The 15th-century nave remains intact and the three bells date from 1423. The church stands in an attractive churchyard with well-maintained lawns and shrubs. To the rear, steps lead down to St Audoen's Arch, the only remaining gateway of the old city. Flanking the gate are restored sections of the 13th-century city walls.

Next door stands St Audoen's Roman Catholic Church, which was built in the 1840s. The two Pacific clam shells by the front door hold holy water. In the basement is an audiovisual presentation on pre-Viking Ireland.

THE VIKINGS IN DUBLIN

Viking raiders arrived in Ireland in the late 8th century and founded Dublin in 841. They built a fort where the River Poddle met the Liffey at a black pool *(Dubh Linn)*, on the site of Dublin Castle. They also established a settlement along the banks of the Liffey at Wood Quay *(see p76)*. Much of their trade was based on silver, slaves and piracy.

Following their defeat by Brian Ború at the Battle of Clontarf in 1014 *(see p32)*, the Vikings integrated fully with the local Irish, adopting Christian beliefs. After Strongbow's Anglo-Norman invasion in 1170 *(see p34)*, the flourishing Hiberno-Viking trading community declined, and many were banished to a separate colony called Oxmanstown, just north of the river.

Artist's impression of a Viking ship in Dublin Bay

Christ Church Cathedral ❼

Arms on Lord Mayor's pew

CHRIST CHURCH CATHEDRAL was established by the Hiberno-Norse king of Dublin, Sitric "Silkbeard", and the first bishop of Dublin, Dunan. It was rebuilt by the Anglo-Norman archbishop, John Cumin in 1186. It is the cathedral for the Church of Ireland (Anglican) diocese of Dublin and Glendalough. By the 19th century it was in a bad state of repair, but was completely remodelled by architect George Street in the 1870s. The vast 12th-century crypt has recently been restored.

★ Medieval Lectern
This beautiful brass lectern was hand-wrought during the Middle Ages. It stands on the north side of the nave, in front of the pulpit. The matching lectern on the south side is Victorian.

The Lord Mayor's pew is usually kept in the north aisle, but is moved to the front of the nave when used by Dublin's civic dignitaries. It features a carving of the city arms and a stand for the civic mace.

Great Nave
The 25-m (68-ft) high nave has some fine early Gothic arches. On the north side, the original 13th-century wall leans out by as much as 50 cm (18 in) due to the weight of the roof.

Entrance

★ Strongbow Monument
The large effigy in chain armour is probably not Strongbow. However, his remains are buried in the cathedral and the curious half-figure may be part of his original tomb.

The bridge to the Synod Hall was added when the cathedral was being rebuilt in the 1870s.

STAR FEATURES
★ **Crypt**
★ **Medieval Lectern**
★ **Strongbow Monument**

Chapel of St Laud
The casket on the wall contains the heart of St Laurence O'Toole. The chapel features original medieval floor tiles.

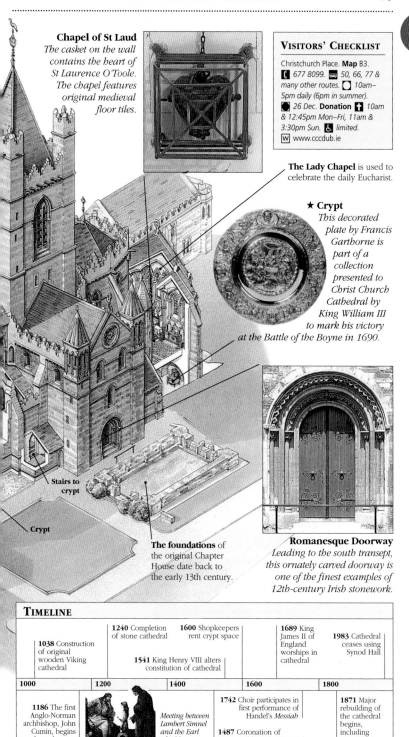

VISITORS' CHECKLIST

Christchurch Place. **Map** B3.
677 8099. 50, 66, 77 & many other routes. 10am–5pm daily (6pm in summer). 26 Dec. **Donation** 10am & 12:45pm Mon–Fri, 11am & 3:30pm Sun. limited.
www.cccdub.ie

The Lady Chapel is used to celebrate the daily Eucharist.

★ Crypt
This decorated plate by Francis Garthorne is part of a collection presented to Christ Church Cathedral by King William III to mark his victory at the Battle of the Boyne in 1690.

Stairs to crypt

Crypt

The foundations of the original Chapter House date back to the early 13th century.

Romanesque Doorway
Leading to the south transept, this ornately carved doorway is one of the finest examples of 12th-century Irish stonework.

TIMELINE

1038 Construction of original wooden Viking cathedral

1186 The first Anglo-Norman archbishop, John Cumin, begins work on the new cathedral.

1240 Completion of stone cathedral

1541 King Henry VIII alters constitution of cathedral

Meeting between Lambert Simnel and the Earl of Kildare (see p35)

1600 Shopkeepers rent crypt space

1487 Coronation of 10-year-old Lambert Simnel as King of England

1689 King James II of England worships in cathedral

1742 Choir participates in first performance of Handel's Messiah

1983 Cathedral ceases using Synod Hall

1871 Major rebuilding of the cathedral begins, including Synod Hall and bridge

1000	1200	1400	1600	1800

Tailors' Hall ⓾

Back Lane. **Map** B4. ⬤ *to the public.*

Dublin's only surviving guildhall preserves a delightful corner of old Dublin in an otherwise busy redevelopment zone. Built in 1706, it stands behind a limestone arch in a quiet cobbled yard. The building is the oldest guildhall in Ireland and was used by various trade groups including hosiers, saddlers and barber-surgeons as well as tailors. It also hosted many political meetings – Wolfe Tone addressed a public United Irishmen rally here before the 1798 rebellion (*see p39*). The building closed in the early 1960s due to neglect, but a successful appeal by Desmond Guinness saw the hall completely refurbished. It is now the home of An Taisce (the Irish National Trust).

Façade of Tailors' Hall, home of the Irish National Trust

St Patrick's Cathedral with Minot's Tower and spire

St Patrick's Cathedral ⓫

St Patrick's Close. **Map** B4.
🅒 *475 4817.* ⬜ *Mar–Oct: 9am–5pm Mon–Sat, 9am–5pm Sun; Nov–Feb: 9am–5pm Mon–Sat, 9am–3pm Sun. Tours are not admitted during services.* 🖾

Ireland's largest church was founded beside a sacred well where St Patrick is said to have baptized converts around AD 450. A stone slab bearing a Celtic cross and covering the well was unearthed over a century ago. It is now preserved in the west end of the cathedral's nave. The original building was just a wooden chapel and remained so until 1192 when Archbishop John Comyn rebuilt the cathedral in stone.

Over the centuries, St Patrick's came to be seen as the people's church, while the older Christ Church Cathedral (*see pp78–9*) nearby was more associated with the British establishment. In the mid-17th century, Huguenot refugees from France arrived in Dublin, and were given the Lady Chapel by the Dean and Chapter as their place of worship. The chapel was separated from the rest of the cathedral and used by the Huguenots until the late 18th century. Today St Patrick's Cathedral is the Protestant Church of Ireland's national cathedral.

Much of the present building dates back to work completed between 1254 and 1270. The cathedral suffered over the centuries from desecration, fire and neglect but, thanks to the generosity of Sir Benjamin Guinness, it underwent extensive restoration during the 1860s. The building is 91 m (300 ft) long; at the western end is a 43-m (141-ft) tower, restored by Archbishop Minot in 1370 and now known as Minot's Tower. The spire was added in the 18th century.

The interior is dotted with memorial busts, brasses and monuments. A leaflet available at the front desk helps identify and locate them. The largest, most colourful and elaborate tomb was dedicated to the Boyle family in the 17th century. Erected by Richard Boyle, Earl of Cork, in memory of his second wife Katherine, it is decorated with painted figures of his family,

Jonathan Swift (1667–1745)

Jonathan Swift was born in Dublin and educated at Trinity College (*see pp60–61*). He left for England in 1689, but returned in 1694 when his political career failed. Back in Ireland he began a life in the church, becoming Dean of St Patrick's in 1713. In addition to his clerical duties, Swift was a prolific political commentator – his best-known work, *Gulliver's Travels*, contains a bitter satire on Anglo-Irish relations. Swift's personal life, particularly his friendship with two younger women, Ester Johnson, better known as Stella, and Hester Vanhomrigh, attracted criticism. In his final years, Swift suffered from Ménière's disease – an illness of the ear which led many to believe him insane.

including his wife's parents. Other famous citizens remembered in the church include the harpist Turlough O'Carolan (1670–1738) *(see p22)* and Douglas Hyde (1860–1949), the first President of Ireland.

Many visitors come to see the memorials associated with Jonathan Swift, the satirical writer and Dean of St Patrick's. In the north transept is "Swift's Corner", containing various memorabilia such as an altar table and a bookcase holding his death mask and various pamphlets. A self-penned epitaph can be found on the wall on the southwest side of the nave. A few steps away, two brass plates mark his grave and that of his beloved Stella, who died in 1728.

At the west end of the nave is an old door with a hole in it – a relic from a feud which took place between the Lords Kildare and Ormonde in 1492. The latter took refuge in the Chapter House, but a truce was soon made and a hole was cut in the door by Lord Kildare so that the two could shake hands in friendship.

Marsh's Library ⑫

St Patrick's Close. **Map** B4.
🕿 454 3511. ⏲ 10am–1pm & 2–5pm Mon & Wed–Fri, 10:30am–1pm Sat. ⏺ Tue & Sun, 10 days at Christmas & public hols. ♿
🖥 www.marshlibrary.ie

THE OLDEST public library in Ireland was built in 1701 for Archbishop Narcissus Marsh, a Dean of St Patrick's Cathedral. It was designed by Sir William Robinson, architect of much of Dublin Castle *(see pp74–5)* and the Royal Hospital Kilmainham *(see p95)*.

Inside, the bookcases are topped by a mitre and feature carved gables with lettering in gold leaf. To the rear of the library are wired alcoves (or "cages") where readers were locked in with rare books. The collection, from the 16th, 17th and early 18th centuries, includes irreplaceable volumes, such as Bishop Bedell's 1685 translation of the Old Testament into Irish and Clarendon's *History of the Rebellion*, with anti-Scottish margin notes by Jonathan Swift.

Statue of Virgin and Child in Whitefriar Street Carmelite Church

Whitefriar Street Carmelite Church ⑬

56 Aungier St. **Map** C4. 🕿 475 8821.
⏲ 8am–6:30pm Mon & Wed–Fri, 8am–9pm Tue, 8am–7pm Sat, 8am–7:30pm Sun, 9:30am–1pm public hols.

DESIGNED by George Papworth, this Catholic church was built in 1827. It stands on the site of a 16th-century Carmelite priory of which nothing remains.

In contrast to the two Church of Ireland cathedrals, St Patrick's and Christ Church, which are usually full of tourists, this church is frequented by local worshippers. Every day they come to light candles to various saints, including St Valentine – the patron saint of lovers. His remains, previously buried in the cemetery of St Hippolytus in Rome, were offered to the church as a gift from Pope Gregory XVI in 1836. Today they rest beneath the commemorative statue of St Valentine, which stands in the northeast corner of the church beside the high altar.

Nearby is a Flemish oak statue of the Virgin and Child, dating from the late 15th or early 16th century. It may have belonged to St Mary's Abbey *(see p91)* and is believed to be the only wooden statue of its kind to escape destruction when Ireland's monasteries were sacked at the time of the Reformation *(see p36)*.

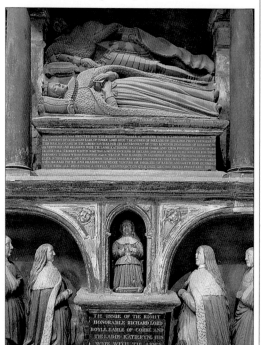

Carved monument (1632) to the Boyle family in St Patrick's Cathedral

NORTH OF THE LIFFEY

DUBLIN'S NORTHSIDE was the last part of the city to be developed during the 18th century. The city authorities envisioned an area of wide, leafy avenues, but the reality of today's heavy traffic has rather spoiled their original plans. Nonetheless, O'Connell Street, lined with fine statues and monuments, is an impressive thoroughfare. This is where Dubliners come to shop and some of the adjacent streets, particularly Moore Street, have a colourful parade of stalls and street vendors offering cut-price tobacco.

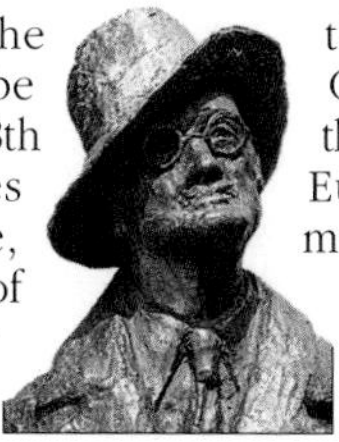

Some public buildings, such as James Gandon's glorious Custom House and majestic Four Courts, together with

Statue of James Joyce on Earl Street North

the historic General Post Office *(see p87)*, add grace to the area. The Rotunda Hospital, Europe's first purpose-built maternity hospital, is another fine building. Dublin's two most celebrated theatres, the Abbey and the Gate, act as a cultural magnet, as do the Dublin Writers Museum and the James Joyce Cultural Centre, two museums dedicated to writers who lived in the city.

Some of the city's finest Georgian streetscapes are found in the north of the city. Many have been neglected for decades, but thankfully some areas, most notably North Great George's Street, are undergoing restoration.

SIGHTS AT A GLANCE

Museums and Galleries
Dublin Writers Museum **9**
Hugh Lane Municipal Gallery
   of Modern Art **10**
Old Jameson's Distillery **13**
James Joyce Cultural Centre **5**

Historic Buildings
Custom House **1**
Four Courts **15**
King's Inns **11**
Rotunda Hospital **7**

Historic Streets and Bridges
Ha'penny Bridge **17**
O'Connell Street **3**
Smithfield **12**

Theatres
Abbey Theatre **2**
Gate Theatre **6**

Churches
St Mary's Abbey **16**
St Mary's Pro-Cathedral **4**
St Michan's Church **14**

Parks and Gardens
Garden of Remembrance **8**

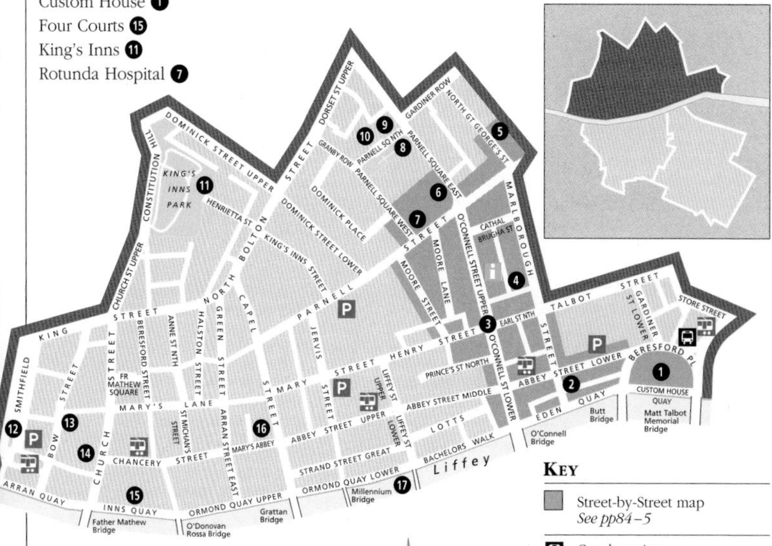

KEY

Street-by-Street map
See pp84–5

Coach station

Luas stop

P Parking

Tourist information

0 metres 250
0 yards 250

◁ **Portico of the Custom House, illuminated at night**

Street-by-Street: Around O'Connell Street

THROUGHOUT THE Georgian era, O'Connell Street was very much the fashionable part of Dublin to live in. However, the 1916 Easter Rising destroyed many of the fine buildings along the street, including much of the General Post Office – only its original façade still stands. Today, this main thoroughfare is lined with shops and businesses. Other attractions nearby include St Mary's Pro-Cathedral and James Gandon's Custom House, overlooking the Liffey.

Detail of pavement mosaic, Moore Street

James Joyce Cultural Centre
This well-restored Georgian town house contains a small Joyce museum ⑤

Parnell Monument (1911)

Gate Theatre
Founded in 1928, the Gate is renowned for its productions of contemporary drama ⑥

Rotunda Hospital
Housed in the Rotunda Hospital is a chapel built in the 1750s to the design of Richard Castle. It features lovely stained-glass windows, fluted columns, panelling and intricate iron balustrades ⑦

Moore Street Market is the busiest of the streets off O'Connell. Be prepared for the shrill cries of the stall holders offering an enormous variety of fresh fruit, vegetables and cut flowers.

The Monument of Light, an elegant stainless steel spire, rises to 120 m (394 ft).

The General Post Office, the grandest building on O'Connell Street, was the centre of the 1916 Rising.

James Larkin Statue (1981)

KEY

— Suggested route

🚈 Luas stop

ℹ Tourist information

0 metres	50
0 yards	50

STAR SIGHTS

★ **Custom House**

★ **O'Connell Street**

St Mary's Pro-Cathedral
Built around 1825, this is Dublin's main place of worship for Catholics. The plaster relief above the altar in the sanctuary depicts The Ascension **4**

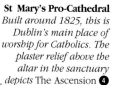

The statue of James Joyce (1990), by Marjorie Fitzgibbon, commemorates one of Ireland's most famous novelists. Born in Dublin in 1882, he catalogued the people and streets of Dublin in *Dubliners* and in his most celebrated work, *Ulysses.*

Abbey Theatre
Ireland's national theatre is known throughout the world for its productions by Irish playwrights, such as Sean O'Casey and JM Synge **2**

★ **O'Connell Street**
This monument to Daniel O'Connell by John Foley took 19 years to complete from the laying of its foundation stone in 1864 **3**

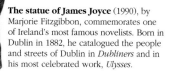

CUSTOM HOUSE QUAY

STREET NORTH

MARLBOROUGH ST

SACKVILLE PL

ABBEY STREET LR

EDEN QUAY

LIFFEY

Butt Bridge

O'Connell Bridge

To Trinity College

★ **Custom House**
This grotesque head, by Edward Smyth, symbolizes the River Liffey. It is one of 14 carved keystones that adorn the building **1**

Illuminated façade of the Custom House reflected in the Liffey

Custom House ❶

Custom House Quay. **Map** E2 **[C**
888 2538. ◯ *mid-Mar–Oct: 10am–*
12.30pm Mon–Fri, 2pm–5pm Sat–Sun
& Bank Holidays; Nov–mid-Mar:
10am–12.30pm Wed–Fri, 2pm–5pm
Sun. ♿ *on weekdays only.*

THIS MAJESTIC BUILDING was
designed as the Custom
House by the English architect
James Gandon. However, just
nine years after its completion,
the 1800 Act of Union *(see p40)*
transferred the customs and
excise business to London,
rendering the building
practically obsolete. In 1921,
supporters of Sinn Féin celebrated their election victory
by setting light to what they
saw as a symbol of British
imperialism. The fire blazed
for five days causing extensive
damage. Reconstruction took
place in 1926, although further
deterioration meant that the
building was not completely
restored until 1991, when it reopened as government offices.
　The main façade is made up
of pavilions at each end with
a Doric portico in its centre.
The arms of Ireland crown the
two pavilions and a series of
14 allegorical heads, by Dublin
sculptor Edward Smyth, form
the keystones of arches and
entrances. These heads depict
Ireland's main rivers and the
Atlantic Ocean. Topping the
central copper dome is a

statue of Commerce, while the
north façade is decorated with
figures representing Europe,
Africa, America and Asia.
The best view of the building
is from the south of the Liffey
beyond Matt Talbot Bridge.

Abbey Theatre ❷

Lower Abbey St. **Map** E2. **[C** *878*
7222. ◯ *for performances only.* **Box**
office ◯ *10:30am–7pm Mon–Sat. See*
also **Entertainment in Dublin** *p107.*

Logo of the Abbey Theatre

FOUNDED in 1898 with WB
Yeats and Lady Gregory as
co-directors, the Abbey staged
its first play in 1904. The early
years of this much lauded
national theatre witnessed
works by WB Yeats, JM Synge
and Sean O'Casey. Many were
controversial: nationalist sensi-
tivities were severely tested in
1926 during the premiere of
O'Casey's *The Plough and the*

Stars when the flag of the Irish
Free State appeared on stage
in a scene which featured a
pub frequented by prostitutes.
　While presenting the work
of eminent foreign authors
from time to time, the prime
objective of the Abbey &
Peacock Theatres is to
provide a performance space
for Irish dramatic writing.
Some of the most acclaimed
performances have been Brian
Friel's *Dancing at Lughnasa*
and *Translations*, Patrick
Kavanagh's *Tarry Flynn*, Dion
Boucicault's *The Colleen
Bawn* and Hugh Leonard's
Love in the Title.

O'Connell Street ❸

Map D1–D2.

O'CONNELL STREET is very
different from the original
plans of Irish aristocrat Luke
Gardiner. When he bought
the land in the mid-18th
century, Gardiner envisioned
a grand residential parade
with an elegant mall running
along its centre. Such plans
were short-lived. The construction of Carlisle (now
O'Connell) Bridge in 1790
transformed the street into the
city's main north-south route.
Also, several buildings were
destroyed during the 1916
Easter Rising and the Irish
Civil War. Since the 1960s

many of the old buildings have been replaced by the plate glass and neon of fast food joints, amusement arcades and chain stores.

A few venerable buildings remain, such as the General Post Office (1818), Gresham Hotel (1817), Clery's department store (1822) and the Royal Dublin Hotel, part of which occupies the street's only original town house.

A walk down the central mall is the most enjoyable way to see the street's mix of architectural styles and take a close look at the series of monuments lining the route. At the south end stands a massive monument to Daniel O'Connell *(see p40)*, unveiled in 1882. The street, which throughout the 19th century had been called Sackville Street, was renamed after O'Connell in 1922. Higher up, almost facing the General Post Office, is an animated statue of James Larkin (1867–1943), leader of the Dublin general strike in 1913. The next statue is of Father Theobald Mathew (1790–1856), founder of the Pioneer Total Abstinence

South end of O'Connell Street with monument to Daniel O'Connell

Statue of James Larkin (1981) in O'Connell Street

Movement. At the north end of the street is the obelisk-shaped monument to Charles Stewart Parnell (1846–91), who was leader of the Home Rule Party and known as the "uncrowned King of Ireland" *(see p41)*. A new addition to O'Connell Street is the Monument of Light, erected on the site where Nelson's column used to be. It is a stainless steel, conical spire which tapers from a 3-metre diameter base to a 10 cm pointed tip of optical glass at a height of 120 metres (394 ft).

St Mary's Pro-Cathedral ➍

Marlborough St. **Map** D2. ☎ 874 5441. ◷ 8:30am–6:30pm Mon–Sat, 10am–6:30pm Sun.

DEDICATED in 1825 before Catholic emancipation *(see p40)*, St Mary's backstreet site was the best the city's Anglo-Irish leaders would allow a Catholic cathedral.

The façade is based on a Greek temple. Doric columns support a pediment with statues of St Mary, St Patrick and St Laurence O'Toole, 12th-century Archbishop of Dublin and patron saint of the city. Inside, one striking feature is the intricately carved high altar.

St Mary's has a great musical tradition and is home to the famous Palestrina Choir, with which the great tenor John McCormack *(see p22)* began his career in 1904. The choir can still be heard every Sunday morning at 11am.

Austere Neo-Classical interior of St Mary's Pro-Cathedral

THE GENERAL POST OFFICE (GPO)

Irish Life **magazine cover showing the 1916 Easter Rising**

Built in 1818 halfway along O'Connell Street, the GPO became a symbol of the 1916 Irish Rising. Members of the Irish Volunteers and Irish Citizen Army seized the building on Easter Monday, and Patrick Pearse *(see p42)* read out the Proclamation of the Irish Republic from its steps. The rebels remained inside for a week, but shelling from the British eventually forced them out. At first, many Irish people viewed the Rising unfavourably. However, as WB Yeats wrote, matters "changed utterly" and a "terrible beauty was born" when, during the following weeks, 14 of the leaders were caught and shot at Kilmainham Gaol *(see p95)*. Inside the building is a sculpture of the mythical Irish warrior Cúchulainn *(see p24)*, dedicated to those who died for their part in the Easter Rising.

James Joyce Cultural Centre ❺

35 North Great George's St. **Map** D1.
📞 878 8547. ⏰ 9:30am– 5pm
Mon–Sat, 12:30–5pm Sun (11am–
5pm Jun–Aug). ● Good Fri &
23–27 Dec. 🖼️ 🎫

THIS AGREEABLE STOP on the literary tourist trail is primarily a meeting place for Joyce enthusiasts, but is also worth visiting for its Georgian interior. The centre is in a 1784 town house which was built for the Earl of Kenmare. Michael Stapleton, one of the greatest stuccoers of his time, contributed to the plasterwork, of which the friezes are particularly noteworthy.

The main literary display is an absorbing set of biographies of around 50 characters from Joyce's novel *Ulysses*, who were based on real Dublin people. Professor Dennis J Maginni, a peripheral character in *Ulysses*, ran a dancing school from this town house. Leopold and Molly Bloom, the central characters of *Ulysses*, lived a short walk away at No. 7 Eccles Street. The centre also organizes walking tours of Joyce's Dublin, so a visit is a must for all Joycean zealots.

At the top of the road, on Great Denmark Street, is the Jesuit-run Belvedere College attended by Joyce between 1893 and 1898. He recalls his unhappy schooldays there in *A Portrait of the Artist as a Young Man*. The college's interior contains some of Stapleton's best and most colourful plasterwork (1785).

JAMES JOYCE (1882–1941)

Born in Dublin, Joyce spent most of his adult life in Europe. He used the city of Dublin as the setting for all his major works including *Dubliners*, *A Portrait of the Artist as a Young Man* and *Ulysses*. Joyce claimed that if the city was ever destroyed it could be re-created through the pages of *Ulysses*. However, the Irish branded the book pornographic and banned it until the 1960s.

Gate Theatre ❻

1 Cavendish Row. **Map** D1.
🚪 for performances only. **Box office**
📞 874 4045. ⏰ 10am–7pm Mon–
Sat. See also **Entertainment in
Dublin** pp102–7.

Entrance to the Gate Theatre

RENOWNED FOR its staging of contemporary international drama in Dublin, the Gate Theatre was founded in 1928 by Hilton Edwards and Mícheál Mac Liammóir. The latter is now best remembered for *The*

Importance of Being Oscar, his long-running one-man show about the writer Oscar Wilde *(see p20)*. An early success was Denis Johnston's *The Old Lady Says No*, so-called because of the margin notes made on one of his scripts by Lady Gregory, founding director of the Abbey Theatre *(see p86)*. Although still noted for staging new plays, the Gate's current output often includes classic Irish plays. Among the young talent to get their first break here were James Mason and a teenage Orson Welles.

Rotunda Hospital ❼

Parnell Square West. **Map** D1.
📞 873 0700.

STANDING in the middle of Parnell Square is Europe's first purpose-built maternity hospital. Founded in 1745 by Dr Bartholomew Mosse, the design of the hospital is similar to that of Leinster House *(see p63)*. German-born architect Richard Castle designed both.

At the east end of the hospital is the Rotunda, after which the hospital is named. It was built in 1764 by John Ensor as Assembly Rooms to host fundraising functions and concerts. Franz Liszt gave a concert here in 1843.

On the first floor is a chapel featuring striking stained-glass windows and exuberant Rococo plasterwork and ceiling (1755) by the stuccoer Bartholomew Cramillion.

Across the road from the hospital is Conway's Pub. Opened in 1745, it is a popular retreat for expectant fathers.

Stained-glass Venetian window (c.1863) in Rotunda Hospital's chapel

Garden of Remembrance ❽

Parnell Square. **Map** C1.
⬜ *dawn–dusk daily.*

AT THE NORTHERN END of Parnell Square is a small, peaceful park, dedicated to the men and women who have died in the pursuit of Irish freedom. The Garden of Remembrance marks the spot where several leaders of the 1916 Easter Rising were held overnight before being taken to Kilmainham Gaol (*see p95*), and was also where the Irish Volunteers movement was formed in 1913.

Designed by Daithí Hanly, the garden was opened by President Eamon de Valera (*see p43*) in 1966, to mark the 50th anniversary of the Easter Rising. In the centre of the garden's well-kept lawns is a cruciform pool. A mosaic on the floor of the pool depicts abandoned, broken swords, spears and shields, symbolizing peace. The focal point at one end of the garden is a large bronze sculpture by Oisín Kelly (1971) of the legendary *Children of Lir*, who were changed into swans by their stepmother (*see p25*).

Children of Lir in the **Garden of Remembrance**

Gallery of Writers at Dublin Writers Museum

Dublin Writers Museum ❾

18 Parnell Sq North. **Map** C1. [872 2077. ⬜ *10am–5pm Mon–Sat (Jun–Aug: 10am–6pm), 11am–5pm Sun & public hols (last adm: 45 min before closing.)* ● *25 & 26 Dec.* 🏷

OPENED IN 1991, the museum occupies a tasteful 18th-century town house. There are displays relating to Irish literature in all its forms from around the 10th century to the present day. The exhibits include paintings, manuscripts, letters, rare editions and mementoes of many of Ireland's finest authors. There are a number of temporary exhibits and a sumptuously decorated Gallery of Writers upstairs. The museum also hosts frequent poetry readings and lectures. A good café and a specialist bookstore, providing an out-of-print search service, add to the relaxed, friendly ambience.

Hugh Lane Municipal Gallery of Modern Art ❿

Charlemont House, Parnell Square North. **Map** C1. [874 1903. ⬜ *9:30am–6pm Tue–Thu (Apr–Sep 8pm Thu), 9:30am–5pm Fri & Sat, 11am–5pm Sun.* ● *23–25 Dec & public hols.* Ⓦ *www.hughlane.ie*

ART COLLECTOR Sir Hugh Lane donated his collection of Impressionist paintings to the Dublin Corporation in 1905. However, the failure to find a suitable location for them prompted Lane to begin the process of transferring his gift to the National Gallery in London. The Corporation then proposed Charlemont House and Lane relented. However, in 1915, before Lane's revised will could be witnessed, he died on board the torpedoed liner *Lusitania* (*see p170*). This led to a 50-year dispute which has been resolved by Dublin Corporation and the National Gallery swapping the collection every five years.

Besides the Lane bequest, which includes paintings by Degas, Courbet and Monet, the gallery has an extensive collection of modern Irish paintings and a sculpture hall with work by Rodin and others. An exciting new addition is a bequest by John Edwards of the contents of Francis Bacon's London studio.

Beach Scene (c.1876) by Edgar Degas, Hugh Lane Municipal Gallery

Detail of wood carving (c.1724) at St Michan's Church

King's Inns ⓫

Henrietta St/Constitution Hill.
Map B1. ◔ *to the public.*

THIS CLASSICALLY proportioned public building was founded in 1795 as a place of residence and study for barristers. To build it, James Gandon chose to seal off the end of Henrietta Street, which at the time was one of Dublin's most fashionable addresses. Francis Johnston added the graceful cupola in 1816, and the building was finally completed in 1817. Inside is a fine Dining Hall, and the Registry of Deeds (formerly the Prerogative Court). The west façade has two doorways flanked by Classical caryatids carved by Edward Smyth. The male figure, with book and quill, represents the law.

Sadly, much of **Caryatid,** the area around **King's Inns** Constitution Hill is less attractive than it was in Georgian times. However, the gardens, which are open to the public, are still pleasing.

Smithfield ⓬

Map A2.

LAID OUT IN THE mid-17th century as a marketplace, Smithfield used to be one of Dublin's oldest residential areas. However, the two and a half acre space received a £3.5 million makeover with a well-designed pedestrian cobbled plaza. It is used as a venue for outdoor civic events and is lit by tall gas lighting masts. The traditional horse fair is still held here on the first Sunday of the month and is well worth seeing.

Old Jameson's Distillery ⓭

Bow St. **Map** A2. 🅒 807 2355.
◔ 9am–5:30pm daily (last tour: 5:30pm). ◕ Good Friday, 25 & 26 Dec. 🖪 🗎 🅗 🅗

PROOF OF recent investment in the emerging Smithfield area is this large exhibition in a restored part of John Jameson's distillery, which produced whiskey from 1780 until 1971. A visit here starts with a video and further whiskey-related facts are then explained on a 40-minute tour. This takes you around displays set out as a working distillery, with different rooms devoted to the various stages of production.

The tour guides show how the Irish process differs from that of Scotch whisky: here the barley is dried with clean air, while in Scotland it is smoked over peat. The claim is that the Irish product is a smoother, less smoky tipple. After the tour, visitors can test this in the bar.

Sampling different brands at Old Jameson's Distillery

St Michan's Church ⓮

Church St. **Map** B3. 🅒 872 4154.
◔ mid-Mar–Oct: 10am–12:45pm & 2–4:45pm Mon–Fri, 10am–12:45pm Sat; Nov–mid-Mar: 12:30–3:30pm Mon–Fri, 10am–12:45pm Sat. 🖪 🗎 🅗 🅗 limited.

LARGELY REBUILT IN 1686 on the site of an 11th-century Hiberno-Viking church, the dull façade of St Michan's hides a more exciting interior. Deep in its vaults lie a number of bodies preserved because of the dry atmosphere created by the church's magnesian limestone walls. Their wooden caskets, however, have cracked open, revealing the intact bodies, complete with skin and strands of hair. Among those thought to have been mummified in this way are the brothers Henry and John Sheares, leaders of the 1798 rebellion (see p39), who were executed that year.

Other less gory attractions include the magnificent wood carving of fruits and violins and other instruments above the choir. There is also an organ (1724) on which Handel is said to have played. It is thought that the churchyard contains the unmarked grave of United Irishman Robert Emmet (see p75), leader of the abortive 1803 Rising.

Four Courts ⓯

Inns Quay. **Map** B3. 🅒 872 5555.
◔ 9:30am–12:30pm, 2–4:30pm Mon–Fri (when courts in session).

COMPLETED IN 1796 by James Gandon, this majestic public building overlooks the River Liffey. It was virtually gutted 120 years later during the Irish Civil War (see pp42–3) when government forces bombarded anti-Treaty rebels into submission. The adjacent Public Records Office, with its irreplaceable collection of historical and legal documents dating back to the 12th century, was destroyed by fire.

By 1932, the main buildings were sympathetically restored using Gandon's original design. An imposing copper-covered lantern dome rises above the six-columned Corinthian portico, which is crowned with the figures of Moses, Justice and Mercy. This central section is flanked by two wings containing the four original courts: Common Pleas, Chancery, Exchequer and King's Bench. It is possible to walk into the central waiting hall under the grand dome; an information panel to the right of the entrance gives details of the building's history and functions.

St Mary's Abbey ⓰

Meetinghouse Lane. **Map** C2.
📞 872 1490. ⭘ mid-Jun–mid-Sep: 10am–5pm Wed & Sun. 🖼

Founded by Benedictines in 1139, but transferred to the Cistercian order just eight years later, this was one of the largest and most important monasteries in medieval Ireland. As well as controlling extensive estates, including whole villages, mills and fisheries, the abbey acted as state treasury and meeting place for the Council of Ireland. It was during a council meeting in St Mary's that "Silken Thomas" Fitzgerald (see p36) renounced his allegiance to Henry VIII and marched out to raise the short-lived rebellion of 1534. The monastery was dissolved in 1539 and during the 17th century the site served as a quarry. Stone from St Mary's was used in the construction of Essex Bridge (replaced by Grattan Bridge in 1874), just to the south of the abbey.

All that remains of the abbey today is the vaulted chamber of the Chapter House. This contains a historical display and a model of how the entire complex would have looked 800 years ago.

The Ha'penny Bridge looking from Temple Bar to Liffey Street

Ha'penny Bridge ⓱

Map D3.

Linking the Temple Bar area (see p76) and Liffey Street, this high-arched cast-iron foot-bridge is used by thousands of people every day. It was built by John Windsor, an ironworker from Shropshire, England. One of Dublin's most photographed sights, it was originally named the Wellington Bridge. It is now officially called the Liffey Bridge, but is also known as the Metal Bridge. Opened in 1816, the bridge got its better known nickname from the halfpenny toll that was levied on it up until 1919. A recent restoration, which included the installation of period lanterns, has made the bridge even more attractive.

James Gandon's Four Courts overlooking the River Liffey

FURTHER AFIELD

THERE ARE many interesting sights just outside the city centre. The best part of a day can be spent exploring the western suburbs taking in the modern art museum housed in the splendid Royal Kilmainham Hospital and the eerie Kilmainham Gaol. Phoenix Park, Europe's largest city park, is a good place for a stroll and also has a zoo. Further north are the National Botanic Gardens, with over 20,000 plant species from around the world. Nearby is Marino Casino, one of Ireland's finest examples of Palladian architecture.

Candelabra at Malahide Castle

The magnificent coastline with its stunning views of Dublin Bay is easily reached by the DART rail network. It encompasses the towering promontory of Howth, while the highlights of the southern stretch are around Dalkey village and Killiney Bay. One of many Martello towers built as defences along this coast is known as the James Joyce Tower and houses a collection of Joyce memorabilia. To the northeast, a bit further from the city centre, is Malahide Castle, former home of the Talbot family.

SIGHTS AT A GLANCE

Museums and Galleries
Collins Barracks ❾
Guinness Storehouse ❹
Irish Museum of Modern Art/
   Royal Hospital Kilmainham ❸
James Joyce Tower ⓭

Kilmainham Gaol ❷
Shaw's Birthplace ❻
Waterways Visitors' Centre ❽

Parks and Gardens
National Botanic Gardens ❺
Phoenix Park ❶

Historic Buildings
Malahide Castle ❿
Marino Casino ❼

Towns and Villages
Dalkey ⓮
Dun Laoghaire ⓬
Howth ⓫
Killiney ⓯

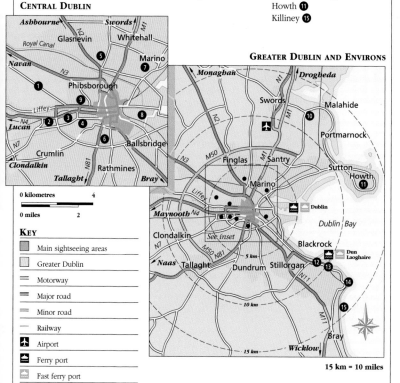

CENTRAL DUBLIN

GREATER DUBLIN AND ENVIRONS

0 kilometres   4
0 miles   2

KEY

   Main sightseeing areas
   Greater Dublin
═ Motorway
═ Major road
═ Minor road
— Railway
✈ Airport
⛴ Ferry port
⛴ Fast ferry port

15 km = 10 miles

◁ **Martello tower at Howth Head**

Phoenix Park ➊

Park Gate, Conyngham Rd, Dublin 8.
🚌 *10, 25, 26, 37, 38, 39 & many other
routes.* 🕐 *7am–11pm daily.* **Phoenix
Park Visitor Centre** 🄲 *677 0095.*
🕐 *Nov–mid March: 9:30am–4:30pm
Sat & Sun only; Apr & May:
9:30am–5:30pm (late Mar & Oct:
5pm) daily; Jun–Sep: 10am–6pm daily.*
📷 🚻 🍴 🚻 *ground floor only.*
Zoo 🄲 *474 8900.* 🕐 *Mar–Sep:
9:30am–6pm Mon–Sat, 10:30am–
6pm Sun; Oct–Feb: 9:30am–dusk
Mon–Sat, 10:30am–dusk Sun.* 📷 🍴
🚻 🚻 📶 *www.dublinzoo.ie*

JUST TO the west of the city
centre, ringed by an 11-km
(7-mile) wall, is Europe's largest
enclosed city park. The name
"Phoenix" is said to be a corruption of the Gaelic *Fionn
Uisce*, or "clear water", referring
to a spring near the **Phoenix
Column**, crowned by a statue
of the mythical bird. Phoenix
Park originated in 1662, when
the Duke of Ormonde turned
the land into a deer park. In
1745 it was landscaped and
opened to the public.

Near Park Gate is the lakeside **People's Garden** – the
only part of the park which
has been cultivated. A little
further on are the **Zoological
Gardens**, established in 1830,
making them the third oldest
zoo in the world. The zoo is
renowned for the successful
breeding of lions, including
the one that appears at the
beginning of MGM movies.
The African Plains savannah
houses the larger residents.

In addition to the Phoenix
Column, the park has two
other conspicuous monuments.
The **Wellington Testimonial**,
a 63-m (206-ft)
obelisk, was begun in
1817 and completed in
1861. Its bronze bas-
reliefs were made
from captured French
cannons. The 27-m
(90-ft) steel **Papal**

**Pope John Paul II celebrating
Mass in Phoenix Park in 1979**

Cross marks the spot where
the pope celebrated Mass in
front of one million people in
1979. Buildings within the
park include two 18th-century
houses: **Áras an Uachtaráin**,
the Irish President's official
residence, for which 525
tickets are issued every
Saturday for a free guided
tour, and **Deerfield**, home of
the US Ambassador. **Ashtown
Castle** is a restored 17th-
century tower house, now
home to the Phoenix Park
Visitor Centre.

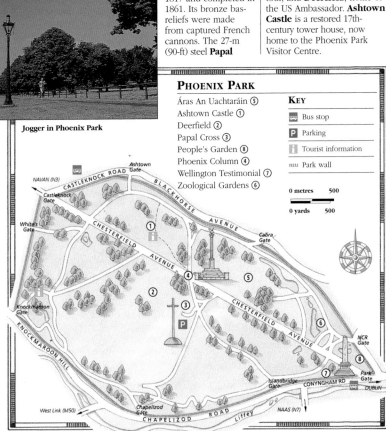

Jogger in Phoenix Park

PHOENIX PARK

Áras An Uachtaráin ⑤
Ashtown Castle ①
Deerfield ②
Papal Cross ③
People's Garden ⑧
Phoenix Column ④
Wellington Testimonial ⑦
Zoological Gardens ⑥

KEY

🚌 Bus stop

🅿 Parking

🛈 Tourist information

⸽⸽⸽⸽ Park wall

0 metres   500

0 yards   500

NAVAN (N3)
Ashtown Gate
CASTLEKNOCK ROAD
Castleknock Gate
BLACKHORSE AVENUE
White's Gate
CHESTERFIELD AVENUE
Cabra Gate
Knockmaroon Gate
CHESTERFIELD AVENUE
KNOCKMAROON HILL
NCR Gate
Park Gate
DUBLIN
CONYNGHAM RD
Islandbridge Gate
West Link (M50)
Chapelizod Gate
CHAPELIZOD ROAD
Liffey
NAAS (N7)

Restored central hall at Kilmainham Gaol

Kilmainham Gaol ❷

Inchicore Rd, Kilmainham, Dublin 8.
📞 453 5984. 🚌 51B, 78A, 79.
🕐 Apr–Sep: 9:30am–6pm Sun–Fri;
Oct–Mar: 9:30am–5pm Mon–Sat,
10am–6pm Sun (last adm: 1 hr
before closing). ● 25 & 26 Dec. 🖼
🎫 📷 📷

A LONG TREE-LINED avenue
runs from the Royal
Hospital Kilmainham to the
grim, grey bulk of Kilmainham
Gaol. The building dates from
1789, but was restored in the
1960s. During its 130 years as
a prison, it housed many of
those involved in the fight for
Irish independence, including
Robert Emmet (see p75) and
Charles Stewart Parnell (p41).
The last prisoner held was
Eamon de Valera (p43), who
was released on 16 July, 1924.

Tours start in the chapel,
where Joseph Plunkett married
Grace Gifford just a few hours
before he faced the firing
squad for his part in the 1916
Rising (see pp42–3). The tours
end in the prison yard where
Plunkett's badly wounded
colleague James Connolly, unable to stand up, was strapped

into a chair before being shot.
You also pass the dank cells
of those involved in the 1798,
1803, 1848 and 1867 uprisings,
as well as the punishment
cells and hanging room.
Exhibits in the central hall
include personal mementos
of some of the former inmates
and depictions of various
events which took place in
the Gaol until it closed in 1924.

Standing in the courtyard is
the *Asgard*, a ship used to
deliver arms from Germany
to the Nationalists in 1914.

Irish Museum of Modern Art – Royal Hospital Kilmainham ❸

Military Road, Kilmainham, Dublin 8.
📞 612 9900. 🚉 Heuston Station.
🚌 26, 51, 51B, 78A, 90, 123. **Irish
Museum of Modern Art** 🕐 10am–
5:30pm Tue–Sat, noon–5:30pm Sun
& public hols (last adm: 5:15pm). ●
Good Fri & 24–26 Dec. 🎫 📷 📷
♿ limited. 🖥 www.modernart.ie

I RELAND'S FINEST surviving 17th-
century building was laid out
in 1680, styled on Les Invalides
in Paris. It was built by Sir
William Robinson as a home
for 300 wounded soldiers – a
role it kept until 1927. When
it was completed, people were
so impressed by its Classical
symmetry that it was suggested it would be better used as
a campus for Trinity College.
The Baroque chapel has fine
carvings and intricate stained
glass. The plaster ceiling is a
replica of the original, which
fell in 1902. The Formal
Gardens, restored using many
of the 17th-century designs,
are now open to the public.

In 1991, the hospital's former
residential quarters became the
Irish Museum of Modern Art.
The collection includes a
cross-section of Irish and
international modern and
contemporary art. Works are
displayed on a rotating basis
and include group and solo
shows, retrospectives and
special visiting exhibitions. A
recent addition is the separate,
multi-screen film theatre.

The Royal Hospital Kilmainham

Drinking Guinness at a local pub

Guinness Storehouse ④

St James's Gate, Dublin 8.
📞 408 4800. 🚌 78A, 51B, 123.
🕐 9:30am–5pm daily.
⬤ Good Fri, 24–26 Dec, 1 Jan.
🎥 ♿ 🏢 🛍 🍴
ⓦ www.guinnessstorehouse.com

THE GUINNESS STOREHOUSE is a new development based in St James's Gate Brewery, the original house of Guinness, now completely remodelled. This 1904 listed building covers nearly four acres of floor space over six floors built around a huge pint glass atrium. The first impression the visitor has is of walking into a large glass pint with light spilling down from above and the original lease signed by Arthur Guinness enshrined on the floor. The Ingredients section is next where visitors can touch, smell and feel the ingredients through interactive displays. The tour continues into an authentic Georgian anteroom to 'meet' Arthur Guinness and see him at work. The Brewing Process is a noisy, steamy and 'hoppy' area giving the impression of brewing all around with full explanation of the process. The historical development of Guinness cooperage is accompanied by a live demonstration of the craft. Models and displays tell the story of Guinness transportation, the appeal of Guinness worldwide, and their popular advertising campaigns. The tour ends with a generous tasting of draught Guinness in the traditional Brewery Bar and the rooftop Gravity Bar.

The Brewing of Guinness

Label from a Guinness bottle

GUINNESS IS A BLACK BEER, known as "stout", renowned for its distinctive malty flavour and smooth creamy head. From its humble beginnings over 200 years ago, the Guinness brewery site at St James's Gate now sprawls across 26 ha (65 acres). It is the largest brewery in Europe and exports beers to more than 120 countries throughout the world. Other famous brands owned by Guinness include Harp Lager and Smithwick's Ale.

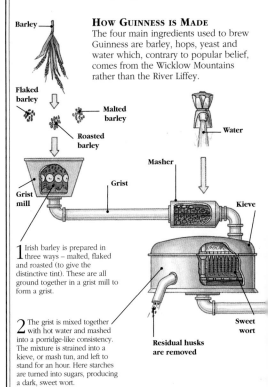

HOW GUINNESS IS MADE

The four main ingredients used to brew Guinness are barley, hops, yeast and water which, contrary to popular belief, comes from the Wicklow Mountains rather than the River Liffey.

Barley

Flaked barley

Malted barley

Roasted barley

Grist mill

Grist

Masher

Water

Kieve

Sweet wort

Residual husks are removed

1 Irish barley is prepared in three ways – malted, flaked and roasted (to give the distinctive tint). These are all ground together in a grist mill to form a grist.

2 The grist is mixed together with hot water and mashed into a porridge-like consistency. The mixture is strained into a kieve, or mash tun, and left to stand for an hour. Here starches are turned into sugars, producing a dark, sweet wort.

Guinness advertising has become almost as famous as the product itself. Since 1929, when the first advertisement announced that *"Guinness is Good for You"*, poster and television advertising campaigns have employed many amusing images of both animals and people.

ARTHUR GUINNESS

Arthur Guinness

In December 1759, 34-year-old Arthur Guinness signed a 9,000-year lease at an annual rent of £45 to take over St James's Gate Brewery, which had lain vacant for almost ten years. At the time the brewing industry in Dublin was at a low ebb – the standard of ale was much criticized and in rural Ireland beer was virtually unknown, as whiskey, gin and poteen were the more favoured drinks. Furthermore, Irish beer was under threat from imports. Guinness started brewing ale, but was also aware of a black ale called porter, produced in London. This new beer was so called because of its popularity with porters at Billingsgate and Covent Garden markets. Guinness decided to stop making ales and develop his own recipe for porter (the word "stout" was not used until the 1920s). So successful was the switch that he made his first export shipment in 1769.

Engraving (c.1794) of a satisfied customer

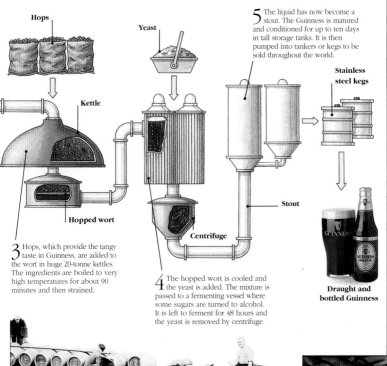

Hops

Yeast

Kettle

Hopped wort

5 The liquid has now become a stout. The Guinness is matured and conditioned for up to ten days in tall storage tanks. It is then pumped into tankers or kegs to be sold throughout the world.

Stainless steel kegs

Stout

Centrifuge

3 Hops, which provide the tangy taste in Guinness, are added to the wort in huge 20-tonne kettles. The ingredients are boiled to very high temperatures for about 90 minutes and then strained.

4 The hopped wort is cooled and the yeast is added. The mixture is passed to a fermenting vessel where some sugars are turned to alcohol. It is left to ferment for 48 hours and the yeast is removed by centrifuge.

Draught and bottled Guinness

The Guinness brewery has relied heavily on water transport since its first export was shipped to England in 1769. The barges, which up until 1961 made the short trip with their cargo up the Liffey to Dublin Port, were a familiar sight on the river. Once at port, the stout would be loaded on to huge tanker ships for worldwide distribution.

Steel kettles used in modern-day brewing

Giant water lilies in the Lily House, National Botanic Gardens

National Botanic Gardens ❺

Botanic Ave, Glasnevin, Dublin 9.
▌ 837 4388. **▦** 13, 19, 19A, 134.
◯ Mar–Oct: 9am–6pm Mon–Sat, 11am–6pm Sun; Nov–Feb: 10am–4:30pm Mon–Sat, 11am–4:30pm Sun.
◯ 25 Dec. **▯ ▮ �* ▮** free on Sun 2:30pm, groups on request.
Glasnevin Cemetery Finglas Rd.
▌ 830 1133. **▦** 40A, 40B from Parnell Street. **◯** 8am–4:30pm daily.

Opened in 1795, the National Botanic Gardens are Ireland's foremost centre of botany and horticulture. They still possess an old-world feel, thanks to the beautiful cast-iron Palm House and other curvilinear glasshouses. These were built between 1843 and 1869 by Richard Turner, the architect who was also responsible for the Palm House at Kew Gardens, London, and the glasshouses at Belfast's Botanic Gardens (see p270).

The 20-ha (49-acre) park contains over 20,000 different plant species. Particularly attractive are the colourful old-fashioned Victorian carpet bedding, the rich collections of cacti and orchids, renowned rose garden, and 30-m (100-ft) high redwood tree.

The gardens back on to the huge Glasnevin or Prospect Cemetery where many of Ireland's political figures are buried, including Charles Stewart Parnell (see p41) and Daniel O'Connell (see p40).

Shaw's Birthplace ❻

33 Synge St, Dublin 8. **▌** 475 0854.
▦ 16, 19, 122. **◯** May–Sep: 10am–5pm Mon–Sat, 2–6pm Sun & public hols. **▯ ▮**

Kitchen at Shaw's Birthplace

Playwright and Nobel prize-winner George Bernard Shaw was born in this house on 26 July 1856. In 1876 he followed his mother to London. She had left four years earlier with her daughters, fed up with her husband's drinking habits. It was in London that Shaw met his wife Charlotte Payne-Townsend. He stayed in England until his death in 1950.

Inside the house visitors can see the young Shaw's bedroom and the kitchen where the author remembered he drank "much tea out of brown delft left to 'draw' on the hob until it was pure tannin". Although there is little on Shaw's productive years, the home gives a fair idea of the lifestyle of a Victorian middle-class family.

Marino Casino ❼

Fairview Park, off Malahide Rd.
▌ 833 1618. **▮** DART to Clontarf.
▦ 20A, 20B, 27, 42, 42C, 123. **◯** May–Oct 10am–5pm daily (Jun–Sep: 6pm); Nov–Apr: noon–4pm Sat & Sun (Apr: 5pm). **▯ ▮** obligatory (last tour 45 min before closing).

This delightful little villa (see pp38–9), built by Sir William Chambers in the 1760s for Lord Charlemont, now sits incongruously next to a busy road and a housing estate. Originally built as a summer house for the Marino Estate, the villa survives although the main house was pulled down in 1921. The Casino is acknowledged to be one of the finest examples of Palladian architecture in Ireland. Some innovative features were used in its construction, including chimneys disguised as urns and hollow columns that accommodate drains. Outside, four carved stone lions, thought to be by English sculptor Joseph Wilton, stand guard at each of the corners.

Carved stone lion at Marino Casino

The building's squat, compact exterior conceals eight rooms built on three floors around a central staircase. The ground floor comprises a spacious hall and a saloon, with beautiful silk hangings, elaborate flooring and a coffered ceiling. On the first floor is the ostentatious State Room.

Waterways Visitors' Centre ⓧ

Grand Canal Quay, Dublin 2.
677 7510. 2,3. ◐ Jun–Sep:
9:30am–5:30pm daily; Oct–May:
12:30pm–5pm Wed–Sun (last adm
45 mins before closing). ● 25 Dec.
on request.

FIFTEEN MINUTES' WALK from Trinity College this building overlooks the Grand Canal Basin. Audiovisual displays and models illustrate Ireland's inland waterways and the wildlife found on and around them. One of the most interesting displays focuses on their construction: in the 18th century, canals were often called "navigations" and the men who built them were "navigators", a term shortened to "navvies".

DUBLIN'S CANALS

The affluent Georgian era witnessed the building of the Grand and Royal canals linking Dublin with the River Shannon and the west coast. These two canals became the main arteries of trade and public transport in Ireland from the 1760s until the coming of the railways, which took much of the passenger business, almost a century later. However, the canals continued to carry freight until after World War II, finally closing to commercial traffic in 1960. Today the canals are well maintained and used mainly for pleasure-boating, cruising and fishing.

Late 18th-century engraving of passenger ferry passing Harcourt Lock on the Grand Canal, taken from a painting by James Barralet

Stretch of the Grand Canal near Waterways Visitors' Centre

National Museum at Collins Barracks ⓧ

Benburb St, Dublin 7. 677
7444. 25, 25A, 66, 67, 90.
◐ 10am–5pm Tue–Sat, 2–5pm Sun.
● Good Fri, 25 Dec.

CLOSE TO Phoenix Park and just across the Liffey from the Guinness Brewery stands the wonderful annexe of the National Museum (see pp64–5). Its setting in this historic building is an inspired move. The massive complex was commissioned by King William III in 1690, just ten years after victory at the Battle of the Boyne, and was the largest barracks in his domain, with living accommodation for over 5,000 people. It was in continuous use right up to

the 1990s. Originally known as Dublin Barracks, the prefix was changed to "Royal" in 1803. After Irish independence the barracks was finally named for Michael Collins, the first commander-in-chief of the Irish Army.

The large central courtyard, measured at one hundred marching paces, is an object lesson in simplicity. In marked contrast to the grey institutional exterior, the museum's interior presents the exhibits in an innovative way that makes use of the latest technology.

Furniture, silver and scientific instrument collections form the bulk of items on show in the South Block. In the West Block, however, visitors get an insight into the

history, work and development of the National Museum. The Out of Storage exhibit brings together a wide array of artifacts from around the world, with background information obtainable from banks of interactive multimedia computers. One of the highlights of the museum is the Curator's Choice section where 25 unusual exhibits – such as, for instance, an early hurling stick and ball – are displayed with a story line that explains their cultural significance.

There is also a large hall set aside for temporary displays. On-going expansion plans incorporate the entire barracks.

An 18th-century, gilded wooden chair on display at Collins Barracks

The oak-beamed Great Hall at Malahide Castle

Malahide Castle ⑩

Malahide, Co Dublin. 🚆 and DART to Malahide. 🚌 42 from Beresford Place, near Busáras. 🛈 846 2184. ⏰ Apr–Oct: 10am–5pm Mon–Sat, 11am–6pm Sun & public hols; Nov–Mar: 10am–5pm Mon–Sat, 11am–5pm Sun & public hols (check for lunchtime closures in winter). 🔲 🎥 obligatory (last tours 4:30pm). **Fry Model Railway** ⏰ Apr–Sep: 10am–1pm 2–6pm Mon–Sat, 2–6pm Sun & public hols; Oct: 10am–1pm 2–5pm Sat, 2–5pm Sun. ⚫ Nov–Mar. 🖼 ♿

Near the seaside dormitory town of Malahide stands a huge castle set in 100 ha (250 acres) of grounds. The castle's core dates from the 14th century but later additions, such as its rounded towers, have given it a classic fairy-tale appearance. The building served as a stately home for the Talbot family until 1973. They were staunch supporters of James II: on the day of the Battle of the Boyne in 1690 *(see p236)*, 14 members of the family breakfasted here; none came back for supper.

Guided tours take you round the castle's collection of 18th-century Irish furniture, the oak-beamed Great Hall and the impressively carved Oak Room. Part of the Portrait Collection, on loan from the National Gallery *(see pp68–9)*, can be seen here. It includes portraits of the Talbot family and other figures such as Wolfe Tone *(see p39)*.

In the old corn store is the Fry Model Railway, started in the 1920s by Cyril Fry, a local railway engineer. The 240 sq m (2,500 sq ft) exhibit contains models of Irish trains, miniatures of stations, streets and local landmarks such as the River Liffey and Howth Head.

Howth ⑪

Co Dublin. 🚆 DART. **Howth Castle grounds** ⏰ 8am–sunset daily.

The commercial fishing town of Howth marks the northern limit of Dublin Bay. Howth Head, a huge rocky mass, has lovely views of the bay. A footpath runs around the tip of Howth Head, which is known as the "Nose". Nearby is Baily Lighthouse (1814). Sadly, much of this area – some of Ireland's prime real estate – has suffered from building development.

To the west of the town is Howth Castle, which dates back to Norman times. Its grounds are particularly beautiful in May and June when the rhododendrons and azaleas are in full bloom.The National Transport Museum in the grounds is worth a visit.

Ireland's Eye, an islet and bird sanctuary where puffins nest, can be reached by a short boat trip from Howth.

Dun Laoghaire ⑫

Co Dublin. 🚆 DART. **National Maritime Museum** 🛈 280 0969. ⚫ closed for renovation. **Comhaltas Ceoltóiri Éireann** 🛈 280 0295. ⏰ music Wed, Fri & Sat nights, céili Fri

Ireland's major passenger ferry port and yachting centre, with its brightly painted villas, parks and palm trees, makes a surprising

Baily Lighthouse on the southeastern tip of Howth Head

Yachts anchored in Dun Laoghaire harbour

introduction to Ireland. On a good day it exudes a decidedly continental feel. Many visitors head straight out of Dun Laoghaire (pronounced Dunleary) but the town offers some magnificent walks around the harbour and to the lighthouse along the east pier. The villages of Sandycove and Dalkey can be reached via "The Metals" footpath which runs alongside the railway line.

In the 1837 Mariners' Church is the National Maritime Museum. Exhibits include a longboat used by French officers during Wolfe Tone's unsuccessful invasion at Bantry in 1796 (*see pp160–61*).

Up the road in Monkstown's Belgrave Square is the Comhaltas Ceoltóirí Éireann, Ireland's main centre for traditional music and dance, with music sessions and *céilís* (dances).

James Joyce Tower ⓭

Sandycove, Co Dublin. 📞 280 9265.
🚉 *DART to Sandycove.* 🚌 59
🕐 *10am–5pm Mon–Sat, 2–6pm Sun & public hols.* ⬤ *1–2pm weekdays.* 📷 🚻

STANDING on a rocky promontory above the village of Sandycove is this Martello tower. It is one of 15 defensive towers erected between Dublin and Bray in 1804 to withstand a threatened invasion by Napoleon. One hundred years later James Joyce (*see p88*) stayed here for a week as the guest of Oliver St John Gogarty, poet and model for the *Ulysses* character Buck Mulligan. Gogarty rented the tower for a mere £8 per year. Inside the squat 12-m (40-ft) tower's granite walls is a small museum with some of Joyce's correspondence, personal belongings, such as his guitar, cigar case and walking stick, and his death mask. There are also photographs and first editions of his works, including a de luxe edition (1935) of *Ulysses* illustrated by Henri Matisse. The roof, originally a gun platform but later used as a sunbathing deck by Gogarty, affords marvellous views of Dublin Bay. Below the tower is Forty Foot Pool, tradition-ally an all-male nude bathing spot, but now open to all.

Guitar at James Joyce Tower

Dalkey ⓮

Co Dublin. 🚉 *DART.*

DALKEY was once known as the "Town of Seven Castles", but only two of these now remain. They are both on the main street of this attractive village whose tight, winding roads and charming villas give it a Mediterranean feel.

A little way offshore is tiny Dalkey Island, a rocky bird sanctuary with a Martello tower and a medieval Benedictine church, both now in a poor state of repair. In summer the island can be reached by a boat ride from the town's Coliemore Harbour.

Killiney ⓯

Co Dublin. 🚉 *DART to Dalkey or Killiney.*

SOUTH OF DALKEY, the coastal road climbs uphill before tumbling down into the village of Killiney. The route offers one of the most scenic vistas on this stretch of the east coast, with views often compared to those across the Bay of Naples. Howth Head is clearly visible to the north, with Bray Head (*see p125*) and the foothills of the Wicklow Mountains (*see pp130–31*) to the south. There is another exhilarating view from the top of Killiney Hill Park, off Victoria Road – well worth tackling the short steep trail for. Down below is the popular pebbly beach, Killiney Strand.

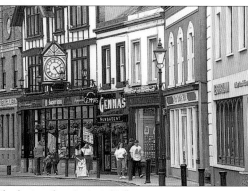

Shopfronts on the main street of Dalkey

ENTERTAINMENT IN DUBLIN

Olympia Theatre façade

Although Dublin is well served by theatres, cinemas, nightclubs and rock venues, what sets the city apart from other European capitals is its pubs. Lively banter, impromptu music sessions and great Guinness are the essential ingredients for an enjoyable night in any one of dozens of atmospheric hostelries.

One of the most popular entertainment districts is the rejuvenated Temple Bar area. Along this narrow network of cobbled streets you can find everything from traditional music in grand old pubs to the latest dance tracks in a postindustrial setting. The many pubs and venues around this area make the city centre south of the Liffey the place to be at night. The north side does, however, boast the two most illustrious theatres, the largest cinemas and the 7,000-seater Point Theatre, a converted 19th-century rail terminal beside the docks. It is now the venue for all major rock concerts and stage musicals as well as a number of classical music performances.

Buskers playing near Grafton Street in southeast Dublin

ENTERTAINMENT LISTINGS

The main listings magazine, *In Dublin*, comes out every two weeks and is readily available from all newsagents. *Hot Press*, a national bimonthly newspaper that covers both rock and traditional music, has comprehensive listings for Dublin. The *Dublin Event Guide* is a free sheet available from pubs, cafés, restaurants and record shops. Also published every two weeks, it is particularly strong on music and nightclubs.

BOOKING TICKETS

Tickets for many events are available on the night, but it is usually safer to book in advance. All the major venues take credit card payment over the telephone. **Ticket Shop** accepts phone bookings by credit card only for many of the major shows and events in and around Dublin, while

HMV and Dublin Tourism (Suffolk Street) sell tickets for most of the top theatres and major rock gigs.

THEATRE

Although Dublin has only a limited number of theatres, there is almost always something worth seeing and productions are of a very high standard. Most of Dublin's theatres are closed on Sunday.

The most famous venue is Ireland's national theatre, the **Abbey** *(see p86),* which concentrates on major new Irish productions as well as revivals of work by Irish playwrights such as Brendan Behan, Sean O'Casey, JM Synge and WB Yeats. The smaller Peacock Theatre downstairs covers more experimental works. Also on the north side is the **Gate Theatre** *(see p88)* founded in 1929 and noted for its interpretations of well-known international plays.

The main venue south of the Liffey, the **Gaiety Theatre**, stages a mainstream mix of plays, emphasizing the work of Irish playwrights. Some of the best fringe theatre and modern dance in Dublin can be seen at the **Project** arts centre in Temple Bar and the **City Arts Centre**, which sometimes has midnight performances. **Andrews Lane Theatre** provides a forum for new writers and directors. The **Olympia Theatre** has the feel of a Victorian music hall. It specializes in comedy and popular drama and occasionally stages rock and Irish music concerts.

Every October the **Dublin Theatre Festival** takes over all the venues in the city with mainstream, fringe, Irish and international plays.

Record shop and ticket office in Crown Alley, Temple Bar

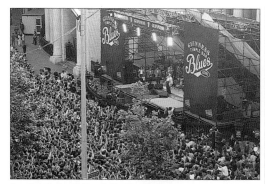
Crowds enjoying the Temple Bar Blues Festival

CLASSICAL MUSIC, OPERA AND DANCE

DUBLIN may not have the range of classical concerts of other European capitals, but it has a great venue in the **National Concert Hall**. In the 1980s, this 19th-century exhibition hall was redesigned, and is where the National Symphony Orchestra plays most Friday evenings. The programme also includes opera, chamber music, jazz, dance and some traditional music.

The **Hugh Lane Municipal Gallery of Modern Art** (see p89) has regular Sunday lunchtime concerts. Other classical venues include the **Royal Hospital Kilmainham** (see p95), **Bank of Ireland Arts Centre** on Dame Street and the **Royal Dublin Society (RDS)** in Ballsbridge. International opera is staged in the **Point Theatre**. The DGOS (Dublin Grand Opera Society) performs every April and November at the Gaiety Theatre.

TRADITIONAL MUSIC AND DANCE

TO MANY IRISH PEOPLE the standard of music in a pub is just as important as the quality of the Guinness. Central Dublin has a host of pubs reverberating to the sound of *bodhráns*, fiddles and uilleann pipes. One of the most famous is **O'Donoghue's**, where the

The listings magazine
In Dublin

legendary Dubliners started out in the early 1960s. The **Cobblestone** and the **Auld Dubliner** are also renowned venues. Established acts play venues such as **Mother Redcap's Tavern**, which is a fun place occupying an old factory. **Jury's Hotel** and the **Castle Inn** stage Irish cabaret (May–October) featuring dancing, singing and music.

ROCK, JAZZ, BLUES AND COUNTRY

DUBLIN has had a thriving rock scene ever since local band Thin Lizzy made it big in the early 1970s. U2's international success has acted as a further catalyst for local bands, and each night there's usually an interesting gig somewhere in the city. **Whelan's** and the **Baggot Inn** feature the best up-and-coming Irish bands

nightly. The upstairs room at the likeable **International Bar** caters mostly for acoustic acts and singer-songwriters, while the **Ha'penny Bridge Inn** has folk and blues on Friday and Saturday nights. Big names play at either the **Point Theatre** or, in summer, local sports stadia. The **Olympia** also attracts top performers. Outside Dublin, **Slane Castle** hosts a big rock event every summer (see p237). **The Temple Bar Music Centre** and **The Sugar Club** offer jazz, salsa, latin and blues all year, with the **Heineken Green Energy Festival** a highlight in May. Country music enjoys a huge following in Ireland, and plays regularly at several Dublin pubs. Check entertainment listings for details.

NIGHTCLUBS

UNTIL A CLUSTER of new dance venues opened in the early 1990s, Dublin's club-life was fairly unremarkable. Nowadays the **POD** (Place of Dance) attracts visiting stars taking time out from their film shoots in the city. Another trendy place is **Spy**, located on South William Street. **Rí-Rá** (Irish for uproar) is at the cutting edge of R&B and dance music, while **River Club** and **Lillie's Bordello** provide a more mainstream dance sound.

Most clubs close at 2am. For further action, head for clubs like **Buck Whaleys** on Leeson Street which stay open until 5am. Admission is free, but drinks prices are high.

A traditional Irish music session in O'Donoghue's

Traditional façade of Doheny & Nesbitt

PUBS AND BARS

DUBLIN'S PUBS are a slice of living history. These are the places where some of the best-known scenes in Irish literature have been set, where rebellious politicians have met and where world-famous music acts have made their debuts. Today, as well as the memorabilia on the walls, it's the singing, dancing, talk and laughter that make a pub tour of Dublin an absolute must.

There are nearly 1,000 pubs inside the city limits. Among the best of the traditional bars are **Neary's**, popular with actors and featuring a gorgeous marble bar, the atmospheric **Long Hall** and the friendly **Stag's Head**, dating from 1770.

Cosy snugs – where drinkers could lock themselves away for private conversation – were an important feature of 19th-century bars. A few remain, notably at the tiny, journalists' haunt of **Doheny & Nesbitt** and the intimate **Kehoe's**.

The **Brazen Head** claims to be the city's oldest pub, dating back to 1198. The present pub, built in the 1750s, is lined with old photographs and dark wood panelling. Every pub prides itself on the quality of its Guinness, though most locals acknowledge that **Mulligan's**, founded in 1782, serves one of the best pints in the city.

The range extends beyond smoky pubs with nicotine-stained ceilings: the splendid decor of the **Shelbourne Bar**, in the Shelbourne Hotel, pulls in a sophisticated crowd. Good bars abound in the Trinity College and Temple Bar areas, including **The Norseman** and **Oliver St John Gogarty**.

A LITERARY PUB CRAWL

PUBS with strong literary associations abound in Dublin, particularly around Grafton Street. **McDaid's**, an old pub with an Art Deco interior, still retains some of the Bohemian air from the time when famous writer-drinkers such as Patrick Kavanagh and Brendan Behan were regulars. **Davy Byrne's** has much plusher decor than when Leopold Bloom dropped in for a gorgonzola and mustard sandwich in *Ulysses*, but it is still well worth paying a visit. These and about six other pubs, once frequented by Ireland's most famous authors and playwrights, are featured on the excellent **Dublin Literary**

GUINNESS TIME

A Guinness sign on the outside of a Dublin pub

Pub Crawl. This is by far the most entertaining way to get a real feel for the city's booze-fuelled literary heritage. The two-and-a-half-hour tours, which are led by actors, start with a beer in **The Duke**. Tours take place daily in summer, but are usually only at weekends in winter.

CINEMA

DUBLIN'S CINEMAS had a boost in the 1990s with the success of Dublin-based films such as *My Left Foot* (1989). Huge growth in the country's movie production industry followed, and hits like *Dancing at Lughnasa* (1998) keep Ireland in the spotlight.

The **Irish Film Centre** opened its doors in 1992 and is a most welcome addition to the city's entertainment scene. Showing mostly independent and foreign films, along with a programme of lectures and seminars, it boasts two screens, as well as a bar and restaurant. Another cinema whose repertoire is mostly art house is the **Screen**, close to Trinity College. The large first-run cinemas are all located on the north side. These usually offer tickets at reduced prices for their afternoon screenings and show late-night films at the weekend. The summer-long **Diversions** festival in Temple Bar includes open air screenings, mainly in Meeting House Square. Tickets are from Temple Bar Properties.

Bustling interior of the Oliver St John Gogarty pub in Temple Bar

DIRECTORY

BOOKING AGENTS

HMV
18 Henry St. **Map** D2.
65 Grafton St. **Map** D4.

Ticketmaster
[1890 925 100.
w www.ticketmaster.ie

THEATRE

Abbey Theatre
Abbey St Lower. **Map** E2.
[878 7222.

Andrews Lane Theatre
9–11 St Andrew's Lane.
Map D3. [679 5720.

City Arts Centre
23–25 Moss St. **Map** E2.
[677 0643.

Dublin Theatre Festival
44 Essex St. East. **Map**
C3. [677 8439.

Focus Theatre
6 Pembroke Place.
Map E5. [676 3071.

Gaiety Theatre
King St South. **Map** D4.
[677 1717.
w www.gaietytheatre.com

Gate Theatre
Cavendish Row. **Map** D1.
[874 4045.

Olympia Theatre
Dame St. **Map** C3
[1890 925 130.

Project
39 East Essex St.
Map C3. [679 6622.
w www.project.ie

CLASSICAL MUSIC, OPERA AND DANCE

Bank of Ireland Arts Centre
Foster Place, College
Green. **Map** D3.
[671 1488.

Hugh Lane Municipal Gallery of Modern Art
Charlemont House, Parnell
Sq North. **Map** C1.
[874 1903.
w www.hughlane.ie

National Concert Hall
Earlsfort Terrace. **Map** D5.
[475 1666.
w www.nch.ie

Point Theatre
East Link Bridge, North
Wall Quay. **Map** D1.
[836 3633.
w www.thepoint.ie

Royal Dublin Society (RDS)
Ballsbridge. [668 0866.
w www.rds.ie

Royal Hospital Kilmainham
Kilmainham.
[612 9900.

TRADITIONAL MUSIC AND DANCE

Auld Dubliner
24–25 Temple Bar.
Map D3. [677 0527.

Castle Inn
5–7 Lord Edward St.
Map C3. [475 1122.

Cobblestone
77 King Street North.
Map A2. [872 1799.

Jury's Hotel
Pembroke Rd, Ballsbridge.
[660 5000. May–Oct.

Mother Redcap's Tavern
Back Lane, Christchurch.
Map B4. [453 8306.

O'Donoghue's
15 Merrion Row.
Map E5. [660 7194.

ROCK, JAZZ, BLUES AND COUNTRY

Ha'penny Bridge Inn
Wellington Quay.
Map C3. [677 0616.

International Bar
23 Wicklow Street.
Map D3. [677 9250.

Temple Bar Music Centre
Curved Street, Temple Bar.
Map E4. [670 9202.
w www.tbmc.ie

Whelan's
25 Wexford St. **Map** C5.
[478 0766.

NIGHTCLUBS

Buck Whaleys
67 Lower Leeson St.
Map E5. [676 1755.

Lillie's Bordello
Adam Court, off Grafton
St. **Map** D4. [679 9204.

POD
Harcourt St. **Map** D5.
[478 0166.

Rí-Rá
11 South Great George's
St. **Map** C3. [671 1220.

River Club
Merchants' Arch. **Map** D3.
[677 2382.

Spy
South William St.
Map D4. [677 0014.

The Sugar Club
8 Lower Leeson Street.
Map E5. [678 7188.

PUBS AND BARS

Brazen Head
20 Bridge St Lower.
Map A3. [677 9549.

Davy Byrne's
21 Duke St. **Map** D4.
[677 5217.

Doheny & Nesbitt
5 Lower Baggot St.
Map E5. [676 2945.

Dublin Literary Pub Crawl
37 Exchequer Street.
Map D3. [670 5602.

The Duke
9 Duke Street.
Map D4. [679 9553.

Kehoe's
9 South Anne St. **Map** D4.
[677 8312.

Long Hall
51 South Great George's
St. **Map** C4. [475 1590.

McDaid's
3 Harry St, off Grafton St.
Map D4. [679 4395.

Mulligan's
8 Poolbeg St. **Map** E3.
[677 5582.

Neary's
1 Chatham St. **Map** D4.
[677 8596.

The Norseman
29 East Essex St, Temple
Bar. **Map** C3.
[671 5135.

The Octagon Bar
The Clarence, 6–8
Wellington Quay.
Map C3. [671 5135.

Oliver St John Gogarty
58–59 Fleet St, Temple Bar.
Map D3. [671 1822.

Queen's
12 Castle St, Dalkey.
[285 4569.

Shelbourne Bar
27 St Stephen's Green
North. **Map** E4.
[676 6471.

Stag's Head
1 Dame Court, off Dame
Lane. **Map** D3.
[679 3701.

Toner's
139 Lower Baggot St.
Map E5. [676 3090.

CINEMA

Diversions
Meeting House Square.
Map C3. [671 5717.
w www.templebar.ie

Irish Film Centre
6 Eustace St, Temple Bar.
Map C3. [679 5744.

Screen
D'Olier St. **Map** D3.
[672 5500.

UGC Cinemas
Parnell St. **Map** C2.
[872 8400.

Dublin's Best: Entertainment

IT'S EASY TO PACK a lot into a night out in Dublin. Most of the best nightspots are situated close to each other and, in the Temple Bar area alone, there are plenty of exciting haunts to try out. The city offers something to suit every taste and pocket: choose from world-class theatre, excellent concert venues, designer café-bars and lively or laid-back clubs hosting nights of traditional, country, jazz or rock music. Even when there is no specific event that appeals, you can simply enjoy Dublin's inexhaustible supply of great traditional pubs.

Gate Theatre
The Gate puts on both foreign plays and Irish classics such as Sean O'Casey's Juno and the Paycock. *(See p88.)*

NORTH OF
THE LIFFEY

Stag's Head
This gorgeous Victorian pub has a long, mahogany bar and has retained its original mirrors and stained glass. Located down an out-of-the-way alley, this atmospheric pub is well worth seeking out. (See p105.)

SOUTHWEST
DUBLIN

0 metres　　　　　500

0 yards　　　　　500

THE TEMPLE BAR AREA

It will take more than a couple of evenings to explore fully all that these narrow streets have to offer. Many of Dublin's best mid-priced restaurants are here, while modern bars sit next to traditional pubs hosting fiddle sessions. There are also theatres and the Irish Film Centre. Later, clubs play music ranging from country to the latest dance sounds.

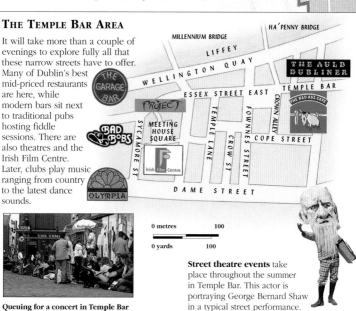

0 metres　　　　　100

0 yards　　　　　100

Queuing for a concert in Temple Bar

Street theatre events take place throughout the summer in Temple Bar. This actor is portraying George Bernard Shaw in a typical street performance.

Abbey Theatre
Despite recurring financial problems, Ireland's prestigious national theatre still manages to stage compelling new drama, such as Dancing at Lughnasa *by Brian Friel. (See p86.)*

Point Theatre
Once a Victorian railway terminus, this is now the country's top live music arena. Major acts, including Van Morrison (above) and Luciano Pavarotti, have appeared here and it's also a popular venue for hit musicals. (See p105.)

LIFFEY

SOUTHEAST DUBLIN

McDaid's
Playwright Brendan Behan (see p21) downed many a pint in this pub, which dates from 1779. Though firmly on the tourist trail, McDaid's retains its bohemian charm, and bars upstairs and downstairs provide space for a leisurely drink. (See p105.)

National Concert Hall
The National Symphony Orchestra performs most Friday evenings. A combination of dance, chamber music and other performance arts makes up a full programme of events. From May to July, inexpensive Tuesday lunch-time concerts are held. (See p103.)

Street Finder Index

KEY TO THE STREET FINDER

Major sight	Coach station	Church
Place of interest	Taxi rank	Post office
Railway station	Main car park	Railway line
DART station	Tourist information office	One-way street
Luas stop	Hospital with casualty unit	Pedestrian street
Main bus stop	Police station	

0 metres 200
0 yards 200
1:11,500

KEY TO STREET FINDER ABBREVIATIONS

Ave	Avenue	**E**	East	**Pde**	Parade	**Sth**	South
Br	Bridge	**La**	Lane	**Pl**	Place	**Tce**	Terrace
Cl	Close	**Lr**	Lower	**Rd**	Road	**Up**	Upper
Ct	Court	**Nth**	North	**St**	Street/Saint	**W**	West

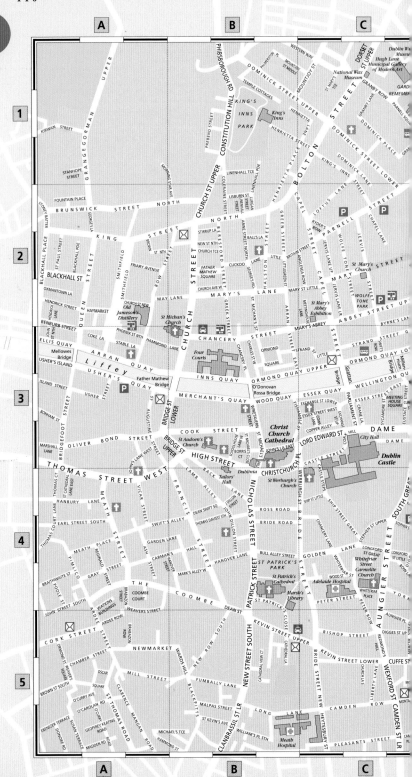

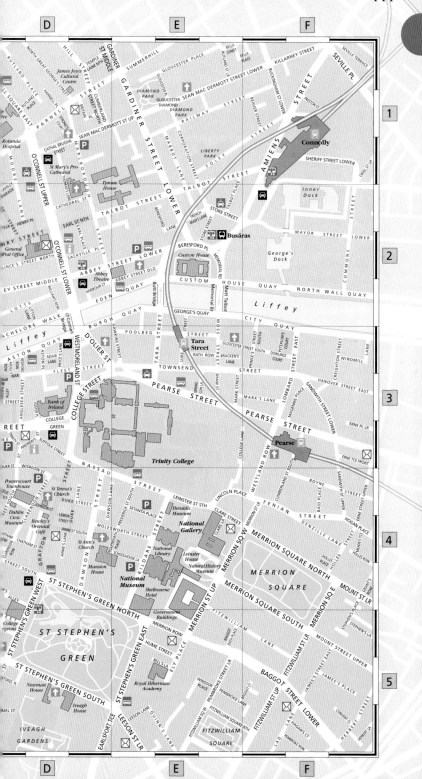

IRELAND REGION BY REGION

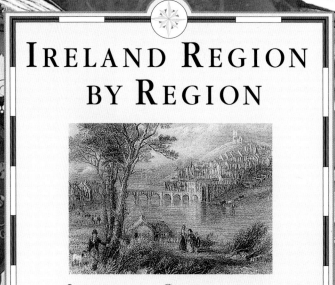

Ireland at a Glance

THE LURE of Ireland's much-vaunted Atlantic shores, from the wild coastline of Cork and Kerry to the remote peninsulas of the Northwest, is strong. However, to neglect the interior would be to miss out on Ireland's equally characteristic landscapes of lush valleys, dark peatlands and unruffled loughs. Most regions are rich in historic sights: from world-famous Neolithic sites in the Midlands to imposing Norman castles in the North and Palladian mansions in the Southeast.

Yeats Country is a charming part of County Sligo closely associated with WB Yeats. The poet was born here and is buried within sight of Ben Bulben's ridge. (See pp224–5.)

NORTHWEST IRELAND
(See pp212–

Connemara National Park in County Galway boasts stunning landscapes in which mountains and lakes are combined with a dramatic Atlantic coastline. The extensive blanket bogs and moorland are rich in wildlife and unusual plants. (See p200.)

THE WEST OF IRELAND
(See pp192–211)

Bunratty Castle
(See pp184–5)

The Rock of Cashel, a fortified medieval abbey, perches on a limestone outcrop in the heart of County Tipperary. It boasts some of Ireland's finest Romanesque sculpture. (See pp188–9.)

THE LOWER SHANNON
(See pp172–91)

CORK AND KERRY
(See pp144–71)

Bantry House
(See pp160–61)

The Lakes of Killarney, flanked by the lush, wooded slopes of some of the country's highest mountains, are the principal attraction in the southwest of Ireland. (See pp154–5.)

The Giant's Causeway, where ancient lava flows have been eroded to reveal columns of unnatural regularity, is Northern Ireland's most curious sight. According to local mythology, the rocks were placed here by a giant called Finn MacCool to enable him to walk across the sea to Scotland. (See pp254–5.)

NORTHERN IRELAND
(See pp246–77)

THE MIDLANDS
(See pp228–45)

Newgrange
(See pp238–9)

Mount Stewart House, a 19th-century mansion, is most renowned for its magnificent gardens. These were created as recently as the 1920s, but a colourful array of exotic plants has thrived in the warm microclimate enjoyed in this part of County Down. (See pp274–5.)

SOUTHEAST IRELAND
(See pp116–43)

Powerscourt is a large estate in superb countryside on the edge of the Wicklow Mountains. Its grounds rank among the last great formal gardens of Europe. Originally planted in the 1730s, they were restored and embellished in the 19th century. (See pp126–7.)

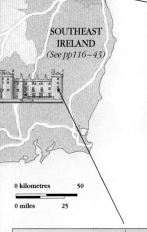

0 kilometres	50
0 miles	25

Kilkenny Castle was for centuries the stronghold of the Butler dynasty, which controlled much of southeast Ireland in the Middle Ages. The vast Norman fortress was remodelled during the Victorian period and still dominates Kilkenny – one of the country's most historic and pleasant towns. (See pp134–6.)

SOUTHEAST IRELAND

KILDARE · WICKLOW · CARLOW · KILKENNY
WATERFORD · WEXFORD

BLESSED WITH *the warmest climate in Ireland, the Southeast has always presented an attractive prospect for settlers. Landscapes of gently rolling hills have been tamed by centuries of cultivation, with lush farmland, imposing medieval castles and great houses enhancing the region's atmosphere of prosperity.*

The Southeast's proximity to Britain meant that it was often the first port of call for foreign invaders. Viking raiders arrived here in the 9th century and founded some of Ireland's earliest towns, including Waterford and Wexford. They were followed in 1169 by the Anglo-Normans *(see pp34–5)*, who shaped the region's subsequent development.

Given its strategic importance, the Southeast was heavily protected, mostly by Anglo-Norman lords loyal to the English Crown. Remains of impressive castles attest to the power of the Fitzgeralds of Kildare and the Butlers of Kilkenny, who between them virtually controlled the Southeast throughout the Middle Ages. English influence was stronger here than in any other part of the island.

From the 18th century, wealthy Anglo-Irish families were drawn to what they saw as a stable zone, and felt confident enough to build fine mansions like the Palladian masterpieces of Russborough and Castletown. English rule was not universally accepted, however. The Wicklow Mountains became a popular refuge for opponents to the Crown, including the rebels who fled the town of Enniscorthy after a bloody battle during the uprising against the English in 1798 *(see p39)*.

This mountainous region is still the only real wilderness in the Southeast, in contrast to the flat grasslands that spread across Kildare to the west. To the east, sandy beaches stretch almost unbroken along the shore between Dublin and Rosslare in Wexford.

Traditional thatched cottages in Dunmore East, County Waterford

◁ **Staircase hall with ornate 18th-century stuccowork in Castletown House, County Kildare**

Exploring Southeast Ireland

THE SOUTHEAST has something for everyone, from busy seaside resorts to quaint canalside villages, Norman abbeys and bird sanctuaries. The Wicklow Mountains, the location of several major sights such as the monastic complex of Glendalough and the magnificent gardens of Powerscourt, provide perfect touring and walking territory. Further south, the most scenic routes cut through the valleys of the Slaney, Barrow and Nore rivers, flanked by historic ports such as New Ross, from where you can explore local waterways by boat. Along the south coast, which is more varied than the region's eastern shore, beaches are interspersed with rocky headlands, and quiet coastal villages provide good alternative bases to the busy towns of Waterford and Wexford. Further inland, the best places to stay include Lismore and Kilkenny, which is one of the finest historic towns in Ireland.

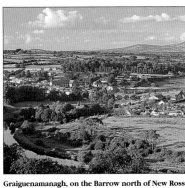

Graiguenamanagh, on the Barrow north of New Ross

SIGHTS AT A GLANCE

Ardmore ⑲
Avondale House ⑭
Bray ⑧
Browne's Hill Dolmen ⑮
Castletown House pp122–3 ❶
Dunmore East ㉑
Enniscorthy ㉔
Glendalough ⑬
Hook Peninsula ㉒
Irish National Heritage Park ㉕
Jerpoint Abbey ⑰
Johnstown Castle ㉗
Kildare ❺
Kilkenny pp134–6 ⑯
Killruddery House ❾
Lismore ⑱
Monasterevin ❹
Mount Usher Gardens ⑫
New Ross ㉓
Peatland World ❸
Powerscourt pp126–7 ❼
Robertstown ❷
Rosslare ㉙

Russborough House ❻
Saltee Islands ㉘
Waterford pp138–9 ⑳
Wexford ㉖
Wicklow Mountains ⑪

Tours
Military Road ⑩

Athlon

PEATLAND WORLD

RATHAN

MONASTEREVIN
❹

Portla

Portlaoise

N8   N77   N78

Casbel

KILKENNY ⑯   N10

CALLAN   N76

JERPOINT ABBEY ⑰

INISTIO

← *Clonmel*

Suir   R678

WATERFORD ⑳

N25

R675

R666

Fermoy   N72   ⑱ **LISMORE**   N72

N72

Blackwater

DUNGARVAN

N25

Cork   ⑲ **ARDMORE**

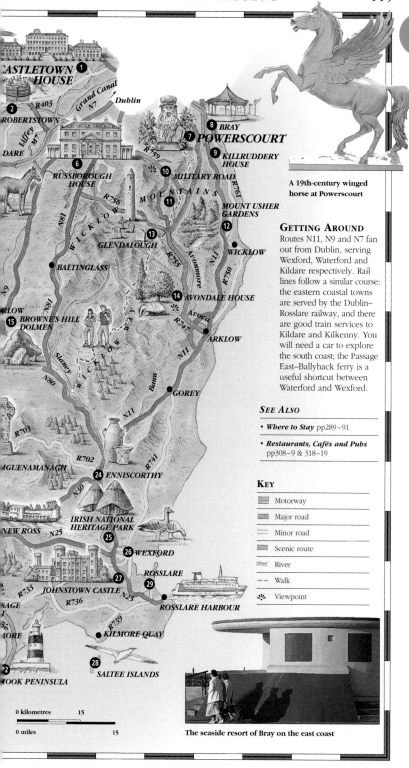

CASTLETOWN HOUSE ❶

❷ **ROBERTSTOWN**

R403 Grand Canal → *Dublin*

N7

KILDARE

Liffey *M7*

RUSSBOROUGH HOUSE

❻

❼ ❽ **BRAY**

POWERSCOURT

❾ **KILLRUDDERY HOUSE**

❿ **MILITARY ROAD**

R759

R756

R761

⓫

WICKLOW MOUNTAINS

MOUNT USHER GARDENS

⓬

⓭ **GLENDALOUGH**

WICKLOW

R755

Avonmore

N11

R750

● **BALTINGLASS**

N81

A 19th-century winged horse at Powerscourt

GETTING AROUND

Routes N11, N9 and N7 fan out from Dublin, serving Wexford, Waterford and Kildare respectively. Rail lines follow a similar course: the eastern coastal towns are served by the Dublin–Rosslare railway, and there are good train services to Kildare and Kilkenny. You will need a car to explore the south coast; the Passage East–Ballyhack ferry is a useful shortcut between Waterford and Wexford.

⓮ **AVONDALE HOUSE**

Avoca

⓯ **BROWNE'S HILL DOLMEN**

CARLOW

N9 *N81*

R747

● **ARKLOW**

Slaney

WICKLOW WAY

Bann

● **GOREY**

N11

N80

R703

R702

GRAIGUENAMANAGH

R741

⓴ **ENNISCORTHY**

N30

IRISH NATIONAL HERITAGE PARK

㉕

NEW ROSS *N25*

㉖ **WEXFORD**

㉗ **ROSSLARE**

㉙

JOHNSTOWN CASTLE

R733

R736

N25

PASSAGE EAST

ROSSLARE HARBOUR

R739

HOOK PENINSULA

● **KILMORE QUAY**

㉘

SALTEE ISLANDS

SEE ALSO

• *Where to Stay* pp289–91

• *Restaurants, Cafés and Pubs* pp308–9 & 318–19

KEY

	Motorway
	Major road
	Minor road
	Scenic route
	River
	Walk
☀	Viewpoint

0 kilometres 15

0 miles 15

The seaside resort of Bray on the east coast

Castletown House ❶

See pp122–3.

Robertstown ❷

Road map D4. Co Kildare. 👥 *240.* 🚌

TEN LOCKS WEST along the Grand Canal from Dublin, Robertstown is a characteristic 19th-century canalside village, with warehouses and cottages flanking the waterfront. Freight barges plied the route until about 1960, but pleasure boats have since replaced them. Visitors can take barge cruises from the quay and the Grand Canal Company's Hotel, built in 1801 for canal passengers, is now used for banquets.

Near Sallins, about 8 km (5 miles) east of Robertstown, the canal is carried over the River Liffey along the **Leinster Aqueduct**, an impressive structure built in 1783.

Peatland World ❸

Road map D4. Lullymore, Co Kildare. 📞 *045 860133.* 🚌 *to Newbridge.* 🚌 *to Allenwood.* 🕐 *all year: 9am– 6pm Mon–Fri; Apr–Oct: 2–6pm Sun; Sat groups by appt.* 🎫 ♿ *limited.*

ANYONE INTERESTED in the natural history of Irish bogs should visit Peatland World. Housed in an old farmhouse at Lullymore, 9 km (6 miles) northeast of Rathangan, Peatland World lies at the heart of the Bog of Allen, a vast expanse of raised bogland *(see p244)* that extends across the counties

The Grand Canal Company's Hotel in Robertstown

of Offaly, Laois and Kildare. An exhibition of flora, fauna and archaeological finds explores the history and ecology of the bog, while guided walks across the peatlands introduce visitors to the bog's delicate ecosystem.

Stacking peat for use as fuel

Monasterevin ❹

Road map D4. Co Kildare. 👥 *2,200.* 🚌

THIS GEORGIAN market town lies west of Kildare, where the Grand Canal crosses the River Barrow. Waterborne trade brought prosperity to Monasterevin in the 18th century, but the locks now see little traffic. However, you can still admire the aqueduct, which is a superb example of canal engineering.

Moore Abbey, next to the church, was built in the 18th century on the site of a monastic foundation, but the grand Gothic mansion owes much to Victorian remodelling. Once the ancestral seat of the Earls of Drogheda, in the 1920s Moore Abbey became the home of the celebrated tenor, John McCormack *(see p22)*. It is now a hospital.

Kildare ❺

Road map D4. Co Kildare. 👥 *4,200.* 🚌 🚌 ℹ️ *Market House (Jun–Sep: 045 522696).* 🛒 *Thu.*

THE CHARMING and tidy town of Kildare is dominated by **St Brigid's Cathedral**, which commemorates the saint who founded a religious community on this site in 480. Unusually, monks and nuns lived here under the same roof, but this was not the only unorthodox practice associated with the community. Curious pagan rituals, including the burning of a perpetual fire, continued until the 16th century. The fire pit is visible in the grounds today. So too is a round tower, which was probably built in the 12th century and has a

St Brigid's Cathedral and roofless round tower in Kildare town

Japanese Gardens at Tully near Kildare

Romanesque doorway. The cathedral was rebuilt in the Victorian era, but the restorers largely adhered to the original 13th-century design.

🔒 St Brigid's Cathedral

Market Square. 📞 045 521229. ⭕ May–Oct: daily. **Donation.** ♿

Environs: Kildare lies at the heart of racing country: the Curragh racecourse is nearby, stables are scattered all around and bloodstock sales take place at Kill, northeast of town.

The **National Stud** is a state-run bloodstock farm at Tully, just south of Kildare. It was founded in 1900 by an eccentric Anglo-Irish colonel called William Hall-Walker. He sold his foals on the basis of their astrological charts, and put skylights in the stables to allow the horses to be "touched" by sunlight and moonbeams. Hall-Walker received the title Lord Wavertree in reward for bequeathing the farm to the British Crown in 1915.

Visitors can explore the 400-ha (1,000-acre) grounds and watch the horses being exercised. Mares are generally kept in a separate paddock from the stallions. Breeding stallions wait in the covering shed: each one is expected to cover 50 mares per season. There is a special foaling unit where the mare and foal can remain undisturbed for a few days after the birth.

The farm has its own forge and saddlery, and also a Horse Museum. Housed in an old stable block, this illustrates the importance of horses in Irish life. Exhibits include the frail skeleton of Arkle, a famous champion steeplechaser in the 1960s.

Sharing the same estate as the National Stud are the **Japanese Gardens** and **St Fiachra's Garden**. The Japanese Gardens were laid out in 1906–10 by Japanese landscape gardener Tassa Eida, with the help of his son Minoru and 40 assistants. The impressive array of trees and shrubs includes maple, bonsai, mulberry, magnolia, sacred bamboo and cherry. The gardens take the form of an allegorical journey through life, beginning with the Gate of Oblivion and leading to the Gateway of Eternity, a contemplative Zen rock garden.

St Fiachra's Garden covers 1.6 ha (4 acres) of woodland, wetland, lakes and islands, and features a Waterford Crystal Garden within the monastic cells.

🏵 National Stud and Japanese and St Fiachra's Gardens

Tully. 📞 045 521617. ⭕ mid-Feb–mid-Nov: 9:30am–6pm daily (last admission 60 mins before closing). 🎫 ♿ 🎦 National Stud only. 🖥 🚻

HORSE RACING IN IRELAND

Ireland has a strong racing culture and, thanks to its non-elitist image, the sport is enjoyed by all. Much of the thoroughbred industry centres around the Curragh, a grassy plain in County Kildare stretching unfenced for more than 2,000 ha (5,000 acres). This area is home to many of the country's studs and training yards, and every morning horses are put through their paces on the gallops. Most of the major flat races, including the Irish Derby, take place at the Curragh racecourse just east of Kildare. Other fixtures are held at nearby Punchestown – most famously the steeplechase festival in April/May – and at Leopardstown, which also hosts major National Hunt races (see pp26–7).

Finishing straight at the Curragh racecourse

Castletown House ❶

BUILT IN 1722–32 for William Conolly, Speaker of the Irish Parliament, the façade of Castletown was the work of Florentine architect Alessandro Galilei and gave Ireland its first taste of Palladianism. The magnificent interiors date from the second half of the 18th century. They were commissioned by Lady Louisa Lennox, wife of William Conolly's great-nephew, Tom, who lived here from 1759. Castletown remained in the family until 1965, when it was taken over by the Irish Georgian Society. The state now owns the house and it is open to the public.

Conolly crest on an armchair

★ **Long Gallery**
The heavy ceiling sections and friezes date from the 1720s and the walls were decorated in the Pompeian manner in the 1770s.

Green Drawing Room

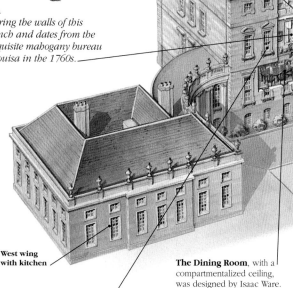

Red Drawing Room
The red damask covering the walls of this room is probably French and dates from the 19th century. This exquisite mahogany bureau was made for Lady Louisa in the 1760s.

West wing with kitchen

The Dining Room, with a compartmentalized ceiling, was designed by Isaac Ware.

Boudoir Wall Paintings
The boudoir's decorative panels, moved here from the Long Gallery, were inspired by the Raphael Loggia in the Vatican.

VISITORS' CHECKLIST

Road map D4. Celbridge, Co
Kildare. **(** 01 628 8252.
67, 67A from Dublin. ◯ Easter
Day–Sep: 10am–6pm Mon–Fri,
1–6pm Sat, Sun & public hols;
Oct: 10am–5pm Mon–Fri, 1–5pm
Sun & public hols; Nov: 1–5pm
Sun. **🔗 🗺 ◻ ✓** obligatory.
Summer concerts.

★ Print Room
In this, the only intact 18th-century print room in Ireland,
Lady Louisa indulged her taste for Italian engravings. It was
fashionable at that time for ladies to paste prints directly on
to the wall and frame them with elaborate festoons.

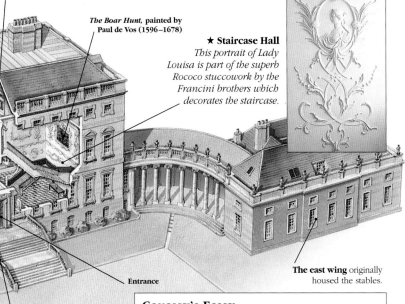

The Boar Hunt, painted by
Paul de Vos (1596–1678)

★ Staircase Hall
This portrait of Lady
Louisa is part of the superb
Rococo stuccowork by the
Francini brothers which
decorates the staircase.

The east wing originally
housed the stables.

Entrance

The Entrance Hall is an
austere Neo-Classical room.
Its most decorative feature is
the delicate carving on the
pilasters of the upper gallery.

STAR FEATURES

★ Long Gallery

★ Print Room

★ Staircase Hall

CONOLLY'S FOLLY

This folly, which lies just
beyond the grounds of
Castletown House, provides
the focus of the view from
the Long Gallery. Speaker
Conolly's widow, Katherine,
commissioned it in 1740
as a memorial to her late
husband, and to provide
employment after a harsh
winter. The unusual structure
of superimposed arches
crowned by an obelisk was
designed by Richard Castle,
architect of Russborough
House *(see p124).*

Saloon in Russborough House with original fireplace and stuccowork

Russborough House ❻

Road map D4. Blessington, Co Wicklow.
📞 045 865239. 🚌 65 from Dublin.
🕐 May–Sep: 10am–5pm daily; Apr &
Oct: 10am–5pm Sun & public hols.
📷 ✔ obligatory. ♿ 🚻 🏪

THIS PALLADIAN MANSION, built in the 1740s for Joseph Leeson, Earl of Milltown, is one of Ireland's finest houses. Its architect, Richard Castle, also designed Powerscourt House *(see pp126–7)* and is credited with introducing the Palladian style to Ireland.

Unlike many grand estates in the Pale, Russborough has survived magnificently, both

inside and out. The house claims the longest frontage in Ireland, with a façade adorned by heraldic lions and curved colonnades. The interior is even more impressive. Many rooms feature superb stucco dec-oration, which was done largely by the Italian Francini brothers, who also worked on Castle-town House *(see pp122–3)*. The best examples are found in the music room, saloon and library, which are embellished with exuberant foliage and cherubs. Around the main staircase, a riot of Rococo plasterwork

depicts a hunt, with hounds clasping garlands of flowers. The stucco mouldings in the drawing room were designed especially to enclose marine scenes by the French artist, Joseph Vernet (1714–89). The paintings were sold in 1926, but were tracked down more than 40 years afterwards and returned to the house.

Russborough has many other treasures, including finely worked fireplaces of Italian marble, imposing mahogany doorways and priceless collections of silver, porcelain and Gobelin tapestries.

Such riches aside, one of the principal reasons to visit Russ-borough is to see the **Beit Art Collection**, famous for its Flemish, Dutch and Spanish Old Master paintings. These include fine works by Gainsborough, Oudry and Belloto. Sir Alfred Beit, who bought the house in 1952, inherited the pictures from his uncle – also named Alfred Beit and co-founder of the de Beers diamond mining empire in South Africa. In 1974, 1986 and 2000 several masterpieces were stolen from the house. Most were later retrieved but, sadly, more dis-appeared in another robbery in 2001. Only a selection of paintings is on view in the house at any one time, while

Vernet seascape in the drawing room

THE HISTORY OF THE PALE

The term "Pale" refers to an area around Dublin which marked the limits of English influence from Norman to Tudor times. The frontier fluctuated, but at its largest the Pale stretched from Dundalk in County Louth to Waterford town. Gaelic chieftains outside the area could keep their lands provided they agreed to bring up their heirs within the Pale.

The Palesmen supported their rulers' interests and considered themselves the upholders of English values. This widened the gap between the Gaelic majority and the Anglo-Irish, a fore-taste of England's doomed involvement in the country. Long after its fortifications were dismantled, the idea of the Pale lived on as a state of mind. The expression "beyond the pale" survives as a definition of those outside the bounds of civilized society.

An 18th-century family enjoying the privileged lifestyle typical within the Pale

Tourist road train on the beachfront esplanade at Bray

others are on permanent loan to the National Gallery in Dublin *(see pp68–9)*.

Russborough enjoys a fine position near the village of **Blessington**, with a good view across to the Wicklow Mountains. The house lies amid wooded parkland rather than elaborate flower gardens. As Alfred Beit said of Irish Palladianism, "Fine architecture standing in a green sward was considered enough."

ENVIRONS: The **Poulaphouca Reservoir**, which was formed by the damming of the River Liffey, extends south from Blessington. The placid lake is popular with watersports enthusiasts, while other visitors come simply to enjoy the lovely mountain views.

Powerscourt **7**

See pp126–7.

Bray **8**

Road map D4. Co Wicklow.
🏃 *33,000.* 🚉 *DART.* 🚌 ℹ️ *Old Court House, Main St (01 286 7128).*

ONCE A REFINED Victorian resort, Bray is nowadays a brash holiday town, with amusement arcades and fish and chip shops lining the seafront. Its beach attracts large crowds in summer, including many young families. Anyone in search of peace and quiet can escape to nearby Bray

Head, where there is scope for bracing cliffside walks. Bray also makes a good base from which to explore Powerscourt Gardens, the Wicklow Mountains and the delightful coastal villages of Killiney and Dalkey *(see p101)*.

Killruddery House and Gardens **9**

Road map D4. Bray, Co Wicklow.
📞 *01 286 2777.* ⏰ *May–Sep: 1pm–5pm daily.* 🎫 ♿ *limited.*
🌐 *www.killruddery.com*

KILLRUDDERY HOUSE lies just to the south of Bray, in the shadow of Little Sugar Loaf Mountain. Built in 1651, it has been the family seat of the Earls of Meath ever since, although the original mansion was remodelled in an Elizabethan Revival style in the early 19th century. The house

contains some good carving and stuccowork, but the real charm of Killruddery lies in the 17th-century formal gardens, regarded as the finest French Classical gardens in the country. They were laid out in the 1680s by a French gardener named Bonet, who also worked at Versailles.

The gardens, planted with great precision, feature romantic parterres, a whole array of different hedges and many fine trees and shrubs, both native and foreign. The sylvan theatre, a small enclosure surrounded by a bay hedge, is the only known example of its kind in Ireland.

The Long Ponds, a pair of canals which extend 165 m (542 ft), were once used to stock fish. Beyond, a pool enclosed by two circular hedges leads to a Victorian arrangement of paths flanked by statues and hedges of yew, beech, lime and hornbeam.

View across the Long Ponds to Killruddery House

Powerscourt ⑦

THE GARDENS AT POWERSCOURT are probably the finest in Ireland, both for their design and their dramatic setting at the foot of Great Sugar Loaf Mountain. The house and grounds were commissioned in the 1730s by Richard Wingfield, the 1st Viscount Powerscourt. New ornamental gardens were completed in 1858–75 by the 7th Viscount, who added gates, urns and statues collected during his travels in Europe. The house was gutted by an accidental fire in 1974, but the ground floor has been beautifully renovated and now accommodates an upmarket shopping centre with an excellent restaurant and café.

Laocoön statue on upper terrace

Bamberg Gate
Made in Vienna in the 1770s, this gilded wrought-iron gate was brought to Powerscourt by the 7th Viscount from Bamberg Church in Bavaria.

The Walled Gardens include a formal arrangement of clipped laurel trees but are also used for growing plants for Powerscourt's nursery.

The Pets' Cemetery contains the graves of Wingfield family dogs, cats and even horses and cattle.

Statue of Laocoön

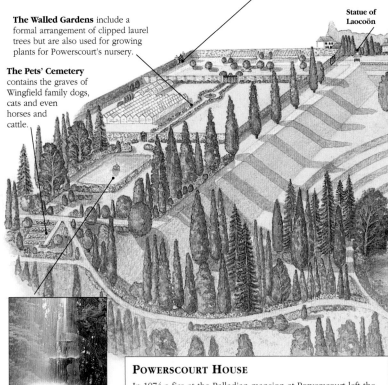

Dolphin Pond
This pool, designed as a fish pond in the 18th century, is enclosed by exotic conifers in a lovely secluded garden.

POWERSCOURT HOUSE

In 1974 a fire at the Palladian mansion at Powerscourt left the fine building a burnt-out shell. In recent years the Slazenger family, who now own the estate, have restored the ground floor and the ballroom upstairs, although much work remains to be done to the rest of the house. Originally built in 1731 on the site of a Norman castle, the house was designed by Richard Castle, who was also the architect of Russborough House (*see p124*).

Powerscourt ablaze in 1974

★ The Perron
Leading down to Triton Lake is the Perron, a beautiful Italianate stairway added in 1874. Beside the lake, it is guarded by two statues of Pegasus – the mythical winged horse and emblem of the Wingfield family.

Pebble Mosaic
Many tonnes of pebbles were gathered from nearby Bray beach to build the Perron and to make this mosaic on the terrace.

The Italian Garden is laid out on terraces which were first cut into the steep hillside in the 1730s.

The Pepper Pot Tower was built in 1911.

★ Triton Lake
Made for the first garden, the lake takes its name from its central fountain, which is modelled on a 17th-century work by Bernini in Rome.

★ Japanese Gardens
These enchanting Edwardian gardens, created out of bogland, contain Chinese conifers and bamboo trees.

STAR FEATURES

★ Japanese Gardens

★ The Perron

★ Triton Lake

Powerscourt Gardens with Great Sugar Loaf Mountain beyond ▷

A Tour of the Military Road ⑩

Rare red squirrel

THE BRITISH BUILT the Military Road through the heart of the Wicklow Mountains during a campaign to flush out Irish rebels after an uprising in 1798 *(see p141)*. Now known as the R115, this road takes you through the emptiest and most rugged landscapes of County Wicklow. Fine countryside, in which deer and other wildlife flourish, is characteristic of the whole of this tour.

Glencree ①
The former British barracks in Glencree are among several found along the Military Road.

Powerscourt Waterfall ⑨
The River Dargle cascades 130 m (425 ft) over a granite escarpment to form Ireland's highest waterfall.

Sally Gap ②
This remote pass is surrounded by a vast expanse of blanket bog dotted with pools and streams.

Glenmacnass ③
After Sally Gap, the road drops into a deep glen where a waterfall spills dramatically over rocks.

Great Sugar Loaf ⑧
The granite cone of Great Sugar Loaf Mountain can be climbed in under an hour from the car park on its southern side.

Lough Tay ⑦
Stark, rocky slopes plunge down to the dark waters of Lough Tay. Though it lies within a Guinness-owned estate, the lake is accessible to walkers.

Roundwood ⑥
The highest village in Ireland at 238 m (780 ft) above sea level, Roundwood enjoys a fine setting. Its main street is lined with pubs, cafés and craft shops.

Glendalough ④
This ancient lakeside monastery *(see pp132–3)*, enclosed by wooded slopes, is the prime historical sight in the Wicklow Mountains.

TIPS FOR DRIVERS

Length: 96 km (60 miles).
Stopping-off points: There are several pubs and cafés in Enniskerry (including Poppies, an old-fashioned tearoom), and also in Roundwood, but this area is better for picnics. There are several marked picnic spots south of Enniskerry. (See also pp355–7.)

0 kilometres   5

0 miles   3

KEY

━━━ Tour route

═══ Other roads

☆ Viewpoint

Vale of Clara ⑤
This picturesque wooded valley follows the River Avonmore. It contains the tiny village of Clara, which consists of two houses, a church and a school.

Wicklow Mountains ⓫

Road map D4. 🚉 to Rathdrum & Wicklow. 🚌 to Enniskerry, Wicklow, Glendalough, Rathdrum & Avoca. 🛈 Rialto House, Fitzwilliam Square, Wicklow (0404 69117).

STANDING AMID the rugged wilderness of the Wicklow Mountains, it can be hard to believe that Dublin is under an hour's drive away. The inaccessibility of the mountains meant that they once provided a safe hideout for opponents of English rule. When much of the Southeast was obedient to the English Crown, within an area known as the Pale *(see p124)*, warlords such as the O'Tooles held sway in the Wicklow Mountains. Rebels who took part in the 1798 uprising *(see p39)* sought refuge here too. One of their leaders, Michael Dwyer, remained at liberty in the hills around Sally Gap until 1803.

The building of the **Military Road**, started in 1800, made the area more accessible, but the mountains are still thinly populated. There is little traffic to disturb enjoyment of the exhilarating scenery of rock-strewn glens, lush forest and bogland where heather gives a purple sheen to the land. Turf-cutting is still a thriving cottage industry, and

---

Bearnas na Diallaite
SALLY GAP

↑ **Bealach Mileata**
MILITARY ROAD ✈

← **Gleann Life**
LIFFEY VALLEY ⤢

Bealach Fheartire →
VARTRY DRIVE

**Road sign in the
Wicklow Mountains**

---

you often see peat stacked up by the road. Numerous walking trails weave through these landscapes. Among them is the **Wicklow Way**, which extends 132 km (82 miles) from Marlay Park in Dublin to Clonegal in County Carlow. It is marked but not always easy to follow, so do not set out without a decent map. Although no peak exceeds 915 m (3,000 ft), the Wicklow Mountains can be dangerous in bad weather.

Hiking apart, there is plenty to see and do in this region. A good starting point for exploring the northern area is the picture-postcard estate village of **Enniskerry**. In summer, it is busy with tourists who come to visit the gardens at Powerscourt *(see pp126–7)*. From Laragh, to the south, you can reach Glendalough *(see pp132–3)* and the **Vale of Avoca**, where cherry trees are laden with blossom in the spring. The beauty of this gentle valley was captured in the poetry of Thomas Moore (1779–1852):

"There is not in the wide world a valley so sweet as that vale in whose bosom the bright waters meet" – a reference to the confluence of the Avonbeg and Avonmore rivers, the so-called **Meeting of the Waters** beyond Avondale House *(see p133)*. Nestled among wooded hills at the heart of the valley is the hamlet of Avoca, where the **Avoca Handweavers** produce colourful tweeds in the oldest hand-weaving mill in Ireland, in operation since 1723.

Further north, towards the coast near Ashford, the River Vartry rushes through the deep chasm of the **Devil's Glen**. On entering the valley, the river falls 30 m (100 ft) into a pool known as the Devil's Punchbowl. There are good walks around here, with fine views of the coast.

🛈 **Avoca Handweavers**
Avoca. 📞 0402 35105. ◯ daily.
● 25 & 26 Dec. ▮▮ 🛈

Mount Usher Gardens ⓬

Road map D4. Ashford, Co Wicklow. 📞 0404 40205. 🚌 to Ashford. ◯ Mar–Oct: daily. ▨ 🛈 🛈 🛈 limited. 📷 call to book.

SET BESIDE the River Vartry just east of Ashford are the Mount Usher Gardens. They were designed in 1868 by a Dubliner, Edward Walpole, who imbued them with his strong sense of romanticism.

The gardens contain many rare shrubs and trees, from Chinese conifers and bamboos to Mexican pines and pampas grass. The Maple Walk is glorious in autumn. The river provides the main focus of the gardens, and amid the exotic vegetation you can glimpse herons on the weirs.

**Mount Usher Gardens, on the
banks of the River Vartry**

Colourful moorland around Sally Gap in the Wicklow Mountains

Glendalough ⓲

Road map D4. Co Wicklow. ⬛ *St Kevin's Bus from Dublin.* **Ruins** ◯ *daily.* ⬛ *in summer.* **Visitors' Centre** ⬛ *0404 45325/45352.* ◯ *daily.* ⬤ *24–27 Dec.* ⬛ ⬛

T HE STEEP, WOODED slopes of Glendalough, the "valley of the two lakes", harbour one of Ireland's most atmospheric monastic sites. Established by St Kevin in the 6th century, the settlement was sacked time and again by the Vikings but nevertheless flourished for over 600 years. Decline set in only after English forces partially razed the site in 1398, though it functioned as a monastic centre until the Dissolution of the Monasteries in 1539 *(see p36).* Pilgrims kept on coming to Glendalough even after that, particularly on St Kevin's feast day, 3 June, which was often a riotous event *(see p28).*

The age of the buildings is uncertain, but most date from the 8th to 12th centuries. Many were restored during the 1870s.

View along the Upper Lake at Glendalough

Remains of the Gatehouse, the original entrance to Glendalough

The main group of ruins lies east of the Lower Lake, but the earliest buildings associated with St Kevin are by the Upper Lake. Here, where the scenery is much wilder, you are better able to enjoy the tranquillity of Glendalough and to escape the crowds which inevitably descend on the site. Try to arrive as early as possible in the day, particularly during the peak tourist season. You enter the monastery through the double stone arch of the **Gatehouse**, the only surviving example in Ireland of a gateway into a monastic enclosure.

A short walk leads to a graveyard with a **Round tower** in one corner. Reaching 33 m (110 ft) in height, this is one of the finest of its kind in the country. Its cap was rebuilt in the 1870s using stones found inside the tower. The roofless **Cathedral** nearby dates mainly from the 12th century and is

St Kevin's Kitchen

the valley's largest ruin. At the centre of the churchyard stands the tiny **Priest's House**, whose name derives from the fact that it was a burial place for local clergy. The worn carving of a robed figure above the door is possibly of St Kevin, flanked by two disciples. East of here, **St Kevin's Cross** dates from the 12th century and is one of the best preserved of Glendalough's various High Crosses. Made of granite, the cross may once have marked the boundary of the monastic cemetery. Below, nestled in the lush valley, a minuscule oratory with a steeply pitched stone roof is a charming sight. Erected in the 11th century or even earlier, it is popularly known as **St Kevin's Kitchen**; this is perhaps because its belfry, thought to be a later addition, resembles a chimney. One of the earliest churches at Glendalough, **St Mary's**, lies across a field to the west.

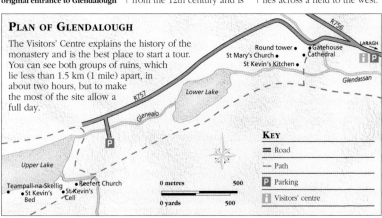

PLAN OF GLENDALOUGH

The Visitors' Centre explains the history of the monastery and is the best place to start a tour. You can see both groups of ruins, which lie less than 1.5 km (1 mile) apart, in about two hours, but to make the most of the site allow a full day.

R756

LARAGH

Round tower ●
St Mary's Church ●   ● Gatehouse
St Kevin's Kitchen ●   ● Cathedral

ℹ P

Glendassan

R757

Lower Lake

Glenealo

P

Upper Lake

Teampall-na-Skellig ●   ● Reefert Church
● St Kevin's   ● St Kevin's
Bed   Cell

0 metres   500

0 yards   500

KEY

▬ Road

-- Path

P Parking

ℹ Visitors' centre

Round tower at Glendalough

Some traces of Romanesque moulding are visible outside the east window. Following the path along the south bank of the river, you reach the Upper Lake. This is the site of more monastic ruins and is also the chief starting point for walks through the valley and to a number of abandoned lead and zinc mines.

Situated in a grove not far from the Poulanass waterfall are the ruins of the **Reefert Church**, a simple Romanesque building. Its unusual name is a corruption of *Righ Fearta*, meaning "burial place of the kings"; the church may mark the site of an ancient cemetery. Near here, on a rocky spur overlooking the Upper Lake, stands **St Kevin's Cell**, the ruins of a beehive-shaped structure which is thought to have been the hermit's home.

There are two sites on the south side of the lake which cannot be reached on foot but are visible from the opposite shore. **Teampall-na-Skellig**, or the "church on the rock", was supposedly built on the site of the first church that St Kevin founded at Glendalough. To the east of it, carved into the cliff, is **St Kevin's Bed**. This small cave, in reality little more than a rocky ledge, may have been used as a tomb in the Bronze Age, but it is more famous as St Kevin's favourite retreat. It was from here that the saint allegedly rejected the advances of a naked woman by tossing her into the lake.

St Kevin at Glendalough

St Kevin was born in 498, a descendant of the royal house of Leinster. He rejected his life of privilege, however, choosing to live instead as a hermit in a cave at Glendalough. He later founded a monastery here, and went on to create a notable centre of learning devoted to the care of the sick and the copying and illumination of manuscripts. St Kevin attracted many disciples to Glendalough during his lifetime, but the monastery became more celebrated as a place of pilgrimage after his death in around 618.

Colourful legends about the saint make up for the dearth of facts about him. That he lived to the age of 120 is just one of the stories told about him. Another tale claims that one day, when St Kevin was at prayer, a blackbird laid an egg in one of his outstretched hands. The saint remained in the same position until it was hatched.

Avondale House ⑭

Road map D4. Co Wicklow. 📞 *0404 46111.* 🚌 🚐 *to Rathdrum.* **House** 🕐 *mid-Mar–Oct: 11am–6pm (Nov–Feb 5pm) daily.* ⬤ *Good Fri & 23–28 Dec; Mar–Apr, Sep–Oct: Mon.* 📷 🔢 🎁 🚻 Limited. **Grounds** 🕐 *daily.*

LYING JUST south of Rathdrum, Avondale House is the birthplace of the 19th-century politician and patriot, Charles Stewart Parnell *(see p41)*. The Georgian mansion is now a museum dedicated to Parnell and the fight for Home Rule.

The grounds are open to the public. Known as **Avondale Forest Park**, they include an impressive arboretum first planted in the 18th century and much added to since 1900. There are some lovely walks through the woods, with pleasant views along the River Avonmore.

Browne's Hill Dolmen ⑮

Road map D4. Co Carlow. 🚌 🚐 *to Carlow.* 🕐 *daily.*

IN A FIELD 3 km (2 miles) east of Carlow, along the R726, stands a dolmen boasting the biggest capstone in Ireland. Weighing a reputed 100 tonnes, this massive stone is embedded in the earth at one end and supported at the other by three much smaller stones. Dating back to 2000 BC, Browne's Hill Dolmen is thought to mark the tomb of a local chieftain. A path leads to it from the road.

Browne's Hill Dolmen, famous for its enormous capstone

Street-by-Street: Kilkenny 🔟

To Irishtown,
St Canice's Cathedral

Kilkenny coat of arms

KILKENNY is undoubtedly Ireland's loveliest inland city. It rose to prominence in the 13th century and became the medieval capital of Ireland. The Anglo-Norman Butler family came to power in the 1390s and held sway over the city for 500 years. Their power has gone but their legacy is visible in the city's historic buildings, many of which have been restored. Kilkenny is proud of its heritage and every August hosts the Republic's top arts festival.

Grace's Castle was built in 1210 and later converted into a jail. Remodelled in the 18th century, it has functioned as a courthouse ever since.

PARLIAMENT STREET

ST KIERAN'S STREET

HIGH STREET

Narrow alleyways, known locally as "slips", are part of Kilkenny's medieval heritage. Several slips survive, and these are currently undergoing restoration.

Marble City Bar

Tholsel (City Hall)

★ **Rothe House**
This fine Tudor merchant's house, built around two court-yards, is fronted by arcades once typical of Kilkenny's main streets. A small museum inside the house contains a display of local archaeological artifacts and a costume collection.

Butter Slip
The alley is named after the butter stalls that once lined this small market place.

View of the High Street
The 18th-century Tholsel, with its distinctive clock tower and arcade, is the main landmark on the High Street. Its elegant Georgian chamber is used by city councillors to this day.

STAR SIGHTS

★ **Kilkenny Castle**

★ **Rothe House**

Kyteler's Inn

This medieval coaching inn (see p318) is named after Dame Alice Kyteler, a 14th-century witch who once lived in the building. Like most of the pubs in the city, Kyteler's Inn sells Smithwick's beer, which has been brewed in Kilkenny since 1710.

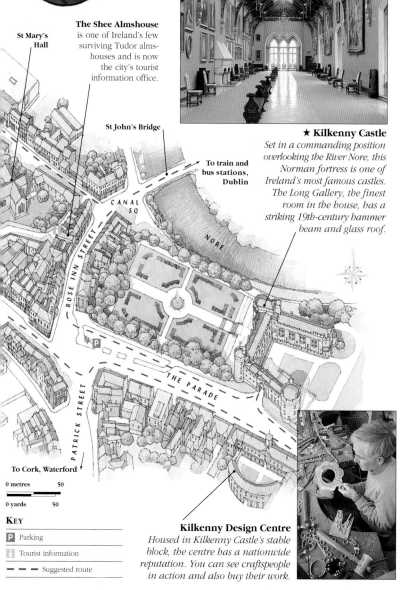

St Mary's Hall

The Shee Almshouse is one of Ireland's few surviving Tudor alms-houses and is now the city's tourist information office.

St John's Bridge

To train and bus stations, Dublin

CANAL SQ

NORE

ROSE INN STREET

★ **Kilkenny Castle**
Set in a commanding position overlooking the River Nore, this Norman fortress is one of Ireland's most famous castles. The Long Gallery, the finest room in the house, has a striking 19th-century hammer beam and glass roof.

P

THE PARADE

PATRICK STREET

To Cork, Waterford

0 metres   50
0 yards   50

KEY

P   Parking

Tourist information

– – –   Suggested route

Kilkenny Design Centre
Housed in Kilkenny Castle's stable block, the centre has a nationwide reputation. You can see craftspeople in action and also buy their work.

Exploring Kilkenny

In a lovely spot beside a kink in the River Nore, Kilkenny is of great architectural interest, with much use made of the distinctive local black limestone, known as Kilkenny marble. A tour of the town also reveals many unexpected treasures: a Georgian façade often seems to conceal a Tudor chimney, a Classical interior or some other surprise.

The survival of the Irishtown district, now dominated by St Canice's Cathedral, recalls past segregation in Kilkenny. The area once known as English-town still boasts the city's grandest public buildings.

As a brewery city, Kilkenny is a paradise for keen drinkers. Not counting the popular private drinking clubs, there are about 80 official pubs.

North side of Kilkenny Castle showing Victorian crenellations

Sign of the Marble City Bar on Kilkenny's High Street

♣ Kilkenny Castle

The Parade. **(** 056 772 1450. ◯ daily. ● Good Fri & 10 days at Christmas. ☒ ▣ ☒ obligatory. ♿ limited. Queues are likely during the summer.

Built in the 1190s, Kilkenny Castle was occupied right up until 1935. The powerful Butler family (see p134) lived in it from the late 14th century, but because of the exorbitant running costs, their descendants eventually donated Kilkenny Castle to the nation in 1967. With its drum towers and

solid walls, the castle retains its medieval form, but has undergone many alterations. The Victorian changes made in Gothic Revival style have had the most enduring impact, and are even more impressive since recent restoration work.

High spots of a tour include the library, the wood-panelled dining room and the Chinese bedroom.

Best of all, however, is the Long Gallery, built in the 1820s to house the Butler art collection. Its elaborate painted ceiling has a strong Pre-Raphaelite feel, with many of the motifs inspired by the *Book of Kells (see p62)*.

The castle grounds have shrunk over the centuries, but the French Classical gardens remain, with terraces opening onto a woodland walk and pleasant rolling parkland.

⛪ St Canice's Cathedral

Irishtown. **(** 056 776 4971 ◯ daily. ☒ ▣ ♿.

The hilltop cathedral, flanked by a round tower, was built in the 13th century in an Early English Gothic style. It was

sacked by Cromwell's forces in 1650, but has survived as one of Ireland's medieval treasures. Walls of the local Kilkenny limestone and pillars of pale sandstone combine to create an interior of simple grandeur. An array of splendid 16th-century tombs includes the beautiful effigies of the Butler family in the south transept. It is worth climbing the round tower for a fine view over Kilkenny.

⛪ Black Abbey

Abbey St. **(** 056 772 1279. ◯ daily. ♿

Lying just west of Parliament Street, this Dominican abbey was founded in 1225. Part of it was turned into a courthouse in the 16th century, but is once again a working monastery. The church has a fine vaulted undercroft, distinctive stonework, and some beautiful stained-glass windows, several of which date back to the 14th century.

ENVIRONS: Just north of the town lies **Dunmore Cave**, a limestone cavern with an impressive series of chambers, noted for its steep descent and curious rock formations.

Bennettsbridge, on the Nore 8 km (5 miles) south of Kilkenny, is famous for its ceramics. The Nicholas Mosse Pottery (see p327) specializes in colourful earthenware made from the local clay.

⛏ Dunmore Cave

Ballyfoyle. **(** 056 67726. ◯ Mar–Oct: daily; Nov–Feb: Sat, Sun & public hols. ☒ ☒ obligatory.

Tomb of 2nd Marquess of Ormonde in St Canice's Cathedral

Jerpoint Abbey ⑰

Road map D5. Thomastown, Co Kilkenny. ☎ 056 772 4623. 🚌 🚌 to Thomastown. 🕐 Mar–May & mid-Sep–Oct: 10am–5pm (Nov 4pm) daily; Jun–mid-Sep: 9:30am–6:30pm daily; Dec: by appt only. 📷 ✓ ♿

O N THE BANKS of the Little Arrigle just south of Thomastown, Jerpoint Abbey is one of the finest Cistercian ruins in Ireland. Founded in 1160, the fortified medieval complex rivalled Duiske Abbey (see p141) in prestige. Jerpoint flourished until the Dissolution of the Monasteries (see pp36–7), when it passed to the Earl of Ormonde.

The 15th-century cloisters have not survived as well as some earlier parts of the abbey. Despite this, they are the highlight of Jerpoint, with their amusing sculptures of knights, courtly ladies, bishops and dragons. The church itself is well preserved. The Irish-Romanesque transepts date back to the earliest period of the Abbey's development and contain several 16th-century tombs decorated with exquisite stylized carvings. The north side of the nave has a rich array of decorated Romanesque capitals and throughout the abbey are tombs and effigies of early bishops and patrons. The battlemented crossing tower was added during the 1400s.

Stylized carving of saints on 16th-century tomb in Jerpoint Abbey

Lismore ⑱

Road map C5. Co Waterford. 🏘 1,200. 🚌 ℹ Lismore Heritage Centre (058 54975). 🛍 craft shop.

T HIS GENTEEL riverside town is dwarfed by **Lismore Castle**, perched romantically above the River Blackwater. Built in 1185 but re-modelled in the 19th century, the castle is the Irish seat of the Duke of Devonshire and is closed to the public. However, you can visit the sumptuous gardens, which include a lovely riverside walk. **Lismore Heritage Centre** tells the story of St Carthage, who founded a monastic centre here in the 7th century. The town has two cathedrals dedicated to him. The Protestant **Cathedral of St Carthage** is the more interesting. It dates from 1633 but incorporates older elements and was later altered to suit the Neo-Gothic tastes of the Victorians. It has fine Gothic vaulting,

Burne-Jones window in St Carthage's Cathedral, Lismore

and two stained-glass windows in the south transept are by the Pre-Raphaelite artist, Sir Edward Burne-Jones.

⛪ **Lismore Castle Gardens** ☎ 058 54424. 🕐 Apr, May, 1–28 Sep: 1:45–4:45pm daily; Jun–Aug: 11am–4:45pm daily. 📷

ENVIRONS: From Lismore you can follow a picturesque route through the **Blackwater Valley** (see p169). This runs from Cappoquin, in an idyllic woodland setting just east of Lismore, down to the estuary at Youghal (see p171).

Ardmore ⑲

Road map C5. Co Waterford. 🏘 450. 🚌 ℹ Jun–Sep: Beach Car Park (024 94444).

A RDMORE is a popular seaside resort with a splendid beach, lively pubs, good cliff walks and some interesting architecture. The hill beside the village is the site of a monastery established in the 5th century by St Declan, the first missionary to bring Christianity to this area.

Most of the buildings, including the ruined **St Declan's Cathedral**, date from the 12th century. The cathedral's west wall has fine Romanesque sculptures, arranged in a series of arcades. The scenes include *The Archangel Michael Weighing Souls* in the upper row, and below this *The Adoration of the Magi* and *The Judgment of Solomon*.

The adjacent round tower is one of the best preserved examples in Ireland, and rises to a height of 30 m (98 ft). An oratory nearby is said to mark the site of St Declan's grave.

St Declan's Cathedral at Ardmore, with its near-perfect round tower

Waterford ⑳

Waterford city coat of arms

WATERFORD, IRELAND'S oldest city, was founded by Vikings in 914. Set in a commanding position by the estuary of the River Suir, it became southeast Ireland's main seaport. From the 18th century, the city's prosperity was consolidated by local industries, including the glassworks for which Waterford is famous. The strong commercial tradition persists today and Waterford's port is still one of Ireland's busiest. In the last few years, following extensive archaeological excavations in the city centre, a new heart and atmosphere has been put into the old city with the creation of pedestrian precincts in the historic quarter and along the quays.

Cathedral Close, looking towards Lady Lane in the heart of the city

Exploring Waterford

The extensive remains of the city walls clearly define the area originally fortified by the Vikings. The best-preserved section runs northwest from the **Watch Tower** on Castle Street, although Reginald's Tower, overlooking the river, is the largest structure in the old defences. In The Reginald Bar (*see p318*) you can see the arches through which boats sailed forth down the river; these sallyports are one of several Viking sections of the largely Norman fortifications.

Although Waterford retains its medieval layout, most of the city's finest buildings are Georgian. Some of the best examples can be seen on the Mall, which runs southwest from Reginald's Tower, and in the lovely Cathedral Square. The latter takes its name from **Christchurch Cathedral**, which was built in the 1770s to a design by John Roberts, a local architect who contributed much to the city's Georgian heritage. It is fronted by a fine Corinthian colonnade. A grim 15th-century effigy of a rotting corpse is an unexpected sight inside. Heading down towards the river, you pass the 13th-century ruins of **Grey Friars**, often known as the French Church after it became a Huguenot chapel in 1693.

West along the waterfront, a Victorian clock tower stands at the top of Barronstrand Street. Rising above the busy shops is **Holy Trinity Cathedral**, which has a rich Neo-Classical interior. George's Street, which runs west from here, is dotted with period houses and cosy pubs. It leads to O'Connell Street, whose partially restored warehouses contrast with the shabbier buildings on the quay. In the summer, you can enjoy another view of the waterfront by taking a cruise on the river.

Reginald's Tower on the quayside

♠ Reginald's Tower

The Quay. 【 *051 304220.*
◯ *Apr–Oct: daily.* 🖾
The Vikings built a fort on this site in 914 but it was the Anglo-Normans who, in 1185, built the stone structure seen today. With impregnable walls 3 m (10 ft) thick, the tower is said to be the first Irish building to use mortar, a primitive concoction of blood, lime, fur and mud. It is the oldest civic urban building in Ireland.

🏛 Waterford Museum of Treasures

The Granary, Merchants Quay. 【 *051 304500.* ◯ *Apr–May, Sep: 9:30am–6pm daily; Jun–Aug: 9:30am–9pm daily; Oct–Mar: 10am–5pm daily.* ● *25 & 26 Dec.* 🖾 🔥 ⅱ 🖾 🛈
🔲 *www.waterfordtreasures.com*
This multi-award-winning interactive museum tells the story of Waterford from its Viking foundation to the late 19th century.

View of the city of Waterford across the River Suir

⛏ Waterford Crystal Factory

Kilbarry. **C** *051 332500.* ☐ *Mar–Oct: 8:30am–6pm daily; Nov–Feb: 9am–5pm Mon–Fri.* 🎫 & 🎥 *Last tour 2 hrs before close.*

A visit to the Waterford Crystal Factory, just 2.5 km (1.5 miles) south of the city, is highly recommended to observe the process of crystal-making.

The original glass factory was founded in 1783 by two brothers, George and William Penrose, who chose Waterford

Craftsman engraving a vase at the Waterford Crystal Factory

because of its port. For many decades their crystal enjoyed an unrivalled reputation, but draconian taxes caused the firm to close in 1851. A new factory was opened in 1947, however, and master blowers and engravers were brought from the Continent to train local apprentices. Competition from Tipperary and Galway Crystal had an effect in the early 1990s, but sales have revived in recent years.

Visitors can follow all stages of production, observing the process by which sand, lead and potash are transformed by fire into sparkling crystal. The main difference between ordinary glass and crystal is the latter's high lead content, 30 per cent in Waterford's case. The glass-blowers require great skill to create walls of the right thickness to take the heavy incisions typical of Waterford Crystal. The factory's other main hallmark is the Waterford signature, which is engraved on the base of each piece.

In the gallery showroom, a crystal chandelier lights up a dining table laden with Wedgwood pottery and Waterford glass, tempting visitors to buy.

VISITORS' CHECKLIST

Road map D5. Co Waterford.
🏠 *44,000.* ✈ *10 km (6 miles) S.*
🚆 *Plunkett Station, The Bridge (051 873401).* 🚌 *The Quay (051 879000).* 🛈 *The Granary, Merchant's Quay (051 875823).* 🚢 *(051 421723): Jun–Aug.* 🚩 *Fri.* 🎭 *Int Festival of Light Opera (Sep).*

Ballyhack port, across Waterford Harbour from Passage East

ENVIRONS: The small port of **Passage East**, 12 km (7 miles) east of Waterford, witnessed the landing of the Normans in 1170 *(see p34),* but little has happened since. A car ferry links the village to Ballyhack in County Wexford, providing a scenic shortcut across Waterford Harbour as well as an excellent entry point to the Hook Peninsula *(see p140).*

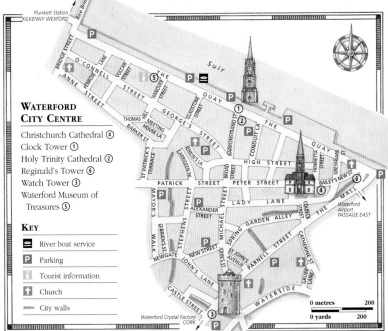

WATERFORD CITY CENTRE

Christchurch Cathedral ④
Clock Tower ①
Holy Trinity Cathedral ②
Reginald's Tower ⑥
Watch Tower ③
Waterford Museum of
   Treasures ⑤

KEY

🚢 River boat service

🅿 Parking

🛈 Tourist information

✚ Church

▬ City walls

0 metres   200
0 yards   200

Dunmore East ㉑

Road map D5. Co Waterford.
🚶 *1,500*. 🚌

THE APPEAL of Dunmore East, Waterford's most charming fishing village, lies chiefly in its red sandstone cliffs and bustling harbour. Paths run along the foot of the cliffs, but for the best views take the road that winds uphill from the beach, past tidy cottages and the ivy-clad Ship Inn to the Haven Hotel. A gate nearby leads to delightful gardens overlooking the fishing boats below. Climbing further, up steps cut into the rock, you are rewarded by views of the cliffs and noisy kittiwake colonies.

Hook Peninsula ㉒

Road map D5. Co. Wexford. 🚌 *to Duncannon*. ⛴ *from Passage East to Ballyhack (051 382480)*. 🛈 *Fethard-on-Sea (051 397502)*.

THIS TAPERING HEADLAND of gentle landscapes scattered with ancient ruins and quiet villages is perfect for a circular tour. The "Ring of Hook" route begins south of New Ross at **Dunbrody Abbey**, the ruins of a 12th-century Cistercian church, but **Ballyhack** is another good place to start. Once a fortified crossing point into County Waterford, the town still has a ferry service to neighbouring Passage East *(see p139)*. **Ballyhack Castle**, built by the Knights Templar in 1450, contains a small museum. About 4 km (2.5 miles) beyond is the small

Busy fishing harbour at Dunmore East

resort of **Duncannon**, with a broad sandy beach and a star-shaped fort, which was built in 1588 in expectation of an attack by the Spanish Armada.

The coast road continues south to **Hook Head**. Here, perched on red sandstone, is Europe's oldest working lighthouse, dating from 1172 and now with its own visitor centre. Paths skirt the coast famous for its fossils, seals and a variety of seabirds.

Just 2 km (1.5 miles) east is the village of **Slade**. A ruined 15th-century tower house, **Slade Castle**, presides over the harbour where fishing boats cluster around the slipways. The road proceeds along the rugged coastline, past the resort of Fethard-on-Sea and Saltmills to the dramatic ruin of **Tintern Abbey**. This 13th-century Cistercian foundation was built by William Marshall, Earl of Pembroke, in fulfilment of a vow made when his boat was caught in a storm off the coast nearby. Fields lead to an old stone bridge and views over **Bannow Bay**, where it

is thought the Normans made their first landing in 1169.

🏛 Dunbrody Abbey
Campile. 📞 *051 388603*.
🕐 *Apr–Sep: daily*. 🎫 ✔ 🛅 🖵
♣ Ballyhack Castle
Ballyhack. 📞 *051 389468*.
🕐 *Jun–Sep: daily*.
🏛 Tintern Abbey
📞 *051 562 6500*.
🎫 *May–Oct: daily*. 🎫 🖵

Norman lighthouse at Hook Head, on the tip of the Hook Peninsula

New Ross ㉓

Road map D5. Co Wexford. 🚶 *6,000*.
🚌 🛈 *mid-Jun–Aug: The Quay (051 421857)*. 🚃 *Tue*. **Galley Cruising Restaurants** *The Quay (051 421723)*.

LYING ON the banks of the River Barrow, New Ross is one of the oldest towns in the county. Its importance, now as in the past, stems from its status as a port. In summer there is much activity on the river. Cruises run by Galley Cruising Restaurants ply the Barrow, Nore and Suir rivers. Traditional shopfronts line the streets, which rise steeply

Castle ruins and harbour at Slade on the Hook Peninsula

from the quayside. The **Tholsel**, now the town hall but originally a tollhouse, was occupied by the British during the 1798 rebellion (*see pp38–9*). Opposite, a monument to a Wexford pikeman commemorates the bravery of the Irish rebels who faced the British cannons.

Nearby is **St Mary's** which, when founded in the 13th century, was the largest parish church in Ireland. A modern church occupies the site, but the original (now roofless) south transept remains, as do many medieval tombstones.

View over Enniscorthy and St Aidan's cathedral from Vinegar Hill

ENVIRONS: A popular trip up the meandering Barrow goes 16 km (10 miles) north to **Graiguenamanagh**. The main attraction of this market town is **Duiske Abbey**, the largest Cistercian church in Ireland. Founded in 1207, it has been extensively restored and now acts as the parish church. The most striking features include a Romanesque door in the south transept, the great oak roof and traces of a medieval pavement below floor level. There is also a cross-legged statue of the Knight of Duiske, which is one of the finest medieval effigies in Ireland. Outside are two 9th-century granite High Crosses.

Trips along the Nore take you to **Inistioge**. Lying in a deep, wooded valley, this is an idyllic village, with neat 18th-century houses, a square planted with lime trees and a ten-arched bridge spanning the Nore. On a rock above the river stands a ruined Norman fort, a popular place for picnics.

From Inistioge you can walk along the river or up to **Woodstock House Demesne**, a national park. Among the

beech woods stands an 18th-century mansion, currently undergoing restoration.

On a hill 12 km (7.5 miles) south of New Ross, a large area of woodland is enclosed within the **John F Kennedy Park and Arboretum**. Founded in 1968, near the late president's ancestral home in Dungans-town (now **The Kennedy Homestead**), the park boasts more than 4,500 types of tree and provides splendid panoramic views. There are marked paths and nature trails.

🛉 **Duiske Abbey**
Graiguenamanagh, Co Kilkenny.
📞 0503 24238. ⬜ daily. &
🛉 **John F Kennedy Park and Arboretum**
New Ross, Co Wexford. 📞 051 388171. ⬜ daily. ⬤ Good Fri & 25 Dec. 🄳 & 🄳 May–Dec.

Enniscorthy ㉔

Road map D5. Co Wexford.
🏯 5,000. 🚉 🚌 🛈 The Castle (054 34699).

THE STREETS of Enniscorthy, on the banks of the River Slaney, are full of character and redolent of the town's turbulent

past. In 1798, Enniscorthy witnessed the last stand of the Wexford pikemen, when a fierce battle was fought against a British force of 20,000 on nearby **Vinegar Hill**. The events of that year are told both at the County Museum inside the imposing **Enniscorthy Castle**, and at the multimedia **National 1798 Visitor Centre**. Enniscorthy's other main sight is the Neo-Gothic **St Aidan's Cathedral**, designed in the 1840s by AWN Pugin (1812–52), better known for his work on London's Houses of Parliament.

Granaries, mills and potteries overlook the Slaney, including Carley's Bridge, founded in 1654 and still operational. Enniscorthy's historic pubs are another attraction. They include the Antique Tavern (*see p318*), which is hung with pikes used during the Battle of Vinegar Hill in 1798.

🛡 **Enniscorthy Castle**
Castle Hill. 📞 054 35926.
⬜ daily (Oct–Dec: pm only).
🄳 & limited.
🏛 **National 1798 Visitor Centre**
Millpark Road. 📞 054 37596.
⬜ daily. 🄳 🄳🛈

The inland port of New Ross seen from the west bank of the River Barrow

View across the harbour to Wexford town

Irish National Heritage Park ㉕

Road map D5. Ferrycarrig, Co Wexford.
🚌 *from Wexford in summer.*
📞 *053 20733.* ⬜ Mar–Oct:
9:30am–6pm daily (last adm 5pm);
Nov–Feb: 9:30am–5:30pm (last adm
3pm). ⬜ week at Christmas. 💷
🅿 Mar–Oct. ⬜ 🍴 ♿

BUILT ON former
marshland near
Ferrycarrig, north of
Wexford, the Irish
National Heritage
Park is a bold open-
air museum. Trails
lead through woods
to replicas of home-
steads, places of
worship and burial
sites, providing a
fascinating lesson on
the country's ancient
history *(see pp30–31)*.
Highlights include the
Viking boatyard, complete
with raiding ship, and a 7th-
century horizontal watermill.

**Sign of a popular
Wexford pub**

Wexford ㉖

Road map D5. Co Wexford.
🏛 17,000. 🚌 🚆 ℹ Crescent Quay
(053 23111).

WEXFORD'S name derives
from *Waesfjord*, a Norse
word meaning "estuary of the
mud flats". It thrived as a port
for centuries but the silting of
the harbour in the Victorian era
put an end to most sea traffic.
Wexford's quays, from where
ships once sailed to Bristol,
Tenby and Liverpool, are now
used mainly by a fleet of
humble mussel dredgers.
    Wexford is a vibrant place,
packed with fine pubs and
boasting a varied arts scene.
The town's singular style is
often linked to its linguistic
heritage. The *yola* dialect,
which was spoken by early
settlers, survives in the local
pronunciation of certain words.
    Wexford retains few traces
of its past, but the Viking fish-
bone street pattern still exists,
with narrow alleys fanning off
the meandering Main
Street. Keyser's Lane,
linking South Main
Street with the lively
Commodore pub on
Paul Quay, is a tiny
tunnel-like Viking
alley which once led
to the Norse water-
front. The Normans
were responsible for
Wexford's town walls,
remnants of which
include one of the
original gateways.
Behind it lies
Selskar Abbey, the
ruin of a 12th-century
Augustinian monastery. King
Henry II is said to have done
penance here for the murder
of Thomas à Becket in 1170.
    Wexford also has several
handsome buildings dating
from a later period, including
the 18th-century market house,
known as the **Cornmarket**,
on Main Street. The nearby
square, the **Bull Ring**, is
notable only for its history: it
was used for bull-baiting in
Norman times and was the
scene of a cruel massacre by
Cromwell's men in 1649.
    Wexford Opera Festival,
held in October, is the leading
operatic event in the country.
Aficionados praise it for its
intimate atmosphere – both
during performances and
afterwards, when artists and
audience mingle together in
the pubs: the Centenary
Stores off Main Street is a
favourite, though the Wren's
Nest, on Custom House Quay,
is better for traditional music.

ENVIRONS: Skirting the shore
just east of the town is the
Wexford Wildfowl Reserve.
It covers 100 ha (250 acres) of
reclaimed land and is noted in
particular for its geese: over a
third of the world's entire
population of Greenland white-
fronted geese winter here
between October and April.
    The mudflats also attract
large numbers of swans and
waders, and provide a rich
hunting ground for birds of
prey. The birds can be viewed
from a number of hides and
an observation tower. Another
way to enjoy the region's
wildlife is to take a boat trip
up the Slaney River to **Raven
Point** to see the seal colony.

🦆 **Wexford Wildfowl
Reserve** 📞 053 23129. ⬜ daily.
💷 at weekends.

Boat Trips
Wexford Harbour. 📞 053 71626 or
086 860 8328. 💷

Johnstown Castle ㉗

Road map D5. Co Wexford. 📞 053
42888. 🚌 🚆 to Wexford. **Gardens**
⬜ daily. ⬜ 24 & 25 Dec. 💷

Façade of Johnstown Castle

JOHNSTOWN CASTLE, a splendid
Gothic Revival mansion, lies
amid gardens and woodland
6 km (4 miles) southwest of
Wexford. In state hands since
1945, the castle is closed for
refurbishment. However, it is

Vast crescent of sand and shingle beach at Rosslare

possible to visit the **Irish Agriculture Museum**, housed in the castle's farm buildings. Reconstructions illustrate traditional trades and there is an exhibition on the Famine.

The real glory of Johnstown Castle are the grounds, from the sunken Italian garden to the ornamental lakes. Azaleas and camellias flourish alongside an array of trees including Japanese cedars and redwoods.

Hidden among the dense woods west of the house lurk the ruins of **Rathlannon Castle**, a medieval tower house.

🏛 **Irish Agriculture Museum**
Johnstown Castle. 📞 053 42888. ⭘ Apr, May & Sep–Nov: 9am–12:30pm & 1:30–5pm Mon–Fri, 2–5pm Sat, Sun & public hols; Jun–Aug: 9am–5pm Mon– Fri, 11am–5pm Sat, Sun & public hols; Nov–Mar: 9am–12:30pm & 1:30–5pm Mon–Fri. 🏞 ☐ ♿ limited.

Saltee Islands ㉘

Road map D5. Co Wexford. 🚌 *from Wexford to Kilmore Quay: Wed & Sat.* 🚢 *from Kilmore Quay: Apr–Sep (weather permitting).* 📞 *053 29684.*

THESE ISLANDS off the south coast of Wexford are a haven for sea birds. Great and Little Saltee together form Ireland's largest bird sanctuary, nurturing an impressive array of birds, from gannets and gulls to puffins and Manx shearwaters. Great Saltee particularly is famous for its colonies of cormorants. It also has more than 1,000 pairs of guillemots and is a popular stopping-off place for spring and autumn migrations. A bird-monitoring and research programme is in progress, and a close watch is also kept on the colony of grey seals.

The two uninhabited islands are privately owned, but visitors are welcome. Boat trips are run in fine weather from **Kilmore Quay**. These leave in late morning and return mid-afternoon.

Kilmore Quay is a fishing village built on Precambrian gneiss rock – the oldest rock in Ireland. Pretty thatched cottages nestle above a fine sandy beach and the harbour, where a moored lightship houses a **Maritime Museum**. The boat's original fittings are just as interesting as the exhibits.

🏛 **Guillemot Maritime Museum**
Kilmore Quay. 📞 053 21572. ⭘ May & Sep: Sat–Sun; Jun–Aug: daily. 🏞 🎦 ☐

Rosslare ㉙

Road map D5. Co Wexford. 🚶 *1,200.* 🚌 🚢 🛈 *Kilrane, Rosslare Harbour (053 33232)* ⭘ *May–Sep.*

ROSSLARE REPLACED Wexford as the area's main port after the decline of the original Viking city harbour. The port is so active today that people tend to associate the name Rosslare more with the ferry terminal for France and Wales than with the town lying 8 km (5 miles) further north.

Rosslare town is one of the sunniest spots in Ireland and draws many holidaymakers. It boasts a fine beach stretching for 9.5 km (6 miles), lively pubs and an excellent golf course fringed by sand dunes. There are good walks north to Rosslare Point.

ENVIRONS: At Tagoat, 6 km (4 miles) south of Rosslare, **Yola Farmstead Folk Park** is a recreated traditional 18th-century village, with thatched roofs and a windmill.

🏛 **Yola Farmstead Folk Park**
Tagoat. 📞 053 32611. ⭘ Mar, Apr & Nov: Mon–Fri; May–Oct: daily. 🏞 🎦 ☐ ♿

Colony of gannets nesting on the cliffs of Great Saltee Island

CORK AND KERRY

CORK · KERRY

MAGNIFICENT SCENERY *has attracted visitors to this region since Victorian times. Rocky headlands jut out into the Atlantic and colourful fishing villages nestle in the shelter of the bays. County Kerry offers dramatic landscapes and a wealth of prehistoric and early Christian sites, whereas County Cork's gentle charm has enticed many a casual visitor into becoming a permanent resident.*

Killarney and its romantic lakes are a powerful magnet for tourists, and so are Cork's attractive coastal towns and villages. Yet the region remains remarkably unspoiled, with a friendly atmosphere and authentic culture still alive in Irish-speaking pockets. There is also a long tradition of arts and crafts in the area.

This corner of Ireland used to be the main point of contact with the Continent. In the 17th century, in response to the threat of invasions from France and Spain, the English built a line of forts along the Cork coast, including the massive Charles Fort at Kinsale.

In the 19th century, the city of Cork was an important departure point for people fleeing from the Famine *(see p211)*, with Cobh the main port for emigrants to the New World. Cork's importance as a port has diminished, but it is still the Republic's second city with a lively cultural scene.

Poverty and temperament helped foster a powerful Republican spirit in the southwest. The region saw much guerrilla action in the War of Independence and the subsequent Civil War. In 1920, the centre of Cork city was burned in an uncontrolled act of reprisal by the notorious Black and Tans *(see pp42–3)*.

Kerry is known as "the Kingdom" on account of its tradition of independence and disregard for Dublin rule. The Irish recognize a distinctive Kerry character, with a boisterous sense of living life to the full. They also make Kerrymen the butt of countless jokes.

As well as the friendliest people in Ireland, the region has some of the finest scenery. Cork has lush valleys and a beautiful coast while Kerry is wilder and more mountainous. The islands off the Kerry coast appear bleak and inhospitable, but many were once inhabited. Remote, rocky Skellig Michael, for example, was the site of a 6th-century Christian monastery.

Puffins on the island of Skellig Michael off the coast of Kerry

◁ Beach at Barley Cove near Mizen Head, County Cork

Exploring Cork and Kerry

K ILLARNEY IS A POPULAR BASE with tourists for exploring
Cork and Kerry, especially for touring the Ring of
Kerry and the archaeological remains of the Dingle
Peninsula. Despite the changeable weather, the region
attracts many visitors who come to see its dramatic
scenery and lush vegetation. As you pass through quiet
fishing villages and genteel towns, such as Kenmare,
you will always encounter a friendly welcome
from the locals. For the adventurous there
are plenty of opportunities to go riding,
hiking or cycling.
Cork city offers a
more cosmopoli-
tan atmosphere,
with its art
galleries and
craft shops.

Newman's Mall in the quaint village of Kinsale

TARBER ❶

CARRIGAFOYLE CASTLE

LISTOWEL

ARDFERT CATHEDRAL ❷

TRALEE ❸

DINGLE PENINSULA

GALLARUS ORATORY

❺

❻

❹

DINGLE

BLASKET ISLANDS

SLIEVE MISH MOUNTAINS

KILLORGLIN

KILLARN ❼

LAKES OF KILLARNEY ❽

DINGLE BAY

CAHERCIVEEN

MACGILLICUDDY'S REEKS

VALENTIA ISLAND ❾

KENMARE ⓬

WATERVILLE

SNEEM

❿ THE SKELLIGS

⓫ RING OF KERRY

CAHA MOUNTAINS

GLENGARIFF

GARINISH ISLAND ⓮

⓯

CASTLETOWNBERE

BANT HOUS

BEARA PENINSULA ⓭

BANTRY BAY ⓰

BALLYDEHOB

SCHULL

MIZEN HEAD

⓱

BALTIMORE

0 kilometres 10

0 miles 10

KEY

▦	Motorway
▦	Major road
▦	Minor road
▦	Scenic route
≈	River
☀	Viewpoint

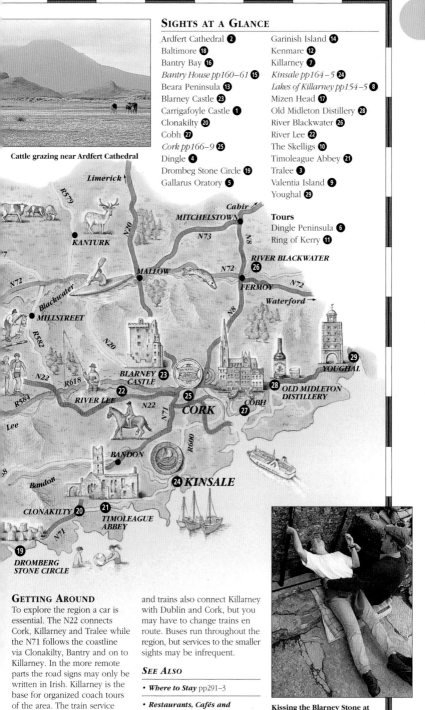

SIGHTS AT A GLANCE

Ardfert Cathedral **2**
Baltimore **18**
Bantry Bay **16**
Bantry House pp160–61 **15**
Beara Peninsula **13**
Blarney Castle **23**
Carrigafoyle Castle **1**
Clonakilty **20**
Cobh **27**
Cork pp166–9 **25**
Dingle **4**
Drombeg Stone Circle **19**
Gallarus Oratory **5**

Garinish Island **14**
Kenmare **12**
Killarney **7**
Kinsale pp164–5 **24**
Lakes of Killarney pp154–5 **8**
Mizen Head **17**
Old Midleton Distillery **28**
River Blackwater **26**
River Lee **22**
The Skelligs **10**
Timoleague Abbey **21**
Tralee **3**
Valentia Island **9**
Youghal **29**

Tours

Dingle Peninsula **6**
Ring of Kerry **11**

Cattle grazing near Ardfert Cathedral

**Kissing the Blarney Stone at
Blarney Castle near Cork**

GETTING AROUND

To explore the region a car is essential. The N22 connects Cork, Killarney and Tralee while the N71 follows the coastline via Clonakilty, Bantry and on to Killarney. In the more remote parts the road signs may only be written in Irish. Killarney is the base for organized coach tours of the area. The train service from Cork to Dublin is efficient, and trains also connect Killarney with Dublin and Cork, but you may have to change trains en route. Buses run throughout the region, but services to the smaller sights may be infrequent.

SEE ALSO

• *Where to Stay* pp291–3

• *Restaurants, Cafés and Pubs* pp310–12 & p319

Ardfert Cathedral and the ruins of Teampall na Hoe and Teampall na Griffin

Carrigafoyle Castle ❶

Road map B5. Co Kerry.
🚌 to Listowel.

Ruined keep of Carrigafoyle Castle

HIGH ABOVE the Shannon estuary, just west of Ballylongford, this 15th-century castle belonged to the O'Connor clan, who ruled much of northern Kerry. The English besieged or sacked it repeatedly but the body blow was delivered in 1649 by Cromwellian forces *(see p37)*. The ruins include a keep and walled bawn, with romantic views of the estuary from the top of the tower.

Ardfert Cathedral ❷

Road map A5. Co Kerry. 🚌 to Ardfert.
📞 066 713 4711. ⏰ Easter–Sep:
daily; rest of year on request. 📷 ♿

THIS COMPLEX of churches is linked to the cult of St Brendan the Navigator *(see p205)*, who was born nearby in 484 and founded a monastery here. The ruined cathedral dates back to the 12th century and retains a delicate Romanesque doorway and blind arcading. The south transept is now restored and houses an exhibition of the history of the site. In the graveyard stand the remains of a Romanesque nave-and-chancel church, Teampall na Hoe, and a late Gothic chapel, Teampall na Griffin. The latter is named after the curious griffins carved beside an interior window.

A short walk away are the ruins of a Franciscan friary. It was founded by Thomas Fitzmaurice in 1253, but the cloisters and south chapel date from the 15th century.

ENVIRONS: Just northwest of Ardfert is **Banna Strand**. Irish patriot Roger Casement landed here in 1916 on a German U-boat, bringing in rifles for the Easter Rising *(see pp42–3)*. He was arrested as soon as he landed and a memorial stands on the site of his capture. This beach was also used for the filming of David Lean's *Ryan's Daughter* (1970).

Tralee ❸

Road map B5. Co Kerry. 👥 23,000.
🚌 🚌 ℹ Ashe Memorial Hall,
Denny St (066 7121288). 🚢 Thu.

HOST TO the renowned Rose of Tralee International Festival *(see p47)*, Tralee has made great strides in promoting its cultural and leisure facilities. The town's main attraction is **Kerry County Museum**. Its theme park, "Kerry the Kingdom", offers a show on Kerry scenery; a display of archaeological finds and interactive models; and a "time travel experience" through Anglo-Norman Tralee, complete with medieval smells.

Also based in Tralee is the **Siamsa Tíre** National Folk Theatre of Ireland, a great ambassador for Irish culture.

Steam train on the narrow gauge railway between Tralee and Blennerville, with Blennerville Windmill in the background

Traditional song and dance performances take place here throughout the summer.

Just outside Tralee is the authentic **Blennerville Windmill**. Built in 1800, it is Ireland's largest working mill and one of Tralee's most popular attractions. The **Steam Railway** connects Blennerville with Tralee along a narrow gauge track. The train also runs from Ballyard Station to the windmill.

🏛 **Kerry County Museum**
Ashe Memorial Hall, Denny St.
🄲 066 7127777. ⬤ mid-Mar–Dec: daily. ⬤ 25 & 26 Dec. 🏷 🔵 🔴 ⬛

🎭 **Siamsa Tíre**
Town Park. 🄲 066 712 3055. ⬤ for performances mid-Apr–Oct. 🏷 🔵

🏛 **Blennerville Windmill**
🄲 066 712 1064. ⬤ Mar–Oct: daily. 🏷 🍴 🔴

🚂 **Steam Railway**
Ballyard Station. 🄲 066 712 1064.
⬤ May–Sep: daily (ring to check times). 🏷 🔵

Dingle ❹

Road map A5. Co Kerry. 🄰 2,100.
⬤ Mar–Oct. ℹ Main St (066 915 1188). ⬤ Fri.

THIS ONCE REMOTE Irish-speaking town is today a thriving fishing port and an increasingly popular tourist

Gallarus Oratory, a dry-stone early Christian church

centre. Brightly painted craft shops and cafés abound, often with slightly hippy overtones.

Dingle Bay is attractive with a somewhat ramshackle harbour lined with fishing trawlers. Along the quayside are lively bars offering music and seafood. The harbour is home to Dingle's biggest star: Fungie, the dolphin, who has been a permanent resident since 1983 and can be visited by boat or on swimming trips.

Although Dingle has few architectural attractions, it makes an engaging base for exploring the archaeological remains on the Dingle Peninsula (see pp150–51).

Gallarus Oratory ❺

Road map A5. Co Kerry.
⬤ to Dingle. 🄲 066 915 5333.

SHAPED LIKE an upturned boat, this miniature church overlooks Smerwick harbour. Gallarus was built some time between the 6th and 9th centuries and is the best preserved early Christian church in Ireland. It represents the apogee of dry-stone corbelling, using techniques first developed by Neolithic tomb-makers. The stones were laid at a slight angle, lower on the outside than the inside, allowing water to run off.

Fishing trawlers moored alongside the quay at Dingle

A Tour of the Dingle Peninsula ❻

GUINNESS
Mar is gnách

Pub sign, Ballyferriter

THE DINGLE PENINSULA offers some of Ireland's most beautiful scenery. To the north rises the towering Brandon Mountain, while the west coast has some spectacular seascapes. A drive around the area, which takes at least half a day, reveals fascinating antiquities ranging from Iron Age stone forts to inscribed stones, early Christian oratories and beehive huts. These are sometimes found on private land, so you may be asked for a small fee by the farmer to see them. Some parts of the peninsula – especially the more remote areas – are still Gaelic speaking, so many road signs are written only in Irish.

View from Clogher Head

Riasc *(An Riasc)* ⑦
This excavated monastic settlement dates from the 7th century. The enclosure contains the remains of an oratory, several crosses and an inscribed pillar stone *(see p235).*

**Ballyferriter
(*Baile an Fheirtéaraigh*) ⑥**
The attractions of this friendly village include the pastel-coloured cottages, Louis Mulcahy's pottery and a museum featuring the cultural heritage of the area.

R559

Clogher Head

**Blasket Centre
(*Ionad an Bhlascaoid*) ⑤**
Overlooking Blasket Sound, the centre explains the literature, language and way of life of the inhabitants of the Blasket Islands. The islanders moved to the mainland in 1953.

*Dunquin
(Dún Chaoin)*

*Mount
Eagle*

*Ve
(Ceann*

R559

Ven

BLASKET ISLANDS

Blasket Sound

❹☀

❺

❷

❸☀

DINGLE BA

**Dunmore Head
(*Ceann an Dúin Mhoir*) ④**
Mainland Ireland's most westerly point offers dramatic views of the Blaskets.

**Slea Head
(*Ceann Sléibe*) ③**
As you round the Slea Head promontory, the Blasket Islands come into full view. The sculpture of the Crucifixion beside the road is known locally as the Cross *(An Cros).*

KEY

▰▰▰ Tour route

═══ Other roads

☀ Viewpoint

0 kilometres   2

0 miles   1

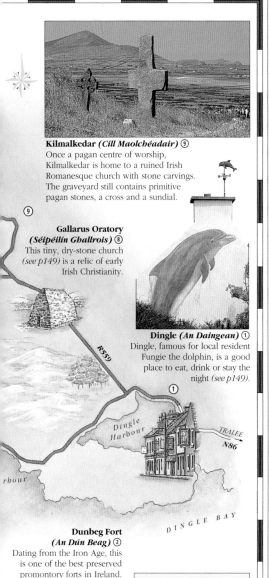

Kilmalkedar (Cill Maolchéadair) ⑨
Once a pagan centre of worship,
Kilmalkedar is home to a ruined Irish
Romanesque church with stone carvings.
The graveyard still contains primitive
pagan stones, a cross and a sundial.

**Gallarus Oratory
(Séipéilín Ghallrois)** ⑧
This tiny, dry-stone church
(*see p149*) is a relic of early
Irish Christianity.

Dingle (An Daingean) ①
Dingle, famous for local resident
Fungie the dolphin, is a good
place to eat, drink or stay the
night (*see p149*).

**Dunbeg Fort
(An Dún Beag)** ②
Dating from the Iron Age, this
is one of the best preserved
promontory forts in Ireland.
Just beyond are the Fahan beehive huts, early Christian huts
thought to have been built
for pilgrims visiting the area.

R559

TRALEE
N86

Dingle Harbour

DINGLE BAY

rbour

TIPS FOR DRIVERS

Length: *40 km (25 miles).*
Stopping-off points: *Most
villages on the route, such as
Dunquin and Ballyferriter, have
friendly bars offering pub meals.
There are also many opportunities
to stop for a picnic. On the
winding coast road around Slea
Head stop only at the safe and
clearly marked coastal viewing
points. (See also pp355–7.)*

**Jaunting cars waiting to take
visitors to sights around Killarney**

Killarney ❼

Road map B5. Co Kerry. 🏘 *9,500.* 🚉
🚌 🛈 *Beech Rd (064 31633).* 🛒 *Sat.*

K ILLARNEY is commonly
derided as "a tourist town"
but this has not dented the
town's open, cheerful atmosphere. The infectious Kerry
humour is personified by the
wise-cracking jarveys whose
families have run jaunting cars
(pony and trap rides) here for
generations. The town does
get crowded in summer but
has much to offer, with shops
open until 10pm in summer,
several excellent restaurants,
and a sprinkling of prestigious
hotels around the lake and
the heights. From the town
visitors can explore the sights
around the Lakes of Killarney
(*see pp154–5*) and the surrounding heather-covered hills.

ENVIRONS: Overlooking the
lakes and a short drive from
Killarney is **Muckross House**.
This imposing Victorian
mansion was built in 1843 in
Elizabethan style. Inside, the
elegant rooms are decorated
with period furnishings. There
is also a museum of Kerry Life,
with displays on the history of
southwest Ireland, and a craft
centre and workshops. The
landscaped gardens are especially beautiful in spring when
the rhododendrons and
azaleas are in bloom. A short
walk away is Muckross Farm,
which still uses traditional
farming techniques.

🏛 Muckross House
4 km (2.5 miles) S of Killarney. 🛈
064 31440. ◻ *July–Aug: 9am–7pm
daily; Sep–Jun: 9am–6pm daily.* ◼ *7
days at Christmas.* 🈲 🅿 🅰 🛗 🚻 🅿

Stunning mountain scenery near Moll's Gap on the Ring of Kerry ▷

Lakes of Killarney ❽

Fruit of the strawberry tree

R ENOWNED FOR ITS splendid scenery, the area is one of Ireland's most popular tourist attractions. The three lakes are contained within Killarney National Park. Although the landscape is dotted with ruined castles and abbeys, the lakes are the focus of attention: the moody watery scenery is subject to subtle shifts of light and colour. The area has entranced many artists and writers including Thackeray, who praised "a precipice covered with a thousand trees ... and other mountains rising as far as we could see". In autumn, the bright red fruits of the strawberry tree colour the shores of the lakes.

Meeting of the Waters
This beauty spot, best seen from Dinis Island, is where the waters from the Upper Lake meet Muckross Lake and Lough Leane. At the Old Weir Bridge, boats shoot the rapids.

Long Range River

Torc Waterfall
The Owengarriff River cascades through the wooded Friars' Glen into Muckross Lake. A pretty path winds up to the top of this 18-m (60-ft) high waterfall, revealing views of Torc Mountain.

Muckross Lake

Dinis Island

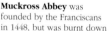

Muckross Abbey was founded by the Franciscans in 1448, but was burnt down by Cromwellian forces in 1653.

Killarney *(see p151)* is the main town from which tourists visit the sights around the lakes.

Lough Leane

Innisfallen Island

N22 to Tralee *(see pp148–9)*

Ross Castle, built around 1420, was the last stronghold under Irish control to be taken by Cromwellian forces in 1653.

★ Muckross House
The 19th-century manor (see p151) enjoys a lovely location overlooking the lakes. Visit the wildlife centre for an introduction to the flora and fauna of the National Park.

Upper Lake
This narrow lake is the smallest of the three lakes. It flows into the Long Range River to the Meeting of the Waters.

Visitors' Checklist

Road map B5. Killarney, Co Kerry. ✈ *Kerry (066 976 4644).* 🚌 🚉 **National Park** 🕐 *9am–6pm (6:30pm Jun–Aug) daily (for access by car).* 🛈 *Killarney (064 31633).* **Muckross House** 📞 *064 31440.* 🕐 *Jul–Aug: 9am–7pm daily; Sep–Jun: 9am–6pm daily.* 🚫 *7 days over Christmas.* **Ross Castle** 📞 *064 35851.* 🕐 *mid-Mar–mid-Nov: daily.* 📷 🎫 *obligatory.* ⛴ *from Ross Castle:* **Pride of the Lakes** *(064 32638): daily (weather permitting);* **The Lily of Killarney** *(064 31068): Mar–Oct.* **Kate Kearney's Cottage** 📞 *064 44146.* 🕐 *Easter–Sep: 9am–midnight daily; Oct–Easter: 9:30am–6pm.* 🍴 🛍

Ladies' View gets its name from the delight it gave Queen Victoria's ladies-in-waiting when they visited the spot in 1861.

N71 to Moll's Gap and Kenmare *(see pp156–8)*

Upper Lake

Purple Mountain, 832 m (2,730 ft)

Tomies Mountain, 735 m (2,411 ft)

Kate Kearney's Cottage was home to a local beauty who ran an illegal drinking house for passing travellers in the mid-19th century.

R562 to Killorglin *(see pp156–7)*

0 kilometres   2

0 miles   1

★ Gap of Dunloe
Glaciers carved this dramatic mountain pass which is popular with walkers, cyclists and horse riders. The route through the gap offers fabulous views of the boulder-strewn gorge and three small lakes.

Star Sights

★ Gap of Dunloe

★ Muckross House

Lough Leane
The largest lake is dotted with un-inhabited islands and fringed with wooded slopes. Boat trips run between Ross Castle and Innisfallen.

Valentia Island ⑨

Road map A5. Co Kerry. 🚌 to Caherciveen. 🛈 Caherciveen (066 947 2589/064 31633).

ALTHOUGH it feels like the mainland, Valentia is an island, albeit linked by a causeway to Portmagee. It is 11 km (7 miles) long and noted for its water sports,

Stairway leading to Skellig Michael monastery

seascapes and views from Geokaun Mountain. Valentia is also popular for its proximity to the Skellig Islands which lie around 15 km (10 miles) southwest of the Iveragh Peninsula.

The **Skellig Experience Centre**, near the causeway linking Valentia to the mainland, houses an audiovisual display about the construction and history of the monastery on Skellig Michael, the largest of the Skellig Islands. Other subjects covered include sea birds and the marine life around the islands, a reminder that the Skellig cliffs lie underwater for a depth of 50 m (165 ft), providing a habitat for giant basking sharks, dolphins and turtles. The centre also operates cruises around the islands.

The main village on Valentia is **Knightstown**, which offers accommodation and lively pubs with music and dancing.

The first transatlantic cable was laid from the southwest point of the island to Newfoundland, Canada, in 1866.

🏛 **Skellig Experience Centre**
Valentia Island. 📞 066 947 6306.
🕐 late-Mar–Sep: daily. 🚫 ♿

The Skelligs ⑩

Road map A6. Co Kerry. 🚤 mid-Mar–Oct: from Valentia Island. 📞 066 947 7156 (ring a few days ahead).

SKELLIG MICHAEL, also known as Great Skellig, is an inhospitable pinnacle of rock rising out of the Atlantic and covering an area of 17 ha (44 acres). Perched on a ledge almost 218 m (714 ft) above sea level and reached by an amazing 1,000-year-old

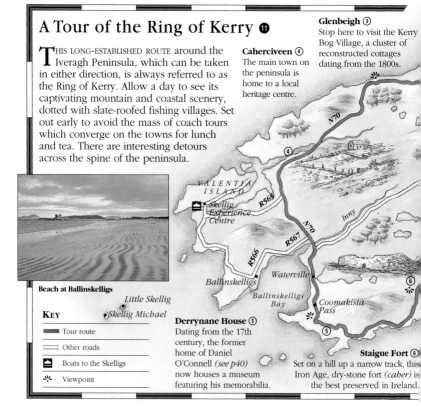

A Tour of the Ring of Kerry ⑪

THIS LONG-ESTABLISHED ROUTE around the Iveragh Peninsula, which can be taken in either direction, is always referred to as the Ring of Kerry. Allow a day to see its captivating mountain and coastal scenery, dotted with slate-roofed fishing villages. Set out early to avoid the mass of coach tours which converge on the towns for lunch and tea. There are interesting detours across the spine of the peninsula.

Glenbeigh ③
Stop here to visit the Kerry Bog Village, a cluster of reconstructed cottages dating from the 1800s.

Caherciveen ④
The main town on the peninsula is home to a local heritage centre.

Beach at Ballinskelligs

Little Skellig
KEY
● *Skellig Michael*

━━ Tour route

═══ Other roads

🚤 Boats to the Skelligs

🌸 Viewpoint

Derrynane House ⑤
Dating from the 17th century, the former home of Daniel O'Connell (*see p40*) now houses a museum featuring his memorabilia.

Staigue Fort ⑥
Set on a hill up a narrow track, this Iron Age, dry-stone fort (*caher*) is the best preserved in Ireland.

stairway is an isolated early
Christian monastery. Monks
settled for solitude on Skellig
Michael during the 6th century, building a cluster of six
corbelled beehive cells and
two boat-shaped oratories.
These dry-stone structures are
still standing, despite being
raked by storms over the
centuries. The monks were
totally self-sufficient, trading
eggs, feathers and seal meat
with passing boats in return
for cereals, tools and animal
skins. The skins were needed
to produce the vellum on
which the monks copied their
religious manuscripts. They
remained on this bleak island
until the 12th century, when
they retreated to the Augustinian priory at Ballinskelligs
on the mainland.

Today the only residents on
Skellig Michael are the thousands of sea birds which nest

Gannets flying around the precipitous cliffs of Little Skellig

and breed on the high cliffs,
including storm petrels, puffins
and Manx shearwaters. The
huge breeding colonies are
protected from predators by
the sea and rocky shores.

Slightly closer to the mainland is Little Skellig. Covering
an area of 7 ha (17 acres), the
island has steep cliffs. Home
to a variety of sea birds, it has
one of the largest colonies of
gannets (about 22,000 breeding
pairs) in the British Isles.

A cruiser from Valentia Island
circles the Skelligs but does
not dock. Except for a pier on
Skellig Michael, there are no
proper landing stages on the
islands. This is to discourage
visitors from disturbing the
birdlife, fragile plant cover
and archaeological remains.

Atlantic gales permitting,
local fishermen may run unofficial trips around the islands
from Portmagee or Ballin-
skelligs, during the summer.

Killorglin ② This pretty village, sitting on the slopes above a river, is famous for its Puck Fair (see p47).

Killarney ① Visitors touring the Ring of Kerry usually start and finish here. The route passes lovely views of the Lakes of Killarney (see pp154–5).

Moll's Gap ⑧ Cutting through bleak bogland and high mountainous terrain, Moll's Gap offers some stunning views.

Sneem ⑦ Brightly painted cottages line the streets of this charming town which also has a quaint village green.

0 kilometres 10

0 miles 5

TIPS FOR DRIVERS

Length: 180 km (112 miles).
Stopping off points: Many towns such as Killorglin and Caherciveen offer pub snacks. Finish the day in one of the excellent gourmet restaurants in Kenmare (see also pp355–7).

Lace making at Kenmare

Kenmare ⑫

Road map B5. Co Kerry. 🚶 *1,400.*
🚌 🏠 *May–Sep: Main St (064
41233).* 🛒 *Wed.*

THIS TOWN, on the mouth of
the River Sheen, was
founded in 1670 by William
Petty, Cromwell's surveyor
general. However, Kenmare's
appearance owes more to his
descendant, the first Marquess
of Lansdowne who, in 1775,
made it a model landlord's
town of neat stone façades
with decorative plasterwork.

Today Kenmare is renowned
for its traditional lace. During
the famine years, nuns from
the local convent, St Clare's,
introduced lace making to
create work for the women
and girls. Other attractions
include the fine hotels *(see
p292)* and gourmet restaurants
(p311). The town is also an

excellent base for exploring
the Beara Peninsula and the
Ring of Kerry *(see pp156–7)*.

Set in a riverside glade off
Market Street is the **Druid's
Circle**, a prehistoric ring of
15 stones associated with
human sacrifice.

Beara Peninsula ⑬

Road map A6. Co Cork & Co Kerry.
🚌 *to Glengarriff (daily) &
Castletownbere (Mon, Wed, Fri & Sun).*
🏠 *Castletownbere (027 70344).*

DOTTED WITH sparsely
populated fishing villages
surrounded by bleak moor-
land, this peninsula is remote.
It used to be a refuge for
smugglers, with the Irish
getting the better deal in their
exchange of pilchards for
contraband French brandy.

The peninsula offers some
spectacular scenery and
wonderful walking country.
From the **Healy Pass**, which
cuts a jagged path across the
spine of the Caha Mountains,
there are some fine views of
Bantry Bay and the rugged
landscape of West Cork. To
the west of the pass is
Hungry Hill, the highest
mountain in the Caha range
and popular with hill walkers.

Encircled by the Caha and
Slieve Miskish Mountains is
Castletownbere, the main
town on the peninsula. This
sheltered port was once a
haven for smugglers, but is
now awash with foreign
fishing trawlers. McCarthey's

Bar on Town Square features
an authentic matchmaking
booth, where Cork families
used to agree marriage terms
until a generation ago.

West of Castletownbere
stands the shell of **Puxley
Mansion**, home of the Puxley
family who owned the mines
at nearby **Allihies**. Centre of
the copper-mining district until
the 1930s, it is now a desolate
place, with tall Cornish-style
chimneys and piles of ochre-
coloured spoil; beware of
unguarded mine shafts.

From the tip of the peninsula
a cable car travels across to
Dursey Island, with its
ruined castle and colonies of
sea birds. Licensed to carry
three passengers and one cow,
the cable car swings across
the strait, offering views of
Bull, Cow and Calf islands.

From the headland the R757
road back to Kenmare passes
through the pretty villages of
Eyeries, noted for its brightly
painted cottages and crafts,
and **Ardgroom**, a centre for
mussel farming and a base for
exploring the scenic glacial
valley around **Glenbeg Lough**.

Garinish Island ⑭

Road map B6. Co Cork. 🚤 *from
Glengarriff.* **Gardens** 🏠 *027 63040.*
🕐 *Mar–Oct: daily.* 🅿 🚻 ♿ *limited.*

ALSO KNOWN as Ilnacullin, this
small island was turned
into an exotic garden in 1910
by Harold Peto for Annan
Bryce, a Belfast businessman.

View of Caha Mountains from the Healy Pass, Beara Peninsula

Italianate garden with lily pool and folly on Garinish Island

Framed by views of Bantry Bay, the gardens are landscaped with Neo-Classical follies and planted with rich subtropical flora. The microclimate and peaty soil provide the damp, warm conditions needed for these ornamental plants to flourish.

Exotic shrubberies abound especially during the summer months. Throughout May and June, visitors can admire the beautiful camellia beds, azaleas and rhododendrons. There is also a New Zealand fernery and a Japanese rockery, as well as a rare collection of Bonsai trees. A Martello tower crowns the island and among the follies are a clock tower and a Grecian temple.

The centrepiece is a colonnaded Italianate garden, with a Classical folly and ornamental lily pool. Much of its charm resides in the contrast between the cultivated lushness of the garden and the glimpses of wild seascape and barren mountains beyond. An added attraction of the boat trip across to this Gulf Stream paradise is the chance to see cavorting seals in Bantry Bay.

Bantry House ⓯

See pp160–61.

Bantry Bay ⓰

Road map A6. Co Cork. 🚌 *to Bantry and Glengarriff.* 🛈 *Mar–Oct: The Square, Bantry (027 50229).*

BANTRY BAY ENCOMPASSES the resorts of **Bantry** and **Glengarriff**. It is also a springboard for trips to Mizen Head and the Beara Peninsula.

Bantry nestles beneath the hills which run down to the bay. Just offshore you can see **Whiddy Island**, the original home of the White family, who moved to Bantry House in the early 18th century. Further along is **Bere Island**, a British base until World War II which still boasts Martello towers on its southern side.

Glengarriff at the head the bay, exudes an air of Victorian gentility with its neatly painted shopfronts and craft shops. On the coast is the Eccles Hotel, a haunt of Queen Victoria and where George Bernard Shaw supposedly wrote *Saint Joan*.

The wooded hinterland to the north of Glengarriff is set in a bowl of the Caha Mountains. There are some pleasant walks leading to waterfalls.

Mizen Head ⓱

Road map A6. Co Cork. 🚌 *to Goleen.* 🛈 *Town Hall, North St, Skibbereen (028 21766).*

MIZEN HEAD, the most southwesterly tip of Ireland, has steep cliffs, often lashed by storms. In a lighthouse, **Mizen Head Visitors' Centre** is reached by a bridge across a rocky chasm. From the car park, a headland walk takes in views of cliffs and Atlantic breakers. The sandy beaches of nearby **Barley Cove** attract bathers and walkers; to the east is **Crookhaven**, a pretty yachting harbour. From here, a walk to Brow Head offers views of the lighthouse.

Mizen Head can be reached either from Bantry via Durrus or from the market town of **Skibbereen**, on the R592, via the charming crafts centre of **Ballydehob** and the village of **Schull**. Trips to Clear Island (*see p162*) leave from Schull.

🏛 Visitors' Centre
Mizen Head. 📞 *028 35115.* 🕐 *Apr–Oct: daily; Nov–Mar: Sat & Sun.* 💷 🎫 ♿ *limited.* 📷 🎁

Rocky cliffs at Mizen Head

Bantry House

BANTRY HOUSE has been the home of the White family, formerly Earls of Bantry, since 1739. The original Queen Anne house was built around 1700, but the north façade overlooking the bay was a later addition. Inside there is an eclectic collection of art and furnishings brought from all over Europe by the 2nd Earl of Bantry. In the carriage house and stable block is the French Armada Centre, which explains the events surrounding Wolfe Tone's attempted invasion in 1796.

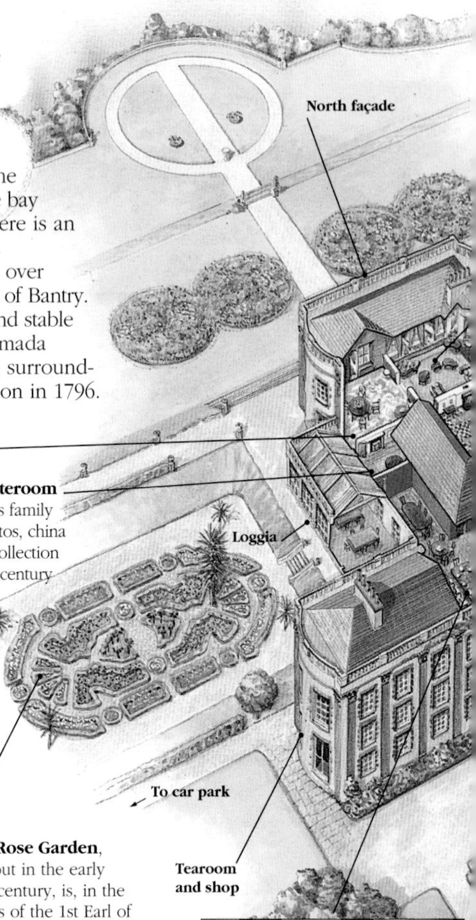

William and Mary clock in anteroom

North façade

The anteroom contains family mementos, china and a collection of 18th-century prints.

Loggia

To car park

Tearoom and shop

Gobelin Room
The subject of this 18th-century Gobelin tapestry is The Bath of Cupid and Psyche. *The room also contains an early 19th-century piano.*

The Rose Garden, laid out in the early 18th century, is, in the words of the 1st Earl of Bantry, "a parterre after the English manner".

1ST EARL OF BANTRY (1767–1851)

Richard White, 1st Earl of Bantry, played a leading role in defending Ireland against an attempted invasion by Wolfe Tone and the United Irishmen *(see pp38–9)*. On 16 December 1796, Tone sailed from Brest in Brittany with a fleet of 43 French ships bound for Ireland. White chose strategic spots around Bantry Bay and mustered volunteers to fight. His efforts proved unnecessary as the French fleet was forced back by bad weather. Nonetheless, White was rewarded with a peerage by George III for his "spirited conduct and important services". In 1801 he was made Viscount Bantry, becoming Earl of Bantry in 1816.

★ Dining Room
This room is dominated by portraits of King George III and Queen Charlotte by court painter Allan Ramsay. The Spanish chandelier is decorated with Meissen china flowers.

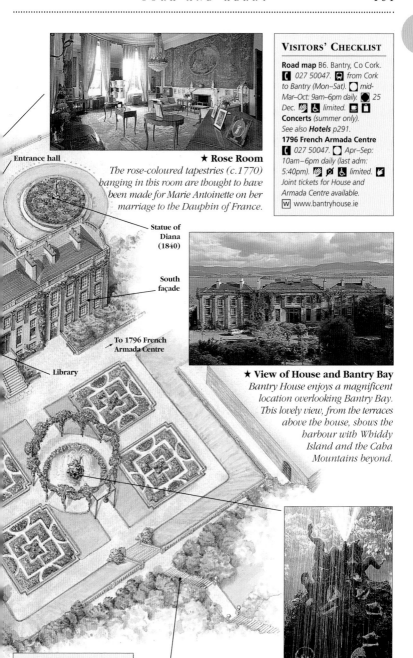

Entrance hall

VISITORS' CHECKLIST

Road map B6. Bantry, Co Cork. 027 50047. from Cork to Bantry (Mon–Sat). mid-Mar–Oct: 9am–6pm daily. 25 Dec. limited. Concerts (summer only). See also **Hotels** p291.
1796 French Armada Centre 027 50047. Apr–Sep: 10am–6pm daily (last adm: 5:40pm). limited. Joint tickets for House and Armada Centre available. W www.bantryhouse.ie

★ **Rose Room**
The rose-coloured tapestries (c.1770) hanging in this room are thought to have been made for Marie Antoinette on her marriage to the Dauphin of France.

Statue of Diana (1840)

South façade

To 1796 French Armada Centre

Library

★ **View of House and Bantry Bay**
Bantry House enjoys a magnificent location overlooking Bantry Bay. This lovely view, from the terraces above the house, shows the harbour with Whiddy Island and the Caha Mountains beyond.

STAR FEATURES

★ **Dining Room**

★ **Rose Room**

★ **View of House and Bantry Bay**

The steps, known as the "Staircase to the Sky", lead to a series of terraces with fabulous views over the house and across the bay.

Italian Garden
Inspired by the Boboli Gardens in Florence, this garden encircles a pool decorated in Classical Grotesque style. It was designed in the early 1850s by the 2nd Earl.

Baltimore ⓲

Road map B6. Co Cork. 🏠 *220.*
🚌 ⛴ *to Sherkin Island (028 20218);*
to Cape Clear Island (028 39135).

BALTIMORE'S most bizarre
claim to fame dates back
to 1631 when more than 100
citizens were carried off as
slaves by Algerian pirates.
Now that the threat of being
kidnapped has gone, this
village appeals to the yachting
fraternity and island-hoppers.
Like neighbouring Schull and
Castletownshend, the town
bustles with summer festivals.
  Overlooking the harbour is
a ruined 15th-century castle,
once the stronghold of the
O'Driscoll clan. Also worth a
visit are the seafood pubs,
including Bushe's Bar, an
atmospheric inn hung with
nautical memorabilia. Behind
the village, cliff walks lead to
splendid views of Carbery's
Hundred Isles – mere specks
on Roaringwater Bay. Baltimore
Beacon is an important marker
for boats in the bay.
  A short ferry ride away is
Sherkin Island with its
sandy beaches in the west,
ruined 15th-century abbey,
marine station and pubs. The
ferry ride to **Cape Clear
Island** is more dramatic, as
the boat weaves between
sharp black rocks to this
remote, Irish-speaking island,
noted for its bird observatory
in the North Harbour. There
are some spectacular views of
the mainland from the island.

**Distinctive white beacon for boats
approaching Baltimore**

Drombeg Stone Circle, erected around the 2nd century BC

Drombeg Stone Circle ⓳

Road map B6. Co Cork. 🚌 *to
Skibbereen or Clonakilty.*

SITUATED ON the Glandore
road 16 km (10 miles) west
of Clonakilty, Drombeg is
the finest of the many
stone circles in
County Cork. Dating
back to about 150
BC, this circle of 17
standing stones is 9
m (30 ft) in diameter.
At the winter solstice,
the rays of the setting
sun fall on the flat
altar stone which
faces the entrance to
the circle, marked by two
upright stones.
  Nearby is a small stream
with a Stone Age cooking pit
(fulacht fiadh), similar to one
at Craggaunowen *(see p182).*
A fire was made in the hearth
and hot stones from the fire
were dropped into the cooking pit to heat the water. Once
the water boiled, the meat,
usually venison, was added.

Clonakilty ⓴

Road map B6. Co Cork. 🏠 *3,000.*
🚌 ℹ️ *25 Ashe Street (023 33226) .*

FOUNDED as an English out-
post around 1588, this
market town has a typically
hearty West Cork atmosphere.
The **West Cork Regional
Museum**, housed in an old
schoolhouse, remembers the
town's industrial heritage. A
number of quayside buildings,
linked to the town's industrial

**Sign for Clonakilty
black pudding**

past, have been restored. Particularly pleasant is the Georgian
nucleus of Emmet Square.
  Until the 19th century
Clonakilty was a noted linen
producer. Today, however, it
is renowned for its rich black
puddings, handpainted Irish
signs and traditional music
pubs. A short walk
from the town
centre is a model
village exhibition,
depicting the
town as it was
during the 1940s.
Just east of town is
the reconstructed
**Lisnagun Ring
Fort**, with earth-
works, huts and
souterrains *(see p18).*
A causeway links Clonakilty
to **Inchydoney** beach.

🏛 **West Cork Regional
Museum**
Western Rd. ⬜ *May–Oct: daily.* 🎫 ♿
♦ **Lisnagun Ring Fort**
📞 *023 33302.* ⬜ *Apr–Oct: daily.*

Timoleague Abbey ㉑

Road map B6. Co Cork.
🚌 *to Clonakilty or Courtmacsherry.*
⬜ *daily.*

TIMOLEAGUE ABBEY enjoys a
waterside setting over-
looking an inlet where the
Argideen estuary opens into
Courtmacsherry Bay. Founded
around the late 13th century,
the abbey is a ruined
Franciscan friary. The buildings have been extended at
various times. The earliest
section is the chancel of the
Gothic church. The most

recent addition, the 16th-century tower, was added by the Franciscan Bishop of Ross. The friary was ransacked by the English in 1642 but much of significance remains, including the church, infirmary, fine lancet windows, refectory and a walled courtyard in the west. There are also sections of cloisters and wine cellars. In keeping with Franciscan tradition, the complex is plain to the point of austerity. Yet

Lancet window in ruined church at Timoleague Abbey

such restraint belied the friars' penchant for high living: the friary prospered on trade in Spanish wines, easily delivered thanks to its position on the then navigable creek.

River Lee ㉒

Road map B6. Co Cork. 🚌 🚐 to Cork. 🛈 Cork (021 427 3251).

CARVING A COURSE through farm- and woodland to Cork city *(see pp166–9)*, the River Lee begins its journey in the lake of the enchanting **Gougane Barra Park**. The shores of the lake are linked by a causeway to **Holy Island**, where St Finbarr, the patron saint of Cork, founded a monastery. The Feast of St Finbarr, on 25 September,

signals celebrations that climax in a pilgrimage to the island on the following Sunday.

The Lee flows through several Irish-speaking market towns and villages. Some, such as **Ballingeary**, with its fine lakeside views, have good angling. The town is also noted for its Irish language college. Further east, near the town of Inchigeela, stand the ruins of **Carrignacurra Castle**. Further downstream lies the Gearagh, an alluvial stretch of marsh and woods which has been designated a wildlife sanctuary.

The river then passes through the Sullane valley, home of the thriving market town of **Macroom**. The hulk of a medieval castle, with its restored entrance, lies just off the main square. In 1654, Cromwell granted the castle to Sir William Penn. His son, who was to found the American state of Pennsylvania, also lived here for a time.

Between Macroom and Cork, the Lee Valley passes through a hydroelectric power scheme surrounded by artificial lakes, water meadows and wooded banks. Just outside Cork, on the south bank of the river is **Ballincollig**, home to the fascinating Royal Gunpowder Mills museum *(see p169)*.

Blarney Castle ㉓

Road map B5. Blarney, Co Cork. 📞 *021 438 5252.* 🚌 *to Cork.* 🚐 *to Blarney.* 🕐 *daily.* ⬤ *24 & 25 Dec.* 📷 ♿ *grounds only, no charge.* 🛈

VISITORS from all over the world flock to this ruined castle to see the legendary Blarney Stone. Kissing the stone is a long-standing tradition, intended to confer a magical eloquence. It is set in the wall below the castle battlements and, in order to kiss it, the visitor is grasped by the feet and suspended backwards under the parapet.

Little remains of the castle today except the keep, built in 1446 by Dermot McCarthy. Its design is typical of a 15th-century tower house *(see p18)*. The vaulted first floor was once the Great Hall. To reach the battlements you need to climb the 127 steps to the top of the keep.

The castle grounds offer some attractive walks, including a grove of ancient yew trees and limestone rock formations at Rock Close. **Blarney House**, a Scottish baronial mansion and the residence of the Colthurst family since the 18th century, is not open to the public.

Just a short walk from the castle, Blarney also has a pretty village green with welcoming pubs and a number of craft shops. The **Blarney Woollen Mills,** selling quality garments and souvenirs, is well worth a visit.

Battlemented keep and ruined towers of Blarney Castle

Street-by-Street: Kinsale 24

Old office sign
in Kinsale

F OR MANY VISITORS to Ireland, Kinsale heads the list of places to see. One of the prettiest small towns in Ireland, it has had a long and chequered history. The defeat of the Irish forces and their Spanish allies in the Battle of Kinsale in 1601 signified the end of the old Gaelic order. An important naval base in the 17th and 18th centuries, Kinsale today is a popular yachting centre. It is also famous for the quality of its cuisine – the town's annual Festival of Fine Food attracts food lovers from far and wide. As well as its many wonderful restaurants, the town has pubs and wine bars to cater for all tastes.

Desmond Castle was built around 1500. It is known locally as the "French Prison".

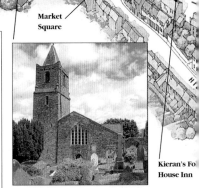

★ **Old Market House**
Incorporating the old courthouse, this museum includes a toll board listing local taxes for 1788.

Market
Square

Kieran's Fo
House Inn

CHARLES FORT

The star-shaped fort is 3 km (2 miles) east of town in Summercove, but can be reached by taking the signposted coastal walk from the quayside, past the village of Scilly. The fort was built in the 1670s by the English to protect Kinsale harbour against foreign naval forces but, because of its vulnerability to land attack, was taken during the siege of 1690 by William of Orange's army. Nonetheless, it remained in service until 1922 when the British forces left the town and handed it over to the Irish Government. Charles Fort remains one of the finest remaining examples of a star-shaped bastion fort in Europe.

Walls and bastions of Charles Fort

★ **St Multose Church**
This much-altered Norman church is named after an obscure 6th-century saint and marks the centre of the medieval town.

| 0 metres | 50 |
| 0 yards | 50 |

KEY

P	Parking
i	Tourist information
– – –	Suggested route

Kinsale Harbour
Situated on the estuary of the Bandon River, this is one of Ireland's most scenic harbours. Kinsale is host to a number of international sailing events throughout the year.

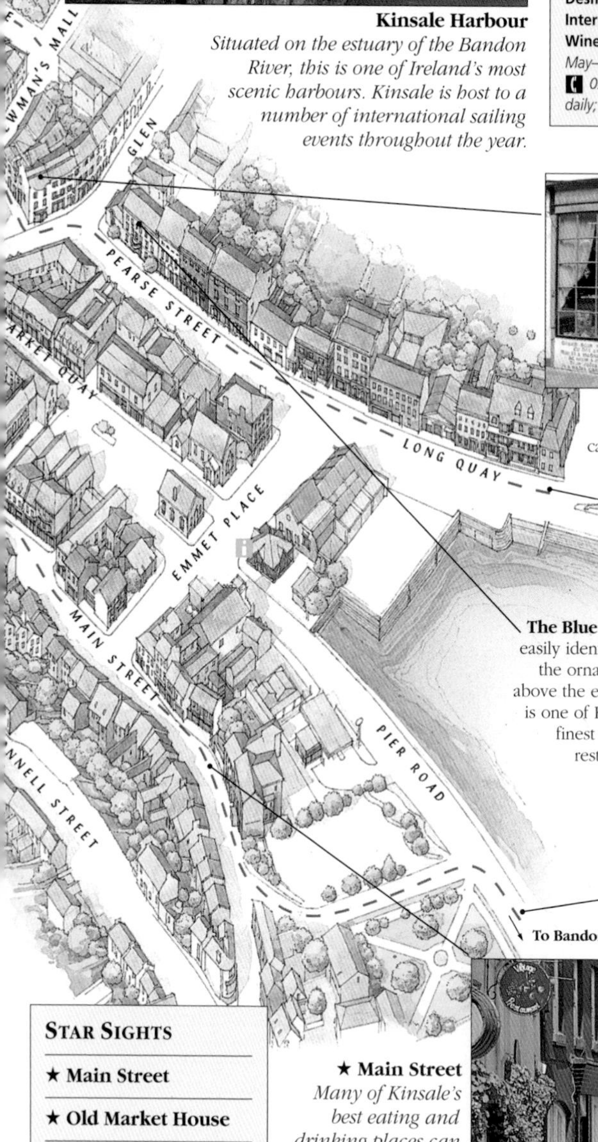

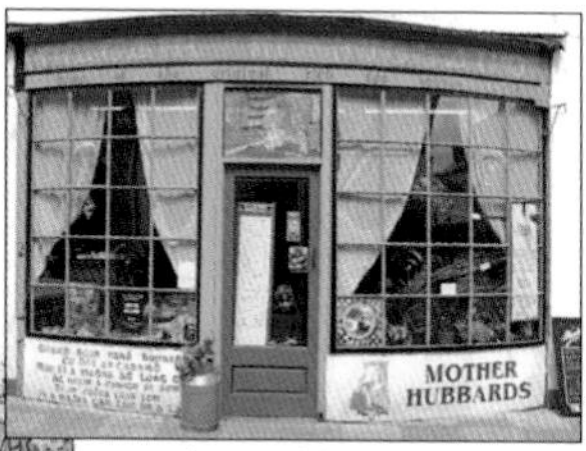

Mother Hubbard's, one of Kinsale's most popular cafés, is situated in the heart of town on Market Street.

To Charles Fort

The Blue Haven, easily identified by the ornate clock above the entrance, is one of Kinsale's finest seafood restaurants.

To Kinsale Harbour, Denis Quay and Compass Hill

To Bandon

STAR SIGHTS

★ **Main Street**

★ **Old Market House**

★ **St Multose Church**

★ **Main Street**
Many of Kinsale's best eating and drinking places can be found on this picturesque street.

Cork ㉕

Sign outside a Cork pub

CORK CITY derives its name from the marshy land on the banks of the River Lee – its Irish name *Corcaigh* means marsh – on which St Finbarr founded a monastery around AD 650. The narrow alleys, waterways and Georgian architecture give the city a Continental feel. Since the 19th century, when Cork was a base for the National Fenian movement *(see p41)*, the city has had a reputation for political rebelliousness. Today this mood is reflected in the city's attitude to the arts and its bohemian spirit, much in evidence at the lively October jazz festival.

Clock tower and weather vane of St Ann's Shandon

♠ St Ann's Shandon

Church St. ☎ 021 450 5906.
☐ daily. ● 25 Dec. ☒ ☐ limited.
This famous Cork landmark stands on the hilly slopes of the city, north of the River Lee. Built in 1722, the church has a façade made of limestone on two sides, and of red sandstone on the other two. The steeple is topped by a weather vane in the shape of a salmon. The clock face is known by the locals as the "four-faced liar" because, up until 1986 when it was repaired, each face showed slightly different times. Visitors can climb the tower and, for a small fee, ring the famous Shandon bells.

♥ Butter Exchange Shandon Craft Centre

John Redman St. ☐ daily. ☐ ☐
The Butter Exchange opened in 1770 and was where butter was graded before it was exported to the rest of the world. It also supplied butter to the British navy. By 1892 the exchange was exporting around 500,000 casks of butter a year, bringing prosperity to the city. The exchange shut in 1924.

Part of the building was re-opened in the 1980s to house the Shandon Craft Centre. Here visitors can watch artists and craft workers, such as crystal cutters and weavers, at work.

⌂ Crawford Municipal Art Gallery

Emmet Place. ☎ 021 427 3377.
☐ 9am–5pm Mon–Sat.
● public hols.
☒ ☐ ☐ ☐
The red brick and limestone building that houses Cork's major art gallery dates back to 1724. Built as the city's original custom house, it became a school of design in 1850. In 1884, a well-known art patron, William Horatio Crawford, extended the building to accommodate studios and sculpture and picture galleries.

The gallery houses some fine examples of late 19th- and early 20th-century Irish

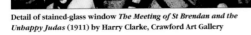

Detail of stained-glass window *The Meeting of St Brendan and the Unhappy Judas* (1911) by Harry Clarke, Crawford Art Gallery

art including paintings by Jack Yeats. There are also three fine windows by Ireland's foremost stained-glass artist, Harry Clarke (1889–1931).

Another attraction is the small collection by British artists and international works by artists such as Joán Miró and Georges Rouault.

The gallery is well known for its excellent restaurant which is run by the Ballymaloe cookery school (see p331), the exponents of authentic Irish cooking with a modern twist.

Richly decorated apse ceiling of St Finbarr's Cathedral

🏠 St Finbarr's Cathedral

Bishop Street. 📞 021 496 3387.
⬤ daily. **Donation**. ♿
Situated in a quiet part of town south of the Lee, St Finbarr's Cathedral is dedicated to the founder and patron saint of the city. Completed in 1878 to the design of William Burges, it is an exuberant

VISITORS' CHECKLIST

Road map C5. Co Cork.
🚶 136,000. ✈ 6 km (4 miles)
S of Cork (021 431 3131).
🚃 Kent Station (021 450 6766).
🚌 Parnell Place (021 450 8188).
ℹ Tourist House, Grand Parade
(021 425 5100). 🎷 Cork Jazz
Festival (Oct); Cork Film Festival
(Oct). 🌐 www.corkkerry.ie

triple-spired edifice built in Gothic Revival style, and decorated with stone tracery. Inside, the painted and gilded apse ceiling shows Christ in Glory surrounded by angels. The stained-glass windows below tell the story of Christ's life.

🏛 Cork City Gaol

Convent Avenue, Sunday's Well.
📞 021 430 5022. ⬤ daily. 📷 📹
♿ 🏠 🛍 🖼
A pretty, 20-minute walk west of the city centre leads to the restored City Gaol, complete with its furnished cells. An exhibition traces the lives of individual inmates imprisoned here during the 19th and 20th centuries.

Conditions were miserable and, for punishment, prisoners were made to run on a human treadmill that would normally be used to grind grain.

The Radio Museum Experience is also housed in this building and chronicles the development of radio in Ireland and across the world.

South Channel of the River Lee, looking towards Parliament Bridge

Exploring Cork

ONE OF CORK's great attractions is that it is a city built on water. Its heart lies on an island between two arms of the River Lee, and many of today's streets were in fact once waterways lined with warehouses and merchants' residences. Although the Dutch canalside appearance has faded, picturesque quays and bridges remain. Steep lanes rise to the north and south of the central island to the city's 19th-century suburbs, offering wonderful views of the city and its fine buildings.

Fitzpatrick's second-hand shop on George's Quay

The Quays

Although the river now plays only a minor part in the city's economy, much of Cork's commercial activity still takes place around the Quays (pronounced "kays" in the Cork accent). The South Mall, which covers an arm of the River Lee, was a waterway until the late 18th century. Boats were once moored at the foot of a series of stone steps, some of which are still intact today. These led to merchants' domestic quarters above. The arches below led to warehouses where goods were unloaded.

Near South Mall is **Parliament Bridge**, built in 1806 to commemorate the Act of Union (see p40). Walk across the bridge to George's Quay to see Fitzpatrick's second-hand shop, with its bizarre display of bicycles, cartwheels, farm implements and other assorted bric-à-brac on its façade. A short walk away, on Sullivan's Quay, is the Quay Co-Op, a popular vegetarian restaurant and meeting place.

From Sullivan's Quay an elegant footbridge, built in 1985, crosses the river to the south end of Grand Parade.

National Monument, Grand Parade

Grand Parade and St Patrick's Street

On Grand Parade, also once a waterway, stands the grandiose **National Monument**, recalling the Irish patriots who died between 1798 and 1867. Bishop Lucey Park, off Grand Parade, has a section of city walls and a fine gateway from the old cornmarket. Between St Patrick's Street and Grand Parade is the **English Market**, a covered fruit and vegetable market established in 1610. Bustling St Patrick's Street, the backbone of the city, was a waterway until 1800 when boats were moored under the steps of gracious houses such as the Chateau Bar (see p319). At the top of the street, near Patrick Bridge, is the **Father Mathew Statue**, a monument to the founder of the Temperance Movement.

Paul Street

Noted for its ethnic restaurants, chic bars, bookshops and trendy boutiques, Paul Street is the hub of the liveliest district in town. Just off Paul Street are the busy backstreets of Carey's Lane and French Church Street. In the early 18th century, Huguenots (French Protestants) settled in these streets and set themselves up as butter exporters, brewers and wholesale merchants. This area is Cork's equivalent to Dublin's Temple Bar (see p76).

Shandon Quarter

Crossing the Christy Ring Bridge to Pope's Quay, you will see on your left **St Mary's Dominican Church**, with its portico of Ionic columns topped by a huge pediment. John Redmond Street leads to the northern slopes of Cork, dominated by the spire of St Ann's Shandon (see p166) with its fine views of the city. To the northeast lies the lofty Montenotte district, once the epitome of Victorian gentility.

St Finbarr's Quarter

South of the river, rising above the city, this area's distinctive landmark is St Finbarr's Cathedral (see p167). Nearby is the ivy-clad **Elizabeth Fort**, a 16th-century structure which was converted into a prison in 1835 and later a Garda (police) station. A short walk to the east lies the **Red Abbey**, a 13th-century relic from an Augustinian abbey – the oldest building in Cork.

Selling fruit and vegetables at the English Market

ENVIRONS: Some beautiful countryside surrounds the city of Cork, especially along the lush valley of the River Lee *(see p163)*. The landscape of East Cork is much gentler than the wild, rocky coastline of West Cork and County Kerry, and the land is much more fertile. Many local attractions make good day trips and there are also plenty of opportunities for outdoor activities such as walking, riding and fishing.

♣ Blackrock Castle

Blackrock. ● *to the public.*
On the banks of the River Lee 1.5 km (1 mile) downstream from the city centre stands Blackrock Castle. Originally built in 1582 by Lord Mountjoy as a harbour fortification, the castle was destroyed by fire in 1827. It was rebuilt in 1830 to the design of architects J and GR Pain. The castle was recently bought by a private company and is no longer open to the public. A little further south at Carrigtwohill, near Fota Wildlife Park *(see pp170–71)*, is the 13th-century Barryscourt Castle, with its two intact towers.

Blackrock Castle standing on the banks of the River Lee

✚ Dunkathel House

Glanmire. 📞 021 482 1014.
○ *May–mid-Oct: Wed–Sun (pm only or by appt). Call to check times.* 📷
🚻 *ground floor.*
Outside Glanmire village, 6 km (3.5 miles) northeast of Cork, is this gracious Neo-Classical country house. It was remodelled around 1785 for Abraham Morris, a wealthy Cork merchant, but retains a few features from an earlier

Copy of *The Three Graces* by Antonio Canova, Dunkathel House

house, including some Italianate stuccowork. The interior is decorated with Adam fireplaces and a fine collection of Irish furniture. In the spacious entrance hall is an elegant Bath stone staircase with an iron balustrade. On the half landing stands a plaster copy of Canova's *The Three Graces,* thought to have been cast in the early 19th century. The drawing room, hung with Victorian watercolours, offers lovely views of the wooded banks of the River Glanmire. Charming parkland surrounds the house.

🏛 Royal Gunpowder Mills

Ballincollig. 📞 *021 487 4430.*
○ *mid-Mar–mid-Apr: Sat & Sun; mid-Apr–Sep: daily. Call to check times.* 📷 📹 🚻
Some 10 km (6 miles) west of Cork, this 320 ha (790 acres) of landscaped grounds is an impressive heritage project featuring canals, weirs, sluice gates, mills and workers' cottages. The mills were established in 1794 and flourished during the Napoleonic Wars, when they were also used as a British military base. By the 1850s, gunpowder production had become one of Cork's foremost industries. The mills finally closed in 1903, at the end of the Boer War. A guided tour covers the production of gunpowder in the main mills, and visitors are free to explore the rest of the complex.

River Blackwater ㉖

Road map B5. Co Cork. 🚌 *to Mallow.* 🚌 *to Fermoy, Mallow or Kanturk.*

THE SECOND LONGEST RIVER in Ireland after the Shannon *(see p177)*, the Blackwater rises in high bogland in County Kerry. It then flows eastwards through County Cork until it reaches Cappoquin, County Waterford, where it changes course south through wooded sandstone gorges to the sea at Youghal *(see p171)*. Much of the valley is wooded, a reminder that the entire area was forested until the 17th century. The river passes some magnificent country houses and pastoral views. However, the region is best known for its fishing – the Blackwater's tributaries are filled with fine brown trout.

The best way to see the valley is to take the scenic Blackwater Valley Drive from Youghal to Mallow. The route passes through **Fermoy**, a town founded by Scottish merchant John Anderson in 1789. Angling is the town's main appeal, especially for roach, rudd, perch and pike. Further west is **Mallow**, a prosperous town noted for its fishing, golf and horse racing, and a good base for tours of the area. Detours along the tributaries include **Kanturk**, a pleasant market town with a castle, on the River Allow.

Weirs and bridge at Fermoy on the River Blackwater

Cobh ㉗

Road map C6. Co Cork. 🚶 *12,000.*
🚉 ℹ *Old Yacht Club (021 4813301).*

COBH (pronounced "cove") lies on Great Island, one of the three islands in Cork harbour which are now linked by causeways. The Victorian seafront has rows of steeply terraced houses overlooked by **St Colman's**, an imposing Gothic Revival cathedral.

Following a visit by Queen Victoria in 1849, Cobh was renamed Queenstown but reverted to its original name in 1921. The town commands one of the world's largest natural harbours – the reason for its rise to prominence as a naval base in the 18th century. It was also a major port for merchant shipping and the main port from which Irish emigrants left for America.

Cobh was also a port of call for luxury passenger liners. In 1838, the *Sirius* made the first transatlantic crossing under steam power from here. Cobh was also the last stop for the *Titanic*, before its doomed Atlantic crossing in 1912. Three years later, the *Lusitania* was torpedoed and sunk by a German submarine just off Kinsale *(see pp164–5)*, southwest of Cobh. A memorial on the promenade is dedicated to all those who died in the attack.

IRISH EMIGRATION

Between 1848 and 1950 almost six million people emigrated from Ireland – two and a half million of them leaving from Cobh. The famine years of 1844–8 *(see p211)* triggered mass emigration as the impoverished made horrific transatlantic journeys in cramped, insanitary conditions. Many headed for the United States and Canada, and a few risked the long journey to Australia. Up until the early 20th century, emigrants waiting to board the ships were a familiar sight in Cobh. However, by the 1930s world recession and immigration restrictions in the United States and Canada led to a fall in the numbers leaving Ireland.

19th-century engraving of emigrants gathering in Cobh harbour

🏛 The Queenstown Story

Cobh Heritage Centre. 📞 *021 481 3591.* ⭕ *daily.* 🅿️ 🍴 ♿ 🚻

Housed in a Victorian railway station, *The Queenstown Story* is an exhibition detailing the town's marine history. Exhibits and audiovisual displays recall the part Cobh played in Irish emigration and the transportation of convicts. Between 1791 and 1853, 40,000 convicts were sent to Australian penal colonies in notorious "coffin ships"; many prisoners were also kept in floating jails in Cork Harbour.

On a happier note, the exhibition also documents Cobh's role as a port of call for glamorous transatlantic liners.

ENVIRONS: North of Cobh is Fota Island, with **Fota House and Gardens**. This glorious Regency mansion, surrounded by landscaped gardens, has a 19th-century arboretum with rare trees and shrubs from Asia, South America, and North America.

Also on the island, the **Fota Wildlife Park** concentrates on breeding and reintroducing

Cobh harbour with the steeple of St Colman's rising above the town

animals to their natural habitat. The white-tailed sea eagle is one native species that has been saved from extinction in Ireland. The park boasts over 70 species, including giraffe, flamingo, and zebra. A train links the sections of the park.

🌳 Fota House and Gardens
Carrigtwohill. **⚫** 021 481 5543.
⚪ daily. 📷 🅿 🏠
🦓 Fota Wildlife Park
Carrigtwohill. **⚫** 021 481 2678.
⚪ mid-Mar–Oct: daily; Nov–mid-Mar: Sat–Sun. 📷 ♿ 🍴 🏠

Old Midleton Distillery ㉘

Road map C5. Distillery Walk, Midleton, Co Cork.
⚫ 021 461 3594. 🚌 to Midleton.
⚪ daily. ⚫ 24 Dec–2 Jan. 📷 ♿
🏠 📷 🍴 in summer only.

A SENSITIVELY RESTORED 18th-century distillery, Old Midleton Distillery is part of the vast Irish Distillers group at Midleton. Bushmills (see p258) is the oldest distillery in Ireland but Midleton is the largest, with a series of distilleries each producing a different whiskey, including Jameson and Tullamore Dew.

The story of Irish whiskey is presented through audiovisual displays, working models and authentic machinery. A tour of the old distillery takes in the mills, maltings, still-houses, kilns, granaries and warehouses. Visitors can take part in whiskey tasting and try to distinguish between various brands of Irish whiskey and Scotch. Highlights of the visit include the world's largest pot still, with a capacity of over 30,000 gallons, and the working water wheel.

Clock tower on the main street of Youghal

Youghal ㉙

Road map C5. Co Cork.
🏘 7,500. 🚌 ℹ Market House, Market Square (024 20170).

Y OUGHAL (pronounced "yawl") is a historic walled town and thriving fishing port. The town was granted to Sir Walter Raleigh by Queen Elizabeth I but later sold to the Earl of Cork. In Cromwellian times, Youghal became a closed borough – an English Protestant garrison town.

The picturesque, four-storey **Clock tower** was originally the city gate, but was recast as a prison. Steep steps beside the tower lead up to a well-preserved section of the medieval town wall and fine views across the Blackwater estuary. Through the tower, in the sombre North Main Street, is the **Red House**, a Dutch mansion built in 1710. Virtually next door are some grim Elizabethan almshouses and, on the far side of the road, a 15th-century tower, known as **Tynte's Castle**.

Nestling in the town walls opposite is **Myrtle Grove** (closed to the public), one of the few unfortified Tudor manor houses to survive in Ireland. It has a triple-gabled façade and exquisite interior oak panelling. Just uphill is the Gothic **Church of St Mary**. Inside are tomb effigies and stained-glass windows depicting the coats of arms of local families.

Grain truck (c.1940) at the Jameson Heritage Centre

THE LOWER SHANNON

CLARE · LIMERICK · TIPPERARY

I N THE THREE COUNTIES *which flank the lower reaches of the Shannon, Ireland's longest river, the scenery ranges from the rolling farmland of Tipperary to the eerie limestone plateau of the Burren. The Shannon's bustling riverside resorts draw many visitors, and there are medieval strongholds and atmospheric towns of great historic interest. The region also boasts a vibrant music scene.*

The River Shannon has long made this area an attractive prospect for settlers. There are several important Stone Age sites, including a major settlement by Lough Gur. From the 5th century, the region lay at the heart of Munster, one of Ireland's four Celtic provinces. The Rock of Cashel, a remarkable fortified abbey in county Tipperary, was the seat of the Kings of Munster for more than 700 years.

The Vikings penetrated the Shannon in the 10th century, but Gaelic clans put up stern resistance. During the Norman period, the chieftains of these clans built Bunratty Castle and other fortresses that were impressive enough to rival the strongholds erected by the Anglo-Irish dynasties. Foremost among the latter families were the Butlers, the Earls of Ormonde, who held much land in Tipperary, and the Fitzgeralds, the main landowners in the Limerick area. From the Middle Ages, Limerick was often at the centre of events in the Lower Shannon. In 1691, the army of William of Orange laid siege to the town, heralding the Treaty of Limerick that triggered the Catholic nobility's departure for Europe – the so-called "Flight of the Wild Geese".

Lush grassland, which has turned the Lower Shannon into prime dairy country, is typical of the region. In places this gives way to picturesque glens and mountains, such as the Galty range in southern Tipperary. The region's most dramatic scenery, however, is found along the coast of Clare, a county otherwise best known for its thriving traditional music scene.

Ruins of Dysert O'Dea monastery in County Clare with an outstanding 12th-century High Cross

◁ Traditional musicians playing at Feakle in County Clare

Exploring the Lower Shannon

T HE CENTRAL LOCATION of Limerick city makes it a natural focus for visitors to the region. However, there are many charming towns that make pleasanter bases, such as Adare, Cashel and also Killaloe, which is well placed for exploring the River Shannon. Most places of interest in Tipperary lie in the southern part of the county, where historic towns such as Clonmel and Cahir overlook the River Suir. By contrast, County Clare has few towns of any size, though it boasts the major attraction of Bunratty Castle. Beyond Ennis, the landscape becomes steadily bleaker until you reach the Burren.

Looking up at the Cliffs of Moher

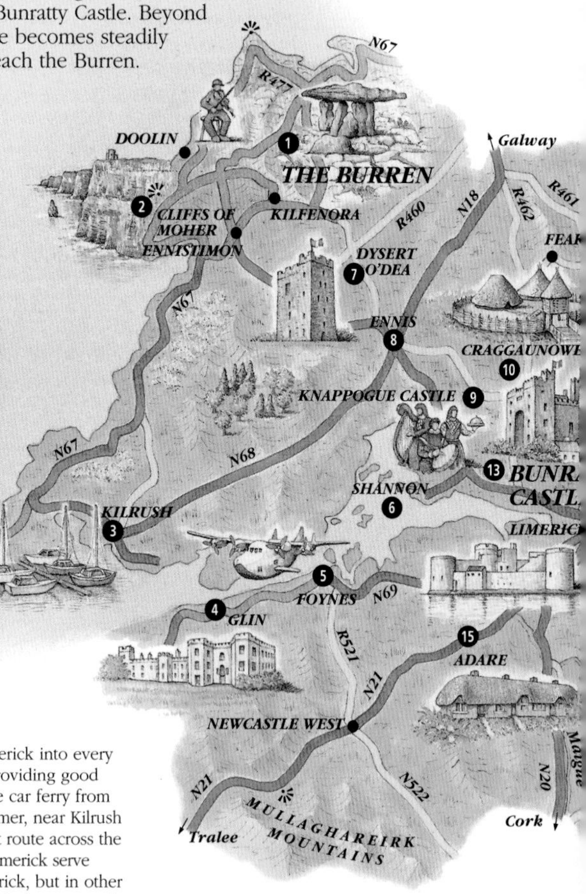

N67 · R477 · DOOLIN · ① THE BURREN · Galway · R461 · R462 · R460 · N18 · ② CLIFFS OF MOHER · KILFENORA · ENNISTIMON · N67 · DYSERT O'DEA · ⑦ · FEAK · CRAGGAUNOWE · ⑩ · ENNIS · ⑧ · KNAPPOGUE CASTLE · ⑨ · N67 · N68 · SHANNON · ⑥ · ⑬ BUNR. CASTL. · KILRUSH · ③ · LIMERIC · R487 · ⑤ · FOYNES · N69 · ④ GLIN · ⑮ ADARE · Marg... · NEWCASTLE WEST · N21 · R521 · N21 · N20 · Tralee · MULLAGHAREIRK MOUNTAINS · N522 · Cork

GETTING AROUND

Roads extend from Limerick into every corner of the region, providing good access for motorists; the car ferry from Tarbert in Kerry to Killimer, near Kilrush in Clare, is a convenient route across the Shannon. Trains from Limerick serve Cahir, Clonmel and Carrick, but in other areas you must rely on the bus network. This is rather limited, especially in County Clare, although buses to the Burren from Limerick pass the Cliffs of Moher. Some of the most popular sights, such as Bunratty Castle and the Burren, can be reached on bus tours from Limerick.

0 kilometres   25

0 miles   25

KEY

▨	Major road
▨	Minor road
▨	Scenic route
▨	River
❀	Viewpoint

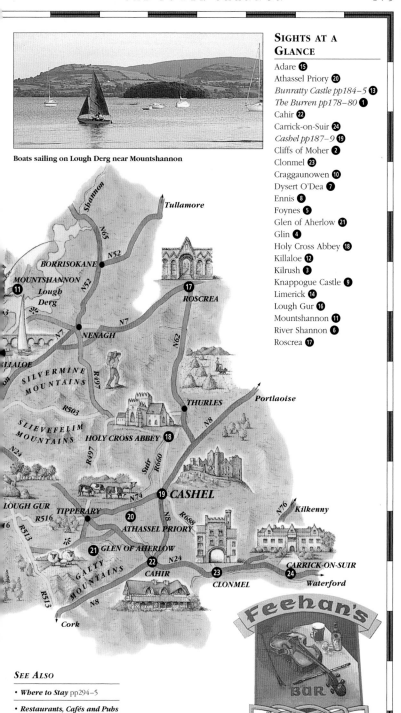

Boats sailing on Lough Derg near Mountshannon

Tullamore

N65

N52

BORRISOKANE

MOUNTSHANNON ⑪
Lough Derg
N52
ROSCREA ⑰
N7
N7
NENAGH
N62
SILVERMINE MOUNTAINS
R497
ILLALOE
R503
THURLES
SLIEVEFELIM MOUNTAINS
R497 Portlaoise
N8
N24
HOLY CROSS ABBEY ⑱
Suir R660
⑲ CASHEL
N74
N76 Kilkenny
LOUGH GUR TIPPERARY
R516 ⑳
ATHASSEL PRIORY
N8 R688
⑳
R46 R513
⑳ GLEN OF AHERLOW ㉑
GALTY MOUNTAINS
㉒ N24
CAHIR
㉓
CARRICK-ON-SUIR ㉔
Waterford
CLONMEL
R513
N8
Cork

Painted pub sign in Cashel

Looking south along the Cliffs of Moher, one of the most dramatic stretches of Ireland's west coast

The Burren ❶

See pp178–9.

Cliffs of Moher ❷

Road map B4. Co Clare. 🚌 *from Ennis & Limerick.* **Visitors' Centre** 【 *061 360788.* 🕐 *daily.* ● *21–27 Dec.* 📷 🚻 **O'Brien's Tower** 【 *061 360788.* 🕐 *Mar–Oct: daily.* 🅿

EVEN WHEN SHROUDED in mist or buffeted by Atlantic gales, the Cliffs of Moher are breathtaking, rising to a height of 200 m (650 ft) out of the sea and extending for 8 km (5 miles). The sheer rock face, with its layers of black shale and sandstone, provides sheltered ledges where guillemots and other sea birds nest.

Well-worn paths lead along the cliffs. From the **Visitors' Centre**, 5 km (3 miles) northwest of Liscannor, you can walk south to **Hag's Head** in an hour. To the north, a good alternative is the three-hour walk along the coast between **O'Brien's Tower** – a viewing point built for the benefit of Victorian tourists – and Fisherstreet near **Doolin** (*see p180*).

Kilrush ❸

Road map B4. Co Clare. 🚶 *2,800.* 🚌 🚹 *Heritage Centre, Market House (065 905 1577).* 🕐 *May–Sep.*

WITH A NEW MARINA and the promotion of Kilrush as a heritage town, the fortunes of this 18th-century estate town have been greatly revived. It now has a **Heritage Centre**, where an exhibition covers the Great Famine (*see p211*) and the landlord evictions of 1888

(*see pp40–41*). A well-marked walking trail around the town's historic sights also starts here.

ENVIRONS: From Kilrush, boats take visitors dolphin-spotting or to nearby **Scattery Island**, site of a medieval monastery. The ruins include five churches and one of the tallest round towers in the country.

The **Loop Head Drive** is a 27-km (17-mile) route which begins at the resort of Kilkee, west of Kilrush. It winds south past dramatic coastal scenery to Loop Head, from where you can enjoy superb views.

Glin ❹

Road map B5. Co Limerick. 🚶 *600.* 🚌 *from Limerick.*

THIS CHARMING village on the banks of the Shannon is the seat of the Knights of Glin, a branch of the Fitzgeralds who have lived in the district for seven centuries. Their first medieval castle is a ruin, but west of the village stands their

Rare 18th-century double "flying" staircase in Glin Castle

newer home, **Glin Castle**. Built in 1780, the manor succumbed to the vogue for Gothic romance in the 1820s, when it acquired battlements and gingerbread lodges. There is fine stuccowork and 18th-century furniture inside. It is now run as a hotel (*see p295*).

♣ **Glin Castle**
【 *068 34173.* 🕐 *by appt.* 🅿 🚷 *obligatory.* 🌐 *www.glincastle.com*

Foynes ❺

Road map B5. Co Limerick. 🚶 *650.* 🚌 *from Limerick.*

FOYNES ENJOYED short-lived fame in the 1930s and 1940s as the eastern terminus of the first airline passenger route across the Atlantic. **Foynes Flying Boat Museum** presents a detailed history of the seaplane service. The original Radio and Weather Room and a 1940s-style tea room are particularly evocative of the era.

🏛 **Foynes Flying Boat Museum**
Aras Ide, Foynes. 【 *069 65416.* 🕐 *Apr–Oct: daily.* 🅿 🖥 🚻 ♿

ENVIRONS: The historic town of **Askeaton**, 11 km (7 miles) east of Foynes, has a castle and Franciscan friary founded by the Fitzgeralds. The friary is particularly interesting, with a 15th-century cloister of black marble. In Rathkeale, 8 km (5 miles) south, **Castle Matrix** is a restored 15th-century tower house renowned for the fine library in the Great Hall.

♣ **Castle Matrix**
Rathkeale. 【 *069 64284.* 🕐 *May–Sep: Sat–Thu.* 🅿

Fishing on Lough Derg, the largest of the lakes on the Shannon

River Shannon ⑥

Road map B4, C4, C3. 🚉 *to Limerick or Athlone.* 🚌 *to Carrick-on-Shannon, Athlone or Limerick.* 🛈 *Arthur's Quay, Limerick (061 317522).*
Ⓦ *www.shannon-dev.ie*

T HE SHANNON IS the longest river in Ireland, rising in County Cavan and meandering down to the Atlantic. Flowing through the heart of the island, it has traditionally marked the border between the provinces of Leinster and Connaught. In medieval times, castles guarded the major fords from Limerick to Portumna, and numerous monasteries were built along the riverbanks, including the celebrated Clonmacnoise *(see pp242–3)*. Work began on the Shannon navigation system in the 1750s, but it fell into disuse with the advent of the railways. It has since been revived with the Shannon–Erne Waterway the latest stretch to be restored *(see p227)*.

There are subtle changes of landscape along the length of the river. South of **Lough Allen**, the countryside is covered with the drumlins or low hills typical of the northern Midlands. Towards **Lough Ree**, islands stud the river in an area of ecological importance which is home to otters, geese, grey herons and whooper swans. Continuing south beyond **Athlone** *(see p241)*, the river flows through flood plains and bog before reaching **Lough**

EXPLORING THE SHANNON

Carrick-on-Shannon is the main centre for boating on the upper reaches of the river, while Portumna and the atmospheric ports of Mountshannon and Killaloe are the principal bases for exploring Lough Derg.

Cruiser on the Shannon

KEY

🛈	Tourist information
🚉	Cruiser hire
🚌	Water-bus tour

(Map of the Shannon showing: Source of the Shannon, NORTHWEST IRELAND, Lough Allen, Shannon–Erne Waterway, Leitrim, Lough Key, Carrick-on-Shannon, Kilglass Lough, THE WEST OF IRELAND, Royal Canal, Lough Ree, Athlone, THE MIDLANDS, Grand Canal, Banagher, Portumna, Lough Derg, Mountshannon, Drominer, THE LOWER SHANNON, Killaloe, Ballina, Shannon Estuary, Limerick)

0 km 20
0 miles 10

Derg, the biggest of the lakes on the Shannon. The scenery is more dramatic here, with the lough's southern end edged by wooded mountains. From **Killaloe** *(see p182)*, the river gains speed on its rush towards **Limerick** *(see p183)* and the sea. The mudflats of the Shannon estuary attract a great variety of birdlife. The port of **Carrick-on-Shannon** *(see p227)* is the cruising centre of Ireland, but there are bases all along the river – especially

Grey heron on the Shannon

around Lough Derg, which is the lake most geared to boating. Water-buses connect most ports south of Athlone. If you hire a cruiser, enquire about the weather conditions before setting out, particularly on Loughs Ree and Derg, which are very exposed. The calm stretch from **Portumna** *(see p205)* to Athlone is easier for inexperienced sailors.

Walkers can enjoy the Lough Derg Way, a signposted route around the lake. The woods by **Lough Key** *(see p211)* also provide good walking territory.

Athlone and the southern reaches of Lough Ree

The Burren ❶

T HE WORD BURREN derives from *boireann*, which means "rocky land" in Gaelic – an apt name for this vast limestone plateau in northwest County Clare. In the 1640s, Cromwell's surveyor described it as "a savage land, yielding neither water enough to drown a man, nor tree to hang him, nor soil enough to bury".

Dark red helleborine

Few trees manage to grow in this desolate place, yet other plants thrive. The Burren is a unique botanical environment in which Mediterranean and alpine plants rare to Ireland grow side by side. From May to August, an astonishing array of flowers adds splashes of colour to the austere landscape. These plants grow most abundantly around the region's shallow lakes and pastures, but they also take root in the crevices of the limestone pavements which are the most striking geological feature of the rocky plateau. In the southern part of the Burren, limestone gives way to the black shale and sandstone that form the dramatic Cliffs of Moher *(see p176)*.

Grazing in the Burren
A quirk in the local climate means that, in winter, the hills are warmer than the valleys – hence the unusual practice in the Burren of letting cattle graze on high ground in winter.

FAUNA OF THE BURREN

The Burren is one of the best places in Ireland for butterflies, with 28 species found in the area. The birdlife is also varied. Sky-larks and cuckoos are common on the hills and in the meadows, while the coast is a good place for razorbills, guillemots, puffins and other sea birds. Mammals are harder to spot. Badgers, foxes and stoats live here, but you are much more likely to see a herd of shaggy-coated wild goats or an Irish hare.

Turloughs are shallow lakes which are dry in summer but flood in winter, when they attract wildfowl and waders.

Spring gentian

The pearl-bordered fritillary, *one of a number of fritillaries found in the Burren, can be seen in no other part of Ireland.*

An Irish hare's *white and brown winter coat turns to reddish-brown in the summer.*

Whooper swans *from Iceland flock to the wetlands of the Burren in winter.*

The hooded crow *is easily identified by its grey and black plumage.*

Bloody Cranesbill
This striking plant, common in the Burren, is a member of the geranium family. It flowers in June.

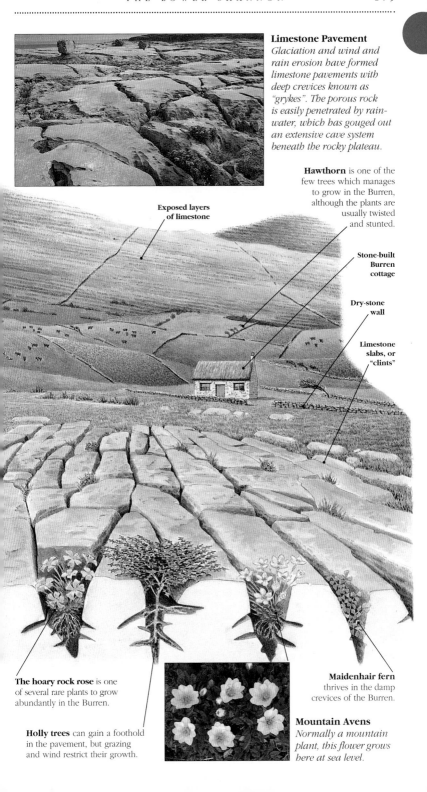

Limestone Pavement
Glaciation and wind and rain erosion have formed limestone pavements with deep crevices known as "grykes". The porous rock is easily penetrated by rainwater, which has gouged out an extensive cave system beneath the rocky plateau.

Hawthorn is one of the few trees which manages to grow in the Burren, although the plants are usually twisted and stunted.

Exposed layers of limestone

Stone-built Burren cottage

Dry-stone wall

Limestone slabs, or "clints"

The hoary rock rose is one of several rare plants to grow abundantly in the Burren.

Holly trees can gain a foothold in the pavement, but grazing and wind restrict their growth.

Maidenhair fern thrives in the damp crevices of the Burren.

Mountain Avens
Normally a mountain plant, this flower grows here at sea level.

Exploring the Burren

If you are interested in the unique geology and natural history of the Burren, head for **Mullaghmore**, to the southeast of the area. This is one of the wildest parts of the plateau and reaches a height of 191 m (626 ft), with some of the best limestone pavements in the area.

A good place to begin a tour of the more accessible parts of the Burren is at the **Cliffs of Moher** (see p176). From here it is a short drive north to **Doolin**, near the port for the Aran Islands (see pp206–7). This rather spread-out village is renowned for its traditional music; Gus O'Connor's pub (see p320) acts as a focus for music-lovers in the area. The coastal road runs north from Doolin to a desolate limestone outcrop at **Black Head**, while turning inland you will reach **Lisdoonvarna**. The Victorians developed the town as a spa, but it is now most renowned for its colourful pubs and its matchmaking festival (see p48).

Poulnabrone Dolmen in the heart of the Burren's limestone plateau

Music shop in Doolin

To the north along the N67 lies **Ballyvaughan**, a fishing village dotted with slate-roofed cottages and busy with tourists in summer. It is well placed for reaching a number of sights. Nearby **Bishop's Quarter** has a sheltered beach with glorious views across a lagoon towards Galway Bay. **Aillwee Cave**, to the south, is just one of thousands of caves in the Burren, but is the only one open to the public. It consists of a tunnel which opens into a series of caverns. In the first, known as Bear Haven, the remains of hibernation pits used by bears are still visible.

Ruined forts and castles and numerous prehistoric sites dot the landscape. Just west of Aillwee Cave is **Cahermore Stone Fort**, with a lintelled doorway, and to the south

Carved capital in Kilfenora Cathedral

Gleninsheen Wedge Tomb, a style of grave which marks the transition between Stone and Bronze Age cultures. The more famous **Poulnabrone Dolmen** nearby is a striking portal tomb dating back to 2500–2000 BC. Continuing south you reach the ghostly shell of **Leamaneagh Castle**, a 17th-century mansion that incorporates an earlier tower house built by the O'Briens.

On the southern fringe of the Burren lies **Kilfenora**, a Catholic diocese which, by a historical quirk, has the Pope for its bishop. The village's modest cathedral, one of many 12th-century churches in the Burren, has a roofless chancel with finely sculpted capitals. Kilfenora, however, is more famous for its High Crosses: there are several in the graveyard. Best preserved is the Doorty Cross, with a carving of a bishop and two other clerics on the east face. Next door, the refurbished **Burren Centre** offers an excellent multi-dimensional exhibition giving information on the geology and fauna of the area and man's impact on the landscape.

🎣 Aillwee Cave
Ballyvaughan. 🄲 06570 77036.
🄾 daily. 💯 🄲 🄲 🄲
🏛 Burren Centre
Kilfenora. 🄲 06570 88030.
🄾 Mar–Oct: daily. 💯 🄲 🄲 🄲
🄦 www.theburrencentre.ie

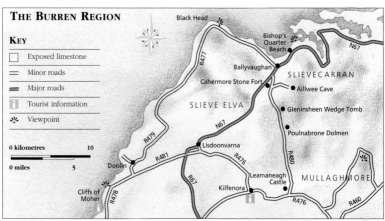

THE BURREN REGION

KEY

☐	Exposed limestone
═	Minor roads
▬	Major roads
🄸	Tourist information
🌟	Viewpoint

0 kilometres 10
0 miles 5

Black Head
Bishop's Quarter Beach
N67
R477
Ballyvaughan
SLIEVECARRAN
Cahermore Stone Fort
Aillwee Cave
SLIEVE ELVA
Gleninsheen Wedge Tomb
N67
Poulnabrone Dolmen
R479
R480
Lisdoonvarna
R481
R476
Doolin
R67
Leamaneagh Castle
MULLAGHMORE
Cliffs of Moher
R478
Kilfenora
R476
R460

Dysert O'Dea ◐

Road map 4B. Corrofin, Co Clare.
🚍 from Ennis. 📞 06568 37722.
🕐 May–Sep: daily. 🅿️

DYSERT O'DEA CASTLE stands on a rocky outcrop 9 km (6 miles) north of Ennis. This tower house, erected in the 15th century, is home to the **Archaeology Centre**, which includes a small museum and also marks the start of a trail around nearby historic sights. A map of the path, designed for both walkers and cyclists, is available from the tea room.

Across a field from the castle is a monastic site said to have been founded by the obscure St Tola in the 8th century. The ruins are overgrown and rather worn, but the Romanesque carving above one doorway is still clear, and there is also an impressive 12th-century High Cross, with a bishop sculpted on the east side *(see p235)*.

Further south, the trail leads past the remains of two stone forts, a ruined castle and the site of a 14th-century battle.

Ennis ◐

Road map 4B. Co Clare. 🏘️ 25,000.
🚍 ℹ️ Clare Rd (06568 28366).

CLARE'S COUNTY TOWN, on the banks of the River Fergus, is a charming place. Narrow, winding lanes are particularly characteristic and recall Ennis's medieval beginnings. The town is also renowned for its painted shopfronts and folk music festivals (known as *fleadh* in Gaelic). It abounds in "singing" pubs and traditional music shops.

Colourful exterior of Michael Kerins pub in Ennis

Ennis can trace its origins to the 13th century and to the O'Briens, Kings of Thomond, who were the area's feudal overlords in the Middle Ages. The Franciscan friary that they founded here in the 1240s is now the town's main attraction. Dating from the 14th and 15th centuries, the ruined **Ennis Friary** is famous for its rich carvings and decorated tombs in the chancel – above all the 15th-century MacMahon tomb with its finely carved alabaster panels. Extensive conservation work is ongoing here.

Next door to the friary is a delightful 17th-century house, now Cruise's restaurant *(see p312)*, and on the corner of nearby Francis Street stands the Queen's Hotel – featured in James Joyce's *Ulysses*. To the south, O'Connell Square has a monument to Daniel O'Connell *(see p40)*, who was elected MP for Clare in 1828. He also gave his name to the town's main street, where, among the pubs and shops, you can spot a medieval tower, a Jacobean chimney stack and an 18th-century arch.

Finely carved Romanesque doorway at Dysert O'Dea

⛪ Ennis Friary
Abbey St. 📞 06568 29100. 🕐 May–Oct: daily. 🅿️ 🚻

ENVIRONS: The area around Ennis is rich in monastic ruins. Just 3 km (2 miles) south of the town is **Clare Abbey**, an Augustinian foundation set up by the O'Briens in 1189 but dating mainly from the 1400s.

Quin Franciscan Friary, set in meadows 13 km (8 miles) southeast of Ennis, was also built in the 15th century, and incorporates the romantic ruins of a Norman castle. The well-preserved cloister is one of the finest of its kind in Ireland.

Knappogue Castle ◐

Road map 4B. Quin, Co Clare. 📞 061 360788. 🚍 to Ennis. 🕐 Apr–Oct; ring for times. 🅿️ 🎧 🚻 limited.

A POWERFUL LOCAL CLAN called the MacNamaras erected Knappogue Castle in 1467. Apart from a ten-year spell in Cromwellian times, it stayed in their hands until 1815. During the War of Independence *(see pp42–3)*, the castle was used by the revolutionary forces.

Knappogue, now owned by Shannon Development, has been well restored and is one of Ireland's most charmingly furnished castles. The central tower house is original, but the rest is Neo-Gothic. Inside are fine Elizabethan fireplaces and linenfold wood panelling.

Medieval banquets are staged in the castle *(see p330)*, with storytelling and singing forming part of the entertainment.

Craggaunowen ⑩

Road map B4. Kilmurry, Co Clare.
🔲 🔲 to Ennis. 【 061 360788.
◯ May–Oct: daily. 📷 ♿ 🔲 🔲

THE CRAGGAUNOWEN PROJECT, known as "Craggaunowen: the Living Past" and designed to bring Bronze Age and Celtic culture to life, is a shining example of a recreated pre-historic site. The centre was created in the grounds of Craggaunowen Castle in the 1960s by John Hunt, a noted archaeologist who had been inspired by his excavations at Lough Gur *(see p186)*. The castle's tower house contains bronzes and other objects from Hunt's archaeological collection, the rest of which can be seen in Limerick.

In summer, people in costume act out particular trades, such as spinning or potting, or serve as guides. A French slave describes how communities lived in the ring fort, a typical early Christian homestead. You can also see meat being prepared in the *fulacht fiadh*, a traditional hunter's cooking hole.

The complex includes part of a *togher*, an original Iron Age timber road that was dis-covered in Longford. The most eye-catching sight, however, is the crannog *(see p31)*, a man-made island enclosing wattle and daub houses – a style of defensive homestead that survived until around 1600.

Another interesting exhibit is a leather-hulled boat built in the 1970s by the explorer, Tim Severin. He used it to retrace

A woman in peasant costume spinning wool at Craggaunowen

the route which legend says St Brendan took in a similar vessel across the Atlantic in the 6th century *(see p25)*.

Mountshannon ⑪

Road map C4. Co Clare. 👫 240.
🔲 to Holy Island. 【 061 921351.

THIS PRETTY VILLAGE on the banks of Lough Derg *(see p177)* seems to have its back turned to the lake but is never-theless a major angling centre. Solid 18th-century stone houses and churches cluster around the harbour, together with some good pubs.

Mountshannon is well placed for exploring the lake's western shores, with plenty of scope for walks and bicycle rides. Fishing boats are available for hire, and in summer you can go by boat to **Holy Island**, the site of a monastery founded in the 7th century. The ruins include four chapels and a graveyard of medieval tombs.

Killaloe ⑫

Road map C4. Co Clare. 👫 950.
🔲 ℹ May–Sep: Brian Ború Heritage Centre, The Bridge (061 376866).

KILLALOE, birthplace of Brian Ború (940–1014), High King of Ireland *(see p32)*, lies close to where the Shannon emerges from Lough Derg, and is the lake's most prospe-rous pleasure port. A 17th-century stone bridge separates Killaloe from its twin town of Ballina on the opposite bank. Ballina has better pubs, such as Goosers on the waterfront *(see p320)*, but Killaloe is the main boating centre *(see p335)* and also offers more of historical interest.

Killaloe's grandest building is **St Flannan's Cathedral**, built around 1182. Its richly carved Romanesque doorway was once part of an earlier chapel. The church also has an ancient Ogham Stone *(see p32)*, unusual because the inscription is carved in both Nordic runes and Ogham. Outside stands St Flannan's Oratory, built around the same time as the cathedral.

The Brian Ború Heritage Centre, in a converted boat-house on the bridge, has an exhibition about the Shannon and Lough Derg, and is the starting point for a marked walk along sections of the old Killaloe Canal. You can also arrange for local fishermen to take you out on the lake.

Bunratty Castle ⑬

See pp184–5.

Bicycle hire and boat trips at Mountshannon

Limerick ⓮

Road map B4. Co Limerick. 🏚 90,000.
👣 Shannon. 🚏 🚇 ℹ️ Arthur's
Quay (061 317522). 🚢 Sat.
W www.visitlimerick.com

THE THIRD LARGEST CITY in the Republic, Limerick was founded by the Vikings. Given its strategic point on the River Shannon, it thrived under the Normans, but later bore the brunt of English oppression. After the Battle of the Boyne (see p236), the rump of the defeated Jacobite army withdrew here. The siege which followed has entered Irish folklore as a heroic defeat, sealed by the Treaty of Limerick in 1691. English treachery in reneging on most of the terms of the treaty still rankles. It is no coincidence that Catholicism and nationalism are strong in the city.

Limerick has a reputation for high unemployment, crime and general neglect. However, it is fast acquiring a new image as a commercial city, revitalized by new industries and restoration projects. Even so, visitors may still have to dig a little to appreciate its charm.

The city centre consists of three historic districts. King's Island was the first area to be settled by the Vikings and was later the heart of the medieval city, when it was known as Englishtown. It boasts Limerick's two main landmarks, King John's Castle and St Mary's Cathedral. The old Irishtown, south of the Abbey River, has its fair share of drab houses and shops, but also has its own

historic buildings and a pocket of Georgian elegance in St John's Square. Near here is Limerick's most conspicuous sight, St John's Cathedral, built in 1861. Its 85-m (280-ft) spire is the tallest in the country.

The most pleasant part of Limerick in which to stroll is Newtown Pery – a grid of gracious Georgian terraces focused on O'Connell Street.

♣ King John's Castle
Nicholas St. 📞 061 411201. ◻
daily ● Good Fri, Dec 24–26. 📷 &
Supposedly founded by King John in 1200, not long after the Normans arrived, this imposing castle has five drum towers and solid curtain walls. Inside, the castle is less interesting architecturally, but it houses a good audiovisual exhibition on the history of the city. Ongoing excavations have unearthed pots and jewellery, and you can also see Viking houses and later fortifications. One of the most dramatic artifacts on display is a soldier's diary recording the horrors of the Siege of Limerick.

Across the nearby Thomond Bridge, the Treaty Stone marks the spot where the Treaty of Limerick was signed in 1691.

Carved misericord in St Mary's Cathedral

🔒 St Mary's Cathedral
Bridge Street. 📞 061 416238.
◻ 9:30am–4:30pm Mon–Fri, 9:30am
–2pm Sat, for services only Sun.
Built in 1172, this is the oldest structure in the city. Except for a fine Romanesque doorway and the nave, however, little remains of the early church. The 15th-century misericords

Characteristic Georgian doorway in St John's Square

in the choir stalls are the pride of St Mary's, with superb carvings in black oak of angels, griffins and other creatures both real and imaginary.

Nearby, George's Quay is a pleasant street with restaurants and outdoor cafés and good views across the river.

🏛 Hunt Museum
Rutland St. 📞 061 312833.
◻ 10am–5pm Mon–Sat, 2pm–5pm
Sun. 📷 🍴 🛍 &
Located in the Old Customs House, this fine museum has one of the greatest collections of antiquities in Ireland, gathered by the archaeologist John Hunt. The best exhibits, dating from the Bronze Age, include gold jewellery and a magnificent shield. Among the other artifacts are Celtic brooches and the Antrim Cross, a masterpiece of 9th-century metalwork.

🏛 Limerick Museum
Nicholas St. 📞 061 417826. ◻
10am–5pm Tue–Sat. ● for lunch,
public hols & 7 days at Christmas. &
The city museum is in a fine 19th-century granary building. Limerick's history and traditions from lace-making to rugby are on display.

View of Limerick showing Thomond Bridge across the Shannon and King John's Castle

Bunratty Castle & Folk Park ⓭

T HIS FORMIDABLE CASTLE, built in the 15th century, is one of Ireland's major tourist attractions. Its most important residents were the O'Briens, Earls of Thomond, who lived here from around 1500 until the 1640s. The present interior looks much as it did under the so-called "Great Earl", who died in 1624. Abandoned in the 19th century, the castle was derelict when Lord Gort bought it in the 1950s, but it has been beautifully restored to its original state. The adjacent Folk Park includes Hazelbrook House, which shows the evolution of ice-cream making. Bunratty is also famous for its splendid medieval banquets.

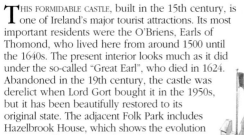

The chimney is a replica in wood of the stone original. It provided a vent for the smoke given off by the fire in the centre of the Great Hall.

★ **North Solar**
This 17th-century German chandelier is the most curious feature in the Great Earl's private apartments. The term "solar" was used during the Middle Ages to describe an upper chamber.

The Murder Hole was designed for pouring boiling water or pitch on to the heads of attackers.

Entrance

North Front
Bunratty Castle is unusual for the high arches on both the north and south sides of the keep. However, the first-floor entrance, designed to deter invaders, was typical of castles of the period.

The basement, with walls 3 m (10 ft) thick, was probably used for storage or as a stable.

STAR FEATURES

★ **Great Hall**

★ **Main Guard**

★ **North Solar**

VISITORS' CHECKLIST

Road map B4. Bunratty, Co Clare.
061 360788. Shannon.
from Ennis, Limerick, Shannon.
Castle & Folk Park
daily. Last adm. to castle:
4pm. Good Friday, 24–26
Dec. to Folk Park.
Banquets see p330.
www.shannonheritage.com

★ **Main Guard**

Now used for medieval-style banquets, this was the room where Bunratty's soldiers ate, slept and relaxed. Music was played to them from the Minstrels' Gallery, and a gate in one corner gave instant access to the dungeons.

Anteroom

The Robing Room
was where the earls put on their gowns before an audience in the Great Hall. They also used it for private interviews.

South Solar

These guest apartments have fine linenfold wood panelling, a form of decoration popular during the Tudor period. The elaborate fan-vaulted ceiling is partly a reconstruction.

A spiral staircase is found in each of the four towers.

★ **Great Hall**

This Tudor standard was among the many furnishings that Lord Gort brought to the castle. It stands in the Great Hall, once the banqueting hall and audience chamber, and still Bunratty's grandest room.

BUNRATTY FOLK PARK

A meticulous recreation of rural life in Ireland at the end of the 19th century, this Folk Park began with the reconstruction of a farmhouse which was saved during the building of nearby Shannon Airport. It now consists of a complete village, incorporating shops and a whole range of domestic architecture from a labourer's cottage to an elegant Georgian house. Other buildings include a farmhouse typical of the Moher region in the Burren *(see p176)* and a working corn mill. During the main summer season, people in authentic costume wander through the streets and demonstrate traditional crafts and trades such as weaving and butter-making.

Main street of Bunratty Folk Park village

Typical thatched cottage in the village of Adare

Adare 🕔

Road map B5. Co Limerick. 🚌 *1,000.*
🏠 ℹ *Heritage Centre, Main St
(061 396255).* ◯ *Feb–Dec: daily.*

A DARE IS BILLED as Ireland's prettiest village. Cynics call it the prettiest "English" village since its manicured perfection is at odds with normal notions of national beauty. Originally a fief of the Fitzgeralds, the Earls of Kildare, Adare owes its present appearance more to the Earls of Dunraven, who restored the estate village in the 1820s and 1830s. The long, thin village is a picture of neat stonework and thatched roofs punctuated by picturesque ruins, all in a woodland setting.

The tourist office is at the new Heritage Centre, which includes a good exhibition on Adare's monastic history. Next

door is the **Trinitarian Priory**, founded by the Fitzgeralds in 1230 and over-restored by the first Earl of Dunraven; it is now a Catholic church and convent. Opposite, by a stone-arched bridge, is the Washing Pool, a restored wash-house site.

By the main bridge, on the Limerick road, is the **Augustinian Priory** which was founded by the Fitzgeralds in 1315. Also known as Black Abbey, this well-restored priory has a central tower, subtle carvings, delightful cloisters and a graceful sedilia – a carved triple seat. Just over the bridge, from where it is best viewed, is **Desmond Castle**, a 13th-century feudal castle set on the banks of the River Maigue.

Nearby stands the main gate to **Adare Manor**, a luxury hotel and golf course *(see p294)*. Within its 900 ha (2,220 acres) of parkland lie two evocative

ruins. The **St Nicholas Church** and **Chantry Chapel** date back to the 12th century; both are accessible by path. The graceful 15th-century **Franciscan Friary**, however, is surrounded by the golf course, though it can be seen clearly from the pathway.

In the heart of the village is the elegant Dunraven Arms Hotel *(see p294)* from where the local hunt rides to hounds. Some of the nearby cottages, originally built by the Earl of Dunraven in 1828 for his estate workers, have been converted into restaurants, including the cosy Inn-Between *(see p312)*.

Lough Gur 🕕

Road map B5. Co Limerick. 🚌
Visitors' Centre 🛈 *061 360788.*
◯ *May–Sep: daily.* 🎦 🛗 *limited.* ◻

T HIS STONE AGE settlement, 26 km (16 miles) south of Limerick, was extensively inhabited in 3000 BC. Today the horseshoe-shaped lough and surrounding hills enclose an intriguing if rather inscrutable archaeological park. All around Lough Gur are standing stones and burial mounds, including megalithic tombs. One of the most impressive sights is the 4,000-year-old **Great Stone Circle**, just outside the park, by the Limerick–Kilmallock road. Excavations in the 1970s unearthed rectangular, oval and rounded Stone Age huts with stone foundations. The

Colourfully painted shopfronts on Main Street in Adare

Façade of Cashel Palace Hotel

interpretive centre, which is housed in mock Stone Age huts on the site of the original settlement, offers a range of audiovisual displays, models of stone circles, burial chambers and tools and weapons.

As well as the various pre-historic sites scattered all over the Knockadoon Peninsula, there are two castle ruins from more recent times beside the lough – the 15th-century **Bourchier's Castle** and **Black Castle**, a 13th-century seat of the Earls of Desmond.

Roscrea ⑰

Road map C4. Co Tipperary.
🏃 5,500. 🚃 🚍 🚹 Heritage Centre, Castle St (0505 21850).
◯ mid-Apr–Oct: daily.

THIS MONASTIC TOWN on the banks of the River Bunnow has an interesting historic centre. The 13th-century Anglo-Norman **Roscrea Castle**, recently fully restored, consists of a gate tower, curtain walls and two corner towers. In the courtyard stands **Damer House**, a Queen Anne-style residence with a magnificent staircase and Georgian garden. Just over the river lies **St Cronan's Monastery** with a High Cross, Romanesque church gable and a truncated round tower. There are remains of a 15th-century **Franciscan Friary** on Abbey Street and nearby in St Cronan's churchyard is **Roscrea Pillar**, an enigmatic early Christian stone.

♣ **Roscrea Castle & Gardens**
Castle Street. 📞 0505 21850. ◯ mid-Mar–Oct: daily. 🎟 🚻 limited. ⏎

Holy Cross Abbey ⑱

Road map C5. Thurles, Co Tipperary.
📞 0504 43241. 🚃 🚍 to Thurles.
◯ 9am–8pm daily.
🎟 🅿 🚻

FOUNDED IN 1169 by the Benedictines, Holy Cross was supposedly endowed with a splinter from the True Cross, hence its name. Now it has been completely re-stored, and the church is once again a popular place of worship and pilgrimage. Most of the present structure dates from the 15th century. It was built by the Cistercians, who took over the abbey in 1180. This gracious cruciform church, embellished with mullioned win-dows and sculpted pillars, is one of the finest examples of late Gothic architecture in Ireland.

The chancel has fine ribbed vaulting and, in the south wall, an exquisitely carved sedilia, which is rather oddly called "the tomb of the Good Woman's son". The abbey complex, set in charming gardens, also houses an old-fashioned pub.

Crucifixion carving at Holy Cross Abbey

Cashel ⑲

Road map C5. Co Tipperary.
🏃 2,500. 🚍 🚹 Heritage Centre, Main St (062 62511).

THE GREAT ATTRACTION of the town is the magnificent medieval **Rock of Cashel** (see pp188–9). Many people stay overnight to enjoy eerie floodlit views of the Rock. A private path leads to it from **Cashel Palace Hotel** (see p294), an opulent Queen Anne residence that was once the Bishop's Palace. Nearby, the remnant of a 12th-century castle has been turned into Kearney Castle Hotel. In the evening you can sample traditional Irish culture at the **Brú Ború Heritage Centre**. Named after Brian Ború, the 10th-century king of Munster (see pp32–3), the centre offers folk theatre, traditional music, banquets, and a craft shop.

At the foot of the Rock is the 13th-century **Dominican Friary**. This austere sandstone church has a fine west door, a 15th-century tower and lancet windows. On farmland outside Cashel lie the scant remains of **Hore Abbey**, a 13th-century Cistercian foundation. The abbey was largely remodelled and a tower added in the 15th century, but the barrel-vaulted sacristy, the nave, choir and chapter house are all original.

🎭 **Brú Ború Heritage Centre**
Cashel. 📞 062 61122. ◯ Jun–Sep: daily; Oct–May: Mon–Fri. 🚻 🚹
🏛 **Dominican Friary**
Dominic Street. 🚻 limited.

Ruins of Hore Abbey (1272) with the Rock of Cashel in the background

Rock of Cashel

THIS ROCKY STRONGHOLD, which rises dramatically out of the Tipperary plain, was a symbol of royal and priestly power for more than a millennium. From the 5th century it was the seat of the Kings of Munster, whose kingdom extended over much of southern Ireland. In 1101, they handed Cashel over to the Church, and it flourished as a religious centre until a siege by a Cromwellian army in 1647 culminated in the massacre of its 3,000 occupants. The cathedral was finally abandoned in the late 18th century. Two hundred years on, the Rock of Cashel is besieged by visitors. A good proportion of the medieval complex is still standing, and Cormac's Chapel is one of the most outstanding examples of Romanesque architecture in the country.

★ St Patrick's Cross
The carving on the east face of this cross is said to be of St Patrick, who visited Cashel in 450. The cross is a copy of the original which stood here until 1982 and is now in the museum.

Hall of the Vicars' Choral
This hall was built in the 15th century for Cashel's most privileged choristers. The ceiling, a modern reconstruction based on medieval designs, features several decorative corbels including this painted angel.

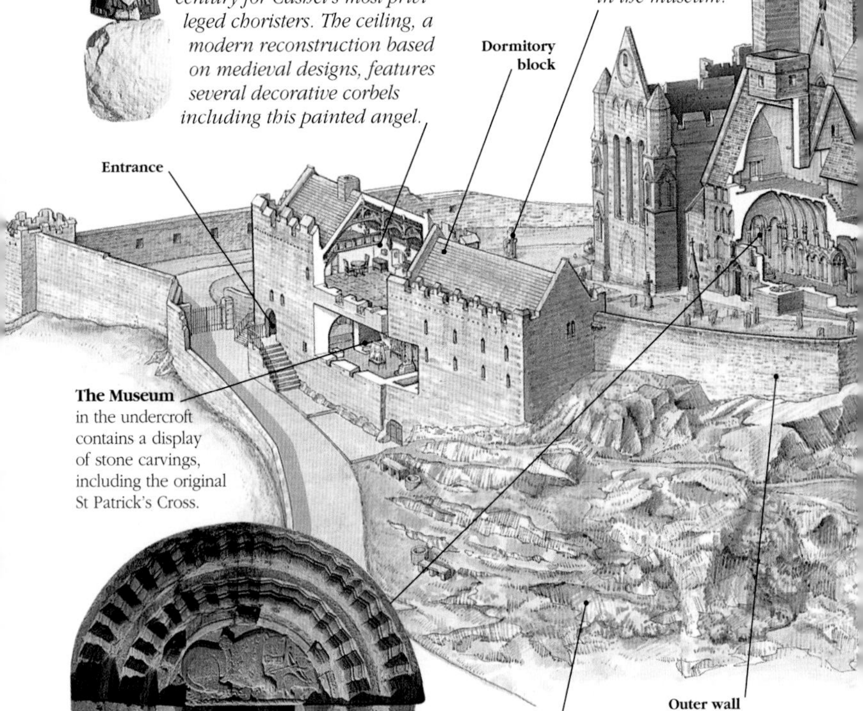

Dormitory block

Entrance

The Museum
in the undercroft contains a display of stone carvings, including the original St Patrick's Cross.

Outer wall

Limestone rock

★ Cormac's Chapel
Superb Romanesque carving adorns this chapel – the jewel of Cashel. The tympanum over the north door shows a centaur in a helmet aiming his bow and arrow at a lion.

STAR FEATURES

★ Cathedral

★ Cormac's Chapel

★ St Patrick's Cross

KEY

☐ **12th Century**
- **4** St Patrick's Cross (replica)
- **12** Cormac's Chapel
- **13** Round tower

☐ **13th Century**
- **6** Cathedral porch
- **7** Nave
- **8** Crossing
- **9** South transept
- **10** Choir
- **11** North transept

☐ **15th Century**
- **1** Ticket office
- **2** Hall of the Vicars' Choral (museum)
- **3** Dormitory
- **5** Castle

0 metres 50
0 yards 50

VISITORS' CHECKLIST

Road map C5. Cashel. **062 61437.** to Thurles. to Cashel. mid-Jun–mid-Sep: 9am–7:30pm: daily; mid-Sep–mid-Mar: 9am–4:30pm; mid-Mar–mid-Jun: 9am–5:30pm. 25–26 Dec.

The Rock
The 28-m (92-ft) round tower, the oldest and tallest building on the rock, enabled Cashel's inhabitants to scour the surrounding plain for potential attackers.

Round tower

Crossing

The Choir contains the 17th-century tomb of Miler Magrath, who caused a scandal by being both a Protestant and Catholic archbishop at the same time.

Graveyard

The O'Scully Monument, an ornate memorial erected in 1870 by a local landowning family, was damaged during a storm in 1976.

North Transept
Panels from three 16th-century tombs in the north transept are decorated with remarkably fresh and intricate carvings. This one, against the north wall, features a vine-leaf design and strange stylized beasts.

★ Cathedral
The roofless Gothic cathedral has thick walls riddled with hidden passages; in the north transept these are seen emerging at the base of the windows.

Athassel Priory ⑳

Road map C5. 8 km (5 miles) W of
Cashel, Co Tipperary. 🚌 *to Tipperary.*
🕐 *daily.*

THIS RUINED Augustinian priory
is situated on the west bank
of the River Suir. The tomb of
William de Burgh, the Norman
founder of the priory, lies in
the church. Established in 1192,
Athassel is believed to have
been the largest medieval priory
in Ireland until it burned down
in 1447. The scattered monastic
site conveys a tranquil atmosphere, from the gatehouse
and church to the remains of
the cloisters and chapter
house. The church has a fine
west doorway, nave and
chancel walls, as well as a
15th-century central tower.

Glen of Aherlow ㉑

Road map C5. Co Tipperary. 🚌 *to
Bansha or Tipperary.* 🛈 *Coach Road
Inn, on R663 8 km (5 miles) E of
Galbally (062 56331).*

THE LUSH VALLEY of the River
Aherlow runs between the
Galty Mountains and the
wooded ridge of Slievenamuck.
Bounded by the villages of
Galbally and **Bansha**, the
glen was historically an important pass between Limerick
and Tipperary and a notorious
hideout for outlaws.

Today there are opportunities
for riding, cycling, rambling
and fishing. Lowland walks

The ruins of Athassel Priory, on the banks of the River Suir

follow the trout-filled river along
the valley floor. More adventurous walkers will be tempted
by the Galty range, which
offers more rugged hill-walking,
past wooded foothills, mountain streams, tiny corrie lakes
and splendid sandstone peaks.

Cahir ㉒

Road map C5. Co Tipperary.
👥 *2,100.* 🚌 🚂 🛈 *May–Sep:
Castle Street (052 41453).* 🚐 *Fri.*

ONCE A GARRISON and mill
town, Cahir is today a
busy market town. The pub-
lined Castle Street is the most
appealing area. It leads to the
Suir River, Cahir Castle and the
well-signposted rural walk to
the Swiss Cottage.

On the edge of town lies
the ruined **Cahir Abbey**, a
13th-century Augustinian
priory. Its fine windows are
decorated with carved heads.

♦ Cahir Castle

Castle Street. 🕻 *052 41011.*
🕐 *daily.* ⬤ *24–30 Dec.* 🌀 🔧
🔧 *limited.*
Built on a rocky island in the
River Suir, Cahir is one of the
most formidable castles in
Ireland and a popular film set.
This well-preserved fortress
dates from the 13th century
but is inextricably linked to its
later owners, the Butlers. A
powerful family in Ireland since
the Anglo-Norman invasion,
they were considered trusty
lieges of the English crown and
were granted the Cahir barony
in 1375. Under their command,
the castle was renovated and
extended throughout the 15th
and 16th centuries. It remained
in the Butler family until 1964.

The castle is divided into
outer, middle and inner wards,
with a barbican at the outer
entrance. The inner ward is on
the site of the original Norman
castle; the foundations are
13th-century, as are the curtain
walls and keep. The restored
interior includes the striking
great hall, which dates largely
from the 1840s, though many of
the walls are original and the
windows are 15th-century.
From the ramparts there are
views of the river and millrace.

⊞ Swiss Cottage

Ardfinnan Road, Cahir. 🕻 *052 41144.*
🕐 *May–Sep: daily; Mar–Apr & Oct–
Nov: Tue–Sun.* 🌀 *obligatory.*
The Swiss Cottage is a superb
example of a *cottage orné*, a
rustic folly. It was designed
for the Butlers by the Regency
architect John Nash in 1810.
Here, Lord and Lady Cahir
played at bucolic bliss, enjoying
picnics dressed as peasants.
Fashion dictated a *cottage*

View across the unspoilt Glen of Aherlow

orné should blend in with the countryside and all designs should be drawn from nature with nothing matching, so the windows and sloping eaves are all of different sizes and design. The beautifully restored cottage contains a tea room, gracious music room and two bedrooms.

Clonmel ㉓

Road map C5. Co Tipperary.
👥 *17,000.* 🚃 🚌 ℹ️ *8 Sarsfield St (052 22960).* 🌐 *www.clonmel.ie*

SET ON THE RIVER SUIR and framed by the Comeragh Mountains, Clonmel is Tipperary's main town. This Anglo-Norman stronghold was a fief of the Desmonds and eventually of the Butlers. Its prosperity was founded on milling and brewing; attractive mills still line the quays. Today, Clonmel is a bustling, brash town with quirky architecture and lively nightlife.

The **Franciscan Friary** by the quays was remodelled in Early English style in Victorian times but retains a 15th-century tower and houses 16th-century Butler tomb effigies. Nearby is O'Connell Street, Clonmel's main shopping street, which is straddled by the West Gate, built in 1831. Visitors to **Hearn's**

Clonmel's mock Tudor West Gate, spanning O'Connell Street

The Swiss Cottage at Cahir, beautifully restored to its original state

Hotel on Parnell Street can see memorabilia of Charles Bianconi (1786 –1875), including pictures of the horse-drawn coach service he established between Clonmel and Cahir. Eventually this developed into a nationwide passenger service.

Carrick-on-Suir ㉔

Road map C5. Co Tipperary.
👥 *5,500.* 🚌 ℹ️ *Heritage Centre (051 640200).*

THIS SLEEPY MARKET TOWN has a distinctly old-fashioned air. In the 15th century, it was a strategic site commanding access west to Clonmel and southeast to Waterford, but after Tudor times the town sank into oblivion. Apart from Ormond Castle, there are few specific sights. However, you can stroll by the old waterside warehouses or shop for Tipperary Crystal *(see p323).*

♠ Ormond Castle

Castle Park. 📞 *051 640787.* 🕐 *mid-Jun–Oct: daily.* 🎫 📷 🚻 ♿ *limited.*
Although once a fortress, Ormond Castle is the finest surviving Tudor manor house in Ireland. It was built by the powerful Butler family, the Earls of Ormonde, who were given their title by the English crown in 1328. The castle has a gracious Elizabethan façade overlaying the medieval original; the battlemented towers on the south side sit oddly with the gabled façade and its mullioned and oriel windows.

The finest room is the Long Gallery, which has a stuccoed ceiling studded with heraldic crests, and two ornately carved fireplaces. The Elizabethan section was added by Black Tom Butler, the 10th Earl of Ormonde, a loyal subject to Elizabeth Tudor. On his death, the Ormondes abandoned Carrick for Kilkenny *(see pp134–6).*

Intricate wood carving on a four-poster bed at Ormond Castle

ENVIRONS: In the churchyard at **Ahenny**, about 10 km (6 miles) north of Carrick, stand two magnificent High Crosses *(see p235).* Both are crowned by "caps" or "bishops' mitres" and have intricate cable, spiral and fret patterns.

At **Kilkieran**, 5 km (3 miles) north of Carrick, are three other interesting High Crosses, dating from the 9th century. The Plain Cross is unadorned but capped; the West Cross is profusely ornamented though weathered; the Long Shaft Cross has an odd design of stumpy arms on a long shaft.

THE WEST OF IRELAND

MAYO · GALWAY · ROSCOMMON

THIS IS THE HEART OF CONNAUGHT, *Ireland's historic western province. The West lives up to its image as a traditional, rural, sparsely populated land, with windswept mountains and countryside speckled with low stone walls and peat bogs. Yet it also encompasses Galway, a fast-growing university town whose youthful population brings life to the medieval streets and snug pubs.*

The rugged Atlantic coastline of the West has been occupied for over 5,000 years. It is rich in prehistoric sites such as the land enclosures of Céide Fields and the ring forts on the Aran Islands. Evidence of the monastic period can be seen in the mysterious and beautiful remains at Kilmacduagh and Clonfert; and the region's religious associations still exert an influence, apparent in the pilgrimages to Knock and Croagh Patrick in County Mayo.

In medieval times, the city of Galway was an Anglo-Norman stronghold, surrounded by warring Gaelic clans. After the Cromwellian victories of the 1640s, many Irish were dispossessed of their fertile lands and dispatched "to hell or Connacht". Landlords made their mark in the 17th and 18th centuries, building impressive country houses at Clonalis, Strokestown Park and Westport. During the Great Famine, the West – especially County Mayo – suffered most from emigration, a trend that continues to this day. In spite of this, strong Gaelic traditions have survived in County Galway, the country's largest Gaeltacht *(see p221)*, where almost half the population speaks Irish as a first language.

The bracken browns and soft violets of Connemara in the west of Galway and the fertile farmland, extensive bogs and placid lakes of County Roscommon are in striking contrast to the magnificent cliff scenery of the remote islands off the coast. This region is often shrouded in a misty drizzle or else battered by Atlantic winds and accompanying heavy downpours.

Summer is a time for festivities: the Galway Races in July, traditional sailing ship races off Kinvarra in August and the Galway Oyster Festival in September are all lively events that attract a stream of visitors.

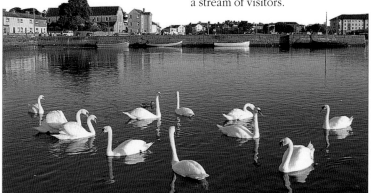

Swans by the quayside of the Claddagh area of Galway

◁ **Typical Connemara landscape dominated by the peaks of the Twelve Bens**

Exploring the West of Ireland

Galway City, Clifden and Westport make the best bases for exploring the region, with cosy pubs, good walks and access to the scenic islands. Connemara and the wilds of County Mayo attract nature lovers, while the islands of Achill, Aran, Clare and Inishbofin appeal to water-sports enthusiasts and ramblers. The lakes of County Roscommon are popular with anglers, and Lough Corrib and Lough Key offer relaxing cruises.

Decorative
stuccowork
in Westport
House

CÉIDE FIELDS ❶

BELMULLET

R314

R313

R315

R314

N59

BALLINA

Lough Conn

CROSSMOLINA

R312

R315

FOXFO ❹

R310

N59

N5

CASTLEBA

N60

R319

ACHILL ISLAND ❷

NEPHIN BEG MOUNTAINS

CLARE ISLAND ❼

WESTPORT ❸

LOUISBURGH

ROONAGH QUAY

CROAGH PATRICK ❻

INISHBOFIN ❽

LEENANE

PARTRY MOUNTAINS

Lough Mask

KYLEMORE ABBEY ❿

CONNEMARA NATIONAL PARK ⓫

CONG ⓬

CLIFDEN ❾

⓭

LOUGH CORRIB

R341

ROUNDSTONE

GORTMORE

OUGHTERARD

N59

R340

See Also

- **Where to Stay** pp295–7

- **Restaurants, Cafés and Pubs**
  pp313–14 & 320–21

ROSSAVEAL

R336

SPIDDAL

GALWA

Enn

Getting Around

The tiny airport near Rossaveal runs flights to the Aran Islands, which can also be reached by ferry from Rossaveal, Galway and Doolin (Co. Clare). Ferries run from Cleggan to Inishbofin and Roonah near Louisburgh to Clare Island. There is no rail service between Galway and Westport but the towns are linked by buses. Bus Éireann runs services to Connemara from Galway and Clifden (via Oughterard or Cong) or the area can be explored on day-long coach tours from Galway or Clifden.

⓯

ARAN ISLANDS

0 kilometres   20

0 miles   10

River valley at Delphi in northern Connemara

SIGHTS AT A GLANCE

**Colourful shopfronts lining
Quay Street, Galway**

KEY

▨	Major road
▨	Minor road
▨	Scenic route
➤	River
☀	Viewpoint

Bogwood centrepiece in Céide Fields interpretative centre

Céide Fields ❶

Road map B2. 8 km (5 miles) W of Ballycastle, Co Mayo. [C] 096 43325. [bus] from Ballycastle. [clock] mid-Mar–Nov: daily. [icons] ground floor.

Surrounded by heather-clad moorlands and mountains along a bleak, dramatic stretch of north Mayo coastline is Europe's largest Stone Age land enclosure. Over 10 sq km (4 sq miles) were enclosed by walls to make fields suitable for growing wheat and barley, and grazing cattle. Remains of farm buildings indicate that it was an extensive community. The fields were slowly buried below the creeping bog formation, where they have been preserved for 5,000 years.

Part of the bog has been cut away to reveal the collapsed stone walls of the ancient fields. The remains are simple rather than spectacular, but excellent guides help visitors to find and recognize key

features. Stone Age pottery and a primitive plough have been found in recent excavations. The striking, pyramid-shaped interpretative centre has a viewing platform overlooking the site, audiovisual presentations and displays on local geology and botany.

ENVIRONS: Scattered around the wilderness of the spectacular north Mayo coast from Ballina to the end of the Mullet peninsula is a series of sculptures forming the **North Mayo Sculpture Trail**. Created by 12 sculptors from three continents, the 15 works, often on a huge scale, are made from earth, stone and other natural materials; additional sculptures are planned. They aim to highlight the coast's grandeur and enduring nature.

Achill Island ❷

Road map A3. Co Mayo. [bus] from Westport. [i] 098 47353. [W] www.achilltourism.com

Ireland's largest island, 22 km (13.5 miles) long and 19 km (12 miles) wide, is reached by a road bridge that can be raised for boats to pass through. Achill offers moorland, mountains, rugged cliffs and long beaches, and is a popular spot for angling and water sports.

For motorists, the best introduction is the **Atlantic Coast Drive**, a circular, signposted route from Achill Sound, by the bridge. The road goes to the island's southern tip, then north around the rest of Achill. Between Doeega and Keel in the southwest run the dramatic

Minaun Cliffs and Cathedral Rocks. In the north is Slievemore, a mountain overlooking the village of Slievemore, which was abandoned during the Great Famine (see p211). Sharks can be spotted off Keem Bay in the west.

Westport ❸

Road map B3. Co Mayo. [icon] 4,700. [icons] [i] James Street (098 25711). [icon] Thu. [W] www.visitmayo.com

The *Angel of Welcome* above the marble staircase at Westport House

Westport is a neat town and has a bustling, prosperous air. In the 1770s, architect James Wyatt laid out the wide, tree-lined streets, including the North and South Mall on either side of Carrowbeg River. The town originally traded in yarn, cloth, beer and slate, but industrialization and the Great Famine (see p211) brought a dramatic decline until the 1950s when new industry and visitors were attracted to the area.

Beyond the South Mall is Bridge Street, lined with cafés and pubs; the most appealing is Matt Molloy's (see p321), named after and owned by the flautist from The Chieftains.

🏠 Westport House
Off Louisburgh Rd. [C] 098 27766. [clock] Easter weekend; May: Sun only; Jun–Sep: daily. [icons] [W] www.westporthouse.ie
Just west of the town is the Carrowbeg estuary and Clew

The deserted village of Slievemore on Achill Island

Statue of St Patrick at the foot of Croagh Patrick, looking out to Clew Bay

Bay. At the head of the bay stands Westport House, the seat of the Earls of Altamont, descendants of the Browne family, who were Tudor settlers. The town of Westport itself was started in the 1750s by John Browne, first Lord Altamont, to complement the house. Designed in 1732 by Richard Castle, and completed by James Wyatt in 1778, the limestone mansion stands on the site of an O'Malley castle. Its imposing interior includes a sweeping marble staircase and an elegant dining room and is adorned with family portraits, antique Waterford chandeliers and 18th-century Chinese wallpaper. The estate has a boating lake, miniature railway, small zoo, museum, amusement arcade and several shops.

Bog oak and silver bowl from Westport House

Foxford **4**

Road map B3. Co Mayo. 👥 *1,000.*
🚌 *from Galway.* 🛈 *Westport (098 25711).*

THIS TRANQUIL market town is known for good angling in nearby Lough Conn and for its woven rugs and tweeds. In the town centre is **Foxford Woollen Mills**, founded in 1892 by an Irish nun, Mother Arsenius (originally named Agnes). The thriving mill now supplies top fashion houses. An audiovisual tour traces the mill's history, and visitors can see craftspeople at work.

🏭 **Foxford Woollen Mills and Visitor Centre**
St Joseph's Place. 📞 *094 56756.*
🕐 *daily.* ⬤ *Good Fri, 24–26 Dec.*
🖼 ✔ 📷 🍴 ♿ *Exhibition Centre.*

Knock **5**

Road map B3. Co Mayo. 👥 *575.*
🚶 *15 km (9 miles) N of Knock.* 🚌
🛈 *May–Sep: Knock (094 88193).*

IN 1879, two local women saw an apparition of the Virgin, St Joseph and St John the Evangelist by the gable of the Church of St John the Baptist. It was witnessed by 13 more onlookers and validated by the Catholic Church amid claims of miracle cures. Every year, a million and a half believers make the pilgrimage to the shrine, including Pope John Paul II in 1979 and Mother Teresa in 1993. Its focal point is the gable where the apparition was seen, which is now covered over to form a chapel. Nearby is the Basilica of Our Lady, a modern basilica and Marian

Bottles of holy water for sale at the shrine in Knock

shrine. **Knock Folk Museum**, beside the basilica, portrays life in 19th-century rural Ireland with reconstructions of a cottage and schoolroom. An Apparition section covers the background to the miracle.

🏛 **Knock Shrine and Folk Museum**
📞 *094 88100.* 🕐 *May–Oct: daily; Nov–Apr: by appt.* 🖼 ✔ ♿

Croagh Patrick **6**

Road map B3. Murrisk, Co Mayo.
🚌 *from Westport.* 🛈 *Murrisk (098 45384), Westport (098 64114).* 🍴

IRELAND's holy mountain, named after the national saint (*see p273*), is one of Mayo's best-known landmarks. From the bottom it seems cone-shaped, an impression dispelled by climbing to its flat peak. This quartzite, scree-clad mountain has a history of pagan worship from 3000 BC. However, in AD 441, St Patrick is said to have spent 40 days on the mountain fasting and praying for the Irish.

Since then, penitents, often barefoot, have made the pilgrimage to the summit in his honour, especially on Reek or Garland Sunday, the last in July. From the start of the trail at Campbell's Pub in Murrisk, where there is huge statue of the saint, it is a two-hour climb to the top, at 765 m (2,510 ft). Mass is celebrated on the peak in a modern chapel. There are panoramic views over Clew Bay and a visitor centre with amenities for exhausted hikers.

Clare Island ❼

Road map A3. Co Mayo. 🚗 165. ⛴
*from Roonagh Quay, 6.5 km (4 miles)
W of Louisburgh* 🕿 098 25045 &
28288. 🛈 *Westport (098 25711).*

The ferry to Inishbofin leaving Cleggan Harbour

CLARE ISLAND, set in Clew Bay, is dominated by two hills, and a square 15th-century castle commands the headland and harbour. In the 16th century the island was the stronghold of Grace O'Malley, pirate queen and patriot, who held sway over the western coast. Although, according to Tudor state papers, she was received at Queen Elizabeth I's court, she stood out against English rule until her death in her seventies in 1603. She is buried here in a tiny Cistercian abbey decorated with medieval murals and inscribed with her motto: "Invincible on land and sea".

The island is dotted with Iron Age huts and field systems as well as promontory forts and Bronze Age cooking sites *(see p162)*. Clare is rich in bog flora and fauna, making it popular with walkers. Animal lovers come to see the seals, dolphins, falcons and otters.

ENVIRONS: The mainland coastal village of **Louisburgh** offers rugged Atlantic landscape, sheltered coves and sea angling. The **Granuaile Centre** tells the story of Grace O'Malley (*Granuaile* in Gaelic) and has displays on Mayo folklore and archaeology.

🏛 Granuaile Centre
St Catherine's Church, Louisburgh.
🕿 098 66195. ◯ *May–Sep: daily.*
🍴 ♿

Inishbofin ❽

Road map A3. Co Galway. 🚗 200. ⛴ *from Cleggan.* 🛈 *Clifden.*

THE NAME Inishbofin means "island of the white cow". This mysterious, often mist-swathed island was chosen for its remoteness by the exiled 7th-century St Colman, English Abbot of Lindisfarne. On the site of his original monastery is a late medieval church, graveyard and holy well. At the sheltered harbour entrance lies a ruined castle, occupied in the 16th century by Spanish pirate Don Bosco in alliance with Grace O'Malley. In 1653 it was captured by Cromwellian forces and used as a prison for Catholic priests. Inishbofin was later owned by a succession of absentee landlords and now survives on farming and lobster-fishing.

Surrounded by reefs and islets, the island's landscape is characterized by stone walls, small abandoned cottages, reed-fringed lakes and hay meadows, where the corn-crake *(see p16)* can be seen, or heard. Inishbofin's beaches offer bracing walks.

Clifden ❾

Road map A3. Co Galway. 🚗 920.
🚌 🛈 *Mar–Nov: Galway Road (095 21163).* ⛴ *Tue & Fri.*

FRAMED by the grandeur of the Twelve Bens mountain range and with a striking skyline dominated by two church spires, this early 19th-century market town passes for the capital of the Connemara region and is a good base for exploring. Clifden was founded in 1812 by John d'Arcy, a local landowner and High Sheriff of Galway, to create a pocket of respect-ability within the lawlessness of Connemara. The family eventually went bankrupt trying to bring prosperity and order to the town. The Prot-estant church contains a copy of the Cross of Cong *(see p65)*.

Today craft shops have taken over much of the town. In the centre is the Square, a place for lively pubs such as EJ Kings *(see p320)*. Nearby is O'Grady's Seafood Restaurant *(see p313)*, one of the finest in Galway. Connemara is noted for its *sean-nos*

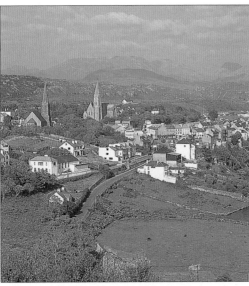

Clifden against a backdrop of the Twelve Bens mountains

CONNEMARA

This wild region in the west of Galway encompasses bogs, mountains and a rugged coastline. Major sights include the Connemara National Park and Kylemore Abbey (*see p200*). For those without a car, coach tours are available from Galway and Clifden (*see p360*).

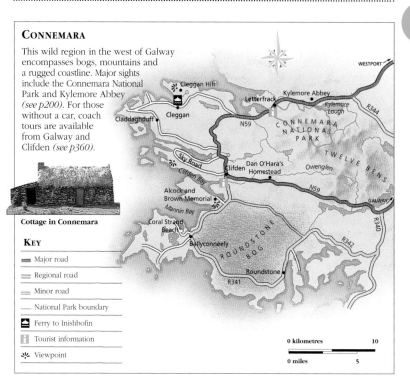

Cottage in Connemara

KEY

▭ Major road

▭ Regional road

▭ Minor road

— National Park boundary

⚓ Ferry to Inishbofin

ℹ Tourist information

☼ Viewpoint

0 kilometres   10

0 miles   5

(unaccompanied singing), but in Clifden, general traditional music is more common.

Jutting out into **Clifden Bay** is a sand spit and beach, signposted from Clifden Square. South of Clifden, at the start of the Roundstone Road, is Owenglen Cascade where, in May, salmon leap on their way to spawn upstream.

ENVIRONS: The **Sky Road** is an 11-km (7-mile) circular route with stunning ocean views. The road goes northwest from Clifden and passes desolate

scenery and the narrow inlet of Clifden Bay. Clifden Castle, John d'Arcy's Gothic Revival ruin, lies just off the Sky Road, as do several beaches.

The coastal road north from Clifden to **Cleggan**, via Claddaghduff, is spectacular, passing former smuggling coves. Cleggan, an attractive fishing village, nestles into the head of Cleggan Bay. From here boats leave for Inishbofin and Inishturk. **Cleggan Hill** has a ruined Napoleonic Martello tower at the top and a megalithic tomb at the foot.

To the south of Clifden, the coastal route to Roundstone skirts a mass of bogland pitted with tiny lakes. The **Alcock and Brown Memorial** overlooks the bog landing site of the first transatlantic flight made by Alcock and Brown in 1919. Nearby is Marconi's wireless station, which exchanged the first transatlantic radio messages with Nova Scotia in 1907. The **Ballyconneely** area has craggy islands and the beautiful **Coral Strand Beach**. The village of **Roundstone** is best seen during the summer regatta of traditional Galway hookers (*see p203*).

A short drive to the east of Clifden is **Dan O'Hara's Homestead**. In a wild, rocky setting, this organic farm recreates the tough conditions of life in Connemara before the 1840s. There is an audiovisual display on the history of Connemara.

🏛 Dan O'Hara's Homestead
Heritage Centre, Lettershea, off N59.
📞 095 21246. ◯ Apr–end Oct: daily.
🅿️ ✦ ▣ 🅰️ &
🆆 www.connemaraheritage.com

View of the coast from the Sky Road

The imposing Kylemore Abbey on the shores of Kylemore Lough

Kylemore Abbey ⑩

Road map A3. Connemara, Co Galway. ☎ 095 41146. 🚌 from Galway and Clifden. ◻ daily. ● Christmas & Good Fri. ☑ call to book. **Walled garden** ◻ Mar–Nov. 🖼 🍴 🛍 ♿ limited. W www.kylemoreabbey.com

SHELTERED BY THE SLOPES of the Twelve Bens, this lakeside castle is a romantic, battlemented Gothic Revival fantasy. It was built as a present for his wife by Mitchell Henry (1826–1911), who was a Manchester tycoon and later Galway MP. The Henrys also purchased a huge area of moorland, drained the boggy hillside and planted thousands of trees as a windbreak for their new orchards and exotic walled gardens. After the sudden deaths of his wife and daughter, Henry left Kylemore and the castle was sold.

It became an abbey when Benedictine nuns, fleeing from Ypres in Belgium during World War I, sought refuge here. The nuns now run the abbey as a girls' boarding school.

Visitors are restricted to the grounds, restaurant and craft shop. The earthenware pottery is painted with a fuchsia motif.

There is also a 2.5 ha (6-acre) restored Victorian walled garden in the abbey grounds, featuring the longest double herbaceous borders in Ireland, a nuttery and a meandering stream-side walk.

Connemara National Park ⑪

Road map A3. Letterfrack, Connemara, Co Galway. ☎ 095 41054. **Visitors' Centre** ◻ Mar–Oct: daily. 🖼 ♿ ▣

A COMBINATION of bogland, lakes and mountains makes up this National Park in the heart of Connemara. Within its more than 2,000 ha (5,000 acres) are four of the Twelve Bens, including Benbaun, the highest mountain in the range at 730 m (2,400 ft), and the peak of Diamond Hill. At the centre is the valley of Glanmore with the Polladirk River flowing through it.

Visitors come for some of the most spectacular landscape in the region and to glimpse the famous Connemara ponies.

Part of the land originally belonged to the Kylemore Abbey estate. In 1980 it became a National Park. There are traces of the land's previous uses all over the park: megalithic tombs, up to 4,000 years old, can be seen as well as old ridges marking former grazing areas and arable fields.

The park is open all year, while the Visitors' Centre near the entrance, just outside Letterfrack, is open only from March to October. It features displays on how the landscape developed and was used and on local flora and fauna. There is also an audiovisual theatre and an indoor picnic area. Two signposted walks start from the Visitors' Centre. In summer there are guided walks, some led by botanists, and various children's activities. Climbing the Twelve Bens should be attempted only by experienced walkers equipped for all weather conditions.

CONNEMARA WILDLIFE

The blanket bogs and moorlands of Connemara are a botanist's paradise, especially for unusual bog and heathland plants. Birdlife is also varied with hooded crows, which can be recognized by their grey and black plumage, stonechats, peregrines and merlins – the smallest falcons in the British Isles. Red deer have been successfully reintroduced into the area and a herd can be seen in the National Park. Badgers, foxes, stoats and otters may also be spotted, as well as grey seals along the rocky coast.

The merlin nests in old clumps of heather and feeds mainly on small birds.

St Dabeoc's heath, a pretty heather, grows nowhere else in Ireland or Great Britain.

Cong @

Road map B3. Co Mayo. 🏃 350.
🚌 ℹ️ Mar–Oct (092 46542).

THIS PICTURESQUE VILLAGE lies on the shores of Lough Corrib, just within County Mayo. Cong means isthmus – the village lies on the strip of land between Lough Corrib and Lough Mask. During the 1840s, as a famine relief project, a canal was built linking the two lakes, but the water drained through the porous limestone bed. Stone bridges and stone-clad locks are still in place along the dry canal.

Cong Abbey lies close to the main street. The Augustinian abbey was founded in the early 12th century by Turlough O'Connor, King of Connaught and High King of Ireland, on the site of a 6th-century monastery established by St Fechin. The abbey has doorways in a style transitional between Romanesque and Gothic, stone carvings and restored cloisters. The Cross of Cong, an ornate processional cross intended for the abbey, is now in Dublin's National Museum (see pp64–5). The most fascinating remains are the Gothic chapter house, stone bridges and the monks' fishing-house overhanging the river – the monks devised a system so that a bell rang in the kitchen when a fish took the bait.

Carved 12th-century doorway of Cong Abbey

Just south of Cong is **Ashford Castle**, rebuilt in Gothic Revival style in 1870 by Lord Ardilaun of the Guinness family. One of Ireland's best hotels (see p284), its grounds can be visited by boat from Galway and Oughterard. Cong was the setting for *The Quiet Man,* the 1950s' film starring John Wayne. "Quiet Man" tours cover locations near the castle.

Lough Corrib @

Road map B3. Co Galway. 🚌 from Galway and Cong. ⛴ from Oughterard and Wood Quay, Galway.
ℹ️ Oughterard (091 552808).

AN ANGLER'S PARADISE, Lough Corrib offers the chance to fish with local fishermen for brown trout, salmon, pike, perch and eels. Despite its proximity to Galway, the lake is a haven of tranquillity, dotted with uninhabited islands and framed by meadows, reed-beds and wooded shores. The waterside is home to swans and coots. On **Inchagoill**, one of the largest islands, stand the ruins of an early Christian monastic settlement and a Romanesque church.

The lake's atmosphere is best appreciated on a cruise. From Galway, the standard short cruise winds through the marshes to the site of an Iron Age fort, limestone

View over Lough Corrib from the shore northwest of Oughterard

quarries and the battlemented Menlo Castle. Longer cruises continue to Cong or include picnics on the islands.

ENVIRONS: On the banks of Lough Corrib, **Oughterard** is known as "the gateway to Connemara". The village has craft shops, thatched cottages and friendly pubs. It is also an important centre for golf, angling, hiking and pony trekking. Other country pursuits include riverside walks, a stroll to a waterfall west of the village and cycle rides.

About 4 km (2.5 miles) southeast of Oughterard (off the N59) is **Aughnanure Castle**. This well-restored six-storey tower house clings to a rocky island on the River Drimneen. The present castle, built by the O'Flaherty clan, is on the site of one dating from 1256. The clan controlled West Connaught from Lough Corrib to Galway and the coast in the 13th to 16th centuries. From this castle the feuding O'Flaherty chieftains held out against the British in the 16th century. In 1545 Donal O'Flaherty married the pirate Grace O'Malley (see p198). The tower house has an unusual double bawn (see p18) and a murder hole from which missiles could be dropped on invaders.

⛪ **Aughnanure Castle**
Oughterard. 📞 091 552214.
🔲 May–Oct: daily. 🚫 ✓
♿ limited.

Connemara ponies roam semi-wild and are fabled to be from Arab stock that came ashore from Spanish Armada wrecks.

Fuchsias grow profusely in the hedgerows of Connemara, thriving in the mild climate.

Galway

Sign with Claddagh ring design

GALWAY IS BOTH THE CENTRE for the Irish-speaking regions in the West and a lively university city. Under the Anglo-Normans, it flourished as a trading post. In 1396 it gained a Royal Charter and, for the next two centuries, was controlled by 14 merchant families, or "tribes". The city prospered under English influence, but this allegiance to the Crown cost Galway dear when, in 1652, Cromwell's forces wreaked havoc. After the Battle of the Boyne (see p236), Galway fell into decline, unable to compete with east-coast trade. In recent years, as a developing centre for high-tech industry, the city's profile has been revived.

Inside The Quays seafood restaurant and pub

Houses on the banks of the Corrib

Exploring Galway

The centre of the city lies on the banks of the River Corrib, which flows down from Lough Corrib (see p201) widening out as it reaches Galway Bay. Urban renewal since the 1970s has led to extensive restoration of the narrow, winding streets of this once-walled city. Due to its compact size, Galway is easy to explore on

foot, and a leisurely pace provides plenty of opportunity to stop off at its shops, pubs and historic sights.

Eyre Square

The square encloses a pleasant park lined with imposing, mainly 19th-century, buildings. On the northwest of the square is the **Browne Doorway**, a 17th-century entrance from a mansion in Abbeygate Street Lower. Beside it are two cannons from the Crimean War and a fountain adorned with a sculpture of a Galway hooker boat. The **Eyre Square Centre**, overlooking the park, is a modern shopping mall built to incorporate sections of the historic city walls. Walkways link Shoemakers and Penrice towers, two of the wall towers that used to ring the city in the 17th century.

Lynch family crest on Lynch's Castle

Latin Quarter

From Eyre Square, William Street and Shop Street are the main routes into the bustling "Latin Quarter". On the corner of Abbeygate Street Upper and Shop Street stands **Lynch's Castle**, now a bank, but still the grandest 16th-century town house in Galway. It was owned by the Lynch family, one of the 14 "tribes".

A side street leads to the **Collegiate Church of St Nicholas**, Galway's finest medieval building. The church, founded in 1320, was extended in the 15th and 16th centuries, but then damaged by the Cromwellians, who used it to stable horses. The west porch is from the 15th century and there are some finely carved gargoyles under the parapet.

Quay Street is lined with restaurants and pubs, including **The Quays** (see p320). Tí Neachtain is a town house which belonged to "Humanity Dick", an 18th-century MP who promoted laws against cruelty to animals. Today, it too is a restaurant and pub (see p320). Nearby are the Taibhdhearc and Druid theatres (see p328).

North Galway

The **Cathedral of St Nicholas** (1965), built of local limestone and Connemara marble, stands on the west bank. From here you can see Wood Quay, where Lough Corrib cruises start (see p201). **University College Galway**, further west,

Outside dining at one of the cosmopolitan cafés in Shop Street

GALWAY HOOKERS

Galway's traditional wooden sailing boats, featured on the city's coat of arms, were known as *pucans* and *gleotogs* – hookers in English. They have broad black hulls, thick masts and white or rust-coloured sails. Once common in the Claddagh district, they were also used along the Atlantic coast to ferry peat, cattle and beer. Hookers can be seen in action at the Cruinniú na mBád festival in Kinvarra *(see p204)*.

Small Galway hooker sailing by the old quays and Spanish Arch

VISITORS' CHECKLIST

Road map B4. Co Galway.
🚶 56,000. ✈ Carnmore, 11 km (7 miles) NE of Galway. 🚊 Ceannt Station (091 561444). 🚌 Ceannt Station (091 562000). 🛈 The Fairgreen, Foster St (091 537700). 🚢 Sat. 🎭 Galway Arts Festival (mid-Jul); Galway Races (late Jul–Aug); Oyster Festival (late Sep).

is a sprawling campus with a 1849 Gothic Revival quad. Salmon Weir Bridge links the two banks. Shoals of salmon rest under the bridge on their way upstream to spawn.

The Old Quays
The **Spanish Arch**, where the river opens out, was built in 1584 to protect the harbour, which was then outside the city walls. Here, Spanish traders unloaded their ships. The old quays are a tranquil spot for a stroll down the Long Walk to the docks.

The Claddagh
Beyond the Spanish Arch, on the west bank of the Corrib, lies the Claddagh. The name comes from *An Cladach*, meaning "flat, stony shore". From medieval times, this fiercely independent fishing community beyond the city walls was governed by a "king" or "mayor", the last of whom died in 1954. The only remnants of this once close-knit, Gaelic-speaking community

are friendly pubs and Claddagh rings, betrothal rings traditionally handed down from mother to daughter *(see p326)*.

ENVIRONS: Just west of the city is **Salthill**, Galway's seaside resort. The beaches at Palmer's Rock and Grattan Road are particularly popular with families in summer. A bracing walk along the promenade is still a Galway tradition.

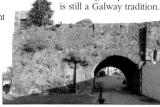

Spanish Arch on the site of the former docks

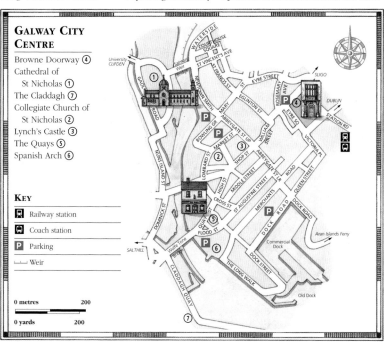

GALWAY CITY CENTRE

Browne Doorway ④
Cathedral of St Nicholas ①
The Claddagh ⑦
Collegiate Church of St Nicholas ②
Lynch's Castle ③
The Quays ⑤
Spanish Arch ⑥

KEY

🚆 Railway station

🚌 Coach station

🅿 Parking

▫▫ Weir

| 0 metres | 200 |
| 0 yards | 200 |

Mural in the centre of Kinvarra depicting a shopfront

Aran Islands ⓑ

See pp206–7.

Kinvarra ⓰

Road map B4. Co Galway. 👥 550.
🚌 ℹ️ *Galway (091 537700).*

ONE OF the most charming fishing villages on Galway Bay, Kinvarra's appeal lies in its sheltered, seaweed-clad harbour and traditional seafaring atmosphere. From medieval times, its fortunes were closely linked to Kilmacduagh, the powerful monastery and bishopric upon which the village depended.

The pier is bordered by a row of fishermen's cottages. Kinvarra remains a popular port of call for sailors of traditional Galway hookers *(see p203)* and is known for the Cruinniú na mBád (gathering of the boats) festival in August. Rambles include historical and nature trails. Bird-watchers may spot teal, curlews and oystercatchers by the shore.

ENVIRONS: North of Kinvarra, on a promontory on the shore of Galway Bay, lies **Dunguaire Castle**. It is perched just beyond some quaint thatched cottages and a stone bridge. The castle is named after the 7th-century King Guaire of Connaught, whose court here was renowned as the haunt of bards and balladeers. Although the medieval earthworks survive, the present castle was built in the 16th century, a quintessential tower house *(see p18)* with sophisticated machicolations. The banqueting hall is still used for "medieval banquets" with Celtic harp music and the recital of Irish poetry.

♣ Dunguaire Castle
📞 *091 637108.* ⭘ *May–Oct: daily.* 📷
🅿️ 🖥️ 🌐 *www.shannonheritage.com*

Kilmacduagh ⓱

Road map B4. Outside Gort on Corofin Rd, Co Galway. 🚌 *to Gort.*
⭘ *daily.*

THIS MONASTIC SETTLEMENT is in a remote location on the borders of Counties Clare and Galway, roughly 5 km (3 miles) southwest of Gort. The sense of isolation is accentuated by the stony moonscape of the Burren to the west *(see pp178–80)*. Reputedly founded by St Colman MacDuagh in the early 7th century, Kilmacduagh owes more to the monastic revival which led to rebuilding from the 11th century onwards.

The centrepiece of the extensive site is a large, slightly leaning 11th- or 12th-century round tower and a roofless church, known as the cathedral or Teampall. The cathedral is a pre-Norman structure, which was later remodelled in Gothic style, with flamboyant tracery and fine tomb carvings. In the surrounding fields lie the remains of several other churches that once depended on the monastery. To the northeast of the Teampall is the late medieval Glebe or Abbot's House, a variant of a 14th- or 15th-century tower house *(see p18)*.

Thoor Ballylee ⓲

Road map B4. Gort, Co Galway.
📞 *091 631436.* 🚌 *to Gort.* ⭘
May–Sep: daily. Call to check times.
📷 🅿️ 🚻 *limited.*

FOR MUCH of the 1920s, this beguiling tower house was a summer home to the poet WB Yeats *(see pp20–21)*. Yeats was a regular visitor to nearby Coole Park, the home of his friend Lady Gregory (1852–1932), who was a cofounder of the Abbey Theatre *(see p86)*.

On one visit Yeats came upon Ballylee Castle, a 14th-century de Burgo tower adjoining a cosy cottage with a walled garden and stream. In 1902, both the tower and the cottage became part of the Gregory estate and Yeats bought them in 1916. From 1919 onwards, his family

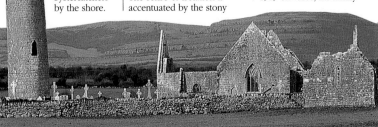

Round tower and cathedral, the most impressive monastic remains at Kilmacduagh

divided their time between Dublin and their Galway tower. Yeats used the name Thoor Ballylee as the address, using the Irish word for tower to "keep people from suspecting us of modern gothic and a deer park". His collection, *The Tower* (1928), includes several poems inspired by the house.

Today, the audiovisual tour includes readings from Yeats's poetry, but the charm of a visit lies in the tower itself, with its spiral stone steps and views from the battlements over forest and farmland.

ENVIRONS: Just to the north of Gort is **Coole Park**, once the home of Lady Gregory. Although the house was demolished in the 1950s, the estate farm has been restored and the fine gardens survive. In particular, there is the "autograph tree", a spreading copper beech carved with the initials of George Bernard Shaw, JM Synge *(see pp20–21)*, Jack Yeats *(see p68)* and other famous visitors. In the farm buildings is an audiovisual display. The emphasis of the visitors' centre is on natural history: it is the start of two signposted walks, one around the gardens and the other through beech, hazel, birch and ash woodland to Coole Lake.

✘ Coole Park
3 km (2 miles) NE of Gort. 【 091 631804. **Visitors' centre** ◯ *Easter–mid-Jun: Tue–Sun; mid-Jun–Sep: daily; park open all year.* 🖼 ▯ ᕼ *limited.*

Thoor Ballylee tower house, the summer home of WB Yeats

Gentle hills and woodland by Coole Lake in Coole Park

Portumna ⑲

Road map C4. Co Galway. 🏘 *1,200.* ▢ ℹ *Galway (091 537700).* ⌂ *Fri.*

PORTUMNA is a historic market town with scattered sights, many of which are newly restored. Situated on Lough Derg, it is a convenient base for cruising the River Shannon *(see p177)* and has a modern marina. **Portumna Castle**, built in the early 17th century, was the main seat of the de Burgo family. Now partially restored, it has a symmetrical façade and some elaborate interior stonework. The façade surveys formal gardens. Near the castle is **Portumna Priory**. Most of the remains date from around 1414 when the priory was founded by the Dominicans, but traces can also be found of the Cistercian abbey that was previously on the site. The large de Burgo estate to the west of the town now forms **Portumna Forest Park**, with picnic sites and signposted woodland trails leading to Lough Derg.

Clonfert Cathedral ⑳

Road map C4. Clonfert, Co Galway. ◯ *daily.* ᕼ

SITUATED near a bleak stretch of the Shannon bordering the boglands of the Midlands, Clonfert is one of the jewels of Irish-Romanesque architecture.

The tiny cathedral occupies the site of a monastery, which was founded by St Brendan in AD 563, and is believed to be the burial place of the saint.

Although a great scholar and enthusiastic founder of monasteries, St Brendan is best known as the "great navigator". His journeys are recounted in *Navigatio Sancti Brendani*, written in about 1050, which survives in medieval manuscripts including Flemish, Norse and French. The account seems to describe a voyage to Wales, the Orkneys, Iceland and conceivably the east coast of North America. His voyage and his boat *(see p182)*, have been re-created by modern explorers in an attempt to prove that St Brendan may have preceded Columbus by about 900 years.

The highlight of Clonfert is its intricately sculpted sandstone doorway. The round arch above the door is decorated with animal and human heads, geometrical shapes, foliage and symbolic motifs. The carvings on the triangular tympanum above the arch are of strange human heads. In the chancel, the 13th-century east windows are fine examples of late Irish-Romanesque art. The 15th-century chancel arch is adorned with sculptures of angels and a mermaid. Although Clonfert was built over several centuries and altered in the 17th century, the church has a profound sense of unity.

Human heads carved on the tympanum at Clonfert Cathedral

Aran Islands ⓯

Jaunting car on Inishmore

Inishmore, Inishmaan and Inisheer, the three Aran Islands, are formed from a limestone ridge. The largest, Inishmore, is 13 km (8 miles) long and 3 km (2 miles) wide. The attractions of these islands include the austere landscape crisscrossed with dry-stone walls, stunning coastal views and several large prehistoric stone forts. In the 5th century, St Enda brought Christianity to the islands, starting a long monastic tradition. Protected for centuries by their isolated position, the islands today are a bastion of traditional Irish culture. Farming, fishing and tourism are the main occupations of the islanders.

Looking over the cliff edge at Dún Aonghasa

Clochán na Carraige is a large, well-preserved beehive hut *(see p19)*, probably built by early Christian settlers on the islands.

The Seven Churches
(Na Seacht dTeampaill)

Clochán na Carraige

Dún Eoghanachta

Dún Eoghanachta
is a 1st-century BC circular stone fort with a single wall terraced on the inside.

Dun Aengus
(Dún Aonghasa)

KILMURVY
(Cill Mhuirbhí)

INISHMORE

Na Seacht dTeampaill
The so-called Seven Churches make up a monastic settlement dedicated to St Brecan. Built between the 9th and 15th centuries, some are probably domestic buildings.

★ **Dún Aonghasa**
This Iron or Bronze Age promontory fort (see p18), has four concentric stone walls. It is also protected by a chevaux de frise, a ring of razor-sharp, pointed stone stakes.

Aran Traditions

Colourful Aran costume

The islands are famous for their distinctive knitwear *(see p324)* and for the traditional Aran costume that is still worn: for women this consists of a red flannel skirt and crocheted shawl; for men it includes a sleeveless tweed jacket and a colourful knitted belt. From time to time you also see a *currach* or low rowing boat, the principal form of transport for centuries. Land-making, the ancient and arduous process of creating soil by covering bare rock with sand and seaweed, continues to this day.

***Currach* made from canvas coated in tar**

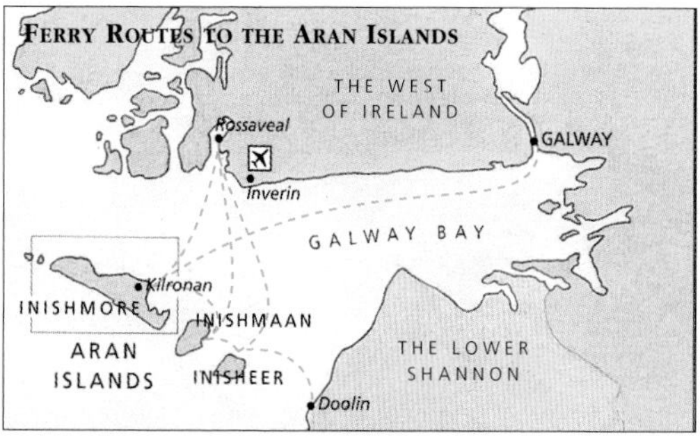
FERRY ROUTES TO THE ARAN ISLANDS
THE WEST OF IRELAND
Rossaveal
GALWAY
Inverin
GALWAY BAY
Kilronan
INISHMORE
INISHMAAN
ARAN ISLANDS
INISHEER
THE LOWER SHANNON
Doolin

Visitors' Checklist

Road map A4, B4. Co Galway. 900. *from Connemara Airport, Inverin (091 593034).* *from Rossaveal:* ***Island Ferries*** *(091 561767),* ***Inis Mór Ferries*** *(www.queenofaran2.com, 091 566535); from Doolin:* ***Doolin Ferry Company*** *(Easter–Oct only; 065 707 4455, 091 567676). Ferries sail throughout the year; some go to all three main islands. Phone for details. Cars cannot be taken to the islands. From Kilronan, you can hire bicycles and jaunting cars, or go on minibus tours (099 61169).* *Kilronan, Inishmore (099 61263).* **Aran Heritage Centre** Kilronan. *099 61355.* *Apr–May, Sep–Oct: 11am–5pm daily; Jun–Aug: 10am–7pm daily.* www.visitaranislands.com

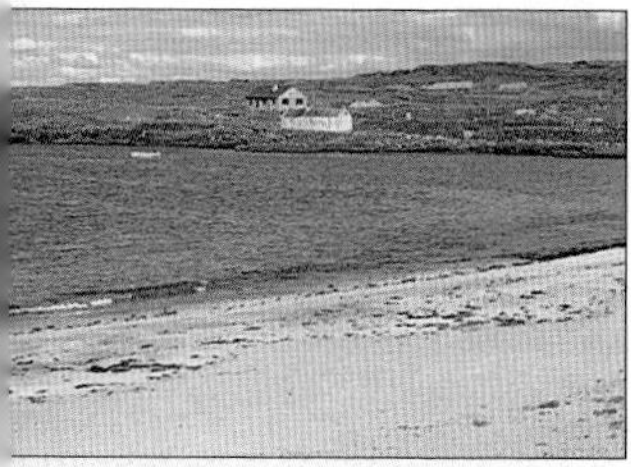

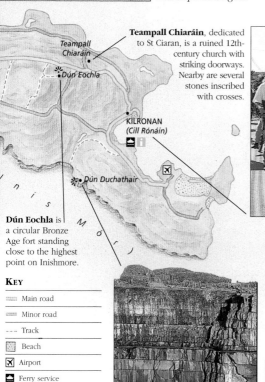

Kilmurvey Beach
The attractive sandy beach east of Kilmurvy offers safe swimming in a sheltered cove. The town itself is a quiet place to stay near a number of the island's most important sights.

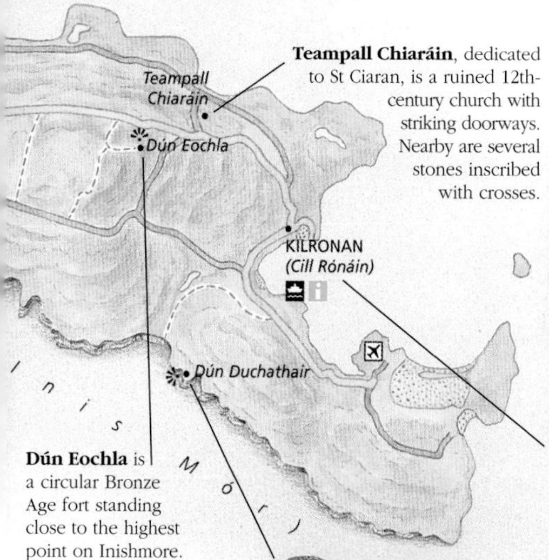
Teampall Chiaráin
Dún Eochla
KILRONAN
(Cill Rónáin)
Dún Duchathair
Inis Mór

Teampall Chiaráin, dedicated to St Ciaran, is a ruined 12th-century church with striking doorways. Nearby are several stones inscribed with crosses.

Dún Eochla is a circular Bronze Age fort standing close to the highest point on Inishmore.

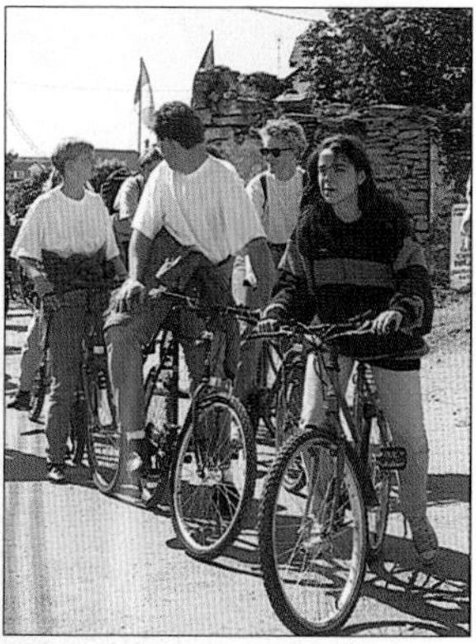

★ Kilronan
The Aran Islands' main port is a busy place, with jaunting cars (ponies and traps) and minibuses waiting by the pier to give island tours; bicycles can also be hired. Nearby, the fascinating Aran Heritage Centre is dedicated to the disappearing Aran way of life.

Key
- Main road
- Minor road
- Track
- Beach
- Airport
- Ferry service
- Tourist information
- Viewpoint

0 kilometres 2

0 miles 1

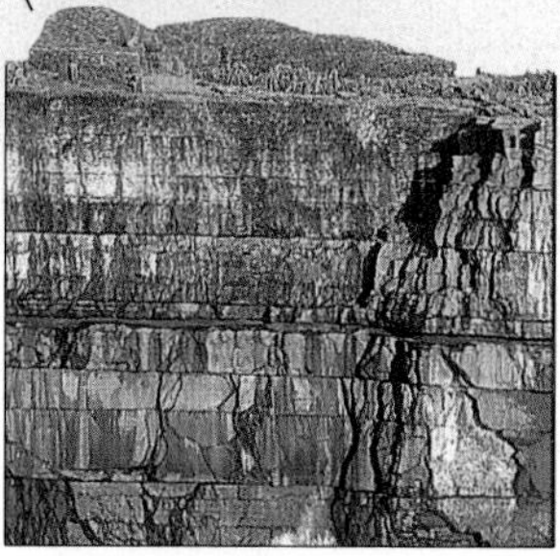

★ Dún Duchathair
Built on a headland, this Iron Age construction is known as the Black Fort. It has dry-stone ramparts.

Star Sights

- ★ **Dún Aonghasa**
- ★ **Dún Duchathair**
- ★ **Kilronan**

Farmer on Inishmore, largest of the Aran Islands ▷

East wall and gatehouse at Roscommon Castle

Turoe Stone ㉑

Road map B4. Turoe, Bullaun, Loughrea, Co Galway. **(** *091 841580.* ⭕ *May–Sep: daily; Oct–Apr: weekends and public hols.* 🏞 ♿ ▭

THE TUROE STONE stands at the centre of a large area of parkland, the Turoe Pet Farm and Leisure Park, near the village of Bullaun (on the R350). The white granite boulder, which stands about 1 m (3 ft) high, dates back to the 3rd or 2nd century BC. Its top half is carved with curvilinear designs in a graceful Celtic style, known as La Tène, also found in Celtic parts of Europe, particularly Brittany. The lower half has a smooth section and a band of step-pattern carving. The stone was originally found at an Iron Age ring fort nearby, and is thought to have been used there in fertility rituals.

The park around the Turoe Stone is designed mainly for children. The Pet Farm has some small fields containing farm animals and a pond with several varieties of ducks and geese. There is also a wooded

The Celtic Turoe Stone carved with graceful swirling patterns

riverside walk, a picnic area, tea rooms, a playground and a 6,000 sq ft (558 sq m) "inflatable city" bouncy castle.

Roscommon ㉒

Road map C3. Co Roscommon. 🏛 *3,500.* ▭ 🚌 ▭ *Jun–Sep: Harrison Hall (090 662 6342).* ⭐ *Fri.* Ⓦ *www.visitroscommon.com*

THE COUNTY CAPITAL is a busy market town. In Main Street is the former gaol, which had a woman as its last executioner. "Lady Betty", as she was known, was sentenced to death for the murder of her son in 1780, but negotiated a pardon by agreeing to become a hangwoman. She continued for 30 years.

South of the town centre, just off Abbey Street, is the **Dominican Friary**, founded in 1253 by Felim O'Conor, King of Connaught. Set in the north wall of the choir is a late 13th-century effigy of the founder. **Roscommon Castle**, an Anglo-Norman fortress north of the town, was built in 1269 by Robert d'Ufford, Lord Justice of Ireland, and rebuilt 11 years later after being destroyed by the Irish led by Hugh O'Conor, King of Connaught. The rectangular castle has 16th-century mullioned windows.

Clonalis House ㉓

Road map B3. Castlerea, Co Roscommon. **(** *094 962 0014.* ⭕ *Jun–mid-Sep: Mon–Sat.* 🏞 ♿ ▭

THIS VICTORIAN manor just outside Castlerea is the ancestral home of the O'Conors, the last High Kings of Ireland

and Kings of Connaught. This old Gaelic family can trace its heritage back 1,500 years. The ruins of their gabled 17th-century home are visible in the grounds. On the lawn lies the O'Conor inauguration stone, dating from 90 BC.

The interior includes a Venetian hallway, a library of many books and documents recording Irish history, a tiny private chapel and a gallery of family portraits spanning 500 years. In the billiard room is the harp once played by Turlough O'Carolan (1670–1738), blind harpist and last of the Gaelic bards *(see p22).*

Strokestown Park House ㉔

Road map C3. Strokestown, Co Roscommon. 🏠 **House, Pleasure Gardens and Museum (** *071 963 3013.* ⭕ *mid-Mar–Oct: daily; Nov–mid-Mar: by appt.* 🏞 🍴 🏠 ♿

STROKESTOWN PARK HOUSE, the greatest Palladian mansion in County Roscommon, was built in the 1730s for Thomas Mahon, an MP whose family was granted the lands by Charles II after the Restoration. It incorporates an earlier 17th-century tower house *(see p18).* The design of the new house owes most to Richard Castle, architect of Russborough *(see p124).* The galleried kitchen, panelled stairwell and groin-vaulted stables are undoubtedly his work, tailoring Palladian principles to the requirements of the Anglo-Irish gentry.

The house stayed in the family's hands until 1979, when major restoration began. In its heyday, the estate included ornamental parkland, a deer park, folly, mausoleum and the town of Roscommon itself. By 1979, the estate's original 12,000 ha (30,000 acres) had dwindled to 120 ha (300 acres), but recent re-creation of the Pleasure Gardens and the Fruit and Vegetable Garden have greatly increased the area. The original interior of the house is intact.

Set in the stable yards, the **Famine Museum** uses the Strokestown archives to tell the story of tenants and landlords during the 1840s Famine. During the crisis, landlords divided into two camps: the charitable, some of whom started up Famine Relief schemes, and the callous, like the Mahons of Strokestown. Major Denis Mahon was murdered after forcing two-thirds of the starving peasantry off his land by a combination of eviction and passages in "coffin ships" to North America. A section of the exhibition deals with continuing famine and malnutrition worldwide.

The Great Famine

The failure of the Irish potato crop in 1845, 1846 and 1848, due to potato blight, had disastrous consequences for the people of Ireland, many of whom relied on this staple crop. More than a million died of starvation and disease, and by 1856 over two and a half million had been forced to emigrate. The crisis was worsened by unsympathetic landlords who often continued collecting rents. The Famine had far-reaching effects: mass emigration became a way of life *(see pp40–41)* and many rural communities, particularly in the far west, were decimated.

Peasants queuing for soup during the Famine (1847)

Boyle 25

Road map C3. Co Roscommon. 2,200. *Apr–Oct: King House (071 966 3242). Fri.*

County Roscommon's most charming town, Boyle is blessed with fine Georgian and medieval architecture. **Boyle Abbey** is a well-preserved Cistercian abbey founded in 1161 as a sister house to Mellifont in County Louth *(see p237)*. It survived raids by Anglo-Norman barons and Irish chieftains, as well as the 1539 suppression of the monasteries. In 1659 it was turned into a castle. The abbey is still remarkably intact, with a church, cloisters, cellars, sacristy and even kitchens. The nave of the church has both Romanesque and Gothic arches and there are well-preserved 12th-century capitals. The visitors' centre in the old gatehouse has exhibits on the abbey's history.

Carved capital in the nave at Boyle Abbey

King House, a Palladian mansion near the centre of town, is the ancestral home of the Anglo-Irish King family, later Earls of Kingston. Inside is a contemporary art gallery, and displays on various subjects, such as Georgian architecture and the mansion's restoration, the history of the surrounding area and the Connaught chieftains.

The gatehouse and remains of the nave at Boyle Abbey

Boyle Abbey
071 966 2604. Apr–Oct.

King House
Main St. *071 966 3242. Apr–Sep: daily; rest of year on request.* *on request.*

Environs: Lough Key is often called the loveliest lake in Ireland. The island-studded lake and surrounding woodland make a glorious setting for the **Lough Key Forest Park**. The 320-ha (790-acre) park formed part of the Rockingham estate until 1957, when Rockingham House, a John Nash design, burned down. The extensive woods were added by 18th-century landlords. Other features of the park include nature trails, an observation tower, a 17th-century ice house, a deer enclosure and, by the lake, a 17th-century gazebo known as the Temple. The park also has several ring forts *(see p18)*. From the jetty, cruisers ply the Boyle River. A river bus visits Church and Trinity Islands, which both contain medieval ruins, and Castle Island, which has a 19th-century folly.

Lough Key Forest Park
N4 8 km (5 miles) E of Boyle.
daily. Easter–Sep.

NORTHWEST IRELAND

DONEGAL · SLIGO · LEITRIM

Towering cliffs, *deserted golden beaches and rocky headlands abound along the rugged coast of Donegal, which incorporates some of Ireland's wildest scenery. To the south, Sligo is steeped in prehistory and Celtic myth, with its legacy of ancient monuments and natural beauty enriched by associations with the poet, WB Yeats. By contrast, Leitrim is a quiet county of unruffled lakes and waterways.*

In Celtic mythology Sligo was the power base of the warrior Queen Maeve of Connaught *(see p24)*, and the county's legacy of prehistoric sites shows that the area was heavily populated in Celtic times. Later, however, both County Sligo and neighbouring County Leitrim often seemed to be little affected by events taking place in the rest of Ireland. The Normans, for example, barely disturbed the rule of local Gaelic clans.

Donegal, on the other hand, was part of Ulster until 1921 and played an active role in that province's history. The O'Donnells held sway over most of Donegal in the Middle Ages, but they fled to Europe in 1607 following their ill-fated stand against the English alongside the O'Neills *(see p247)*. Protestant settlers moved on to land confiscated from the two clans, but they left much of Donegal and its poor soil to the native Irish, who lived there in isolation from the rest of Ulster. This remote corner of the province remained largely Catholic and, at the time of Partition in 1921, Donegal was excluded from the new Protestant Northern Ireland.

County Donegal has little in common with its neighbours in the Republic, either geographically or historically. It is one of the most remote parts of Ireland, and it is no coincidence that Donegal boasts the country's largest number of Gaelic speakers.

While the beauty of Donegal lies mainly along the coast, Sligo's finest landscapes are found inland, around Lough Gill and among the sparsely populated Bricklieve Mountains.

The 19th-century interior of Hargadon's bar in Sligo town, with its original counter and stout jars

◁ **View across to Falcarragh from Bloody Foreland in County Donegal**

Exploring Northwest Ireland

THE SUPREME APPEAL of Donegal lies in the natural beauty of its coast, with windswept peninsulas, precipitous cliffs and a host of golden beaches. There is a scattering of small seaside resorts which make good bases, and Donegal town is well placed for exploring the southern part of the county. The cultural heartland of the Northwest lies in and around Sligo, the only sizeable town in the region, from where you can reach several prehistoric remains and other historic sights. Further south, lovely scenery surrounds Lough Gill and the more remote Lough Arrow. In Leitrim, a county of lakes and rivers, the main centre of activity is the lively boating resort of Carrick-on-Shannon.

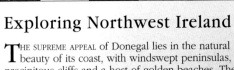

TORY ISLAND ❶

BLOODY FORELAND   HORN H

❷   R257   DUNFANA

BUNBEG   ❸

A R A N M O R E
I S L A N D   THE ROSSES
BURTONPORT   ❿

DUNGLOE   D E R R Y V E A G
M O U N T A I N

N56

R253

Procession during the Mary of Dungloe beauty contest in July

SEE ALSO

- **Where to Stay** pp297–8

- **Restaurants, Cafés and Pubs** pp314–15 & p321

❶❶ ARDARA

❶❷ GLENCOLUMBKILLE   B L U E S T A
M O U N T A

SLIEVE LEAGUE
❶❸   KILLYBEGS   DONEG
❶❹   ❶❺

ROSSNOWLAGH   ❶❼

R231   BALLYSHANNO
❶❽

BUNDORAN   Lough Melvin

LISSADELL HOUSE ❶❾   ❷⓿   C O U N T R Y

DRUMCLIFF   N16   Enniskill
N15

❷❷ SLIGO   MANORHAMILTON
❷❶
PARKE'S CASTLE

N59

Ballina   O X   M O U N T A I N S   N17   N4   Lough Allen

R280

LOUGH ARROW ❷❸

B R I C K L I E V E
M O U N T A I N S   CARRICK-ON-SHANNON
❷❹

KEY

▨	Major road
▤	Minor road
▨	Scenic route
≈	River
⚡	Viewpoint

0 kilometres   20

0 miles   10

Shann

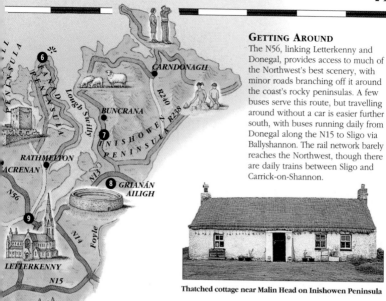

GETTING AROUND

The N56, linking Letterkenny and Donegal, provides access to much of the Northwest's best scenery, with minor roads branching off it around the coast's rocky peninsulas. A few buses serve this route, but travelling around without a car is easier further south, with buses running daily from Donegal along the N15 to Sligo via Ballyshannon. The rail network barely reaches the Northwest, though there are daily trains between Sligo and Carrick-on-Shannon.

Thatched cottage near Malin Head on Inishowen Peninsula

SIGHTS AT A GLANCE

Ardara **11**
Ballyshannon **18**
Bloody Foreland **2**
Carrick-on-Shannon **24**
Derryveagh Mountains **3**
Donegal **15**
Fanad Peninsula **6**
Glencolumbkille **12**
Grianán Ailigh **8**
Horn Head **4**
Killybegs **14**
Letterkenny **9**
Lissadell House **19**
Lough Arrow **23**

Lough Derg **16**
Lough Rynn Estate **25**
Parke's Castle **21**
Rosguill Peninsula **5**
The Rosses **10**
Rossnowlagh **17**
Slieve League **13**
Sligo **22**
Tory Island **1**

Tours
Inishowen Peninsula **7**
Yeats Country **20**

View from Carrowkeel Bronze Age cemetery above Lough Arrow

Quartzite cone of Errigal, the highest of the Derryveagh Mountains

Tory Island ❶

Road map C1. Co Donegal. 🏃 175.
⛴ from Magheraroarty Pier near
Gortahork (074 913 5061) and
Bunbeg (074 953 1991): daily in
summer, weather permitting in winter.

THE TURBULENT Tory Sound
separates this windswept
island from the northwestern
corner of mainland Donegal.
Given that rough weather can
cut off the tiny island for days,
it is not surprising that Tory's
inhabitants have developed a
strong sense of independence.
Most of the islanders speak
Gaelic and they even have
their own monarch: the powers
of this non-hereditary position
are minimal, but the current
incumbent is heavily involved
in promoting the interests of
his "subjects" and in attracting
visitors to the island.

During the 1970s, the Irish
government tried to resettle
most of the islanders on the
mainland, but they refused to
move. Their campaign of
resistance was led by Tory's
school of Primitive artists. This
emerged after 1968, inspired
by a local man called James
Dixon who claimed he could
do better than a visiting
English painter, Derek Hill.
Since then, the school of artists
has drawn a growing number
of tourists; the **Dixon Gallery**
opened in 1992 in the main
village of West Town. There

are ruins of a monastery
founded by St Columba *(see
p32)* nearby, or else you can
explore the island's dramatic
cliffs and seabird rookeries.

🏛 Dixon Gallery
West Town. 【 074 913 5011.
◯ Easter–Sep: daily.

Bloody Foreland ❷

Road map C1. Co Donegal. 🚌 to
Bunbeg from Letterkenny or Dungloe.

BLOODY FORELAND, which gets
its name from the rubescent
glow of the rocks at sunset,
boasts magnificent scenery.
The R257 road skirts the coast
around the headland, providing lovely views. The most
scenic viewpoint is on the
north coast and looks across
to the cliffs of nearby offshore
islands, including **Tory**. A short
distance further south, the tiny
village of **Bunbeg** has a pretty
harbour, but elsewhere the
rocky landscape is spoiled by a
blanket of holiday bungalows.

Derryveagh Mountains ❸

Road map C1. Co Donegal.

THE WILD BEAUTY of these
mountains provides one of
the high spots of a visit to
Donegal. Errigal Mountain, the
range's tallest peak at 751 m
(2,466 ft), attracts keen hikers,
but the cream of the mountain
scenery lies within **Glenveagh
National Park**. Covering
nearly 16,500 ha (40,000 acres),
this takes in the beautiful
valley occupied by Lough
Veagh, and Poisoned Glen, a
marshy valley enclosed by
dramatic cliffs. The park also
protects the largest herd of
red deer in the country.

Glenveagh Castle stands on
the southern shores of Lough
Veagh, near the visitors' centre.
This splendid granite building
was constructed in 1870 by
John Adair, notorious for his
eviction of many families from
the area after the Famine *(see
p211)*. The castle was given
to the nation in the 1970s by
its last owner, a wealthy art
dealer from Pennsylvania.

Minibuses whisk you up the
private road to the castle from
the visitors' centre. You can
go on a guided tour of the
sumptuous interior or just stroll

Glenveagh Castle overlooking Lough Veagh

Looking across to Dunfanaghy, gateway to the Horn Head peninsula

through the formal gardens and rhododendron woods. Trails weave all around the castle grounds; one path climbs steeply to reward you with a lovely view over Lough Veagh.

Glebe House and Gallery overlooks Lough Gartan 6 km (4 miles) south of the visitors' centre. This modest Regency mansion was the home of the painter, Derek Hill, who was also a keen collector. The house reveals his varied tastes, with William Morris wallpapers, Islamic ceramics and paintings by Tory Island artists. The gallery contains works by Picasso, Renoir and Jack B Yeats among others.

Fountain at Glenveagh

The **Colmcille Heritage Centre**, a short distance south, uses stained glass and illuminated manuscripts to trace the life of St Columba (Colmcille in Gaelic), who was born in nearby Church Hill in AD 521 *(see p32)*. A flagstone in the village is said to mark the site of the saint's birthplace.

♣ **Glenveagh National Park and Castle**
Off R251, 16 km (10 miles) N of Churchill.
📞 074 913 7090. **Park** and **Castle**
🕐 Mar–Nov: daily. 🔲 🗓 ⅰⅰ 🔲 ♿
limited. 🆆 www.heritageireland.ie
🏛 **Glebe House and Gallery**
📞 074 913 7071. 🕐 Easter & May–
Sep: Sat–Thu. 🔲 ♿ limited. 🔲 🔲
🏛 **Colmcille Heritage Centre**
📞 074 913 7306. 🕐 Easter &
May–Sep: daily. 🔲

Horn Head ❹

Road map C1. Co Donegal. 🚌 to
Dunfanaghy from Letterkenny.
ⅰ The Workhouse, Dunfanaghy (074 913 6540) mid-Mar–mid-Oct.

Carpeted in heather and rich in birdlife, Horn Head is the most scenic of the northern Donegal headlands. It rises 180 m (600 ft) straight out of the Atlantic and gives lovely views out to sea and inland towards the mountains. The appeal of the area is enhanced by **Dunfanaghy**, a delightful town with an air of affluence and Presbyterianism unusual in this area. The local beach, **Killahoey Strand**, offers excellent swimming.

Rosguill Peninsula ❺

Road map C1. Co Donegal.

Rosguill peninsula juts out into the Atlantic Ocean between Sheephaven and Mulroy bays. The simplest way to see it is to follow the 11-km (7-mile) Atlantic Drive, a circular route which skirts the clifftops at the tip of the headland.

Doe Castle, 5 km (3 miles) north of Creeslough village, is worth a visit as much for its setting on a pro-montory overlooking Sheephaven Bay as for its architectural or historical interest. Even so, it is still a substantial ruin – the remains of a castle erected in the 16th century by the MacSweeneys, a family of Scottish mercenaries.

Fanad Peninsula ❻

Road map C1. Co Donegal. 🚌 to
Rathmelton & Portsalon from
Letterkenny.

A panoramic route winds between the hilly spine and rugged coast of this tranquil peninsula. The eastern side is by far the most enjoyable and begins at **Rathmelton,** a charming Plantation town founded in the 17th century. Elegant Georgian homes and handsome old warehouses flank its tree-lined Main Street.

Further north, **Portsalon** offers safe bathing and great views from nearby Saldanha Head. Near **Doaghbeg**, on the way to Fanad Head in the far north, the cliffs have been eroded into arches and other dramatic shapes.

Doe Castle on Rosguill Peninsula, with its 16th-century battlements

A Tour of the Inishowen Peninsula ❼

INISHOWEN, THE LARGEST of Donegal's northern peninsulas, is an area laden with history, from early Christian relics to strategically positioned castles and forts. The most rugged scenery lies in the west and north, around the the steep rock-strewn landscape of the Gap of Mamore and the spectacular cape of Malin Head, the northern-most point in Ireland. Numerous beaches dot the coastline and cater for all tastes, from the remote Isle of Doagh to the busy family resort of Buncrana. From the shores, there are views to Donegal's Derryveagh Mountains to the west and the Northern Ireland coast in the east. The Inishowen Peninsula can be explored by car as a leisurely day trip.

Tower on Banba's Crown, Malin Head

Carndonagh Cross ④
This 7th-century early Christian cross is carved with human figures and interlacing lines.

Gap of Mamore ③
The road between Mamore Hill and the Urris Hills is 250 m (820 ft) above sea level and offers panoramic views.

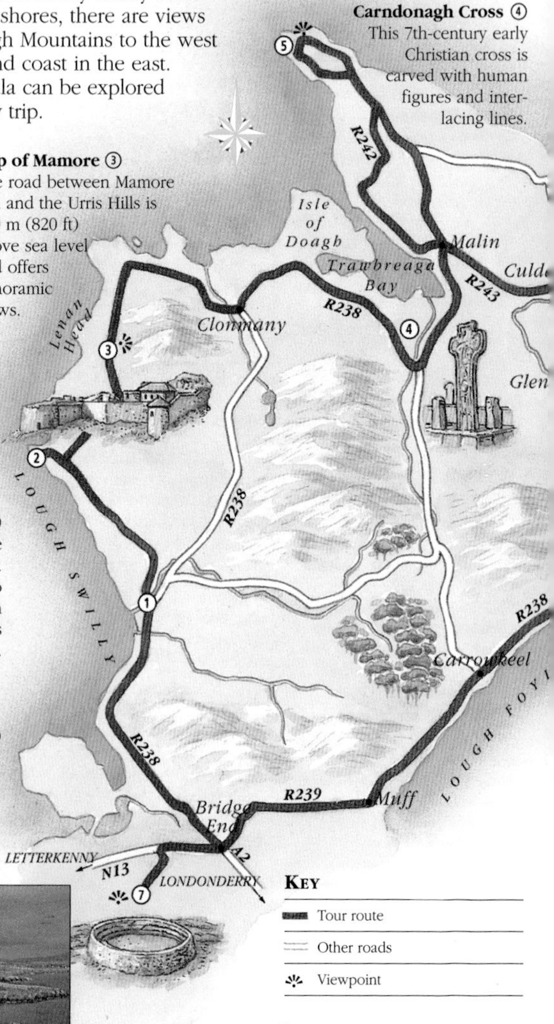

Dunree Head ②
On the headland, Dunree Fort overlooks Lough Swilly. It was built in 1798 to counter the threat of French invasion. Since 1986, it has been a military museum.

Buncrana ①
Buncrana has 5 km (3 miles) of sandy beaches and two castles. Buncrana Castle was rebuilt in 1718 and the intact keep of O'Doherty Castle dates from Norman times.

KEY

Tour route

Other roads

☀ Viewpoint

Shores of Lough Swilly near Dunree Fort

Grianán Ailigh ⑦
At the neck of the Inishowen Peninsula, perched on a hilltop, stands this formidable circular stone fort. The solid structure that can be seen today is the result of extensive restoration in the 1870s.

Enjoying the views from the ramparts of the Grianán of Ailigh

Malin Head ⑤
This traditional cottage makes a good stop for tea after enjoying the superb Atlantic views from Malin Head. At the highest point, Banba's Crown, stands a tower built in 1805 to monitor shipping.

Greencastle ⑥
A resort and fishing port, Greencastle is named after the overgrown castle ruins just outside town. Built in 1305 by Richard de Burgo, Earl of Ulster, the castle guarded the entrance to Lough Foyle.

0 kilometres   5

0 miles   5

Grianán Ailigh ⑧

Road map C1. Co Donegal. 🚌 from Letterkenny or Londonderry. ℹ️ Burt (074 936 8512).

DONEGAL'S most impressive and intriguing ancient monument stands just 10 km (6 miles) west of the city of Londonderry (see pp250–51) at the entrance to the lovely Inishowen Peninsula.

Overlooking Lough Swilly and Lough Foyle, the circular stone structure, measuring 23 m (77 ft) in diameter, is believed to have been built as a pagan temple around the 5th century BC, although the site was probably a place of worship before this date. Later, Christians adopted the fort: St Patrick is said to have baptized Owen, founder of the O'Neill dynasty, here in AD 450. It became the royal residence of the O'Neills, but was damaged in the 12th century by the army of Murtagh O'Brien, King of Munster.

The fort was restored in the 1870s. Two doorways lead from the outside through 4-m (13-ft) thick defences into a grassy arena ringed by three terraces. The most memorable feature of the fort, however, is its magnificent vantage point, which affords stunning views in every direction.

At the foot of the hill stands an attractive church, dedicated to St Aengus and built in 1967. Its circular design echoes that of the Grianán.

Letterkenny ⑨

Road map C1. Co Donegal. 👥 12,000. 🚌 ℹ️ Blaney Rd (074 912 1160). 🌐 www.donegaldirect.ie

STRADDLING the river Swilly, with the Sperrin Mountains to the east and the Derryveagh Mountains (see pp216–17) to the west, Letterkenny is Donegal's largest town. It is also the region's main business centre, a role it took over from Londonderry after partition in 1921. The likeable town makes a good base from which to explore the northern coast of Donegal and, for anglers, is well placed for access to the waters of Lough Swilly.

Letterkenny has one of the longest main streets in Ireland, which is dominated by the 65-m (215-ft) steeple of **St Eunan's Cathedral**. A Neo-Gothic creation built in the late 19th century, it looks particularly impressive when floodlit at night. It contains Celtic-style stonework, a rich marble altar and vivid stained-glass windows. The **County Museum** has increased in size over the last couple of years and offers informative displays on local history from the Stone Age to the 20th century. It also has a collection of archaeological artifacts found in Donegal, some of them dating from the Iron Age.

🏛 County Museum

High Rd. 📞 074 912 4613. ⭕ Mon–Sat. ⬤ 10 days at Christmas and public hols. ♿

The imposing spire of St Eunan's Cathedral in Letterkenny

Isolated cottage near Burtonport in the Rosses

The Rosses ❿

Road map C1. Co Donegal. 🚌 *to Dungloe or Burtonport from Letterkenny.* 🛈 *Jun–Sep: Main St, Dungloe (074 952 1297).* ⛴ *to Aranmore from Burtonport (074 952 0532).*

A ROCKY HEADLAND dotted with more than 100 lakes, the Rosses is one of the most picturesque and unspoilt corners of Donegal. It is also a strong Gaeltacht area, with many people speaking Gaelic.

The hub of the Rosses, at the southern end of the headland, is **Dungloe**, a bustling market town and major angling centre.

ENVIRONS: There is a glorious sheltered beach 8 km (5 miles) west of Dungloe at **Maghery Bay**. From here you can also walk to nearby **Crohy Head**, known for its caves, arches and unusual cliff formations. From Burtonport, 8 km (5 miles) north of Dungloe, car ferries sail daily to Donegal's largest island, **Aranmore**. The rugged northwest coast is ideal for clifftop walks, and from the south coast you can enjoy fine views across to the Rosses. Most of Aranmore's population of 700 lives in Leabgarrow. The village's thriving pub culture is due partly to the granting of 24-hour licences, for the benefit of fishermen returning from sea.

Ardara ⓫

Road map C2. Co Donegal. 🏠 *700.* 🚌 *from Killybegs or Donegal.* 🛈 *Tourist office, Killybegs Rd (074 954 1422) Easter–Sep: Heritage Centre, The Diamond (074 954 1704).*

A RDARA, THE weaving capital of Donegal, proliferates in shops selling locally made tweeds and hand-knitted sweaters. Some larger stores put on displays of hand-loom weaving. Ardara is also worth a stop for its pubs, much loved for their fiddle sessions.

ENVIRONS: There is superb scenery between Ardara and **Loughros Point**, 10 km (6 miles) west of the town: the drive along the narrow peninsula provides dramatic coastal views. Another picturesque route runs southwest from Ardara to Glencolumbkille, going over **Glengesh Pass**, a series of bends through a wild, deserted landscape.

Hand-loom worker in Ardara

Glencolumbkille ⓬

Road map B2. Co Donegal. 🏠 *260.* 🚌 *from Killybegs.* 🛈 *Cashel St (074 973 0116) or Donegal (074 972 1148).*

G LENCOLUMBKILLE, a quiet, grassy valley scattered with brightly coloured cottages, feels very much like a backwater, in spite of the sizeable number of visitors who come here.

The "Glen of St Colmcille" is a popular place of pilgrimage due to its associations with the saint more commonly known as St Columba. Just north of the valley's main village of Cashel, on the way to Glen Head, there is a tiny church where St Columba worshipped: it is said that between prayers the saint slept on the two stone slabs still visible in one corner.

Another attraction here is the **Folk Village Museum**, which depicts rural Donegal lifestyles through the ages. It was started in the 1950s by a local priest called Father James

Old irons at the Folk Village Museum in Glencolumbkille

Slieve League, the highest sea cliffs in Europe

MacDyer. Concerned about the high rate of emigration from this poor region, he sought to provide jobs and a sense of regional pride, partly by encouraging people to set up craft cooperatives. The Folk Village shop sells local wares, and has a good stock of wine – made of anything from seaweed to fuchsias.

There is plenty to explore in the valley, which is littered with cairns, dolmens and other ancient monuments. The nearby coast is lovely too, the best walks taking you west across the grassy foreland of **Malinbeg**. Beyond the small resort of Malin More, steps drop down to an idyllic sandy cove hemmed in by cliffs.

🏛 **Folk Village Museum**
Cashel. 🏛 074 973 0017. ⭕ Easter–Sep: daily. 🏷 📷 💺 🚻 ♿

Slieve League ⓭

Road map B2. Co Donegal. 🚌 to Carrick from Glencolumbkille or Killybegs.

T HE HIGHEST cliff face in Europe, Slieve League is spectacular not just for its sheer elevation but also for its colour: at sunset the rock is streaked with changing shades of red, amber and ochre. The 8-km (5-mile) drive to the eastern end of Slieve League from **Carrick** is bumpy but well worth enduring. Beyond Teelin, the road becomes a

series of alarming switchbacks before reaching **Bunglass Point** and Amharc Mor, the "good view". From here, you can see the whole of Slieve League, its sheer cliffs rising dramatically out of the ocean.

Only experienced hikers should attempt the treacherous ledges of **One Man's Pass**. This is part of a trail which climbs westwards out of Teelin and up to the highest point of Slieve League – from where you can admire the Atlantic Ocean shimmering 598 m (1,962 ft) below. The path then continues on to Malinbeg, 16 km (10 miles) west. During the summer, for a less strenuous but safer and equally rewarding excursion, pay a boat-owner from Teelin to take you out to see Slieve League from the sea.

Killybegs ⓮

Road map C2. Co Donegal. 🏠 1,700. 🚌 from Donegal. 🛈 Donegal (074 972 1148).

N ARROW WINDING streets give Killybegs a timeless feel, which contrasts sharply with the industriousness of this small town. The sense of prosperity stems in part from the manufacture of the Donegal carpets for which the town is famous, and which adorn Dublin Castle *(see pp 74–5)* and other palaces around the world.

Killybegs is one of Ireland's busiest fishing ports and the quays are well worth seeing when the trawlers arrive to off-load their catch: gulls squawk overhead and the smell of fish fills the air. Trawlermen come from far and wide – so do not be surprised if you hear Eastern European voices as you wander around the town.

Trawler crew in Killybegs relaxing after unloading their catch

THE IRISH GAELTACHTS

The term "Gaeltacht" refers to Gaelic-speaking areas of Ireland. Up to the 16th century, virtually the entire population

Gaelic pub sign in Gaeltacht region

spoke the native tongue. British rule, however, undermined Irish culture, and the Famine *(see p211)* drained the country of many of its Gaelic-speakers. The use of the local language has fallen steadily since. Even so, in the Gaeltachts 75 per cent of the people still speak it, and road signs are exclusively in Irish – unlike in most other parts of Ireland.

The Donegal Gaeltacht stretches almost unbroken along the coast from Fanad Head to Slieve League and boasts the largest number of Irish-speakers in the country. Ireland's other principal Gaeltachts are in Galway and Kerry.

Donegal town, overlooked by the ruins of its 15th-century castle

Donegal ⑮

Road map C2. Co Donegal. 👥 2,300.
🚌 🛈 Quay St (074 972 1148).

DONEGAL MEANS "Fort of the Foreigners", after the Vikings who built a garrison here. However, it was under the O'Donnells that the town began to take shape. The ruins of **Donegal Castle** in the town centre incorporate the gabled tower of a fortified house built by the family in the 15th century. The adjoining house and most other features are Jacobean – added by Sir Basil Brooke, who moved in after the O'Donnells were ousted by the English in 1607 (see pp36–7). The castle has recently been partly restored.

Brooke was also responsible for laying out the market square, which is known as the **Diamond**. An obelisk in the centre commemorates four Franciscan monks who wrote the Annals of the Four Masters in the 1630s, tracing the history of the Gaelic people from 40 days before the Great Flood up until the end of the 16th century. Part of it was written at **Donegal Abbey**, south of the market square along the River Eske. Built in 1474, little now remains of the abbey but a few Gothic

windows and cloister arches. About 1.5 km (1 mile) further on is **Donegal Craft Village**, a showcase for the work of local craftspeople.

Donegal town has some pleasant hotels (see p298) and makes a good base for exploring the southern part of the county.

⚜ **Donegal Castle**
Tirchonaill St. ☎ 074 972 2405. ◯ Easter–Jun: Sat & Sun; Jun–Aug: daily. 🎨 🎫 ♿ limited.

🏛 **Donegal Craft Village**
Ballyshannon Rd. ☎ 074 972 2015. ◯ May–Sep: Mon–Sat; Jun–Aug: daily. 🖳 ♿ limited.

Lough Derg ⑯

Road map C2. Co Donegal. ⛴ Jun–mid-Aug (pilgrims only). 🚌 to Pettigo from Donegal.

PILGRIMS HAVE made their way to Lough Derg ever since St Patrick spent 40 days praying on one of the lake's islands in an attempt to rid Ireland of all evil spirits. The Pilgrimage of St Patrick's Purgatory began in around 1150 and still attracts thousands of Catholics every summer. Their destination is the tiny **Station Island**, close to Lough Derg's southern shore and reached by boat from a jetty

8 km (5 miles) north of the border village of Pettigo. The island is completely covered by a religious complex, which includes a basilica, built in 1921, and hostels for pilgrims.

The pilgrimage season runs from June to mid-August. People spend three days on the island, eating just one meal of dry bread and black tea per day. Although only pilgrims can visit Station Island, it is interesting to go to the jetty to savour the atmosphere and get a good view of the basilica near the shore.

Rossnowlagh ⑰

Road map C2. Co Donegal. 👥 55.
🚌 from Bundoran & Donegal.
🛈 Apr–Oct: Main St, Bundoran (071 984 1350).

Holiday-makers enjoying the fine sandy beach at Rossnowlagh

AT ROSSNOWLAGH, Atlantic waves break on to one of Ireland's finest beaches, drawing crowds of both bathers and surfers to this tiny place. Even so, the village remains far more peaceful than the resort of Bundoran, 14 km (9 miles) south. In addition, the cliffs at Rossnowlagh provide scope for exhilarating coastal walks. Away from the sea, you can visit the **Donegal Historical Society Museum**, housed in a striking Franciscan friary

Basilica on Station Island viewed from the shores of Lough Derg

Lissadell House dining room with Gore-Booth family portraits

Lissadell House ⑲

Road map B2. Carney, Co Sligo.
📞 *071 916 3150.* 🚌 *or* 🚂 *to Sligo.* ⏰ *Jun–Sep: Mon–Sat.* ⛔

A GREEK REVIVAL mansion built in the 1830s, Lissadell is famous more for its occupants than its architecture. It is still the home of the Gore-Booths who, unlike some of the Anglo-Irish gentry, have contributed much to the region over the four centuries they have been in County Sligo. During the Famine *(see p211)*, Sir Robert mortgaged the house to help feed his employees.

The most famous member of the Gore-Booth family is Sir Robert's granddaughter, Constance Markievicz (1868–1927), a leading nationalist who took part in the 1916 Rising *(see pp42–3)*. She was the first woman to be elected to the British House of Commons and later became Minister for Labour in the first Dáil. WB Yeats, who first visited the house in 1894, immortalized Constance and her sister, Eva, in one of his poems, describing them as "Two girls in silk kimonos, both beautiful, one a gazelle". Built in grey limestone, the exterior of Lissadell House is rather austere. The interior, on the other hand, has an appealing atmosphere of faded grandeur, with peeling paintwork and copious memorabilia of the building's former occupants. The finest rooms are the gallery and the dining room, decorated with extraordinary full-length murals of the Gore-Booth family, their famous butler Thomas Kilgallon, the gamekeeper, head woodman and a dog. Painted directly on to the wall, they were the work of Constance's husband, adventurer and self-styled "Count" Casimir Markievicz.

Both the house and the overgrown estate are slowly being restored. You can already explore along paths skirting the seashore, and there is also a wildlife reserve which is a popular winter refuge for barnacle geese.

---

built in the 1950s. The tiny but fascinating collection includes displays of Stone Age flints, Irish musical instruments and other local artifacts.

Rossnowlagh never fails to make the news in July, when it hosts the only parade to take place in the Republic by the Protestant organization, the Orange Order *(see p47)*.

🏛 **Donegal Historical Society Museum**
📞 *071 985 1267.* ⚫ *25 Dec.*

Ballyshannon ⑱

Road map C2. Co Donegal. 👥 *2,600.* 🚌 *from Bundoran & Donegal.*

IN BALLYSHANNON, well-kept Georgian homes jostle for space along hilly streets on the banks of the River Erne, near where it flows into Donegal Bay. This is a bustling town, full of character and off the main tourist track – though it gets packed during August's festival of traditional music, which is one of the best of its kind in the country.

The festival apart, Ballyshannon is most famous as the birthplace of poet William Allingham (1824–89), who recalled his home town in the lines "Adieu to Ballyshanny and the winding banks of the Erne". He lies buried in the graveyard of St Anne's Church, off Main Street. There is a fine view over the river from here: you can see the small island of **Inis Saimer** where, according to legend, Greeks founded the first colony in Ireland after the Great Flood. Beyond, you can glimpse a large Irish Army base: Ballyshannon's position on a steeply rising bluff overlooking the River Erne has always made the town a strategic military site.

Mural of the family dog in Lissadell's dining room

About 1.5 km (1 mile) northwest of town lie the scant ruins of **Assaroe Abbey**, founded by Cistercians in 1184. A graveyard with some ancient burial slabs and headstones is all that remains. Nearby, two water wheels installed by the monks have been restored. **Water Wheels** has a small heritage centre as well as a café.

🏛 **Water Wheels**
Assaroe Abbey. 📞 *071 985 1580.*
⏰ *Mar–Sep: daily.* 🏪 🚻 ♿
Heritage centre ⏰ *Mar–Sep: daily.*

A Tour of Yeats Country ⑳

EVEN FOR PEOPLE unfamiliar with the poetry of WB Yeats, Sligo's engaging landscapes are reason enough to make a pilgrimage. This tour follows a varied route, taking you past sandy bays and dramatic limestone ridges, through forest and alongside rivers and lakes. Lough Gill lies at the heart of Yeats country, enclosed by wooded hills crisscrossed by walking trails. In summer, boats ply the length of the lough, or you can head to one of the northwest's best beaches, at Rosses Point.

Yeats tour sign

Ben Bulben ⑤
The eerie silhouette of Ben Bulben rises abruptly out of the plain. You can climb to the top, but go with great care.

Lissadell House ④
Yeats was a close friend of the Gore-Booth sisters who lived at Lissadell. You can see the room where the poet slept as a guest (*see p223*).

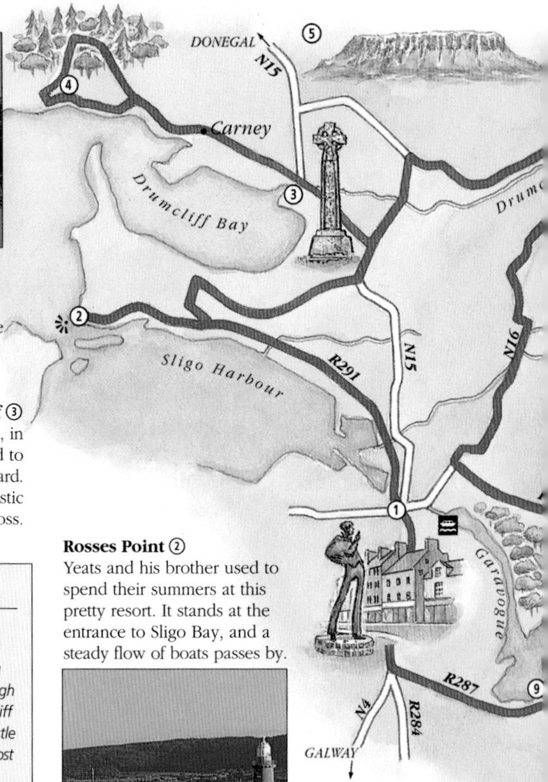

Drumcliff ③
Although he died in France, in 1948 Yeats's body was laid to rest in Drumcliff churchyard. The ruins of an old monastic site include a fine High Cross.

Rosses Point ②
Yeats and his brother used to spend their summers at this pretty resort. It stands at the entrance to Sligo Bay, and a steady flow of boats passes by.

TIPS FOR DRIVERS

Length: 88 km (55 miles).
Stopping-off points: Outside Sligo, the best choice of eating places is at Rosses Point, although there are good pubs in Drumcliff and Dromahair, and Parke's Castle has a café. Lough Gill provides most picnic spots.
Boat trips: Wild Rose Water Bus (071 916 4266 or 087 259 8869). (See also pp355–7.)

KEY

▬▬▬ Tour route

═══ Other roads

🚤 Boat trips

☀ Viewpoint

Sligo ①
This town is a good place to begin a tour of Yeats country. It has many connections with the poet and his family, whose literary and artistic legacy has helped to inspire Sligo's thriving arts scene (*see p226*).

Map labels: DONEGAL, N15, Carney, Drumcliff Bay, Sligo Harbour, R291, N15, N16, Garaogue, R287, R284, N4, GALWAY, Drum

WB YEATS AND SLIGO

As a schoolboy in London, Yeats *(see p21)* longed for his native Sligo, and as an adult he often returned here. He lovingly describes the county in his *Reveries over Childhood and Youth*, and the lake-studded landscape haunts his poetry. "In a sense", Yeats said, "Sligo has always been my home", and it is here that he wished to be buried. His gravestone in Drumcliff bears an epitaph he penned himself: "Cast a cold eye on life, on death. Horseman pass by."

WB Yeats (1865–1939)

Parke's Castle viewed from across the calm waters of Lough Gill

Parke's Castle ㉑

Road map C2. 6 km (4 miles) N of Dromahair, Co Leitrim. **[** 071 916 4149. **🚌** or **🚌** to Sligo. **○** mid-Mar–Oct: 10am–6pm daily. **☞** **ᐃ** ground floor only. **☞** **▯**

THIS FORTIFIED manor house dominates the eastern end of Lough Gill. It was built in 1609 by Captain Robert Parke, an English settler who later became MP for Leitrim. It has been beautifully restored by the Office of Public Works using 17th-century building methods and native Irish oak.

Parke's Castle was erected on the site of a 16th-century tower house belonging to the O'Rourkes, a powerful local clan, and stones from this earlier structure were used in the new building. The original foundations and part of the moat were incorporated, but otherwise Parke's Castle is the epitome of a Plantation manor house *(see p37)*. It is protected by a large enclosure or bawn, whose sturdy wall includes a gatehouse and two turrets as well as the house itself.

Among the most distinctive architectural features of Parke's Castle are the diamond-shaped chimneys, mullioned windows and the parapets. There is also a curious stone hut, known as the "sweathouse", which was an early Irish sauna. Inside, an exhibition and audiovisual display cover Parke's Castle and various historic and prehistoric sites in the area, with photos and archaeological finds. There is also a working forge.

Boat trips around sights on Lough Gill that are associated with the poet, WB Yeats, leave from outside the castle walls.

Glencar Lough ⑥

"There is a waterfall ... that all my childhood counted dear", wrote Yeats of the cataract which tumbles into Glencar Lough. A path leads down to it from the road.

N16 ENNISKILLEN

Parke's Castle ⑦

This 17th-century fortified manor house commands a splendid view over the tranquil waters of Lough Gill. It is a starting point for boat trips around the lough.

LOUGH GILL

R288

Dromahair

R289

CARRICK-ON-SHANNON

R287

Isle of Innisfree ⑧

"There midnight's all a glimmer, and noon a purple glow", is how Yeats once described Innisfree. There is not much to see on this tiny island but it is a romantic spot. In summer, a boatman ferries visitors here.

Dooney Rock ⑨

A steep path leads from the road to Dooney Rock, from where glorious views extend over the lough to Ben Bulben. Trails weave through the surrounding woods and by the lake.

0 kilometres   3

0 miles   2

Hargadon's bar, one of Sligo town's most famous watering holes

Sligo ②

Road map C2. Co Sligo. 🕌 20,000.
✈ 071 916 8280. 🚌 🚆 🛈 *Aras
Reddan, Temple St (071 916 1201).*
🛍 *Fri.* ⓦ *www.irelandnorthwest.ie*

THE PORT of Sligo sits at the mouth of the River Gara-vogue, sandwiched between the Atlantic and Lough Gill. The largest town in the north-west, it rose to prominence under the Normans, being well placed as a gateway between the provinces of Ulster and Connaught. The appearance of Sligo today is mainly the result of growth during the late 18th and 19th centuries.

Sligo is perfectly situated for touring the ravishing countryside nearby, and it is also a good centre for traditional music. While at first sight it can seem a bit sombre, the town is thriving as the arts capital of northwest Ireland.

Sligo's link with the Yeats family is the main source of the town's appeal. WB Yeats *(see pp224–5)*, Ireland's best-known poet, was born into a prominent local family. The Pollexfen warehouse, at the western end of Wine Street, has a rooftop turret from which the poet's grandfather would observe his merchant fleet moored in the docks.

The town's sole surviving medieval building is **Sligo Abbey**, founded in 1253. Some original features remain, such as the delicate lancet windows in the choir, but this ruined Dominican friary dates mainly from the 15th century. The best features are a beautifully carved altar and the cloisters.

A short distance west from the abbey is O'Connell Street, with the town's main shops and Hargadon's bar – an old Sligo institution complete with a dark, wooden interior, snugs and a grocery counter. Near the junction with Wine Street, overlooking Hyde Bridge, is the Yeats Memorial Building. This houses the Yeats Society and the **Sligo Art Gallery**, which puts on shows by foreign and Irish artists. The Yeats International Summer School is held here too: a renowned annual festival of readings and lectures on the poet's life and work.

Just the other side of Hyde Bridge is a statue of the poet, engraved with lines from his own verse. **Sligo County Museum** has a collection of Yeatsian memorabilia and local artifacts but the entire Niland Collection including the paintings by Jack B Yeats have been moved to the **Model Arts & Niland Gallery** in The Mall. This outstanding new centre also puts on temporary exhibitions of major Irish and international contemporary art.

Bronze statue of WB Yeats

🔒 **Sligo Abbey**
Abbey St. 🅲 071 914 6406. 🔆
Easter–Oct: daily; winter: Fri–Sun.
🅿 *Easter–Oct.*
🏛 **Sligo Art Gallery**
Hyde Bridge. 🅲 071 914 5847.
🔆 *Mon–Sat.*
🏛 **Sligo County Museum**
Stephen St. 🅲 071 914 7190.
🔆 *Tue–Sat daily (Oct–May: pm only).*
🏛 **Model Arts & Niland
Gallery** The Mall. 🅲 071 914
1405. 🔆 *Tue–Sun.*

ENVIRONS: Improbably set in the suburbs of Sligo, **Carrow-more Megalithic Cemetery** once held the country's largest collection of Stone Age tombs. Quarrying destroyed much, but about 40 passage tombs *(see pp238–9)* and dolmens *(see p30)* survive among the abandoned gravel pits, with some in private gardens and even protruding from cottages.

The huge unexcavated cairn atop **Knocknarea** mountain dates back 5,000 years and is said to contain the tomb of the legendary Queen Maeve of Connaught *(see p24)*. It is an hour's climb starting 4 km (2.5 miles) west of Carrowmore.

Tobernalt, by Lough Gill 5 km (3 miles) south of Sligo, means "cliff well", after a near-by spring with alleged curative powers. It was a holy site in Celtic times and later became a Christian shrine. Priests came here to celebrate Mass in secret during the 18th century, when Catholic worship was illegal. The Mass rock, next to an altar erected around 1900, remains a place of pilgrimage.

🔒 **Carrowmore Cemetery**
🅲 071 916 1534. 🔆 *May–Sep.* 🖾

Altar by the holy well at Tobernalt, overlooking Lough Gill in Sligo

Lough Arrow ㉓

Road map C3. Co Sligo. 🚌 to Ballinafad. 🚏 May–Oct: Boyle (071 966 2145).

PEOPLE GO to Lough Arrow to sail and fish for the local trout, and also simply to enjoy the glorious countryside. You can explore the lake by boat, but the views from the shore are the real joy of Lough Arrow. A full circuit of the lake is recommended, but for the most breathtaking views head for the southern end around **Ballinafad**. This small town lies in a gorgeous spot, enclosed to the north and south by the Bricklieve and Curlew Mountains.

The **Carrowkeel Passage Tomb Cemetery** occupies a remote and eerie spot in the Bricklieve Mountains to the north of Ballinafad. The best approach is up the single track road from Castlebaldwin, 5 km (3 miles) northeast of the site.

The 14 Neolithic passage graves, which are scattered around a hilltop overlooking Lough Arrow, are elaborate corbelled structures. One is comparable with Newgrange *(see pp238–9)*, except that the burial chamber inside this cairn is lit by the sun on the day of the summer solstice (21 June) as opposed to the winter solstice. On a nearby ridge are the remains of Stone Age huts, presumably those occupied by the farmers who buried their dead in the Carrowkeel passage graves.

Passage tomb in Carrowkeel cemetery above Lough Arrow

Carrick-on-Shannon ㉔

Road map C3. Co Leitrim. 🏘 2,500. 🚌 🚏 🛈 Apr–Sep: The Marina (071 962 0170).
ⓦ www.leitrimtourism.com

THE TINY CAPITAL of Leitrim, one of the least populated counties in Ireland (although this is changing), stands in a lovely spot on a tight bend of the River Shannon.

The town's location by the river and its proximity to the Grand Canal were crucial to Carrick's development. They are also the main reasons for its thriving tourist industry. There is a colourful, modern marina, which in summer fills up with private launches and boats available for hire.

Already a major boating centre, Carrick has benefited from the reopening of the Shannon-Erne Waterway, one end of which begins 6 km (4 miles) north at Leitrim. The channel was restored in a cross-border joint venture billed as a symbol of peaceful cooperation between Northern Ireland and the Republic.

Away from the bustle of the marina, Carrick is an old-fashioned place, with 19th-century churches and convents, refined Georgian houses and shopfronts. The town's most curious building is the quaint **Costello Chapel** on Bridge Street, one of the smallest in the world. It was built in 1877 by local businessman Edward Costello, to house the tombs of himself and his wife.

Lough Rynn Estate ㉕

Road map C3. Mohill, Co Leitrim. 🚌 or 🚌 to Carrick-on-Shannon. ⭕ gardens only, Apr–mid-Sep: daily.

THIS VAST ESTATE, lying 3 km (2 miles) south of Mohill, was the ancestral seat of the Clements family, Earls of Leitrim. The baronial-style house, constructed in 1832, is currently closed and at the centre of a development dispute. It is still possible to visit the grounds, however, which extend across 40 ha (100 acres) of land and more than 240 ha (600 acres) of lakes. Although there is plenty to explore, including ornamental gardens, water meadows, lush woodland, the ruins of a 16th-century castle and a Neolithic burial site, the grounds have been neglected recently and may still be in a state of disarray.

SHANNON-ERNE WATERWAY

This labyrinthine system of rivers and lakes passes through unspoiled border country, linking Leitrim on the Shannon and Upper Lough Erne in Fermanagh. It follows the course of a canal which was completed and then abandoned in the 1860s. The channel was reopened in 1993, enabling the public to enjoy both the Victorian stonework (including 34 bridges) and the state-of-the-art technology used to operate the 16 locks.

Cruiser negotiating a lock on the Shannon-Erne Waterway

THE MIDLANDS

CAVAN · MONAGHAN · LOUTH · LONGFORD · WESTMEATH
MEATH · OFFALY · LAOIS

THE CRADLE *of Irish civilization and the Celts' spiritual home,
the Midlands encompass some of Ireland's most sacred and
symbolic sites. Much of the region is ignored, but the ragged
landscapes of lush pastures, lakes and bogland reveal ancient Celtic
crosses, gracious Norman abbeys and Gothic Revival castles.*

The fertile Boyne Valley in County Meath was settled during the Stone Age and became the most important centre of habitation in the country. The remains of ancient sites from this early civilization fill the area and include Newgrange, the finest Neolithic tomb in the country. In Celtic times, the focus shifted south to the Hill of Tara, the seat of the High Kings of Ireland and the Celts' spiritual and political capital. Tara's heyday came in the 3rd century AD, but it retained its importance until the Normans invaded in the 1100s.

Norman castles, such as the immense fortress at Trim in County Meath, attest to the shifting frontiers around the region of English influence known as the Pale *(see p124).* By the end of the 16th century, this area incorporated nearly all the counties in the Midlands.

The Boyne Valley returned to prominence in 1690, when the Battle of the Boyne ended in a landmark Protestant victory over the Catholics *(see pp36–7).*

Although part of the Republic since 1921, historically Monaghan and Cavan belong to Ulster, and the former retains strong links with the province. The rounded hills called drumlins, found in both counties, are typical of the border region between the Republic and Northern Ireland.

Grassland and bog dotted with lakes are most characteristic of the Midlands, but the Slieve Bloom Mountains and the Cooley Peninsula provide good walking country. In addition to Meath's ancient sites, the historical highlights of the region are monasteries like Fore Abbey and Clonmacnoise, this last ranking among Europe's greatest early Christian centres.

Carlingford village and harbour, with the hills of the Cooley Peninsula rising behind

◁ Temple Finghin round tower at Clonmacnoise monastery on the banks of the River Shannon

Exploring the Midlands

DROGHEDA IS THE OBVIOUS BASE from which to explore the Boyne Valley and neighbouring monastic sites, such as Monasterboice. Trim and Mullingar, to the southwest, are less convenient but make pleasanter places in which to stay. The northern counties of Monaghan, Cavan and Longford are quiet backwaters with a patchwork of lakes that attract many anglers. To the south, Offaly and Laois are dominated by dark expanses of bog, though there is a cluster of sights around the attractive Georgian town of Birr. For a break by the sea, head for the picturesque village of Carlingford on the Cooley Peninsula.

West doorway of Nuns' Church at Clonmacnoise

KEY

▨	Motorway
▨	Major road
▨	Minor road
▨	Scenic route
～	River
✲	Viewpoint

SEE ALSO

• *Where to Stay* p299

• *Restaurants, Cafés and Pubs* pp315–16 & p321

GETTING AROUND

In the Midlands, there is an extensive network of roads and rail lines fanning out across the country from Dublin. As a result, getting around on public transport is easier than in most other areas. The Dublin–Belfast railway serves Dundalk and Drogheda, while Mullingar and Longford town lie on the Dublin–Sligo route. The railway and N7 road between Dublin and Limerick give good access to Laois and Offaly. For motorists, roads in the Midlands are often flat and straight but also potholed.

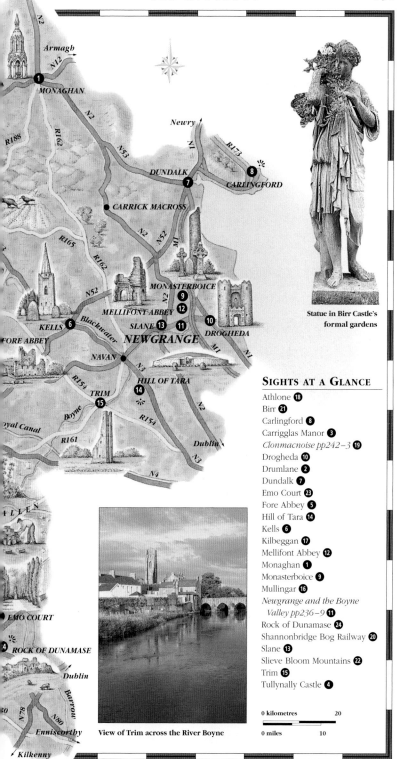

MONAGHAN

DUNDALK

CARRICK MACROSS

CARLINGFORD

MONASTERBOICE

MELLIFONT ABBEY

KELLS

FORE ABBEY

SLANE

NEWGRANGE

DROGHEDA

NAVAN

HILL OF TARA

TRIM

EMO COURT

ROCK OF DUNAMASE

*Statue in Birr Castle's
formal gardens*

SIGHTS AT A GLANCE

View of Trim across the River Boyne

| 0 kilometres | 20 |
| 0 miles | 10 |

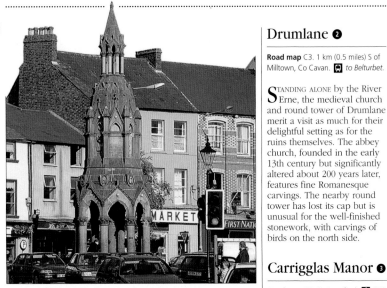

Rossmore Memorial drinking fountain in Monaghan

Monaghan ❶

Road map D2. Co Monaghan.
🏠 6,000. 🚌 🛈 *Market House,
Market Square (047 81122).*

T HE SPRUCE AND THRIVING town of Monaghan is the urban highlight of the northern Midlands. Planted by James I in 1613 *(see p37),* it developed into a prosperous industrial centre, thanks mainly to the local manufacture of linen. A crannog *(see p31)* off Glen Road is the sole trace of the town's Celtic beginnings.

Monaghan centres on three almost contiguous squares. The main attraction in Market Square is the 18th-century **Market House**, a squat but charming building with the original oak beams still visible. It is now home to the tourist office. To the east lies Church Square, very much the heart of modern Monaghan and lined with dignified 19th-century buildings, such as the Classical-style courthouse. The third square, which is known as the Diamond, was the original marketplace. It contains the **Rossmore Memorial**, a large Victorian drinking fountain with an ornate stone canopy supported by marble columns.

Do not miss the excellent **County Museum**, just off Market Square, which tells the story of Monaghan's linen and lace-making industries. The pride of its historical collection is the Cross of Clogher, an ornate bronze altar cross which dates from around 1400.

The Gothic Revival Cathedral of St Macartan perches on a hilltop south of the town, from where you can enjoy a fine view over Monaghan.

🏛 **County Museum**
Hill St. ☎ 047 82928. ◯ Tue–Sat.
⬤ *public hols.* ♿ *limited.*

Drumlane ❷

Road map C3. 1 km (0.5 miles) S of Milltown, Co Cavan. 🚌 *to Belturbet.*

S TANDING ALONE by the River Erne, the medieval church and round tower of Drumlane merit a visit as much for their delightful setting as for the ruins themselves. The abbey church, founded in the early 13th century but significantly altered about 200 years later, features fine Romanesque carvings. The nearby round tower has lost its cap but is unusual for the well-finished stonework, with carvings of birds on the north side.

Carrigglas Manor ❸

Road map C3. Co Longford. ☎ 043 45165. 🚌 *to Longford.* ◯ 1 Jun–12 Aug: 11am–5pm Sun–Fri. 🖾 🗳 🗋 ♿ *limited.*

C ARRIGGLAS MANOR has been the seat of the Lefroys, a family of Huguenot descent, ever since its construction in 1837. It has changed little in the intervening years and is a fine example of the Tudor Revival style. The Victorian atmosphere is still very much alive inside, where the rooms are decorated with pseudo-

Drawing room in Carrigglas Manor with original 19th-century features

Authentic Victorian kitchen in Tullynally Castle

Gothic panelling and ornate plasterwork ceilings. The stable block, by contrast, is a grand Neo-Classical building by James Gandon, the architect of Dublin's Custom House *(see p86)*. The manor grounds are primarily woodland but include a wild flower garden.

ENVIRONS: Just 14 km (9 miles) south of Carrigglas Manor, **Ardagh** is considered the most attractive village in Longford, with pretty stone cottages gathered around a green.

Tullynally Castle ❹

Road map C3. Castle Pollard, Co Westmeath. ☎ 044 61159. ➡ to Mullingar. **Castle** ◯ mid-Jun–Jul: daily (pm only). ✦ ✦ obligatory. ♿ **Gardens** ◯ May–Aug: daily (pm only). ✦ ♿ limited. ▢ ▯ ⓦ www.tullynallycastle.com

THIS HUGE STRUCTURE, adorned with numerous turrets and battlements, is one of Ireland's largest castles. The original 17th-century tower house was given a Georgian gloss, but this was all but submerged under later Gothic Revival changes. The Pakenham family have lived at Tullynally since 1655. Thomas Pakenham, son of the present Earl of Longford, now manages the estate.

The imposing great hall leads to a fine panelled dining room hung with family portraits. Of equal interest are the Victorian kitchen, laundry room and the adjacent drying room.

The 8,000-volume library looks out on to rolling wooded parkland, much of which was landscaped in the 1760s. The grounds include Victorian terraces, walled kitchen and flower gardens, and two small lakes where black swans have recently been introduced.

Fore Abbey ❺

Road map C3. Fore, Castle Pollard, Co Westmeath. ➡ to Castle Pollard. ◯ daily.

THE RUINS of Fore Abbey lie in glorious rolling countryside about 8 km (5 miles) east of Tullynally Castle. St Fechin set up a monastery here in 630, but what you see now are the remains of a large Benedictine priory founded around 1200. Located on the northern border of the Pale *(see p124)*, Fore Abbey was heavily fortified in the 15th century as protection against the native Irish.

The ruined church was part of the original Norman priory, but the cloister and refectory date from the 1400s. On the hill opposite lies St Fechin's Church, a Norman building said to mark the site of the first monastery. The tiny church nearby incorporates a 15th-century anchorite's cell.

Kells ❻

Road map D3. Co Meath. 🏚 5,500. 🚌 🚂 ⓘ Kells Heritage Centre, Navan Road (046 924 7840). ● Dec–Jan.

SIGNPOSTED by its Irish name, Ceanannus Mór, this modest town provides an unlikely backdrop to the monastery for which it is so famous.

Kells Monastery was set up by St Columba in the 6th century, but its heyday came after 806, when monks fled here from Iona. They may have been the scribes who illuminated the superb *Book of Kells,* now kept at Trinity College, Dublin *(see p62).*

Lying in the west of town, the monastery centres on a rather gloomy 18th-century church beside which stands a decapitated round tower. There are several 9th-century High Crosses; the South Cross is in the best condition.

Just north of the enclosure is **St Columba's House**, a tiny steep-roofed stone oratory, similar to St Kevin's Kitchen at Glendalough *(see p132).*

The Market Cross, a High Cross that once marked the entrance to the monastery, now stands outside the Heritage Centre in the Old Courthouse. It was used as a gallows during the uprising in 1798 *(see p39).* The battle scene on the base is a subject rarely used in High Cross art.

Ruins of Fore Abbey, a medieval Benedictine priory

Thatched cottage in Carlingford on the mountainous Cooley Peninsula

Dundalk **❼**

Road map D3. Co Louth. 👥 32,000.
🚌 🚉 🛈 Jocelyn Street
(042 933 5484). 🚌 Fri.

DUNDALK once marked the northernmost point of the Pale, the area controlled by the English during the Middle Ages (see p124). Now it is the last major town before the Northern Irish border.

Dundalk is also a gateway to the magnificent countryside of the Cooley Peninsula. The **County Museum**, which is housed in an 18th-century distillery in the town, gives an imaginative history of the county, including a section on some of Louth's traditional industries such as beer-making.

🏛 **County Museum**
Jocelyn St. 🛈 042 932 7056.
◯ May–Sep: daily; Oct–Apr: Tue–Sat.
● 25 & 26 Dec, 1 Jan. 🖼 🚻

Carlingford **❽**

Road map D3. Co Louth. 👥 950. 🚌
🛈 Holy Trinity Heritage Centre
Churchyard Rd (042 937 3454).
Carlingford Adventure Centre
Tholsel St (042 937 3100).
● 2 weeks at Christmas.

THIS IS A PICTURESQUE fishing village, located between the mountains of the Cooley Peninsula and Carlingford Lough. The border with Northern Ireland runs through the centre of this drowned river valley, and from the village you can look across to the Mountains of Mourne on the Ulster side (see pp276–7). Carlingford is an interesting place to explore, with its

pretty whitewashed cottages and ancient buildings clustered along medieval alleyways. The ruins of **King John's Castle**, built by the Normans to protect the entrance to the lough, still dominate the village, and there are other impressive fortified buildings, including the Mint. The **Holy Trinity Heritage Centre**, which is housed in a medieval church, traces the history of the port from Anglo-Norman times.

Carlingford is the country's oyster capital, and often holds an oyster festival in August, which draws a large crowd. The lough is a popular watersports centre too, and in summer you can go on cruises around the lough from the village quayside where there is a smart new marina.

The **Carlingford Adventure Centre** organizes walking tours, plus sailing, kayaking, canoeing and windsurfing.

Detail from a tomb in Monasterboice graveyard

ENVIRONS: A scenic route weaves around the **Cooley Peninsula**, skirting the coast and then cutting right through the mountains. The section along the north coast is the most dramatic: just 3 km (1.8 miles) northwest of Carlingford, in the **Slieve Foye Forest Park**, a corkscrew road climbs to give a gorgeous panoramic view over the hills and lough.

The Tain Trail, which you can join at Carlingford, is a 30-km (19-mile) circuit through some of the peninsula's most rugged scenery, with cairns and other prehistoric sites scattered over the moorland. Keen hikers will be able to walk it in a day.

Monasterboice **❾**

Road map D3. Co Louth. 🚌 to Drogheda. ◯ daily.

FOUNDED in the 5th century by an obscure disciple of St Patrick called St Buite, this monastic settlement is one of the most famous religious sites in the country. The ruins of the medieval monastery are enclosed within a graveyard in a lovely secluded spot north of Drogheda. The site includes a roofless round tower and two churches, but Monasterboice's greatest treasures are its 10th-century High Crosses.

Muiredach's High Cross is the finest of its kind in Ireland, and its sculpted biblical scenes are still remarkably fresh. They depict the life of Christ on the west face, while the east face, described in detail opposite, features mainly Old Testament scenes. The cross is named after an inscription on the base – "A prayer for Muiredach by whom this cross was made" – which is perhaps a reference to the abbot of Monasterboice. The 6.5-m (21ft) West Cross, also known as the Tall Cross, is one of the largest in Ireland. The carving has not lasted as well as on Muiredach's Cross, but you can make out scenes from the Death of Christ. The North Cross, which is the least notable of the three, features a Crucifixion and a carved spiral pattern.

Round tower and West High Cross at Monasterboice

Ireland's High Crosses

HIGH CROSSES exist in Celtic parts of both Britain and Ireland. Yet in their profusion and craftsmanship, Irish High Crosses are exceptional. The distinctive ringed cross has become a symbol of Irish Christianity and is still imitated today. The beautiful High Crosses associated with medieval monasteries were carved between the 8th and 12th centuries. The early crosses bore only geometric motifs, but in the 9th to 10th centuries a new style emerged when sculpted scenes from the Bible were introduced. Referred to as "sermons in stone", these later versions may have been used to educate the masses. In essence, though, the High Cross was a status symbol for the monastery or a local patron.

Pillar stones inscribed with crosses, like this 6th-century example at Riasc (see p150), were precursors of the High Cross.

Capstone, showing St Anthony and St Paul meeting in the desert

The High Cross at Abenny (see p191) is typical of 8th-century "ornamental" crosses. These were carved with interlacing patterns and spirals similar to those used in Celtic metalwork and jewellery.

Tenon

MUIREDACH'S CROSS
Each face of this 10th-century cross at Monasterboice features scenes from the Bible, including the east face seen here. The 5.5-m (18-ft) cross consists of three blocks of sandstone fitted together by means of tenons and sockets.

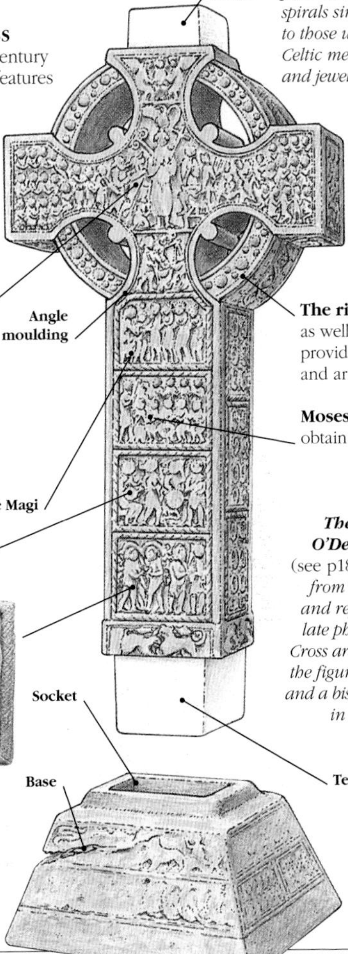

The Last Judgment shows Christ in Glory surrounded by a crowd of resurrected souls. The devil stands on his right clutching a pitchfork, ready to chase the damned souls into Hell.

Angle moulding

The ring served a functional as well as a decorative purpose, providing support for the head and arms of the stone cross.

Moses smites the rock to obtain water for the Israelites.

Adoration of the Magi

David struggling with Goliath

The Dysert O'Dea Cross (see p181) dates from the 1100s and represents the late phase of High Cross art. It features the figures of Christ and a bishop carved in high relief.

Socket

Tenon

The Fall of Man shows Adam and Eve beneath an apple-laden tree, with Cain slaying Abel alongside. Both scenes are frequently depicted on Irish High Crosses.

Base

Drogheda ⑩

Road map D3. Co Louth. 🏠 *30,000.*
🚌 🚆 🛈 *Donore Rd (041 983 7070);
Hillmount (041 984 5684).* 🛒 *Sat.*

IN THE 14TH CENTURY, this
historic Norman port near
the mouth of the River Boyne
was one of Ireland's most
important towns. However,
the place seems never to have
recovered from the trauma of
a vicious attack by Cromwell in
1649 *(see p37)*, in which 2,000
citizens were killed. Although
it now looks rather dilapidated,
the town has retained its original street plan and has a rich
medieval heritage.

Little remains of Drogheda's
medieval defences but **St
Lawrence Gate**, a fine 13th-
century barbican, has survived.
Nearby, there are two churches
called **St Peter's**. The one
belonging to the Church of
Ireland, built in 1753, is the
more striking and has some
splendid grave slabs. The
Catholic church is worth
visiting to see the embalmed
head of Oliver Plunkett, an
archbishop martyred in 1681.

South of the river you can
climb Millmount, a Norman
motte topped by a Martello
tower. As well as providing a
good view, this is the site of
the **Millmount Museum**,

Drogheda viewed from Millmount across the River Boyne

which contains an interesting
display of historical artifacts,
as well as craft workshops.

🏛 **Millmount Museum**
Millmount Square. 📞 *041 983 3097.*
⭘ *daily (Sun pm only).* ⬤ *7 days at
Christmas.* 📷 ✔ ♿ *limited.*

Newgrange and
the Boyne Valley ⑪

Road map D3. Co Meath. 🚆 *to
Drogheda.* 🚌 *to Slane or Drogheda.*
🛈 *Brú na Bóinne Interpretative
Centre (041 988 0300).* ⭘ *daily.*

KNOWN AS Brú na Bóinne,
the "Palace of the Boyne",
this river valley was the cradle
of Irish civilization. The fertile
soil supported a sophisticated
society in Neolithic times.
Much evidence survives, in
the form of ring forts, passage

graves and sacred enclosures.
The most important Neolithic
monuments in the valley are
three passage graves: supreme
among these is **Newgrange**
(see pp238–9), but **Dowth**
and **Knowth** are significant
too. The Boyne Valley also
encompasses the Hill of Slane
and the Hill of Tara *(see p240)*,
both of which are major sites
in Celtic mythology. Indeed,
this whole region is rich in

**River Boyne near the site of the
Battle of the Boyne**

THE BATTLE OF THE BOYNE

In 1688, the Catholic King of England, James
II, was deposed from his throne, to be replaced by his Protestant daughter, Mary, and
her husband, William of Orange.
Determined to win back the
crown, James sought the
support of

Irish Catholics, and challenged William at
Oldbridge by the River Boyne west of
Drogheda. The Battle of the Boyne took
place on 1 July 1690, with James's poorly
trained force of 25,000 French and Irish
Catholics facing William's hardened army of
36,000 French Huguenots, Dutch, English
and Scots. The Protestants triumphed and
James fled to France, after a battle that
signalled the beginning of total Protestant
power over Ireland. It ushered in the
confiscation of Catholic lands and the
suppression of Catholic interests,
sealing the country's fate for the
next 300 years.

William of Orange leading his troops at the Battle of the Boyne, 1 July 1690

associations with Ireland's prehistory. With monuments predating Egypt's pyramids, the Boyne Valley is marketed as the Irish "Valley of the Kings".

Newgrange and Knowth can only be seen on a tour run by **Brú na Bóinne Interpretive Centre** near Newgrange. The centre also has displays on the area's Stone Age heritage and a reconstruction of Newgrange.

Dowth

Off N51, 3 km (2 miles) E of Newgrange. ● *to the public.*
The passage grave at Dowth was plundered by Victorian souvenir hunters and has not been fully excavated. You cannot approach the tomb, but it can be seen from the road.

Knowth

1.5 km (1 mile) NW of Newgrange. ● *as Newgrange (see pp238–9).*
Knowth outdoes Newgrange in several respects, above all in the quantity of its treasures, which form the greatest concentration of megalithic art in Europe. Also, the site was occupied for a much longer period – from Neolithic times right up until about 1400.

Unusually, Knowth has two passage tombs rather than one. The excavations begun in 1962 are now complete and the site is open. The tombs can only be viewed externally to prevent further decay. Keep a look out for the finely carved kerbstones. Visitors sign up for tours via Brú na Bóinne.

Ruined lavabo at Mellifont Abbey

Slane Castle in grounds landscaped by Capability Brown

Mellifont Abbey ⑫

Road map D3. Cullen, Co Louth.
【 041 982 6459. ▣ to Drogheda.
▣ to Drogheda or Slane. ◯ May–Oct: daily; Nov–Apr: by appt. ▨

ON THE BANKS of the River Mattock, 10 km (6 miles) west of Drogheda, lies the first Cistercian monastery to have been built in Ireland. Mellifont was founded in 1142 on the orders of St Malachy, the Archbishop of Armagh. He was greatly influenced by St Bernard who, based at his monastery at Clairvaux in France, was behind the success of the Cistercian Order in Europe. The archbishop introduced not only Cistercian rigour to Mellifont, but also the formal style of monastic architecture used on the continent. His new monastery became a model for other Cistercian centres built in Ireland, retaining its supremacy over them until 1539, when the abbey was closed and turned into a fortified house. William of Orange used Mellifont as his headquarters during the Battle of the Boyne in 1690. The abbey is now a ruin, but it is still possible to appreciate the scale and ground

Glazed medieval tiles at Mellifont Abbey

plan of the original complex. Not much survives of the abbey church, but to the south of it, enclosed by what remains of the Romanesque cloister, is the most interesting building at Mellifont: a unique 13th-century lavabo where monks came to wash their hands in a fountain before meals. Four of the building's original eight sides survive, each with a graceful Romanesque arch. On the eastern side of the cloister stands the 14th-century chapter house. It has an impressive vaulted ceiling and a floor laid with glazed medieval tiles taken from the abbey church.

Slane ⑬

Road map D3. Co Meath. ⚘ 950. ▣

SLANE IS AN ATTRACTIVE estate village, centred on a quartet of Georgian houses. The Boyne flows through it and skirts **Slane Castle Demesne**, set in glorious grounds laid out in the 18th century by Capability Brown. The castle was damaged by fire in 1991 but reopened in 2001 after a decade of restoration.

Just to the north rises the **Hill of Slane** where, in 433, St Patrick is said to have lit a Paschal (Easter) fire as a challenge to the pagan High King of Tara *(see p240)*. The event symbolised the triumph of Christianity over paganism.

Newgrange

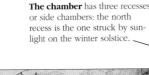

T HE ORIGINS of Newgrange, one of the most important passage graves in Europe, are steeped in mystery. According to Celtic lore, the legendary kings of Tara *(see p240)* were buried here, but Newgrange predates them. Built in around 3200 BC, the grave was left untouched by all invaders until it was

Tri-spiral carving on stone in chamber rediscovered in 1699. When it was excavated in the 1960s, archaeologists discovered that on the winter solstice (21 December), rays of sun enter the tomb and light up the burial chamber – making it the world's oldest solar observatory. All visitors to Newgrange and Knowth *(see pp236–7)* are admitted through the visitors' centre from where tours of the historic site are taken. Early arrival is advised in summer to avoid long queues.

Basin Stone
The chiselled stones, found in each recess, would have once contained funerary offerings and the bones of the dead.

The chamber has three recesses or side chambers: the north recess is the one struck by sunlight on the winter solstice.

Chamber Ceiling
The burial chamber's intricate corbelled ceiling, which reaches a height of 6 m (20 ft) above the floor, has survived intact. The overlapping slabs form a conical hollow, topped by a single capstone.

CONSTRUCTION OF NEWGRANGE

The tomb at Newgrange was designed by people with clearly exceptional artistic and engineering skills, who had use of neither the wheel nor metal tools. About 200,000 tonnes of loose stones were transported to build the mound, or cairn, which protects the passage grave. Larger slabs were used to make the circle around the cairn (12 out of a probable 35 stones have survived), the kerb and the tomb itself. Many of the kerbstones and the slabs lining the passage, the chamber and its recesses are decorated with zigzags, spirals and other geometric motifs. The grave's corbelled ceiling consists of smaller, unadorned slabs and has proved completely waterproof for the last 5,000 years.

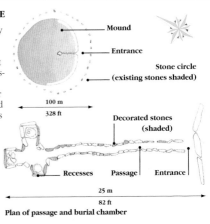

Mound

Entrance

Stone circle
(existing stones shaded)

100 m
328 ft

Decorated stones
(shaded)

Recesses   Passage   Entrance

25 m
82 ft
Plan of passage and burial chamber

Restoration of Newgrange

Located on a low ridge north of the Boyne, Newgrange took more than 70 years to build. Between 1962 and 1975 the passage grave and mound were restored as closely as possible to their original state.

The standing stones in the passage are slabs of slate which would have been collected locally.

Passage
At dawn on 21 December, a beam of sunlight shines through the roof box (a feature unique to Newgrange), travels along the 19-m (62-ft) passage and hits the central recess in the burial chamber.

The retaining wall around the front of the cairn was rebuilt using the white quartz and granite stones found scattered around the site during excavations.

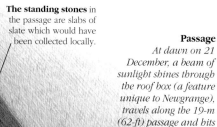

Roof box

Entrance
The opening was originally blocked by the stone standing to its right. Newgrange's most elaborately carved kerbstone is in front, part of the kerb of huge slabs around the cairn.

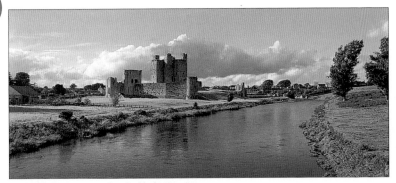

Trim Castle set in water meadows beside the River Boyne

Hill of Tara ⑭

Road map D3. Nr Killmessan Village, Co Meath. 📞 046 902 5903 (May–Oct), 041 988 0300 (Nov–Apr). 🚌 to Navan. ⏰ May–Oct: daily; Nov–Apr: by appt. 🖼 Interpretative Centre. 🎫

A SITE of mythical importance, Tara was the political and spiritual centre of Celtic Ireland and the seat of the High Kings until the 11th century. The spread of Christianity, which eroded the importance of Tara, is marked by a statue of St Patrick. The symbolism of the site was not lost on Daniel O'Connell *(see p40)*, who chose Tara for a rally in 1843, attended by over one million people.

Tours from the Interpretative Centre take in a Stone Age passage grave and Iron Age hill forts, which, to the untutored eye, look like mere hollows and grassy mounds. Clearest is the Royal Enclosure, an oval fort, in the centre of which is Cormac's House containing the "stone of destiny" *(Liath Fáil)*, fertility symbol and inauguration stone of the High Kings. Most moving, however, is the poignant atmosphere and views over the Boyne Valley.

Trim ⑮

Road map D3. Co Meath. 🏘 6,500. 🚌 ℹ Mill St (046 943 7111). 🛍 Fri.

TRIM IS ONE of the most pleasing Midlands market towns. A Norman stronghold on the River Boyne, it marked a boundary of the Pale *(see p124)*. Trim runs efficient heritage and genealogy centres

while the **Dúchas Trim Folk Theatre** provides rousing summer entertainment. (This popular company is at present in search of new premises.)

The dramatic **Trim Castle** was founded in the 12th century by Hugh de Lacy, a Norman knight, and is one of the largest medieval castles in Europe. It makes a spectacular backdrop for films and was used in Mel Gibson's film *Braveheart* in 1995.

Over the river is **Talbot Castle**, an Augustinian abbey converted to a manor house in the 15th century. Just north of the abbey, **St Patrick's Cathedral** incorporates part of a medieval church with a 15th-century tower and sections of the original chancel.

Butterstream Gardens, on the edge of town, are the best in the county. A luxuriant herbaceous bed is the centrepiece, but equally pleasing are the exotic woodland, rose and white gardens. The design is enhanced by pergolas, pools and bridges.

🏰 **Trim Castle**
📞 046 943 8619. ⏰ Easter–Oct: daily; Nov–Easter: weekends. ℹ Mill St (046 943 7111). 🖼 🎫 obligatory.
🌺 **Butterstream Gardens**
Kildalkey Rd. 📞 046 943 6017. ⏰ May–Sep: daily. 🖼

Mullingar ⑯

Road map C3. Co Westmeath. 🏘 25,000. 🚌 🚉 ℹ Market Square (044 48650).

THE COUNTY TOWN of Westmeath is a prosperous but unremarkable market town encircled by the Royal Canal

Aerial view of Iron Age forts on the Hill of Tara

(see p99), which with its 46 locks links Dublin with the River Shannon. The cost of building the canal bankrupted its investors and it was never profitable. Although Mullingar's main appeal is as a base to explore the surrounding area, pubs such as Con's and the cheery Canton Casey's can make a pleasant interlude.

ENVIRONS: The Dublin to Mullingar stretch of the Royal Canal has attractive towpaths for walkers, and fishing.

Just off the Kilbeggan road from Mullingar stands **Belvedere House**, a romantic Palladian villa overlooking Lough Ennel. The house, built in 1740 by Richard Castle, is decorated with Rococo plasterwork and set in beautiful grounds.

Shortly after the house was built, the first Earl of Belvedere accused his young wife of having an affair with his brother, and imprisoned her for 31 years in a neighbouring house. In 1760, the Earl built a Gothic folly – the Jealous Wall – to block the view of his second brother's more opulent mansion across the lake. The Jealous Wall remains as does an octagonal gazebo and other follies.

Charming terraces descend to the lake. On the other side of the house is a picturesque walled garden, enclosed by an arboretum and parkland.

⚘ Belvedere House
6.5 km (4 miles) S of Mullingar. ☎ 044 49060. ◯ May–Aug: 10:30am–7pm daily; Sep–Oct: 10:30am–6pm daily; Nov–Apr: 10:30am–4:30pm daily (last adm 1hr before closing). ⚘ ◻ ◻ ⚘ theatre & interpretative centre.

The Jealous Wall at Belvedere House, near Mullingar

Athlone Castle below the towers of the church of St Peter and St Paul

Kilbeggan ⓱

Road map C4. Co Westmeath.
⚘ 1,000. ◻

Situated between Mullingar and Tullamore, this pleasant village has a small harbour on the Grand Canal. However the main point of interest is **Locke's Distillery**. Founded in 1757, it claims to be the oldest licensed pot still distillery in the world. Unable to compete with Scotch whisky manufacturers, the company went bankrupt in 1954, but the aroma hung in the warehouses for years and was known as "the angel's share". The distillery was reopened as a museum in 1987. The building is authentic, a solid structure complete with water wheel and inside steam engine. A tour traces the process of Irish whiskey-making, from the mash tuns to the vast fermentation vats and creation of wash (rough beer) to the distillation and maturation stages. At the tasting stage, workers would sample the whiskey in the can pit room. Visitors can still taste whiskeys in the bar but, unlike the original workers, cannot bathe in the whiskey vats.

Miniature whiskey bottles at Locke's Distillery in Kilbeggan

🏛 Locke's Distillery
Main Street. ☎ 0506 32134. ◯ Apr–Oct: 9am–6pm daily; Nov–Mar: 10am–4pm daily. ⚘ ⚘ ⚘ ⚘ ⚘

Athlone ⓲

Road map C3. Co Westmeath.
⚘ 16,000. ◻ ◻ ◻ **i** Market Square (090 649 4630). ◻ Fri.

The town owes its historical importance to its position by a natural ford on the River Shannon. **Athlone Castle** is a much altered 13th-century fortress, which was badly damaged in the Jacobite Wars *(see pp36–7)*. It lies in the shadow of the 19th-century church of St Peter and St Paul. The neighbouring streets offer several good pubs. Across the river from the castle, boats depart for Clonmacnoise *(see pp242–3)* or Lough Ree.

♠ Athlone Castle
Visitors' Centre ☎ 090 649 2912. ◯ May–Oct: daily; Nov–Apr: by appt. ⚘ ⚘ limited.

ENVIRONS: The **Lough Ree Trail** starts 8 km (5 miles) northeast of Athlone, at Glasson. The route passes picturesque views and unspoilt countryside. The trail is a popular cycling tour.

Clonmacnoise ❶

Detail on a grave slab

THIS MEDIEVAL MONASTERY, in a remote spot by the River Shannon, was founded by St Ciaran in 545–548. Clonmacnoise lay at a crossroads of medieval routes, linking all parts of Ireland. Known for its scholarship and piety, it thrived from the 7th to the 12th century. Many kings of Tara and of Connaught were buried here. Plundered by the Vikings and Anglo-Normans, it fell to the English in 1552. Today, a group of stone churches (temples), a cathedral, two round towers and three High Crosses remain.

Last Circuit of Pilgrims at Clonmacnoise
This painting (1838), by George Petrie, shows pilgrims walking the traditional route three times around the site. Pilgrims still do this every year on 9 September, St Ciaran's Day.

The Pope's Shelter was where John Paul II conducted Mass during his visit in 1979.

Cross of the Scriptures
This copy of the original 9th-century cross (now in the museum) is decorated with biblical scenes, but the identity of most of the figures is uncertain.

VISITING CLONMACNOISE

The Visitors' Centre is housed in three buildings modelled on beehive huts *(see p19)*. The museum section contains early grave slabs and the three remaining High Crosses, replicas of which now stand in their original locations. The Nuns' Church, northeast of the main site, has a Romanesque doorway and chancel arch.

KEY

1 South Cross	**7** Cathedral
2 Temple Dowling	**8** North Cross
3 Temple Hurpan	**9** Cross of the Scriptures
4 Temple Melaghlin	**10** Round Tower
5 Temple Ciaran	**11** Temple Connor
6 Temple Kelly	**12** Temple Finghin

0 metres	50
0 yards	50

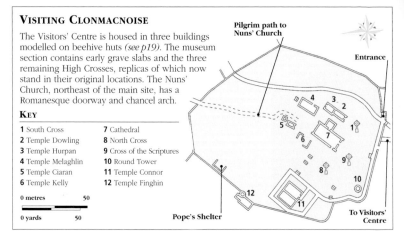

Pilgrim path to Nuns' Church

Entrance

Pope's Shelter

To Visitors' Centre

VISITORS' CHECKLIST

Road map C4. 7 km (4 miles) N of
Shannonbridge, Co Offaly. 090
967 4195. to Athlone,
then minibus (090 647 4839/087
240 7706). from Athlone.
daily. Pre-book for groups. 25
Dec. in summer. Enquire at
reception.

Whispering Door
*Above the cathedral's 15th-
century north doorway are
carvings of saints Francis,
Patrick and Dominic. The
acoustics of the doorway are
such that even a whisper is
carried inside the building.*

**The Shannonbridge Bog Railway
passing an area of cut bog**

Shannonbridge
Bog Railway ⑳

Road map C4. 5 km (3 miles) E of
Shannonbridge, Co Offaly. 090
967 4114. to Athlone.
Apr–Oct: daily; Nov–Mar: groups by
appt. www.bnm.ie

STARTING near Shannonbridge,
this guided tour by train is
run by the Irish Peat Board
(Bord na Móna). The 45-minute
tour covers 9 km (6 miles) of
bogland and gives a fascinating
insight into the history and
development of the Blackwater
raised bogs – an area of great
ecological importance, parts
of which are protected.

Tour guides describe the
transformation from lake to
marshy fen and thence to bog
(see p244), and explain that
in several hundred years the
bog will become fields and
woodland. They also point out
the area's distinctive flora and
fauna, from dragonflies to bog
cotton, bog asphodel and
sphagnum moss. The small
lakes and pools that punctuate
the bog provide excellent
habitats for wetland birds.

Bog oaks – old trees which
have been preserved in the
bog – are visible in the places
where the peat has been har-
vested. For centuries, peat has
been the main source of fuel
in rural Ireland, and visitors
can watch peat being cut by
hand using the traditional tool
known as a "slane". Modern
peat-harvesting machines in
use nearby supply the power
station at Shannonbridge.
There is a craft shop and also a
machinery museum here.

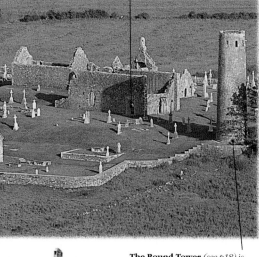

The Round Tower *(see p18)* is
over 19 m (62 ft) high with its
doorway above ground level.

Temples Dowling, Hurpan and Melaghlin
*Built as a family crypt, Temple Hurpan was a 17th-century
addition to the early Romanesque Temple Dowling. The 13th-
century Temple Melaghlin has two fine round-headed windows.*

The Raised Bogs of the Midlands

PEATLAND OR BOG, which covers about 15 per cent of the Irish landscape, exists in two principal forms. Most extensive is the thin blanket bog found chiefly in the west, while the dome-shaped raised bogs are more characteristic of the Midlands – notably in an area known as the Bog of Allen.

Four-spotted chaser dragonfly

Although Irish boglands are some of the largest in Europe, the use of peat for fuel and fertilizer has greatly reduced their extent, threatening not only the shape of the Irish landscape but also the survival of a unique habitat and the unusual plants and insects it supports.

Unspoiled expanse of the Bog of Allen

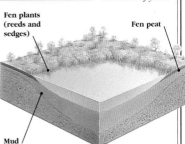

Peat cutters still gather turf (as peat is known locally) by hand in parts of Ireland. It is then set in stacks to dry. Peat makes a good fuel, because it is rich in partially decayed vegetation, laid down over thousands of years.

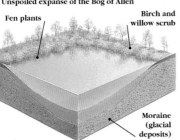

Fen plants

Birch and willow scrub

Moraine (glacial deposits)

8000 BC: *Shallow meltwater lakes that formed after the Ice Age gradually filled with mud. Reeds, sedges and other fen plants began to dominate in the marshy conditions which resulted.*

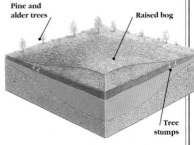

Fen plants (reeds and sedges)

Fen peat

Mud

6000 BC: *As the fen vegetation died, it sank to the lake bed but did not decompose fully in the waterlogged conditions, forming a layer of peat. This slowly built up and also spread outwards.*

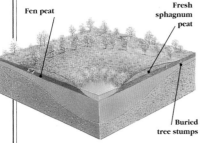

Fen peat

Fresh sphagnum peat

Buried tree stumps

3000 BC: *As the peat built up and the lake slowly disappeared, plant life in the developing bog had to rely almost exclusively on rainwater, which is acid. Fen plants could not survive in these acidic conditions and gave way to bog mosses, mainly species of sphagnum. As these mosses died, they formed a layer of sphagnum peat on the surface of the bog which, over the centuries, attained a distinctive domed shape.*

Pine and alder trees

Raised bog

Tree stumps

Present day: *Few raised bogs are actively growing today. Those that remain contain a fascinating historical record of the landscape. The survival of ancient tree stumps shows how well plants are preserved in peat.*

Sphagnum moss

Birr ㉑

Road map 4C. Co Offaly. 🏛 *4,100*.
🚌 🛈 *May–Sep: Rosse Row (0509 20110)*.

BIRR, A GENTRIFIED estate town, grew up in the shadow of the castle where the Earls of Rosse have resided for almost four centuries. It is famous for its authentic Georgian layout, with houses displaying original fanlights, door panelling and iron railings. Two particularly elegant streets are Oxmantown Mall, designed by the 2nd Earl of Rosse, and John's Mall. Emmet Square may have sold its Georgian soul to commerce, but Dooly's Hotel is still a fine example of an old coaching inn. Foster's bar, in nearby Connaught Street, is one of many traditional shopfronts to have been restored in Birr.

🏰 Birr Castle Demesne
Rosse Row. 📞 *0509 20336*.
Gardens 🔲 *daily.* 🖼 ♿ 🛍 🛒
🌐 www.birrcastle.com

Birr Castle was founded in 1620 by the Parsons, later Earls of Rosse, and is still the family seat. They are most noted for their contribution to astronomy – a telescope, built by the 3rd Earl in 1845, was the largest in the world at the time. The 17-m (56-ft) wooden tube, supported by two walls, can be seen in the grounds, fully restored. The Historic Science Centre traces the family's pioneering work.

The castle is closed to the public, but the glory of Birr lies in its grounds. First landscaped in the 18th century, these are famous for their 9-m (30-ft) box hedges and for the

An alcove in the front hall of Emo Court with a *trompe l'oeil* ceiling

exotic trees and shrubs from foreign expeditions sponsored by the 6th Earl. The magnolias and maples are particularly striking. The gardens overlook the meeting of two rivers.

The National Country Fair is held here in early June.

Slieve Bloom Mountains ㉒

Road map D4. Co Offaly and Co Laois.
🚌 *to Mountmellick.* 🛈 *May–Sep: Rosse Row, Birr (0509 20110)*.

THIS LOW RANGE of mountains rises unexpectedly from the bogs and plains of Offaly and Laois, providing a welcome change in the predominantly flat Midlands. You can walk along the **Slieve Bloom Way**, a 30-km (19-mile) circular trail through an unspoiled area of open vistas, deep wooded glens and mountain streams. There are other marked paths too. Good starting points are **Cadamstown**, with an attractive old mill, and the pretty village of **Kinnitty** – both in the northern foothills.

Emo Court ㉓

Road map D4. 13 km (8 miles) NE of Portlaoise, Co Laois. 📞 *0502 26573*.
🚌 *to Monasterevin or Portlaoise.*
House 🔲 *mid-Jun–mid-Sep: Tue–Sun.*
Gardens 🔲 *daily.* 🖼 ♿ *limited.*

EMO COURT, commissioned by the Earl of Portarlington in 1790, represents the only foray into domestic architecture by James Gandon, designer of the Custom House in Dublin *(see p86)*. The monumental Neo-Classical mansion has a splendid façade featuring an Ionic portico. Inside are a magnificent gilded rotunda and fine stuccowork ceilings.

Emo Court became the property of the Office of Public Works in 1994 but the previous owner, who restored the house, is still resident and is now working on the grounds. These are adorned with fine statuary and include a lakeside walk.

Rock of Dunamase ㉔

Road map D4. 5 km (3 miles) E of Portlaoise, Co Laois. 🚌 *to Portlaoise.*

THE ROCK OF DUNAMASE, which looms dramatically above the plains east of Portlaoise, has long been a military site. Originally crowned by an Iron Age ring fort, the 13th-century castle which succeeded it is now more prominent – though it was virtually destroyed by Cromwellian forces in 1650. You can reach the battered keep by climbing up banks and ditches through two gateways and a fortified courtyard.

Rock of Dunamase viewed from Stradbally to the east

NORTHERN IRELAND

LONDONDERRY · ANTRIM · TYRONE · FERMANAGH
ARMAGH · DOWN

NORTHERN IRELAND *has sights from every era of Ireland's history as well as magnificently varied coastal and lakeland scenery. In the past, it has received fewer visitors than the Republic as a result of the "Troubles". Following recent moves towards peace, there seems every chance that it will at last attract the attention it deserves.*

The province of Northern Ireland was created after partition of the island in 1921. Its six counties (plus Donegal, Monaghan and Cavan) were part of Ulster, one of Ireland's four traditional kingdoms. It was most probably in Ulster that Christianity first ousted the old Celtic pagan beliefs. In 432 St Patrick landed at Saul in County Down, later founding a church at Armagh, which is still the spiritual capital of Ireland.

The dominant political force in early Christian times was the Uí Néill clan. Their descendants, the O'Neills, put up fierce resistance to English conquest in the late 16th century. Hugh O'Neill, Earl of Tyrone, had some notable successes against the armies of Elizabeth I, but was defeated and in 1607 fled to Europe with other Irish lords from Ulster, in what became known as the "Flight of the Earls". Vacant estates were granted to individuals and companies, who planted them with English and Scottish Protestants *(see p37)*. Many Plantation towns, such as Londonderry, preserve their 17th-century layout around a central square or "diamond". The arrival of new settlers meant that Irish Catholics were increasingly marginalized, thereby sowing the seeds of 400 years of conflict.

In the relative tranquillity of the 18th century, the Anglo-Irish nobility built stately homes, such as Mount Stewart House on the Ards Peninsula and Castle Coole near Enniskillen. Ulster also enjoyed prosperity in the 19th century through its ship-building, linen and rope-making industries.

Though densely populated and industrialized around Belfast, away from the capital the region is primarily agricultural. It also has areas of outstanding natural beauty, notably the rugged Antrim coastline around the Giant's Causeway, the Mountains of Mourne in County Down and the Erne lakeland in the west of the region.

Belfast's City Hall (1906), symbol of the city's civic pride

◁ **Carrick-a-rede Rope Bridge, an unusual tourist attraction on the Causeway Coast**

Exploring Northern Ireland

THE STARTING POINT for most visitors to the province is
Belfast, with its grand Victorian buildings, good pubs and
the excellent Ulster Museum. However, Northern Ireland's
greatest attractions lie along its coast. These range from the
extraordinary volcanic landscape of the Giant's Causeway to
Carrickfergus, Ireland's best preserved Norman castle. There
are also Victorian resorts, like Portstewart, tiny fishing
villages and unspoiled sandy beaches, such as Benone
Strand. Ramblers are drawn to the Mountains of
Mourne, while anglers and boating enthusiasts
can enjoy the lakeland of Lower Lough Erne.

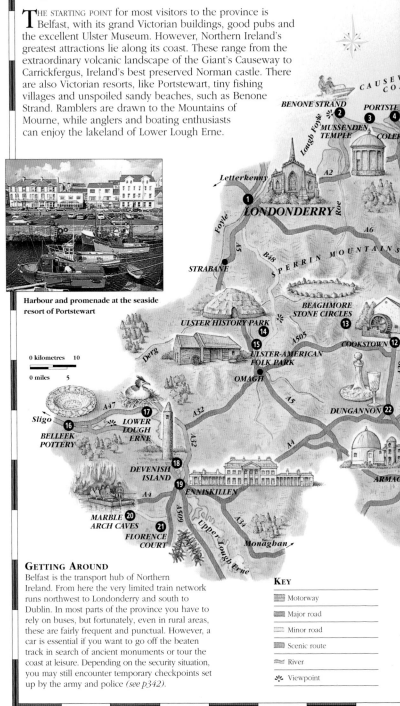

Harbour and promenade at the seaside resort of Portstewart

0 kilometres   10

0 miles   5

GETTING AROUND

Belfast is the transport hub of Northern
Ireland. From here the very limited train network
runs northwest to Londonderry and south to
Dublin. In most parts of the province you have to
rely on buses, but fortunately, even in rural areas,
these are fairly frequent and punctual. However, a
car is essential if you want to go off the beaten
track in search of ancient monuments or tour the
coast at leisure. Depending on the security situation,
you may still encounter temporary checkpoints set
up by the army and police (see p342).

KEY

▨ Motorway

▨ Major road

▨ Minor road

▨ Scenic route

〜 River

⚹ Viewpoint

SIGHTS AT A GLANCE

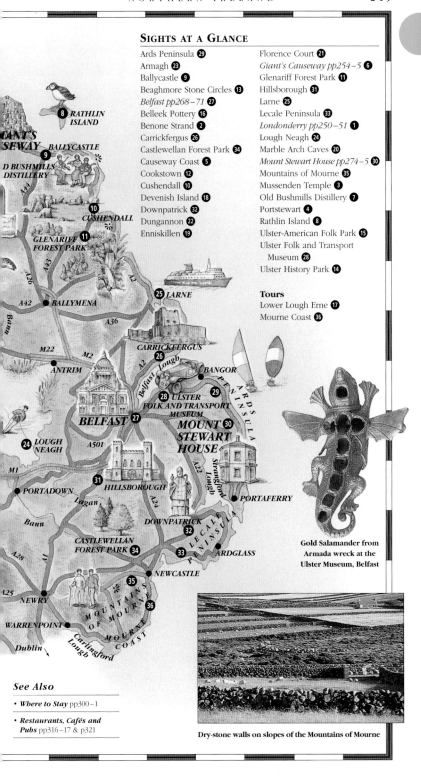

8 RATHLIN ISLAND

GIANT'S
SEWAY   BALLYCASTLE
9
D BUSHMILLS
DISTILLERY

10
CUSHENDALL

11 GLENARIFF
FOREST PARK

A26

A43

A42 BALLYMENA

A36

A2

25 LARNE

CARRICKFERGUS
26

M2

ANTRIM

A2   Belfast Lough   BANGOR

28 ULSTER
FOLK AND TRANSPORT
MUSEUM

BELFAST **27**

MOUNT
30
STEWART
HOUSE

24 LOUGH
NEAGH

A501

29

31 HILLSBOROUGH

A24

Strangford Lough

A22

PORTAFERRY

M1

PORTADOWN

Lagan

Bann

CASTLEWELLAN
FOREST PARK **34**

DOWNPATRICK
32

33 ARDGLASS

A28   A1

35

NEWCASTLE

NEWRY

36

WARRENPOINT

Carlingford Lough

Dublin

**Gold Salamander from
Armada wreck at the
Ulster Museum, Belfast**

Dry-stone walls on slopes of the Mountains of Mourne

Londonderry ❶

S<small>T</small> C<small>OLUMBA</small> founded a monastery here beside the River Foyle in 546. He called the place Doire or "oak grove", later anglicized as Derry. In 1613, the city was selected as a major Plantation project *(see pp36–7)*, organized by

Carving on Shipquay Gate

London livery companies. As a result, it acquired the prefix London, though most people still call it Derry. When British troops shot dead 13 demonstrators in 1972, Derry hit the world's headlines. Today, with an end to the Troubles in sight, the city council has undertaken several admirable heritage projects.

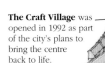

★ Tower Museum
The excellent displays on local history in this new museum include one on the mapping of the area during the reign of Elizabeth I.

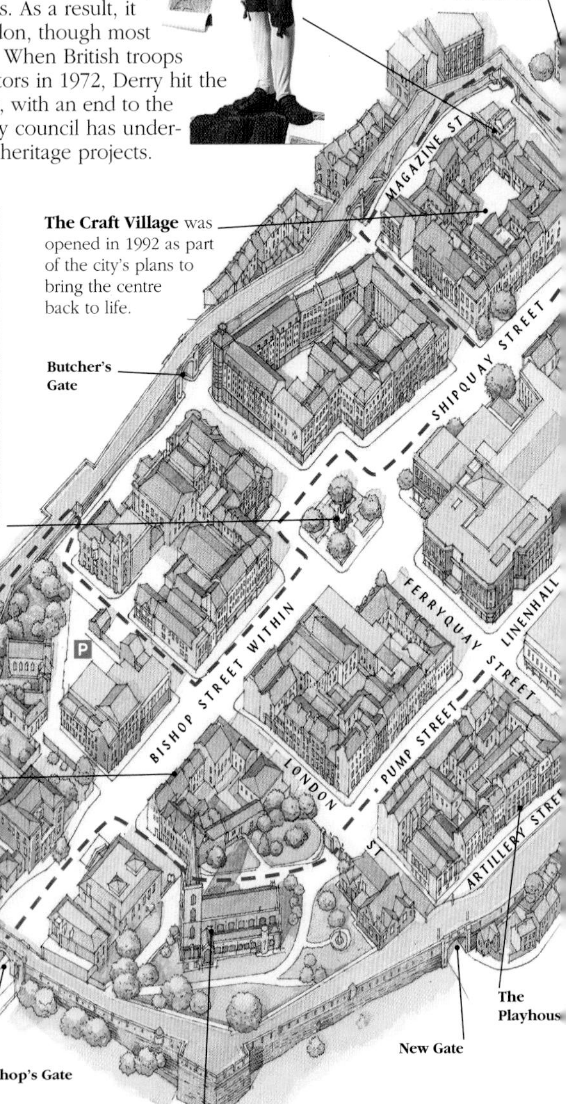

Shipquay Gate

The Craft Village was opened in 1992 as part of the city's plans to bring the centre back to life.

Butcher's Gate

The Diamond
The war memorial in the Diamond or main square was erected in 1927. It was originally made for the city of Sheffield in England.

Court House

Bishop's Gate

The Playhouse

New Gate

★ St Columb's Cathedral
The nave's wooden ceiling dates from 1862. The corbels are carved with the heads of former bishops and deans.

KEY

🅿 Parking

— Suggested route

VISITORS' CHECKLIST

Road map C1. Co Londonderry.
106,000. 11 km (7 miles) E.
Waterside, Duke St (028 7134
2228). Foyle St (028 7126
2261). 44 Foyle St (028 7126
7284). Walled City Festival
(June); Hallowe'en Festival (Oct).
Sat. www.derryvisitor.com

★ Guildhall
*This stained-glass
window shows
St Columba.
Others feature
incidents from
the siege of Derry,
including the
apprentice boys
shutting the city
gates in 1688.*

Ferryquay
Gate

To Craigavon Bridge
and River Foyle

0 metres   100

0 yards   100

STAR SIGHTS

★ **Guildhall**

★ **St Columb's
Cathedral**

★ **Tower Museum**

St Columb's Cathedral
St Columb's Court. 028 7126
7313. Mon–Sat. donation.
on request.

Built between 1628 and 1633,
in "Planters' Gothic" style, St
Columb's was the first
cathedral to be
founded in the
British Isles after
the Reformation.
The interior was
extensively restored
in the 19th century.
A small museum in the
Chapter House has
relics from the siege
of 1689 *(see pp36
–7)*, including the 17th-century
locks and keys of the city. In
the vestibule is a hollow mortar
cannonball that was fired into
the city by James II's army. It
carried terms for capitulation,
but the reply of the Protestants
within the walls was a defiant
"No surrender", a phrase used
by Loyalists to this day.

**Lock of city gate in
St Columb's Cathedral**

Tower Museum
Union Hall Place. 028 7137 2411.
Jul & Aug: daily; Sep–Jun: Tue–Sat;
bank hols.
Housed in O'Doherty Tower
(a replica of the original 16th-
century building on this site),
the museum traces the history
of the city from its foundation
to the recent Troubles using
multimedia displays. Upstairs,
an exhibition about the 1688
Spanish Armada includes
artifacts from ships wrecked
in nearby Kinnagoe Bay.

Walls of Derry
Access from Magazine Street.
Among the best preserved city
fortifications in Europe, the
city walls rise to a height of
8 m (26 ft) and in places are
9 m (30 ft) wide. Completed
in 1618 to defend the new
merchant city from Gaelic
chieftains in Donegal, the walls
have never been breached, not
even during the siege of 1689,
when 7,000 out of a population
of 20,000 perished from
disease or starvation.
Restoration work
means that it should
soon be possible to
walk right around
the walls for the first
time in decades. Just
outside the old fortifications, beyond Butcher's
Gate, is the Bogside,
a Catholic area with
a famous mural that
announces "You are now
entering Free Derry".

Guildhall
Guildhall Square. 028 7137 7335.
Mon–Fri.
Standing between the walled
city and the River Foyle, this
Neo-Gothic building was constructed in 1890, but a fire in
1908 and a bomb in 1972 both
necessitated substantial repairs.
Stained-glass windows – copies
of the originals – recount the
history of Derry. To the rear
of the Guildhall is Derry Quay,
from where Irish emigrants
sailed to America in the 18th
and 19th centuries.

ENVIRONS: Just off the B194,
on the way to Muff, is the
Earhart Museum containing
a small exhibition on American
aviator Amelia Earhart, the first
woman to complete a
transatlantic solo flight. She
had intended to fly to Paris,
but in May 1932 landed in a
field outside Derry. The nearby
park is lovely for picnics.

Earhart Museum
Ballyarnet. 028 7135 4040.
Mon–Fri. Fri pm.

The old walled city viewed across the River Foyle

Terraced houses behind the promenade at Portrush

Benone Strand ❷

Road map D1. Co Londonderry.
🅸 Benone Tourist Complex, 53
Benone Ave, Seacoast Rd, Magilligan
(028 7775 0555). ◐ daily.

THE WIDE, golden sands of Ireland's longest beach, also known as Magilligan Strand, sweep along the Londonderry coastline for more than 10 km (6 miles). The magnificent beach has been granted EU Blue Flag status for its cleanliness. Marking the western extremity of the beach is **Magilligan Point** where a Martello tower, built during the Napoleonic wars, stands guard over the bottleneck entrance to Lough Foyle. To get to the point, renowned for its rare shellfish and sea birds, you have to drive over ramps below the watchtowers and listening devices of a huge army base. The experience is rather unsettling, but well worth the trouble.

Mussenden Temple ❸

Road map D1. Co Londonderry.
🅲 028 7084 8728. ◐ Jun–Aug:
11am–7:30pm daily ; Mar–May &
Sep–Oct: 11am–6pm Sat, Sun &
public hols. 🅱 limited.

THE ODDEST SIGHT along the Londonderry coast is this small, domed rotunda perched precariously on a windswept headland outside the family resort of Castlerock. The temple

was built in 1785 by Frederick Augustus Hervey, the eccentric Earl of Bristol and Protestant Bishop of Derry, as a memorial to his cousin Mrs Frideswide Mussenden. The design was based on the Temple of Vesta at Tivoli outside Rome.

The walls, made of basalt faced with sandstone, open out at the four points of the compass to three windows and an entrance. Originally designed for use as a library (or, as some stories go, an elaborate boudoir for the bishop's mistress), the structure is now maintained by the National Trust and remains in excellent condition.

The bishop allowed the local priest to say Mass for his Roman Catholic tenants in the basement. The bishop's former residence, the nearby Downhill Castle, was gutted by fire and is now little more than an impressive shell.

The surrounding area offers some good glen and cliff walks and there are some magnificent views of the Londonderry and Antrim coastline. Below the temple is Downhill Strand, where the bishop sponsored horseback races between his clergy.

Portstewart ❹

Road map D1. Co Londonderry.
🅺 6,000. 🅿 to Coleraine or Portrush.
🅲 🅸 Jul & Aug: Town Hall, The
Crescent (028 7034 4723).

A POPULAR HOLIDAY destination for Victorian middle-class families, Portstewart is still a family favourite today. Its long, crescent-shaped seafront promenade is sheltered by rocky headlands. Just west of town, and accessible by road or by a cliffside walk, stretches **Portstewart Strand**, a magnificent, long, sandy beach, protected by the National Trust.

On Ramore Head, just to the east, lies **Portrush**, a brasher resort with an abundance of souvenir shops and amusement arcades. The East Strand is backed by sand dunes and runs parallel with the world-class **Royal Portrush Golf Links**. You can stroll along the beach to White Rocks – limestone cliffs carved by the wind and waves into caves and arches.

To the south is the university town of **Coleraine**. The North West 200 (see p26), the world's fastest motorcycle road race, is run between Portstewart, Coleraine and Portrush. The race is held in May in front of 100,000 people.

Mussenden Temple set on a cliff top on the Londonderry coast

Causeway Coast **❻**

Road map D1. Co Antrim. **ℹ** *Giant's Causeway (028 2073 1855).* **Carrick-a-rede Rope Bridge** **☎** *028 2073 1582.* **◯** *17 Mar–Sep: daily, weather permitting.* **🅿** *for car park.* **🏠 ♿**

THE RENOWN of the **Giant's Causeway** *(see pp254–5),* Ireland's only World Heritage Site, overshadows the other attractions of this stretch of North Antrim coast. When visiting the Causeway, it is well worth investigating the sandy bays, craggy headlands and dramatic ruins that punctuate the rest of this inspirational coastline.

Approaching the Causeway from the west, you pass the eerie ruins of **Dunluce Castle** perched vulnerably on a steep crag – a storm once blew its kitchen into the sea. Dating back to the 13th century, it was the main fortress of the MacDonnells, chiefs of Antrim. Although the roof has gone, it is still well preserved, with its twin towers, gateway and some original cobbling intact.

Dunseverick Castle can be reached by road or a lengthy hike from the Causeway. It is a much earlier fortification than Dunluce and only one massive

The roofless ruins of 13th-century Dunluce Castle

wall remains. Once the capital of the kingdom of Dalriada, it was linked to Tara *(see p240)* by a great road and was the departure point for 5th-century Irish raids on Scotland.

Just past the attractive, sandy **White Park Bay**, a tight switchback road leads down to the picturesque harbour of **Ballintoy**, reminiscent – on a good day – of an Aegean fishing village. **Sheep Island**, a rocky outcrop just offshore, is a cormorant colony. Boat trips run past it in the summer.

Just east of Ballintoy is one of the most unusual and scary tourist attractions in Ireland, the **Carrick-a-rede Rope Bridge**. The bridge hangs 25 m (80 ft) above the sea and wobbles and twists as soon as you stand on it. Made of planks strung between wires, it provides access to the salmon

fishery on the tiny island across the 20-m (65-ft) chasm. There are strong handrails and safety nets, but it's definitely not for those with vertigo. Further east along the coast lies **Kinbane Castle**, a 16th-century ruin with spectacular views.

♣ Dunluce Castle
☎ *028 2073 1938.* **◯** *daily.* **🅿**
📷 *in summer and by appt.*

Fishing boats moored in the shelter of Ballintoy harbour

Carrick-a-rede Rope Bridge

THE NORTH ANTRIM COASTLINE

KEY

═ Minor road	**P** Parking
▬ Major road	**ℹ** Tourist information

Giant's Causeway · B146 · Dunseverick Castle · White Park Bay · Sheep Island · Carrick-a-rede Rope Bridge · Ballintoy · Kinbane Castle · A2 · B15 · Dunluce Castle · Portballintrae · Bushmills · B17 · B147 · B17 · A2 · Ballycastle · Portrush · A2 · B62 · B17 · B66 · B67 · Portstewart

0 kilometres 5
0 miles 3

Giant's Causeway

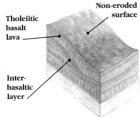

Chimney stacks

THE SHEER STRANGENESS of this place and the bizarre regularity of its basalt columns have made the Giant's Causeway the subject of numerous legends. The most popular tells how the giant, Finn MacCool *(see pp24–5)*, laid the causeway to provide a path across the sea to his lady love, who lived on the island of Staffa in Scotland – where similar columns are found. The Giant's Causeway attracts many tourists, who are taken by the busload from the visitors' centre down to the shore. Nothing, however, can destroy the magic of this place, with its looming grey cliffs and shrieking gulls; paths along the coast allow you to escape the crowds.

Aird's Snout
This nose-shaped promontory juts out from the 120-m (395-ft) basalt cliffs that soar above the Giant's Causeway.

THE FORMATION OF THE CAUSEWAY

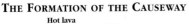

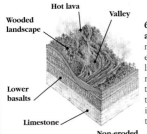

Wooded landscape / Hot lava / Valley / Lower basalts / Limestone

61 million years ago: In a series of massive volcanic eruptions molten lava poured from narrow fissures in the ground, filling in the valleys and burning the vegetation that grew there.

Tholeiitic basalt lava / Non-eroded surface / Inter-basaltic layer

60 million years ago: This layer of tholeiitic basalt lava cooled rapidly. In the process it shrank and cracked evenly into polygonal-shaped blocks, forming columnar jointing beneath the surface.

Steam and gas clouds / New lava flows

58 million years ago: New volcanic eruptions produced further lava flows. These had a slightly different chemical composition from earlier flows and, once cool, did not form such well defined columns.

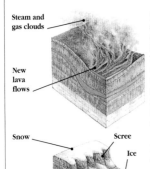

Snow / Scree / Ice / Sea water

15,000 years ago: At the end of the Ice Age, when the land was still frozen, sea ice ground its way slowly past the high basalt cliffs, eroding the foreshore and helping to form the Giant's Causeway.

Inter-basaltic layer

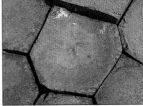

Shape of the Columns
Most columns are hexagonal, but some have four, five, eight or even ten sides. They generally measure about 30 cm (12 in) across.

Giant's Causeway and the North Antrim Coast

Millions of years of geological activity can be witnessed in the eroded cliffs flanking the Causeway. The striking band of reddish rock is the inter-basaltic layer, which formed during a long period of temperate climatic conditions. The high iron content explains the rock's rich ochre colour.

Road

Little Causeway

Middle Causeway

This section of the Middle Causeway is known as the Honeycomb. Like other unusual rock formations along the coast, it was christened by local guides during Victorian times.

GIANT'S CAUSEWAY TODAY

It has been estimated that 37,000 basalt columns extend from the cliffs down into the sea. Close to the shore, they have been eroded to form the Grand, Middle and Little Causeways.

Plant debris is trapped between the lava flows.

Wishing Chair

Myth has it that this rocky seat was made for Finn MacCool when he was a boy, and that wishes made here will come true.

Lower basalts

Grand Causeway

Visitors exploring the Giant's Causeway at low tide ▷

Old Bushmills Distillery ❼

Road map D1. Bushmills, Co Antrim.
📞 *028 2073 1521.* 🚌 *from Giant's Causeway & Coleraine.* ⏰ *daily.* ⬤ *2 weeks at Christmas. Oct–Apr: Sat & Sun am.* 📷 📹 *obligatory.* 🏪 🍴 ♿ *limited.* 🌐 *www.whiskeytours.ie*

THE SMALL TOWN of Bushmills has an attractive square and a great river for salmon and trout fishing, but its main claim to fame is whiskey. The Old Bushmills plant on the edge of town prides itself on being the world's oldest distillery. Its Grant to Distil dates from 1608, but the spirit was probably made here at least 200 years before that.

In 1974 Bushmills joined the Irish Distillers Group based at the Jameson plant *(see p171)* in Midleton, but its products have retained their own character. Most are a blend of different whiskeys; Old Bushmills, in contrast, is made from a blend of a single malt and a single grain.

The tour of the distillery ends with a whiskey sampling session in the 1608 Bar in the former malt kilns, which are also home to a small museum with old distilling equipment on display.

Murlough Bay, on the coast facing Scotland to the east of Ballycastle

Rathlin Island ❽

Road map D1. Co Antrim. 🚶 *75.* ⛴ *daily from Ballycastle (028 2076 9299).* ℹ *Ballycastle (028 2076 2024).*

RATHLIN IS SHAPED rather like a boomerang – 11 km (7 miles) in length and at no point more than 1.6 km (1 mile) wide. The island is just a 50-minute boat ride from Ballycastle. About 30 families remain on Rathlin Island, making a living from fishing, farming and a little tourism. Facilities are limited to a café, a pub, a guesthouse, a hostel and a campground. The fierce, salty Atlantic winds ensure that the landscape on Rathlin is virtually treeless.

Whiskey barrel at Bushmills Distillery

High white cliffs encircle much of the island, and at craggy **Bull Point** on the westerly tip, tens of thousands of seabirds, including kittiwakes, puffins and razorbills, make their home. A local minibus service will take visitors to view the birds. At the opposite end of the island is **Bruce's Cave**, where, in 1306, Robert Bruce, King of Scotland, supposedly watched a spider climbing a thread. The spider's perseverance inspired the dejected Bruce to return and win back his kingdom.

Ballycastle ❾

Road map D1. Co Antrim. 🚶 *4,800.* 🚌 ⛴ *to Campbeltown (Scotland)* ℹ *Sheskburn House, 7 Mary St (028 2076 2024).* 🎉 *Lammas Fair (end Aug), Apple Fair (end Oct).*

A MEDIUM-SIZED resort town, Ballycastle boasts an attractive harbour and a central sandy beach. Near the harbour is a memorial to Guglielmo Marconi, whose assistant sent the first wireless message across water from here to Rathlin Island in 1898.

Ballycastle's Oul' Lammas Fair, held in late August, is one of the oldest traditional fairs in Ireland, featuring stalls selling dulce (dried, salted seaweed) and yellowman (honeycomb toffee) .

On the outskirts of town, the ruined 15th-century **Bonamargy Friary** houses the remains of Sorley Boy MacDonnell, former chieftain of this part of Antrim. Sections of the church, gatehouse and cloisters are well preserved.

IRISH WHISKEY

The word whiskey comes from the Gaelic *uisce beatha*, meaning water of life. Distillation was probably introduced to Ireland by monks from Asia over 1,000 years ago. Small-scale production became part of the Irish way of life, but in the 17th century, the English introduced a licensing system and started to close down stills. In the 19th century, post-famine poverty and the Temperance movement combined to lower demand. The result was that Scotch whisky (with no "e") stole an export march on the Irish, but in recent years, thanks to lower production costs, improved marketing and the rise in popularity of Irish coffee, sales have been increasing.

Poster showing the Old Bushmills Distillery beside the River Bush

Environs: Off the A2, 5 km (3 miles) east of town, a narrow scenic road starts to wind its way along the coast to Cushendall. First stop is **Fair Head**, where a poorly marked path meanders across heathery marshland to towering cliffs 200 m (650 ft) above the sea. From here there are stunning views of Rathlin and the islands off the Scottish coast.

To the lee side of the headland lies **Murlough Bay**, the prettiest inlet along the coast. This can be reached by road. Further to the southeast stands **Torr Head**, a peninsula that reaches to within 21 km (13 miles) of the Mull of Kintyre making it the closest point in Ireland to Scotland.

Cushendall ⑩

Road map D1. Co Antrim. 👣 *2,400.* 🚌 👤 *4b Mill St (028 2177 1180).* ⊙ *all year; Oct–June: mornings only.*

Three of the nine Glens of Antrim converge towards Cushendall, earning it the unofficial title of "Capital of the Glens". This attractive village has brightly painted houses and a distinctive edifice known as Curfew Tower,

Carnlough harbour, a popular stop south of Cushendall

built of local red sandstone in the early 19th century as a lock-up for thieves and idlers.

Environs: About 1.5 km (1 mile) north of the village stands **Layde Old Church**. It can be reached by a pretty walk along the cliffs. Founded by the Franciscans, it was a parish church from 1306 to 1790 and contains many monuments to the local chieftains, the MacDonnells.

Just over 3 km (2 miles) west of Cushendall, on the slopes of Tievebulliagh mountain, lies **Ossian's Grave**, named after the legendary warrior-poet and son of the giant Finn MacCool *(see pp24–5)*. It is in fact a Neolithic court

tomb: the area was a major centre of Stone Age tool-making and axeheads made of Tievebulliagh's hard porcellanite rock have been found at a wide range of sites all over the British Isles.

Other attractive villages further south along the coast road include **Carnlough**, which has a fine sandy beach and a delightful harbour, and **Ballygally**, whose supposedly haunted 1625 castle is now a hotel *(see p300)*.

Glenariff Forest Park ⑪

Road map D1. Co Antrim. 📞 *028 2175 8232.* ⊙ *daily.* 🅿 *for car park.* ♿ *limited.*

Nine rivers have carved deep valleys through the Antrim Mountains to the sea. Celebrated in song and verse, the Glens of Antrim used to be the wildest and most remote part of Ulster. This region was not "planted" with English and Scots settlers in the 17th century and was the last place in Northern Ireland where Gaelic was spoken.

Today the Antrim coast road brings all the glens within easy reach of the tourist. Glenariff Forest Park contains some of the most spectacular scenery. The main scenic path runs through thick woodland and wildflower meadows and round the sheer sides of a gorge, past three waterfalls. There are also optional trails to distant mountain viewpoints. William Makepeace Thackeray, the 19th-century English novelist, called the landscape "Switzerland in miniature".

Glenariff Forest Park

Stone circle and stone rows at Beaghmore

Cookstown ⑫

Road map D2. Co Tyrone. ⚄ 12,000. 🚉 🛈 Burnavon, Burn Road (028 8676 6727). ⬥ Sat. 🌐 www.cookstowngov.uk

COOKSTOWN STICKS in the memory for its grand central thoroughfare – 2 km (1.25 miles) long and perfectly straight. The road is about 40 m (130 ft) wide and, as you look to the north, it frames the bulky outline of Slieve Gallion, the highest of the Sperrin Mountains. A 17th-century Plantation town *(see pp36–7)*, Cookstown takes its name from its founder Alan Cook.

Ardboe Cross

ENVIRONS: The countryside around Cookstown is rich in Neolithic and early Christian monuments. To the east, on a desolate stretch of Lough Neagh shoreline, the **Ardboe Cross** stands on the site of a 6th-century monastery. Although eroded, the 10th-century cross is one of the best examples of a High Cross *(see p235)* in Ulster: its 22 sculpted panels depict Old Testament scenes on the east side and New Testament ones on the west. The **Wellbrook Beetling Mill**, west of Cookstown, is a relic of Ulster's old linen industry. "Beetling" was the process of hammering the cloth to give it a sheen. Set amid trees beside the Ballinderry River, the mill dates from 1768 and is now a popular tourist attraction. The National Trust has restored the whitewashed two-storey building and its water wheel. Inside, working displays demonstrate just how loud "beetling" could be. From the mill, there are pleasant walks along the river banks.

⛫ Ardboe Cross
Off B73, 16 km (10 miles) E of Cookstown.

⚒ Wellbrook Beetling Mill
Off A505, 6.5 km (4 miles) W of Cookstown. 📞 028 8675 1735. ◯ *(pm only) Jul & Aug: Wed–Mon; Apr–Jun & Sep: Sat, Sun & public hols.* 📷

Beaghmore Stone Circles ⑬

Road map D2. Co Tyrone. Off A505, 14 km (9 miles) NW of Cookstown.

ON A STRETCH of open moorland in the foothills of the Sperrin Mountains lies a vast collection of stone monuments, dating from between 2000 and 1200 BC. There are seven stone circles, several stone rows and a number of less prominent features, possibly collapsed field walls of an earlier period. Their exact purpose remains unknown, though in some cases their alignment correlates with movements of the sun, moon and stars. Three of the rows, for example, are clearly aligned with the point where the sun rises at the summer solstice.

The individual circle stones are small – none is more than 1.20 m (4 ft) in height – but their sheer numbers make them a truly impressive sight. As well as the circles and rows, there are a dozen round cairns (burial mounds). Up until 1945, the whole complex, one of Ulster's major archaeological finds, had lain buried beneath a thick layer of peat.

ULSTER'S HISTORIC LINEN INDUSTRY

The rise in Ulster's importance as a linen producer was spurred on by the arrival from France of refugee Huguenot weavers at the end of the 17th century. Linen remained a flourishing industry for a further two centuries, but today it is produced only in small quantities for the luxury goods market. Hundreds of abandoned mills dot the former "Linen Triangle" bounded by Belfast, Armagh and Dungannon. One of the reasons why the material diminished in popularity was the expensive production process: after cutting, the flax had to be retted, or soaked, in large artificial ponds so that scutching – the separation of the fibres – could begin. After combing, the linen was spun and woven before being bleached in the sun, typically in fields along river banks. The final stage was "beetling", the process whereby the cloth was hammered to give it a sheen.

18th-century print, showing flax being prepared for spinning

Copy of Iron Age Celtic stone head at the Ulster History Park

Ulster History Park ⓮

Road map C2. Co Tyrone. 📞 *028 8164 8188.* 🚌 *from Omagh.* ⏱ *Apr–Sep: daily; Oct & Mar: Mon–Fri.* ⏺ *23–29 Dec, Jan–Feb.* 📷 🅿 ♿ 🏬 🚻

NESTLING AT THE EDGE of the Sperrin Mountains, the Ulster History Park is filled with full-scale models of structures built by successive waves of settlers in Ireland. They range from a Mesolithic hunter/gatherer's hut covered with animal pelts, dating from 7000 BC, to a 17th-century Plantation village *(see pp36–7)*. There are also megalithic burial tombs, a crannog *(see p31)* from the early Christian period and a Norman motte and bailey (a wooden fortress built on a high mound). An exhibition centre helps put the exhibits in perspective.

Ulster-American Folk Park ⓯

Road map C2. Co Tyrone. 📞 *028 8224 3292.* 🚌 *from Omagh.* ⏱ *Easter–Sep: daily; Oct–Easter: Mon–Fri.* 📷 🍴 🅿 ♿ 🆆 www.folkpark.com

ONE OF THE BEST open-air museums of its kind, the Folk Park grew up around the restored boyhood home of Judge Thomas Mellon (founder of the Pittsburgh banking dynasty). The Park's permanent exhibition, called "Emigrants", examines why two million people left Ulster for America during the 18th and 19th centuries. It also shows what became of them, following stories of both fortune and failure, including the grim lives of indentured servants and the 15,000 Irish vagrants and convicts transported to North America in the mid-18th century.

The park has more than 30 historic buildings, some of them original, some replicas. There are settler homesteads (including that of John Joseph Hughes, the first Catholic Archbishop of New York), churches, a schoolhouse and a forge, some with craft displays, all with costumed interpretative guides. There's also an Ulster streetscape, a reconstructed emigrant ship and a Pennsylvania farmstead, complete with log barn, corn crib and smokehouse. The six-roomed farmhouse is based on one built by Thomas Mellon and his father in the early years of their new life in America.

A fully stocked library and database allow visitors to trace their family roots. Popular American festivals such as Independence Day and Hallowe'en are celebrated at the park and there is an Appalachian-Bluegrass music festival in early September.

Belleek Pottery ⓰

Road map C2. Belleek, Co Fermanagh. 📞 *028 6865 8501.* 🚌 ⏱ *Apr–Sep: daily; Oct–Mar: Mon–Fri.* ⏺ *17 Mar & 10 days at Christmas.* 📷 ♿ 🏬 🚻 🆆 www.belleek.ie

Worker at the Belleek factory making a Parian ware figurine

THE LITTLE BORDER VILLAGE of Belleek would attract few visitors other than anglers were it not for the world-famous Belleek Pottery, founded in 1857. The company's pearly coloured china is known as Parian ware. Developed in the 19th century, it was supposed to resemble the famous Parian marble of Ancient Greece.

Belleek is now best known for its ornamental pieces of fragile lattice work decorated with pastel-coloured flowers. These are especially popular in the USA. Several elaborate showpieces stand on display in the visitors' centre and small museum. There's also a 20-minute video presentation on the company's history, a gift shop and ample parking space for tour buses.

Pennsylvania log farmhouse at the Ulster-American Folk Park

A Tour of Lower Lough Erne ⑰

Kingfisher

THE AREA AROUND Lower Lough Erne boasts a rich combination of both natural and historic sights. From pre-Christian times, settlers sought the security offered by the lough's forests and inlets. Monasteries were founded on several of its many islands in the Middle Ages, and a ring of castles recalls the Plantation era *(see p37)*. The lake is a haven for water birds such as ducks, grebes and kingfishers, and the trout-rich waters attract many anglers. Lough Erne is a delight to explore by land or by boat. In summer, ferries serve several islands, and cruisers are available for hire.

View across Lower Lough Erne

Belleek ⑦
Northern Ireland's most westerly village, Belleek is famous for its pottery *(see p261)*. There is also a museum, ExplorErne, which covers most aspects of the region.

Castle Caldwell Forest Park ⑥
The park's wooded peninsulas are a sanctuary for birds, and you can watch waterfowl from hides on the shore. You may see great crested grebes, the common scoter duck and perhaps even otters.

Boa Island ⑤
Two curious double-faced figures stand in Caldragh cemetery, a Christian graveyard on Boa Island. While little is known about the stone idols, they are certainly pre-Christian.

Lough Navar Forest Drive ⑧
An 11-km (7-mile) drive through pine forest leads to a viewpoint atop the Cliffs of Magho, with a magnificent panorama over Lough Erne and beyond. Trails weave through the woods.

Tully Castle ⑨
A delightful 17th-century-st* herb garden has recently been planted and is maturing well alongside th fortified Plantation house.

TIPS FOR DRIVERS

Length: 110 km (68 miles).
Stopping-off points: Outside Enniskillen, the best places to eat are the pubs in Kesh and Belleek; in summer, a café opens in Castle Archdale Country Park. There are good picnic places all along the route of this tour, including at the Cliffs of Magho viewpoint. (See also pp355–7.)

KEY

▬▬▬ Tour route

═══ Other roads

🚢 Boats to islands

🏞 Viewpoint

White Island ④
The Romanesque church on White Island has bizarre pagan-looking figures set into one wall. Of uncertain origin, they probably adorned an earlier monastery on this site. Ferries to the island leave from Castle Archdale Marina in summer.

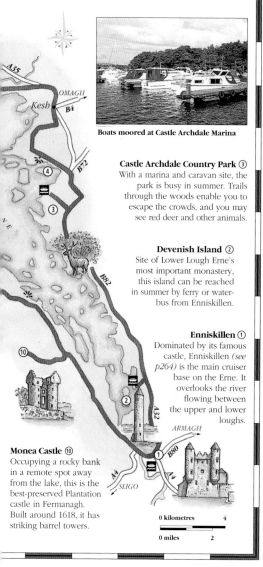

Boats moored at Castle Archdale Marina

Castle Archdale Country Park ③
With a marina and caravan site, the park is busy in summer. Trails through the woods enable you to escape the crowds, and you may see red deer and other animals.

Devenish Island ②
Site of Lower Lough Erne's most important monastery, this island can be reached in summer by ferry or water-bus from Enniskillen.

Enniskillen ①
Dominated by its famous castle, Enniskillen (see p264) is the main cruiser base on the Erne. It overlooks the river flowing between the upper and lower loughs.

Monea Castle ⑩
Occupying a rocky bank in a remote spot away from the lake, this is the best-preserved Plantation castle in Fermanagh. Built around 1618, it has striking barrel towers.

0 kilometres 4

0 miles 2

Beautifully constructed round tower on Devenish Island

Devenish Island ⑱

Road map C2. Co Fermanagh. Devenish Ferry (028 6862 1588 & 077 020 52873) from Trory Point, 5 km (3 miles) N of Enniskillen: Easter –Sep: daily. for museum and tower.

St MOLAISE, who had 1,500 scholars under his tutelage, founded a monastery on this tiny windswept island in the 6th century. Though raided by Vikings in the 9th century and burned in 1157, it remained an important religious centre up to the early 17th century.

Several fine buildings from the medieval monastery have survived, including **Teampall Mor** near the jetty. Built in 1225, this church displays the transition between Romanesque and Gothic styles. On the highest ground stands **St Mary's Priory**, an Augustinian church that was erected in the 15th century. An intricately carved stone cross close by dates from the same period.

The most spectacular sight on Devenish Island, however, is the 12th-century round tower, which stands some 25 m (82 ft) tall. From the high windows the monks could spot approaching strangers. It is perfectly preserved, and the five floors can be reached by internal ladders. Supporting the roof is an elaborate cornice with a human face carved above each of the four windows; this is a unique feature in an Irish round tower. A small museum covers both the history and architecture of the island, and contains a collection of antiquities discovered at the site.

Enniskillen ⑲

Road map C2, Co Fermanagh.
🏠 *14,000.* 🚍 ℹ️ *Wellington Road
(028 6632 3110).* 🚌 *Thu.*

THE BUSY tourist centre of
Enniskillen occupies an
island between Upper and
Lower Lough Erne. The town
gained fame for the wrong
reason in 1987, when 11
people died in an IRA bomb
attack, but it deserves a visit
for its setting and sights.

At the west end of town
stands **Enniskillen Castle**,
dating from the 15th century.
It houses **Fermanagh County
Museum** and the Inniskilling
Regimental Museum. Its most
stunning feature, however, is
the Watergate, a fairy-tale twin-
turreted tower, best admired
from the far bank of the river.
Further west, **Portora Royal
School**, founded in 1618,
counts among its old boys the
playwrights Oscar Wilde and
Samuel Beckett *(see pp20–21)*.

The **Cole Monument**
stands on a little hill in a
pretty Victorian park on the
east side of town. It is a tall
Doric column with a spiral

Enniskillen Castle seen from across the River Erne

staircase that can be climbed
for views of the lake country.

⚓ Enniskillen Castle

📞 *028 6632 5000.* ⏱️ *Jul & Aug:
10am–5pm Tue–Fri, 2–5pm Sat–Mon;
May–Jun & Sep: 10am–5pm Tue–Fri,
2–5pm Mon & Sat; Oct–Apr: 10am–
5pm Tue–Fri, 2–5pm Mon.* ♿
● *1 Jan, 25 & 26 Dec.* 🏠 ♿ *limited.*
W *www.enniskillencastle.co.uk*

ENVIRONS: Just outside town,
set in a park with mature oak
woodland overlooking a lake,
is **Castle Coole**, one of the

finest Neo-Classical homes in
Ireland. It has a long Portland
stone façade, with a central
portico and small pavilions at
each end. The stone was
shipped from Dorset to
Ballyshannon in Co Donegal.
The first Earl of Belmore, who
commissioned the house in
the 1790s, was almost bankrupted by the cost of it. The
original design was by Irish
architect Richard Johnston, but
the Earl then commissioned a
second set of drawings by the
fashionable English architect
James Wyatt. The extravagant
Earl died, deep in debt, in 1802
and it was left to his son to
complete the decorating and
furnishing during the 1820s.

The glory of Castle Coole is
that almost all the house's
original furniture is still in
place. Family portraits from
the 18th century line the walls
of the dining room. In the
lavish State Bedroom there is
a bed made specially for King
George IV on the occasion of
his visit to Ireland in 1821,
though in the end he never
came here to sleep in it. One
of the finest rooms is the oval
saloon (or ballroom) at the
back of the house. The heavy
curtains and richly gilded
Regency furniture may not be
to everyone's taste, but the
spacious oak-floored room
produces a magnificent effect
of unostentatious luxury.

🏛️ Castle Coole

Off A4, 1.6 km (1 mile) SE of Enniskillen.
📞 *028 6632 2690.* **House** ⏱️ *Jun–
Aug: Fri–Wed (pm only); Mar–May &
Sep: Sat, Sun & public hols (pm only)*
♿ ♿ 🏠 🅿️ **Park** ⏱️ *daily.*

The saloon at Castle Coole, with original Regency furnishings

Marble Arch Caves  20

Road map C2. Marlbank Scenic Loop, Florence Court, Co Fermanagh. **C** *028 6634 8855.* ⏺ *Apr–Sep: daily (phone first as bad weather can cause closure).* 🅿 🅿 *obligatory.* 🍽 🔌

THE MARBLE ARCH CAVES are cut by three streams which flow down the slopes of Cuilcagh Mountain, unite underground and emerge as the Cladagh River. Tours lasting 75 minutes consist of a boat ride into the depths of the cave complex and a guided walk that leads past stalagmites, calcite cascades and other curious limestone formations. The 9-m (30-ft) "Marble Arch" itself stands outside the cave system in the glen where the river gushes out from below ground.

The caves are very popular, so it's best to book ahead. It is also advisable to ring to check the local weather conditions before setting out; the caves may be closed because of rain. Whatever the weather, bring a sweater and sensible walking shoes.

Boat trip through Marble Arch Caves

Florence Court 21

Road map C2. Co Fermanagh. **C** *028 6634 8249.* 🚌 *from Enniskillen (Jul & Aug).* **House** ⏺ *Apr–May & Sep: Sat, Sun & public hols (pm only); Jun–Aug: (pm only) daily.* 🅿 ♿ 🍽 🔌 **Grounds** ⏺ *daily.* 🅿 *for car park.*

THIS THREE-STOREY Palladian mansion was built for the Cole family in the mid-18th century. The arcades and pavilions, which are of a later date than the main house, were probably added around 1770 by William Cole, first Earl of Enniskillen. The house features flamboyant Rococo plasterwork said to be by the Dublin stuccodore Robert West. Sadly, however, not much of what you see today is original as most of the central block was seriously damaged by fire in 1955. Much of the furniture was lost, but the plasterwork was painstakingly recreated from photographs. The finest examples are in the dining room, the staircase and the small Venetian room.

Perhaps more spectacular are the grounds, which occupy a natural mountain-ringed amphitheatre. The area is fairly wild and there are many enjoyable walks around the house. One woodland trail leads to the famous Florence Court yew tree, whose descendants are to be found all over Ireland. Closer to the house is a walled garden where pink and white roses make an attractive sight in summer.

Dungannon 22

Road map D2. Co Tyrone. 🏠 *10,000.* 🚌 🅸 *Killymaddy Tourist Centre, Ballygawly Rd, 8 km (5 miles) W of town (028 8776 7259).* 🚍 *Thu.*

DUNGANNON'S HILLY location made an ideal site for the seat of government of the O'Neill dynasty from the 14th century until Plantation *(see pp36–7),* when their castle was razed. The town's **Royal School** claims to be the oldest school in Northern Ireland. Opened in 1614, it moved to its present site on Northland Row in 1789.

Once a major linen centre, this busy market town's best-known factory is now **Tyrone Crystal**, the largest concern of its kind in Northern Ireland. Tours of its modern complex cover all stages of production, including glass-blowing.

⚒ Tyrone Crystal Coalisland Road. **C** *028 8772 5335.* ⏺ *9am–6pm Mon–Sat; 1–5 pm Sun.* ⚫ *10 days Christmas.* 🅿 *fee.* ♿ 🍽

Florence Court, the former seat of the Earls of Enniskillen

View of Armagh dominated by St Patrick's Roman Catholic Cathedral

Armagh ㉓

Road map D2. Co Armagh.
🏠 17,000. 🚌 🛈 40 English St
(028 3752 1800). 🚲 Tue & Fri.

ONE OF IRELAND's oldest cities, Armagh dates back to the age of St Patrick *(see p273)* and the advent of Christianity. The narrow streets in the city centre follow the ditches that once ringed the church, founded by the saint in 455. Two cathedrals, both called **St Patrick's**, sit on opposing hills. The more visually striking is the huge Roman Catholic one, a twin-spired Neo-Gothic building with seemingly every inch of wall covered in mosaic. The older Protestant Cathedral dates back to medieval times. It boasts the bones of Brian Ború, the King of Ireland who defeated the Vikings in 1014 *(see pp32–3)*, and an 11th-century High Cross.

Armagh's gorgeous oval, tree-lined Mall, where cricket is played in summer, is surrounded by dignified Georgian buildings. One of these houses the small **Armagh County Museum**, which has a good exhibition on local history. Off the Mall, **St Patrick's Trian** is a heritage centre telling the story of the city. It also has a "Land of Lilliput" fantasy centre for children, based on *Gulliver's Travels* by Jonathan Swift *(see p80)*. Ireland's only planetarium is on College Hill in the **Observatory Grounds**, from where there are splendid views over the city.

🏛 **Armagh County Museum**
The Mall East. 🎧 028 3752 3070.
◯ Mon–Sat. ● some public hols.
🎫 by arrangement.

🏛 **St Patrick's Trian**
40 English St. 🎧 028 3752 1801.
◯ daily. ● 25, 26 Dec. 🎫
🍴 ♿ 🅿

🌿 **Observatory Grounds**
College Hill. 🎧 028 3752 2928.
◯ daily, pm only. **Planetarium**
🎧 028 3752 3689. 🎫 for shows.
📷 ♿

ENVIRONS: To the west of Armagh stands **Navan Fort**, a large earthwork on the summit of a hill. In legend, Navan was Emain Macha, ceremonial and spiritual capital of ancient Ulster, associated with tales of the warrior Cúchulainn *(see p24)*. The site may have been in use as much as 4,000 years ago, but seems to have been most active around 100 BC when a huge timber building, 40 m (130 ft) across, was erected over a giant cairn. The whole thing was then burned

Skull of Barbary ape from Navan Fort

and the remains covered with soil. Archaeological evidence indicates that this was not an act of war, but a solemn ritual performed by the inhabitants of Emain Macha themselves.

Below the fort, the grass-roofed **Navan Centre** interprets the site, but is now only open for groups of 25 or more. One unexpected exhibit is the skull of a Barbary ape, found in the remains of a Bronze Age house. The animal must come from Spain or North Africa, evidence that by 500 BC Emain Macha was already a place with far-flung trading links.

🏛 **Navan Centre**
On A28 4 km (2.5 miles) W of Armagh.
🎧 028 3752 1800. ◯ large groups only. Call to book. 🎫 ♿

Lough Neagh ㉔

Road map D2. Co Armagh, Co Tyrone, Co Londonderry, Co Antrim.

LEGEND HAS IT that the giant Finn MacCool *(see pp24–5)* created Lough Neagh by picking up a piece of turf and hurling it into the Irish Sea, thus forming the Isle of Man in the process. At 400 sq km (153 sq miles), the lake is the largest in Britain. Bordered by sedgy marshland, it has few roads along its shore. The best recreational areas lie in the south: Oxford Island, actually a peninsula, has walking trails, bird lookouts and the informative **Lough Neagh Discovery Centre**. In the southwest corner, a narrow-gauge railway runs through the bogs of **Peatlands Park**. Salmon and trout swim in the

Navan Fort, the site of Emain Macha, legendary capital of Ulster

Hide for birdwatchers at Oxford Island on the southern shore of Lough Neagh

rivers that flow from Lough Neagh. The lake is famous for its eels, with one of the world's largest eel fisheries at **Toome** on the north shore.

Lough Neagh Discovery Centre
Oxford Island. Exit 10 off M1. 028 3832 2205. *Apr–Sep: daily; Oct–Mar: Wed–Sun.* *25, 26 Dec.*

Peatlands Park
Exit 13 off M1. 028 3885 1102. **Park** *daily.* *25 Dec.* **Visitors' centre** *Jun–Aug: daily (pm only); Easter–end May & Sep: Sat, Sun & public hols (pm only).*
www.nics.gov.uk/ehs

Larne 25

Road map D1. Co Antrim. *20,000.* *Narrow Gauge Rd (028 2826 0088).*

INDUSTRIAL LARNE is the arrival point for ferries from Scotland *(see pp352–4)*. The town is not the finest introduction to Ulster scenery, but it lies on the threshold of the magnificent Antrim coastline *(see p259)*.

The sheltered waters of Larne Lough have been a landing point since Mesolithic times – flint flakes found here provide some of the earliest evidence of human presence on the island – nearly 9,000 years ago. Since then, Norsemen used the lough as a base in the 10th century, Edward Bruce landed his Scottish troops in the area in 1315, and in 1914 the Ulster Volunteer Force landed a huge cache of German arms here during its campaign against Home Rule *(see pp42–3)*.

Carrickfergus 26

Road map E2. Co Antrim. *38,500.* *Antrim St (028 9336 6455).* *Thu.*
www.carrickfergus.org

CARRICKFERGUS grew up around the massive castle begun in 1180 by John de Courcy to guard the entrance to Belfast Lough. De Courcy was the leader of the Anglo-Norman force which invaded Ulster following Strongbow's conquest of Leinster in the south *(see pp34–5)*.

Carrickfergus Castle was shaped to fit the crag on which it stands overlooking the harbour. The finest and best-preserved Norman castle in Ireland, it even has its original portcullis *(see pp34–5)*. Many changes have been made since the 12th century, including wide ramparts to accommodate the castle's cannons. Arms and armour are on display in the large keep, while life-size model soldiers are posed along the ramparts. In continuous use up to 1928, the castle has changed hands several times over the years. Under Edward Bruce, the Scots took it in 1315, holding it for three years. James II's army was in control of the castle from 1688 until General Schomberg took it for William III in 1690. William himself stayed here before the Battle of the Boyne *(see p236)* in 1690.

De Courcy also founded the pretty **St Nicholas' Church**. Inside are rare stained-glass work and a "leper window", through which the afflicted received the sacraments.

Other attractions include the **Andrew Jackson Centre**, which celebrates the town's link to the seventh president of the USA, and **Flame**, a museum based around a Victorian coal gasworks.

Carrickfergus Castle
028 9335 1273. *daily (Sun pm).* *25 Dec.*

Flame
44 Irish Quarter West. 028 9336 9575. www.gasworksflame.com

The massive Norman keep of Carrickfergus Castle

Belfast ㉗

B ELFAST WAS THE ONLY CITY in Ireland to experience the full force of the Industrial Revolution. Its ship-building, linen, rope-making and tobacco industries caused the population to rise to almost 400,000 by the end of World War I. The

Red Hand of Ulster, Linen Hall Library

Troubles and the decline of traditional industries have since damaged economic life, but regeneration

projects, such as the Odyssey complex at Queen's Quay, are breathing new life into run-down areas. Belfast remains a handsome city and visitors are agreeably surprised by the friendliness of the "Big Smoke".

Mosaic in St Anne's Cathedral, showing St Patrick's journey to Ireland

Interior of the Grand Opera House

🏛 City Hall

Donegall Square. **[** 028 9032 0202 ext 2346. **🗓** 11am and 2:30pm daily; all other times by appointment.

Most of Belfast's main streets (and many major bus routes) radiate out from the hub of Donegall Square. In the centre of the square stands the vast rectangular Portland stone bulk of the 1906 City Hall. It has an elaborate tower at each corner and a central copper dome that rises to a height of 53 m (173 ft). Highlight of the tour of the interior is the sumptuous oak-panelled council chamber.

Statues around the building include a glum-looking Queen Victoria outside the main entrance and, on the east side, Sir Edward Harland, founder of the Harland and Wolff shipyard, which built the *Titanic*. A memorial to those who died when the *Titanic* sank in 1912 stands close by.

Detail of *Titanic* Memorial outside City Hall

🎭 Grand Opera House

Great Victoria St. **[** 028 9024 0411.

Designed by Frank Matcham, the renowned theatre-architect, this exuberant late-Victorian building opened its doors in 1894. The sumptuous interior, with its gilt, red plush and intricate plasterwork, was restored to its full glory in 1980. On occasions, bombings of the adjacent Europa Hotel disrupted business at the theatre, but it survives as a major venue for plays and concerts. In 1984, Belfast-born singer Van Morrison recorded a famous live album here.

⛪ St Anne's Cathedral

Donegall St. **[** 028 9032 8332.

The Neo-Romanesque façade of this Protestant cathedral, consecrated in 1904, fails to make much of an impression. The interior is far more attractive, especially the vast, colourful mosaics executed by the two Misses Martin in the 1920s. The one covering the baptistry ceiling contains over 150,000 pieces. The wide nave is paved with Canadian maple and the aisles with Irish marble. Lord Carson (1854–1935), implacable leader of the campaign against Home Rule (*see p42*), is buried in the south aisle.

SIGHTS AT A GLANCE

0 metres	500
0 yards	500

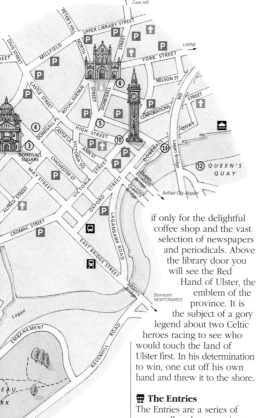

VISITORS' CHECKLIST

Road map D2. Co Antrim. 🏃
500,000. ✈ Belfast City, 6.5 km
(4 miles) E; Belfast International, 29
km (18 miles) NW. 🚉 Central
Station, East Bridge St (028 9089
9400); Great Victoria St Station
(028 9066 6630). 🚌 Europa Bus
Centre, Great Victoria St; Laganside Bus Centre, Victoria Sq (028
9066 6630). ℹ 47 Donegall Pl
(028 9024 6609). 🌐 www.goto
belfast.com ⚙ Royal Agricultural
Show & Lord Mayor's Show (May).

🍺 Linen Hall Library

17 Donegall Square North.
📞 028 9032 1707. ○ Mon–Sat. 📧
Founded as the Belfast Society
for Promoting Knowledge in
1788, the library has thousands
of rare, old books in its dark
wooden stacks. There is also
extensive documentation of
political events in Ireland since
1968 and a vast database of
genealogical information. Even
if you have no special reason
for visiting the library, it is
still well worth going inside,
if only for the delightful
coffee shop and the vast
selection of newspapers
and periodicals. Above
the library door you
will see the Red
Hand of Ulster, the
emblem of the
province. It is
the subject of a gory
legend about two Celtic
heroes racing to see who
would touch the land of
Ulster first. In his determination
to win, one cut off his own
hand and threw it to the shore.

🍺 The Entries

The Entries are a series of
narrow alleys between Ann
Street and High Street. They
feature some of the best pubs
in the city, including White's
Tavern (see p321), reputedly
the oldest bar in Belfast. The
Globe in Joy's Entry and the
Morning Star on Pottinger's
Entry both serve excellent
lunches. In 1791, the United
Irishmen, a radical movement
inspired by the new ideas of
the French Revolution, was
founded in a tavern on Crown
Entry. Its most famous member
was Wolfe Tone (see pp38–9).

🍺 Crown Liquor Saloon

Great Victoria St. 📞 028 9027 9901.
○ daily.
Even teetotallers should make
a detour to the tiled façade of
this flamboyant Victorian
drinking palace. The Crown,
which dates back to the 1880s,
is one of only two pubs owned
by the National Trust. The
lovingly restored interior
features stained glass, marbling,
mosaics and a splendid ceiling
with scrolled plasterwork. The
wooden snugs facing the long
bar have their original gas
lamps: the perfect place for a
pint of Guinness or Bass and
some Strangford Lough oysters.

KEY

🚉	Railway station
🚌	Coach station
⛴	Ferry port
🅿	Parking
ℹ	Tourist information
✝	Church

The ornate Victorian interior of the Crown Liquor Saloon

Exploring Belfast

AWAY FROM THE CITY CENTRE, Belfast has many pleasant suburbs unaffected by the civil strife of recent times. The area around Queen's University to the south of the city has two major attractions in the Ulster Museum and the Botanic Gardens. To the north, there are splendid views to be enjoyed from the heights of Cave Hill, while visitors interested in Belfast's industrial heritage will be keen to see both the old docks and the Harland and Wolff working shipyards.

🏛 Ulster Museum

Botanic Gardens. **(** *028 9038 3000.*
⬤ *daily (Sat & Sun: pm only).*
⬤ *public hols.* ♿ ▢ ▢
This four-floor bunker of a museum covers all aspects of Ulster, from local history, arch-aeology, antiquities and art to geology, natural history and technology. Especially prized treasures include gold and silver jewellery recovered from the *Girona*, a Spanish Armada ship that sank off the Giant's Causeway in 1588 *(see p249)*. One of the most interesting exhibits is of Belfast industry, featuring some crude turn-of-the-century textile machinery.

In the top-floor gallery is a collection of paintings mostly by British and Irish artists, including a large number by Belfast-born Sir John Lavery (1856–1941).

In addition to the Irish collections, there are exhibits ranging from ancient Egyptian mummies to dinosaurs. The museum also mounts frequent temporary exhibitions on a wide variety of themes.

Interior of the Victorian Palm House at the Botanic Gardens

♣ Botanic Gardens

Stranmills Rd. **(** *028 9032 4902.*
⬤ *daily.*
Backing on to the university, the Botanic Gardens provide a quiet refuge from the bustle of campus. The 1839 Palm House is a superb example of curvilinear glass and cast-iron work. The Tropical Ravine, or Fernery, is another fine piece of Victorian garden archi-tecture. Visitors can look down from the balcony to a sunken glen of exotic plants.

🎓 Queen's University

University Rd. **(** *028 9024 5133.*
A 15-minute stroll south from Donegall Square, through the lively entertainment district known as the Golden Mile, leads to Northern Ireland's most prestigious university. The main building, designed in Tudor-style red and yellow brick by Charles Lanyon in 1849, bears similarities to Magdalene College, Oxford. A towered gateway leads to a colonnaded quadrangle.

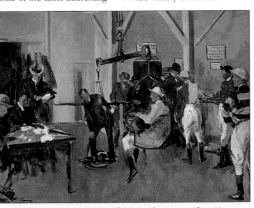

Weighing Room, Hurst Park (1924) by Sir John Lavery, Ulster Museum

THE POLITICAL MURALS OF WEST BELFAST

Republican mural in the Falls Road

Ever since the onset of the "Troubles" in 1968, popular art has played a conspicuous role in pro-claiming the loyalties of Belfast's two most intransigent working-class communities, on the Protestant Shankill Road and the Catholic Falls Road. The gable walls of dozens of houses in these areas have been decorated with vivid murals expressing local political and paramilitary affiliations. Likewise, kerbstones on certain streets are painted either in the red, white and blue of the United Kingdom or the green, white and gold of Ireland. Even with the successes of the current peace process, many are likely to remain. Some tourists make the journey out to West Belfast just to see the murals. The simplest way to do this is to pre-book a "Black Cab Tour" through the Belfast Welcome Centre. Call 028 9024 6609.

Protestant Loyalist mural

🏛 W5

Odyssey, 2 Queen's Quay. 📞 028
9046 7788. ⏰ 10am–6pm Mon–Sat,
noon–6pm Sun (last adm: 5pm).

W5, short for "whowhatwhere
whenwhy", is an award-
winning interactive museum,
which presents science as an
exciting process of discovery.

There are sections on the
elements (including the Fire
Tornado, a huge column of
twisting fire), perception
experiments, and problem
solving. Visitors can try
working a replica of a Port of
Belfast crane, designing and
building a boat, forensically
examining replica bones, or
composing music.

**Belfast cityscape showing the
giant cranes, Samson and Goliath**

🏛 Albert Memorial Clock Tower

Queen's Square.

One of Belfast's best-known
monuments, today the clock
tower leans slightly as a result
of subsidence. Beyond it,
facing the river, stands the
Custom House (1854) by
Charles Lanyon, architect of
Queen's University.

🏛 Lagan Weir Lookout

Donegall Quay. 📞 028 9031 5444.
⏰ daily (Sat & Sun: pm only). 🅿 ♿
🔌 📷 W www.laganside.com

Belfast's once thriving harbour
area can best be viewed from
the footbridge alongside the
Lagan Weir development. Five
computer-controlled steel gates
maintain a fixed water level,
getting rid of the mudbanks
produced by varying tide
levels and allowing for
angling and watersports along
the river. The visitors' centre,
on the footbridge, explains how
it all works and tells some
good tales of modern Belfast
folklore. At night, the weir is

The unmistakable profile of Cave Hill above the roofs of Belfast

lit by gas-filter blue light that
shimmers across the water.

There is a partly obscured
view across to the giant
yellow cranes – appropriately
named Samson and Goliath –
of the once-mighty Harland
and Wolff shipyards.

🐾 Cave Hill

Antrim Rd, 6.5 km (4 miles) N of city.
Belfast Castle visitors' centre 📞 028
9077 6925. ⏰ daily. ● 25 Dec. ♿
🍴 📷 W www.belfastcastle.co.uk
Zoo 📞 028 9077 4625. ⏰ daily.
● 25 Dec. 🅿 ♿ 🍴 🎁 📷

It was on Cave Hill, next to
the remains of MacArt's Fort
(named after an Iron Age
chieftain), that Wolfe Tone
(see p39) and the northern
leaders of the United Irishmen
met in 1795 to pledge
themselves to rebellion. The
five artificial caves near the
fort were carved out during
the Neolithic period.

On the wooded eastern
slopes of the hill stands the
baronial pile of Belfast Castle,
built in 1870. Previously home
to the Earl of Shaftesbury, the
castle now belongs to the city
and houses a restaurant and a
visitors' centre that interprets
the area's history. A little
further along the road past
the castle is Belfast Zoo.

⋔ Giant's Ring

Off B23, 5 km (3 miles) S of city centre.

Little is known about this awe-
inspiring prehistoric enclosure
almost 200 m (660 ft) in
diameter. It is surrounded by
a grassy bank averaging
almost 6 m (20 ft) in width
and 4.5 m (15 ft) in height.
Bones from a Stone Age burial
were found under the dolmen
in the centre. During the 18th
century the ring was a popular
venue for horse races.

🏛 Stormont

Newtownards Rd, 8 km (5 miles) SE of
city centre. ● to the public. 📷 by
arrangement only.

Built between 1928 and 1932, at
a cost of £1,250,000, Stormont
was designed to house the
Northern Ireland Parliament.
The huge Anglo-Palladian mass
of Portland stone and Mourne
granite stands at the end of a
majestic avenue, 1.6 km (1 mile)
long, bordered by parkland. A
statue of Lord Carson (see p42)
stands near the front entrance.

Since the parliament was dis-
banded in 1972, the building
has been used as government
offices. Its future depends very
much on the outcome of the
ongoing peace process. The
debating chamber was badly
damaged in a fire in 1994.

Stormont in its parkland setting outside Belfast

Ulster Folk and Transport Museum ❷❽

Road map E2. Cultra, near Holywood, Co Down. ☎ *028 9042 8428.* 🚌 🚗 🅿 *daily.* ● *24–25 Dec.* 💷 *(free for the disabled).* ⚕ 🛒 🚻

DOZENS OF old buildings, including flax-, corn- and sawmills, have been plucked from the Ulster countryside and re-erected in this absorbing folk park. Demonstrations of traditional crafts, industries and farming methods are given all year round.

The A2 road splits the folk museum from the transport section. This is dominated by a hangar that houses the Irish Railway Collection. The smaller Transport Gallery exhibits machinery made in Ulster, including a saloon carriage from the tram service that ran from Portrush to Giant's Causeway *(see pp254–5)*. Of particular note is a test model of the spectacularly unsuccessful De Lorean car, made in the early 1980s with a huge government subsidy. There's also a popular exhibit on another ill-fated construction – the *Titanic*. It's best to allow half a day to take in most of the attractions.

1883 tram carriage at the Ulster Folk and Transport Museum

Ards Peninsula ❷❾

Road map E2. Co Down. 🚌 🚗 *to Bangor.* 🏛 *Newtownards (028 9182 6846).* **Heritage Centre** ☎ *028 9127 1200.*

THE PENINSULA – and some of Northern Ireland's finest scenery – begins east of Belfast at **Bangor**. This resort town has a modern marina and some well-known yacht clubs. A little way south is **Donaghadee**, from where boats sail to the three **Copeland Islands**,

Scrabo Tower, a prominent landmark of the Ards Peninsula

inhabited only by seabirds since the departure of the last human residents in the 1940s. The **Ballycopeland Windmill** (1784) is Northern Ireland's only working windmill and stands on the top of a small hill a little further south, near the town of Millisle.

Just across the peninsula is **Newtownards**. On a hill above the town is the pleasant and shady **Scrabo Country Park**. In the park stands the **Scrabo Tower**, built in 1857 as a memorial to the third Marquess of Londonderry.

Past the grounds of **Mount Stewart House** *(see pp274–5)* is the hamlet of Greyabbey, with its antique shops and Cistercian abbey ruins. Founded in 1193, **Grey Abbey** was used as a parish church until the 17th century. It is idyllically set in lush meadows by a stream and some of its features, particularly the finely carved west doorway, are well preserved.

On the tip of the peninsula, **Portaferry** overlooks the Strangford Narrows across from the Lecale Peninsula *(see p.76)*. Portaferry's large aquarium, **Exploris**, displays

the diversity of life in the Irish Sea and Strangford Lough.

🏯 **Ballycopeland Windmill**
On B172 1.6 km (1 mile) W of Millisle. ☎ *028 9054 3037.* ○ *Jul–Aug: Tue–Sun; winter on request.* 💷

🏯 **Scrabo Country Park**
Near Newtownards. ☎ *028 9181 1491.* ○ *daily.* **Tower** ○ *Easter–Sep: Sat–Thu or by appt.*

⛪ **Grey Abbey**
Greyabbey ☎ *summer: 028 4278 8585; winter: 028 9054 3037 .* ○ *Apr–Sep: Tue–Sun; Oct–Mar: Sat and Sun only or on request.* ⚕

🐠 **Exploris**
Castle Street, Portaferry. ☎ *028 4272 8062.* ○ *daily.* ● *25 Dec.* 💷 ⚕ 🛒

Ballycopeland Windmill, which dates back to 1784

Mount Stewart House ㉚

See pp274–5.

Hillsborough ㉛

Road map D2. Co Down. 🏘 2,600.
🚌 🛈 *The Square (028 9268 9717).*

DOTTED WITH craft shops and restaurants, this Georgian town lies less than 16 km (10 miles) from Belfast. **Hillsborough Castle**, with its elaborate wrought-iron gates and coat of arms, is where visiting dignitaries to Northern Ireland normally stay.

Across from the 18th-century Market House in the town square, and next to the pleasant Forest Park, is **Hillsborough Fort**. An artillery fort dating from 1650, it was remodelled in the 18th century for feasts held by the descendants of Arthur Hill, founder of the town.

♠ Hillsborough Castle
🛈 *028 9268 1309.* ⬜ *Easter–Sep: Sat only (call to check times).*
♠ Hillsborough Fort
Access from town square or car park at Forest Park. 🛈 *028 9268 3285.* ⬜ *daily.*

Downpatrick ㉜

Road map E2. Co Down. 🏘 10,300.
🚌 🛈 *53a Market St (028 4461 2233).* 🚏 *Sat.*

WERE IT NOT for its strong links with St Patrick, Downpatrick would attract few visitors. The Protestant **Down Cathedral**, high on the Hill of Down, dates in its present form from the early 19th century – many previous incarnations have been razed to the ground. In the churchyard is a well-worn 10th-century cross and the reputed burial place of St Patrick, marked by a 20th-century granite slab with the inscription "Patric".
Down County Museum, which is housed in the 18th-century Old County Gaol, features refurbished cells and exhibits relating to St Patrick, while close by is the **Mound of Down**, a large Norman motte and bailey.

Terraced houses in the town of Hillsborough

🏛 Down County Museum
English Street, The Mall. 🛈 *028 4461 5218.* ⬜ *daily.* ● *25–26 Dec; Sat & Sun am* ♿ *limited.* 🖻 🖿 📷

ENVIRONS: There are several sights associated with St Patrick on the outskirts of Downpatrick. **Struell Wells**, believed to be a former pagan place of worship that the saint blessed, has a ruined church, 17th-century bath houses and good potential for a picnic. Further out and to the north at **Saul**, where St Patrick landed and began his Irish mission in 432, is a small memorial church.

The nearby hill of **Slieve Patrick** is an important place of pilgrimage and has a granite figure of the saint at its summit. An open-air mass is celebrated here every June.

Not far from the banks of the River Quoile is the Cistercian **Inch Abbey**, founded by John de Courcy in about 1180. Its attractive marshland setting is probably more memorable than its scant remains, but it's worth a visit nonetheless.

🔒 Inch Abbey
5 km (3 miles) NW of Downpatrick. ⬜ *daily.* 🖾 *donation.*

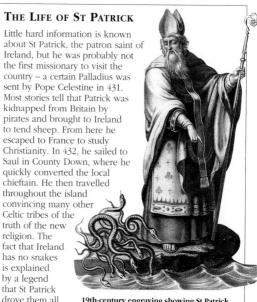

THE LIFE OF ST PATRICK

Little hard information is known about St Patrick, the patron saint of Ireland, but he was probably not the first missionary to visit the country – a certain Palladius was sent by Pope Celestine in 431. Most stories tell that Patrick was kidnapped from Britain by pirates and brought to Ireland to tend sheep. From here he escaped to France to study Christianity. In 432, he sailed to Saul in County Down, where he quickly converted the local chieftain. He then travelled throughout the island convincing many other Celtic tribes of the truth of the new religion. The fact that Ireland has no snakes is explained by a legend that St Patrick drove them all into the sea.

19th-century engraving showing St Patrick banishing all snakes from Ireland

Mount Stewart House ㉚

Lord Castlereagh (1769–1822)

THIS GRAND 19TH-CENTURY HOUSE has a splendid interior, but it is the magnificent gardens which are the main attraction. These were planted only in the 1920s, but the exotic plants and trees have thrived in the area's subtropical microclimate. Now owned by the National Trust, Mount Stewart used to belong to the Londonderry family, the most famous of whom was Lord Castlereagh, British Foreign Secretary from 1812 until his death in 1822.

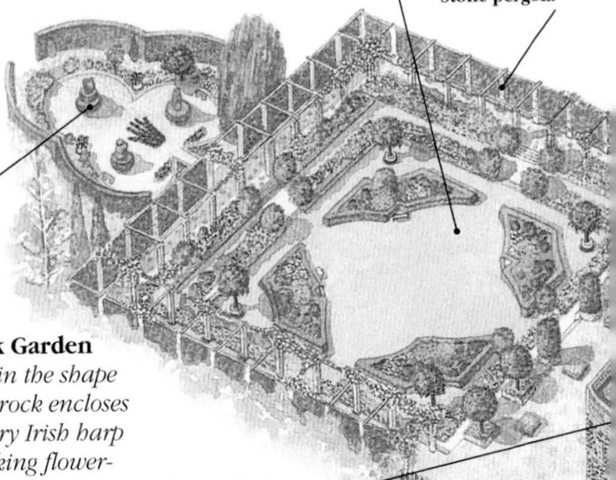

The Sunk Garden comprises symmetrical beds which in summer are full of rich blue, yellow and orange flowers, complemented by purple foliage.

Stone pergola

★ **Shamrock Garden**
A yew hedge in the shape of a shamrock encloses this topiary Irish harp and a striking flower-bed designed in the form of a red hand, emblem of Ulster.

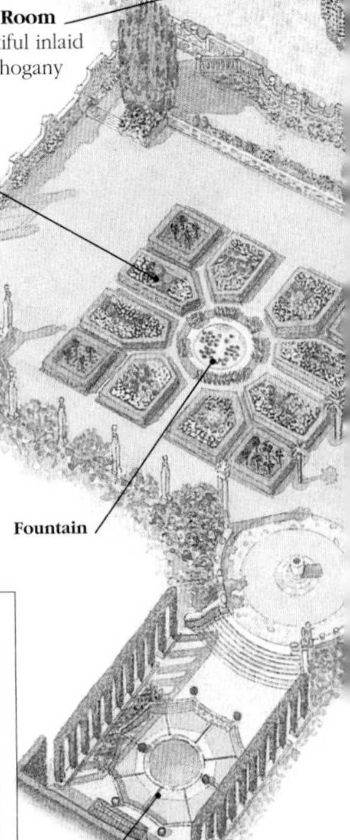

The Music Room has a beautiful inlaid floor of mahogany and oak.

Italian Garden
The flowers in the Italian Garden, the largest of the formal gardens, are planted so that strong oranges and reds on the east side contrast with the softer pinks, whites and blues on the west.

Fountain

THE TEMPLE OF THE WINDS

This banqueting pavilion looks over Strangford Lough to the east of the house. It was built in 1785 by James "Athenian" Stuart, a renowned pioneer of Neo-Classical architecture, who took his inspiration from the Tower of the Winds in Athens. Restored in the 1960s and now being worked on once more, the building's finest features are the spiral staircase and the upper room's plasterwork ceiling and exquisite inlaid floor.

The Spanish Garden is framed by a neat arcade of clipped cypress trees.

★ **Hambletonian by George Stubbs**
This picture of the celebrated racehorse at Newmarket, painted in 1799, hangs halfway up the main staircase.

VISITORS' CHECKLIST

Road map E2. 3 km (2 miles) N of Greyabbey, Co Down. 028 4278 8387. 🚌 from Belfast. **House** ◯ Easter, Apr & Oct: noon–6pm Sat, Sun & public hols; May–Sep: daily. **Temple** ◯ Apr–Oct: daily (Sat & Sun pm only). **Gardens** ◯ Mar & Oct: Sat–Sun; Apr–Sep: 10am–5pm (Apr: 4pm) daily. **Lake** ◯ all year. 🚫 ⌀ in house. ♿ 🅿 🚻 🛒

Entrance

The Dining Room contains 22 chairs used at the Congress of Vienna (1815) and given to Lord Castlereagh in recognition of his role in the talks.

Entrance Hall
The most austere room in the house, this hall features Ionic stone pillars which have been painted to resemble green marble. It is lit by an impressive glass dome.

The Chapel, converted from a sitting room in 1884, is still used by the Londonderry family.

STAR FEATURES

★ **Dodo Terrace**

★ **Hambletonian by George Stubbs**

★ **Shamrock Garden**

★ **Dodo Terrace**
The stone dodos and ark on this terrace relate to the Ark Club, a social circle set up by Lady Londonderry in London during World War I. Each member was given an animal nickname.

Lady Bangor's Gothic boudoir in Castle Ward on the Lecale Peninsula

Lecale Peninsula **㉝**

Road map E2. Co Down. 🚌 *to Ardglass.* 🛈 *Downpatrick (028 4461 2233).* 🎭 *Castle Ward Opera Festival (Jun; 028 9066 1090).*

A GOOD WAY to get to this part of County Down is to take the car ferry from Portaferry on the Ards Peninsula to Strangford. Just outside this tiny port is **Castle Ward**, the estate of Lord and Lady Bangor, who seemed to argue about everything – including the design of their 18th-century mansion. His choice, Palladian, can be seen at the front, while her favourite Gothic style influences the garden façade. Likewise, the interior is a mix of Classical and Gothic fantasy. Look out for Lady Bangor's cluttered boudoir, with its extravagant fan-vaulted ceiling based on Henry VIII's chapel in Westminster Abbey. Around the grounds are fine gardens, walking trails, children's play areas and a lakeside farmyard with a working corn mill.

About 4 km (2.5 miles) south of Strangford, the A2 passes **Kilclief Castle**, dating from the 15th century, one of the oldest tower houses *(see p18)* in Ireland. The road continues to **Ardglass**, now a small fishing village but once Ulster's busiest harbour. A cluster of castles was erected between the 14th and 16th centuries to protect the port, of which six remain. Only one of these is open to the public, **Jordan's Castle**.

The finest view in the area is from **St John's Point**, 6 km (3.5 miles) southwest of Ardglass, offering a sweeping panorama over Dundrum Bay.

🏛 Castle Ward
On A25, 2.5 km (1.5 miles) W of Strangford. 📞 *028 4488 1204.*
House ⭕ *mid-Mar–Apr: Sat, Sun, & public hols (pm only); May: Wed–Mon (pm only); Jun–Aug: daily (pm only); Sep–Oct: Sat–Sun (pm only).* 🎫 ♿
🅿 🚻 **Grounds** ⭕ *daily.* 🎫 *car park.*
⚓ Jordan's Castle
Ardglass. ⭕ *Jul–Aug: Tue–Sun.* 🎫

Castlewellan Forest Park **㉞**

Road map D2. Main St, Castlewellan, Co Down. 📞 *028 4377 8664.*
⭕ *daily.* 🎫 *for car park.*

T HE OUTSTANDING FEATURE of Castlewellan Forest Park, in the foothills of the Mourne Mountains, is its magnificent arboretum. This has grown far beyond the

original walled garden, begun in 1740, and now comprises hothouses, dwarf conifer beds and a rhododendron wood.

Elsewhere in the park are a 19th-century Scottish baronial-style castle (now a conference centre), a lake and pleasant woodlands; these are at their most colourful in autumn.

Mountains of Mourne **㉟**

Road map D2. Co Down. 🚌 *to Newry.* 🚌 *to Newcastle.*
🛈 *10–14 Central Promenade, Newcastle (028 4372 2222).*
🌐 *www.kingdomsofdown.com*

T HESE MOUNTAINS occupy just a small corner of County Down, with no more than a dozen peaks surpassing 600 m (2,000 ft), and yet they attract thousands of visitors each year.

Only one road of any size, the B27 between Kilkeel and Hilltown, crosses the Mournes, making this ideal territory for walkers. A popular but tough trail runs from **Newcastle**, the main gateway to the area, up to the peak of **Slieve Donard**: at 848 m (2,781 ft), this is the highest mountain in the range. Part of the route follows the **Mourne Wall**, which was erected in 1904–22 to enclose the catchment area of the two reservoirs in the **Silent Valley**.

Over 20 short hikes are to be enjoyed in the area. These range from easy strolls around Rostrevor Forest to rather more arduous treks up Slieve Muck and other Mourne peaks. Tourist offices will have details.

Some 35 km (22 miles) north of Newcastle, the **Legananny Dolmen** *(see p30)* is one of the finest and most photo-graphed ancient sights in the country.

Rounded peaks of the Mountains of Mourne

A Tour of the Mourne Coast ㊱

NEWCASTLE, where, in the words of the 19th-century songwriter Percy French, "the Mountains of Mourne sweep down to the sea", makes a good base from which to explore this area. Driving up and down the dipping roads of the Mournes is one of the highlights of a trip to Northern Ireland. Along the coast, the road skirts between the foothills and the Irish Sea, providing lovely views and linking a variety of fishing villages and historic castles. Heading inland, you pass through an emptier landscape of moorland, purple with heather. The Silent Valley, with a visitors' centre and well-marked paths, is the only area to have been developed especially for tourists.

Dundrum ②
The town is overlooked by the ruins of a Norman castle, and from the nearby bay you can see the mountains rising in the distance.

Tollymore Forest Park ③
This attractive park is dotted with follies like the Gothic Gate that formed part of the original 18th-century estate.

Spelga Dam ④
There are stunning views north from the Spelga Dam over the Mourne foothills.

Rostrevor with Slieve Martin behind

Newcastle ①
A popular resort since the early 19th century, Newcastle has a promenade overlooking a sweeping, sandy beach.

Silent Valley ⑦
The valley is closed to traffic, but you can walk to the top of Ben Crom Mountain from the car park, or in summer go by bus.

Rostrevor ⑤
This tranquil and leafy Victorian resort nestles below the peak of Slieve Martin, on the shores of Carlingford Lough.

Green Castle ⑥
Erected in the 13th century, Green Castle lies at the end of a single track road on a rocky outcrop at the entrance to Carlingford Lough.

TIPS FOR DRIVERS

Length: 85 km (53 miles).
Stopping-off points: Newcastle has the biggest choice of pubs and restaurants. Dundrum, Annalong, Kilkeel and Rostrevor all have pubs, and a café opens in the Silent Valley in summer. The Spelga Dam and Tollymore Forest Park are good picnic spots.
(See also pp355–7.)

0 kilometres   5

0 miles   3

KEY

 Tour route

--- Other roads

✵ Viewpoint

TRAVELLERS' NEEDS

WHERE TO STAY

WHETHER YOU ARE STAYING in exclusive luxury or modest self-catering accommodation, one thing you can be certain of in Ireland is that you'll receive a warm welcome. The Irish are renowned for their friendliness. Even in big corporate hotels, where you might expect the reception to be more impersonal, the staff go out of their way to be hospitable. The choice is enormous: you can stay in an elegant 18th-century country house, a luxurious (or slightly run-down) castle, a Victorian town house, an old-fashioned commercial hotel, a cosy village inn, or

Waterford Castle doorman

on a working farm. For the hardier visitor there are good hostels, plenty of trailer and camping sites, or even your own horse-drawn caravan. We give details here of the types of accommodation available, tourist board ratings and the choices for house or apartment rental. Our listings on pages 286–301 recommend over 200 hotels around the country – all places of quality, ranging from simple bed-and-breakfast to unashamed luxury accommodation. Fáilte Ireland (the Irish Tourist Board) and the Northern Ireland Tourist Board both publish comprehensive guides.

Entrance hall of the Delphi Lodge *(see p296)* in Connemara

HOTELS

AT THE TOP of the price range there are a handful of expensive, luxury hotels in castles and stately country houses. Magnificently furnished and run, they offer maximum comfort, delicious food and a wide range of sports facilities – either owned by the hotel or available close by. Salmon-fishing, fox-hunting and shooting can be arranged as well as riding, golf, sailing and cycling.

If your priority is a full range of indoor facilities, such as a gym, sauna and swimming pool, the modern hotel chains will best cater to your needs. **Jury's** and **Great Southern Hotels** offer this standard of accommodation in the Republic, as does **Hastings Hotels** in Northern Ireland. However, these establishments can

sometimes lack the charm and individuality of privately run hotels.

Coastal resort hotels usually offer a range of sports activities or can advise you on the best places to go. In smaller towns, the main hotel is often the social centre of the area with a lively public bar, popular with locals and guests alike.

The shamrock symbols of both the Northern Ireland Tourist Board and Fáilte Ireland are displayed by hotels (and other forms of accommodation) that have been inspected and officially approved.

COUNTRY HOUSE ACCOMMODATION

VISITORS WISHING to stay in a period country home and sample authentic Irish country life can contact a specialist

organization called **Hidden Ireland**. However, this type of accommodation may not suit everybody, as the houses are not guesthouses, hotels or bed-and-breakfast establishments, but something quite different. You should therefore not expect the same facilities and service usually found in a hotel, such as a swimming pool, elevators, televisions, porters and room service. Instead, the experience is a very intimate one; guests dine together with their host and hostess as if at a private dinner party. Many of the houses have been in the same family for hundreds of years and the history attached to them can be fascinating. Prices reflect the type of house and the standard of accommodation, but all offer excellent value for money and

The entrance to the Shelbourne Hotel in Dublin *(see p287)*

Bar at the Hunter's Hotel *(see p290)* in Rathnew, County Wicklow

a first-hand experience of an aspect of the Irish way of life.

There are many other private residences that also take paying guests. Two useful publications, *Friendly Homes of Ireland* and *Ireland's Blue Book*, provide listings and information and are available from tourist offices and bookshops. Tourist boards throughout Ireland also supply listings and make reservations.

GUESTHOUSES

M OST GUESTHOUSES are found in cities and large towns. They are usually converted family homes and have an atmosphere all of their own. Most offer a good-value evening meal and all give you a delicious full Irish breakfast *(see p304)*. Top-of-the-range guesthouses can be just as good, and sometimes even better, than hotels. You will see a much more personal side of a town or city while staying at a guesthouse. If you are looking for anonymity, however, a guesthouse may not suit you – both the proprietor and your fellow guests are likely to try and draw you into conversation.

There are plenty of good guesthouses to choose from in the Dublin area and the prices are usually reasonable. The **Irish Hotels Federation** publishes a useful booklet with guesthouse listings that cover the whole of Ireland including Dublin. The Northern Ireland Tourist Board publishes its own

similar booklet, called *Where to Stay in Northern Ireland*. This includes a comprehensive list of approved guesthouses which is updated annually. However, it is hard to beat personal recommendations you might receive from fellow guests.

Bedroom at Enniscoe House *(see p296)*, Crossmolina in County Mayo

PRICES

R OOM RATES advertised in both Northern Ireland and the Republic are inclusive of tax and service. In general, prices in the Republic are marginally cheaper than

in the North. Hotel rates can vary by as much as 40 per cent depending on the time of year; country house rates also vary a great deal according to the season. Guesthouse prices are influenced more by their location in relation to tourist sights and public transport.

For those on a tight budget, farmhouse accommodation represents excellent value for money, though the cheapest option is self-catering in a rented cottage *(see p282)*.

TIPPING

T IPPING IN IRELAND is a matter of personal discretion but is not common practice, even at the larger hotels. Tasks performed by staff are considered part of the service. Tipping is not expected, for example, for carrying bags to your room or for serving drinks. However, it is usual to tip the waiting staff in hotel restaurants: the standard tip is around 10 per cent and anything over 15 per cent of the bill would be considered generous.

BOOKING

I T IS WISE to reserve your accommodation during the peak season and public holidays *(see p49)*, particularly if your visit coincides with a local festival or major sporting event *(see pp26–7)*. Fáilte Ireland can offer advice and make reservations through its nationwide accommodation service; the Northern Ireland Tourist Board runs a similar service. Central reservation facilities are available at the hotel chains that have been listed here.

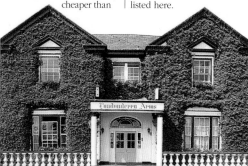

Façade of the Londonderry Arms *(see p300)* in Carnlough, County Antrim

A bed-and-breakfast on the River Corrib in Galway

BED-AND-BREAKFAST ACCOMMODATION

IRELAND has the reputation for the best B&Bs in Europe. You will never be far from a place to stay, even in the remotest spots. Your welcome will always be friendly and the food and company excellent. Even if the house is no architectural beauty, the comfort and atmosphere will more than compensate. Not all bedrooms have bathrooms *en suite*. When one is available, you may have to pay a little extra, but considering the inexpensive rates, the surcharge is negligible.

The Irish swear by their B&Bs and many stay in them by choice rather than suffer the impersonality and prices of the mainstream hotels; frequent visitors to Ireland agree. The **Town and Seaside House Association** will provide details of bed-and-breakfast accommodation in Northern Ireland, while the **Town and Country Homes Association** covers the Republic.

FARMHOUSES

FARMHOUSE VACATIONS are a popular tradition in Ireland. **Irish Farmhouse Holidays Ltd** has a list of farmhouses in the Republic that take paying guests. You can stay for one night or longer and they make an excellent base for touring the countryside. As with most things in Ireland, it is the hospitality and friendliness of the people that makes staying on a farm so memorable. You get a feel of rural Ireland with its rich agricultural heritage, and the families are determined you will enjoy every moment of your stay.

HOUSE AND APARTMENT RENTALS

VACATIONS SPENT in rental houses are an increasingly popular option in Ireland and there are properties to rent all over the country. You are likely to have more choice in the south and west as these areas have traditionally attracted the majority of tourists. Fáilte Ireland has a small section in its accommodation guide, but local tourist offices have lists of apartments and houses to rent in their area. It is also worth looking for ads in the newspapers, both local and international. Accommodation can range from quaint, stone cottages, converted barns and stable yards to more modern, purpose-built bungalows. All will generally have adequate facilities, with simple but comfortable furnishings, modern kitchen equipment and televisions.

The properties available through the popular organization **Rent an Irish Cottage** are built in traditional style with whitewashed walls inside and out, and painted roofs and windows; the decor is also traditional – simple and attractive. Locations are generally superb; the only possible criticism is, if you wanted to be "away from it all", they are built in clusters of about ten, so there isn't a great deal of privacy.

At the other end of the scale, you could rent a castle or country house, furnished with paintings and antiques. In some cases, the properties are fully staffed. A company called **Elegant Ireland** has a selection of such properties.

CAMPING, TRAILERS AND MOTOR HOMES

A LIST of fully inspected camping and trailer parks is given in the Fáilte Ireland accommodation guide. Many of the camp sites and parks offer additional facilities – these might include a shop, restaurant or café/snack bar, an indoor games room, laundry, tennis court and minature golf course. The standard and con-

A farmhouse in Clonakilty, County Cork

Traditional painted horse-drawn caravan from Slattery's in Tralee

dition of these facilities will vary but you can be reliably guided by the tourist board's star ratings: four-star parks have an extensive range of facilities with a high standard of management; three-star parks have good facilities and management; two-star parks offer limited facilities and good management and the one-star parks have the minimum facilities required for registration with Fáilte Ireland. A complete list of approved camping sites in the North is produced by the Northern Ireland Tourist Board.

If you want to experience the Irish countryside at a more leisurely pace, it is possible to hire a traditional horse-drawn caravan. Two of the best companies specializing in this type of trip are **Kilvahan Caravans**, based at Portlaoise in the Midlands, and **Slattery's Travel Agency** in Tralee, County Kerry.

Fáilte Ireland sign for approved accommodation

YOUTH HOSTELS

THERE ARE 31 youth hostels registered with **An Óige** (the Irish Youth Hostel Association), set in some wonderfully scenic areas of Ireland in buildings ranging from castles to military barracks. Accommodation is generally provided in simple dormitories with comfortable beds and basic cooking facilities. You can only use these hostels if you are a member of An Óige or

another youth organization affiliated to the International Youth Hostel Federation. Charges vary according to the standard of accommodation, location and season. Northern Ireland is covered by the **Youth Hostel Association of Northern Ireland**, which has 8 registered hostels.

Independent Holiday Hostels of Ireland publishes a guide to 151 independent hostels, and places such as universities offer similar inexpensive accommodation. Tourist boards have listings of those they recommend.

DISABLED TRAVELLERS

A FACT SHEET for disabled visitors can be obtained from tourist offices, Dublin Tourism, and Fáilte Ireland, and in their main accommodation guide there is a symbol for wheelchair accessibility. A similar symbol is used in the accommodation listings in this book (see pp286–301). Comhairle (see pp340–41) is another body that offers information on accommodation for the disabled.

The annual publication *Holidays in the British Isles* caters specifically for the disabled traveller and covers Northern Ireland. There is also a guide, with comprehensive listings, available from the Northern Ireland Tourist Board entitled *Accessible Accommodation*.

Typical bed-and-breakfast sign in Pettigo, County Donegal

Ireland's Best: Hotels

THE HOTELS featured here are a selection from our lists of recommended places to stay on pages 286–301. They give an indication of the very best that Ireland has to offer, ranging from private establishments which are members of the Hidden Ireland group *(see p280)* to the efficiency and luxury of five-star hotels and the romance of historic castles. All are impressive places, both for their setting and the buildings themselves.

St Ernan's House
This elegant, pink Regency country house is situated on its own private island not far from Donegal.
(See p298.)

Delphi Lodge
The atmosphere at this comfortable, well-run fishing lodge is extremely relaxing. The River Delphi and nearby loughs provide plenty of sport. (See p296.)

NORTHWEST IRELAND

Ashford Castle
This huge Gothic-style edifice is set on the shores of Lough Corrib. The standard of service is impeccable and the food is excellent.
(See p296.)

THE WEST OF IRELAND

THE LOWER SHANNON

Adare Manor
Set in a large estate beside one of the prettiest villages in the country, this luxurious hotel occupies a magnificent Victorian Gothic mansion.
(See p294.)

CORK AND KERRY

Bantry House
The spacious library in this 18th-century house looks out on to the gardens. Many of the bedrooms enjoy superb views of Bantry Bay. (See pp160–61 and p291.)

Streeve Hill
This 18th-century dower house is a member of the Hidden Ireland group. A stay here gives access to the stunning gardens of Drenagh House, which include the hidden Moon Garden. (See p301.)

Hunter's Hotel
Cobbled courtyards, paddocks and a magnificent garden are only a few of the attractions of this friendly and comfortable inn. The building dates back to 1720, and is owned and run by the fourth generation of the Hunter family. (See p290.)

NORTHERN
IRELAND

THE
MIDLANDS

SOUTHEAST
IRELAND

Roundwood House
This fine, small Palladian house is set in chestnut and beech woods. The Slieve Bloom Mountains are close by and you can fish and play golf locally. The lovely rooms are filled with antiques, books and pictures and the atmosphere is one of relaxed informality. (See p299.)

| 0 kilometres | 50 |
| 0 miles | 25 |

Waterford Castle
The ultimate in "getting away from it all", this 15th-century castle sits on a beautifully located island in the estuary of the River Suir. The hotel is reachable only by its own private ferry. (See p291.)

Choosing a Hotel

THESE HOTELS have been selected across a wide price range for their good value, facilities and location; they are listed by region, starting with Dublin. Use the colour-coded thumb tabs, which indicate the regions covered on each page, to guide you to the relevant section of the chart. For Dublin map references see pages 110–11; for road map references see the inside back cover.

	CREDIT CARDS	CHILDREN'S FACILITIES	PARKING FACILITIES	RESTAURANT	PUBLIC BAR
DUBLIN					
SOUTHEAST DUBLIN: *Fitzwilliam Guest House* €€ 41 Fitzwilliam St Upper, Dublin 2. **Map** E5. **(** *01 660 0448.* **FAX** *01 676 7488.* A friendly, unpretentious guesthouse in an attractive Georgian street, with simple, elegant decor and comfortable bedrooms. **TV** *Rooms: 13*	MC V AE DC	●	■	●	
SOUTHEAST DUBLIN: *Kilronan House* W www.dublinn.com €€ 70 Adelaide Rd, Dublin 2. **(** *01 475 5266.* **FAX** *01 478 2841.* A small cosy guesthouse in a quiet street near St Stephen's Green. Delicious breakfasts. **TV** *Rooms: 15*	MC V AE	●	■		
SOUTHEAST DUBLIN: *Leeson Court* €€ 26 Leeson St Lower, Dublin 2. **Map** E5. **(** *01 676 3380.* **FAX** *01 661 8273.* Spread across two Georgian houses, this cheerfully decorated hotel has a relaxed, informal atmosphere and the service is good. St Stephen's Green is only a few minutes' walk away. **TV** *Rooms: 20*	MC V AE DC	●	■	●	■
SOUTHEAST DUBLIN: *Buswells* €€€ 25 Molesworth St, Dublin 2. **Map** E4. **(** *01 676 4013.* **FAX** *01 676 2090.* A short walk from Grafton Street, this smart, newly refurbished hotel is a listed Georgian building with a fine interior. **TV** *Rooms: 69*	MC V AE DC	●		●	■
SOUTHEAST DUBLIN: *Clarion Stephen's Hall* €€€ 14–17 Leeson St Lower, Dublin 2. **Map** E5. **(** *01 638 1111.* **FAX** *01 638 1122.* All the rooms are suites and represent good value for families who want smart, comfortable accommodation in the centre of the city near St Stephen's Green. There are cooking facilities in rooms. **TV** **&** *Rooms: 38*	MC V AE DC	●	■		
SOUTHEAST DUBLIN: *Georgian Hotel* €€€ 18 Baggot St Lower, Dublin 2. **Map** F5. **(** *01 634 5000.* **FAX** *01 634 5100.* A short walk from St Stephen's Green, this hotel is a good base for exploring Dublin. The bedrooms are large and comfortable and there's a good traditional restaurant in the basement. **TV** *Rooms: 75*	MC V AE DC	●	■	●	
SOUTHEAST DUBLIN: *Harcourt* €€€ 60 Harcourt St, Dublin 2. **Map** D5. **(** *01 478 3677.* **FAX** *01 475 2013.* Just off St Stephen's Green, this hotel is close to many of the city's main sights. The bedrooms are modern and well-equipped, there is a popular bar, a restaurant for evening meals and a nightclub. **TV** *Rooms: 106*	MC V AE DC	●		●	■
SOUTHEAST DUBLIN: *Russell Court* €€€ 21–25 Harcourt St, Dublin 2. **Map** D5. **(** *01 478 4066.* **FAX** *01 478 1576.* Jolly, welcoming hotel with young staff and a lively atmosphere in the evenings. There's a choice of bars and a more formal restaurant. Bedrooms are neat and well-equipped. **TV** *Rooms: 46*	MC V AE DC	●	■	●	■
SOUTHEAST DUBLIN: *Temple Bar Hotel* €€€ Fleet St, Temple Bar, Dublin 2. **Map** D3. **(** *01 677 3333.* **FAX** *01 677 3088.* This hotel, situated in a trendy area of Dublin, is a popular meeting place with its theme bar "Buskers" attracting a lively crowd. Bedrooms are comfortable but lack character. **TV** **&** *Rooms: 129*	MC V AE DC	●		●	■
SOUTHEAST DUBLIN: *Conrad Hotel* W www.conradhotels.com €€€€ Earlsfort Terrace, Dublin 2. **Map** D5. **(** *01 676 5555.* **FAX** *01 676 5424.* This international-style hotel by St Stephen's Green is geared to business people, but has a jolly pub with a large terrace. **TV** **&** *Rooms: 192*	MC V AE DC	●	■	●	■
SOUTHEAST DUBLIN: *Longfields* €€€€ 10 Fitzwilliam St Lower, Dublin 2. **Map** F5. **(** *01 676 1367.* **FAX** *01 67 61542.* Two Georgian town houses have been knocked together to create this stylish hotel with an attractive sitting room and smart, pretty bedrooms. There is a very good restaurant in the basement. **TV** *Rooms: 26*	MC V AE DC	●		●	

	Price & description		CREDIT CARDS	CHILDREN'S FACILITIES	PARKING FACILITIES	RESTAURANT	PUBLIC BAR

Price categories are for a standard double room (not per person) for one night, including tax, service charges and breakfast.
€ under 65 euros
€€ 65–130 euros
€€€ 130–190 euros
€€€€ 190–260 euros
€€€€€ over 260 euros

CHILDREN'S FACILITIES
Cots and high chairs are available and some hotels will also provide a baby-sitting service.

PARKING FACILITIES
Parking provided by the hotel in either a private car park or a private garage close by.

RESTAURANT
The hotel has a restaurant for residents which also welcomes non-residents – usually only for evening meals.

PUBLIC BAR
The hotel has a bar that is open to non-residents and residents alike.

SOUTHEAST DUBLIN: *Mont Clare* W www.ocallaghanhotels.ie €€€€
Merrion Square, Dublin 2. **Map** F4. (01 607 3800. **FAX** 01 661 5663.
Not as grand as the Davenport opposite, but with the same club-like feel. A busy, traditional pub takes up most of the ground floor. *Rooms: 80*
Credit Cards: MC V AE DC · Children's Facilities · Parking Facilities · Restaurant · Public Bar

SOUTHEAST DUBLIN: *Davenport* W www.ocallaghanhotels.ie €€€€€
Merrion Square, Dublin 2. **Map** F4. (01 607 3500. **FAX** 01 661 5663.
The grand proportions of the Neo-Classical façade are carried through into the lobby – a vast, marble-floored atrium. Opened in 1993, it is elegant and rather like a gentleman's club. *Rooms: 118*
Credit Cards: MC V AE DC · Children's Facilities · Parking Facilities · Restaurant

SOUTHEAST DUBLIN: *The Merrion* W www.merrionhotel.com €€€€€
Merrion Street Upper, Dublin 2. **Map** E4. (01 603 0600. **FAX** 01 603 0700.
This top-class hotel was created from four Georgian townhouses. Its elegant interior is full of antiques and it has an outstanding art collection. It is highly civilised and relaxing. *Rooms: 145*
Credit Cards: MC V AE DC · Children's Facilities · Restaurant · Public Bar

SOUTHEAST DUBLIN: *Shelbourne Hotel* W www.shelbourne.ie €€€€€
27 St Stephen's Green, Dublin 2. **Map** D4. (01 676 6471. **FAX** 01 661 6006.
The Shelbourne has been the city's most distinguished hotel since it opened in the 19th century. Although it has every facility for the business traveller, it retains a personal atmosphere. *Rooms: 190*
Credit Cards: MC V AE DC · Children's Facilities · Parking Facilities · Restaurant · Public Bar

SOUTHEAST DUBLIN: *Westbury Hotel* €€€€€
Grafton St, Dublin 2. **Map** D4. (01 679 1122. **FAX** 01 679 7078.
You couldn't get much closer to the centre of things than here, only seconds from Dublin's major shopping street. It is a smart, ritzy hotel decorated in traditional style. *Rooms: 204*
Credit Cards: MC V AE DC · Children's Facilities · Parking Facilities · Restaurant · Public Bar

SOUTHWEST DUBLIN: *Avalon House* W www.avalon-house.ie €
55 Aungier St, Dublin 2. **Map** C4. (01 475 0001. **FAX** 01 475 0303.
This cheap and cheerful accommodation has over 300 beds. It is centrally located and has clean bedrooms and a communal kitchen. *Rooms: 60*
Credit Cards: MC V AE DC

SOUTHWEST DUBLIN: *Jury's Christchurch Inn* W www.jurysdoyle.com €€
Christchurch Place, Dublin 8. **Map** B4. (01 454 0000. **FAX** 01 454 0012.
The Jury's group "inns" offer spruce modern facilities. This "inn", 15 minutes from St Stephen's Green, has a good bar and restaurant, and neat, well-equipped rooms at reasonable prices. *Rooms: 182*
Credit Cards: MC V AE DC · Children's Facilities · Restaurant · Public Bar

SOUTHWEST DUBLIN: *Blooms Hotel* W www.blooms.ie €€€
Anglesea St, Temple Bar, Dublin 2. **Map** D3. (01 671 5622. **FAX** 01 671 5997.
Situated near Trinity College, this modern hotel is very convenient for exploring, but its reception areas are slightly limited. *Rooms: 97*
Credit Cards: MC V AE DC · Restaurant · Public Bar

SOUTHWEST DUBLIN: *Central Hotel* W www.centralhotel.ie €€€
1–5 Exchequer St, Dublin 2. **Map** D5. (01 679 7302. **FAX** 01 679 7303.
As its name suggests, one of the great advantages of this hotel is its position. The Exchequer Bar has live music at the weekends, so choose your neat, functional bedroom carefully. *Rooms: 70*
Credit Cards: MC V AE DC · Children's Facilities · Restaurant · Public Bar

SOUTHWEST DUBLIN: *Grafton Capital Hotel* €€€€
Lower Stephen's Street, Dublin 2. **Map** D4. (01 475 0888. **FAX** 01 648 1122.
W www.capital-hotels.com
This neat hotel with a Georgian façade is neat and tastefully decorated throughout. Only a few minutes' walk from Grafton Street, it makes an excellent city base. *Rooms: 75*
Credit Cards: MC V AE DC · Children's Facilities · Restaurant · Public Bar

SOUTHWEST DUBLIN: *Clarence* W www.theclarence.ie €€€€€
6–8 Wellington Quay, Dublin 2. **Map** C3. (01 407 0800. **FAX** 01 407 0820.
The hotel is owned by the rock band U2 and has been completely refurbished. A stylish restaurant sets the standard for the rest of the hotel – one of the trendiest places to stay in town. *Rooms: 50*
Credit Cards: MC V AE DC · Children's Facilities · Parking Facilities · Restaurant · Public Bar

<table>
<tr><td colspan="2">

Price categories are for a standard double room (not per person) for one night, including tax, service charges and breakfast.
€ under 65 euros
€€ 65–130 euros
€€€ 130–190 euros
€€€€ 190–260 euros
€€€€€ over 260 euros

CHILDREN'S FACILITIES
Cots and high chairs are available and some hotels will also provide a baby-sitting service.
PARKING FACILITIES
Parking provided by the hotel in either a private car park or a private garage close by.
RESTAURANT
The hotel has a restaurant for residents which also welcomes non-residents – usually only for evening meals.
PUBLIC BAR
The hotel has a bar that is open to non-residents and residents alike.

</td></tr>
</table>

	CREDIT CARDS	CHILDREN'S FACILITIES	PARKING FACILITIES	RESTAURANT	PUBLIC BAR
NORTH OF THE LIFFEY: *Isaacs Hotel* W www.isaacs.ie €€ Store St, Dublin 1. **Map** E2. ☎ 01 855 0067. **FAX** 01 836 5390. Recently developed alongside an older hostel of the same name, the hotel is reasonably priced, well-run and centrally located. ⊟ TV ♿ *Rooms: 58*	MC V AE	●	●	●	●
NORTH OF THE LIFFEY: *Royal Dublin* W www.royaldublin.com €€€ 40–42 O'Connell St Upper, Dublin 1. **Map** D1. ☎ 01 873 3666. **FAX** 01 873 3120. Modern hotel in one of Dublin's most famous streets. It has well-equipped rooms and is smart, though lacking in atmosphere. ⊟ TV ♿ *Rooms: 117*	MC V AE DC	●	●	●	●
NORTH OF THE LIFFEY: *Gresham Hotel* W www.gresham-hotels.com €€€€€ 23 O'Connell St Upper, Dublin 1. **Map** D1. ☎ 01 874 6881. **FAX** 01 878 7175. One of Dublin's oldest and best known hotels. It is a popular rendezvous spot so the public areas are always busy. The bedrooms are comfortable and there is ample safe parking. ⊟ TV ♿ ▮ *Rooms: 288*	MC V AE DC	●	●	●	●
NORTH OF THE LIFFEY: *The Morrison* W www.morrisonhotel.ie €€€€€ Ormond Quay, Dublin 1. **Map** C3. ☎ 01 878 2999. **FAX** 01 878 3185. Built in 1999 with John Rocha as design consultant, this is the ultimate cool but comfortable hotel. ⊟ TV ▮▮ ♿ *Rooms: 95*	MC V AE DC	●	●	●	●
BALGRIFFIN: *Belcamp Hutchinson* W www.belcamphutchinson.com €€€ Carrs Lane, Malahide Rd, Balgriffin, Dublin 17. ☎ 01 846 0843. **FAX** 01 848 5703. Only ten minutes from the airport, a Georgian house on 20 acres of its own land. A comfortable, pleasant place to stay. ⊟ TV *Rooms: 8*	MC V		●		
BALLSBRIDGE: *Bewleys Hotel* W www.bewleyshotels.com €€ Merrion Road, Ballsbridge, Dublin 4. ☎ 01 668 1111. **FAX** 01 668 1999. This magnificent redbrick building used to be a school but is now part of the reliable Bewleys chain. It offers very good value for families. ⊟ TV ♿ *Rooms: 300*	MC V AE DC	●	●	●	
BALLSBRIDGE: *Glenogra Guesthouse* W www.glenogra.com €€ 64 Merrion Rd, Ballsbridge, Dublin 4. ☎ 01 668 3661. **FAX** 01 668 3698. Attractive, stylish guesthouse convenient for both Dun Laoghaire and the centre. The bedrooms are charming and very comfortable. ⊟ TV ⚡ *Rooms: 13*	MC V AE DC .	●	●		
BALLSBRIDGE: *Anglesea Town House* €€€ 63 Anglesea Rd, Dublin 4. ☎ 01 668 3877. **FAX** 01 668 3461. This Edwardian house is beautifully decorated and furnished. It has a lovely drawing room, very comfortable bedrooms and offers a superb breakfast – all within ten minutes' drive of the centre. ⊟ TV *Rooms: 6*	MC V AE	●	●		
BALLSBRIDGE: *Mount Herbert Hotel* W www.mountherberthotel.ie €€€ 7 Herbert Rd, Lansdowne Rd, Ballsbridge, Dublin 4. ☎ 01 668 4321. **FAX** 01 660 7077. A Victorian hotel close to Lansdowne Road stadium. The rooms are light with modern furnishings and it is reasonably priced. ⊟ TV ♿ *Rooms: 185*	MC V AE DC	●	●	●	●
BALLSBRIDGE: *Herbert Park Hotel* W www.herbertparkhotel.ie €€€€ Ballsbridge, Dublin 4. ☎ 01 667 2200. **FAX** 01 667 2595. This award-winning hotel adjoins Herbert Park, close to the RDS. Public areas are light and spacious. ⊟ TV ♿ ▮ *Rooms: 153*	MC V AE DC	●	●	●	
BALLSBRIDGE: *Hibernian* W www.hibernianhotel.com €€€€ Eastmoreland Place, Ballsbridge, Dublin 4. ☎ 01 668 7666. **FAX** 01 660 2655. Tucked away in a quiet street but close to the centre, this smart, comfortable hotel offers elegant, luxurious rooms. ⊟ TV ♿ *Rooms: 42*	MC V AE DC	●	●	●	●
BALLSBRIDGE: *Berkeley Court Hotel* W www.jurysdoyle.com €€€€€ Lansdowne Rd, Dublin 4. ☎ 01 660 1711. **FAX** 01 661 7238. The very smart lobby area sets the standard for this luxury hotel, which is well located for Lansdowne Road stadium. ⊟ TV ▮ ♿ *Rooms: 187*	MC V AE DC	●	●	●	●

BALLSBRIDGE: *Jury's Hotel & The Towers at Jury's* €€€€€ MC V AE DC
Pembroke Rd, Ballsbridge, Dublin 4. (01 660 5000. w www.jurysdoyle.com
A modern hotel, popular with business people and tourists, a short distance
from the centre with all the facilities you'd expect from a five-star hotel. The
adjacent Towers is the hotel's luxury wing. 🔲 TV 🍴 ≋ 🔲 *Rooms:* 400

BOOTERSTOWN: *Doyle Tara* w www.jurysdoyle.com €€€ MC V AE DC
Merrion Rd, Dublin 4. (01 269 4666. FAX 01 269 1027.
Conveniently situated for Dun Laoghaire, the hotel has recently undergone
refurbishment with a number of new rooms added. 🔲 TV 🔲 *Rooms:* 113

RATHMINES: *Clara House* €€ MC V
23 Leinster Rd, Rathmines, Dublin 6. (01 497 5904. FAX 01 497 5904.
In an attractive area, ten minutes' walk from the centre, this Georgian
house is a comfortable B&B with a friendly atmosphere. 🔲 TV *Rooms:* 13

SOUTHEAST IRELAND

BAGENALSTOWN: *Lorum Old Rectory* w www.lorum.com €€ MC V AE
Co Carlow. **Road map** D4. (059 977 5282. FAX 059 977 5455.
Set beneath the Blackstairs Mountains with a cosy atmosphere and log fires
and an inspired six-course dinner. Member of Hidden Ireland. 🔲 *Rooms:* 5

BALLYMACARBRY: *Clonanav Farm Guesthouse* €€ MC V AE DC
Clonmel, Co Waterford. **Road map** C5. (052 36141. FAX 052 36294.
A friendly welcome and lots of outdoor activities at this bungalow
farmhouse. A delicious full Irish breakfast is provided. 🔲 TV 🔲
Rooms: 14

BALLYMURN: *Ballinkeele House* w www.ballinkeele.com €€€ MC V AE
Enniscorthy, Co Wexford. **Road map** D5. (053 38105. FAX 053 38468.
The comfortable rooms overlook its parkland setting. Delicious dinners are
served in the original dining room. Member of Hidden Ireland. 🔲 *Rooms:* 5

BLESSINGTON: *Tulfarris Hotel and Golf Resort* w www.tulfarris.com €€€€ MC V AE DC
Blessington Lakes, Co Wicklow. **Road map** D4. (045 867555. FAX 045 867561.
In a lovely position overlooking Blessington Lake, the hotel offers stylish
comfort and lots of facilities. 🔲 TV ≋ *Rooms:* 80

CAPPOQUIN: *Richmond House* w www.richmondhouse.net €€€ MC V AE DC
Co Waterford. **Road map** C5. (058 54278. FAX 058 54988.
A delightful 18th-century, Georgian country house, charmingly decorated
and furnished with antiques, set in peaceful parkland. 🔲 TV *Rooms:* 9

CASTLEDERMOT: *Kilkea Lodge* €€ MC V AE
Co Kildare. **Road map** D4. (& FAX 059 914 5112.
This attractive house is popular with racegoers as the Curragh, Punchestown
and Naas are within easy reach. 🔲 *Rooms:* 5

CLONEA: *Clonea Strand Hotel* w www.clonea.com €€€ MC V AE DC
Dungarvan, Co Waterford. **Road map** C5. (058 42416. FAX 058 42880.
A large, modern resort hotel without huge charm but located next to a lovely
beach and with lots of facilities – great for families. 🔲 TV 🔲 *Rooms:* 59

DUNLAVIN: *Rathsallagh House* w www.rathsallagh.com €€€€ MC V AE DC
Dunlavin, Nr. Naas, Co. Wicklow. **Road map** D4 (045 403112. FAX 045 403343.
Open fires, comfortable furnishings, an excellent restaurant and a relaxed
atmosphere, make this large country house 15 miles outside Naas a great
place to stay. Closed January. 🔲 TV 🔲 *Rooms:* 29

DUNMORE EAST: *Church Villa* €
Co Waterford. **Road map** D5. (051 383390. FAX 051 383023.
Situated in the village, this attractive house offers excellent-value, simple
B&B. Very friendly owners and neat, comfortable bedrooms. 🔲 TV *Rooms:* 6

ENNISCORTHY: *Salville House* €€
Enniscorthy, Co Wexford. **Road map** D5. (& FAX 054 35252.
Spacious rooms with huge windows give views over wooded countryside.
Delicious breakfasts. Dinner available if pre-booked. 🔲 *Rooms:* 5

INISTIOGE: *Cullintra House* w indigo.ie/~cullhse €€
The Rower, Inistioge, Co Kilkenny. **Road map** D5. (051 423614.
An attractive farmhouse set in beautiful scenery with woods and farmland all
around. It is a very cosy place with log fires. Dinner available. 🔲 *Rooms:* 6

		Price categories			CREDIT CARDS	CHILDREN'S FACILITIES	PARKING FACILITIES	RESTAURANT	PUBLIC BAR

Price categories are for a standard double room (not per person) for one night, including tax, service charges and breakfast.
€ under 65 euros
€€ 65–130 euros
€€€ 130–190 euros
€€€€ 190–260 euros
€€€€€ over 260 euros

CHILDREN'S FACILITIES
Cots and high chairs are available and some hotels will also provide a baby-sitting service.

PARKING FACILITIES
Parking provided by the hotel in either a private car park or a private garage close by.

RESTAURANT
The hotel has a restaurant for residents which also welcomes non-residents – usually only for evening meals.

PUBLIC BAR
The hotel has a bar that is open to non-residents and residents alike.

KILKENNY: Lacken House ⓦ www.lackenhouse.ie €€
Dublin Rd, Kilkenny, Co Kilkenny. **Road map** C4. ☎ 056 776 1085. FAX 056 776 2435.
Only five minutes walk from the city centre, this Victorian house is a very comfortable place to stay with a highly regarded restaurant. 🚗 TV ♿
Rooms: 11
Credit cards: MC V AE · Children's Facilities ● · Parking Facilities ■ · Restaurant ● · Public Bar ■

KILKENNY: Butler House ⓦ www.butler.ie €€€
16 Patrick St, Kilkenny, Co Kilkenny. **Road map** C4. ☎ 056 776 5707. FAX 056 776 5626.
The former dower house of Kilkenny Castle right in the heart of town has been restored by the Civic Trust. The 18th-century building has fine proportions and is stylishly decorated throughout. 🚗 TV *Rooms: 13*
Credit cards: MC V AE DC · Children's Facilities ● · Parking Facilities ■

MACREDDIN VILLAGE: The BrookLodge ⓦ www.brooklodge.com €€€€
Macreddin Village, Co. Wicklow. **Road map** D4. ☎ 0402 36444. FAX 0402 36580.
This is a new hotel in a new village in the middle of the Wicklow countryside. Evan Doyle of The Strawberry Tree restaurant in Killarney has masterminded the project and the restaurant has relocated here.
🚗 TV ♿ *Rooms: 40*
Credit cards: MC V AE DC · Children's Facilities ● · Parking Facilities ■ · Restaurant ● · Public Bar ■

RATHASPECK: Rathaspeck Manor ⓦ www.iol.ie/ecuddiny €€
Co Wexford. **Road map** D5. ☎ 053 42661/45148.
This 300-year-old Georgian manor has an 18-hole, par three golf course and a tennis court. Offering B&B only, the bedrooms are large and comfortable and the breakfast excellent. 🚗 TV *Rooms: 6*
Parking Facilities ■

RATHNEW: Hunter's Hotel ⓦ www.hunters.ie €€€
Co Wicklow. **Road map** D4. ☎ 0404 40106. FAX 0404 40338.
This inn on the old Dublin coaching road dates from 1720 and is run by the fifth generation of the Hunter family. It is a very relaxing place to stay with delicious food and a lovely garden. 🚗 TV ♿ *Rooms: 16*
Credit cards: MC V AE DC · Children's Facilities ● · Parking Facilities ■ · Restaurant ● · Public Bar ■

RATHNEW: Tinakilly House, Hotel and Restaurant €€€€
Co Wicklow. **Road map** D4. ☎ 0404 69274. FAX 0404 67806. ⓦ www.tinakilly.ie
The many outstanding features of this Victorian house include lovely views over the coast and large, attractive gardens. Comfort is assured with a mix of antiques and modern facilities. 🚗 TV ♿ *Rooms: 51*
Credit cards: MC V AE DC · Children's Facilities ● · Parking Facilities ■ · Restaurant ● · Public Bar ■

ROSSLARE: Kelly's Resort Hotel ⓦ www.kellys.ie €€€
Co Wexford. **Road map** D5. ☎ 053 32114. FAX 053 32222.
This hotel on the beach is ideal for families who don't mind any lack of character but want lots of leisure and sports facilities. 🚗 TV 🏊 ♿
Rooms: 99
Credit cards: MC V AE · Children's Facilities ● · Parking Facilities ■ · Restaurant ● · Public Bar ■

STRAFFAN: Kildare Hotel & Country Club ⓦ www.kclub.ie €€€€€
Co Kildare. **Road map** D4. ☎ 01 627 3333. FAX 01 601 7299.
Parts of this exclusive hotel building date back to the 17th century. As well as luxurious bedrooms and a grand drawing room, it boasts a one-star Michelin restaurant, The Byerley Turk. Facilities include a championship golf course and extensive fishing. 🚗 TV 🏊 ♿ *Rooms: 79*
Credit cards: MC V AE DC · Children's Facilities ● · Parking Facilities ■ · Restaurant ● · Public Bar ■

THOMASTOWN: Mount Juliet Conrad €€€€
Co Kilkenny. **Road map** D5. ☎ 056 772 4455. ⓦ www.mountjuliet.com
One of Ireland's luxury hotels but retaining the character and style of a grand family house. Set in an estate of over 450 ha (1,100 acres) with lots of sports facilities including an 18-hole golf course. 🚗 TV 🏊 ♿
Rooms: 59
Credit cards: MC V AE DC · Children's Facilities ● · Parking Facilities ■ · Restaurant ● · Public Bar ■

WATERFORD: Foxmount Country House €€
Passage East Rd, off Dunmore Rd, Waterford, Co Waterford. **Road map** D5.
☎ 051 874308. FAX 051 854906. ⓦ www.iol.ie/tipp/foxmount.htm
An attractive, 17th-century house, full of antiques and personality. The atmosphere is homely and you can bring your own wine to dinner. 🚗 *Rooms: 5*
Parking Facilities ■

WATERFORD: *Waterford Castle Hotel* €€€€€
The Island, Ballinakill, Waterford, Co Waterford. **Road map** D5.
051 878203. FAX 051 879316. www.waterfordcastle.com
Guests are ferried across the river to this romantically sited, 15th-century castle. Log fires blaze in lofty rooms and both the large suites and the smaller cosy bedrooms are truly luxurious. TV *Rooms: 19*
MC V AE DC

WEXFORD: *Newbay Country House Hotel* €€
Newbay, Wexford, Co Wexford. **Road map** D5. 053 42779. FAX 053 46318.
Part Georgian and part early Victorian, the house feels very much like a private home and guests are given a great welcome. It is a very comfortable and relaxing hotel with peat fires and interesting antiques. TV *Rooms: 14*
MC V AE DC

WEXFORD: *White's Hotel* www.whiteshotel.ie €€
George St, Wexford, Co Wexford. **Road map** D5. 053 22311. FAX 053 45000.
Centrally located, this former coaching inn is neat and reasonably comfortable with a gothic-style restaurant. There is also a fitness and leisure centre with gym and solarium. TV *Rooms: 82*
MC V AE DC

CORK AND KERRY

BALLINADEE: *Glebe Country House* €€
Bandon, Co Cork. **Road map** B6. 021 477 8294. FAX 021 477 8456.
Only ten minutes from Kinsale with lots of sports opportunities close by, this attractive Georgian rectory is beautifully furnished and makes a great base for the area. Book by noon if you want dinner. *Rooms: 4*
MC V

BALLYLICKEY: *Ballylickey Manor House* €€€€
Bantry Bay, Co Cork. **Road map** B6. 027 50071. www.ballylickeymanorhouse.com
A 17th-century shooting lodge which has been completely refurbished over recent years. It's an attractive place to stay with lovely, comfortable rooms and delicious food. TV *Rooms: 14*
MC V AE DC

BANTRY: *Bantry House* €€€€
Co Cork. **Road map** B6. 027 50047. FAX 027 50795.
An outstanding, 18th-century, stately home *(see pp160–61)*, open to the public since 1946 and a member of the Hidden Ireland Group. It has a fine collection of pictures, furniture and works of art. The comfortable bedrooms have *en suite* bathrooms. Open March to October. *Rooms: 8*
MC V

CARAGH LAKE: *Caragh Lodge* www.caraghlodge.com €€€
Co Kerry. **Road map** A5. 066 976 9115. FAX 066 976 9316.
Colonial-style fishing lodge in magnificent, award-winning gardens bordering the lake. All rooms are neatly decorated and furnished with antique furniture. Open mid-April to mid-October. *Rooms: 15*
MC V AE DC

CARAGH LAKE: *Ard-na-Sidhe* €€€€
Co Kerry. **Road map** A5. 066 976 9105. FAX 066 976 9282.
This attractive Victorian mansion enjoys a wonderfully peaceful setting beside the lake. The ambience is somewhat old-fashioned, reinforced by the neat period furnishings. Open May to September. *Rooms: 20*
MC V AE DC

CASTLELYONS: *Ballyvolane House* €€€
Co Cork. **Road map** B6. 025 36349. FAX 025 36781.
A lovely 18th & 19th-century house surrounded by very attractive gardens and parkland. All of the large rooms have a view and are very comfortable, furnished with the family antiques. Fishing available. *Rooms: 6*
MC V AE DC

CLONAKILTY: *O'Donovan's Hotel* www.odonovanhotel.com €€
Co Cork. **Road map** B6. & FAX 023 33250.
A traditional, centrally located, family-run hotel in the old commercial mould with unremarkable decor but a very friendly welcome. TV *Rooms: 21*
MC V AE

CORK: *Jury's Cork Inn* www.jurysdoyle.com €€
Anderson's Quay, Cork, Co Cork. **Road map** C5. 021 427 6444. FAX 021 427 6144.
A fixed room-rate hotel with modern, attractive furnishings and good facilities at reasonable prices – ideal for families. TV *Rooms: 133*
MC V AE DC

CORK: *Lotamore House* www.lotamorehouse.com €€
Tivoli, Cork, Co Cork. **Road map** C5. 021 482 2344. FAX 021 482 2219.
This Georgian Manor converted into a guesthouse is surrounded by lovely grounds with good views of the harbour and Blackrock Castle. Five minutes' drive from the city centre. TV *Rooms: 20*
MC V AE

For key to symbols see back flap

Price categories are for a standard double room (not per person) for one night, including tax, service charges and breakfast.
€ under 65 euros
€€ 65–130 euros
€€€ 130–190 euros
€€€€ 190–260 euros
€€€€€ over 260 euros

CHILDREN'S FACILITIES
Cots and high chairs are available and some hotels will also provide a baby-sitting service.
PARKING FACILITIES
Parking provided by the hotel in either a private car park or a private garage close by.
RESTAURANT
The hotel has a restaurant for residents which also welcomes non-residents – usually only for evening meals.
PUBLIC BAR
The hotel has a bar that is open to non-residents and residents alike.

	CREDIT CARDS	CHILDREN'S FACILITIES	PARKING FACILITIES	RESTAURANT	PUBLIC BAR
CORK: *Seven North Mall* W www.sevennorthmall.com €€ 7 North Mall, Cork, Co Cork. **Road map** C5. 📞 021 439 7191. FAX 021 430 0811. This smart 18th-century house overlooks the River Lee and is a convenient base for exploring the city and surrounding areas. 🚗 TV ♿ **Rooms:** 7	MC V		■		
COURTMACSHERRY: *Travara Lodge* € Courtmacsherry, Co Cork. **Road map** C5. 📞 023 46493. Sea views from some of the rooms in this comfortable, house. Simple and extremely tasty food served in the small restaurant. 🚗 ♿ **Rooms:** 6	MC V		■	●	
DINGLE: *Doyle's Seafood Bar and Townhouse* W www.doylesofdingle.com €€ John St, Dingle, Co Kerry. **Road map** A5. 📞 066 915 1174. FAX 066 915 1816. Famous for its delicious seafood, Doyle's also provides first-class accommodation. Smart and stylish bedrooms with luxurious bathrooms and an attractive sitting room. Informal, relaxed atmosphere. 🚗 TV **Rooms:** 8	MC V AE				
DINGLE: *Benners Hotel* €€€€ Main St, Dingle, Co Kerry. **Road map** A5. 📞 066 915 1638. FAX 066 915 1412. American-owned hotel right in the centre of town. The old building has been converted to provide an efficient hotel with a choice of bars, a restaurant and comfortable bedrooms. 🚗 TV **Rooms:** 52	MC V AE DC	●	■	●	■
INISHANNON: *Inishannon House Hotel* W www.inishannonhouse.ie €€ Co Cork. **Road map** B6. 📞 021 477 5121. FAX 021 477 5609. This 18th-century house is very romantic with lovely gardens and parkland leading down to the River Bandon. The bedrooms are individual both in shape and decor. 🚗 TV **Rooms:** 17	MC V AE DC	●	■	●	■
KANTURK: *Assolas Country House* W www.assolas.com €€€ Co Cork. **Road map** B5. 📞 029 50015. FAX 029 50795. An elegant, 17th-century house, with cosy decor and an excellent restaurant. Open mid-March to November. 🚗 **Rooms:** 9	MC V	●	■	●	
KENMARE: *Park Hotel* W www.parkkenmare.com €€€€€ Co Kerry. **Road map** B5. 📞 064 41200. FAX 064 41402. Built in 1897 in a stunning setting by Kenmare Bay, the Park is rated one of Ireland's finest hotels, luxurious with an individual style and lots of original touches. The facilities include an 18-hole golf course. Open mid-April to November, Christmas and New Year. 🚗 TV **Rooms:** 46	MC V AE DC	●	■	●	■
KENMARE: *Sheen Falls Lodge* W www.sheenfallslodge.ie €€€€€ Co Kerry. **Road map** B5. 📞 064 41600. FAX 064 41386. The new hotel blends in well with the original 17th-century house. Luxurious, spacious bedrooms with great views over the falls or the huge grounds. Closed January. 🚗 TV ♿ **Rooms:** 66	MC V AE DC	●	■	●	■
KILLARNEY: *Dunloe Castle Hotel* W www.killarneyhotels.ie €€€€ Co Kerry. **Road map** B5. 📞 064 44111. FAX 064 44583. A member of the Historic Castles and Gardens Association. The modern buildings are in lovely grounds by the ruins of the 13th-century castle. Excellent facilities. Open April to September. 🚗 TV ♨ ♿ **Rooms:** 102	MC V AE DC	●	■	●	■
KILLARNEY: *Hotel Europe* W www.killarneyhotels.ie €€€€ Co Kerry. **Road map** B5. 📞 064 31900. FAX 064 32118. Huge five-star resort hotel with stunning views of the Lakes of Killarney and the mountains, with every facility from beauty salon to 25 metres pool and lots of outdoor sports. Open March to October. 🚗 TV ♨ ♿ **Rooms:** 206	MC V AE DC	●	■	●	■
KILLARNEY: *Killarney Park Hotel* W www.killarneyparkhotel.ie €€€€€ Kenmare Place, Killarney, Co Kerry. **Road map** B5. 📞 064 35555. FAX 064 35266. This tasteful, modern hotel is conveniently located in the centre of town. It also has a fully equipped leisure centre. 🚗 TV ♿ ♨ **Rooms:** 71	MC V AE	●	■	●	■

KILLARNEY: *Killarney Royal Hotel* w www.killarneyroyal.ie €€€€€
College St, Killarney, Co Kerry. **Road map** B5. 064 31853. **FAX** 064 34001.
A short walk from the centre of town, this traditional hotel is a smart,
comfortable place to stay. TV Rooms: 29
MC V AE DC

KILLEAGH: *Ballymakeigh House* €€€
Youghal, Co Cork. **Road map** C5. 024 95184. **FAX** 024 95370.
This attractive 18th-century farmhouse is a comfortable, reasonably priced
base from which to explore the area. It offers cosy bedrooms and good,
home-cooked food. Rooms: 7
MC V

KINSALE: *The Blue Haven* w www.bluehavenkinsale.com €€€
3–4 Pearse St, Kinsale, Co Cork. **Road map** B6. 021 477 2209. **FAX** 021 477 4268.
Attractive, small hotel right in the centre of Kinsale, built on the site of
the old fish market. It is smart throughout and has a very popular
restaurant. TV Rooms: 17
MC V AE DC

KINSALE: *Old Bank House* w www.oldbankhousekinsale.com €€€
11 Pearse St, Kinsale, Co Cork. **Road map** B6. 021 477 4075. **FAX** 021 477 4296.
Right in the centre of town, the Old Bank House used to be a branch of
the Munster and Leinster Bank. A listed Georgian building, it has finely
proportioned, comfortable rooms and excellent staff. TV Rooms: 17
MC V AE

KINSALE: *Old Presbytery* w www.oldpres.com €€€
43 Cork St, Kinsale, Co Cork. **Road map** B6. 021 477 2027. **FAX** 021 477 2166.
A comfortable, relaxing place to stay in a quiet street in the town centre.
Bedrooms are simple but stylish, furnished mainly with Victorian pieces.
Closed Dec–Jan. TV Rooms: 6
MC V AE

KINSALE: *Sovereign House* w www.sovereignhouse.com €€€
Newman's Mall, Kinsale, Co Cork. **Road map** B6. 021 477 2850. **FAX** 021 477 4728.
This comfortable small hotel, in the old heart of Kinsale, has a Queen
Anne exterior and an interior full of Jacobean furniture. Three of the
rooms have four-poster beds. TV Rooms: 4
MC V

MALLOW: *Longueville House* €€€€
Co Cork. **Road map** B5. 022 47156. **FAX** 022 47459. w www.longuevillehouse.ie
The main part of the house is Georgian; the rooms are elegant and
individually decorated, many with huge old-style beds. The hotel's
Presidents' Restaurant has won a number of awards. TV Rooms: 20
MC V AE DC

PARKNASILLA: *Great Southern Hotel* w www.gshotels.com €€€
Sneem, Co Kerry. **Road map** A6. 064 45122. **FAX** 064 45323.
Set in acres of sub-tropical gardens, the main building is Victorian.
Leisure and conference facilities have been added, including a 9-hole golf
course. All the rooms are smartly co-ordinated. TV Rooms: 83
MC V AE DC

SHANAGARRY: *Ballymaloe House* w www.ballymaloe.com €€€€
Midleton, Co Cork. **Road map** C6. 021 465 2531. **FAX** 021 465 2021.
This has become one of the most famous country house hotels in
Ireland. It is not only a charming farmhouse with plenty of places to
relax, but is also the home of the famous Tim and Darina Allen cookery
school, and one of Ireland's best restaurants. Rooms: 32
MC V AE DC

TAHILLA: *Tahilla Cove Country House* w www.tahillacove.com €€
Nr Sneem, Co Kerry. **Road map** A6. 064 45204. **FAX** 064 45104.
A friendly guesthouse spread over two houses and set in lovely gardens.
Views from the rooms are either of the sea or mountains. The bar is open
to non-residents and is a great focus of hospitality. TV Rooms: 9
MC V AE

WATERVILLE: *The Smugglers' Inn* w www.welcome.to/thesmugglersinn.ie €€
Cliff Rd, Waterville, Co Kerry. **Road map** A6. 066 947 4330. **FAX** 066 947 4422.
A 100-year-old, modernized, whitewashed inn on the Ring of Kerry right
next door to Waterville championship golf course and overlooking a fine
sandy beach. It is an unpretentious, jolly place with comfortable
bedrooms, friendly bar and good restaurant. TV Rooms: 17
MC V AE DC

YOUGHAL: *Aherne's Seafood Restaurant* w www.ahernes.com €€€
163 North Main St, Youghal, Co Cork. **Road map** C5. 024 92424. **FAX** 024 93633.
Aherne's is run by the third generation of the Fitzgibbon family. The
outstanding reputation of this place is due as much to the family's
incredible hospitality and friendliness as it is to the delicious food and
luxuriously appointed bedrooms. TV Rooms: 13
MC V AE DC

For key to symbols see back flap

| | | CREDIT CARDS | CHILDREN'S FACILITIES | PARKING FACILITIES | RESTAURANT | PUBLIC BAR |

Price categories are for a standard double room (not per person) for one night, including tax, service charges and breakfast.

€ under 65 euros
€€ 65–130 euros
€€€ 130–190 euros
€€€€ 190–260 euros
€€€€€ over 260 euros

CHILDREN'S FACILITIES
Cots and high chairs are available and some hotels will also provide a baby-sitting service.

PARKING FACILITIES
Parking provided by the hotel in either a private car park or a private garage close by.

RESTAURANT
The hotel has a restaurant for residents which also welcomes non-residents – usually only for evening meals.

PUBLIC BAR
The hotel has a bar that is open to non-residents and residents alike.

THE LOWER SHANNON

	Credit Cards	Children's Facilities	Parking Facilities	Restaurant	Public Bar
ADARE: *Dunraven Arms* W www.dunravenhotel.com €€€€ Co Limerick. **Road map** B5. 061 396633. FAX 061 396541. Set in the extremely pretty village of Adare, this inn was established in 1792 and is a great touring base for the southwest. The bedrooms are luxurious and the restaurant is outstanding. TV *Rooms: 74*	MC V AE DC	●	▪	●	▪
ADARE: *Adare Manor* W www.adaremanor.com €€€€€ Co Limerick. **Road map** B5. 061 396566. FAX 061 396124. This huge, Victorian-Gothic mansion was the former seat of the Earls of Dunraven. Built in 1720, it was enhanced and enlarged in the 19th century. It's both tasteful and luxurious throughout. TV *Rooms: 138*	MC V AE DC	●	▪	●	▪
AGLISH: *Ballycormac House* W www.ballyc.com €€ Borrisokane, Co Tipperary. **Road map** C4. 067 21129. FAX 067 21200. Located in a quiet rural setting this cosy, 300-year-old house has a relaxed, informal atmosphere with lots of activities on offer, including riding and golf. Dinner is by reservation only. TV *Rooms: 5*	MC V	●	▪		
AHERLOW: *Aherlow House* W www.aherlowhouse.com €€€ Glen of Aherlow, Co Tipperary. **Road map** C5. 062 56153. FAX 062 56212. Set in the middle of a pine forest with a view of the mountains, this is a comfortable and welcoming hunting lodge. TV *Rooms: 29*	MC V AE	●	▪	●	
BALLYVAUGHAN: *Hylands* W www.hylandburren.com €€ Co Clare. **Road map** B4. 065 707 7037. FAX 065 707 7131. Dating back to the 18th century, this family-run hotel is traditional in style, with simple but pretty bedrooms. Irish music in the bar. TV *Rooms: 30*	MC V AE DC	●	▪	●	▪
BALLYVAUGHAN: *Gregans Castle Hotel* W www.gregans.ie €€€€ Co Clare. **Road map** B4. 065 707 7005. FAX 065 707 7111. This is a marvellous hotel in the middle of the Burren, with views towards Galway Bay. Open April to October. *Rooms: 22*	MC V AE	●	▪	●	
BUNRATTY: *Bunratty Castle Hotel* W www.bunrattycastlehotel.com €€€ Co Clare. **Road map** B4. 061 478700. FAX 061 364891. This Georgian hotel is situated in its own grounds opposite Bunratty Castle. It has been fully modernised inside. TV *Rooms: 79*	MC V AE DC	●	▪	●	▪
CASHEL: *Legends Townhouse & Restaurant* €€ Co Tipperary. **Road map** C5. 062 61292. W www.legendsguesthouse.com This small townhouse and restaurant is just beside the great Rock of Cashel and has great views from both the bedrooms and the dining room. Bedrooms are simply furnished with good bathrooms. Open all year except two weeks in February and November. *Rooms: 7*	MC V	●	▪	●	
CASHEL: *Cashel Palace Hotel* W www.cashel-palace.ie €€€€ Main St, Cashel, Co Tipperary. **Road map** C5. 062 62707. FAX 062 61521. Beautiful Palladian house originally built as an archbishop's palace in the 1730s. Right in the centre of town but surrounded by a peaceful garden, it is an extremely civilized place to stay. TV *Rooms: 23*	MC V AE DC	●	▪	●	▪
CLARECASTLE: *Carnelly House* W www.carnelly-house.com €€€€ Co Clare. **Road map** B4. 065 682 8442. FAX 065 682 9222. A lovely Queen Anne house designed by Francis Bindon and set in delightful grounds. A member of Hidden Ireland, it is elegantly and tastefully furnished and has a relaxed atmosphere. TV *Rooms: 5*	MC V AE		▪		
CLONMEL: *Clonmel Arms Hotel* W www.clonmelarmshotel.com €€ Sarsfield St, Clonmel, Co Tipperary. **Road map** C5. 052 21233. FAX 052 21526. A predictable but comfortable central hotel. The bars and restaurants are popular with the locals. Particularly helpful staff. TV *Rooms: 30*	MC V AE DC	●	▪	●	▪

GLIN: *Glin Castle* W www.glincastle.com €€€€€
Co Limerick. **Road map** B5. (068 34173. FAX 068 34364.
Built in the 1780s, this magnificent yet intimate building owned by the Knight of Glin is surrounded by formal gardens. It is also a member of Ireland's Blue Book (*see p176*). **Rooms:** *15*
Credit cards: MC V AE DC

KILNABOY: *Fergus View* €
Corrofin, Co Clare. **Road map** B4. (065 683 7606. FAX 065 683 7192.
Very good-value, friendly guesthouse and a useful base for exploring the Burren. Recently refurbished, it is pristine and comfortable. Dinner is available Monday to Thursday, but only if pre-booked. **Rooms:** *6*

LIMERICK: *Jury's Hotel* W www.jurysdoyle.com €€€
Ennis Rd, Limerick, Co Limerick. **Road map** B4. (061 327777. FAX 061 326400.
Reliable part of the Jury's chain with good quality furnishings and dependable service. Lovely location in 2 ha (5 acres) of gardens on the banks of the River Shannon. **Rooms:** *98*
Credit cards: MC V AE DC

LIMERICK: *Woodfield House* W www.woodfieldhousehotel.com €€€
Ennis Rd, Limerick, Co Limerick. **Road map** B4. (061 453022. FAX 061 326755.
This traditional hotel has a friendly, informal family atmosphere. The bedrooms are smartly co-ordinated and well-equipped. **Rooms:** *26*
Credit cards: MC V AE DC

LISDOONVARNA: *Sheedy's Country House Hotel* €€€
Co Clare. **Road map** B4. (065 707 4026. W www.sheedys.com
This house has been in the Sheedy family for five generations and has now been converted into a very comfortable, efficient hotel by the present owners. **Rooms:** *11*
Credit cards: MC V AE

LISMACUE: *Lismacue House* W www.lismacue.com €€€
Bansha, Co Tipperary. **Road map** C5. (062 54106. FAX 062 54055.
The house is part of the Hidden Ireland group. It is a classically beautiful, Irish country house built at the beginning of the 19th century; it has particularly fine reception rooms and comfortable bedrooms. **Rooms:** *5*
Credit cards: MC V AE

NEWMARKET-ON-FERGUS: *Dromoland Castle* €€€€€
Co Clare. **Road map** B4. (061 368144. FAX 061 363355. W www.dromoland.ie
Sister hotel to Ashford Castle in Cong, you can expect a high standard of luxury here, too. The castle dates back to the 16th century and has a fascinating history and acres of grounds. **Rooms:** *100*
Credit cards: MC V AE DC

THE WEST OF IRELAND

BALINA: *Teach Iorrais* W www.teachiorrais.com €€
Geesala, Ballina, Co Mayo. **Road map** B2. (097 86888. FAX 097 86855.
This small and functional modern hotel (opened 1999) in the Gaeltacht has good value rooms and excellent facilities that include conference and banqueting. The hotel has its own garden and offers good fishing and walking nearby. **Rooms:** *31*
Credit cards: MC V AE

BALLYNAHINCH: *Ballynahinch Castle Hotel* €€€€
Recess, Connemara, Co Galway. **Road map** A3. (095 31006. FAX 095 31085.
W www.ballynahinch-castle.com
A magnificent castle, once owned by a maharajah, in a superb location. The hotel is well-run, and friendly. There is an excellent restaurant and lots of sporting possibilities. Closed Christmas and February. **Rooms:** *40*
Credit cards: MC V AE DC

CASHEL BAY: *Zetland House* W www.zetland.com €€€€
Connemara, Co Galway. **Road map** A3. (095 31111. FAX 095 31117.
A stylishly decorated, 19th-century shooting lodge. Set on the edge of Cashel Bay in lovely gardens, most of the bedrooms and the dining room share the superb views. Open February to November. **Rooms:** *19*
Credit cards: MC V AE DC

CASHEL BAY: *Cashel House* W www.cashel-house-hotel.com €€€€€
Connemara, Co Galway. **Road map** A3. (095 31001. FAX 095 31077.
In a stunning position at the head of Cashel Bay, this is a hotel with comfortable, relaxing rooms, full of interesting antiques. Closed January. **Rooms:** *32*
Credit cards: MC V AE

CLIFDEN: *Erriseask House* W www.erriseask.com €€
Ballyconneely, Connemara, Co Galway. **Road map** A3. (095 23553. FAX 095 23639.
This modern farmhouse is stylishly decorated, with light, comfortable bedrooms. It's set in a beautiful spot, only a short walk away from the sea and the food is superb. **Rooms:** *12*
Credit cards: MC V AE DC

For key to symbols see back flap

Price categories are for a standard double room (not per person) for one night, including tax, service charges and breakfast.

€ under 65 euros
€€ 65–130 euros
€€€ 130–190 euros
€€€€ 190–260 euros
€€€€€ over 260 euros

CHILDREN'S FACILITIES
Cots and high chairs are available and some hotels will also provide a baby-sitting service.

PARKING FACILITIES
Parking provided by the hotel in either a private car park or a private garage close by.

RESTAURANT
The hotel has a restaurant for residents which also welcomes non-residents – usually only for evening meals.

PUBLIC BAR
The hotel has a bar that is open to non-residents and residents alike.

	Credit Cards	Children's Facilities	Parking Facilities	Restaurant	Public Bar
CLIFDEN: *Ardagh Hotel & Restaurant* W www.commerce.ie/ardaghhotel €€€ Connemara, Co Galway. Road map A3. 095 21384. FAX 095 21314. Many rooms at this modern, chalet-style hotel look out onto Ardbear Bay. The gardens are beautiful. Open April to October. TV *Rooms: 21*	MC V AE DC	●	■	●	■
CLIFDEN: *Rock Glen Country House Hotel* €€€€ Connemara, Co Galway. Road map A3. 095 21035. FAX 095 21737. This traditional hotel used to be a shooting lodge for Clifden Castle. Comfortable rooms and reliable, friendly service. Open mid-February to October. TV *Rooms: 26*	MC V AE	●	■		
CONG: *Ashford Castle* W www.ashford.ie €€€€€ Co Mayo. Road map B3. 092 954 6003. FAX 092 954 6260. A mixture of 13th-century and Gothic Revival, this magnificent castle is set on the shore of Lough Corrib. Rich wall-to-wall carpeting kills a lot of the historical atmosphere, but it is undoubtedly luxurious. TV *Rooms: 83*	MC V AE DC	●	■		
CROSSMOLINA: *Enniscoe House* W www.enniscoe.com €€€ Castlehill, Nr Crossmolina, Ballina, Co Mayo. Road map B2. 096 31112. FAX 096 31773. This fine Georgian house, set in magnificent grounds which lead down to Lough Conn, is full of beautiful antiques and has a relaxed, lived-in feel with attractive bedrooms and good food. Member of Hidden Ireland. *Rooms: 6*	MC V AE	●	■		
GALWAY: *Brennan's Yard Hotel* W www.brennansyardhotel.com €€€ Lower Merchant's Rd, Galway, Co Galway. Road map B4. 091 568166. FAX 091 568262. Converted from a stone warehouse, and now decked with designer fabrics and Irish art, it offers comfortable rooms with city views. TV *Rooms: 45*	MC V AE DC	●	■	●	■
GALWAY: *Ardilaun House* W www.ardilaunhousehotel.ie €€€€ Taylor's Hill, Galway, Co Galway. Road map B4. 091 521433. FAX 091 521546. A short distance from the city centre and quite close to Salthill, this hotel is popular with business people and tourists. Smart decor, friendly, efficient service and comfortable rooms. TV *Rooms: 89*	MC V AE DC	●	■		
GALWAY: *Great Southern Hotel* W www.gshotels.com €€€€€ Eyre Sq, Galway, Co Galway. Road map B4. 091 564041. FAX 091 566704. The rooftop swimming pool is an unusual feature of this large and rambling Victorian hotel in the heart of the city. The rooms are comfortable and there are plenty of facilities. TV *Rooms: 99*	MC V AE DC	●	■	●	■
KNOCKFERRY: *Knockferry Lodge* W www.knockferrylodge.com € Roscahill, Co Galway. Road map B3. 091 550122. FAX 091 550328. Situated in a tranquil spot on the western shore of Lough Corrib; the prices reflect the simple accommodation with plain decor and furnishings. The atmosphere is very friendly and the food good. *Rooms: 10*	MC V AE DC	●			
LEENANE: *Delphi Lodge* W www.delphilodge.ie €€€ Co Galway. Road map B3. 095 42222. FAX 095 42296. A sporting lodge in a lovely setting by a lough surrounded by mountains. Informal atmosphere with plenty of fishing on the loughs and River Delphi. A member of Hidden Ireland. Open Feb to mid-Dec. *Rooms: 12*	MC V AE		■		
LETTERFRACK: *Rosleague Manor House* W www.rosleague.com €€€€ Connemara, Co Galway. Road map A3. 095 41101. FAX 095 41168. A substantial Georgian house overlooking Ballinakill Bay and well placed for the Connemara National Park. Comfortable and relaxed with an excellent restaurant. Open Easter to end-October. TV *Rooms: 20*	MC V AE	●	■	●	■
MOYARD: *Crocnaraw Country House* W www.crocnaraw.itgo.com €€ Connemara, Co Galway. Road map A3. 095 41068. FAX 095 41068. Beautifully furnished Georgian house on Ballinakill Bay with award-winning gardens. Relaxed atmosphere and comfortable bedrooms. *Rooms: 6*	MC V AE	●	■		

NEWPORT: *Newport House* W www.newporthouse.ie €€€€
Co Mayo. **Road map** B3. (098 41222. FAX 098 41613.
A stay at this historic, creeper-covered Georgian house is extremely
comfortable and civilized. It stands beside the River Newport, renowned
as a great fishing centre. Open 19-March to 6-October. **Rooms:** 18

MC
V
AE
DC

OUGHTERARD: *Currarevagh House* W www.currarevagh.com €€€
Connemara, Co Galway. **Road map** B3. (091 552312. FAX 091 552731.
In an isolated, peaceful spot on the shores of Lough Corrib and surrounded
by woods, parkland and gardens, this Victorian country house is traditionally run with a cosy, slightly old-fashioned atmosphere. **Rooms:** 15

MC
V

OUGHTERARD: *Ross Lake House* W www.rosslakehotel.com €€€
Rosscahill, Oughterard, Co Galway. **Road map** B3.
(091 550109. FAX 091 550184.
This 19th-century house feels spruce and efficient. Fishing is available in
nearby loughs and you can play tennis in the hotel grounds. Open mid-
March to end-October. **Rooms:** 13

MC
V
AE
DC

PONTOON: *Healy's* W www.healyspontoon.com €€
Foxford, Co Mayo. **Road map** B3. (094 925 6443. FAX 094 925 6572.
In a stunning position on the shores of Lough Conn and Lough Cullen,
this traditional old stone house is a great spot for bird-watchers. Simple,
neat bedrooms and good Irish cooking. **Rooms:** 14

MC
V
AE
DC

RENVYLE: *Renvyle House* W www.renvyle.com €€€€
Connemara, Co Galway. **Road map** A3. (095 43511. FAX 095 43515.
A very relaxed, family hotel on the edge of the Atlantic, it offers lots of
sporting activities as well as comfort and good food. Beams and polished
wooden floors with rugs give atmosphere and style. **Rooms:** 65

MC
V
AE
DC

ROSTURK: *Rosturk Woods* W www.rosturk-woods.com €€
Mulrany, Westport, Co Mayo. **Road map** B3. (098 36264. FAX 098 36264.
In a wonderfully quiet spot by the sea, 11 km (7 miles) from Newport,
this stylishly furnished guesthouse is an extremely attractive and
comfortable place to stay. **Rooms:** 3

WESTPORT: *Olde Railway* W www.anu.ie/railwayhotel €€€
The Mall, Westport, Co Mayo. **Road map** B3. (098 25166. FAX 098 25090.
Situated in the centre of town, this traditional hotel is comfortable and
reliable and has recently been attractively refurbished. It makes an
excellent base for the area. **Rooms:** 26

MC
V
AE
DC

NORTHWEST IRELAND

ARDARA: *The Green Gate* €
Ardvally, Co Donegal. **Road map** C2. (074 954 1546.
This highly original bed and breakfast can be found at the end of a steep,
winding lane. The accommodation is spread over three cottages and the
place is run in unique style by Paul Chatenoud. **Rooms:** 5

BALLYMOTE: *Temple House* W www.templehouse.ie €€
Co Sligo. **Road map** B3. (071 918 3329. FAX 071 918 3808.
This lovely Georgian house is set in extensive parkland. A member of
Hidden Ireland, the house is open April to end-November. Guests are
asked not to use scented products, due to allergy in host. **Rooms:** 6

MC
V
AE

BRUCKLESS: *Bruckless House* W www.iol.ie/~bruck/bruckless €€
Co Donegal. **Road map** C2. (074 973 7071. FAX 074 973 7070.
Set in 7 ha (17 acres) of attractive grounds on the shores of Bruckless
Bay, this 18th-century farmhouse is a comfortable and relaxing place to
stay with friendly hosts and good food. Two rooms are *en suite*. **Rooms:** 4

MC
V
AE

CASTLEBALDWIN: *Cromleach Lodge Country House* €€€€€
Boyle, Co Sligo. **Road map** C3. (071 916 5155. FAX 071 916 5455. W www.cromleach.com
Superbly positioned in the hills above Lough Arrow, the hotel has
spacious bedrooms, an excellent restaurant and a high standard of
comfort. **Rooms:** 11

MC
V
AE
DC

COLLOONEY: *Markree Castle* W www.markreecastle.ie €€€€
Co Sligo. **Road map** C2. (071 916 7800. FAX 071 916 7840.
In the Cooper family since 1640, the castle has recently been restored and
turned into a hotel. Stately rooms and lovely grounds make this a
civilized and relaxing experience. **Rooms:** 30

MC
V
AE
DC

For key to symbols see back flap

Price categories are for a standard double room (not per person) for one night, including tax, service charges and breakfast. €€ under 65 euros €€ 65–130 euros €€€ 130–190 euros €€€€ 190–260 euros €€€€€ over 260 euros	**CHILDREN'S FACILITIES** Cots and high chairs are available and some hotels will also provide a baby-sitting service. **PARKING FACILITIES** Parking provided by the hotel in either a private car park or a private garage close by. **RESTAURANT** The hotel has a restaurant for residents which also welcomes non-residents – usually only for evening meals. **PUBLIC BAR** The hotel has a bar that is open to non-residents and residents alike.			

	CREDIT CARDS	CHILDREN'S FACILITIES	PARKING FACILITIES	RESTAURANT	PUBLIC BAR
DONEGAL: *St Ernan's House* W www.sainternans.com €€€€ Co Donegal. **Road map** C2. 074 972 1065. FAX 074 972 2098. Set on a small island, linked to the mainland by a causeway, this pink-painted, 19th-century house is elegantly furnished but retains an informal atmosphere. Open mid-April–end-October. **Rooms: 10**	MC V		■	●	
DRUMCLIFF: *Urlar House* € Co Sligo. **Road map** C2. 071 916 3110. In a peaceful, secluded position in the shadow of Ben Bulben, this attractive farmhouse offers good, simple *en suite* accommodation and makes a perfect base for exploring Yeats Country. **Rooms: 5**		●	■		
DUNKINEELY: *Castle Murray House* W www.castlemurray.com €€ St John's Point, Co Donegal. **Road map** C2. 074 973 7022. FAX 074 973 7330. Stunningly located with views of McSweeney Bay, this small hotel is a wonderful place to stay. The decor is simple but smart and the restaurant offers a delicious menu. **Rooms: 10**	MC V	●	■	●	
LETTERKENNY: *Castle Grove Country House Hotel* €€€ Co Donegal. **Road map** C1. 074 915 1118. FAX 074 915 1384. W www.castlegrove.com Approached down a long avenue through lovely parkland, this 17th-century house looks out on to Lough Swilly and is a peaceful and relaxing place to stay. **Rooms: 15**	MC V AE DC	●	■		
LOUGH ESKE: *Harvey's Point* W www.harveyspoint.com €€€ Donegal Town, Co Donegal. **Road map** C2. 074 972 2208. FAX 074 972 2352. Swiss-style hotel on the banks of Lough Eske. Neat, modern furnishings, excellent restaurant and lots of sports facilities. Most rooms overlook the lough. **Rooms: 33**	MC V AE DC		■	●	■
LOUGH ESKE: *Ardnamona House* €€€€ Co Donegal. **Road map** C2. 074 972 2650. FAX 074 972 2819. A member of Hidden Ireland, this Edwardian house is in a beautiful spot, surrounded by famous gardens and backed by the Blue Stack Mountains. Comfortable rooms and a hospitable, informal atmosphere. **Rooms: 6**	MC V AE DC	●	■		
MOHILL: *Glebe House* W www.glebehouse.com €€ Ballinamore Rd, Mohill, Co Leitrim. **Road map** C3. 071 963 1086. FAX 071 963 1886. This early 19th-century former rectory is set in 20 ha (50 acres) of parkland, woods and farmland, and is peaceful and attractive. **Rooms: 10**	MC V AE	●	■		
RIVERSTOWN: *Coopershill House* €€€ Co Sligo. **Road map** C2. 071 916 5108. FAX 071 916 5466. Very civilized, elegant 17th-century house surrounded by a vast estate. Fine rooms with lovely antiques, huge bedrooms and excellent food. **Rooms: 8**	MC V AE DC	●	■	●	
ROSSNOWLAGH: *Smuggler's Creek* €€ Co Donegal. **Road map** C2. 071 985 2366. FAX 071 982 2000 This is a very cosy place in a wonderful position on top of the cliff looking down over the Rossnowlagh beach. There's a choice of bar food or the restaurant, and three of the bedrooms have sea views. **Rooms: 5**	MC V	●	■	●	■
ROSSNOWLAGH: *Sand House Hotel* W www.sandhouse-hotel.ie €€€ Co Donegal. **Road map** C2. 071 985 1777. FAX 071 985 2100. An imposing, white castellated building right on a sandy beach overlooking Donegal Bay, this long-established hotel is very comfortable and well decorated and has a relaxed atmosphere. **Rooms: 60**	MC V AE DC	●	■	●	■
STRANORLAR: *Kee's Hotel and Leisure Club* W www.keeshotel.ie €€€ Ballybofey, Co Donegal. **Road map** C2. 074 913 1018. FAX 074 913 1917. A coaching inn and mail staging post in the 19th century, the hotel maintains a tradition of generous hospitality. It has an excellent leisure centre and is well located for exploring Donegal. **Rooms: 53**	MC V AE DC	●	■	●	■

THE MIDLANDS

ARDEE: *Grove House* € MC V
Grove Rd, Carlingford, Co Louth. **Road map** D3. 📞 *042 937 3494.*
This comfortable, homely B&B has some views of the Mourne mountains
and is a five-minute walk from Carlingford Lough. 🔒 TV ⚡ **Rooms:** 5

CARLINGFORD: *McKevitt's Village Hotel* 🆆 www.mckevittshotel.com €€ MC V AE DC
Market Sq, Carlingford, Co Louth. **Road map** D3. 📞 *042 937 3116.* FAX *042 937 3144.*
Popular village inn at the heart of the local scene. Rooms have real fires
and a great atmosphere, bedrooms are pristine and pretty. 🔒 TV **Rooms:** 13

CARLINGFORD: *Viewpoint* 🆆 www.omeath.net/viewpoint.htm €€ V
Omeath Rd, Carlingford, Co Louth. **Road map** D3. 📞 *042 937 3149.*
Motel-style, modern accommodation. Well-equipped bedrooms with
wonderful views across Carlingford Lough. B&B only. 🔒 TV **Rooms:** 8

CARRICK-ON-SHANNON: *Hollywell Country House* €€ MC V AE
Co Leitrim. **Road map** C3. 📞 *& FAX 071 962 1124.*
Set on the hillside close to the town, there are great views across the
Shannon and surrounding countryside from the house. It is a very
welcoming and relaxing place to stay. 🔒 **Rooms:** 4

CLONES: *Hilton Park* 🆆 www.hiltonpark.ie €€€€ MC V
Co Monaghan. **Road map** C2. 📞 *047 56007.* FAX *047 56033.*
Superb mansion in magnificent parkland. The rooms have a relaxed
grandeur. Self-catering gate lodge also available. 🔒 ⚡ **Rooms:** 6

CROSSDONEY: *Lisnamandra Farmhouse* € MC V
Lisnamandra, Crossdoney, Co Cavan. **Road map** C3. 📞 *049 433 7196.*
Simple but comfortable accommodation in hospitable 17th-century
farmhouse. 🔒 **Rooms:** 4

DROGHEDA: *Boyne Valley Hotel & Country Club* €€€ MC V AE DC
Co Louth. **Road map** D3. 📞 *041 983 7737.* 🆆 www.boyne-valley-hotel.ie
A much extended and refurbished 18th-century manor house. Although
most of the decor and furnishings are modern, the hotel preserves much
of the house's traditional feel. 🔒 TV ♿ **Rooms:** 71

DULEEK: *Annesbrook* 🆆 www.annesbrook.com €€ MC V
Co Meath. **Road map** D3. 📞 *041 982 3293.* FAX *041 982 3024.*
This fine 17th-century house is a lovely, welcoming place to stay with
spacious bedrooms. Open April to end-September. 🔒 **Rooms:** 5

KILMESSAN: *Station House Hotel and Restaurant* €€€ MC V AE DC
Co Meath. **Road map** D3. 📞 *046 902 5239* FAX *046 902 5588.*
The railway used to run through Kilmessan, but now this Victorian station
building is a comfortable hotel with a good restaurant. 🔒 TV **Rooms:** 20

MOUNTRATH: *Roundwood House* €€€ MC V AE DC
Co Laois. **Road map** C4. 📞 *0502 32120.* FAX *0502 32711.*
A beautiful, 18th-century Palladian villa set in lovely grounds close to the
Slieve Bloom Mountains. Civilized but informal atmosphere. 🔒 **Rooms:** 10

MULLINGAR: *Greville Arms* 🆆 www.grevillearms.com €€ MC V AE DC
Pearse Street, Co Westmeath. **Road map** C3. 📞 *044 48563.* FAX *044 48052.*
Centrally located, this traditional hotel caters for both locals and tourists. It
has two large and very welcoming bars. 🔒 TV **Rooms:** 39

MULLINGAR: *Bloomfield House Hotel* 🆆 www.bloomfieldhouse.com €€€ MC V AE DC
Co Westmeath. **Road map** C3. 📞 *044 40894.* FAX *044 43767.*
A manor house on Lough Ennell with great views. Traditional in atmosphere
but recently refurbished, it's comfortable and friendly. 🔒 TV 🏊 ♿ **Rooms:** 65

MULLINGAR: *Crookedwood House* 🆆 www.crookedwoodhouse.com €€€ MC V AE DC
Crookedwood, Co Westmeath. **Road map** C3. 📞 *044 72165.* FAX *044 72166.*
This handsome house started life as an 18th-century rectory and is now a
leading hotel and restaurant. There are some lovely views over Lough
Derravaragh. Smoking is not allowed in the restaurant. 🔒 TV **Rooms:** 8

SLANE: *Conyngham Arms* 🆆 www.conynghamarms.com €€ MC V
Co Meath. **Road map** D3. 📞 *041 982 4155.* FAX *041 982 4205.*
In the heart of the estate village, this traditional family hotel is welcoming
and comfortable. Good base for touring the Boyne Valley. 🔒 TV **Rooms:** 15

For key to symbols see back flap

<table>
<tr><td rowspan="2">

Price categories are for a standard double room (not per person) for one night, including tax, service charges and breakfast.

£ under £50
££ £50–100
£££ £100–150
££££ £150–200
£££££ over £200

</td><td rowspan="2">

CHILDREN'S FACILITIES
Cots and high chairs are available and some hotels will also provide a baby-sitting service.

PARKING FACILITIES
Parking provided by the hotel in either a private car park or a private garage close by.

RESTAURANT
The hotel has a restaurant for residents which also welcomes non-residents – usually only for evening meals.

PUBLIC BAR
The hotel has a bar that is open to non-residents and residents alike.

</td><td>CREDIT CARDS</td><td>CHILDREN'S FACILITIES</td><td>PARKING FACILITIES</td><td>RESTAURANT</td><td>PUBLIC BAR</td></tr>
</table>

NORTHERN IRELAND

ANNALONG: *Glassdrumman Lodge* W www.glassdrummanlodge.co.uk £££ Mill Rd, Annalong, Co Down. **Road map** D2. 028 4376 8451. FAX 028 4376 7041. Set deep in the "Kingdom of Mourne", the hotel looks out on the region's famous dry-stone walls. Excellent reputation for food. 🖥 TV 🔊 *Rooms:* 10 MC V AE DC	●	■	●	
ARMAGH: *Charlemont Arms* W www.charlemontarmshotel.com ££ 57–65 English St. Co Armagh. **Road map** D2. 028 3752 2028. FAX 028 3752 6979. A country-style hotel perfectly located for the major attractions. What it lacks in luxury it makes up for in the warmth of its welcome. 🖥 TV 🔊 *Rooms:* 30 MC V	●	●	●	●
BALLYGALLY: *Hastings Ballygally Castle* W www.hastings.com £££ 274 Coast Rd, Ballygally, Co Antrim. **Road map** D1. 028 2858 1066. FAX 028 2858 3681. Reputedly haunted, the castle showpiece is the Ghost Room, a tiny old tower bedroom with a macabre legend. The hotel bar provides a jolly atmosphere in a modern setting. 🖥 TV *Rooms:* 44 MC V AE DC	●	■	●	●
BALLYMENA: *Galgorm Manor* W www.galgorm.com £££ Co Antrim. **Road map** D1. 028 2588 1001. FAX 028 2588 0080. The River Maine sweeps past the hotel, enhancing the view from many of the rooms. Fishing is available on the magnificent estate. There is a first-rate restaurant and a traditional, Irish-style bar. 🖥 TV 🔊 *Rooms:* 24 MC V AE DC	●	■	●	●
BANGOR: *Clandeboye Lodge* W www.clandeboyelodge.com ££ 10 Estate Rd, Bangor, Co Down. **Road map** E2. 028 9185 2500. FAX 028 9185 2772. Resembling a Victorian church school, the hotel has reasonably priced rooms and a stylish dining room with a great menu. 🖥 TV 🔊 *Rooms:* 43 MC V AE DC	●	■	●	
BELFAST: *Duke's Hotel* W www.dukeshotel.com ££ 65 University St, Belfast BT7 1HL. **Road map** D2. 028 9023 6666. FAX 028 9023 7177. A modern hotel offering comfort, style and international cuisine in the heart of the city. It has a good public bar. 🖥 TV 🔊 *Rooms:* 20 MC V AE DC	●		●	●
BELFAST: *Hastings Stormont Hotel* W www.hastingshotels.com £££ 587 Upper Newtownards Rd, Belfast BT4 3LP. **Road map** D2. 028 9065 1066. FAX 028 9048 0240. Close to Stormont and the airport, it's excellent for business people. Modern and functional with an award-winning restaurant. 🖥 TV 🔊 *Rooms:* 109 MC V AE DC	●	■	●	●
BELFAST: *Malone Lodge Hotel* W www.malonelodgehotel.com £££ 60 Eglantine Ave, Belfast BT9 6DY. **Road map** D2. 028 9038 8000. FAX 028 9038 8088. Centrally located, it's ideal for business people and tourists and offers comfortable, modern facilities. 🖥 TV 🔊 🍴 *Rooms:* 51 MC V AE DC	●	■	●	●
BELFAST: *The Europa Hotel* W www.hastingshotels.com ££££ Great Victoria St, Belfast BT2 7AP. **Road map** D2. 028 9027 1066. FAX 028 9032 7800. An imposing building in the heart of the Golden Mile, ideal for business people and tourists, with very good restaurants. 🖥 TV 🔊 *Rooms:* 240 MC V AE DC	●		●	●
CARNLOUGH: *Londonderry Arms Hotel* W www.glensofantrim.com ££ 20 Harbour Rd, Carnlough, Co Antrim. **Road map** D1. 028 2888 5255. FAX 028 2888 5263. Winston Churchill once owned this ivy-covered inn next to the harbour of Carnlough in a breathtaking setting at the foot of Glencloy. Family owned, it has a genuine warmth of welcome. 🖥 TV 🔊 *Rooms:* 35 MC V AE DC	●	■	●	●
CRAWFORDSBURN: *The Old Inn at Crawfordsburn* W www.theoldinn.com ££ Co Down. **Road map** E2. 028 9185 3255. FAX 028 9185 2775. One of Ireland's oldest hostelries, this thatched 16th-century inn offers quality and comfort with roaring log fires and four-poster beds in some rooms. A good Irish menu and an excellent wine list. 🖥 TV 🔊 *Rooms:* 32 MC V AE DC	●	■	●	●

DUNGANNON: *Grange Lodge* ££
Grange Rd, Dungannon, Co Tyrone. **Road map** D2.
028 8778 4212. FAX 028 8778 4313. @ grangelodge@nireland.com
The hotel is set in pleasant surroundings and offers good Ulster home-style cooking and a hospitable family welcome. 🚗 TV *Rooms: 5*
Cards: MC V

ENNISKILLEN: *Killyhevlin Hotel* £££
Dublin Rd, Enniskillen, Co Fermanagh. **Road map** C2.
028 6632 3481. FAX 028 6632 4726. W www.killyhevlin.com
The grounds sweep down to Lower Lough Erne and many bedrooms look out on the lough, but you must pay extra for the view. 🚗 TV ♿ *Rooms: 42*
Cards: MC V AE DC

ENNISKILLEN: *Manor House Country Hotel* £££
Killadeas, Enniskillen, Co Fermanagh. **Road map** C2.
028 6862 1561. FAX 028 6862 1545. W www.manor-house-hotels.com
Situated on the shores of Lough Erne, this country hotel has a rich interior, with antiques and paintings, a warm atmosphere and friendly staff. The emphasis is on healthy eating using local seasonal produce. 🚗 TV 🏊 *Rooms: 81*
Cards: MC V AE

HOLYWOOD: *Hastings Culloden Hotel* W www.hastingshotels.com ££££
142 Bangor Rd, Holywood, Co Down. **Road map** E2.
028 9042 1066. FAX 028 9042 6777.
A very fine hotel, set in gardens and woodlands by Belfast Lough. Originally the palace of the Bishops of Down, it retains its opulence with many fine antiques and valuable paintings. 🚗 TV 🏊 ♿ *Rooms: 79*
Cards: MC V AE DC

IRVINESTOWN: *Mahon's Hotel* W www.mahonshotel.co.uk ££
Hill Street, Co Fermanagh. **Road map** C2. 028 6862 1656. FAX 028 6862 8344.
A family-run hotel offering very pleasant service and accommodation in well-maintained surroundings. An eclectic collection of bric-à-brac adorns the bar and restaurants. 🚗 TV *Rooms: 16*
Cards: MC V AE

KILKEEL: *The Kilmorey Arms Hotel* W www.kilmoreyarmshotel.co.uk £
41 Greencastle St, Kilkeel, Co Down. **Road map** D3.
028 4176 2220. FAX 028 4176 5399.
An excellent base for the Mourne area. The rooms are well furnished and the Smugglers' Bar's ambience fits well with the area. 🚗 TV *Rooms: 30*
Cards: MC V AE

LIMAVADY: *Streeve Hill* ££
Co Londonderry. **Road map** D1. 028 7776 6563. FAX 028 7776 8285.
This 18th-century dower house on the Drenagh estate is a good base for the area. The gardens at Drenagh House are exquisite. Plenty of golf, riding and fishing nearby. 🚗 *Rooms: 3*
Cards: MC V AE

LONDONDERRY: *Beech Hill Country House Hotel* £££
32 Ardmore Rd, Londonderry, Co Londonderry. **Road map** C1.
028 7134 9279. FAX 028 7134 5366. W www.beech-hill.com
Good service and food and a real "home from home" atmosphere. The bedrooms, some with beautiful pieces of Victorian furniture, give the feel of a grand old country home. 🚗 TV ♿ 🍴 *Rooms: 27*
Cards: MC V AE

NEWCASTLE: *Burrendale Hotel and Country Club* £££
51 Castlewellan Rd, Co Down. **Road map** E2.
028 4372 2599. FAX 028 4372 2328. W www.burrendale.com
An excellent base for climbing, horse riding and golf. Good facilities for the disabled with a comfortable bar and restaurant. 🚗 TV ♿ *Rooms: 69*
Cards: MC V AE DC

NEWCASTLE: *Hastings Slieve Donard Hotel* ££££
Downs Rd, Newcastle, Co Down. **Road map** E2.
028 4372 1066. FAX 028 4372 4830. W www.hastingshotels.com
A stunning red-brick building overlooking the beach and the Royal County Down Golf Course. Good efficient service. 🚗 TV ♿ 🍴 🏊 *Rooms: 124*
Cards: MC V AE DC

NEWTOWNARDS: *Edenvale Country House* W www.edenvalehouse.com £
130 Portaferry Road, Newtownards, Co Down. **Road map** E2.
028 9181 4881. FAX 028 9182 6192.
Set in extensive grounds next to a wildfowl reserve, this Georgian house is a haven for nature lovers, and provides croquet on the lawns. 🚗 *Rooms: 4*
Cards: MC V

PORTAFERRY: *Portaferry Hotel* W www.portaferryhotel.com ££
The Strand, Portaferry, Co Down. **Road map** E2.
028 4272 8231. FAX 028 4272 8999.
This waterside inn on the Ards Peninsula overlooks Strangford Lough. A pleasant atmosphere and an award-winning restaurant. 🚗 TV *Rooms: 14*
Cards: MC V AE DC

For key to symbols see back flap

RESTAURANTS, CAFÉS AND PUBS

ALTHOUGH the highest concentration of top gourmet restaurants is in Ireland's main cities, equally fine cuisine can be found in some very unlikely, remote locations around the country. Good, plain cooking is on offer at moderately priced, family-style restaurants all over Ireland. The restaurants listed on pages 306–17 are recommended for their high standards of service, quality of food and value

Restaurant sign in Kinsale

for money. To supplement these listings, look out for the *Dining in Ireland* booklet published by Fáilte Ireland, the Irish Tourist Board. Pub lunches are one of Ireland's top travel bargains, offering generous portions of fresh vegetables and prime meats, and can often serve as the main meal of the day for a very reasonable price. Light meals, bar food and a variety of take-out dishes are also widely available.

IRISH EATING PATTERNS

TRADITIONALLY, the Irish have started the day with a huge breakfast: bacon, sausages, black pudding, eggs, tomatoes and brown bread. In Northern Ireland this, plus potato cakes and soda farls *(see p304)*, is known as an "Ulster Fry". The main meal, dinner, was served at midday, with a lighter "tea" in the early evening.

Although continental breakfasts are now available, you will be hard-pressed to escape the traditional breakfast, which is included in most hotel and bed-and-breakfast rates. Increasingly, however, even the Irish settle for a light salad or soup and sandwiches at midday and save their main meal for the evening. Vestiges of the old eating patterns remain in the huge midday platefuls still served in pubs.

Enjoying breakfast at Adare Manor Hotel *(see p294)*

Arriving at a café in Kinvarra *(see p204)*

TIPS ON EATING OUT

ELEGANT DINING becomes considerably more affordable when you make lunch your main meal of the day. In many of the top restaurants, the fixed-price lunch and dinner menus offer much the same, but lunch will usually come to about half the price. House wines are quite drinkable in most restaurants and can reduce the total cost of your meal. If you are travelling with children, shop around for one of the many restaurants that provide a less expensive children's menu.

Lunch is usually served between noon and 2:30pm, with dinner between 6:30 and 10pm, although many ethnic and city-centre restaurants stay open later, particularly in Temple Bar. Bed-and-breakfast hosts will often provide an ample home-cooked evening meal, and many will serve tea and scones in the late evening at no extra charge.

In top restaurants, men are expected to wear a jacket, though not necessarily a tie, and women to wear a dress or suit. Elsewhere, the dress code is pretty informal, stopping short of bare chests and very short shorts.

Visa (V) and MasterCard/Access (MC) are the most commonly accepted credit cards, with Diners Club (DC) and American Express (AE) also in use. The abbreviations in brackets are used in the restaurant listings to indicate which cards are accepted.

GOURMET AND ETHNIC DINING

THIS ONCE gourmet-poor land now sports restaurants that rank among Europe's very best, with chefs trained in outstanding domestic and continental institutions. There is a choice of Irish, French, Italian, Chinese, Indonesian and even Russian and Cuban cuisines, with styles ranging from traditional to regional to *nouvelle cuisine*. Locations vary as widely as the cuisine, from hotel dining rooms, town house basements and city mansions to castle hotels and tiny village cafés. The small County Cork town of Kinsale has established itself as the "Gourmet Capital of Ireland". Outstanding chefs also reign over the gracious houses listed in *Ireland's Blue Book of Country Houses and Restaurants*, available from tourist offices.

BUDGET DINING

IT IS QUITE POSSIBLE to eat well on a small budget wherever you are in Ireland. In both city and rural locations, there are small cafés, tea rooms and family-style restaurants with inexpensive meals. Even if a café or tea room is at a main tourist attraction, such as Bantry House, you can still expect good, home-made food and freshly baked bread and cakes. Sandwiches are usually made with thick, tasty slices of cheese or meat (not processed); salad plates feature smoked salmon, chicken, ham, pork and beef; and hot meals usually come with large helpings of vegetables, with the beloved potato often showing up roast, boiled and mashed, all on one plate.

PUB FOOD

IRELAND'S PUBS have moved into the food field with a vengeance. In addition to bar snacks (soup, sandwiches and

Selection of cakes served at Bantry House café *(see pp160–61)*

so on), available from noon until late, salads and hot meals are served from midday to 2:30pm. At rock-bottom prices, hot plates all come heaped with mounds of fresh vegetables, potatoes in one or more versions, and good portions of local fish or meat. Particularly good bargains are the pub carveries that offer a choice of joints, sliced to your preference. In recent years, the international staples of spaghetti, lasagne and quiche have also appeared on pub menus. For a list of recommended pubs, see pages 318–21.

Café sign at Baltimore

FISH AND CHIPS AND OTHER FAST FOODS

THE IRISH, from peasant to parliamentarian, love their "chippers", immortalized in Roddy Doyle's novel *The Van*, and any good pub night will end with a visit to the nearest

fish-and-chip shop. At virtually any time of day, however, if you pass by Leo Burdock's in Dublin, there will be a long queue for this international institution *(see p307)*. With Ireland's long coastline, wherever you choose, the fish will usually be the freshest catch of the day – plaice, cod, haddock, whiting or ray (a delicacy). The many other fast-food outlets include a host of familiar international names, such as McDonald's and Kentucky Fried Chicken, as well as a wide variety of burger and kebab shops. Relatively new arrivals on the scene are several quite good pasta and pizza chains, such as Pizza Express and Milano.

PICNICS

IRELAND IS GLORIOUS picnic country. Farmhouse cheeses and flavoursome tomatoes are picnic treats, or stop by one of the many small shops that offer sandwiches made with fresh local ingredients. As for where to picnic, the long, indented coast is ringed with sandy beaches and over 400 forest areas, many with picnic tables; great views add to the pleasure of mountainside picnics; and there are often places to pull off the road in scenic spots. Turn off a main road onto almost any lane and you will find a picnic spot by a lakeside, riverbank or the shady edge of a field.

The 1601 pub in Kinsale *(see p319)*

What to Eat in Ireland

IRELAND'S rich pastureland, unpolluted rivers and extensive coastline provide tender lamb, beef and pork, an array of fish and seafood and fresh fruit and vegetables. From hearty rural fare that makes the most of the ingredients available, Irish cooking has evolved into the gourmet cuisine created by internationally trained chefs. Often you will find the best of both worlds, with Irish stew or ham and cabbage on the same menu as more exotic dishes. The ideal end to a meal is an Irish coffee – coffee, cream and whiskey.

Irish coffee

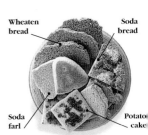

Wheaten bread　Soda bread　Soda farl　Potato cake

Bread, *invariably baked daily, comes in different guises. Soda bread may be brown or white. In Northern Ireland, brown soda bread is called wheaten bread.*

Sausage　Bacon　Grilled tomato　Soda farl　Potato cake　Fried egg　Black pudding

An Ulster fry *consists of home-baked soda farls (soft bread cakes leavened with soda and buttermilk) and potato cakes (bread made from mashed potato, butter and flour), as well as the basic ingredients of a fried meal. The ultimate Irish breakfast, the "fry" is a perfect way to set yourself up for the day. Without the soda farls and potato cakes, meals like this are consumed with relish all over Ireland at any time of day.*

Mushroom soup *makes a wholesome appetizer or snack. It is normally made with freshly picked local mushrooms and a generous amount of cream.*

Smoked salmon *is very popular all over Ireland and is generally served as simply as possible. Eat wild salmon, rather than farmed, for a truly wonderful flavour.*

Mussel soup *is a substantial dish made with fresh local mussels in a creamy fish stock flavoured with vegetables and herbs. Try it with wheaten bread.*

Fresh oysters, *here served on a bed of seaweed and cracked ice, make a light but delicious lunch – especially when accompanied by a glass of Guinness.*

Dublin coddle, *a traditional Saturday night supper dish, consists of chopped sausages and ham or bacon cooked in stock with potatoes and onions.*

Irish stew, originally a peasant dish, is a thick casserole made with lamb or mutton, onions, and parsley, topped with potatoes.

Fresh salmon is often poached in fish stock or wine and herbs. Galway salmon is particularly sought after for its fine taste.

Lamb cutlets are usually served with mint sauce or jelly. Lamb from Kerry and Wicklow is renowned for its tenderness.

Mashed potato   Roast potatoes

Vegetables are served in generous portions, usually as an accompaniment to the main course. It is not uncommon to be given potatoes in a number of different forms – roast, boiled, mashed, baked or chipped – together with whichever vegetables happen to be fresh and in season.

Broccoli

Boiled potatoes   Carrots

Baked ham, coated with cloves and brown sugar, is commonly served with boiled cabbage in butter and eaten at Christmas and on other festive occasions.

Strawberries and cream are the archetypal summer dessert. They are sometimes sweetened with honey rather than sugar.

Porter cake, a classic Irish cake made with dried fruit, is most famous for the inclusion of stout, usually in the form of Guinness.

Apple tart, or "cake" as the Irish often call it, is eaten all year round but is traditionally associated with Hallowe'en.

CHEESES

For centuries, cheese has been made in farms and monasteries throughout Ireland. Cheese-making has expanded in the last 25 years and Ireland now produces cheeses with a worldwide reputation, from semi-soft ones such as Cashel Blue and St Killian, which is similar to Camembert, to Gouda-like Carrigaline and smoked Durrus.

St Killian

Carrigaline

Cashel Blue

Durrus

Tea-time favourites include sponge cakes, fruit cakes and white or brown scones, made with or without fruit. Barm brack, a doughy, fruity bread, is traditionally eaten at Hallowe'en and on All Saints' Day, when a ring is hidden in the cake. According to tradition, the finder of the ring will marry by the following Easter.

Brown scone   Fruit scone

Plain scone   Barm brack

Choosing a Restaurant

THIS CHART LISTS restaurants, selected for their good value, food and location, by region, starting with Dublin. Use the colour-coded thumb tabs, which indicate the regions covered on each page, to guide you to the relevant section of the chart. For Dublin map references, see the map on pages 110–11; for road map references, see the inside back cover.

	CREDIT CARDS	OPEN LUNCH TIME	OPEN LATE	FIXED-PRICE MENU	GOOD WINE LIST

DUBLIN

SOUTHEAST DUBLIN: *Bewley's Oriental Café* €€
78–79 Grafton St, Dublin 2. **Map** D4. (*01 677 6761*.
This Dublin institution is open from breakfast time onwards. Its breads, pastries and home-made soups are superb, but most people come here for a coffee and a chat. ♿ ⚡ ⭐ V

| MC V AE DC | ● | ■ | ● | |

SOUTHEAST DUBLIN: *Kilkenny Shop Restaurant* €€
The Kilkenny Shop, 6–10 Nassau St, Dublin 2. **Map** E4. (*01 677 7066*.
A busy restaurant, overlooking Trinity College playing fields, offering traditional Irish cooking, homemade quiches and salads. ⚡ ⭐ V

| MC V AE DC | ● | | ● | |

SOUTHEAST DUBLIN: *Gotham Café* €€€
8 Anne St South, Dublin 2. **Map** D4. (*01 679 5266*.
The American-style menu at this bright, funky café includes "Bowery", "Upper East Side" and "Central Park" gourmet pizzas. ♿ ⚡ ⭐ V

| MC V AE | ● | ■ | | ■ |

SOUTHEAST DUBLIN: *Rajdoot Tandoori* €€€
26–28 Clarendon St, Dublin 2. **Map** D4. (*01 679 4274*.
This authentically decorated North Indian restaurant serves mildly spiced curries and, from the clay oven, tandoori barbecued dishes. ♿ ⭐ V

| MC V AE DC | ● | ■ | ● | |

SOUTHEAST DUBLIN: *Celts Banquet* €€€€
20 Baggot St Lower, Dublin 2. **Map** F5. (*01 661 8832*.
As the name suggests, traditional Irish food is served in this cosy basement restaurant in the Georgian House Hotel. ⚡ ⭐

| MC V AE DC | ● | ■ | | |

SOUTHEAST DUBLIN: *The Commons* €€€€
85–6 Newman House, St Stephen's Green South, Dublin 2. **Map** D5. (*01 478 0530*.
Specially commissioned paintings by Irish artists share the honours in this tasteful restaurant with gourmet specialities. On sunny days, aperitifs can be taken in the pretty courtyard. ⭐ V

| MC V AE DC | ● | ■ | ● | ■ |

SOUTHEAST DUBLIN: *Dobbin's Wine Bistro* €€€€
15 Stephen's Lane, Mount St, Dublin 2. **Map** F5. (*01 676 4679*.
An intimate, friendly bistro with an innovative monthly menu and one of Dublin's best wine lists. ⚡ ⭐ V

| MC V AE DC | ● | ■ | | ■ |

SOUTHEAST DUBLIN: *L'Ecrivain* €€€€
109 Baggot St Lower, Dublin 2. **Map** F5. (*01 661 1919*.
In the heart of Georgian Dublin, French classics here have an Irish touch, such as breast of guinea fowl with a black pudding mousse. ⚡ ⭐ V

| MC V AE DC | ● | ■ | | ■ |

SOUTHEAST DUBLIN: *Fadó* €€€€
Mansion House, Dawson Street, Dublin 2. **Map** D4. (*01 676 7200*.
Part of the Mansion House, this stunning dining room is in the Belle Epoque Style. The cuisine is Irish with French influence. ♿ ⚡ ⭐ V

| MC V AE DC | ● | ■ | | ■ |

SOUTHEAST DUBLIN: *Pearl Brasserie* €€€€
20 Upper Merrion St, Dublin 2. **Map** D4. (*01 661 3627*.
A classical French brasserie serving traditional French cuisine and combining charm, friendly service and affordable prices. ⭐ V

| MC V AE | ● | | | ■ |

SOUTHEAST DUBLIN: *Pier 32* €€€€
22–23 Pembroke St Upper, Dublin 2. **Map** D4 . (*01 676 1494*.
Open fires and a great atmosphere are the hallmark of this warm and friendly place. Their specialities are seafood and regional dishes. ⭐ V

| MC V AE DC | | ■ | | ■ |

SOUTHEAST DUBLIN: *Sandbank Bistro Café* €€€€
Westbury Hotel, Grafton St, Dublin 2. **Map** D4. (*01 679 1122*.
Completely refurbished, this smart but simple bistro has beech tables and a minimalist feel to the decor. ♿ ⭐ V

| MC V AE DC | ● | ■ | | ■ |

		CREDIT CARDS	OPEN LUNCH TIME	OPEN LATE	FIXED-PRICE MENU	GOOD WINE LIST

Average prices for a three-course meal for one, half a bottle of house wine and all extra service and cover charges:
€ under 14 euros
€€ 14–20 euros
€€€ 20–32 euros
€€€€ 32–66 euros
€€€€€ over 66 euros

OPEN LUNCH TIME
Many restaurants open only in the evening, but those in large towns and attached to pubs often open at lunch time.
OPEN LATE
Restaurant remains open with the full menu available after 10pm.
FIXED-PRICE MENU
A good-value fixed-price menu on offer at lunch, dinner or both, usually with three courses.
GOOD WINE LIST
Denotes a wide range of good wines, or a more specialized selection of wines.

Restaurant	Price	Credit Cards	Open Lunch Time	Open Late	Fixed-Price Menu	Good Wine List
SOUTHEAST DUBLIN: *La Stampa* — 35 Dawson St, Dublin 2. **Map** D4. ☎ 01 677 8611. This up-market restaurant in the heart of Dublin is noted for its sumptuous, highly ornate Georgian decor. Service is efficient and there is a lively atmosphere. Book at weekends.	€€€€	MC V AE DC		■		■
SOUTHWEST DUBLIN: *Leo Burdock's* — 2 Werburgh St, Dublin 8. **Map** C4. ☎ 01 454 0306. Dublin's oldest fish-and-chip takeaway attracts a mix of patrons. The fish is fresh, and the chips made from top-grade Irish potatoes.	€		●	■		
SOUTHWEST DUBLIN: *Elephant and Castle* — 18 Temple Bar, Dublin 2. **Map** D3. ☎ 01 679 3121. This boisterous American-style restaurant serves up-market fast food from tortillas to hamburgers. It is open for breakfast from 8am Monday to Friday and is popular for brunch at weekends.	€€€€	MC V AE DC	●	■		■
SOUTHWEST DUBLIN: *Les Frères Jacques* — 74 Dame St, Dublin 2. **Map** C3. ☎ 01 679 4555. This French restaurant next to the Olympia Theatre adds Irish flair to many of its dishes. Live piano music on Friday and Saturday. Closed Sunday.	€€€€	MC V AE	●	■	●	■
SOUTHWEST DUBLIN: *Lord Edward* — 23 Christchurch Place, Dublin 8. **Map** B4. ☎ 01 454 2420. Dublin's oldest seafood restaurant serves lunch in the ground-floor pub and evening meals in the upstairs restaurant. Service is courteous.	€€€€	MC V AE DC	●	■	●	■
SOUTHWEST DUBLIN: *Mermaid Café* — 69-70 Dame Street, Dublin 2. **Map** C3. ☎ 01 670 8236. This popular café serves delicious, trendy, European dishes. Decor is simple but smart with wooden polished tables.	€€€€	MC V	●			■
NORTH OF THE LIFFEY: *101 Talbot* — 100–102 Talbot St, Dublin 1. **Map** E2. ☎ 01 874 5011. A cheerful and relaxed restaurant close to the Abbey Theatre – good for pre-theatre meals. Excellent choice of vegetarian dishes.	€€€	MC V AE DC		■		■
NORTH OF THE LIFFEY: *Chapter One Restaurant* — Below Dublin Writers Museum, Parnell Square, Dublin 1. **Map** C1. ☎ 01 873 2266. Across the square from the Gate Theatre, this excellent restaurant does pre–theatre dinners. Cuisine is modern European.	€€€€	MC V AE DC	●	■	●	■
NORTH OF THE LIFFEY: *Flanagan's Restaurant* — 61 O'Connell St Upper, Dublin 1. **Map** D2. ☎ 01 873 1388. Popular Flanagan's is great value for money with an extensive menu ranging from burgers and salads to vegetarian and pasta choices.	€€€€	MC V	●	■	●	■
NORTH OF THE LIFFEY: *The Halo* — The Morrison Hotel, Ormond Quay, Dublin 1. **Map** C3. ☎ 01 887 2421. The Morrison is a chic, minimalist designed hotel and The Halo is its excellent restaurant. The style of cooking is modern European with Asian influence and the ingredients are predominantly organic.	€€€€	MC V AE DC	●	■	●	■
BALLSBRIDGE: *Palmcourt Café* — Berkeley Court Hotel, Lansdowne Rd, Dublin 4. ☎ 01 660 1711. In this bright, conservatory-style room in one of the city's most luxurious hotels, meals from the extensive menu are excellent value for money. Very popular with Dubliners.	€€€€	MC V AE DC	●	■	●	■
BALLSBRIDGE: *Roly's Bistro* — 7 Ballsbridge Terrace, Dublin 4. ☎ 01 668 2611. Lively bistro with Irish cuisine, including seasonal delights such as venison pie with juniper berries and wood mushrooms. Book ahead.	€€€€	MC V AE DC	●		●	■

For key to symbols see back flap

<table>
<tr><td colspan="2">
<table>
<tr><td>
Average prices for a three-course meal for one, half a bottle of house wine and all extra service and cover charges:
€ under 14 euros
€€ 14–20 euros
€€€ 20–32 euros
€€€€ 32–66 euros
€€€€€ over 66 euros
</td><td>
OPEN LUNCH TIME
Many restaurants open only in the evening, but those in large towns and attached to pubs often open at lunch time.
OPEN LATE
Restaurant remains open with the full menu available after 10pm.
FIXED-PRICE MENU
A good-value fixed-price menu on offer at lunch, dinner or both, usually with three courses.
GOOD WINE LIST
Denotes a wide range of good wines, or a more specialized selection of wines.
</td></tr>
</table>
</td></tr>
</table>

	CREDIT CARDS	OPEN LUNCH TIME	OPEN LATE	FIXED-PRICE MENU	GOOD WINE LIST
DUN LAOGHAIRE: *Brasserie Na Mara* €€€€ 1 Harbour Rd. ☎ 01 280 6767. This restaurant, overlooking the harbour, serves the best just-caught seafood in the area. Non-fish dishes are also available. ♿ 🍴 ⚡ 🅅	MC V AE DC	●		●	▣
HOWTH: *Abbey Tavern* €€€€ Abbey St. ☎ 01 839 0307. A 16th-century tavern just off Howth Harbour and specializing in seafood. Its Irish music session is an institution. Book ahead. ♿ 🍴 ⚡ 🅅	MC V AE DC	●			▣
HOWTH: *King Sitric Fish Restaurant* €€€€ East Pier. ☎ 01 832 5235. Howth crab and lobster star on the menu of this well-known, recently refurbished, restaurant. Reserve for dinner. 🍴 ⚡ 🅅	MC V AE DC	●	▣	●	▣
SANDYCOVE: *Caviston's* €€€ 58 Glasthule Road. ☎ 01 280 9120. This fish restaurant serves fresh mouthwatering dishes and has a great deli. Open noon to 3pm only. Booking recommended. Non-smoking. ♿ 🍴 ⚡	MC V AE DC	●		●	▣
SOUTHEAST IRELAND					
BRAY: *The Tree of Idleness* €€€ Seafront. **Road map** D4. ☎ 01 286 3498. This attractive and very welcoming restaurant serves outstanding Greek-Cypriot cooking such as their delicious roast suckling pig. ♿ ⚡ 🅅	MC V AE DC		▣		▣
CAPPOQUIN: *Richmond House* €€€€ Cappoquin. **Road map** C5. ☎ 058 54278. On the banks of the Blackwater River, this 18th-century country home serves French dishes and local salmon and trout. ♿ 🍴 ⚡ 🅅	MC V AE DC			●	▣
CARLOW: *The Beams Restaurant* €€€€ 59 Dublin St. **Road map** D4. ☎ 059 913 1824. A family-run restaurant with beamed ceilings and an old wall oven. Dishes include wild Atlantic salmon with white wine sauce, plus a huge choice of Irish cheeses. Closed Sunday and Monday. 🍴 ⚡ 🅅	MC V				▣
DUNGARVAN: *Merry's Restaurant* €€€€ Main St. **Road map** C5. ☎ 058 41974. Set in an atmospheric 19th-century wine merchant's shop, Merry's menu features shellfish and other seafoods, plus game in season. ♿ 🍴 ⚡ 🅅	MC V	●		●	▣
FERRYCARRIG BRIDGE: *Tides Restaurant* €€€€€ Ferrycarrig Hotel. **Road map** D5. ☎ 053 20999. One of the best restaurants in County Wexford, this relaxed room filled with greenery overlooks the Slaney estuary. Book ahead. ♿ ⚡ 🅅	MC V AE DC				
GOREY: *Marlfield House* €€€€€ Courtown Rd. **Road map** D4. ☎ 055 21124. This Regency mansion houses one of the Southeast's premier dining rooms. Organically grown vegetables are used. 🍴 ♿ ⚡ 🅅	MC V AE DC	●		●	▣
GREYSTONES: *The Hungry Monk* €€€€ Greystones. **Road map** D4. ☎ 01 287 5759. This attractive monk-themed restaurant has a very welcoming atmosphere. Excellent wine list and seafood specials. Closed Monday. 🍴 ⚡ 🅅	MC V AE	●	▣		▣
KILDARE: *Silken Thomas* €€€ The Square. **Road map** D4. ☎ 045 522232. Located near the Norman castle keep in the town centre, this restaurant includes beef stroganoff and Gaelic steak on its menu. 🍴 ♿ ⚡ 🅅	MC V AE	●			▣

KILKENNY: *Kilkenny Design Centre Restaurant* €€
Castle Yard. **Road map** C4. **[** 056 772 2118.
A bright, self-service restaurant with home-cooked casseroles and other hot dishes, plus salads, quiches, soups and patés. 🏃 ⫶ V ♿
MC V AE DC

KILKENNY: *Langtons Restaurant and Bar* €€€€
69 John St. **Road map** C4. **[** 056 776 5133.
At Langton's, each of several small rooms has its own distinctive decor. Stuffed mussels are among local favourites. ♿ 🏃 ⫶ V
MC V AE DC

LEIGHLINBRIDGE: *Lord Bagenal Inn* €€€€
Main St. **Road map** D4. **[** 059 972 1668.
This riverside restaurant has an old-world air and award-winning wine list. Wild Irish salmon and game dishes in season. Five course meal. ♿ 🏃 ⫶ V
MC V AE DC

LISMORE: *Eamonn's Place* €€€€
Main St. **Road map** C5. **[** 058 54025.
In summer, dinners in the stone-walled beer garden are delightful, while a cheerful turf fire adds a glow to winter meals (lunch only) inside. ♿ 🏃 V

NAAS: *Manor Inn* €€€€
Main St. **Road map** D4. **[** 045 897471.
A haunt of punters en route to and from the nearby Curragh racecourse. Fish, steaks, pasta and grills feature on the menu. ♿ 🏃 ⫶ V
MC V AE DC

RATHNEW: *Hunter's Hotel* €€€€
Rathnew. **Road map** D4. **[** 0404 40106.
Cheerful hotel dining room attracting patrons from Dublin and nearby, with its friendly ambience and superb meat and fish dishes. ♿ 🏃 ⫶ V
MC V AE DC

ROSSLARE: *The Lobster Pot* €€€€
Carne, Sore Point. **Road map** D5. **[** 053 31110.
Lobster and oysters come straight from sea tanks in this traditional pub and restaurant near Rosslare ferry harbour. Closed Jan–Feb. ♿ 🏃 ⫶ V
MC V AE

THOMASTOWN: *Kendals Restaurant* €€€€
Mount Juliet Conrad Hotel. **Road map** D5. **[** 056 777 3073.
Bright and spacious, this modern restaurant offers delicious dishes that are a fusion of Modern Irish and international cuisine. 🏃 ⫶ V ♿
MC V AE DC

THOMASTOWN: *Lady Helen Restaurant* €€€€€
Mount Juliet Conrad Hotel. **Road map** D5. **[** 056 777 3000.
The menu, as elegant as the decor, includes chicken breast with fennel stuffing in a tomato and red pepper sauce. Book ahead. ♿ ⫶ V
MC V AE DC

WATERFORD: *The Munster Bar* €€
Bailey's New St. **Road map** D5. **[** 051 874656.
This restaurant is open at lunch time only. One popular speciality at The Munster Bar is a "blaa" (meat, onion, tomato and lettuce on a roll), found only in Waterford City. Other traditional dishes feature on the extensive menu. ♿ 🏃 ⫶ V
MC V

WATERFORD: *O'Grady's* €€€€
Cork Rd. **Road map** D5. **[** 051 378851.
Innovative use of fresh local ingredients characterizes the delectable fare at this bright restaurant near the Waterford Crystal factory. ⫶ V
MC V AE DC

WATERFORD: *The Stand Pub and Red's Restaurant* €€€€
45 Michael St. **Road map** D5. **[** 051 879488.
A glowing fireplace adds to the ambience upstairs in this cosmopolitan restaurant. More casual meals are served downstairs. Skip dessert and indulge in one of their connoisseur coffees. 🏃 ⫶ V
MC V AE

WATERFORD: *Waterford Castle Hotel* €€€€€
The Island, Ballinakill. **Road map** D5. **[** 051 878203.
A small car ferry crosses to Waterford Castle on its River Suir estuary island. Fish and seafood are the specialities in the magnificent wood-panelled dining room. ♿ 🏃 ⫶ V
MC V AE DC

WEXFORD: *La Dolce Vita* €€€€
Westgate. **Road map** D5. **[** 053 23935.
Originally a grain store, this attractive building now houses an inviting restaurant specializing in modern Italian dishes and fresh seafood. 🏃 ⫶ V
MC V

<table>
<tr><td colspan="2">

Average prices for a three-course meal for one, half a bottle of house wine and all extra service and cover charges:

€ under 14 euros
€€ 14–20 euros
€€€ 20–32 euros
€€€€ 32–66 euros
€€€€€ over 66 euros

</td><td>

OPEN LUNCH TIME
Many restaurants open only in the evening, but those in large towns and attached to pubs often open at lunch time.

OPEN LATE
Restaurant remains open with the full menu available after 10pm.

FIXED-PRICE MENU
A good-value fixed-price menu on offer at lunch, dinner or both, usually with three courses.

GOOD WINE LIST
Denotes a wide range of good wines, or a more specialized selection of wines.

</td></tr>
</table>

	CREDIT CARDS	OPEN LUNCH TIME	OPEN LATE	FIXED-PRICE MENU	GOOD WINE LIST
CORK AND KERRY					
BALLYDEHOB: *Annie's* €€€€ Main St, Ballydehob. **Road map** B6. **(** 028 37292. Annie's is popular with locals and resident stars such as Jeremy Irons. The food is a fusion of French and contemporary Irish. Book ahead. 👤 🏃 ⚡ **V**	MC V	●		●	▪
BALLYLICKEY: *Sea View House Hotel* €€€€ Bantry Bay. **Road map** B6. **(** 027 50073. The award-winning cuisine at this charming spot centres on local produce and fish from Bantry Bay. Open from 17 Mar–Sep. 👤 🏃 ⚡ **V**	MC V AE DC			●	▪
BANTRY: *O'Connor's Seafood Restaurant* €€€€ The Square. **Road map** B6. **(** 027 50221. Right in the centre of town, Bantry Bay's famed mussels and live lobsters take pride of place in this established restaurant. 👤 🏃 ⚡ **V**	MC V	●			▪
BLARNEY: *Phelan's Woodview House* €€€€ Tweedmount. **Road map** B5. **(** 021 438 5197. This intimate restaurant often draws diners from nearby Cork to sample chef Billy Phelan's hot seafood parcel. Closed Sun and Mon. 👤 🏃 ⚡ **V**	MC V		▪	●	▪
CASTLETOWNSHEND: *Mary Ann's Bar* €€€€ Skibbereen. **Road map** B6. **(** 028 36146. Local seafood features prominently on the menu of this 150-year-old bar and restaurant. Try the baked brill with prawns. 👤 🏃 ⚡ **V**	MC V			●	▪
CORK: *Arbutus Lodge Hotel* €€€€ Montenotte. **Road map** C5. **(** 021 450 1237. This informal bar provides some of the best-value lunchtime food in Cork. The more formal restaurant in the same hotel offers gourmet dinners mixing Irish, French and other international cuisine. 🏃 ⚡ **V**	MC V AE DC	●			▪
CORK: *Isaac's Restaurant* €€€€ 48a MacCurtain St. **Road map** C5. **(** 021 450 3805. The menu in this converted warehouse in the centre of Cork is extensive, offering both continental and world cuisine. 👤 🏃 ⚡ **V**	MC V AE DC	●			▪
CORK: *The Ivory Tower* €€€€€ The Exchange Buildings, 35 Princes St. **Road map** C5. **(** 021 427 4665. Unusual and delicious combinations grace the menu of this attractive and rather trendy restaurant. 🏃 *by arrangement.* ⚡ **V**	MC V		▪	▪	▪
DINGLE: *Fentons Bistro* €€€€ Green St. **Road map** A5. **(** 066 915 2172. This bright popular bistro, open for the summer season, serves local produce including lamb, lobster and catch of the day. 👤 🏃 ⚡ **V**	MC V AE DC			●	▪
DINGLE: *Half Door Restaurant* €€€€ 3 John St. **Road map** A5. **(** 066 915 1600. A combination of stone and light woods creates a relaxed ambience at the Half Door. The day's catch determines the menu. 👤 🏃 ⚡ **V**	MC V DC	●			▪
DURRUS: *Blair's Cove House Restaurant* €€€€ Blair's Cove. **Road map** B6. **(** 027 61127. In this romantic waterside restaurant on the shores of Dunmanus Bay, both wine list and cheeseboard are exceptional. 👤 🏃 ⚡ **V**	MC V			●	▪
INNISHANNON: *Innishannon Hotel & Restaurant* €€€€ Innishannon. **Road map** B6. **(** 021 477 5121. The setting of this lovely 18th-century house beside the river makes it a very romantic spot. The owners' son, Pearse, is the excellent chef producing modern Irish and classical French dishes. 👤 🏃 **V**	MC V AE			●	▪

KENMARE: *The Purple Heather*   €€
Henry St. **Road map** B5.   064 41016.
This town-centre pub and restaurant serves up tasty, hearty food. Dishes
include chicken liver terrine and Cumberland sauce.

KENMARE: *Lime Tree Restaurant*   €€€€   MC V
Shelburne St. **Road map** B5.   064 41225.
Housed in a charming 1830s school, the Lime Tree offers imaginative
dishes like goat's cheese potato cakes. Open April to October.

KENMARE: *Packie's*   €€€€   MC V
35 Henry St. **Road map** B5.   064 41508.
The emphasis is on seafood, but you're likely to find touches of California
or Mediterranean cuisine along with traditional Irish dishes, such as a
delicious Irish lamb stew with fresh herbs.

KILLARNEY: *The Cooperage Restaurant*   €€€€   MC V
Old Market Lane. **Road map** B5.   064 37716.
A very attractive modern restaurant in the centre of town. The menu is
simple but delicious making the most of seasonal produce.

KILLARNEY: *The Old Presbytery*   €€€€   MC V AE DC
Cathedral Place. **Road map** B5.   064 30555.
Located in a Georgian building opposite St Mary's Cathedral and beside
Killarney National Park, this restaurant is contemporary and elegant. The
modern European cuisine reflects the decor. Closed Tuesday.

KILLARNEY: *Gaby's*   €€€€€   MC V AE DC
27 High St. **Road map** B5.   064 32519.
Gaby's is undoubtedly the best seafood restaurant in town. Its interior
incorporates seafaring memorabilia. Specialities include lobster, shellfish,
oysters and Atlantic salmon. Closed Sunday.

KILLORGLIN: *Nick's Restaurant*   €€€€   MC V AE DC
Lower Bridge St. **Road map** A5.   066 976 1219.
Chef Nick Foley's background as a butcher ensures that only the best cuts
of meat reach the table. The same care goes into seafood offerings. There
are open fires and a pianist plays regularly. limited.

KINSALE: *The Blue Haven Hotel*   €€€€   MC V AE DC
3–4 Pearse St. **Road map** B6.   021 477 2209.
A pleasant family restaurant, the Blue Haven offers a wide variety of food,
from bar lunches to substantial meals. There's always a good selection of
farmhouse cheeses.

KINSALE: *Man Friday*   €€€€   MC V AE DC
Scilly. **Road map** B6.   021 477 2260.
Overlooking Kinsale Harbour, this restaurant has won culinary awards
galore. No wonder, with specialities such as grilled turbot with crab
peppercorn sauce and hot seafood platter.

KINSALE: *Max's Wine Bar*   €€€€   MC V AE
Main St. **Road map** B6.   021 477 2443.
For more than 20 years, Max's has been in the forefront of Kinsale's
gourmet restaurants. The emphasis here is on fresh, locally sourced
ingredients. Open March to October.

LEAP: *Friskey's Restaurant*   €€€   MC V
The Leap Inn. **Road map** B6.   028 33307.
Traditional Irish dishes (Irish stew, bacon and cabbage, roast stuffed
chicken) feature on lunchtime menus in this delightful country inn. Locally
caught seafoods are also a speciality. Open only during the summer.

MALLOW: *Presidents' Restaurant*   €€€€   MC V AE DC
Longueville House. **Road map** B5.   022 47156.
Portraits of Irish presidents line the walls in this Georgian mansion. The
modern cuisine uses local farm produce.

MONKSTOWN: *Bosun*   €€€€   MC V AE DC
Monkstown. **Road map** B5.   021 484 2172.
About six miles outside of Cork city along the river Lee, this well-known
bar and restaurant serves local produce, including mussels and lobster.
There are tables outside and good views of the river.

For key to symbols see back flap

Average prices for a three-course meal for one, half a bottle of house wine and all extra service and cover charges:
€ under 14 euros
€€ 14–20 euros
€€€ 20–32 euros
€€€€ 32–66 euros
€€€€€ over 66 euros

OPEN LUNCH TIME
Many restaurants open only in the evening, but those in large towns and attached to pubs often open at lunch time.
OPEN LATE
Restaurant remains open with the full menu available after 10pm.
FIXED-PRICE MENU
A good-value fixed-price menu on offer at lunch, dinner or both, usually with three courses.
GOOD WINE LIST
Denotes a wide range of good wines, or a more specialized selection of wines.

		CREDIT CARDS	OPEN LUNCH TIME	OPEN LATE	FIXED-PRICE MENU	GOOD WINE LIST
PARKNASILLA: *Pygmalion Restaurant* — €€€€ Great Southern Hotel. **Road map** A6. (064 45122. Overlooking Kenmare Bay on the Ring of Kerry, the Pygmalion's elegant decor and polished service set off a gourmet cuisine. 🚻 ♿ ✹ **V**		MC V AE DC			●	▦
SHANAGARRY: *Ballymaloe House* — €€€€€ Shanagarry, Midleton. **Road map** C6. (021 465 2531. At Ballymaloe House, acclaimed for its Irish and French classics, vegetables and meats come from their own farm, and seafood is local. ♿ ✹ **V**		MC V AE DC	●		●	▦
YOUGHAL: *Aherne's Seafood Restaurant* — €€€€ 163 North Main St. **Road map** C5. (024 92424. Chef David Fitzgibbon's seafood chowder is positively addictive. His sumptuous platter of six fish and four shellfish won Aherne's the prestigious Seafood Dish of the Year Award. 🚻 ♿ ✹ **V**		MC V AE DC	●		●	▦

THE LOWER SHANNON

		CREDIT CARDS	OPEN LUNCH TIME	OPEN LATE	FIXED-PRICE MENU	GOOD WINE LIST
ADARE: *The Mustard Seed at Echo Lodge* — €€€€ Ballingarry. **Road map** B5. (069 68508. In a Victorian-style building the Mustard Seed has wonderful views over a vast expanse of countryside. The modern Irish cuisine includes seasonal dishes prepared with the freshest of ingredients. 🚻 ♿ ✹ **V**		MC V AE			●	▦
ADARE: *The Inn-Between* — €€€€€ Dunraven Arms Hotel, Main St. **Road map** B5. (061 396633. A charming restaurant in a thatched cottage, with informal service and a cosy atmosphere. The cooking is modern cuisine. 🚻 ♿ ✹ **V**		MC V AE DC				▦
BUNRATTY: *Muses Restaurant* — €€€€ Bunratty House Mews. **Road map** B4. (061 364082. Downstairs in this 1846 mansion, the original kitchen, staff quarters and wine cellars form one of the best restaurants in the country. ♿ ✹ **V**		MC V AE DC			●	▦
CAHIR: *Malone's* — €€€ The Galtee Inn, The Square. **Road map** C5. (052 41247. The all-day menu in this family-run restaurant offers prime beef with rich sauces, roasts and seafood dishes as well as light meals. 🚻 ♿ ✹ **V**		MC V AE	●			▦
CASHEL: *Chez Hans* — €€€€ Rockside. **Road map** C5. (062 61177. At the foot of the Rock of Cashel, Chez Hans occupies a former Wesleyan chapel. For several years, Hans-Peter Matthiä has created wonderfully innovative versions of traditional dishes. 🚻 ♿ ✹ **V**		MC V				▦
CLONMEL: *The Old Bank Restaurant* — €€€€ Clonmel Arms Hotel, Sarsfield St. **Road map** C5. (052 21233. The Old Bank is a bright, airy hotel dining room, decorated with strong colours, lots of brass and some interesting art. The European-influenced menu changes with the seasons. 🚻 ♿ ✹ **V**		MC V AE DC			●	▦
DOOLIN: *Bruach na hAille* — €€ Roadford. **Road map** B4. (065 707 4120. This charming, cottage-style restaurant (its name means "banks of the river") uses local produce in unexpected ways, such as fillets of sole in cider served with shellfish in a cream sauce. 🚻 ♿ ✹ **V**		MC V AE			●	▦
ENNIS: *Cruise's Pub and Restaurant* — €€€€ Abbey St. **Road map** B4. (065 684 1800. The 17th-century building's low, beamed ceilings and the open fires in winter create a cosy ambience. There is traditional music in the bar every night which filters through into the restaurant. 🚻 ♿ ✹ **V**		MC V AE DC			●	▦

ENNISTIMON: *Byrnes Restaurant* €€€€ MC V AE DC
Main St. **Road map** B4. 065 707 1080.
This smart restaurant is housed in a fine 18th-century building on the town's main street. Drinks are served on terraces overlooking the river, waterfall and a stone-arched bridge.

LIMERICK: *Chez O'Shea* €€€€ MC V DC
74 O'Connell St. **Road map** B4. 061 316311.
In a Georgian building with roaring open fires, this city-centre restaurant serves modern Irish dishes with Mediterranean influences.

LIMERICK: *Soral's Restaurant* €€€€ MC V AE DC
Jury's Hotel, Ennis Rd. **Road map** B4. 061 327777.
All-day service makes this bright hotel restaurant one of the most con-venient in Limerick. Light snacks share the menu with full meals. The more formal Copper Room serves gourmet and traditional Irish dishes.

NEWMARKET-ON-FERGUS: *Earl of Thomond Room* €€€€€ MC V AE DC
Dromoland Castle. **Road map** B4. 061 368144.
A traditional Irish harper accompanies evening meals in this elegant dining room. The "Taste of Ireland" set menu has no fewer than six courses. Try the hot brown-bread soufflé and the creamy lamb ravioli.

THURLES: *Inch House* €€€€ MC V AE
Thurles. **Road map** B4. 0504 51261.
A mixture of traditional and more adventurous dishes in a fine country house setting. limited by arrangement.

THE WEST OF IRELAND

ACHILL ISLAND: *Ferndale Restaurant* €€€€ MC V AE
Crumpaun, Keel. **Road map** A3. 098 43908.
On an elevated site with wonderful views of the cliffs, beach and across the whole island, Ferndale produces exotic international cuisine. There is sometimes live music in the summer.

ARAN ISLANDS: *Dún Aonghasa & Aran Fisherman Restaurant* €€€€ MC V
Kilronan, Inishmore. **Road map** B4. 099 61104.
Overlooking the harbour, in a setting of stone, wood and open fires, owner Grace Flaherty bases her menu on fish fresh from Galway Bay. Choices include creamy seafood chowder and grilled shark.

BARNA: *Donnelly's Seafood Restaurant and Bar* €€€€ MC V AE DC
Freeport. **Road map** B4. 091 592487.
Fresh seafood is a speciality in this rustic-style restaurant. Among non-seafood dishes is chicken supreme.

CLARINBRIDGE: *Moran's Oyster Cottage* €€€€ MC V AE
The Weir. **Road map** B4. 091 796113.
Known as "Moran's of the Weir", this 200-year-old restaurant in a thatched cottage is loved by both locals and celebrities, especially during the annual Clarinbridge Oyster Festival in the second week in September.

CLIFDEN: *O'Grady's Seafood Restaurant* €€€€€ MC V
Market St. **Road map** A3. 095 21450.
Award-winning O'Grady's offers wonderful seafood, plus superb vegetarian choices. Open late-March to November.

CLIFDEN: *Rock Glen Restaurant* €€€€ MC V AE
Rock Glen Manor House. **Road map** A3. 095 21035.
A converted Connemara shooting lodge is the setting for gracious dining here, with friendly service enhancing an excellent cuisine.

CONG: *Connaught Room* €€€€€ MC V AE DC
Ashford Castle. **Road map** B3. 094 954 6003.
Only the best local ingredients come to table in this wood-panelled dining room. Its menu includes rack of Connemara hill lamb and fillet of turbot with scallops. Open May to October.

GALWAY: *McDonagh's Seafood Bar* €€€€ MC V AE DC
22 Quay St. **Road map** B4. 091 565001.
Not surprisingly, the speciality in this popular and relaxed establishment is the seafood platter. The fish and chips section stays open till midnight.

Average prices for a three-course meal for one, half a bottle of house wine and all extra service and cover charges:

€ under 14 euros
€€ 14–20 euros
€€€ 20–32 euros
€€€€ 32–66 euros
€€€€€ over 66 euros

OPEN LUNCH TIME
Many restaurants open only in the evening, but those in large towns and attached to pubs often open at lunch time.

OPEN LATE
Restaurant remains open with the full menu available after 10pm.

FIXED-PRICE MENU
A good-value fixed-price menu on offer at lunch, dinner or both, usually with three courses.

GOOD WINE LIST
Denotes a wide range of good wines, or a more specialized selection of wines.

	Credit Cards	Open Lunch Time	Open Late	Fixed-Price Menu	Good Wine List
GALWAY: *Kirwan's Lane Restaurant* €€€€ Kirwan's Lane. **Road map** B4. (091 568266. Just beside the Hotel Spanish Arch, this smart, sophisticated restaurant is run by Michael O'Grady of Clifden fame. The freshest local ingredients are used in a huge choice of international and New Irish dishes. & ⚥ ⚡ V	MC V AE	●	■		■
GALWAY: *The Park Room* €€€€ Park House Hotel, Forster St, Eyre Sq. **Road map** B4. (091 564924. Inside the Park House Hotel, this restaurant offers a well-priced menu of Irish specialities, all prepared with local ingredients. & ⚥ ⚡ V	MC V AE DC	●		●	■
MOYCULLEN: *Moycullen House* €€€€ Moycullen. **Road map** B4. (091 555621. This house was built as a sporting lodge and is surrounded by over 30 acres of grounds. The restaurant is well run and the food excellent. & ⚡ V	MC V AE			●	■
ROSCOMMON: *Abbey Hotel* €€€€ Galway Rd. **Road map** C3. (090 662 6250. Set dinners in this 18th-century turreted mansion feature steak prepared in different ways, grilled sea trout and other fish dishes. & ⚥ ⚡ V	MC V AE DC	●		●	■
WESTPORT: *The Lemon Peel* €€€€ The Octagon. **Road map** B3. (098 26929. This small modern restaurant has an informal atmosphere but the service is very professional and the food delicious. & ⚥ ⚡ V	MC V	●		●	■

NORTHWEST IRELAND

	Credit Cards	Open Lunch Time	Open Late	Fixed-Price Menu	Good Wine List
BALLYSHANNON: *Sweeney's White Horse Bar* €€€€ Assaroe Rd. **Road map** C2. (071 985 1452. Sweeney's set bar menu offers good food in an inviting atmosphere. There is traditional music in the Cellar Bar on Friday nights in summer. ⚥ ⚡ V		●			■
CASTLEBALDWIN: *Cromleach Lodge Country House* €€€€€ Castlebaldwin, Boyle. **Road map** C3. (071 916 5155. Fabulous views of Lough Arrow and the Bricklieve Mountains form a backdrop for gourmet dining in this hilltop country house. & ⚥ ⚡ V	MC V AE DC			●	■
COLLOONEY: *Glebe House Restaurant* €€€€ Collooney. **Road map** C2. (071 916 7787. At this Georgian house, there's an emphasis on organically grown produce and imaginative use of local fish and meats. Friendly service. & ⚥ ⚡ V	MC V AE DC			●	■
DUNKINEELY: *Castlemurray House* €€€€ Dunkineely. **Road map** C2. (074 973 7022. There are wonderful views across the bay from the relaxed restaurant – perfect surroundings for you to enjoy classic dishes expertly prepared. & ⚡ V	MC V			●	■
INISHOWEN PENINSULA: *Bree Inn* € Malin Head. **Road map** C1. (074 937 0161. At the northernmost point in Ireland, this lively country inn serves home-cooked meals all day in summer. The place is popular with locals. & ⚥ V		●	■		
INISHOWEN PENINSULA: *Kealey Seafood Bar* €€€€ The Harbour, Greencastle. **Road map** C1. (074 938 1010. Right by the harbour, Kealey's uses fresh seafood catch and organic farm produce to make award-winning cuisine. There's sometimes traditional music. & ⚥ ⚡ V	MC V AE	●	■	●	■
KILLYBEGS: *The Fleet Inn* €€€€ Bridge St. **Road map** C2. (074 973 1664. The restaurant is upstairs from the inn in the centre of town. Award-winning seafood is the speciality, with a French twist. ⚥ ⚡ V					■

RATHMULLAN: *Pavilion Restaurant*   €€€€   MC V AE DC
Rathmullan Country House. **Road map** C1. **☎** *074 915 8188.*
The Pavilion offers gourmet food in a glass-walled setting. Sample the
unusual seaweed-based dessert of carrageen moss with stewed fruits.
& ♣ ≠ V

ROSSES POINT: *The Austies*   €€€€   MC V
Rosses Point Road. **Road map** B2. **☎** *071 917 7111.*
High above Sligo Bay, The Austies offers fresh seafood dishes such as crab
au gratin. Open evenings only. **♣ ≠ V**

SLIGO: *Garavogue*   €€€   MC V
Rear 15-16 Stephens Street. **Road map** C2. **☎** *071 914 0100.*
This excitingly-designed restaurant is named after the river flowing past it.
Dishes include Thai and Spanish, with bar-food portions downstairs and
full menu available in the restaurant. **& ♣ ≠ V**

TOBERCURRY: *Killoran's Traditional Restaurant*   €€€   MC V AE DC
Teeling St. **Road map** B3. **☎** *071 918 5679.*
Irish stew, boxty (potato pancakes) and crubeens (pigs' feet) are on the
traditional menu. Snacks and full meals served all day. **& ♣ ≠ V**

THE MIDLANDS

ATHLONE: *L'Escale Restaurant*   €€€€   MC V AE DC
The Hodson Bay Hotel. **Road map** C3. **☎** *090 649 2444.*
Cuisine is an international mix. A typical dish is Dublin Bay prawns with
shallots, mushrooms and tomato, flamed in whiskey. **& ♣ ≠ V**

ATHLONE: *Wineport Lakeshore Restaurant*   €€€€€   MC V AE DC
Glassan. **Road map** D3. **☎** *090 648 5466.*
This lakeside restaurant has a very loyal clientele who find the view, the
atmosphere and the food irresistible. Awards galore. **& ♣ ≠ V**

BUTLER'S BRIDGE: *Derragarra Inn*   €€€€   MC V
Butler's Bridge. **Road map** C3. **☎** *049 433 1003.*
A thatched cottage inn decorated with relics of rural Ireland by the River
Annalea. The restaurant menu is available in the bar all day. **& ♣ ≠ V**

CARLINGFORD: *Jordan's Town House Restaurant*   €€€€   MC V AE
Newry St. **Road map** D3. **☎** *042 937 3223.*
A renovated 19th-century warehouse overlooking the harbour is the setting
for culinary gems with organically grown ingredients. **& ♣ ≠ V**

CARRICKMACROSS: *Nuremore Hotel*   €€€€   MC V AE DC
Carrickmacross. **Road map** D3. **☎** *042 966 1438.*
This beautiful restaurant has an imaginative menu, including French and
Irish cuisine, served in a tranquil setting. **& ♣ ≠ V**

DUNDALK: *Quaglino's Restaurant*   €€€€   MC V AE DC
88 Clanbrassil St. **Road map** D3. **☎** *042 933 8567.*
This bright, town-centre restaurant features superb Continental and Modern
Irish cuisine using local produce. **♣ ≠ V**

KELLS: *Carrick House*   €€   MC V
Carrick St. **Road map** D3. **☎** *046 924 0100.*
Carrick House is a moderately priced family restaurant. Only locally-farmed
meats are used. Children welcome until 9pm. **& ♣ V**

MONAGHAN: *Andy's Restaurant*   €€€€   MC V
Market St. **Road map** D2. **☎** *047 82277.*
This cheerful, airy restaurant in Monaghan town centre is above an award-
winning pub. The extensive menu includes sirloin steak in mushroom and
cider sauce. **& ♣ ≠ V**

MOUNTRATH: *Roundwood House*   €€€€   MC V AE DC
Mountrath. **Road map** C4. **☎** *0502 32120.*
Pre-booking is a must in this gracious Palladian mansion. The compulsory
four-course set menu changes daily. **♣ ≠ V**

MULLINGAR: *Crookedwood House*   €€€€   MC V AE DC
Crookedwood. **Road map** C3. **☎** *044 72165.*
This 200-year-old restaurant changes its menu with the seasons. A summer
speciality is River Moy salmon with hollandaise sauce. **& ♣ ≠ V**

For key to symbols see back flap

		CREDIT CARDS	OPEN LUNCH TIME	OPEN LATE	FIXED-PRICE MENU	GOOD WINE LIST

Average prices for a three-course meal for one, half a bottle of house wine and all extra service and cover charges:
£ under £10
££ £10–£15
£££ £15–£20
££££ £20–£25
£££££ over £25

OPEN LUNCH TIME
Many restaurants open only in the evening, but those in large towns and attached to pubs often open at lunch time.
OPEN LATE
Restaurant remains open with the full menu available after 10pm.
FIXED-PRICE MENU
A good-value fixed-price menu on offer at lunch, dinner or both, usually with three courses.
GOOD WINE LIST
Denotes a wide range of good wines, or a more specialized selection of wines.

NORTHERN IRELAND

	CREDIT CARDS	OPEN LUNCH TIME	OPEN LATE	FIXED-PRICE MENU	GOOD WINE LIST
ARMAGH: *Pilgrim's Table* ££ 38–40 English St. **Road map** D2. (028 3752 1814. This restaurant creates fine home cooking with fresh local produce. Non-fussy dishes, especially the soups, are tasty, filling and superb value. No wine licence. ⓺ ⚶ ⚐ V		●			
BALLYCASTLE: *Wysner's Restaurant* £££££ 16 Anne St. **Road map** D1. (028 2076 2372. Downstairs at Wysner's is a French-style café, while upstairs is a restaurant where the Bushmills Malt cheesecake is a must. ⓺ ⚶ ⚐ V	MC V	●		●	■
BELFAST: *Crown Liquor Saloon* £ 46 Great Victoria St. **Road map** D2. (028 9024 9476. This bar's snug-like booths include table space for a bowl of Irish stew and champ – a local speciality of potatoes, spring onions and butter. ⚶ V	MC V AE	●			■
BELFAST: *Manor House Restaurant* ££ 43–47 Donegall Pass. **Road map** D2. (028 9023 8755. Run by the Wong family since 1982, this Cantonese restaurant is a reliable and popular place. The menu is extensive. ⓺ ⚶ V	MC V	●	■	●	■
BELFAST: *Duke of York* £££ 11 Commercial Court. **Road map** D2. (028 9024 1062. This very reasonably priced restaurant offers typical pub grub. Near St Anne's Cathedral, it is Irish in style and cluttered with Belfast memorabilia. Open from noon to 3pm only. ⚶ V		●			
BELFAST: *Malone House* ££££ Barnett Demesne. **Road map** D2. (028 9068 1246. Only the highest quality Ulster produce is used in the Brasserie-style menu served at this local favourite. Vegetarian dishes are often the house speciality. ⓺ ⚶ ⚐ V	MC V AE DC	●		●	■
BELFAST: *Cayenne* £££££ 7 Lesley House, Shaftesbury Sq. **Road map** D2. (028 9033 1532. Celebrity chefs Paul and Jeanne Rankin opened this restaurant in 1999, and serves a delicious mixture of Thai, Japanese and other Asia-influenced dishes. ⓺ ⚶ ⚐ V	MC V AE DC	●	■	●	■
BELFAST: *Metro Brasserie* £££££ 13 Lower Crescent. **Road map** D2. (028 9032 3349. This is a trendy modern version of the traditional brasserie. The interior design is striking and unusual and gives the place a sophisticated but relaxed atmosphere. ⓺ ⚶ ⚐ V	MC V AE DC	●		●	■
BELFAST: *Nick's Warehouse* £££££ 35–39 Hill St. **Road map** D2. (028 9043 9690. Nick and Kathy Price's converted warehouse, tucked away in the cobbled backstreets of city-centre Belfast, gets top marks for atmosphere. The menu regularly includes Nick's latest culinary innovations. ⓺ ⚶ V	MC V AE DC	●			■
BELFAST: *Restaurant Michael Deane* £££££ 38–40 Howard St. **Road map** D2. (028 9056 0000. You have a choice here of smart and elegant formal dining on the first floor or the more informal brasserie on the ground floor. The food is excellent in both. ⓺ ⚶ V	MC V AE	●	■		■
BUSHMILLS: *Bushmills Inn* £££££ 9 Dunluce Rd. **Road map** D1. (028 2073 2339. Originally an old coaching inn, this popular hostelry is only a few miles from the Giant's Causeway and close to Bushmills Distillery. ⓺ ⚶ ⚐ V		●		●	■

DUNDRUM: *The Buck's Head*   £££££   MC V AE
77 Main St. **Road map** E2. [028 4375 1868.
Open fires and hospitable, friendly service make this an excellent stop for
either lunch or dinner. The cuisine is a mix of traditional and modern.
& ⚦ ⚡ V

DUNGANNON: *Viscount's Restaurant*   £££££   MC V
10 Northland Row. **Road map** D2. [028 8775 3800.
A Victorian church has been converted into a medieval-style banqueting
hall with the emphasis on fun as much as food. The large menu caters to
all appetites and is popular with families in the daytime. & ⚦ ⚡ V

ENNISKILLEN: *Arch Tullyhona House Restaurant*   £££
59 Marble Arch Rd, Florencecourt. **Road map** C2. [028 6634 8452.
Beside Marble Arch caves, this farm restaurant offers great food and
service. Produce fresh from the farm is used, and desserts such as lemon
soufflé and fresh fruit pavlova are a speciality. & ⚦ ⚡ V

ENNISKILLEN: *The Sheelin*   ££££   MC V
Bellanaleck. **Road map** C2. [028 6634 8232.
This thatched cottage restaurant on the shores of Lower Lough Erne is a
gourmet experience. The menu is a mixture of French and continental
cuisine presenting an eclectic range of dishes. & ⚦ ⚡ V

ENNISKILLEN: *Franco's Restaurant*   £££££   MC V AE
Queen Elizabeth Rd. **Road map** C2. [028 6632 4424.
A warren of nooks and crannies, this hospitable pizzeria often has live
traditional music. The vast menu offers Italian food with an Irish influence.
Seafood dishes include fresh lobster and mussels. & ⚦ ⚡ V

HILLSBOROUGH: *Hillside Restaurant and Bar*   £££££   MC V AE DC
21 Main St. **Road map** D2. [028 9268 2765.
This attractive country-style pub and restaurant has an excellent seasonal
menu. The bar serves a good selection of real ales. & ⚦ ⚡ V

HOLYWOOD: *Bistro Iona*   ££££   MC V
27 Church Rd. **Road map** E2. [028 9042 5655.
Roughcast walls and tightly packed tables make this restaurant, homely,
welcoming and bright. "Early bird" menus are great value. There's no wine
licence so bring your own bottle. ⚦ V

LIMAVADY: *The Lime Tree*   £££££   MC V AE
60 Catherine Street. **Road map** D1. [028 7776 4300.
Right on the main street in this attractive town, the restaurant is small and
quite simply decorated. The interesting menu offers unusual and subtle
tasting dishes put together with local ingredients. & ⚦ ⚡ V

LONDONDERRY: *The Metro*   ££   MC V
3–4 Bank Pl. **Road map** C1. [028 7126 7401.
Shadowed by Derry's city walls, this is a local favourite. The food, from
soup and sandwiches to Guinness beef stew, is first rate. Lunch only. & ⚦ V

PORTAFERRY: *The Narrows*   £££££   MC V AE
8 Shore Rd. **Road map** E2. [028 4272 8148.
A bright, light restaurant with delicious, locally sourced ingredients.
Seafood is a speciality. & ⚦ ⚡ V

PORTBALLINTRAE: *Sweeny's Wine Bar*   ££££
6b Seaport Ave. **Road map** D1. [028 2073 2404.
Prices here are cheap and cheerful and the food creatively prepared.
Situated on the Causeway Coast, Sweeny's occupies a converted stable
block overlooking Portballintrae Harbour. & ⚦ ⚡ V

PORTRUSH: *The Harbour Bar*   £££   MC V AE DC
The Harbour. **Road map** D1. [028 7082 2430.
The traditional pub area on the ground floor has roaring fires and a great
atmosphere. The restaurant is also informal and offers a good selection of
à la carte dishes. & ⚦ V

STRANGFORD: *The Lobster Pot Bar & Restaurant*   £££££   MC V AE DC
The Square. **Road map** E2. [028 4488 1288.
Only the finest local catches are served in this predominantly fish restaurant
overlooking Strangford Lough. & ⚦ ⚡ V

Pubs in Ireland

THE ARCHETYPAL IRISH PUB is celebrated for its convivial atmosphere, friendly locals, genial bar staff and the "crack" – the Irish expression for fun. Wit is washed down with whiskey or Guinness, the national drinks. Irish pubs date back to medieval taverns, coaching inns and shebeens, illegal drinking dens which flourished under colonial rule. In Victorian times, brewing and distilling were major industries. The sumptuous Edwardian or Victorian interiors of some city pubs are a testament to these times, furnished with mahogany and marble bar counters. Snugs, partitioned-off booths, are another typical feature of Irish pubs. Traditional pubs can be boldly painted, thatched or "black-and-white" – beamed with a white façade and black trim. Some rural pubs double as grocers' shops.

Good pubs are not evenly distributed throughout the country: in the Southeast, Kilkenny is paradise for pub-lovers, while Cork and Kerry possess some of the most picturesque pubs. The Lower Shannon region is noted for its boisterous pubs, especially in County Clare where spontaneous music sessions are common. The West has an abundance of typical Irish pubs, and the many tourists and students guarantee a profusion of good pubs in Galway. The listings below cover a selection of pubs throughout Ireland; for Dublin pubs, see pages 104–7.

SOUTHEAST IRELAND

Dunmore East: *The Ship Inn*
Road map D5. **(** 051 383141.
This old, ivy-clad pub lies above the harbour, away from the crowds on the beach. It is noted both for its seafood and its seafaring links. Inside, nautical memorabilia and half-barrel seats abound in the front bar. The small garden is an appealing spot for drinking in the summer. Lemon sole, turbot and brill are on the menu. 🍴 🛏

Enniscorthy: *The Antique Tavern*
14 Slaney St. **Road map** D5.
(054 33428.
This traditional, timbered, black-and-white pub is charming. The dark, intimate bar contains relics such as pikestaffs from Vinegar Hill, the decisive battle in the 1798 uprising that was fought outside town. Pub lunches and local chat are on offer. In good weather, you can sit on the balcony. 🛏 🍴

Enniscorthy: *Holohan*
Slaney Place. **Road map** D5.
(054 33179.
At the back of the Castle Museum, this is essentially a workaday pub with few pretensions. Its unusual location makes it worth a visit for a few pints – it is built right into the base of an old quarry and a vertical cliff forms part of the back wall of the bar.

Kilkenny: *Kyteler's Inn*
27 St Kieran's St. **Road map** C4.
(056 772 1064.
In good weather you can sit in the courtyard of this historic coaching inn and cellar bar. Food is served all day, and meals are served in the restaurant downstairs until 9:45pm (last orders). An effigy of a witch sits in the window frame, a reminder of the story of a former resident, Dame Alice Kyteler. In 1324, Alice and her maid were pronounced guilty of witchcraft after four of Alice's husbands had died in mysterious circumstances; although pardoned, Alice was again accused but escaped, leaving her maid to burn at the stake. 🍴 🛏

Kilkenny: *Langton's*
69 John St. **Road map** C4.
(056 776 5133.
Langton's is noted for its black-and-white exterior, Edwardian ambience and the stylish glass interior at the back. The front bar is cosy with a low ceiling. Pub food is on offer, and there's music and dancing three or four nights a week; Tuesday, Thursday and Saturday are disco nights. 🍴

Kilkenny: *Maggie Holland's*
St Kieran's St. **Road map** C4.
(056 776 2273.
In a central spot near the river, this is a dimly lit but welcoming pub. Traditional music on Tuesday evenings draws plenty of locals. 🎵 🍴

Kilkenny: *Marble City Bar*
66 High St. **Road map** C4.
(056 776 1143.
Marble City Bar, the most famous pub in town, is named after the local limestone, which becomes black when polished. This four-storey building has an Art Deco facade and has recently been restored. Bar food till 8:30pm. 🎵

Kilkenny: *Tynan's Bridge House Bar*
2 John's Bridge. **Road map** C4.
(056 772 1291.
This is the most genuine old-world pub in town, with an intimate interior lit by charming lamps. Quaint relics of the former grocery store and pharmacy are on display, from a set of old scales to the drawers labelled with names of nuts and spices. No music, no TV; as publican Michael puts it, this is "a chat bar". 🍴

Kilmore Quay: *The Wooden House Lodge*
Road map D5. **(** 053 29804.
This traditional – if over-restored – thatched pub is full of nautical memorabilia and quirky sayings while the small terrace is decorated with anchors. Hearty pub fare is served. 🍴 🛏 🎵

Waterford: *Axis Mundi*
The Mall. **Road map** D5.
(051 855087.
Set beside Reginald's Tower, the pub incorporates part of the Viking city walls and the medieval sallyports (attack exits), which are still visible. The service is rather brusque. There is an adjoining nightclub. 🍴 🎵

Waterford: *T and H Doolin*
George's St. **Road map** D5.
(051 841504.
Set in the city's most charming pedestrianized street, this traditional, 18th-century black-and-white pub offers an intimate atmosphere and good "crack". Traditional folk music sessions are held every night. 🍴 🛏 🎵

Wexford: *Centenary Stores*
Charlotte St. **Road map** D5.
(053 24424.
Tucked away in a converted warehouse, this cosy, dimly lit pub is the most charming in Wexford. The friendly bar staff and a mixed local and bohemian crowd chat in the wood-panelled bar. Drinkers are entertained with sessions of traditional music every Sunday morning, and on Monday and Wednesday evenings in summer. 🍴 🛏 🎵

Wexford: *Westgate Tavern*
Westgate. **Road map** D5.
[053 22086.
Licensed since 1761, this distinctive tavern faces the path leading to the famous Selskar Abbey and Westgate Heritage Centre. Lunch menu and bar snacks are available in the welcoming bar and there are music sessions on Sunday and Monday evenings. 🎵 🍴

CORK AND KERRY

Clonakilty: *De Barra's*
Road map B6. [023 33381.
This is one of the best-known pubs in West Cork, with a traditional folk club most nights; many musicians come from the Gaeltacht *(see p221)*. The bar is lovingly restored, with hand-painted signs and traditional whiskey jars. Simple snacks and full lunches are served from noon to 3pm. 🍴 🎵

Cork: *Chateau Bar*
St Patrick's St. **Road map** C5.
[021 427 0370.
This bar in the heart of the city occupies a striking building that was once on the quayside. Founded in 1793, this elegant pub has a stylish Victorian interior and offers good quality bar fare. 🍴 ♿

Cork: *Chimes*
27 Church St. **Road map** C5.
[021 430 4136.
Set in the hilly, old-world Shandon district, this convivial working-class pub attracts a mixed, friendly crowd, from local pensioners to sports fans and students. On Saturday and Sunday nights there's music, usually in the form of accordion or keyboard soloists. 🎵

Cork: *Henchy's*
40 St Luke's Cross. **Road map** C5.
[021 450 7833.
This traditional pub, situated close to Chimes *(see above)*, dates from 1884 and has retained much of its Victorian ambience, enhanced by the mahogany bar, stained glass and a snug (a private room, in this case, with a separate entrance). It has long been associated with poets and is where young hopefuls come to recite their work to a largely sympathetic audience.

Cork: *The Oyster Tavern*
Market Lane, off St Patrick's St.
Road map C5. [021 427 2716.
Founded in the 18th century, this tavern was sympathetically refurbished by the new management in 1994. Lunches are served between noon and 3pm; Saturdays until 5pm. Occasional music. There is a DJ performing Thursday–Sunday.

Dingle: *Dick Mack's*
Green St. **Road map** A5.
[066 915 1960.
This individualistic spot is part shoe shop, part pub, and retains the original shop and drinking counters. The pub is a haunt of local artists, eccentrics and extroverts. In the evening, regulars often congregate around the piano. 🎵

Dingle: *Doyle's Townhouse*
John St. **Road map** A5.
[066 915 1174.
This bar and restaurant is celebrated for its delicious freshly caught seafood, and the bar's rustic, yet cosy, stone interior is an appealing place for dinner. Doyle's is open mid-March to mid-November. 🍴

Dunquin: *Krugers*
Road map A5. [066 915 6127.
Situated close to the quays for the Blasket Islands, this well-known family pub is also a guesthouse from March to September. The pub is decorated with family memorabilia and stills from films made in the area, such as *Ryan's Daughter*. 🎵 🍴

Killarney: *Buckley's Bar*
College St. **Road map** B5.
[064 31037.
This oak-panelled bar is noted for its regular traditional music sessions and its filling meals. The pub was opened in 1926 when Tom Buckley, a homesick emigrant, returned from New York. Bar food is served until 2:30pm. 🍴 🎵

Killarney: *The Laurels*
Main St. **Road map** B5.
[064 31119.
This claims to be Killarney's liveliest pub and is popular with the young locals as well as Irish-Americans who enjoy listening to the ballads and singing along. The pub provides excellent bar snacks and good meals (steak, mussels, oysters, fish) in a separate restaurant area. Ballads are performed nightly from 9:15pm between February and November, and more sporadically in winter. 🍴 🎵

Killorglin: *The Old Forge*
Road map A5. [066 976 1231.
Set on the popular Ring of Kerry, this thatched pub is delightfully old-fashioned and authentic. Expect to be packed during the Puck Fair in August *(see p47)*. Music is played in summer. 🎵

Kinsale: *Kieran's Folk House Inn*
Guardwell. **Road map** B6.
[021 477 2382.
This convivial corner of old Kinsale draws locals and visitors

alike. The interior is snug and welcoming, with live music every night during the season. The inn also houses a pleasant guesthouse and a noted restaurant, the Shrimps Seafood Bistro, open for lunch and dinner all year. 🍴 🎵

Kinsale: *The Lord Kingsale*
Main St. **Road map** B6.
[021 477 2371.
This beamed, old-fashioned pub attracts a quiet, genteel crowd. The pub is several hundred years old but the interior is, in part, a clever fake. In summer, live music is performed at weekends and on Mondays. Bar food is served from noon to 3pm 🍴 🎵

Kinsale: *The 1601*
Pearse St. **Road map** B6.
[021 477 2529.
The front bar is bedecked as a tribute to the Battle of Kinsale *(see p164)* while the back bar incorporates an ever-changing art gallery. On summer evenings you might find live modern and traditional music performed in the pub. 🍴 🎵

Kinsale: *The Spaniard Inn*
Scilly. **Road map** B6. [021 477 2436.
Set on a hairpin bend above the village of Scilly, this popular fishermen's pub has the air of a smugglers' inn. There is often live traditional music in one of the bars every night during the summer and it is particularly popular at weekends. The restaurant (open in the summer season) and bar offer simple, but excellent fare. 🍴 🍴 🎵

THE LOWER SHANNON

Ballyvaughan: *Monk's Pub*
The Pier. **Road map** B4.
[065 707 7059.
This quaint, cosy pub is situated on the quay. Inside, country furniture and peat fires are matched by local seafood including chowder, served until 8pm. There's live music every Saturday and traditional music on Wednesdays in summer – ring for details. 🍴 🍴 🎵

Bunratty: *Durty Nelly's*
Road map B4. [061 364072.
Set beside Bunratty Castle, this touristy, extremely commercialized pub appeals to locals as well as tourists. The 17th-century atmosphere is sustained by the warren of rooms, inglenook fireplaces and historical portraits. Traditional music is performed most evenings, and wholesome food is available both from the bar and from the two restaurants. 🍴 🎵

Doolin: *O'Connor's*
Road map B4. 065 707 4168.
This famous pub is known to lovers of traditional music the world over. The pub has been in the O'Connor family for over 150 years and combines an authentic grocery store with a lively pub. This is the place for spontaneous music, simple bar food, young company and great "crack". There is music here every night.

Ennis: *The Cloister*
Abbey St. **Road map** B4.
065 682 9521.
This recently refurbished historic pub is situated by the famous Ennis Friary. The pub's cosy, atmospheric interior is complemented by a patio in summer, and by traditional music on some nights.

Killaloe: *Goosers*
Ballina. **Road map** C4.
061 376791.
This delightfully picturesque waterfront pub on the Ballina side of the river has a thatched roof, traditional interior and a welcoming atmosphere. Noted for its cuisine, Goosers serves fairly pricey seafood in the restaurant and more reasonably priced but satisfying "pub grub" in the rustic bar.

Kilrush: *Crotty's Pub*
Market Square. **Road map** B4.
065 905 2470.
This popular pub is named after the concertina player Lizzie Crotty, and hosts live traditional music four nights of the week in summer. Tasty bar food is available noon–3pm weekdays.

Limerick: *The Locke*
3 George's Quay. **Road map** B4.
061 413733.
Set on a quay on the Shannon, this is a typical black-and-white pub. In summer, it is a favourite port of call for riverside strollers. In winter, blazing fires and snugs make it a cosy spot. Traditional music is played on Monday, Tuesday and Sunday nights. The restaurant is open all day

Limerick: *Nancy Blake's*
Upper Denmark St. **Road map** B4.
061 416443.
Limerick's best-known bar, Nancy Blake's has much to offer in the way of good "crack" and traditional music. If you prefer rhythm and blues, try the adjoining Outback Bar. The cosy main bar serves soup and sandwiches at lunchtime. Music is played from Monday to Wednesday, and Saturday.

THE WEST OF IRELAND

Aran Islands: *Joe Watty's Pub*
Kilronan, Inishmore. **Road map** B4.
099 61155.
Set along the road between Kilronan and Kilmurvy Bay, this island pub is noted for its informality and huge, hearty portions of food. Passers-by appreciate the lamb stews, soups, sandwiches and stout.

Clarinbridge: *Moran's Oyster Cottage*
The Weir, Kilcolgan. **Road map** B4.
091 796113.
Set in a thatched cottage, this bar was a regular port of call for crews from passing "hookers" (traditional ships). Nowadays, you can sample all kinds of seafood here, though Moran's is best known as an oyster bar – the owner holds the local speed record for shelling oysters. You can watch fishermen at work from the terrace tables.

Clarinbridge: *Paddy Burke's Oyster Inn*
Road map B4. 091 796226.
Founded in 1835, this authentic thatched pub has leaded windowpanes and a charming beamed interior. Apart from the renowned Clarinbridge oysters and buffet lunches, gourmet menus are also available at lunch and dinner.

Clifden: *EJ Kings*
The Square. **Road map** A3.
095 21330.
This spacious, bustling pub is situated on several floors, with the ground floor the most appealing. Seafood platters or varied pub fare can be enjoyed by the peat fire. In summer, live music is often on offer, especially folk and ballads. The staff, mainly students, are exceptionally friendly.

Galway: *Cooke's Thatch Bar*
Cooke's Corner, 2 Newcastle Rd.
Road map B4. 091 521749.
Situated on the outskirts of Galway, this traditional thatched inn has been in the same family for seven generations and is renowned for its friendliness. Recently refurbished, the pub now includes an off-licence with over 20 wines on sale as well as beer and spirits.

Galway: *The King's Head*
15 High St. **Road map** B4.
091 566630.
Founded in 1649, this historic pub is adorned with a bow-fronted façade. The homely interior contains authentic 17th-century

fireplaces. Simple lunch snacks are served in the main bar. In the back bar there are jazz sessions on Sunday lunch times, and various live bands playing in the evenings attract a youthful crowd.

Galway: *O'Flaherty's*
Great Southern Hotel, 15 Eyre Sq.
Road map B4. 091 564041.
This solid cellar bar began as wine cellars but now offers cosy snugs and railway memorabilia. The popular pub provides a contrast to the more sophisticated hotel cocktail bar on the floor above. A carvery lunch is on offer daily in the bar, while at weekends live popular music sessions (from traditional music to jazz) draw large audiences of locals and visitors.

Galway: *The Quays*
11 Quay St. **Road map** B4.
091 568347.
This cavernous pub is the highlight of a Galway pub crawl. Set in an old stone mansion in Galway's "Latin Quarter", the sprawling pub is noted for its old-world charm, choice of bars and live music every night. The quaint front bar retains its authenticity while the rest of the pub has been sensitively converted, using old materials. The tasty and filling cooked pub meals are popular with locals.

Galway: *The Slate House*
Cross St Upper. **Road map** B4.
091 563377.
This barn-like city pub occupies several storeys, including the shell of a 16th-century convent on the top floor. Busker Brown's, the pub next door, is under the same management, and both are popular with local students. There are jazz sessions on Sundays.

Galway: *Tí Neachtain*
Quay St. **Road map** B4.
091 568820.
Set in the "Latin Quarter", this 18th-century town house boasts a distinctive oriel window. Inside, a musty wood interior is home to old-world snugs and friendly service. Traditional music can often be heard here and, if you get peckish, just upstairs is Periwinkles restaurant.

Maam Cross: *Peacocks Hotel*
Road map B3. 091 552306.
Next to a replica of the traditional cottage used in the 1950s John Wayne film *The Quiet Man* is a brand new hotel complex with a modern pub. It is highly popular with locals and a good choice of pub food is available daily. Music every weekend.

Westport: *The Asgard Tavern*
The Quay. **Road map** B3.
[098 25319.
This old inn facing the pier and Clew Bay is decorated with a nautical theme. Both the main downstairs back bar and the up-stairs restaurant provide excellent seafood and salads. The small downstairs front bar is the most atmospheric. 🍴 🎵

Westport: *Matt Molloy's*
Bridge St. **Road map** B3.
[098 26655.
Founded by the flautist from the traditional Irish folk band The Chieftains, this deceptively spacious pub is designed along equally traditional lines. There is live music in the back room every evening, when the pub is packed. No children after 9pm. 🍴 🎵

NORTHWEST IRELAND

Crolly: *Leo's Tavern*
Menaleck. **Road map** C1.
[074 954 8143.
Owned by the father of modern folk musicians Clannad and of the singer Enya, this friendly pub attracts locals and tourists for its sing-songs round the accordion, and traditional music nights. 🍴 🎵

Dromahair: *Stanford's Inn*
Main St. **Road map** C2.
[071 916 4140.
Set in a picturesque village, this traditional pub has been in the same family for generations. The tiny, quaint Biddy's Bar remains unchanged, adorned with family portraits and old grocery jars. The main bar has mellow brickwork and flagstones from a ruined castle. Delicious food is on offer all day in the restaurant, and in summer there are often impromptu evening music sessions. 🍴 🎵

Rossnowlagh: *Smugglers' Creek Inn*
Road map C2. [071 985 2366.
On a clifftop overlooking Donegal Bay, this pub is popular with surfers and other water sports enthusiasts. There is traditional music at weekends and the beer garden offers panoramic views. The pub is closed Monday and Tuesday and on Sunday evening. 🍴 🍴 🎵

Sligo: *Beezie's*
Tobbergal Lane. **Road map** C2.
[071 914 3031.
The pub is dedicated to Beezie Gallagher, a much-loved character who regularly rowed from her home on Cottage Island to Sligo until her death in 1951. A Victorian mood is recreated by the stained glass, skylights and fireplaces. 🍴

Sligo: *Hargadon's*
4–5 O'Connell St. **Road map** C2.
[071 917 0933.
A scruffy, rather ramshackle exterior reveals the most tradi-tional pub in town. The timeless atmosphere is enhanced by the old-fashioned stove, uneven floors and wooden grocery drawers. The pub is lined with cosy snugs, all individually designed. During the summer, dinner is served in the beer garden. 🍴 🍴

THE MIDLANDS

Abbeyleix: *Morrissey's*
Main St. **Road map** C4.
[0502 31233.
If driving through County Laois, it is worth stopping at this genuinely traditional pub. The 18th-century inn was remodelled in the Victorian era and has stayed the same ever since. The grocery section survives while the plain but unpretentious bar serves simple bar snacks.

Carlingford: *PJ O'Hare's Anchor Bar*
Tholsel St. **Road map** D3.
[042 937 3106.
Known locally as PJ's, this atmos-pheric pub and grocery store is popular with sailors and locals alike. A friendly and often eccentric wel-come is matched by bar food such as oysters and sandwiches. Music is played in the summer. 🍴 🎵

Kilbeggan: *Locke's Distillery Museum*
Mullingar. **Road map** C3.
[0506 32307.
As well as being the oldest licensed pot still distillery in the world (established in 1757), this historic complex has a tiny whiskey bar – the ideal place to sample a few brands before buying *(see p241).* There is an adjoining restaurant. 🍴

Portlaoise: *Tracey's Pub and Restaurant*
The Heath. **Road map** C4.
[0502 46539.
This charming thatched cottage pub and restaurant is 5 km (3 miles) outside of the town, but is well worth the drive. It is the oldest family-run pub in these parts, and there is a good range of pub grub (roasts, fish, salads) as well as prime steak at amazingly reasonable prices. 🍴 🍴

NORTHERN IRELAND

Bangor: *Jenny Watt's*
41 High St. **Road map** E2.
[028 9146 0682.
Likeable and very popular, this bar with Victoriana trimmings is found in the centre of town. The walls

are adorned with local photos and memorabilia. There's live jazz at Sunday lunch times, traditional on Tuesday and folk music on Thursday nights. Bar food is served until 7pm, and there's a beer garden. 🍴 🎵

Belfast: *Crown Liquor Saloon*
46 Great Victoria St. **Road map** D2.
[028 9024 9476.
This Victorian gin palace ranks as one of the most gorgeous bars in Ireland *(see p269).* Lunch includes several local specialities including Strangford Lough oysters which are almost too good to believe. The recently renovated Robinson's pub next door is particularly lively in the evening. 🍴

Belfast: *Lavery's Gin Palace*
12–14 Bradbury Place. **Road map** D2.
[028 9087 1106.
Yet another of Belfast's fine old gin palaces. Bar food served at lunch and discos in the evenings. It is popular with students from Queen's University. 🎵

Belfast: *White's Tavern*
Winecellar Entry. **Road map** D2.
[028 9024 3080.
Just one of several daylight-free pubs tucked away in the Entries *(see p269)* sector of Belfast city that are best at lunch time when decent, reasonably priced pub food is served. White's lays claim to be the oldest bar in the city. Other pubs in this series of alleys that are worth a look include the Morning Star and the Globe. 🎵 🍴

Bushmills: *Bushmills Inn*
9 Dunluce Rd. **Road map** D1.
[028 2073 2339.
Set in an old coaching inn, this cosy bar is lit by gaslights. There is also an excellent restaurant on the premises. 🍴

Enniskillen: *Blake's of the Hollow*
6 Church St. **Road map** C2.
[028 6632 2143.
One of a number of popular town-centre pubs, Blake's dates back to Victorian days and has many of its original fittings. 🍴 🎵

Hillsborough: *Plough Inn*
The Square. **Road map** D2.
[028 9268 2985.
Dating back to the 1750s, this quintessential village pub has wooden ceiling beams and a selection of crockery, china and other ornaments on the walls. There's a bistro upstairs open during the day, serving oysters, and a good beer garden. The Hillside, just down the main street, is also worth a visit. 🍴 🍴

SHOPPING IN IRELAND

IRELAND OFFERS a wide range of handmade goods, usually regionally based and highly individual. Its most renowned products include chunky Aran sweaters, Waterford crystal, demure Irish linen, hand-loomed Donegal tweed and tasty farmhouse cheeses. The thriving crafts industry is based on traditional products with an innovative twist. Typical of contemporary Irish crafts are good design, quality craftsmanship and a range spanning

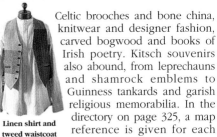

Linen shirt and tweed waistcoat

Celtic brooches and bone china, knitwear and designer fashion, carved bogwood and books of Irish poetry. Kitsch souvenirs also abound, from leprechauns and shamrock emblems to Guinness tankards and garish religious memorabilia. In the directory on page 325, a map reference is given for each address. Dublin references are to the map on pages 110–11; road map references are to the towns and cities shown on the inside back cover.

Fruit and vegetable market in Moore Street, Dublin

WHERE TO SHOP

THE CHOICE of places to shop in Ireland ranges from tiny workshops to large factory outlets, from elegant boutiques to high-street chain stores. Bargains can often be had at bric-a-brac shops and local markets, although the banter is sometimes the best thing available. This guide lists market days for every town featured.

SHOPPING IN DUBLIN

IN DUBLIN there are two major shopping quarters: the north side of the Liffey, centred around O'Connell and Henry Streets, where there are large shopping centres with many of the UK chains and department stores; and the more prestigious south side, around Grafton and Nassau Streets. The Temple Bar area contains a number of trendy craft shops. The two main markets are Mother Redcap's indoor flea market in Christchurch at weekends, and the

fruit and vegetable market in Moore Street from Monday to Saturday. One of Dublin's largest shopping centres is **St Stephen's Green Shopping Centre,** full of clothes and craft shops. Near chic Grafton Street is the Powerscourt Townhouse Shopping Centre *(see p76)* in its Georgian shell. Traditional department stores in the city include **Brown Thomas** and **Clery's**.

WHEN TO SHOP

MOST SHOPS are open from Monday to Saturday, 9am to 5:30 or 6pm. In shopping centres and large towns, shops tend to have at least one late-night opening, usually Thursday or Friday (Thursday in Dublin). In tourist areas, craft shops are generally open on Sundays too. Shops are closed at Easter and Christmas and on St Patrick's Day but are open on most other public holidays. In Killarney, Ireland's tourist capital, most shops are open until 10pm in summer.

HOW TO PAY

MAJOR CREDIT CARDS are generally accepted in department stores and larger retail outlets, but smaller shops prefer cash. Most traveller's cheques are accepted in major stores with a passport as identification. Eurocheques are no longer being issued by Irish banks and so will not be accepted in the shops.

SALES TAX AND REFUNDS

MOST PURCHASES are subject to VAT (sales tax) at 21 per cent, a sum included in the sales price. However, visitors from outside the European Union (EU) can reclaim VAT prior to departure. If you are shipping goods overseas, refunds can be claimed at the point of purchase. If taking your goods with you, look for the CashBack logo in shops, fill in the special voucher, then visit CashBack offices at Dublin or Shannon Airport.

A traditional fiddle maker in his workshop in Dingle

Colourful bric-a-brac shop in Kilkenny

BOOKS

READING is a national passion so bookshops are generally good. In larger shops expect solid sections on Irish archaeology and architecture, folklore, history, politics and cuisine. **Eason and Son** is one of the biggest bookshops in Dublin with a wide range of Irish literature and national and international newspapers; seek out the smaller, "Irish interest" shops too. In Galway, **Kennys Bookshop and Art Gallery** is full of both new and secondhand Irish books.

MUSIC

TRADITIONAL MUSICAL instruments *(see pp22–3)* are made in many regions, especially County Clare, known as "the singing county". Handmade harps are a speciality in Mayo and Dublin. In Dublin, several shops sell musical instruments, such as handcrafted *bodhráns* (traditional goatskin hand-held drums) and uilleann pipes (bagpipes). **Waltons** sells traditional instruments and sheet music, while **Claddagh Records** sells Irish folk and traditional music.

CRAFTS

CRAFTS are a flourishing way of life in rural Ireland. The **Crafts Council of Ireland**, with branches in Dublin where it is part of **DESIGNyard**, and in Kilkenny, recommends good small-scale outlets. Tourist offices also provide lists of local workshops, where you can often watch the production process. Many craft shops, such as the **Kilkenny Design Centre** and **Bricín**, sell good examples of several different crafts. Some regions are associated with specific crafts. In Cork and Kerry there is an abundance of workshops; the *Guide to Craft Outlets* is available from local tourist offices. Distinctive products from this area are traditional tiles based on designs found in Kilkenny Cathedral and nearby medieval abbeys. Further west, green Connemara marble is made into "worry stones", small charms much like worry beads. Also made in Connemara, particularly Clifden, are wall hangings, hand-knits and woollen rugs.

Other crafts in Ireland include metalwork, leatherwork and carpentry. Local woods are used for ash or beech furniture, blackthorn walking sticks and sculptures made of 1,000-year-old bogwood.

Kylemore Abbey teapot

CERAMICS AND CHINA

ESTABLISHED in 19th-century Ulster, the Belleek Pottery *(see p261)* produces creamy china with a lustrous sheen and subtle decorative motifs, including shamrocks and flowers. **Royal Tara China**, in Galway, is Ireland's leading fine bone china manufacturer, with designs incorporating Celtic themes. Also in County Galway, Kylemore Abbey produces handpainted pottery *(see p200)*. **Louis Mulcahy's Pottery** in Ballyferriter is noted for its fine decorative glazes, while **Nicholas Mosse Pottery** in Bennettsbridge, County Kilkenny, is well known for its colourful handpainted designs. Enniscorthy in County Wexford is another centre for ceramics.

CRYSTAL AND GLASSWARE

IN THE WAKE of Waterford Crystal *(see p139)*, the brand leader, come countless followers. The price depends on reputation, the quantity of lead used in the glass and the labour-intensiveness of the design. In the North, **Tyrone Crystal** is rated almost as highly as Waterford and is less expensive. Like Waterford, the factory runs an illuminating tour. **Tipperary Crystal** offers a number of lines, including trophies, lamps and gifts. **Galway Irish Crystal** is another elegant brand.

In County Kilkenny, the famous Jerpoint Abbey inspires local designs by **Jerpoint Glass**. Decorated with simple yet stylish motifs, the small vases, candlesticks, jugs and bowls make pleasing gifts. Most stores will pack and send glassware overseas for you.

Pottery display in Kilkenny Design Centre

Sign for the linen department at Dublin's Brown Thomas store

JEWELLERY

I**N ITS GOLDEN AGE**, Celtic metalwork was the pride of Ireland *(see pp30–33)*, and many contemporary crafts-people are still inspired by traditional Celtic designs. Hand-crafted or factory-made silver, gold, enamel and ceramic jewellery is produced all over Ireland in a huge variety of designs. The Claddagh ring from Galway is the most famous – the lovers' symbol of two hands cradling a crowned heart. **DESIGNYARD** in Temple Bar sells the best contemporary Irish jewellery. Dublin's Powerscourt Townhouse Shopping Centre *(see p76)* is home to Ceramic Design, a studio producing Celtic-influenced brooches. Gold- and silversmiths can also be seen at work here.

KNITWEAR AND TWEED

A**RAN SWEATERS** are sold all over Ireland, but particularly in County Galway and on the Aran Islands themselves. One of Ireland's best

buys, these oiled, off-white sweaters used to be handed down through generations of Aran fishermen. Legend has it that each family used its own motifs so that if a fisherman was lost at sea and his body unidentifiable, his family could recognize him by his sweater.

Given the Irish experience of wet weather, warm and waterproof clothes are generally of good quality, from waxed jackets and duffel coats to sheepskin jackets. Knitwear is on sale all over Ireland, with **Avoca Handweavers** and **Blarney Woollen Mills** the best-known outlets. Good buys include embroidered sweaters and waistcoats and hand-woven shawls and scarves.

Donegal tweed is a byword for quality, noted for its texture, tension and subtle colours (originally produced by dyes made from lichens, local plants and minerals). Tweed caps, hats, scarves, ties, jackets and suits are sold in outlets such as **Magee and Co** in Donegal.

Secondhand furniture shop in Kenmare

LINEN

D**AMASK LINEN** was brought to Armagh by Huguenot refugees fleeing French persecution. As a result, Belfast became the world linen capital. Ulster is still the place for linen, with sheets and double-damask table linen on sale in Belfast – at **Smyth's Irish**

Linen, for example – and in other towns. There are also outlets in the Republic. Hand-embroidered linen is made in County Donegal. Linen-making can be seen at Wellbrook Beetling Mill *(see p260)*.

FASHION

I**NSPIRED** by a predominantly young population, Ireland is fast acquiring a name for fashion. Conservatively cut tweed and linen suits continue to be models of classic good taste, while younger designers are increasingly experimental, using bold lines and mixing traditional fabrics.

A-Wear is a quality boutique that has branches in major cities. Here, and in the **Design Centre** in Powerscourt Town-house Shopping Centre in Dublin, are clothes by the best Irish designers including John Rocha, Paul Costelloe, Louise Kennedy, Quin and Donnelly and Mariad Whisker. Clothing and shoe sizes are identical to British fittings.

FOOD AND DRINK

S**MOKED SALMON**, home-cured bacon, farmhouse cheeses, soda bread, preserves and handmade chocolates make perfect last-minute gifts. Several shops will package and send Irish salmon overseas.

Bewley's teas and coffees are sold in **Bewley's Oriental Café** and Bewley shops all over Ireland. Guinness travels less well and is best drunk in Ireland. Irish whiskey is hard to beat as a gift or souvenir. Apart from the cheaper Power and Paddy brands, the big names are Bushmills *(see p258)* and Jameson *(see p171)*. Rich Irish liqueurs include Irish Mist and Baileys Irish Cream.

Selection of hand-knitted sweaters at a craft shop in Dingle

DIRECTORY

DEPARTMENT STORES AND SHOPPING CENTRES

Brown Thomas
88–95 Grafton St, Dublin 2.
Dublin map D4.
[01 605 6666.

Clery's
18–27 O'Connell St
Lower, Dublin 1.
Dublin map D2.
[01 878 6000.

St Stephen's Green Shopping Centre
St Stephen's Green West,
Dublin 2. **Dublin map** D4.

BOOKS

Eason and Son
80 Middle Abbey St,
Dublin 1. **Dublin map** D2.
[01 873 3811.

Eason Hanna
27–29 Nassau St, Dublin 2.
Dublin map E4.
[01 677 1255.

Kennys Bookshop and Art Gallery
High St, Galway.
Road map B4.
[091 562739.

Waterstone's
7 Dawson St, Dublin 2.
Dublin map D4.
[01 679 1415.

MUSIC

Claddagh Records
2 Cecilia St, Temple Bar,
Dublin 2. **Dublin map** C3.
[01 677 0262.

J McNeill
140 Capel St, Dublin 1.
Dublin map C2.
[01 872 2159.

Waltons
3–5 Frederick St North,
Dublin 1.
[01 874 7805.

CRAFTS

Bricín
26 High Street, Killarney,
Co Kerry. **Road map** B5.
[064 34902.

Connemara Marble Factory
Moycullen, Co Galway.
Road map B4.
[091 555102.

Crafts Council of Ireland
Castle Yard, Kilkenny.
Road map C4.
[056 61804.

Craftworks Shop
Bedford House, Bedford
Street, Belfast.
Road map D2.
[028 9024 4465.

DESIGNyard
12 Essex Street East,
Dublin 2.
Dublin map C3.
[01 677 8453.

Doolin Crafts Gallery
Ballyvoe, Doolin, Co Clare.
Road map B4.
[065 707 4309.

Kilkenny Design Centre
Castle Yard, Kilkenny.
Road map C4.
[056 22118.

The Kilkenny Shop
6 Nassau St, Dublin 2.
Dublin map E4.
[01 677 7066.

Standuin
Spiddal, Co Galway.
Road map B4.
[091 553357.

Tower Enterprise Centre
Pearse St, Dublin 2.
[01 677 5655.

The Whichcraft Gallery
Cow's Lane, Temple Bar,
Dublin 2. **Dublin map** C3.
[01 474 1011.

CERAMICS AND CHINA

Louis Mulcahy's Pottery
Clogher, Ballyferriter, Tralee,
Co Kerry. **Road map** A5.
[066 915 6229.

Michael Kennedy Ceramics
Bolands Lane, Gort, Co
Galway. **Road map** B4.
[091 632245.

Nicholas Mosse Pottery
Bennettsbridge, Co
Kilkenny. **Road map** D5.
[056 27105.

Royal Tara China
Tara Hall, Mervue, Galway.
Road map B4.
[091 751301.

Treasure Chest
31-33 William St, Galway.
Road map B4.
[091 567237.

CRYSTAL AND GLASSWARE

Galway Irish Crystal
Merlin Park, Galway.
Road map B4.
[091 757311.

Jerpoint Glass
Stoneyford, Co Kilkenny.
Road map D5.
[056 24350.

Sligo Crystal
2 Hyde Bridge, Sligo,
Co Sligo. **Road map** C2.
[071 914 3440.

Tipperary Crystal
Ballynoran, Carrick-on-
Suir, Co Tipperary.
Road map C5.
[051 641188.

Tyrone Crystal
Killybrackey, Coal Island Rd,
Dungannon, Co Tyrone.
Road map D2.
[028 8772 5335.

Waterford Crystal
Kilbarry, Waterford.
Road map D5.
[051 373311.

JEWELLERY

Brian de Staic
18 High St, Killarney,
Co Kerry. **Road map** B5.
[064 33822.

Hilser Brothers
Grand Parade, Cork.
Road map C5.
[021 427 0382.

Saller's Jewellers
Williamsgate St, Galway.
Road map B4.
[091 561226.

KNITWEAR AND TWEED

Avoca Handweavers
Kilmacanogue, Bray, Co
Wicklow. **Road map** D4.
[01 286 7466.

Blarney Woollen Mills
Blarney, Co Cork.
Road map B5.
[021 438 5280.

House of Ireland
37–38 Nassau Street,
Dublin 2. **Dublin map** D4.
[01 671 1111.

Magee and Co
The Diamond, Donegal.
Road map C2.
[074 972 2660.

Quills Woollen Market
1 High St, Killarney, Co
Kerry. **Road map** B5.
[064 32277.

Studio Donegal
The Glebe Mill, Kilcar,
Co Donegal. **Road map**
B2. [074 973 8194.

LINEN

Forgotten Cotton
Savoy Centre,
St Patrick's St, Cork.
Road map C5.
[021 427 6098.

Smyth's Irish Linen
65 Royal Ave, Belfast.
Road map D2.
[028 9024 2232.

FASHION

A-Wear
26 Grafton St, Dublin 2.
Dublin map D4.
[01 671 7200.

FOOD AND DRINK

Bewley's Oriental Café
78 Grafton St, Dublin 2.
Dublin map D4.
[01 677 6761.

Butler's Chocolate Café
51a Grafton St, Dublin 2.
Dublin map D4.
[01 671 0599.

What to Buy in Ireland

St Brigid's cross

Hundreds of gift and craft shops scattered throughout Ireland make it easy to find Irish specialities to suit all budgets. The best buys include linen, tweeds and crystal from factory shops which invariably offer an extensive choice of good quality products. Local crafts make unique souvenirs, from hand-made jewellery and ceramics to traditional musical instruments. Religious artifacts are also widely available. Irish food and drink are evocative reminders of your trip.

Traditional hand-held drum (bodhrán) and beater

Connemara marble "worry stone"

Traditional Claddagh ring

Modern jewellery and metalwork draw on a long and varied tradition. Craftspeople continue to base their designs on sources such as the Book of Kells (see p62) and Celtic myths. Local plants and wildlife are also an inspiration. County Galway produces Claddagh rings – traditional betrothal rings – in gold and silver as well as "worry stones".

Enamel brooch

Fuchsia earring from Dingle

Celtic-design enamel brooch

Bronzed resin Celtic figurine

Donegal tweed jacket and waistcoat

Tweed skirt and jacket

Clothing made in Ireland is usually of excellent quality. Tweed-making still flourishes in Donegal where tweed can be bought ready-made as clothing and hats or as lengths of cloth. Knitwear is widely available all over the country in large factory outlets and local craft shops. The many hand-knitted items on sale, including Aran sweaters, are not cheap but should give years of wear.

Tweed cap

Tweed fisherman's hat

Aran sweater

Irish linen is world-famous and the range unparalleled. There is a huge choice of table and bed linen, including extravagant bedspreads and crisp, formal tablecloths. On a smaller scale, tiny, intricately embroidered hand-kerchiefs make lovely gifts as do linen table napkins. Tea towels printed with colourful designs are widely available. You can also buy linen goods trimmed with fine lace, which is still hand-made in Ireland, mainly in Limerick and Kenmare.

Set of linen placemats and napkins

Nicholas
Mosse
plate

Fine linen handkerchiefs

Belleek
teapot

Nicholas
Mosse
cup

Irish ceramics come in traditional and modern designs. You can buy anything from a full dinner service by established factories, such as Royal Tara China or the Belleek Pottery, to a one-off contemporary piece from a local potter's studio.

Irish crystal, hand-blown and hand-cut, can be ordered or bought in many shops in Ireland. Visit the outlets of the principal manu-facturers, such as Waterford Crystal, Tyrone Crystal and Jerpoint Glass, to see the full range – from glasses and decanters to elaborate chandeliers.

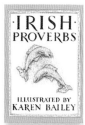

Book of Irish Proverbs

Books and stationery are often beautifully illustrated. Museums and bookshops stock a wide range.

**Celtic-design
cards**

**Waterford crystal tumbler
and decanter**

Food and drink will keep the distinctive tastes of Ireland fresh long after you arrive home. Whiskey connoisseurs should visit the Old Bushmills Distillery (see p258) or the Jameson Heritage Centre (see p171) to sample their choice of whiskeys. Good regional food can be found at local shops all over Ireland. Try the dried seaweed, which is eaten raw or added to cooked dishes.

| Jameson whiskey | Bushmills whiskey | Fruit cake made with Guinness | Jar of Irish marmalade | Packet of dried seaweed |

ENTERTAINMENT IN IRELAND

I F THERE IS ONE SPHERE in which Ireland shines, it is entertainment. For details about entertainment in Dublin, see pages 102–7. Elsewhere in Ireland, nightclubs and concerts by international entertainers tend to be concentrated in large cities, but many other events including theatre, arts festivals, traditional music and dance, cultural holidays and even medieval banquets take place all over the country. Most towns and cities also have one or two cinemas showing the latest movies on release. Not to be overlooked

Morris Minor van advertising the Clonakilty Folk Club

is the free entertainment (planned or spontaneous) provided by a night in a pub. For more active forms of entertainment, covered on pages 332–5, the list is even longer, from golf to pony trekking and cycling to scuba diving. Those who prefer their sports sitting down can go along as spectators to Ireland's famous horse race meetings, as well as Gaelic football, hurling, soccer and rugby matches. Best of all, a happy mix of these activities can easily be put together with almost any itinerary.

Ulster Symphony Orchestra at the Ulster Hall in Belfast

INFORMATION SOURCES

T HE TOURIST BOARD for the Republic, **Fáilte Ireland**, and the **Northern Ireland Tourist Board** (*see p339*) both publish a yearly *Calendar of Events* that lists major fixtures around the country, and all the regional tourist offices have information about happenings in each locality. To supplement these listings, check regional newspapers and inquire locally.

BOOKING TICKETS

T ICKETS can usually be bought at the door on the day or evening of most events. Advance booking is a must, however, for popular concerts and plays. Many cultural and arts festivals require tickets only for the key performances, but for internationally famous festivals, such as the Wexford Opera Festival, you will need to book well in advance through the festival office for all performances.

Credit-card bookings for plays, concerts and other events around Ireland can be made by telephone through **Keith Prowse Travel (IRL) Ltd** and **Ticketmaster** in Dublin.

MAJOR VENUES

I N MANY IRISH CITIES, the main theatres host a huge variety of events. In Cork, the **Opera House** presents predominantly Irish plays during the summer months, with musical comedy, opera and ballet at other times of year. The city's **Everyman Palace Theatre** stages plays by local and visiting companies interspersed with concerts of both classical and popular music. Sligo's **Hawks Well Theatre** and Limerick's **Belltable Arts Centre** are venues for drama and concerts. In the centre of Belfast, the **Grand Opera House**, **Waterfront Hall** and **Lyric Theatre** present a varied programme, including Irish and inter–national plays, experimental drama, pantomime and opera.

THEATRE

F ROM INTERNATIONAL TOURS to amateur productions, there is excellent theatre to be seen in virtually every location in Ireland. In Galway, the **Druid Theatre** specializes in avant-garde plays, new Irish plays and Anglo-Irish classics, with frequent lunchtime and late-night performances, while Gaelic drama, Irish music, singing and dancing have all thrived at the **Taibhdhearc Theatre** since 1928. Waterford boasts its resident Red Kettle Theatre Company which performs at the **Garter Lane Theatre**, while the **Theatre Royal** brings amateur drama and musicals to the city.

Keep an eye out for small theatre groups performing in local halls around the country. Many of them are superb and they have spawned several of Ireland's leading actors.

Home of the Druid Theatre Company in Galway (*see p202*)

The Moscow Ballet at Belfast's Grand Opera House *(see p268)*

CLASSICAL MUSIC, OPERA AND DANCE

MAJOR VENUES for classical music include the **Crawford Art Gallery**, Opera House and Everyman Palace in Cork; the Theatre Royal in Waterford; the Hawks Well Theatre in Sligo; and the Belltable Arts Centre in Limerick. Belfast's **Ulster Hall** hosts concerts from rock bands to the Ulster Symphony Orchestra.

Opera lovers from around the world come to Ireland for the **Wexford Festival of Opera** in October and November and the **Waterford Festival of Light Opera** in late September and early October. At Wexford, neglected operas are revived, while Waterford selects more mainstream operas and musicals. Elsewhere, opera is performed in Cork's Opera House and in Belfast's Grand Opera House.

Ireland has no resident ballet or avant-garde dance companies, but leading international companies perform occasionally at the major venues around the country.

ROCK, JAZZ AND COUNTRY

WHEN INTERNATIONAL music stars tour Ireland, concerts outside Dublin are held at large outdoor sites. **Semple Stadium** in County Tipperary and Slane Castle *(see p237)* in County Meath are popular venues. Tickets and information are available from Ticketmaster.

Musical pubs *(see pp318–21)* are your best bet for good rock and jazz performed by Irish groups. Check local tourist offices and newspapers for rock and jazz nights, which usually take place midweek, with country and traditional music at weekends. For some

of Ireland's "big band" jazz music, keep an eye out for Waterford's Brass and Co who play at dances around the country. Jazz lovers have a field day at the **Cork Jazz Festival** in late October, when music pours from every pub and international jazz greats play in the city's theatres.

Pub scene at Feakle Traditional Music Weekend, County Clare

TRADITIONAL MUSIC AND DANCE

THE COUNTRY PUB has helped keep Irish music alive and provided the setting for the musical revival that began in the 1960s. Today, sessions of informal or impromptu music are still commonplace. In pubs, traditional music embraces ballads and rebel songs, as well as the older *sean-nos* – unaccompanied, understated stories, often sung in Irish.

Nights of Irish music and song are scheduled in many pubs, such as The Laurels and the Danny Mann in Killarney, the Yeats Tavern in Drumcliff, near Sligo, and An Phoenix and The Lobby in Cork. In Derry, the Gweedore Bar, Castle Bar and Dungloe Bar are among the cluster of musical pubs along Waterloo Street. Wherever you are, a query to the locals will send you off to the nearest musical pub. For more pub listings, see pages 318–21.

In Tralee, **Siamsa Tíre**, the National Folk Theatre, stages marvellous folk drama incorporating traditional music, singing and dance. The Barn, in Bunratty Folk Park, is the setting for the **Shannon Ceilí** – traditional music nights during the summer months.

Comhaltas Ceoltóirí Éireann, in Monkstown *(see p100)* has branches around the country and organizes traditional music and dance nights all year. Traditional Irish dancing can be stylish step dancing or joyous set dancing. Visitors are usually encouraged to join in the fun.

The **Fleadh Cheoil** (national traditional music festival) is a weekend of music, dance, song and stage shows that spill over into colourful street entertainment. It takes place at the end of August in a different town each year. Earlier in August, the **Feakle Traditional Music Weekend** in County Clare is a more intimate celebration of traditional music, song and dance.

A large audience for open-air music at the Cork Jazz Festival

Knappogue banquet at Knappogue Castle, County Clare

FESTIVALS

THE IRISH are experts at organizing festivals, staging a week of street entertainment, theatre, music and dance to celebrate almost everything under the sun *(see pp46–9)*.

In mid-July the lively town of Galway is host to the **Galway Arts Festival**, one of the largest festivals in Ireland. Here you will find Irish and international theatre and music, street entertainment and events for children. Taking place over two weeks in late July and early August is the **Boyle Arts Festival**. The events here include art exhibitions, poetry and drama performances as well as classical, traditional, folk and jazz concerts. Creative workshops are run for both adults and children.

Kilkenny Arts Festival in August, another major festival, features poetry, classical music concerts, movies and a range of crafts. The **Cork Film Festival** takes place within the first two weeks of October when international feature, documentary and short films are screened at venues all over the city. The **Belfast Festival at Queen's** is held for two weeks in October to late November. The lively and cosmopolitan programme includes a mixture of drama, ballet, comedy, cabaret, music and film. These take over the Queen's University campus plus theatres and other venues throughout Belfast.

In May, June, and July the **County Wicklow Gardens Festival** entices gardening enthusiasts to wander around the county's most beautiful gardens. In mid-June, the **Music in Great Irish Houses** festival opens the doors to many of Ireland's historic homes to which the public seldom has access, with classical music performed by top-rate musicians. Venues include Mount Stewart House *(see pp274–5)* and University College, Cork.

Kilkenny Arts Week street theatre

TRADITIONAL BANQUETS WITH ENTERTAINMENT

IRELAND'S BANQUETS have gained international fame and are great fun. Each of the banquets features costumed waiters and performers, as well as traditional food and drink of the chosen period.

Most famous are the medieval banquets – the one at Bunratty Castle *(see pp184–5)* was the first and is the liveliest, with year-round performances. From April to October, there is a medieval banquet at Knappogue Castle *(see p181)*, and at Dunguaire Castle *(see p204)* there is a quieter, more intimate programme of music and poetry. From March until November, the highly enjoyable Killarney Manor Banquet, held at the stately manor on the Loreto road just south of Killarney, creates an early 19th-century atmosphere.

CULTURAL BREAKS

A BREAK IN IRELAND focused on any one of the cultural aspects of Irish life is enriching as well as fun. Choose from a variety of cultural topics and study courses: Irish music and literature, great houses and gardens, Irish language and folklore, crafts and cookery.

One of the most fascinating possibilities is the exploration of Ireland's 5,000-year history as revealed in the many relics strewn across the landscape. The **Achill Archaeological Summer School** in County Mayo, for example, runs a course that includes the active excavation of ancient sites.

To learn the secret of Irish cooking, there is no better place than the **Ballymaloe School of Cookery** in County Cork; it is run by Darina Allen, Ireland's most famous cook.

For literature enthusiasts, the **Yeats International Summer School** studies the works of Yeats and his contemporaries, while **Listowel Writers' Week** brings together leading writers for lectures and workshops.

Folk dancers in traditional Irish costume

DIRECTORY

BOOKING TICKETS

Keith Prowse Travel (IRL) Ltd
10 St Stephen's Green, Dublin 2. 〔 *01 679 5333.*

Ticketmaster
Grafton House, 70 Grafton St, Dublin 2.
〔 *01 456 9569.*

MAJOR VENUES

Belltable Arts Centre
69 O'Connell St, Limerick.
〔 *061 319866.*
ⓦ *www.belltable.ie*

Everyman Palace Theatre
MacCurtain St, Cork.
〔 *021 450 1673.* ⓦ
www.everymanpalace.com

Grand Opera House
Great Victoria St, Belfast.
〔 *028 9024 0411.*
ⓦ *www.goh.co.uk*

Hawks Well Theatre
Temple St, Sligo.
〔 *071 916 1526.*

Lyric Theatre
55 Ridgeway St, Belfast.
〔 *028 9038 1081.*

Opera House
Emmet Place, Cork.
〔 *021 427 4308.*
ⓦ *www.corkopera-house.com*

Waterfront Hall
2 Lanyon Place, Belfast.
〔 *028 9033 4400.*

THEATRE

Druid Theatre
Chapel Lane, Galway.
〔 *091 568617.*
ⓦ *www.druidtheatre.com*

Garter Lane Theatre
22A O'Connell St, Waterford.
〔 *051 877153.*
ⓦ *www.garterlane.ie*

Taibhdhearc Theatre
Middle St, Galway.
〔 *091 562024.*

Theatre Royal
The Mall, Waterford.
〔 *051 874402.*

CLASSICAL MUSIC, OPERA AND DANCE

Crawford Art Gallery
Emmet Place, Cork. 〔
021 427 3377. ⓦ *www.-crawfordartgallery.com*

Ulster Hall
Bedford St, Belfast.
〔 *028 9032 3900.*
ⓦ *www.ulsterhall.co.uk*

Waterford Festival of Light Opera
Theatre Royal, Waterford.
〔 *051 874402.*

Wexford Festival of Opera
Theatre Royal, High St, Wexford. 〔 *053 22144.*
ⓦ *www.wexfordopera.com*

ROCK, JAZZ AND COUNTRY

Cork Jazz Festival
20 South Mall, Cork.
〔 *021 427 0463.*

Semple Stadium
Thurles, Co Tipperary.
〔 *0504 21308*

TRADITIONAL MUSIC AND DANCE

Comhaltas Ceoltóirí Éireann
32 Belgrave Sq, Monkstown, Co Dublin.
〔 *01 280 0295.*

Feakle Traditional Music Weekend
Maghera, Caher, Co Clare.
〔 *061 925125.*

Shannon Ceili
Bunratty Castle and Folk Park, Bunratty, Co Clare.
〔 *061 360788.*

Siamsa Tíre
National Folk Theatre, The Town Park,Tralee, Co Kerry. 〔 *066 712 3055.*
ⓦ *www.siamsatire.com*

FESTIVALS

Belfast Festival at Queen's
Festival House, 25 College Gardens, Belfast.
〔 *028 9066 7687.*
ⓦ *www.belfastfestival.com*

Boyle Arts Festival
Festival Office, Great Meadow, Boyle, Co Roscommon.
〔 *071 966 3085.*

Cork Film Festival
10 Washington St, Cork.
〔 *021 427 1711.*
ⓦ *www.corkfilmfest.org*

County Wicklow Gardens Festival
St Manntan's House, Kilmantin Hill, Wicklow.
〔 *0404 20070.*

Galway Arts Festival
Black Box Theatre, Dyke Rd, Terryland, Galway.
〔 *091 509700.*
ⓦ *www.galwayarts-festival.com*

Kilkenny Arts Festival
92 High St, Kilkenny.
〔 *056 63663.*
ⓦ *www.kilkennyarts.ie*

Music in Great Irish Houses
1st floor Blackrock Post Office, Blackrock, Co Dublin (open from March).
〔 *01 278 1528.*
ⓦ *www.musicirish-houses.com*

CULTURAL BREAKS

Archaeology
Achill Archaeological Summer School
Folk Life Centre, Dooagh, Achill Island, Co. Mayo.
〔 *098 43564.*
ⓦ *www.achill-field school.com*

Gerard Manley-Hopkins Summer School
Drogheda Street, Monasterevin, Co. Kildare.
〔 *045 525416.*

Oideas Gael
Gleanncholmcille, Co Donegal.
〔 *074 973 0248.*

Cookery
Ballymaloe School of Cookery
Shanagarry, Midleton, Co. Cork.
〔 *021 464 6785.*
ⓦ *www.cookingisfun.ie*

Crafts
Ardess Craft Centre
Ardess House, Kesh, Co Fermanagh.
〔 *028 6863 1267.*

Houses, Castles & Gardens of Ireland
〔 *01 288 9114.* ⓦ
www.gardensireland.com;
ⓦ *www.castlesireland.com*

National Trust
Rowallane House, Saintfield, Ballynahinch, Co Down.
〔 *028 9751 0721.*

Irish Language
Conversation Classes
Oidhreacht Chorca Dhuibhne, Ballyferriter, Co Kerry.
〔 *066 915 6100.*

Literary
Goldsmith Summer School
Rathmore, Ballymahon, Co Longford.
〔 *090 643 2374.*

James Joyce Summer School
University College Dublin, Belfield, Dublin 4.
〔 *01 706 8480.*

Listowel Writers' Week
24 The Square, Listowel, Co Kerry.
〔 *068 21074.* ⓦ *www.writersweek.ie*

William Carleton Summer School
Dungannon District Council, Circular Rd, Dungannon, Co Tyrone.
〔 *028 8772 5311.*

Yeats International Summer School
Yeats Society, Yeats Memorial Building, Douglas Hyde Bridge, Sligo.
〔 *071 914 2693.*
ⓦ *www.yeats-sligo.com*

Music
South Sligo School of Traditional Music, Song and Dance
Tubbercurry, Co Sligo.
〔 *071 918 5010.*
ⓦ *www.sssschool.org*

Willie Clancy Summer School
Miltown Malbay, Co Clare.
〔 *065 708 4148.*

Sports and Outdoor Activities

EVEN IN THE LARGEST CITIES, the country-side is never far away, and it beckons to all lovers of the outdoors. Topping the list of spectator sports is Ireland's famous horse racing, while hurling, Gaelic football and soccer also make for exciting viewing. Those who want to do more than just watch can choose between fishing, golf, horse riding, cruising, cycling, walking and water sports. Entire vacations can be based around any of these activities. In addition to the contacts on page 335, Fáilte Ireland in the Republic, the Northern Ireland Tourist Board and all local tourist offices have information on spectator and participant sports. For details of the main events in Ireland's sporting calendar, see pages 26–7.

Horse riding in Killarney

Fishing in the canal at Robertstown, County Kildare *(see p120)*

SPECTATOR SPORTS

THE IRISH PASSION for horse racing is legendary. Major courses include the Curragh *(see p121)*, where the Irish Derby is held; Fairyhouse, the venue for Ireland's Grand National; Leopardstown and Punchestown. Apart from these major courses, there are smaller ones all over the Republic (and two in Northern Ireland), where the atmosphere is exciting and informal. Galway Race Week in late July is a great social event. A racing calendar for the whole of Ireland, available from the **Irish Horse Racing Authority**, allows you to choose either National Hunt or flat race meets, which take place on 230 days of the year.

Sign outside a fishing tackle shop in Donegal

In Dublin, **Croke Park** hosts Gaelic football and hurling matches *(see pp26–7)*, while international rugby and soccer matches are held at Lansdowne Road Stadium. Ticket details for soccer internationals are available from the **Football Association of Ireland**.

For keen golfers, the annual highlight is the Irish Open Golf Championship in July. The venue varies from year to year. For tickets and the latest information, contact the **Irish Open Office**.

FISHING

THE CLAIM that Ireland is a paradise for anglers is no exaggeration. Coarse, game and sea fishing all enjoy widespread popularity. The lakes and rivers are home to bream, pike, perch and roach. Coastal rivers yield the famous Irish salmon, and, among other game fish, sea trout and brown trout also offer anglers a real challenge.

Flounder, whiting, mullet, bass and coalfish tempt the sea angler; deep-sea excursions chase abundant supplies of dogfish, shark, skate and ling. You can organize sea-angling trips from many different places – the Cork and Kerry coastline being a particularly popular starting point. Contact the **Irish Federation of Sea Anglers** for information on planning a sea fishing trip or to book organized trips and courses.

Maps and information on fishing locations are provided by the **Central Fisheries Board** and Fáilte Ireland in the Republic, and the **Department of Agriculture (Fisheries)** and Northern Ireland Tourist Board. Check permit requirements before you go.

GOLF

OF THE 300 or more golf courses in the whole of Ireland, over 50 are championship class, and many are by spectacular stretches of coast. Mount Juliet's world-class, Jack Nicklaus-designed course in County Kilkenny has won international acclaim, and many others are also kept in top condition. Northern Ireland's best-known courses are Royal Portrush and Royal

Golfers at Portstewart in Northern Ireland *(see p252)*

Walking in the Gap of Dunloe, Killarney *(see p155)*

County Down. The **Golfing Union of Ireland**, the **Irish Ladies Golfing Union** and the tourist boards have information on courses, conditions and green fees throughout the Republic and Northern Ireland. Some have clubs for rent, but it is better to bring your own.

Golfers Abroad organizes customized golfing trips for individuals and groups in Northern Ireland.

CYCLING

CYCLING is one of Ireland's most popular sports. There is an exhilarating range of countryside to be explored and the comparatively traffic-free roads make cycling a pleasure. Limerick, Waterford and Galway make good bases for cycling trips. Several organizations, such as **Celtic Cycling**, will plan an itinerary and book accommodation.

If you bring your own bike, you can transport it around the country fairly cheaply by train or bus.

Alternatively, try the many **Raleigh Rent-a-Bike** dealers with depots in the Republic and Northern Ireland, or **Cycleways**, based in Parnell Street, Dublin.

HORSE RIDING AND PONY TREKKING

THE IRISH ARE rightly proud of their fine horses. Many riding centres, both residential and non-residential, offer trail riding and trekking along woodland trails, deserted beaches, country lanes and mountain routes. Dingle, Donegal, Connemara, and Killarney are all renowned areas for trail riding. There are two types of trail riding – post-to-post and based. Post-to-post trails follow a series of routes with accommodation in a different place each night. Based trail rides follow different routes in one area and you stay at the same

place for the whole holiday. Also on offer at many riding centres are lessons for every-one from beginners to more advanced riders to those who want to learn show jumping.

The Northern Ireland Tourist Board and Fáilte Ireland have details of centres and courses. **Equestrian Holidays Ireland** organizes trips for riders of various abilities.

HIKING AND MOUNTAINEERING

A HIKING TRIP puts you in the very middle of the glorious Irish landscape. The network of waymarked trails all over the country takes you to some of the loveliest areas. Information on long-distance walks is available from Fáilte Ireland and the Northern Ireland Tourist Board. Routes include the Wicklow Way *(see p131)*, Dingle Way, Munster Way, Kerry Way and Barrow Towpath. All may be split into shorter sections for less experi-enced walkers or those short of time. The 800-km (500-mile) Ulster Way encircles Northern Ireland, taking in the spectac-ular scenery around the Giant's Causeway *(see pp254–5)* and the peaks of the Mountains of Mourne *(see pp276–7)*.

Sign for the Ulster Way, the trail around Northern Ireland

Irish Ways offers walking trips in the Republic. For activities in Northern Ireland, call the **Ulster Federation of Rambling Clubs**.

Hill walking, rock climbing and mountaineering holidays are also available. For informa-tion, contact the **Mountain-eering Council of Ireland**. Be sure to go well-equipped for the notoriously changeable Irish weather.

Cycling through the Muckross House estate near Killarney *(see p151)*

Surfing at Bundoran *(see p222)*

WATER SPORTS

WITH A COASTLINE of over 4,800 km (3,000 miles), small wonder that water sports are among Ireland's favourite recreational activities. Surfing, windsurfing, water-skiing, scuba diving and canoeing are the most popular, and there are facilities for all of these right around the coastline.

Conditions in Sligo are the best in Ireland for surfing, but many other coastal locations offer good conditions. The **British Surfing Association** has information about surfing all over Europe.

Windsurfing centres are mainly found near Dublin, Cork and Westport in County Galway.

There is a wide range of diving conditions off the coast of Ireland – visibility is particularly good on the west coast. The **Irish Underwater Council** will put you in touch with courses and facilities. **DV Diving** organizes scuba diving courses and offers accommodation near Belfast Lough and the Irish Sea where there are a number of historic wrecks to be explored.

Inland, Lower Lough Erne *(see pp262–3)* and Killaloe by Lough Derg *(see p182)* are popular centres. The **Lakeland Canoe Centre**, between Upper and Lower Lough Erne, gives canoeing courses and organizes canoeing trips (with overnight camping), including one down

the Shannon-Erne Waterway *(see p227)*. From March **Atlantic Sea Kayaking** has daily and two to eight-day tours round Castlehaven and Baltimore, amongst others.

CRUISING AND SAILING

A TRANQUIL CRUISING trip is an ideal alternative to the stress and strain of driving, and Ireland's 14,500 km (9,000 miles) of rivers and some 800 lakes offer a huge variety of conditions for those who want a waterborne experience. Stopping over at waterside towns and villages puts you in touch with the Irish on their home ground. Whether you opt for Lough Derg or elsewhere on the Shannon *(see p177)*, or the Grand Canal *(see p99)* from Dublin to the Shannon, a unique view of the Irish countryside opens up all along the way.

Running between Carrick-on-Shannon in County Leitrim and Upper Lough Erne in Fermanagh is the **Shannon-Erne Waterway** *(see p227)*, a disused canal reopened in 1993. From here it is simple to continue through Upper and Lower Lough Erne to Belleek *(see p262)*. **Emerald Star** has a fleet of cruisers for use on the waterway.

A popular sailing area is between Cork and the Dingle Peninsula. The **International Sailing Centre**, near Cork, offers tuition. In Carrickfergus the **Ulster Cruising School** provides lessons at all levels; more experienced sailors can charter a yacht and sail up to the western coast of Scotland.

HUNTING AND SHOOTING

IRELAND'S HUNTING season runs from October to March, and although fox-hunting predominates, stag and hare hunts also take place. For details, contact the **Irish Master of Foxhounds Association** in the Republic and, in Northern Ireland, the **Countryside Alliance**. Clay-pigeon (year-round) and pheasant (from November to January) shooting are also popular. **Mount Juliet Estate**, in County Kilkenny, offers both with guns and cartridges for rent.

Yachting off Rosslare *(see p143)*

SPORTS FOR THE DISABLED

SPORTS ENTHUSIASTS with a disability can obtain details of facilities for the disabled from the **Irish Wheelchair Association**. Central and local tourist boards and many of the organizations listed in the directory under each sport will also advise on available facilities. The **Share Centre** provides a range of activity breaks for people with and without disabilities.

Boats moored at Carnlough Harbour on the Antrim coast *(see p259)*

DIRECTORY

SPECTATOR SPORTS

Croke Park
Dublin 3. 01 836 3222. W www.gaa.ie

Football Association of Ireland
80 Merrion Sq, Dublin 2.
01 676 6864.

Horse Racing
The Curragh, Co Kildare.
045 445645. W www.horseracingireland.ie

Irish Open Office
Dartmouth House, Grand Parade, Dublin 6.
01 498 0300.

FISHING

Central Fisheries Board
Mobhi Boreen, Glasnevin, Dublin 9. 01 837 9206.

Department of Agriculture
Annex 5, Castle buildings, Stormont, Belfast.
028 9052 0100.

Irish Federation of Sea Anglers
Mr Hugh O'Rorke, 67 Windsor Dr, Monkstown, Co Dublin.
01 280 6873.

GOLF

Golfers Abroad
45 Rectory Rd, Duckmanton, Chesterfield, Derbyshire.
01246 240836.

Golfing Union of Ireland
Glencar House, 81 Eglinton Rd, Dublin 4.
01 269 4111.
W www.goi.ie

Irish Ladies Golfing Union
1 Clonskeagh Sq, Dublin 14. 01 269 6244.
W www.ilgu.ie

Professional Golf Association
01 932 1193.
W www.pga.org.uk

CYCLING

Ardclinis Activity Centre
High St, Cushendall, Co Antrim.
028 2577 1340.

Celtic Cycling
Lorum Old Rectory, Bagenalstown, Co Carlow.
059 977 5282.
W www.celticcycling.com

Cycleways
185-6 Parnell St, Dublin 1.
01 873 4748.
W www.cycleways.com

Raleigh Rent-a-Bike
58 Gardiner St, Dublin 1.
01 872 5399.

RIDING AND PONY TREKKING

Association of Irish Riding Establishments
11 Moore Park, Newbridge, Co Kildare.
045 431584.
W www.aire.ie

British Horse Society
House of Sport, Upper Malone Rd, Belfast.
028 9038 1222.

Equestrian Holidays Ireland
1 Sandyford Office Park, Foxrock, Dublin 18.
01 295 8928.

WALKING AND MOUNTAINEERING

Irish Ways
Old Rectory, Ballycanew, Gorey, Co Wexford.
055 27479.
W www.irishways.com

Mountaineering Council of Ireland
House of Sport, Longmile Rd, Dublin 12.
01 450 7376.
W www.mountaineering.ie

Ulster Federation of Rambling Clubs
12B Breda House, Drumart Drive, Belfast.
028 9064 8041.

WATER SPORTS

Atlantic Sea Kayaking
Union Hall, Co Cork.
028 21058.

Baltimore Diving & Watersports Centre
Baltimore, Co. Cork.
028 20300. W www.baltimorediving.com

British Surfing Association
Champions Yard, Penzance, Cornwall.
01736 360250.

DV Diving
138 Mountstewart Rd, Newtownards, Co Down.
028 9186 1686.

Irish Underwater Council
78a Patrick St, Dun Laoghaire, Co Dublin.
01 284 4601.
W www.scubaireland.com

Lakeland Canoe Centre
Castle Island, Enniskillen, Co Fermanagh.
028 6632 4250.

Out and Out Activities
Garrison, Co Fermanagh.
028 6865 8072.

Outside World
Parnell Place, Cork.
021 427 8833.

Schull Watersports Centre
Schull, Co Cork.
028 28554.

CRUISING AND SAILING

Athlone Cruisers
Jolly Mariner, Athlone, Co Westmeath. 090 647 2892. W www.acl.ie

Emerald Star
The Marina, Carrick-on-Shannon, Co Leitrim.
071 962 0234.
W www.emeraldstar.ie

Erne Marine
Bellanaleck, Enniskillen, Co Fermanagh.
028 6634 8267.
W www.ernemarine.com

International Sailing Centre
East Beach, Cobh, Cork.
021 481 1237.
W www.sailcork.com

Ireland Line Cruisers
Derg Marina, Killaloe, Co Clare. 061 375011.
W www.ireland linecruisers.com

Lough Melvin Holiday Centre
Garrison, Co Fermanagh.
028 6865 8142.
W www.loughmelvin centre.com

Shannon-Erne Waterways
Ballinamore, Co Leitrim.
071 964 5185.

Silver Line Cruisers
The Marina, Banagher, Co Offaly. 0509 51112.
W www.silverline cruisers.com

Ulster Cruising School
The Marina, Carrickfergus, Co Antrim. 028 9336 8818. W www.ulster cruising.com

HUNTING

Countryside Alliance
47 Whiterock Rd, Killinchy, Co Down.
028 9754 1871.

Irish Master of Foxhounds Association
051 853981.

Mount Juliet Estate
Thomastown, Co Kilkenny.
056 772 4455.
www.conradhotels.com

SPORTS FOR THE DISABLED

Irish Wheelchair Association
Blackheath Dr, Clontarf, Dublin 3. 01 833 8241. W www.iwa.ie

Share Centre
Smith's Strand, Lisnaskea, Co Fermanagh.
028 6772 2122.
W www.sharevillage.org

SURVIVAL
GUIDE

PRACTICAL INFORMATION

Ireland
Tourist Board logo

ALTHOUGH IRELAND is quite a small island, visitors should not expect to see everything in a short time, since many of the country's most magnificent attractions are in rural areas. In remote parts of the island the roads are narrow and winding, the pace of life is very slow, banks often open for only one or two days of the week and public transport tends to be infrequent. However, although the Republic of Ireland remains one of

Europe's most unspoiled destinations, its economy is developing fast. Any decent-sized town in the Republic is likely to have a tourist information centre and offer a full range of facilities for the visitor. Northern Ireland has its own tourist board which also has offices in most towns. The standard of facilities available to those travelling in the North equals that across the border and, as with the Republic, the level of hospitality is first-rate.

TOURIST INFORMATION

IN BOTH THE REPUBLIC and Northern Ireland there is an impressive network of tourist information offices. As well as providing lots of free local information, the tourist offices in large towns sell maps and guide books and can reserve accommodation for a nominal charge. There are also tourist information points in some of the smaller towns and villages. The opening hours can be somewhat erratic and many are open only during the summer season. The local museums and libraries often stock a selection of useful tourist literature.

Before leaving for Ireland you can get brochures and advice from **Tourism Ireland**, which has information on both Northern Ireland and the Republic. Their offices can be found in major cities all over the world – a reflection of the universal appeal of Ireland. **Fáilte Ireland** (the Irish Tourist Board) and the **Northern Ireland Tourist Board** (NITB) can also supply you with maps and leaflets. For more local information on sights, accommodation and car rental, it's worth contacting the regional tourist offices in Dublin, Cork, Galway and Limerick.

If you pick up a list of places to stay in a tourist office, it's worth noting that not every local hotel and guesthouse will be included – these lists recommend only those establishments that have been approved by the Tourist Board.

The Dúchas-run Parke's Castle in County Leitrim *(see p225)*

ADMISSION CHARGES

MOST OF IRELAND'S major sights, including ancient monuments, museums and national parks, have an admission fee. For each place of interest in this guide, we specify whether or not there is a charge. The entrance fees in the Republic of Ireland are normally between 1.50 euros and 6.50 euros, with some offering discounts for students and seniors.

Dúchas, the Irish heritage service, manages and maintains national parks, museums, monuments and gardens. At most Dúchas sites you can buy a Heritage Card, which allows unlimited, free admission to all sites managed by Dúchas for a year. At 20

Heritage Card giving access to historic sites

euros for adults, 15 euros for senior citizens, 7.60 euros for children and students, and 50 euros for a family ticket, the card is a good investment. Popular Dúchas sites include Céide Fields *(see p196)*, Cahir Castle *(see p190)* and the Blasket Centre *(see p150)*. Entrance fees in Northern Ireland are about the same as in the Republic, also with discounts offered to students and senior citizens.

North of the border the **National Trust** has a scheme similar to the Heritage Card, but membership costs more (just under £35 per annum per person or under £50 for a family ticket) and there are fewer sites to see. It is only good value for money if you are also planning to visit National Trust sites across the water in Great Britain.

Interpretative centre at Connemara National Park *(see p200)*

OPENING TIMES

Opening HOURS are usually between 10am and 5pm, though some sights close for lunch. Few places are open on Sunday morning. Some museums shut on Monday.

From June to September all the sights are open but crowds are at their biggest. July is the marching season in the North *(see p47)* and tensions can run high in Belfast and Derry; many shops and restaurants close at this time.

Some attractions close for winter, while others keep shorter hours. Many places open for public holidays such as Easter and then close again until summer.

INTERPRETATIVE CENTRES

Many OF IRELAND's major sights are ruins or Stone Age archaeological sites and can be difficult to appreciate. In recent years, however, money has become available for building interpretative or visitors' centres which explain the historical significance of sites. Entry to the site may be free, but you have to pay to visit the interpretative centre.

In areas of natural beauty, such as Connemara National Park, an interpretative centre acts as a useful focal point. The centre typically provides information leaflets and has reconstructions of sights. Connemara has 3D models and displays, as well as an audiovisual presentation on the development of the local landscape over the last 10,000 years. There is also a shop for postcards, books and posters.

RELIGIOUS SERVICES

IRELAND is a deeply religious country and for much of the population, churchgoing is a way of life. Because the Republic of Ireland is 95 per cent Roman Catholic, finding a non-Catholic church may sometimes be difficult. In the Republic and Northern Ireland, the tourist offices, hotels and B&Bs all keep a list of local church service times.

DIRECTORY

TOURISM IRELAND OFFICES ABROAD

United Kingdom
For Republic of Ireland:
Ireland Desk, British Visitor Centre, 1 Regent St, London SW1Y 4XT.
(0800 039 7000.
For Northern Ireland:
Tourism Ireland UK, Nations House, 103 Wigmore St, London W1U 1QS. (020 7518 0800.
w www.tourismireland.com

United States
345 Park Avenue, New York, NY 10154. (800 223 6470.
w www.tourismireland.com

TOURIST BOARD OFFICES IN IRELAND

Fáilte Ireland
Baggot St Bridge, Dublin 2.
(01 602 4000.
w www.ireland.ie

Northern Ireland Tourist Board
St Anne's Court, 59 North St, Belfast BT1 1NB.
(028 9023 1221.
Belfast Welcome Centre:
47 Donegall Place. (028 9024 6609. w www.discovernorthern ireland.com

OTHER ADDRESSES

National Trust
Rowallane House, Saintfield, Ballynahinch, Co Down BT24 7LH. (028 9751 0721.
w www.nationaltrust.org.uk

Dúchas
6 Upper Ely Place, Dublin 2.
(01 647 2461/1890 321421.
w www.duchas.ie

LANGUAGE

The Republic of Ireland is officially bilingual – almost all road signs have place names in both English and Irish. English is the spoken language everywhere apart from a few parts of the far west, called Gaeltachts *(see p221)*, but now and then you may find signs written only in Irish. Here are some of the words you are most likely to come across.

USEFUL WORDS

an banc – **bank**
an lár – **town centre**
an trá – **beach**
ar aghaidh – **go**
bád – **boat**
bealach amach – **exit**
bealach isteach – **entrance**
bus – **bus**
dúnta – **closed**
fáilte – **welcome**
fir – **men**
gardaí – **police**
leithreas – **toilet**

Sign using old form of Gaelic

mná – **women**
oifig an phoist – **post office**
oscailte – **open**
óstán – **hotel**
siopa – **shop**
stop/stad – **stop**
ticéad – **ticket**
traein – **train**

Additional Information

European Youth Card

IRELAND IS DIVIDED between the state of the Republic of Ireland, and Northern Ireland – a part of the United Kingdom. Each has a separate currency, postal service and telecommunications system *(see pp344–9)*. However, there are many similarities between them: they are part of the European Union, English is their first language and, both north and south of the border, the tourist industry is well established. These two pages describe the regulations that affect the Republic and Northern Ireland, and the special facilities that are available to travellers, including students and the disabled. There is also a general guide to the media in both the North and South as well as a directory of useful names and addresses.

Students at Trinity College, Dublin

VISAS

VISITORS FROM THE EU, US, Canada, Australia and New Zealand require a valid passport but not a visa for entry into the Republic or Northern Ireland. All others, including those wanting to study or work, should check with their local Irish or British Embassy first. UK nationals born in Britain or Northern Ireland do not need a passport to enter the Republic of Ireland but should take one with them for car rental, medical services, cashing of traveller's cheques or if travelling by air.

DUTY-FREE GOODS AND CUSTOMS ALLOWANCES

IN 1999 THE duty-free allowances on goods bought between the Republic of Ireland and other countries were abolished. However, a wide range of items may still be purchased at airport shops

and on ferries, including goods that were previously duty-free, such as beers, wines, spirits, perfume and cigarettes. Electrical goods and camera equipment, items which were traditionally considerably cheaper in duty-free, are still on sale at the airport shops but travellers should have some idea of comparative prices for the goods and know the different exchange rates before making an expensive purchase.

STUDENT INFORMATION

STUDENTS WITH a valid ISIC card (International Student Identity Card) benefit from a range of travel discounts as well as reduced admission to museums and concerts. Buy a Travelsave stamp from any branch of **USIT** and affix it to your ISIC card to get a good discount on Irish Rail, NIR train services and Irish Ferries. A Travelsave stamp

will also get you discounts on various rail and bus services in the South and special rates on commuter tickets (Sep–Jun only) in Dublin, Limerick, Cork, Galway and Waterford. In the North, an ISIC card gives a 15 per cent discount on Ulsterbus services and 20 per cent on Belfast Citybus "Gold Card" commuter services. ISIC cards can be obtained from branches of USIT travel in Dublin, Belfast and other college towns.

USIT will also supply non-students under 26 with an EYC (European Youth Card) for discounts on air fares, and in restaurants, shops and theatres. Recognized in over 20 European states, the card varies from country to country but can be identified by its distinctive logo.

FACILITIES FOR THE DISABLED

MOST SIGHTS in Ireland have access for wheelchairs. This book gives basic information about disabled access for each sight, but it's worth phoning to check details. **Comhairle** provides information for the Republic, publishing county guides to accommodation, restaurants and amenities. In the North, **Disability Action** can advise on accessibility, while **ADAPT** provides information and a book on disabled access to over 400 venues in the cultural sector. Both **tourist boards** also have guides to accommodation and amenities.

Shop at Shannon Airport

Relaxing with newspapers in Eyre Square, Galway

RADIO AND TELEVISION

IRELAND has three state-controlled television channels, RTE 1, Network 2 and the Irish-language Teilifís na Gaelige (TG4), and one privately run channel, TV3. There are six national radio stations and many local ones.

The five British TV channels can be picked up in most parts of Ireland on Cable TV, which is commonly available in hotels in the Republic.

A selection of daily newspapers from North and South

NEWSPAPERS AND MAGAZINES

THE REPUBLIC of Ireland has six national daily papers and five Sunday papers. Quality dailies include the *Irish Independent*, the *Examiner* and the *Irish Times*, the latter being well known for its journalistic excellence. The broadsheets are useful for up-to-date information on theatre and concerts. Ireland's daily

tabloid is the *Star*. The North's top local paper is the *Belfast Telegraph*, on sale in the afternoon. The province's morning papers, the *News Letter* and *Irish News*, are less rewarding.

In larger towns throughout Ireland, British tabloids are on sale. Newspapers such as *The Times* are also available and cost less than the quality Irish press. Most towns have a local or regional paper, which will tell you what's on and where.

USA Today, *Newsweek* and *Time* magazine are sold in major cities but are very hard to find in rural areas.

IRISH TIME

THE WHOLE of Ireland is in the same time zone as Great Britain, i.e. five hours ahead of New York and Toronto, one hour behind Germany and France, and ten hours behind Sydney. In both the North and the South, clocks go forward one hour for summer time.

CONVERSION CHART

Imperial to Metric
1 inch = 2.5 centimetres
1 foot = 30 centimetres
1 mile = 1.6 kilometres
1 ounce = 28 grams
1 pound = 454 grams
1 pint = 0.6 litres
1 gallon = 4.6 litres

Metric to Imperial
1 millimetre = 0.04 inches
1 centimetre = 0.4 inches
1 metre = 3 feet 3 inches
1 kilometre = 0.6 miles
1 gram = 0.04 ounces
1 kilogram = 2.2 pounds
1 litre = 1.8 pints

DIRECTORY

EMBASSIES

Australia
Fitzwilton House, Wilton Terrace, Dublin 2. (01 664 5300.

Canada
65–68 St Stephen's Green, Dublin 2. (01 417 4100.

UK
29 Merrion Rd, Dublin 4.
(01 205 3700.

US
42 Elgin Rd, Ballsbridge, Dublin 4.
(01 668 7122.

USEFUL ADDRESSES

ADAPT
109–113 Royal Avenue, Belfast.
(028 9023 1211.
W www.adapt.ni.org

Comhairle
44 North Great George's St, Dublin 1. (01 874 7503.
W www.comhairle.com

Disability Action
189 Airport Rd West, Belfast.
(028 9029 7880.
W www.disabilityaction.org

USIT
19/21 Aston Quay, Dublin 2.
(01 602 1600. Fountain Centre, College St, Belfast BT1 6ET. (
028 9032 7111. W www.usit.ie

METRICATION

THE CHANGE towards metrication is slow in Ireland, particularly the North, where distances are still measured in miles. In the Republic, all new road signs show distances in kilometres, but there are still many old ones left that use miles (*see p356*). However, throughout Ireland all speed limits are shown in miles. In both Northern Ireland and the Republic, fuel is sold in litres but draught beer is always sold in pints. And just to add to the confusion, food may be weighed out either in imperial or in metric measures.

$$\boxed{\text{km} \begin{array}{l} 4 \ \textit{Ceann Trá} \\ 17 \ \textit{Dún Chaoin} \end{array}}$$

One of the new metric road signs used in the Republic of Ireland

Personal Security and Health

IRELAND IS PROBABLY one of the safest places to travel in Europe. Petty theft, such as pickpocketing, is seldom a problem outside certain parts of Dublin and a few other large towns. Tourist offices and hoteliers gladly point out the areas to be avoided. In the recent past, the main security risk in Northern Ireland has been the threat of bombings, though this has hardly ever affected tourists. In fact, crimes against the individual tend to be fewer than in other parts of the UK and Europe.

Pharmacy in Dublin showing old-fashioned snake and goblet symbol

Pearse Street Garda Station, Dublin

PERSONAL SECURITY

THE POLICE, should you ever need them, are called the Gardaí in the Republic of Ireland and the Police Service of Northern Ireland (PSNI) in the North. Violent street crime in Ireland – North or South – is relatively rare but it's still advisable to take suitable precautions, such as avoiding poorly lit streets in the cities and larger towns. Poverty and a degree of heroin addiction

Garda   PSNI policeman

in inner-city Dublin has been known to cause a few problems, and Limerick isn't the most inviting of places after dark. There have also been a number of racial attacks recently in Dublin. But if you take sensible precautions, avoiding back-streets at night and keeping to the popular and busy areas, there should be little cause for concern. In some of the larger southern towns you may be approached in the street by people asking for money. This rarely develops into a troublesome situation, but it is still best to avoid eye contact and leave the scene as quickly as possible.

PERSONAL SAFETY IN NORTHERN IRELAND

Even at the height of the Troubles in Northern Ireland, there was never a significant threat to the tourist, and travelling around the province was deemed to be as safe as in the Republic. As long as peace prevails, no extra precautions need to be taken here, but in the event of the Troubles resurfacing, first-time visitors should be prepared for certain unfamiliar situations. When driving, if you see a sign that indicates you are approaching a checkpoint, slow down and use dipped headlights. To keep fuss down to a minimum in these situations, it is a good idea to keep a passport or some other form of identification close at hand. If you are walking around the city centres of Belfast and Londonderry, you may notice

Garda station

PSNI badge

a strong police or military presence. This is unlikely to inconvenience you. Occasionally, you may be asked by shop security to reveal the contents of your bags – don't be alarmed, this is a routine procedure.

Try to avoid visiting in July, as tensions are higher during the Orange marches *(see p47)*.

PERSONAL PROPERTY

BEFORE YOU LEAVE, make sure that your possessions are insured, as it might be difficult and more expensive to do this in Ireland. Travel insurance for the UK may not cover you for the Republic, so make sure you have an adequate policy. As pickpocketing and bag-snatching can be a problem in some of the larger towns, it's best not to carry around your passport or large amounts of cash, or leave them in your room. Most hotels have a safe and it makes sense to take advantage of this facility. Those carrying large amounts of money around should use traveller's cheques *(see pp346–7)*. When out and about, use a bag that can be held securely, and be alert in crowded places and restaurants. A money belt may be a good investment.

If travelling by car, ensure all valuables are locked in the boot and always lock the car, even when leaving it for just a few minutes. If visiting Northern Ireland, do not leave any of your bags or packages unattended, as they are likely to result in a security scare.

LOST PROPERTY AND BAGGAGE ROOMS

REPORT ALL LOST or stolen items at once to the police. In order to make a claim against your insurance company you need to send in a copy of the police report. Most train and bus stations in the Republic operate a lost-property service but there is no such service in Northern Ireland.

If you wish to do a day's sightseeing unencumbered by baggage, most hotels and some main city tourist offices, both in the Republic and Northern Ireland, offer baggage storage facilities.

MEDICAL TREATMENT

RESIDENTS OF COUNTRIES in the European Union can claim free medical treatment in Ireland by getting form E111 before setting out. You'll need to show your E111 and identification, such as a driver's licence or passport. Also, be sure to let the doctor know that you want treatment under the EU's social security regulations. In Northern Ireland, British citizens need no documentation.

Non-EU travellers should either have their own travel insurance or be willing to pay for any treatment received.

Private health insurance policies may include a certain level of travel coverage. US visitors in particular should check before leaving home whether they are covered by their insurance companies for

Small rural health centre in County Donegal

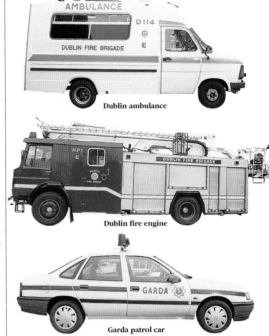

Dublin ambulance

Dublin fire engine

Garda patrol car

medical care abroad. You may have to pay first and reclaim costs; if so, be sure to get an itemized bill.

PHARMACIES

A WIDE RANGE of medical supplies is available over the counter at pharmacies. However, many medicines are available only with a prescription authorized by a local doctor. If you are likely to require specialized drugs during your stay, take your own supplies with a copy of the original prescription. You can also ask your doctor to write a letter with the generic name of the medicine you require. Always obtain a receipt for insurance claims.

Until recently, condoms were not freely available in the Republic but are now relatively easy to obtain in the big cities at least. In some of the small towns you may discover that the pharmacist is opposed to contraception and does not sell condoms, but this is becoming a fairly rare occurrence. There are no such difficulties in Northern Ireland.

Local Currency

T HE REPUBLIC and Northern Ireland have different currencies. The euro is the currency in the Republic and the pound sterling is the currency in Northern Ireland, the same as in Great Britain. When travelling between Northern Ireland and the Republic, there's no shortage of money-changers in towns on either side of the border. Look in the daily newspapers for the standard rate of exchange to give yourself a guideline. Some tourist attractions offer money changing facilities but for the best exchange rates use the banks or *bureaux de change.*

Ulster Bank sub-office in Delvin, County Westmeath

CURRENCY IN NORTHERN IRELAND

N ORTHERN IRELAND uses British currency – the pound sterling (£), which is divided into 100 pence (p). As there are no exchange controls in the UK, there is no limit to the amount of cash you can take into and out of Northern Ireland. In addition to the British currency, four provincial banks issue their own banknotes (bills), worth the same as their counterparts. To tell them apart, look for the words "Bank of England" on British notes. It is best to use the provincial banknotes in Northern Ireland rather than in Britain – some shops may be reluctant to accept notes that are unfamiliar to them.

Banknotes

British banknotes are issued in the denominations £50, £20, £10 and £5. Their different colours help make them easily distinguishable.

£50 note

£20 note

£10 note

£5 note

Coins

Coins come in the following denominations: £2, £1, 50p, 20p, 10p, 5p, 2p and 1p. All have the Queen's head on one side and are the same as those elsewhere in the UK, except that the pound coin has a different detail – a flax plant – on the reverse side.

£2

£1

50p

20p

10p

5p

2p

1p

The Euro

THE SINGLE European currency, the euro, has been adopted by 12 of the 15 member states of the EU. Austria, Belgium, Finland, France, Germany, Greece, Ireland, Italy, Luxembourg, Netherlands, Portugal and Spain chose to join the new currency; the UK, Denmark and Sweden stayed out, with an option to review their decision at a later date.

The euro was introduced on 1 January 1999, but only for banking purposes. Notes (bills) and coins came into circulation on 1 January 2002.

Irish euro notes and coins can be used in any of the 12 member states listed. However, with the high cost of living in Ireland, they go less far here than in some neighbouring European countries.

Banknotes

Euro banknotes have seven denominations. The 5-euro note (grey in colour) is the smallest, followed by the 10-euro note (pink), 20-euro (blue), 50-euro (orange), 100-euro (green), 200-euro (yellow) and 500-euro (purple). All notes show the 12 stars of the EU and a specific style of European architecture.

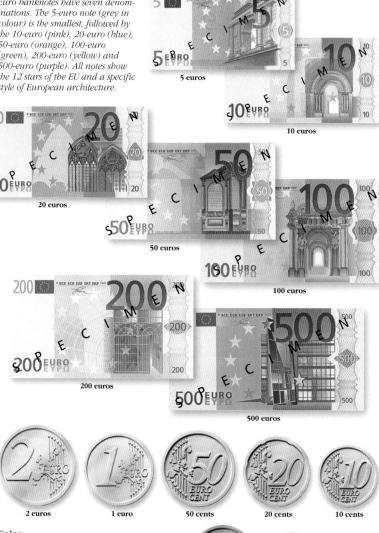

5 euros

10 euros

20 euros

50 euros

100 euros

200 euros

500 euros

2 euros

1 euro

50 cents

20 cents

10 cents

Coins

The euro has eight coin denominations: 2 euros and 1 euro (gold and silver); 50 cents, 20 cents, 10 cents (gold); 5 cents, 2 cents and 1 cent (bronze). The reverse sides of all coins are the same in all euro-zone countries, while the obverse sides are different in each state.

5 cents

2 cents

1 cent

Banks in Ireland

THE OPENING TIMES of banks in Ireland vary depending on whether the banks are situated in the town or country, in the Republic or Northern Ireland. Both north and south of the border, banks in small towns are often sub-offices where banking services may be provided on only one or two days of the week, so it's advisable to make the most of facilities in the bigger towns whenever you can. Banks throughout Ireland generally provide a very good service and, along with many of the larger post offices, will exchange traveller's cheques, often without charging commission.

Bank of Ireland sub-office in Sneem, County Kerry

USING BANKS

THE FIVE RETAIL BANKS in the Republic of Ireland are the Bank of Ireland, the Allied Irish Bank (AIB), the Ulster Bank, the National Irish Bank and the Permanent tsb. In Northern Ireland there are four retail banks: the Ulster Bank, the Bank of Ireland, the Northern Bank and the First Trust Bank.

Bank machine

In the Republic of Ireland the usual banking hours are Monday to Friday from 10am to 12:30pm and from 1:30 to 4pm, but most branches now stay open during lunch time. There is extended opening (till 5pm) on one day of the week. In Dublin, Cork and most other cities and towns, late opening is on

Thursdays but in rural areas banks often stay open late on market day instead. Some rural areas are visited once or twice a week by a mobile bank. Check locally for days and times. Branches of the Permanent tsb re-main open at lunch time and till 7pm on Thursdays and up to 5pm on other week-days. Most banks in Northern Ireland open from 10am till 4pm, though a few close for lunch between 12:30 and 1:30pm. In both the Republic and in Northern Ireland, all banks close on public holidays, which differ from North to South *(see p49)*. Banks in the cities and most towns have automated teller machines (ATMs), or cash dispensers, so if the local bank is closed, it isn't necessarily a major catastrophe.

CREDIT CARDS

THROUGHOUT IRELAND you can pay by credit card in most hotels, petrol (gas) stations, large shops and supermarkets. VISA and MasterCard (known also as Access) are the most commonly accepted credit cards. Fewer businesses take American Express and Diners Club cards. Cash can be with-drawn from banks displaying the appropriate sign.

TRAVELLER'S CHEQUES

TRAVELLER'S CHEQUES are the safest way to carry around large amounts of money. These are best changed at one of the main banks but, failing this, many shops and restaurants accept them – usually for a small charge.

Traveller's cheques can be bought before setting out at American Express, Travelex,

Ornate post office and *bureau de change* in Ventry, County Kerry

or your own bank.
In Ireland, traveller's cheques can be purchased at banks and from *bureaux de change*, which can be found in the larger cities and at airports.

TRANSFERRING MONEY

THE CHEAPEST way to get money from home is to have your own bank wire funds to a bank in Ireland. This process is very slow, often taking several days; it's much faster, though expensive, to get money sent through a dedicated money transfer company such as Western Union (tel: 1800 395395).

**Drawing money from an
Allied Irish Bank ATM**

BUREAUX DE CHANGE

IN ADDITION to the foreign exchange counters at the main banks, there are some private *bureaux de change* in Dublin. As with most other exchange facilities, *bureaux de change* stay open later than banks. However, it's worth checking their rates before undertaking any transactions.

BUREAUX DE CHANGE

American Express
41 Nassau Street, Dublin 2.
▌ *01 679 9000.*
Branches also at Dublin Tourism Centre, Suffolk Street & Killarney.

Thomas Cook
51 & 118 Grafton Street, Dublin 2.
▌ *01 677 1721.*
11 Donegall Place, Belfast.
▌ *028 9088 3900.*

Travelex
Belfast International Airport.
▌ *028 9444 7510.*
Ⓦ www.travelex.com

Sending a Letter

**Northern Ireland
Post Office sign**

MAIN POST OFFICES in the Republic and Northern Ireland are usually open from 9am to 5:30pm during the week and from 9am to around 1pm on Saturdays, although times do vary. Some smaller offices close for lunch on weekdays and do not open on Saturdays. Standard letter and postcard stamps can also be bought from some corner shops. The Republic of Ireland does not have a first- and second-class system, but sending a postcard is a few cents less expensive than a letter.

Though it is improving all the time, the postal service in the Republic is still quite slow – allow three to four days when sending a letter to Great Britain and at

Republic of Ireland Post Office logo

least six days for the United States. Swiftpost guarantees delivery within two working days. In Northern Ireland, letters to other parts of the UK can be sent either first- or second-class, with most first-class letters reaching their UK destination the next day. The cost of a letter from Northern Ireland is the same to all EU countries.

POSTBOXES

POSTBOXES in Ireland come in two colours – green in the Republic and red in the North. Many of Ireland's postboxes are quite historic. Some of those in the Republic even carry Queen Victoria's monogram on the front, a relic from the days of British rule. Even the smallest towns in Ireland have a postbox, from which the mail is collected regularly – anything from once to four times daily.

**Letter stamps used in the
Republic of Ireland**

**First-class and second-class
stamps used in the North**

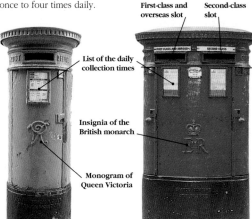

**First-class and
overseas slot**

**Second-class
slot**

**List of the daily
collection times**

**Insignia of the
British monarch**

**Monogram of
Queen Victoria**

Postbox in the Republic

Northern Ireland double postbox

Using Ireland's Telephones

THE REPUBLIC'S national telephone company, eircom (previously Telecom Eireann), once ran all the telephone services in the country, but changes in the law have meant that other companies can now provide public phones. Eircom's service includes up-to-date coin, card and credit card telephones that provide a modern, efficient service. For those intending to spend more than 5 euros on calls during their stay, it is worth using a phonecard, as these offer discounts. Northern Ireland uses British Telecom public phones. Both BT and eircom phonecards are available from post offices, supermarkets and other retail outlets.

eircom phonebox

Coffee and computers at the Central Cyber Café in Dublin

ACCESSING THE INTERNET

THE MAIN CITIES in the Republic have plenty of public access to computers and the Internet. Public facilities are available free of charge from public libraries, but you may have to book in advance. The easiest and fastest way to access the Internet is at one of the ever-increasing number of Internet cafés found all over Dublin and throughout the country in major towns and cities. The cafés generally charge by the minute for computer use, so costs build up quickly especially when including the cost of printed pages. Internet access is often cheaper during off-peak times so check charges beforehand.

PHONING FROM THE REPUBLIC OF IRELAND

CHEAP CALL RATES within the Republic and to the UK are from 6pm to 8am on weekdays and all day at weekends. Off-peak times for international calls vary from country to country, but are generally as above.
• To call Northern Ireland: dial 048, then the area code, followed by the number.
• To call the UK: dial 00 44, the area code (minus the

leading 0), then the number.
• To call other countries: dial 00, followed by the country code (for example, 1 for the USA, 61 for Australia), the area code (minus the leading 0), then the number.
• Credit cards issued in certain countries including the USA, Australia and Canada are accepted as payment for calls to the country in which the card was issued.

USING AN EIRCOM PHONE

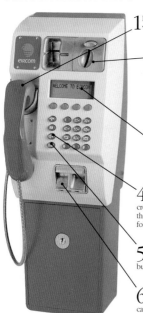

1 Lift the receiver and wait for the dial tone.

2 Insert your phonecard or credit card into the slot, or deposit any of the following coins: 10c, 20c, 50c, 1, 2. The minimum amount is 40c. Dial the number and wait to be connected.

3 The display indicates how much credit you have left. A rapid bleeping noise means your credit has run out. Insert more coins or another card.

4 If you want to make a further call and you have credit left, do not replace the receiver, press the follow-on-call button instead.

5 To redial the number you have just called, press the button marked "R".

6 After you have replaced the receiver, retrieve your card or collect your change. Only wholly unused coins are refunded.

paying by credit card

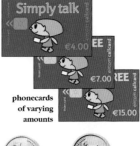

phonecards of varying amounts

€4.00

€7.00

€15.00

1 euro

50 cents

20 cents

10 cents

Phoning from Northern Ireland

CHEAP CALL RATES within and from the Province are as for the Republic.
• For calls within Great Britain and Northern Ireland: dial the area code and the number required.
• For calls to the Republic of Ireland: dial 00 353, then the area code minus the first 0, then the number.
• For international calls: dial 00, then the country code (for example, 1 for Canada, 64 for New Zealand), then the area code minus the first 0, and finally the number you require.

In addition to using coins and pre-paid phonecards in the BT phone boxes as indicated below, credit card boxes are also available.

In 1999, all phone numbers in Northern Ireland changed from having a prefix of 01 and an area code, to having an area code of 028, followed by an 8-digit local number.

Using a BT Phone

1 Lift the receiver and wait for the dial tone.

3 Dial the number and wait to be connected.

2 Insert your phonecard into the slot or deposit any of the following coins: 10p, 20p, 50p, £1, £2. The minimum amount is 20p.

4 The display indicates how much credit you have left. A rapid bleeping noise means your money has run out. Deposit more coins or insert another phonecard.

5 If you want to make another call and you have money left in credit, do not replace the receiver, press the follow-on-call button.

6 When you have finished speaking, replace the receiver and retrieve your card or collect your change. Only wholly unused coins are refunded.

£1   50p   20p   10p

Phone Booths in Northern Ireland

Most of the phone booths in the Republic are modern. In Northern Ireland there are two different types of BT phone booths: traditional red phone booths and a newer modern style. Both are issued with the same type of telephone. In both Northern Ireland and in the Republic, the wording around the top of each booth shows whether it is a coin, phonecard or credit card phone.

Old BT phone booth   **New BT phone booth**

TRAVEL INFORMATION

I RELAND'S THREE main airports, Dublin, Shannon and Belfast, are well served by flights from Britain, the United States and an increasing number of countries around the world. If you are travelling by sea from the UK, there is a very good choice of ferry routes from ports in Britain to both the Republic and Northern Ireland. Instead of buying separate tickets, you can purchase combined coach/ferry and rail/ferry tickets from almost all of the towns in mainland Britain. The less-than-comprehensive public transport systems in both the North and South reflect the rural nature of the island. With this in mind, travelling around Ireland is probably best enjoyed if you embrace the Irish way of thinking and just take your time.

Aer Lingus Airbus in flight

Information signs in the main concourse of Shannon Airport

GETTING TO AND FROM THE AIRPORT

T HE REPUBLIC'S three main airports are all served by regular bus services, whereas the smaller airports depend mainly on local taxi services. Two express bus services run between Dublin Airport, the city's main rail and bus stations and the city centre every 15 to 20 minutes, from early morning to around midnight. The journey takes 30 minutes.

At Cork, the Bus Éireann service takes 15 minutes from the airport into the city. Buses run every 45 minutes on weekdays and hourly at the weekends. At Shannon Airport, Bus Éireann runs a regular service into Limerick which takes 35 minutes to the city centre. In addition, several buses a day go to the town of Ennis, about 30 km (18 miles) away. All airports in the Republic have both long- and short-stay parking facilities.

The modern exterior of Dublin International Airport

FLYING TO THE REPUBLIC OF IRELAND

F LIGHTS from most of the major cities in Europe arrive at **Dublin Airport**, which is the country's busiest airport. Regular services to the Republic depart from all five of the London airports (Heathrow, City, Gatwick, Luton and Stansted) and 15 other cities in Britain, plus the Channel Islands and the Isle of Man.

The major airline operating scheduled flights between Britain and the Republic is **Aer Lingus**. However since deregulation, the rival company **Ryanair** has grown fast, with cheap fares from several airports in Britain and around Europe, including Barcelona, Brussels, Paris, Faro and Malaga.

Aer Lingus and **Continental Airlines** fly direct from the US to Dublin Airport and

Shannon Airport, ten miles outside Limerick – gone is the old ruling that all planes flying eastward to Dublin must first touch down at Shannon, but **Delta Air Lines** does serve both airports.

Cork Airport is served by flights from London (Heathrow and Stansted), Birmingham, Manchester, Bristol, Plymouth, Cardiff, Leeds, Glasgow, Paris, Amsterdam and Dublin. None of the airlines flies direct to Ireland from Australia or New Zealand, but there are plenty of connections via London and other capitals.

The Republic's other airports have fewer flights. There are many charter flights for pilgrims to **Knock International Airport** in Co Mayo, which also has flights from Dublin, London (Stansted) and Manchester. There are flights into Kerry from Dublin and Stansted airports and Waterford Airport has flights from both London and Luton. Galway is well served with five daily flights from Dublin.

One of the Airlink buses which take passengers from Dublin Airport into the city centre

Passengers checking in at Belfast International Airport

FLYING TO NORTHERN IRELAND

THERE ARE HOURLY flights, operated by either **British Airways** or **British Midland**, from London Heathrow to **Belfast International Airport**, 30 km (18 miles) northwest of Belfast city centre. The airport is also served by flights from Luton and some regional airports like Stansted, Bristol, Liverpool and Glasgow. There are also **easyJet** flights from Amsterdam.

Belfast City Airport is used by smaller aircraft, but is favoured by many because of its location – it is just 6.5 km (4 miles) from the city centre. The airport also has more flights from the UK – around 15 cities plus London Gatwick, Stansted and Luton – than Belfast International. The City of Derry Airport is Northern Ireland's smallest, with flights from Stansted, Manchester and Glasgow.

AIRPORT CONNECTIONS IN NORTHERN IRELAND

THE ARRANGEMENTS for getting to and from the airports in Northern Ireland are generally good. BIA's Airbus service will take you from the airport to the Europa Bus centre via Oxford Street Bus Station and Central Railway Station. This runs every half hour and takes about 30 minutes from end to end. At Belfast City Airport the number 21 bus passes every half hour, taking around 10 minutes to get to the Belfast City Hall bus depot. There are trains from the airport to Central Station about every 30

minutes. Derry's airport is on a local bus route: the number 143 goes into the city centre once an hour (less frequently at weekends). All airports in Northern Ireland have taxi ranks and both long- and short-term parking facilities.

AIR FARES

AIRLINE OPTIONS between the United States and Ireland have increased in the last few years, with frequent flights now from both the East and West coasts.

It's quite easy to get a round-trip flight to Shannon from the East Coast for under US$700 (prices are so competitive now it could cost as little as US$200), but these tickets often restrict your visit to between 7 and 30 days. The best bargains are on flights with fixed dates.

Air fares from the US are at their highest in the peak season which runs from July to September.

Many UK airports serve Ireland and airlines offer a host of options on fares. It's not difficult to get a round-trip flight from mainland UK to Dublin for well under £100. The cheapest place to fly from is usually London, especially Luton and Stansted airports. Prices are fairly constant all year except at Christmas, during summer and on public holidays, when there are few discounted fares.

Many airlines offer discounts to those under 25, while USIT (see p340), Campus Travel and other specialist travel agents often have cheaper rates for students and under-26s.

Airport sign in English and Gaelic

← Arrivals ✈
↑ Shops 🛒 Siopaí
↑ Bar 🍺 Beár
↑ Snacks ✕ Sólaistí

DIRECTORY

MAJOR AIRPORTS

Belfast City Airport
028 9093 9093.
Belfast International
028 9442 2888.
Cork International
021 431 3131.
Dublin Airport
01 844 6166.
Knock International
094 936 7222.
Shannon Airport
061 472299.

AIRLINES

Aer Lingus
01 886 8888 (Ireland).
1 800 IRISH AIR (US).
0845 084 4444 (UK).
www.aerlingus.com

Continental Airlines
01 672 7070 (Ireland).
1 800 523 3273 (US).
www.continental.com

British Airways
1800 626 747 (Ireland).
0845 773 3377 (UK).
1 800 247 9297 (US).
www.ba.com

British Midland (bmi)
0870 607 0555 (UK).
www.flybmi.com

Cityjet
01 844 5566 (Ireland).
www.cityjet.com

Delta Air Lines
1800 768080 (Ireland).
1 800 221 1212 (US).
0800 414767 (UK).
www.delta.com

easyJet
0870 600 0000 (UK).
www.easyjet.com

KLM
01 284 3823 (Ireland).
20 474 7747 (Netherlands).
1 800 447 4747 (US).
www.klmuk.com

Qantas
01 407 3278 (Ireland).
02 691 3636 (Aus).
1 800 227 4500 (US).
www.qantas.com.au

Ryanair
01 609 7800 (Ireland).
0870 333 1250 (UK).
www.ryanair.com

Arriving by Sea

Travelling by ferry is a popular way of getting to Ireland, especially for groups or families intending to tour the country by car. Nine ports in Great Britain and two in France provide ferry crossings to Ireland's six ports. Nowadays, all ferries are of the modern drive-on/drive-off variety with lounges, restaurants and, if you're sailing to the Republic, tax-free shops. Crossing the Irish Sea is now faster than ever before, thanks to a new generation of high-speed ferries.

Logo of Irish Ferries

Stena HSS on the Dun Laoghaire to Holyhead crossing

FERRIES TO DUBLIN AND DUN LAOGHAIRE

There is a good choice of ferry services running between Wales and Ireland. **Irish Ferries**, the country's largest shipping company, operates on the Holyhead–Dublin Port route and has up to six crossings a day. The high-speed service takes 1 hour 49 minutes, while the conventional ferry takes about 3¼ hours. **Stena Line** also operates two conventional ferry crossings each day on this route. Like most ferry companies, Irish Ferries does not operate on Christmas Day or on Boxing Day.

The service from Holyhead to the Dublin suburb of Dun Laoghaire – traditionally the busiest port in Ireland – is operated by Stena Line. This route is served by the Stena HSS (High-speed Sea Service). As the largest ferry on the Irish Sea, the HSS has the same passenger and vehicle capacity as the conventional ferries but its jet-engine propulsion gives it twice the speed.

Vehicle loading and unloading times on the fast ferries are considerably shorter than with other ferries. Passengers requiring special assistance at ports or on board the ship

should contact the company they are booked with at least 24 hours before the departure time. Like most other ferry companies, Irish Ferries and Stena Line take bicycles free of charge, but this should be mentioned when making your reservation. **P&O Irish Sea** operates an 18-hour crossing from Dublin Port to Cherbourg every Saturday between March and November.

FERRIES TO ROSSLARE

Rosslare, in County Wexford, is the main port for crossings from South Wales to Ireland. Stena Line runs a service from Fishguard using both the conventional ferry and the speedier Sea Lynx

Irish Ferries ship loading up at Rosslare Harbour

catamaran-style ferries. Those intending to take a car on Sea Lynx should make sure the measurements of their vehicle, when fully loaded, are within those specified by Stena Line. The maximum dimensions allowable per vehicle are 3 m (10 ft) high by 6 m (20 ft) long and up to 3 tonnes.

Irish Ferries operates two crossings to Rosslare from Pembroke (4 hours) all year round. They also run a service from Roscoff in France (17 hours) between April and September. Both Irish Ferries and P&O run services to Rosslare from Cherbourg (18 hours). Cabins and berths are available on all crossings to Rosslare and should be booked in advance

FERRIES TO CORK

The prospect of a 10-hour sea journey could be enough to deter some from taking the ferry to Cork, but for those heading for south-west Ireland, sailing to the small town of Ringaskiddy, near Cork, can help cut out a cross-Ireland car journey of up to 250 miles. During the high season, **Swansea Cork Ferries** has up to six crossings per week between the two cities but the service doesn't operate between the end of January and mid-March. The crossing takes about 10 hours.

There is also one route direct to Cork from Roscoff in France operated by **Brittany Ferries**. The ferry runs once a week leaving from Cork on a Saturday and from Roscoff on a Friday. The service is only available from April to early October and the crossing time is 14 hours. Cabins and berths are available on routes to Cork but

Gallery overlooking the quayside at Rosslare Harbour

need to be booked well in advance in high season. There is a small charge for taking bicycles on Swansea Cork Ferries and it should be mentioned when booking.

PORT CONNECTIONS

ALL IRELAND'S PORTS have adequate bus and train connections. At Dublin Port, Bus Éireann buses meet ferry arrivals and take passengers into the city centre for a small charge. From Dun Laoghaire, DART trains run into Dublin every 10 to 15 minutes calling at Pearse Street, Tara Street and Connolly Stations. These go from the railway station near the main passenger concourse. Buses run from Dun Laoghaire to Eden Quay and Fleet Street in the city centre every 10 to 15 minutes. At all ports, taxis are there to meet arrivals. For those interested in car hire, Hertz has a desk at Dun Laoghaire. Passengers arriving at Dublin Port have to rent cars from the city centre.

TRAIN AND BUS THROUGH-TICKETS

IT IS POSSIBLE TO TRAVEL from any train station in Great Britain to any specified destination in Ireland on a combined sea/rail ticket. Combined tickets can be bought from most train stations throughout Britain.
  Eurolines runs a through-bus service from about 35 towns in Britain to over 100 destinations in the Republic. **Ulsterbus/Translink** offers the same service to destinations in Northern Ireland.
  Tickets for both these bus companies can be booked through **National Express**, which has over 2,000 agents in Great Britain. Travellers from North America, Australia, New Zealand and certain countries in Asia can buy a Brit Ireland pass. As well as including the return ferry crossing to Ireland, it allows unlimited rail travel throughout Great Britain and Ireland on any five or ten days during one month.

Directions for ferry passengers

DIRECTORY

FERRY COMPANIES

Brittany Ferries
📞 021 427 7801 (Cork).
📞 0870 536 0360 (UK).
W www.brittany-ferries.com

Irish Ferries
📞 1890 313131 (ROI).
📞 0870 517 1717 (UK).
W www.irishferries.com

Isle of Man Steam Packet and SeaCat
📞 1800 805055 (ROI).
📞 0870 552 3523 (UK).
W www.seacat.co.uk

Norse Merchant Ferries
📞 028 9077 9090 (Belfast).
📞 0870 600 4321 (UK).
W www.norsemerchant.com

P&O Irish Sea
📞 1800 409049 (ROI).
📞 0870 242 4777 (UK).
W www.poirishsea.com

Stena Line
📞 01 204 7777 (Dublin).
📞 0870 570 7070 (UK).
W www.stenaline.co.uk

Swansea Cork Ferries
📞 021 427 1166 (Cork).
📞 01792 456116 (UK).
W www.swansea-cork.ie

BUS COMPANIES

Eurolines
📞 01 836 6111(Dublin).
📞 0870 514 3219 (UK).
W www.eurolines.ie

National Express
📞 0870 580 8080 (UK).
W www.gobycoach.com

Ulsterbus/Translink
📞 028 9089 9400 (Belfast).

FERRY ROUTES TO THE REPUBLIC OF IRELAND	OPERATOR	LENGTH OF JOURNEY
Fishguard–Rosslare	Stena Line Stena Line	3hrs 30min (Stena Europe) 1hr 50min (Fastcraft)
Holyhead–Dublin	Irish Ferries Stena Line	1hr 49min (Jonathan Swift) 3hrs (Stena Forwarder)
Holyhead–Dun Laoghaire	Stena Line	1hr 49min (Stena HSS)
Liverpool–Dublin	Norse Merchant Ferries P&O SeaCat Dublin Maritime	8hrs 8hrs (Norbay) 3hrs 55min (Super Seacat 3)
Mostyn–Dublin	P&O P&O	6hrs (European Ambassador) 7hrs 30min (European Envoy)
Pembroke–Rosslare	Irish Ferries	3hrs 45min (Isle of Inishmore)
Swansea–Cork	Swansea Cork Ferries	10hrs (Superferry)

FERRIES TO BELFAST AND LARNE

THE FASTEST CROSSING to Belfast is the 90-minute **SeaCat** service from Stranraer in Scotland. This catamaran-style ferry sails up to four times per day, all year round. On the same route, Stena Line has introduced the second of their new HSS ferries. On these the sailing time is only 15 minutes longer than that of the SeaCat.

A Liverpool to Belfast service is run by **Norse Merchant Ferries**, leaving Liverpool (Birkenhead) every evening and five mornings a week, and taking over 7½ hours to reach Belfast. Crossing the Irish Sea with the **Isle of Man Steam Packet Co** lets you visit the Isle of Man en route. Leaving from both Liverpool and Heysham, this service provides the added advantage of allowing you to disembark at Dublin and return from Belfast or vice versa.

There are now three routes to Larne (north of Belfast): from the Scottish ports of Cairnryan (1 hour 45 minutes) and Troon (4 hours); and from Fleetwood in Lancashire, (8 hours). The services are operated by **P&O Irish Sea**, who run both conventional ferries and the high-speed Superstar Express on the Larne–Cairnryan route. This service runs from mid-April to mid-September and takes only an hour. During the week in high season there are four sailings a day to Cairnryan.

Cars and lorries disembarking at Larne Port

PORT CONNECTIONS

ALTHOUGH it takes only ten minutes on foot into the city centre from Belfast Port, Flexibus shuttles are on hand to take ferry passengers into the city centre via the Europa Buscentre and Central Railway Station. A regular bus service connects Larne Harbour to the town's bus station, and from here, buses run every hour into Belfast city centre. From Larne Port, there are trains to take ferry passengers to Belfast's Yorkgate and Central train stations. Taxis are available at both ports.

Port of Belfast logo

FARES AND CONCESSIONS

FARES ON FERRY CROSSINGS to Ireland vary dramatically according to the season – prices on certain days during the peak period of mid-June to mid-September can be double those at other times of the year. Prices increase greatly during the Christmas and New Year period, too. It is advisable to book your journey both ways before setting out. Those travelling to ports without a reservation should always check availability before setting out.

Often, the cheapest way for families or groups of adults to travel is to buy a ticket that allows you to take a car plus a maximum number of passengers. At certain times of the year on particular routes, the return ticket for a car and five adults (two children count as one adult) can cost less than 65 euros. The cheapest crossings are usually those where the passenger must depart and return within a specified period. Fares are normally reduced for mid-week travel and early-morning or late-night crossings. Ferry companies offer discounts for students bearing an ISIC card *(see p340)* and some have cut-price deals for those with InterRail tickets *(see p359)*.

FERRY ROUTES TO NORTHERN IRELAND	OPERATOR	LENGTH OF JOURNEY
Cairnryan–Larne	P&O P&O P&O	1hr 45min (European Causeway) 1hr (Superstar Express) 1hr 45min (European Highlander)
Fleetwood–Larne	P&O P&O	8hrs (European Pioneer) 8hrs (European Leader)
Heysham–Belfast	SeaCat Scotland	4hrs (Seacat Rapide)
Liverpool–Belfast	Norse Merchant Ferries	9hrs
Stranraer–Belfast	Stena Line	1hr 45 (Stena HSS) 3hrs 15min (Stena Caledonia)
Troon–Belfast	SeaCat Scotland	2hrs 30min
Troon–Larne	P&O	1hr 50 min (Superstar Express)

On the Road

ONE OF THE BEST WAYS to see Ireland's magnificent scenery and ancient sites is by car. Driving on the narrow, twisting country roads can be a pleasure; often you don't see another vehicle for miles. It can also be frustrating, especially if you find yourself stuck behind a slow-moving tractor or a herd of cows. If you don't want to take your own vehicle, car rental in Ireland is no problem. All the international car rental firms operate in the Republic and are also well represented in the North. Touring by bicycle is another enjoyable way of seeing the best parts of the island at your own leisurely pace.

Gaelic road sign instructing motorists to yield or give way

TAKING YOUR OWN CAR

IF YOU INTEND to take your own car across on the ferry *(see pp352–4)* check your car insurance to find out how well you are covered. To prevent a fully comprehensive policy being downgraded to third-party coverage, ask your insurance company for a Green Card. Carry your insurance certificate, Green Card, proof of ownership of the car and, importantly, your driver's licence. If your licence was issued in Great Britain, you should also bring your passport with you for ID.

Membership of a reputable automobile club like the **AA**, **RAC** or **Green Flag National Breakdown** is advisable unless you are undaunted by the prospect of breaking down in remote parts. Non-members can join up for just the duration of their trip. Depending on the type of coverage, automobile clubs may offer only limited services in Ireland.

RENTING A CAR

CAR RENTAL FIRMS do good business in Ireland, so in summer it's wise to book ahead. Rental – particularly in the Republic – is quite expensive and the best rates are often obtained by renting in advance. Broker companies, such as **Holiday Autos**, will shop around to get you the best deal. Savings can also be made by choosing a fly-drive or even a rail-sail-drive vacation, but always check for hidden extras.

Car rental usually includes unlimited mileage plus passenger indemnity

One for the road

insurance and coverage for third party, fire and theft, but not damage to the vehicle. If you plan to cross the border in either direction, however briefly, you must tell the rental company, as there may be a small insurance premium.

To rent a car, you must show a full driver's licence, held for two years without violation. US visitors are advised to obtain an international licence through AAA before leaving the States to facilitate dealing with traffic officials should problems occur.

BUYING FUEL

UNLEADED PETROL (gas) and diesel fuel are available just about everywhere in Ireland. Although prices vary from station to station, fuel in the Republic is quite expensive; in Northern Ireland it costs even more. Almost all the stations accept VISA and MasterCard, although it is worth checking before filling up, particularly in rural areas.

ROAD MAPS

THE ROAD MAP on the inside back cover shows virtually all the towns and villages mentioned in this guide. In addition, each chapter starts with a map of the region showing all the major sights and tips on getting around. However, if you plan to do much driving or cycling, you should equip yourself with a more detailed map. Ordnance Survey Holiday Maps are among the best road maps. You can usually get town plans free from tourist offices *(see p338)*. The tourist boards of the Republic and Northern Ireland both issue free lists of suggested routes for cyclists.

A busy Hertz car rental desk at Dublin Airport

The familiar sight of a farmer and cattle on an Irish country road

RULES OF THE ROAD

Even for those unused to driving on the left, driving in Ireland is unlikely to pose any great problems. For many, the most difficult aspect of it is getting used to over-taking on the right and giving way to traffic on the right at roundabouts (traffic circles). On both sides of the border, the wearing of seat belts is compulsory for drivers and all front-seat passengers; where provided, rear seat belts must also be worn. Children must have a suitable restraint system. Motorcyclists and passengers must wear helmets. Northern Ireland uses the same Highway Code as Great Britain. The Republic of Ireland's Highway Code is very similar – copies of both

Speed limit signs in mph on a country road in County Cork

are available from bookstores. In Northern Ireland, you will notice some cars carrying a red "R" plate. These identify "restricted" drivers who have passed their driving test within the previous 12 months and have to keep to lower speeds.

SPEED LIMITS

In the Republic and Northern Ireland the maximum speed limits, which are shown in miles per hour, are much the same as those in Britain:
• 30 mph (50 km/h) in built-up areas.
• 60 mph (100 km/h) outside built-up areas.
• 70 mph (110 km/h) on motorways.
On certain roads, which are clearly marked, the speed limits are either 40 mph (65 km/h) or 50 mph (80 km/h). Where there is no indication, the speed limit is 60 mph (95 km/h). In the Republic, vehicles towing caravans (trailers) must not exceed 55 mph (90 km/h). Speed limits are strictly enforced in both the North and the Republic.

ROAD SIGNS

Most road signs in the Republic are in both Gaelic and English. Ireland is striving toward metrication so all the new-style green and white signs are in kilometres. However, nothing's quite that simple in Ireland, so expect to come across some black-on-white signs showing distances in miles. As in Britain, road signs in the North are always

in miles. One road sign that is unique to the Republic is the "Yield" sign – in the UK this is worded "Give Way". Through-out both the Republic and Northern Ireland, brown signs with white lettering indicate places of historic, cultural or leisure interest.

SIGNS IN THE REPUBLIC

Unprotected quay or river ahead

Junction ahead

Children or school ahead

Dangerous bends ahead

SIGNS IN NORTHERN IRELAND

Motorway direction sign

Primary route sign

ROAD CONDITIONS

Northern Ireland's roads are well surfaced and generally in better condition than those in the Republic, though there are just as many winding stretches requiring extra caution. The volume of traffic, particularly in the South, is much lower than in Britain. On some of the more rural roads you may not come across another driver for miles. Even the major roads can be surprisingly quiet. There are only a few sections of motorway in the whole of Ireland, though recent years have seen extensive construction of two-lane highways in the Republic, including rural areas such as County Donegal.

PARKING

Finding parking in Ireland used to be easy, but this has changed in recent years. Due to increased congestion, the majority of towns now have paid parking on and off street. Dublin, Belfast and a few other cities have either parking meters or (fairly expensive) parking lots. Parking on the street is allowed, though a single yellow line along the edge of the road means there are some restrictions (there should be a sign nearby showing the permitted parking times). Double yellow lines indicate that no parking is allowed at any time.

Parking disc sign

Disc parking – a version of "pay & display" – operates in most large towns and cities in the Republic and the North. Discs can be purchased from fuel stations, tourist offices and many small shops. In Northern Ireland, almost all towns and villages have Control Zones, which are indicated by large yellow or pink signs. For security reasons, unattended parking in a Control Zone is not permitted at any time of the day.

Warning sign in Northern Ireland

CYCLING

The quiet roads of Ireland help to make touring by bicycle a real joy. The **Raleigh** **Rent-a-Bike** network of bike dealers operates a reasonably priced rental scheme throughout Ireland. Also local shops, such as **Cycle Ways** in Dublin, rent bikes to tourists and are open at least six days a week. You can often rent a bike in one town and drop it off at another for a small charge. Many dealers can also provide safety helmets, but bring your own lightweight waterproof clothing to help cope with the unpredictable weather. Buses and trains will carry bikes for a surcharge.

SECURITY ROADBLOCKS IN NORTHERN IRELAND

In the late 1960s, when the Northern Ireland troubles began, roadblocks were introduced on to the roads of the province. These days if you are travelling by road, whether in the centre of Londonderry or the remote Sperrin Mountains, you are very unlikely to come across a roadblock, depending on the political climate at the time. Checkpoints can be staffed by either the army or the police, who will ask for proof of identity. In the unlikely event of your being stopped, show your driver's licence and insurance certificate or rental agreement when asked.

Cyclists checking their directions in Ballyvaughan, County Clare

Travelling by Train

THE REPUBLIC OF IRELAND'S RAIL NETWORK is run by **Irish Rail** (Iarnród Éireann) and is state-controlled. The rail network is far from comprehensive and quite expensive, but the trains are generally reliable and comfortable and can be a good way of covering long distances. The service provided by **Northern Ireland Railways** (NIR) is more limited but fares are slightly cheaper. There is an excellent train service between Dublin and Belfast, with a journey time of just under two hours. Fares can be as little as 43 euros round trip.

Train at Killarney station on the southwest rail network

TRAIN SERVICES IN THE REPUBLIC OF IRELAND

ALTHOUGH the more rural areas in the Republic of Ireland are not served by train, Irish Rail operates a satisfactory service to most of the large cities and towns. Taking the train is probably the fastest and most convenient way of going from Dublin to places like Cork, Waterford, Limerick and Galway. However, there are glaring gaps in the network; for example, Donegal is totally devoid of train services, so if you are planning to explore the west coast of Ireland using public transport, you will have to continue westward from towns such as Galway, Sligo, Limerick and Westport using the local bus services.

The two main train stations in Dublin are Connolly Station, for trains to the north, northwest and Rosslare, and Heuston Station, which serves the west, midlands and southwest. These two stations are connected by the No. 90 bus service which runs every 10 to 15 minutes and takes a quarter of an hour – traffic permitting. All trains in the Republic of Ireland have standard and super-standard (first-class) compartments.

Bicycles can be taken on intercity trains but there is a fee of up to 10 euros.

OUTER DUBLIN RAIL SERVICES

THE HANDY electric rail service known as DART (Dublin Area Rapid Transit) serves 30 stations between Malahide and Greystones with several stops in Dublin city centre. A Rail/Bus ticket allows three consecutive days' travel on DART trains as well as Dublin Bus services. Tickets can be purchased at any of the DART stations. The Luas light rail service connects central Dublin with the suburbs. The first lines are set for completion in 2004, and will eventually interconnect with the DART.

TRAIN SERVICES IN NORTHERN IRELAND

OTHER THAN an express service out to Larne Harbour and a commuter line to Bangor, there are only two main routes out of Belfast: a line westward to Londonderry via Coleraine (for the Giant's Causeway) and Ireland's only cross-border service, operating a high-speed link between Belfast and Dublin eight times a day. All trains leave from Central Station. Great Victoria Street station opened in 1995 and brings rail travellers right to the heart of the city's business and shopping district. Bear in mind that there are no baggage rooms at any of Northern Ireland's train or bus stations.

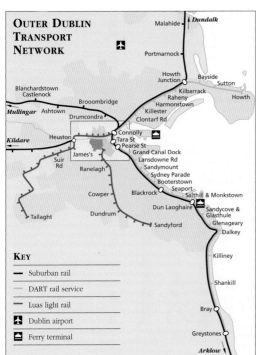

OUTER DUBLIN TRANSPORT NETWORK

Malahide · Dundalk

Portmarnock

Howth Junction
Bayside
Sutton
Blanchardstown
Castleknock
Brooombridge
Kilbarrack
Raheny
Harmonstown
Howth
Mullingar Ashtown
Drumcondra
Killester
Clontarf Rd
Kildare
Heuston
Connolly
Tara St
Pearse St
Grand Canal Dock
Lansdowne Rd
James's
Suir Rd
Ranelagh
Sandymount
Sydney Parade
Booterstown
Seapoint
Cowper
Blackrock
Salthill & Monkstown
Tallaght
Dundrum
Dun Laoghaire
Sandycove & Glasthule
Sandyford
Glenageary
Dalkey

Killiney

Shankill

Bray

Greystones

Arklow

KEY

— Suburban rail

— DART rail service

— Luas light rail

✈ Dublin airport

⛴ Ferry terminal

TICKETS AND FARES

THROUGHOUT IRELAND, train tickets are generally quite expensive, but there are lots of bargain incentives and concessionary passes. Most of these include bus travel, so you can get virtually anywhere in Ireland on one ticket.

The most comprehensive ticket available is the Emerald Card, which can be used on all Irish Rail, Northern Ireland Railways, Dublin Bus and Ulsterbus services. For around 180 euros the Emerald Card gives eight days' unlimited travel in a 15-day period. An 8-day Irish Explorer ticket is slightly cheaper and is valid on all Irish Rail and Bus Éireann transport. For rail travellers, the Irish Rover ticket can be a bargain. It is valid on all Irish Rail and Northern Ireland Railways journeys for five days within a 15-day period.

The modern ticket office at Belfast's Central Station

CONCESSIONS

STUDENTS CAN BUY a Travel-save Stamp *(see p340)* to affix to their ISIC cards for discounts on train fares. For those under 26, Faircards give good discounts on all Irish Rail single journeys, and can be bought from USIT *(see p340).*

Under-26 InterRail passes allow unlimited rail travel for 15 days or one month in the Republic and 25 other European countries. Older travellers can get InterRail Plus 26 cards costing slightly more. However, InterRail cards allow only a one-third discount on Northern Ireland Railways.

IRELAND'S RAIL NETWORK

Irish Rail (Iarnród Éireann)
35 Abbey St Lower, Dublin 1. **C** *01 836 6222.*
W www.irishrail.ie

Northern Ireland Railways
Central Station, East Bridge St,
Belfast BT1 3PB. **C** *028 9066 6630.*
W www.translink.co.uk

KEY

═══ Irish Rail

═══ NIR

Travelling by Bus and Taxi

THE BUS SERVICES THROUGHOUT IRELAND are quite good, for such a rural island. However, longer journeys often involve changing buses en route so extra travelling time should be allowed for. Touring by bus is also a good way to see Ireland – local tourist offices have details of tours as well as prices and often take bookings. Taxi services are available in all major cities and towns in Ireland. In the Republic, taxis can be four or eight-seater cars and are identified by a yellow light on the roof. In the North, cities like Belfast and Londonderry have both mini-cabs and London-style black cabs.

Boarding a bus at the Europa Buscentre in Belfast

Logo on Bus Éireann local and express buses

GETTING AROUND BY BUS

THE REPUBLIC OF IRELAND'S national bus company, **Bus Éireann**, operates a countrywide network of buses serving all the cities and most of the towns. In Dublin, the main bus station is the Busáras on Store Street, a short walk from O'Connell Street. There are a number of private bus companies which either compete with the national network or provide services on routes not covered by Bus Éireann. In rural Donegal, for example, there are several private bus services. Some are not fully licensed, so check whether you would be covered in the event of an accident. Local tourist offices should be able to point out the most reputable firms.

Ulsterbus runs an excellent service throughout Northern Ireland including express links between all the major

towns. Belfast has two main bus stations – the Europa Buscentre off Great Victoria Street and Laganside Station. Check before setting out that you are going to the right one. Note that for reasons of security, there are no baggage rooms at any of the stations in Northern Ireland.

FARES AND TICKETS

IN THE REPUBLIC, long-distance buses are about half the price of the equivalent train trip. If you are making the return trip on the same day, ask for a day-return ticket, which is much cheaper than the normal round-trip fare. Also, between Monday and Thursday you can buy a "period" return ticket for the price of a one-way fare. Under 16s pay half the adult fare. Students with a Travelsave stamp *(see p340)* get a 30 per cent reduction. For those intending to do a lot of travelling it is cheaper to buy

a "Rambler" ticket. This allows unlimited bus travel throughout the Republic for a certain number of days in a set period, for example, 15 days' travel out of 30 consecutive days.

A "Freedom of Northern Ireland" ticket gives you unlimited travel on all Ulsterbus routes for either a day or a week. Ulsterbus also offers cheap day-return tickets. Students can get a 15 per cent discount by showing their ISIC card. There are also a number of period passes available that combine bus and rail travel *(see p359)*.

BUS TOURS

WHILE THE BUS SERVICES in Ireland are generally adequate for getting from town to town, using public transport isn't a very practical way of exploring specific areas or regions in great detail, unless you have a lot of time on your hands. If you find yourself in a remote area like Connemara *(see pp198–201)* but have only a very limited amount of time in which to see its main attractions, a local guided tour of the area is a good idea. For about 25 euros per adult you can do the picturesque "figure of eight" circuit by bus, starting from Galway and taking in Spiddal, Kylemore, Letterfrack, Oughterard and then returning to Galway. The bus sets out at 10am and returns at about 5:30pm, making regular stops at places of interest. The price does not include admission fees or

Express service bus in Northern Ireland

lunch. Bookings are made at Galway Tourist Information Centre and can be arranged in advance or on the day. Four-hour or one-day tours such as this are available in many of Ireland's main tourist areas. Other popular tours of rural Ireland include Glendalough *(see pp132–3)*, Donegal *(see pp216–23)*, and the Ring of Kerry *(see pp156–7)*. In Dublin and other cities in the Republic, Bus Éireann and some local companies run half- and one-day excursions. **Dublin Bus** (Bus Átha Cliath) runs a Dublin City tour, which leaves from O'Connell Street Upper. This guided tour takes in the city's most famous sights.

In Northern Ireland, Ulsterbus operates tours from the Europa Buscentre in Belfast to all the major places of interest. These tours include the Causeway Coast, the Glens of Antrim and the Ulster-American Folk Park near Omagh. Ulsterbus prefers bookings to be made in person at their Belfast office. In summer, **Belfast Citybus** operates up to two guided bus tours per day around the city; in winter there are tours on Thursday and Saturday.

Local Transport

Local bus services throughout the Republic are generally well-run and reasonably priced. **Dublin Bus** runs the bus services in the Greater Dublin area. Buses in the city centre run from about 6am until 11:30pm with an

Passengers alighting from a Waterford city bus

extended "nitelink" service at weekends. One-day passes, costing 5 euros, are good value. The new on-street light rail service, **Luas**, provides an easy way to reach suburban areas previously only accessible by bus. The Luas lines will eventually connect with the DART rail service *(see p358)* and a proposed Metro system. In the rest of the Republic the bus services, including city buses in Galway, Limerick, Waterford and Cork, are operated mainly by Bus Éireann; a comprehensive timetable is available at tourist offices and bus stations. Some bus routes connecting towns and villages are served by private companies as well as Bus Éireann. For bus times (and stops) in more remote areas, try asking the locals.

Except for Belfast, Northern Ireland's bus network is run by **Ulsterbus/Translink**. In the province's capital the local service is operated by **Citybus**. A wide variety of travel passes are available for Citybus and Ulsterbus/Translink lines. Regional timetables are available at bus stations.

Taxis in the Republic

Except in the most rural of places, there is usually a local taxi service – your hotel or B&B will provide details. In Dublin, taxis range from four-seater cars to minivans. Cruising taxis are a rarity: the best places to find taxis are at train or bus stations, hotels and taxi ranks. Prices are usually based on metered mileage; if not, always ask the fare to your destination.

Taxis in Northern Ireland

Taxis in Northern Ireland are reasonably priced. Journeys within the centre of Belfast usually cost no more than £4 by mini-cab or black cab. In most decent-sized towns in the North you will find at least one taxi office or rank where you can wait for a cab. Otherwise, ask for the number of a taxi firm at a local hotel or B&B.

DIRECTORY

CITY TRANSPORT

Citybus (Belfast)
(028 9024 6485.
DART (Dublin)
(01 836 6222.
W www.irishrail.ie
Dublin Bus
(01 873 4222.
W www.dublinbus.ie
Luas (Dublin)
(01 703 2029. W www.luas.ie

NATIONAL BUS COMPANIES

Bus Éireann
(01 836 6111.
W www.buseireann.ie
Ulsterbus/Translink
(028 9066 6630.
W www.translink.co.uk

BUS TOURS

Guide Friday
Dublin Tourist Office, Dublin 2.
(01 605 7705.
McGeehan Coaches
Fintown PO, Co Donegal.
(074 954 6101.

Taxis lined up outside the arrivals building at Dublin Airport

General Index

Page numbers in **bold** type refer to main entries.

Acknowledgments

DORLING KINDERSLEY would like to thank the following people whose contributions and assistance have made the preparation of this book possible.

MAIN CONTRIBUTORS
LISA GERARD-SHARP is a writer and broadcaster who has contributed to numerous travel books, including the *Eyewitness Travel Guide to France*. She is of Irish extraction, with roots in County Sligo and County Galway, and a regular visitor to Ireland.

TIM PERRY, from Dungannon, County Tyrone, writes on travel and popular music for various publishers in North America and the British Isles.

ADDITIONAL CONTRIBUTOR
Douglas Palmer.

ADDITIONAL PHOTOGRAPHY
Peter Anderson, Joe Cornish, Andy Crawford, Michael Diggin, Steve Gorton, Anthony Haughey, Mike Linley, Stephen Oliver, Magnus Rew, Clive Streeter, Matthew Ward.

ADDITIONAL ILLUSTRATIONS
Richard Bonson, Brian Craker, John Fox, Paul Guest, Stephan Gyapay, Ian Henderson, Claire Littlejohn, Gillie Newman, Chris Orr, Kevin Robinson, John Woodcock, Martin Woodward.

ADDITIONAL PICTURE RESEARCH
Miriam Sharland.

EDITORIAL AND DESIGN
MANAGING EDITORS Vivien Crump, Helen Partington
MANAGING ART EDITOR Steve Knowlden
DEPUTY EDITORIAL DIRECTOR Douglas Amrine
DEPUTY ART DIRECTOR Gaye Allen
PRODUCTION David Proffit, Hilary Stephens
PICTURE RESEARCH Sue Mennell, Christine Rista
DTP DESIGNER Adam Moore
MAPS Gary Bowes, Margaret Slowey, Richard Toomey (ERA-Maptec, Dublin, Ireland)
MAP CO-ORDINATORS Michael Ellis, David Pugh

Marion Broderick, Margaret Chang, Martin Cropper, Guy Dimond, Fay Franklin, Yael Freudmann, Sally Ann Hibbard, Annette Jacobs, Erika Lang, Michael Osborn, Polly Phillimore, Caroline Radula-Scott.

INDEX
Hilary Bird.

REVISIONS
REVISIONS CO-ORDINATOR Kathryn Lane
FACTCHECKER Oenone Luke
EDITOR Christina Park
PROOFREADER Stewart J. Wild
DESIGNER Rachel Symons

SPECIAL ASSISTANCE
Dorling Kindersley would like to thank all the regional and local tourist offices in the Republic and in Northern Ireland for their valuable help. Particular thanks also to: Ralph Doak and Egerton Shelswell-White at Bantry House, Bantry, Co Cork; Vera Greif at the Chester Beatty Library and Gallery of Oriental Art, Dublin; Alan Figgis at Christ Church Cathedral, Dublin; Labhras Ó Murchu at Comhaltas Ceoltóirí Éireann; Catherine O'Connor at Derry City Council; Patsy O'Connell at Dublin Tourism; Tanya Cathcart at Fermanagh Tourism, Enniskillen; Peter Walsh at the Guinness Hop Store, Dublin; Gerard Collet at the Irish Shop, Covent Garden, London; Dónall P Ó Baoill at ITE, Dublin; Pat Cooke at Kilmainham Gaol, Dublin; Angela Shanahan at the Kinsale Tourist Office; Bill Maxwell, Adrian Le Harivel and Marie McFeely at the National Gallery of Ireland, Dublin; Philip McCann at the National Library of Ireland, Dublin; Willy Cumming at the National Monuments Divison, Office of Public Works, Dublin; Eileen Dunne and Sharon Fogarty at the National Museum of Ireland, Dublin; Joris Minne at the Northern Ireland Tourist Office, Belfast; Dr Tom MacNeil at Queen's University, Belfast; Sheila Crowley at St Mary's Pro-Cathedral, Dublin; Paul Brock at the Shannon Development Centre; Tom Sheedy at Shannon Heritage and Banquets, Bunratty Castle, Co Clare; Angela Sutherland at the Shannon-Erne Waterway, Co Leitrim; Máire Ní Bháin at Trinity College, Dublin; Anne-Marie Diffley at Trinity College Library, Dublin; Pat Maclean at the Ulster Museum, Belfast; Harry Hughes at the Willie Clancy School of Traditional Music, Miltown Malbay, Co Clare.

ADDITIONAL ASSISTANCE
Kathleen Crowley, Rory Doyle, Peter Hynes, David O'Grady, Mary O'Grady, Madge Perry, Poppy.

PHOTOGRAPHY PERMISSIONS
THE PUBLISHER would like to thank all those who gave permission to photograph at various cathedrals, churches, museums, restaurants, hotels, shops, galleries and other sights too numerous to list individually.

PICTURE CREDITS
tl = top left; tc = top centre; tr = top right; cla = centre left above; ca = centre above; cra = centre right above; cl = centre left; c = centre; cr = centre right; clb = centre left below; cb = centre below; crb = centre right below; bl = bottom left; bc = bottom centre; br = bottom right.

Every effort has been made to trace the copyright holders and we apologize in advance for any unintentional omissions. We would be pleased to insert the appropriate acknowledgments in any subsequent edition of this publication.

Works of art have been reproduced with the permission of the following copyright holders:
© DACS, London 1995 68tr, 88tr.

The publisher would like to thank the following individuals, companies and picture libraries for permission to reproduce their photographs:

AER LINGUS/AIRBUS INDUSTRIE: 350tc; AKG, LONDON: National Museum, Copenhagen/Erich Lessing 24cl; ALLSPORT: David Rogers 26cb; Steve Powell 45tc; APPLETREE PRESS LTD, BELFAST (*Irish Proverbs* © illustrations Karen Bailey) 327cl.

© BRISTOL CITY MUSEUMS AND ART GALLERY: 30bl; © BRITISH LIBRARY: *Richard II's Campaigns in Ireland* Ms.Harl.1319, f.18 35tl; © BRITISH MUSEUM: 31bl; BT PAYPHONES: 349cl, 349cr, 349b; BUS ÉIREANN: 360cl; © BUSHMILLS LTD: 258bl.

© CENTRAL BANK OF IRELAND: *Lady Lavery as Cathleen ni Houlihan*, John Lavery 13ca, 344 (all banknotes and coins except for tr), 345; CENTRAL CYBER CAFÉ, DUBLIN: Finbarr Clarkson 348tr; © CHESTER BEATTY LIBRARY, DUBLIN: 75t; © CLASSIC DESIGNS/LJ YOUNG LTD, BLARNEY: 327c; Mark Boulton 17tr; Patrick Clement 16clb, 16bl; Adrian Davies 16br; Rodney Dawson 17cl; Frances Furlong 16tl; David Green 200bl; Pekka Helo 17cr; Jan Van de Kam 178bl; Gordon Langsbury 16cl, 178cr; John Markham 244br; George McCarthy 17tl, 17bl,17br, 130tl, 201bl; MR Phicon 16crb; Eckhart Pott 17cb; Hans Reinhard 17tcb, 154tl, 262tl; Kim Taylor 17tc, 244t; R Wanscheidt 17cbr; Uwe Walz 16cr, 177cb; G Ziesler 201bl; © CORK EXAMINER: 27tl; © CORK PUBLIC MUSEUM: 33cla; JOE CORNISH: 17cla, 204b, 262tr, 336–7; CRAWFORD MUNICIPAL ART GALLERY: *The Meeting of St Brendan and the Unhappy Judas*, Harry Clarke 166bl.

DAVISON & ASSOCIATES, LTD, IRELAND: 79cra; DERRY CITY COUNCIL: 250tr; MICHAEL DIGGIN: 18tl, 145b, 155cr, 156cla, 157tr, 177tl, 198bl, 217t, 218tr, 218cl, 219cra, 332tl, 333tl, 333b, 339br, 341b, 343cl, 346b; BILL DOYLE: 206bl; GA DUNCAN: 44cb, 44bl; © DUNDEE ART GALLERIES AND MUSEUMS: *The Children of Lir*, John Duncan 25tc.

eircom: 348tl, 348bl, 348cr; ET ARCHIVE: 25bl; MARY EVANS PICTURE LIBRARY: 9 (inset), 22tl, 24tr, 24bl, 24br, 25cla, 32bl, 35bc, 36bl; 42bl, 51 (inset), 75cl, 87bl, 113 (inset), 273br, 279 (inset), 337 (inset).

FÁILTE IRELAND/IRISH TOURIST BOARD: Brian Lynch 22–23, 23tl, 238tl, 238tr, Pat Odea 330c; © STEPHEN FALLER LTD, GALWAY: 326cla; © FAMINE MUSEUM CO ROSSCOMMON: 211tr; JIM FITZPATRICK: 77bl.

GILL AND MACMILLAN PUBLISHERS, DUBLIN: 43bl; RONALD GRANT ARCHIVE: *The Commitments*, Twentieth Century Fox 21br; © GUINNESS IRELAND LTD: 96bl, 96br, 97tl, 97tr, 97bl, 97br.

HULTON DEUTSCH COLLECTION: 20clb, 21tr, 37t, 40br, 40cbl, 44crb, Reuter 45crb, 60bl.

IMAGES COLOUR LIBRARY: 46bl, 53tl; 221bc; INPHO, DUBLIN: 26cla, Billy Stickland 26br, Lorraine O'Sullivan 27br; IRISH PICTURE LIBRARY, DUBLIN: 36cla, 39tl, 42tl; IRISH RAIL (IARNRÓD ÉIREANN): 358tr; © IRISH TIMES: 126br; © IRISH TRADITIONAL MUSIC ARCHIVE, DUBLIN: 23bl.

JARROLD COLOUR PUBLICATIONS: JA Brooks 60br; MICHAEL JENNER: 235cr.

TIMOTHY KOVAR: 76bl; 103tl, 106bl.

© LAMBETH PALACE LIBRARY, LONDON: Plan of the London Vintners' Company Township of Bellaghy, Ulster, 1622 (ms. Carew 634 f.34) (detail) 37cra; FRANK LANE PICTURE AGENCY: Roger Wilmshurst 178bc; © LEEDS CITY ART GALLERY: *The Irish House of Commons*, Francis Wheatley 38cla.

HUGH MCKNIGHT PHOTOGRAPHY: 99t; MANDER AND MITCHESON THEATRE COLLECTION: 22cl; MANSELL COLLECTION: 38bl, 43cra, 79bl, 260bc; ARCHIE MILES: 200br; JOHN MURRAY: 49bl, 94cl, 120c; © MUSEUM OF THE CITY OF NEW YORK: Gift of Mrs Robert M Littlejohn, *The Bay and Harbor of New York 1855*, Samuel B Waugh 40–41.

NATIONAL CONCERT HALL, DUBLIN: Frank Fennell 107bl; © NATIONAL GALLERY OF IRELAND, DUBLIN: *WB Yeats and the Irish Theatre*, Edmund Dulac 20tr, *George Bernard Shaw*, John Collier 20cr, *Carolan the Harper*, Francis Bindon 22tr, *Leixlip Castle*, Irish School 39cla, *The Custom House, Dublin*, James Malton 39bc, *Queen Victoria and Prince Albert Opening the 1853 Dublin Great Exhibition*, James Mahoney 41bl, *The Houseless Wanderer*, JH Foley 68tl, *Pierrot*, Juan Gris 68tr, *For the Road*, JB Yeats 68cla, *The Taking of Christ*, Caravaggio 69cra, *Judith with the Head of Holofernes*, Andrea Mantegna 69cra, *The Sick Call*, Matthew James Lawless 69crb, *Jonathan Swift, Satirist*, Charles Jerval 80bc, *James Joyce*, Jacques Emile Blanche 88t, *Interior with Members of a Family*, P Hussey 124br; *William Butler Yeats, Poet*, JB Yeats 225tl, *The Last Circuit of Pilgrims at Clonmacnoise*, George Petrie 242tr; © NATIONAL GALLERY, LONDON: *Beach Scene*, Edgar Degas 89br; © NATIONAL LIBRARY OF IRELAND, DUBLIN: 21cla, 21crb, 29b, 32tl, 32clb, 34bl, 36tl, 36clb, 38clb, 40tl, 40cla, 40bl, 41crb, 41tl, 42clb, 43tl, 43crb, *St Stephen's Green*, James Malton 50–51, 133tr, 170cra, 236b; © NATIONAL MUSEUM OF IRELAND, DUBLIN: 3, 30tl, 30clb, 30cb 30crb, 30–31, 31c 31clb, 31br, 32cla, 33cb, 33br, 53bl, 57cr, all 64–5, 99b; THE NATIONAL TRUST, NORTHERN IRELAND: *Lord Castlereagh* after

Lawrence 274tl, *Hambletonian,* George Stubbs 275tl, 275cra; THE NATIONAL TRUST PHOTOGRAPHIC LIBRARY: Mathew Antrobus 265b, John Bethell 276tl, Patrick Pendergast 264bl, Will Webster 269br, 278–9; NATURE PHOTOGRAPHERS: B Burbridge 179bc, Paul Sterry 178clb; NORTHERN IRELAND TOURIST BOARD: 26tr, 250cl, 265tr, 328cl, 329tl; NORTON ASSOCIATES: 72 clb.

KYRAN O'BRIEN 107tr; © THE OFFICE OF PUBLIC WORKS, IRELAND: 164bl, 238cl, 239tl, 239cr, 240br, 242tl; OXFORD SCIENTIFIC FILMS: Frithjof Skibbe 178tl. PACEMAKER PRESS INTERNATIONAL, LTD: 342bc, 342br; WALTER PFEIFFER STUDIOS, DUBLIN: 23tr, 23cra, 23c, 23cr, 23crb, 23br; PHOTO FLORA: Andrew N Gagg 178br; PHOTOSTAGE: Donald Cooper 106tr, 107tl; POPPERFOTO: 44cla, 44br, 45tl, Reuter/Crispin Rodwell 45tr; POWERSCOURT ESTATE, ENNISKERRY: 127c.

RANGE PICTURES: 41cra; THE REFORM CLUB, LONDON: 40cla; REPORT/DEREK SPIERS, DUBLIN: 44tl, 44tr, 270bl, 270br; RETNA PICTURES: Chris Taylor 22bl, Jay Blakesberg 22br; RETROGRAPH ARCHIVE, LONDON: © Martin Ranicar-Breese 63br; REX FEATURES: 45ca; Sipa Press 45clb, 45br, 45bl.

SHANNON DEVELOPMENT PHOTO LIBRARY: 330tl; SHANNON-ERNE WATERWAY: 227bc; THE SLIDE FILE, DUBLIN: 14bc, 15t, 15c, 16cla, 16cra, 20cla, 27cra, 27clb, 27bl, 30cla, 46cla, 46bl, 47cb, 48cla, 48cra, 48cb, 48bl, 49cra, 75tr, 75br, 106br, 114cla, 121br, 130cl 130br, 143br, 177br, 203tl, 205tr, 206cb, 206br, 207bc, 216br, 219tr, 222tl, 222b, 224tr, 229b, 232tl, 234tl, 240tl, 242–3, 244cra, 262clb, 329br, 330br; SPORTSFILE, DUBLIN: 27tc; STENA LINE: 352cl; DON SUTTON INTERNATIONAL PHOTO LIBRARY: 282br. © TATE GALLERY PUBLICATIONS: *Captain Thomas Lee, Marcus Gheeraedts* 36br; TOPHAM PICTURE SOURCE: 39br, Tim Graham 94t; TRANSLINK: 360bl; © TRINITY

COLLEGE, DUBLIN: Ms.1440 (Book of Burgos) f.20v 35clb; Ms.58 (Book of Kells) f.129v 4tr, *The Marriage of Princess Aoite and the Earl of Pembroke,* Daniel Maclise 34cla, Ms.57 (Book of Durrow) f.84v 53cr, Ms.57 (Book of Durrow) f.85v 61cr, Ms.58 (Book of Kells) f.129v 62cra, Ms.58 (Book of Kells) f.34r 62cl, Ms.58 (Book of Kells) f.28v 62crb, Ms.58 (Book of Kells) f.200r 62b; TRIP: R Drury 15br, 132c.

© ULSTER MUSEUM, BELFAST: *The Festival of St Kevin at the Seven Churches, Glendalough,* Joseph Peacock 28, *The Relief of Derry,* William Sadler II 36–7, 37crb, 42cla, 249crb, 270clb.

VIKING SHIP MUSEUM, STRANDENGEN, DENMARK: watercolour by Flemming Bau 33tl.

© WATERFORD CORPORATION: 33bl, 34tl, 34clb, 35bl; © WRITERS MUSEUM, DUBLIN: 20tl.

PETER ZÖLLER: 12, 14tl, 46tc, 46cr, 47cra, 47bl, 138br, 192, 208–9, 211bl, 212, 228, 241tr, 334tl.

Front endpaper: all commissioned photography with the exception of PETER ZÖLLER: tl, tc, cb.

JACKET
Front - DK PICTURE LIBRARY, Peter Anderson crb; ROBERT HARDING PICTURE LIBRARY bla, Roy Rainford main image; TRINITY COLLEGE, DUBLIN: Courtesy of the Board of Trinity College Dublin bc. Back - COLLECTIONS, Michael St. Maur Sheil t; CORBIS, Richard Cummins b. Spine - ROBERT HARDING PICTURE LIBRARY, Roy Rainford.

All other images © DORLING KINDERSLEY. For further information see www.DKimages.com

DORLING KINDERSLEY SPECIAL EDITIONS

DORLING KINDERSLEY books can be purchased in bulk quantities at discounted prices for use in promotions or as premiums. We are also able to offer special editions and personalized jackets, corporate imprints, and excerpts from all of our books, tailored specifically to meet your own needs.

To find out more, please contact: (in the United Kingdom) Sarah.Burgess@dk.com or Special Sales, Dorling Kindersley Limited, 80 Strand, London WC2R 0RL; (in the United States) Special Markets Dept, DK Publishing, Inc., 375 Hudson Street, New York, NY 10014.

EYEWITNESS TRAVEL INSURANCE

FOR PEACE OF MIND ABROAD,
WE'VE GOT IT COVERED

DK INSURANCE PROVIDES YOU
WITH QUALITY WORLDWIDE
INSURANCE COVER

For an instant quote
go to **www.dk.com/travel-insurance**

Organised by Columbus Travel Insurance Services Ltd, 17 Devonshire Square, London EC2M 4SQ, UK.
Underwritten by certain underwriters at Lloyd's and Professional Travel Insurance Company Ltd.

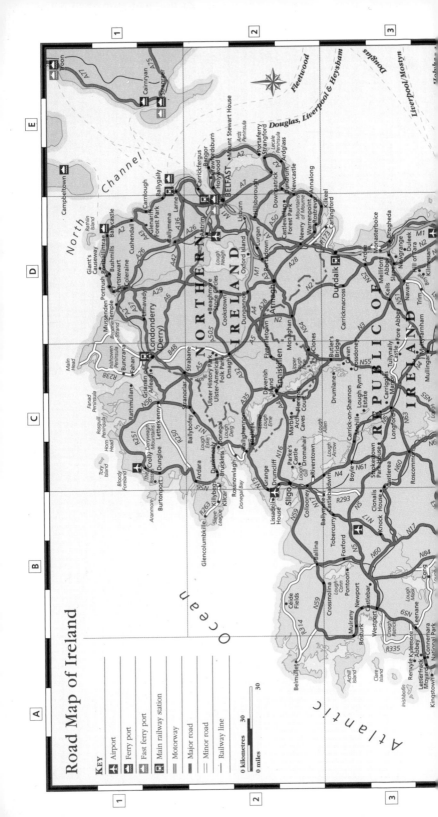

Road Map of Ireland

Key

- ✈ Airport
- ⚓ Ferry port
- ⚓ Fast ferry port
- 🚉 Main railway station
- Motorway
- Major road
- Minor road
- Railway line

0 kilometres 30

0 miles 30